TEACH YOURSELF BOOKS

GUIDE TO MODERN WORLD LITERATURE
Volume 2

'A quite remarkable feat . . . this is an astounding and outstanding book. He doesn't just copy out accepted opinions. Drama is there as well. I'm very much afraid he'll prove indispensable.'

CYRIL CONNOLLY, *Sunday Times*

'I have greatly enjoyed it, and I admire it immensely. I can think of no comparably prodigious effort of literary evaluation ... altogether a noble achievement.'

ANTONY QUINTON, *Sunday Telegraph*

'The word "indispensable" is the only one that will do, and if only because there is surely no other book which deals so thoroughly with so many different national literatures.'

PHILIP TOYNBEE, *Observer*

'The energy of writing hardly flags, author after author is characterised in terms which a student may easily grasp, but which also satisfy readers wanting something more than teachers usually say . . . this book will become a critical classic.'

ROBERT NYE, *Spectator*

'I have read it from cover to cover, and feel an infinitely better informed man.'

ANTHONY POWELL, *Daily Telegraph*

'Mr. Seymour-Smith's commentary exemplifies at almost every point an active engagement with the works he is discussing . . . (his) book embodies both the myths of literature and a sense of what it is like to encounter the thing itself. That is the merit—indeed, the distinction—of his excellent book.'

MARTIN DODSWORTH, *Encounter*

'Essential if reading (or writing) is your essence of life; a book for exploration and discovery, an excited book, and one which stimulates argument and controversy, as well as agreement.'

GEOFFREY GRIGSON, *Country Life*

Martin Seymour-Smith, son of the distinguished librarian and bibliographer Frank Seymour-Smith, was born in London in 1928. Educated at Highgate School and St Edmund Hall, Oxford, he taught abroad and in Britain from 1954 to 1960, when he became a full-time writer. He is married, and lives on the Sussex coast. He has written, compiled or edited over twenty-five books, among them his distinguished collections of poetry, *Tea With Miss Stockport* (1963) and *Reminiscences of Norma* (1971); the subject of much controversy, these have led to his being hailed by C. H. Sisson and others as the best English poet to emerge since the war. His innovatory old-spelling edition of *Shakespeare's Sonnets* (1963) was acclaimed by such scholars as John Dover Wilson, Robert Graves and William Empson. *Poets Through Their Letters* (1969), also highly praised, elicited from Anthony Burgess a comparison of the author to Dr Johnson. The writer's other publications include an annotated edition of Ben Jonson's *Every Man in his Humour* (1966), the anthology *Longer Elizabethan Poems* and *Sex and Society*. His wittily irreverent *The Bluffer's Guide to Literature* (1966, rev. 1972) was a best-seller. An illustrated edition of *Who's Who in Twentieth Century Literature* is at the press.

In 1971–2 he was Visiting Professor of English at Wisconsin University. At present fiction and poetry reviewer for the *Financial Times*, he is currently engaged on several projects, including *Fifty Great European Novels*, and a critical biography of Percy Wyndham Lewis.

Seymour-Smith's growing reputation is based on his erudition, his humour and his stimulatingly different approach to literary criticism. As the critics' evaluations quoted on the first page of this book suggest, both students and the general reader will find this attitude as refreshing as it is illuminating.

BY THE SAME AUTHOR

Poetry:
Poems (with Rex Taylor, Terence
    Hards), 1952
All Devils Fading, 1954
Tea With Miss Stockport, 1963
Reminiscences of Norma, 1971

Satire:
The Bluffer's Guide to Literature
    (1966), 1972

With James Reeves:
A New Canon of English Poetry, 1967
Selected Poems of Andrew Marvell, 1969
Inside Poetry, 1970
Selected Poems of Walt Whitman, 1975

Criticism:
Robert Graves (1956), 1971
Poets Through Their Letters, I: Wyatt
    to Coleridge, 1969
Fallen Women, 1969
Sex and Society, 1975

Editions:
Shakespeare's Sonnets (1963), 1966
Ben Jonson's *Every Man in his
    Humour*, 1966
Longer Elizabethan Poems, 1972

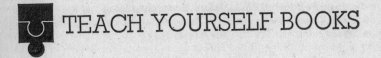 TEACH YOURSELF BOOKS

GUIDE TO MODERN WORLD LITERATURE
Volume 2

Martin Seymour-Smith

'Real literature can be created only by madmen, hermits, heretics, dreamers, rebels, and sceptics, not by diligent and trustworthy functionaries.'

Evgeny Zamyatin

TEACH YOURSELF BOOKS
HODDER & STOUGHTON
ST PAUL'S HOUSE   WARWICK LANE   LONDON EC4P 4AH

First published in one volume by Wolfe Publishing Ltd 1973
Teach Yourself Books, Hodder & Stoughton, corrected and revised edition in
four volumes 1975

ISBN 0 340 19505 3

Printed and bound in Great Britain
for Teach Yourself Books, Hodder & Stoughton,
by Hazell Watson & Viney Ltd, Aylesbury, Bucks

To the Memory of My Father
and
To My Mother

When Scaliger, whole years of labour past,
Beheld his Lexicon complete at last,
And weary of his task, with wond'ring eyes,
Saw from words pil'd on words a fabric rise,
He curs'd the industry, inertly strong,
In creeping toil that could persist so long,
And if, enrag'd he cried, heav'n meant to shed
Its keenest vengeance on the guilty head,
The drudgery of words the damn'd would know,
Doom'd to write lexicons in endless woe.

(From Dr. Johnson's Latin poem 'Know Yourself', written after revising and enlarging his lexicon, or dictionary; translated into English by Arthur Murphy, in his *Life*, 1772.)

Contents

	page
Preface to the Second Edition	ix
Introduction	xi
Abbreviations	xxiii
Dutch Literature	1
Finnish Literature	19
French and Belgian Literature	29
German Literature	189
Scandinavian Literature	363
Select Bibliography	419
Index	425

Preface to the Second Edition

This second edition, in four paperback volumes, contains revisions, corrections and some additions. The introduction, the abbreviated references, and the bibliography, are printed in their entirety in each volume. When the abbreviation q.v. refers to an author, concept or literary movement that is discussed in another volume it is followed by the number of that volume; otherwise it appears alone. Each of the volumes has been given a new and separate index.

For criticism of and corrections to this edition I am indebted to the following: Ronald Bottrall (most especially), Geoffrey Grigson, Miron Grindea, Peter Jay, Dr. S. Jacobson, Professor A. H. Johns, Anthony Rudolf, Jorge Silva, Istvan Siklos (especially), C. H. Sisson (again), I. D. Waldie, Graeme Wilson (especially).

As in the case of the first edition, some of these names appear in the text of the book: in no instance were any of the persons involved aware of any changes or additions that I may have made in my discussions of their own work. None, of course, sought to influence my views in any way. All errors remain my sole responsibility.

I must also gratefully thank the printers of this re-set edition for their skill and forbearance.

Since the publication of the first edition I have received many helpful letters from all parts of the world. I invite more, not the least because they help to improve a work of reference that by its very nature cannot be perfect—but which, so far as my own imperfections allow, can be improved with each successive edition. Would those who wish to write to me please do so in care of the present publishers, Teach Yourself Books.

Bexhill-on-Sea,   25 November 1974
Sussex.

Introduction

I

The scope of this book extends to writers, of all nationalities, who survived 31 December 1899. In certain instances (e.g. Hopkins, Mallarmé) I have had, for obvious reasons, to discuss writers who died before that; but I have strictly limited these. I have given an account of the major literary movements of the past century and a half; the names of these will be found in the respective indexes. The system of putting 'q.v.' after names of literary movements, authors, and titles of books, is intended to be a practical aid to the reader: if he turns to the indicated index he will find the main entry he requires in **bold** type. If no number follows 'q.v.' he will find the entry in the volume he is reading. This should make cross-reference quick and simple. Such philosophers and concepts and so on (e.g. Bergson, *Künstlerschuld*) as are not dealt with at length in the body of the text are discussed or explained in this introduction, which appears at the beginning of each volume.

Complete accuracy in a comprehensive work such as this is, alas, impossible: errors of dating are repeated from reference-book to reference-book; it is frequently impossible to check the dates of first publication of books without seeing the original editions. . . . I have made every effort to give correct information (e.g. my dates of birth for Tennessee Williams and E. Lasker-Schüler differ from most authorities, but are right). I shall be glad to correct any errors, with acknowledgements, in future editions—as I have done in this second revised edition.

The dates given for dramatic works are of publication, not first production.

Dates after individual books are of earliest publication, wherever or in whatever form this took place.

The list of abbreviations consists mainly of books in which translations into English of works by writers (other than English-language) discussed in the text are conveniently available. It cannot pretend to completeness, since more and more such collections are being published each year; all libraries and bookshops in large cities stock them. Not all books listed are currently in print.

Unsigned translations are by me.

The emphasis, since in the interests of space I have had to place emphases, is on the more universal areas of interest and language-knowledge (English, German, French, Spanish, Russian, Italian); and on the earlier rather than the later part of the period, which may less surely be assessed. But I have discussed some authors I believe to be neglected or misunderstood or underrated (e.g. George Moore, Céline, Ford) at length; and one great literature that is neglected, at least in Great Britain, the Japanese, has received a fuller treatment.

II

All Western literature has developed, with some national exceptions and variations, to a consistent pattern. In the succeeding brief sketch I have kept definitions as broad as possible: our understanding of literature does not benefit from attempts to narrow down the meanings of terms too precisely: the terms themselves lose their value.

By the mid-century *realism*, particularly in the novel, was well established. Realism in its broadest sense is an essential aim of any work of literature: it simply means verisimilitude to actuality—and points to the aspects of life the author selects as meaningful. But this leaves entirely open the question of how actuality is regarded—as an outward or an inward phenomenon, or both, or whatever. Nineteenth-century realism, the method out of which modern literature developed, does, even though it remains one of the broader literary concepts, have a less vague connotation.

First, realism is essentially a part of romanticism—however much it may sometimes look like a reaction against it, and however certainly the romantic movement may have seemed, in the positivist Fifties, to have collapsed. We are still living in a romantic period—nor, indeed, will there ever be any return to the limitations and artificialities of classicism.

Realism has no significant relationship to the literary classicism of antiquity or to the neo-classicism of the eighteenth century. It originates in the age-old tendency towards accuracy of representation (usually manifesting itself as an anti- or non-classical depiction of plebeian life—Cervantes, Jonson, Shakespeare, Smollett—or as regionalism), and in philosophical empiricism and all proto-pragmatic and proto-utilitarian inclinations. Nineteenth-century realism, at various times and in various writers, exhibited the following characteristics: objectivity (in the sense of concentration on facts rather than on interpretations of them); lucidity (rather than style or rhetoric); 'ordinary', quotidian experience; a search for an immediate, verifiable, truth, even if this be no more than relativistic; secularism; emphasis on the psychological motivations of the characters, often at the expense of 'plot'. In general the good realist authors (for example, George Eliot, Howells, Henry James) had good, or even idealistic, intentions towards their audience; but they refused to uplift their hearts, thus raising false hopes. A few realists (to some extent Flaubert; certainly Maupassant) had more aggressive intentions towards the bourgeois. But the milieu chosen was emphatically middle-class.

In many countries(but most notably in France) realism turned into *naturalism*. This term is frequently used, particularly by journalists and reviewers of plays (but also by critics who should know better) as a synonym for realism. This is seriously misleading. Naturalism is a more precise term than realism: a narrowing-down of it. (Zola's program—described in the account of him—is entirely naturalist; his practice is not.) Naturalist fiction is guided, or thinks it is guided, by the principles of scientific determinism. This arose largely from 'Darwinism', a movement or climate of thought that has less connection with Charles Darwin, from whom it derives its name, than might seem apparent. Darwin had in fact given a new and viable interpretation of the theory of transformism; according to 'Darwinism' he invented and 'proved' it. Actually it went back, as a theory, to at least 550 B.C. The naturalists extracted from Darwinism the notion of man-as-animal, of his life as a bloody struggle (they could have found this more definitely and confidently stated in Hobbes' *Leviathan*, as distinct from hypothetically in Darwin; but Darwin seemed *scientifically* respectable)—'the strongest, the swiftest and the cunningest live to fight another day', said T. H. Huxley. This persistent fallacy has been given the name of 'Social Darwinism'. The lives of the poor, to the depiction of which the naturalists turned, gave ample justification for such a view. However, in practice the best naturalists (e.g. Zola, Dreiser) have transcended their deterministic programs. Zola is as romantic as he is naturalistic, and Dreiser is massively puzzled as well as sentimental: both are naturalists, it is true; but both gain their ultimate effects from their power of psychological penetration.

The so-called *neo-romanticism*, and then *decadence*, that manifested itself in nearly all the Western literatures between about 1885 and 1905 was not as remote from either realism or naturalism as may have seemed apparent at the time.

All great literary movements eventually deteriorate: into preciosity,

over-aestheticism, over-self-consciousness, trivial scholarship, cultivation of debility and whatever society may at the time determine as
perverse behaviour. . . . The decadent movement (it is more of a
tendency) at the end of the nineteenth century is sometimes called
fin de siècle, a term I have occasionally employed. It is as much a
development, or etiolation, of *Parnassianism* and *Symbolism* (both these
terms are discussed in the section on French literature) as a reaction
against positivism and naturalism. Symbolism had contained the
religious or 'Platonic' impulses inherent in human beings, never
completely submergeable, during the realist-naturalist period. The
decadent writers—they range from the only partly decadent, like
Verlaine, to the wholly decadent, like Dowson—were nearly all
'religious' (if only in the sense that they embraced 'Satanism' or
aspects of it and died incense-sniffing Catholics); but they viewed
civilization as a decay rather than growth: they worshipped entropy,
degeneration, disorder; they transformed the romantic cult of the
individual into the romantic-decadent cult of the self (narcissism)—
hence their interest in or cultivation of homosexuality. They made a
cult of the erotic and hurled themselves into hopeless loves. They
worshipped the urban and the ugliness it offered—but in a deliberately perverse spirit. They romanticized the then dominant principle
of the Second Law of Thermodynamics, seeing it as operative in the
evolutionary sphere.

The foregoing are the chief characteristics of decadence in general;
no single writer manifests all of them—except, possibly, some entirely
trivial one. In its least extreme form this neo-romantic spirit began to
pervade the works of realists and naturalists—for example, Zola's
novels are increasingly full of deliberate symbolization.

In the course of literary history movements (or tendencies) provoke
reactions to themselves; but these reactions absorb the essences, the
genuine discoveries, of the movements that have engendered them.
To give an over-simple illustration: romanticism at is best contains
the essence of classicism. The best neo-romantic writers had learned
the important lessons of realism. And it was essentially from neo-
romanticism that modernism arose.

Expressionism, which I have fully described in the section on German
literature, was a specifically German movement. However, literary
modernism can most usefully be described as expressionism: every
modern movement after Symbolism (which was in any case nineteenth-
century in origin) may conveniently be described as a form of
expressionism.

Modernism, which often arouses great hostility, has a number of
characteristics (the writer who combines every one of them in his

work is likely to be a charlatan). Realism remains committed—more or less subtly—to a *mimetic* theory: literature is an imitation, a photograph, of life. Modernism (in the sense used in this book) is fundamentally non- or anti-mimetic. In its extremest form, modernism may resolutely omit what is 'essential' in societal, communal or simply representational terms. On the other hand, it will stress precisely what is 'unessential' in such terms. This amounts to an emphasis on inner life, and therefore on the life of the individual. Causality, carefully observed in the nineteenth century, may be deliberately deleted. This does not mean, of course, that it is rejected. It means that it is not an essential part of what the modernist writer is trying to say.

An even more important aspect of modernist writing—and one which puzzles many of its readers, for whom 'time' remains, consciously, a means of manipulating reality into acceptable forms—is its jettisoning of conventional chronology. I have explained this at some length in my treatment of the French *nouveau roman* (q.v.).

It is here that the French philosopher, Henri Bergson, is relevant. Bergson did not 'discover' either unconventional time or *stream-of-consciousness*; but his philosophy reflected much contemporary thinking. Bergson is part of the neo-romantic reaction against positivism; he also complements the phenomenology of the German philosopher Husserl (discussed with the French *nouveau roman*) inasmuch as he concentrates upon the concrete rather than the abstract (Husserl was not himself at all interested in this problem; but the effect of his work has been to draw attention to perceptual actualities). It is appropriate that Bergson, although not an imaginative writer, should have received the Nobel Prize for Literature (1928): his influence on literature has been wide and deep. He demanded a return to the 'immediate data of consciousness', and he believed that this could be grasped by means of what he called 'intuition'. Like a number of modern novelists he saw character not as 'personality' but as a process of ceaseless becoming.

The actual term *stream-of-consciousness* originated with Henry James' brother William James; stream-of-consciousness fiction tends to lay emphasis on pre-verbal types of experience; by implication, therefore, this type of fiction regards internal experience as more 'important' than external. (However, stream-of-consciousness can be used simply as an extension of realist technique: the fact that mental minutiae are recorded is not in itself guarantee of a phenomenological approach.) Bergson's attitude was similar: for him consciousness was *duration* (*la durée*); intellect conceptualizes this flow into something static; intuition *thinks in duration*. Sartre has summarized Bergson's position well: 'on going into the past an event does not cease to be; it merely ceases to act and remains "in its place" at its date for eternity. In this way being has been restored to the past, and it is very well done; we even affirm that duration is a multiplicity of interpenetration and that the past is continually organized with the present'.

Bergson is important above all for his anti-intellectuality and his continual suggestion of new ways of seeing ourselves in the world. 'There is one reality, at least', he wrote, 'which we all seize from within, by intuition and not by simple analysis. It is our own personality in its flowing through time—our self which endures'. The relevance of this to the work of Proust (q.v.) is immediately clear.

III

I have referred throughout to a number of concepts, and used certain terms, which require initial definition.

I have categorized some writers as *naïve* and others as *sentimentive*. In 1795 Goethe's friend and contemporary, the German poet, dramatist and critic Friedrich Schiller published his essay *On Naïve and Sentimentive Poetry* (*Über naive und sentimentalische Dichtung*)—I have followed the sensible practice of translating 'sentimentalische' as 'sentimentive'; 'naïve' is misleading, too, but 'simple' does not help; 'sentimentive' is less hopelessly misleading, if only because less familiar, than 'sentimental'. This great essay has not had, in the English-speaking world, the recognition that it deserves. However, the questions of Schiller's exact intentions and of its significance in its time are not relevant here. What I have done is to borrow Schiller's terms and to simplify them for the purposes of this book. For, even in my modified and restricted usage, they convey indispensable information that is not contained in the more familiar romantic-classical opposition.

For Schiller the naïve poet is one who is in perfect harmony with nature—with, indeed, the universe; his personality cannot be found in his poetry. He may even seem 'repulsive', 'callous', 'invisible'. The sentimentive poet, on the other hand, has lost his contact with and even his faith in nature, for which he yearns. Naïve poetry (Schiller says) is characteristic of the ancients: an immediate, inspired, detailed representation of the sensuous surface of life. In sentimentive poetry the author is everywhere present; he is self-conscious. The object does 'not possess him utterly'.

On Naïve and Sentimentive Poetry was originally prompted by the example of Goethe, whom Schiller saw, as he saw Shakespeare, as a serene and naïve poet born out of his time. It was Goethe, too, who made the most profound comment on the essay: '. . . he plagued himself with the design of perfectly separating sentimentive from naïve poetry. . . . As if . . . sentimentive poetry could exist at all without the naïve ground in which . . . it has its root'.

Schiller was contrasting the objective (naïve) poetry written in the early (progressive) stages of a culture, and the subjective (self-conscious, sentimentive) poetry written in its decline. Goethe, again, summed the matter up: 'All eras in a state of decline and dissolution are subjective . . . all progressive eras have an objective tendency'. Thus, in the poetry of Shakespeare there is a centrifugal tendency (called 'healthy' by Goethe), an inwards-outwards movement; in most of the poetry of Schiller's contemporaries, and more of that of our century, there is a centripetal tendency, an outwards-inwards movement.

Now Schiller wished to justify his own kind of (sentimentive) poetry in the light of what he felt to be Goethe's naïve poetry. As I have remarked, his precise concerns and (in particular) his program need not—in this context—be ours.

Here I mean by the naïve writer the writer whose inspiration is above all drawn from his unsophisticated, uncomplicated, *direct* view of the universe. His view is uncluttered by intellectualization. The naïve writers of the nineteenth and twentieth centuries have been poor thinkers—this is a point of which I have made a good deal. Hardy, Dreiser and Sherwood Anderson (for example) were all writers of great power—but poor thinkers. (True, Anderson was something of a sage: but sages are not thinkers.) The naïve writer does not proceed by thought. The phenomenon can still only be explained by recourse to Schiller's distinction. And even where a writer—Pablo Neruda, pioneer explorer of the unconscious, comes immediately to mind—neither wants or tries to 'think', Schiller's essay immediately enriches our understanding.

I mean by the sentimentive writer—but always bearing in mind Goethe's stipulation that no work that has not roots in the naïve has any creative status—the writer who is sophisticated, trained in thinking, self-conscious. Thomas Mann is perhaps the prime example in the twentieth century.

Of course there is no such thing as a purely naïve writer—any more than there can be a purely sentimentive writer. But this applies to the romantic-classical opposition as well. Schiller's distinction is essential; and very important for our time. It reveals not only how the naïve writer can wreck and corrupt his work and himself by betraying his impulses, but also how sentimentive writing is becoming increasingly sterile as it draws cunningly away from the naïve; it reveals, too, the terrible predicament of the sophisticated creative writer in this second half of our century. It is towards the truly mysterious—and yet authentic—that the creative writer must now aim. This is why much of the newest poetry and fiction is coming from Latin America: an exotic and largely unexplored region of the world that well matches our own even more exotic, even less explored regions. Recourse to the purely surreal can lead to nothing better than the raw material of the dream—which, as it comes into consciousness, is censored, screened. What is needed—we have had it in Rilke, Vallejo and some others—is the *real dream*: the meaning of the dream in terms of *its own original, unknown, mysterious, day-haunting images*—not in those of (say) a psycho-analytical interpretation. This truth contains, absorbs and accepts death.

The problem is one of control as well as of inspiration: what kind of control must the writer exercise over his immediate impulses to return to his naïve realm? Here the animal cunning of sentimentive writers such as Vallejo or Rilke can be useful. One thinks in this connection of the cunning art of the 'primitive' man who hunts, for food, animals he loves: this is nearer to the required sentimentive than is the cleverness of the regular academic critic—for all the ancient wisdom that is locked up—one might say fossilized—inside the notions with which he plays.

*

Another concept that I have used freely is what I have christened *Künstlerschuld*: 'artist-guilt'. Increasingly in this century poets and writers (Rilke, Mann and Broch are examples) have been beset by fear that literature fulfils no useful, but only a selfish function. The writers who feel this particular kind of anguish have been or are almost invariably dedicated to literature to the exclusion of everything else (Broch is an exception). The question is, of course, as old as Plato (this was how Aristotle and others understood Plato); but for some writers of the past hundred or so years it has become crucial. Broch tried not to be a writer. At one point Rilke wanted to be a country doctor. Laura Riding has repudiated poetry. Mann portrayed the writer as a sick Faustus. . . .

This is of course a relevant theme in an age of 'committed literature' and *socialist realism* (this is discussed fully in the section devoted to Russian literature; it must, of course, be distinguished from mere *social realism*, which means no more than it implies). The naïve writer has no doubts: Neruda, the most substantial modern naïve poet, had no difficulty in reconciling his poetry with what he called his communism. But the more sentimentive the writer the more wracked he is by doubts. . . .

*

I have very often spoken of *midcult* and *middlebrow*. This is a dangerous but essential concept in an age that is desperate to reject the wildness of the imagination by absorbing it (hence literary prizes, government-sponsored culture-feasts, and so on). One of the chief features of the truly middlebrow literature is that, however 'tragic' or 'modern' it may seem, it consists of material manipulated to satisfy the *conscious* desires of a pseudo-cultured (some would simply say cultured) audience: an audience that still thinks of the world-as-it-is as essentially the best; an audience of individuals who, in varying degrees, reject their endogenous suffering ('decent', externally prompted grief is allowed: in midcult novels relatives die young, girls get raped or crippled, babies are murdered by 'beasts' and/or so on, and it is 'very sad'): that suffering they experience as a result of their failure to attain authenticity. Middlebrow literature is, in Sartre's existentialist sense, *slimy, viscous*: it helps us to remain *filthy swine* (*salauds*). Some middlebrow literature is apparently *avant garde*; at its worst it may not even be intended for reading, but simply for display (hence the phrase 'coffee-table book'). The great midcult successes are seldom, probably never, planned. They arise from the innate vulgarity and ignorance or (usually) pretentiousness of their progenitors.

Of course few works are entirely middlebrow; equally, some works are merely tainted with middlebrowism in one or another aspect. Some of the characteristics of the kind of midcult literature with which I have been concerned here (where this has not been taken seriously by critics regarded as serious I have happily ignored it), though they never co-exist all together, are: 'uncanniness', 'weirdness', 'occultness'; 'profundity' in the sense that dictionaries of 'great ideas that have changed the world' are profound; fashionableness—whether in the matter of being sexy or using 'dirty' language or whatever; slickness of technique; pseudo-complexity, conferring upon the reader the sense that he is reading a 'difficult' (and therefore 'worthwhile', 'deep') book; potential for discussion at lounge-, drawing-room-, or pub-level (or in the foyers of theatres); liability to excite certain reviewers.

*

The useful term *objective correlative* was first used by the American painter Washington Allston in 1850; T. S. Eliot revived it in 1919. It has been much criticized as putting either too much or too little emphasis on the objectivity of works of literature. . . . I am not concerned with this: here I mean by it simply: *objective equation for personal emotion*. If the writer, in expressing a personal emotion about having killed his wife, composes a work about a toad eating dry, red eggs, then that situation is the *objective correlative* for his emotion at killing his wife. I imply absolutely nothing more by my use of the term: it is purely descriptive.

*

For a truly viable (non-commercial) theatre to exist there has to be a truly viable audience. This certainly exists—or existed until a few years ago—in Belgium. The theatre of today is largely in the hands of the directors (hence the term, used pejoratively by me, *director's theatre*), who do not work in true conjunction with the authors of plays, but rather as more or less commercial *entrepreneurs*, 'realists' who manipulate such dramatic texts as they decide to exploit to meet the needs of their (alas, mostly middlebrow) audiences. The genuine dramatist has to survive this and to assert himself. All he has on his side is the spirit of the genuine theatre—but this, fortunately, survives along with (and often in the purveyors of) the commercial theatre. There are two tests of a genuine dramatist: his work must be playable on the stage, in some form, at any time during or after his lifetime; and it must stand the test of reading as well as viewing. Perhaps there are a score of twentieth-century dramatists who will fulfil these requirements. I have discussed these and a number of other interesting ones. But it must be remembered that this is a guide to literature and not to the entertainment industry or the history of intelligently motivated socio-anthropological phenomena.

IV

Finally, many people have helped me in many ways with the writing of this book. None is of course in any way whatever responsible for any of the opinions expressed in it, or for any errors. The following have given me aid, of kinds too various to mention, that I found invaluable: of my colleagues on the English Faculty at the University of Wisconsin-Parkside, where I am currently spending a happy and instructive year as Visiting Professor: James and Angelica Dean, Andrew Maclean, James Mehoke; my family, which has worked harder than I have—

and suffered much: my wife, my daughters Miranda Britt and Charlotte Seymour-Smith, my son-in-law Colin Britt (in particular), who made things memorably cheerful at a time when they were difficult; Ivar Ivask, for generously overlooking some of the material —and correcting me on a number of points; Toby Zucker, for help with the German section; S. K. Pearce, my bank manager, without whose practical understanding and help I could not have proceeded; and B. H. Bal, George Barker, Robert Bly, Edward Charlesworth, Sally Chilver, Tony Gottlieb, Robert Graves, Fujio Hashima, Wing-Commander Vernon 'Coils' Pocock, James Reeves, C. H. Sisson, Hilary Spurling, Anthony Thwaite, David Wright. I should also like to thank the printers, who have performed a difficult task (and not the first one composed by me) with exemplary intelligence and fortitude. My greatest debt is expressed in my dedication; the greatest sorrow of my life in its first part. Libraries have as always been helpful and courteous beyond the line of duty: The London Library; the East Sussex County Library, both at Bexhill-on-Sea and at Lewes (this is in process of being destroyed by faceless bureaucrats as I prepare this revision for the press); and the Library at the University of Wisconsin-Parkside.

The University of Wisconsin-Parkside,   18 April 1972
Kenosha, Wisconsin, U.S.A.

Abbreviations

AD: *Absurd Drama*, P. Meyer, 1965
ad.: adapted
add.: with additional matter
AL: *Albanian Literature*, S. E. Mann, 1955
AMEP: *Anthology of Modern Estonian Poetry*, W. K. Matthews, 1955
AMHP: *Anthology of Modern Hebrew Poetry*, A. Birman, 1968
AMYP: *Anthology of Modern Yugoslav Poetry*, J. Lavrin, 1963
ANZP: *Anthologyy of New Zealand Poetry*, V. O'Sullivan, 1970
AP: *Africa in Prose*, O. R. Dathorne and W. Feuser, 1969
ARL: *Anthology of Russian Literature in the Soviet Period*, B. G. Guerney, 1960
ASP: Apollinaire: *Selected Poems*, O. Bernard, 1965
AU: *Agenda*, Vol. 8, No. 2, Ungaretti Special Issue, Spring 1970
AW: *Australian Writing Today*, C. Higham, 1968
AWT: *African Writing Today*, E. Mphahlele, 1967
BAP: Bella Akmadulina: *Fever and Other Poems*, G. Dutton and I. Mezhakov-Koriakin, 1970
BAV: *Book of Australian Verse*, J. Wright, 1956
BEJD: Josef Brodsky: *Elegy for John Donne and Other Poems*, N. Bethell, 1967
BISS: *Penguin Book of Italian Short Stories*, G. Waldman, 1969
BP: Bert Brecht: *Plays*, 2 vols, J. Willett and E. Bentley, 1960–2
BRV: *Book of Russian Verse*, C. M. Bowra, 1943
BRV2: *Second Book of Russian Verse*, C. M. Bowra, 1948
BSP: André Breton: *Selected Poems*, K. White, 1969
CCD: *Chief Contemporary Dramatists*, 3 vols, T. H. Dickinson, 1915–30
CFP: *Contemporary French Poetry*, A. Aspel and D. Justice, 1965
CGP: *Contemporary German Poetry*, J. Bithell, 1909
CGPD: *Contemporary German Poetry*, B. Deutsch and A. Yarinolinsky, 1923
CIP: *Contemporary Italian Poetry*, C. L. Golino, 1962
CIV: *Contemporary Italian Verse*, G. Singh, 1968
CLP: *Century of Latvian Poetry*, W. K. Matthews, 1957
CP: Anton Chekhov, *Plays*, 1959

CRP: *Anthology of Contemporary Rumanian Poetry*, R. MacGregor-Hastie, 1969

CTP: Albert Camus: *Caligula and Three Other Plays*, S. Gilbert, 1958

CV: *Caribbean Verse*, O. R. Dathorne, 1967

CWT: *Canadian Writing Today*, M. Richler, 1970

DFP: Friedrich Dürrenmatt: *Four Plays*, G. Nellhaus et al, 1964

ed.: edited by

ESW: Paul Éluard: *Selected Writings*, L. Alexander, 1951

FBS: Marcel Raymond: *From Baudelaire to Surrealism*, 1950

FCP: *Five Centuries of Polish Poetry*, J. Peterkiewicz, Burns Singer and J. Stallworthy, 1970

FGP: *Four Greek Poets*, E. Keeley and P. Sherrard, 1966

FMR: *From the Modern Repertoire*, 3 vols, E. Bentley, 1949–56

FTP: Max Frisch: *Three Plays*, M. Bullock, 1962

FTS: Frank Wedekind: *Five Tragedies of Sex*, B. Fawcett and S. Spender, 1952

FWT: *French Writing Today*, S. W. Taylor, 1968

GED: *Anthology of German Expressionist Drama*, W. H. Sokel, 1963

GMS: *Plays of Gregorio Martínez Sierra*, H. Granville-Barker and J. G. Underhill, 1923

GSP: Michel de Ghelderode: *Seven Plays*, G. Hauger and G. Hopkins, 1960

GSS: *German Short Stories*, R. Newnham, 1964

GWT: *German Writing Today*, C. Middleton, 1967

HE: *Heart of Europe*, T. Mann and H. Kesten, 1943

HW: René Char: *Hypnos Waking*, J. Matthews, 1956

HWL: Joseph Reményi, *Hungarian Writers as Literature*, 1964

IMPL: *Introduction to Modern Polish Literature*, A. Gillon and L. Krzyzanowski, 1964

IMSL: *Introduction to Modern Spanish Literature*, K. Schwartz, 1968

IN: P. J. Jouve: *An Idiom of Night*, K. Bosley, 1968

IP4: Eugene Ionesco: *4 Plays*, D. Watson, 1958

IQ: *Italian Quartet*, R. Fulton, 1966

ISS: *Italian Short Stories*, R. Trevelyan, 1965

ISS2: *Italian Short Stories 2*, D. Vittorini, 1972

IWT: *Italian Writing Today*, R. Trevelyan, 1967

JDP: Max Jacob: *Drawings and Poems*, S. J. Collier, 1951

JLME: Y. Okazakix: *Japanese Literature in the Meija Era*, V. H. Vigliemo, 1955

LAP: *Anthology of Latin-American Poetry*, D. Fitts, 1942

LTT: Federico García Lorca: *Three Tragedies*, J. Graham-Luján and R. L. O'Connell, 1961

LWLF: *An Anthology of Byelorussian Poetry from 1928 until the Present Day*, 1971

LWT: *Latin-American Writing Today*, J. M. Cohen, 1967

MAP: *Modern African Prose*, R. Rive, 1964

MBL: *Introduction to Modern Bulgarian Literature*, N. Kirilov and F. Kirk, 1969

MBSP: V. Mayakovsky: *The Bedbug and Selected Poetry*, P. Blake, 1961

MEP: *Modern European Poetry*, W. Barnstone, 1966

MFC: *Four Modern French Comedies*, A. Bermel, 1960

MGL: *Introduction to Modern Greek Literature*, M. P. Gianos, 1969

MGP: *Modern German Poetry*, M. Hamburger and C. Middleton, 1962

MHP: *Mayakovsky and his Poetry*, H. Marshall, 1965

MJL: *Modern Japanese Literature*, D. Keene, 1956

MJS: *Modern Japanese Stories*, I. Morris, 1961

MPA: *Modern Poetry from Africa*, G. Moore and U. Beier, 1963

MRD: *Masterpieces of Russian Drama*, 1933

MRP: *Modern Russian Poetry*, V. Markov and M. Sparks, 1966

MSP: Oscar Venceslas de Lubicz Milosz: *14 Poems*, K. Rexroth, 1952

MST: *Modern Spanish Theatre*, M. Benedikt and G. E. Wellwarth, 1968

MSW: Henri Michaux: *Selected Writings*, R. Ellmann, 1968

MT: *Modern Theatre*, 6 vols, E. Bentley, 1955–60

NVSP: *Selected Poems of Neruda and Vallejo*, R. Bly, 1970

NWC: *New Writing in Czechoslovakia*, G. Theiner, 1969

NWP: *New Writing from the Philippines*, L. Caspar, 1966

NWSD: *The New Wave Spanish Drama*, G. E. Wellwarth, 1970

NWY: *New Writing in Yugoslavia*, B. Johnson, 1970

OBCV: *The Oxford Book of Canadian Verse*, A. J. M. Smith, 1960

PBAV: *Penguin Book of Australian Verse*, H. Heseltine, 1972

PBFV3, PBFV4: *Penguin Book of French Verse 3, 4*, A. Hartley, 1957, 1959

PBGV: *Penguin Book of Greek Verse*, C. Trypanis, 1971

PC: Anton Chekhov: *Plays*, E. Fen, 1959

PGV: *Penguin Book of German Verse*, L. Forster, 1957

PI: *Poem Itself*, S. Burnshaw, 1960

PIV: *Penguin Book of Italian Verse*, G. Kay, 1965

PJV: *Penguin Book of Japanese Verse*, G. Bownas and A. Thwaite, 1964

PKM: Kai Munk: *Five Plays*, R. P. Keigwin, 1953

PLAV: *Penguin Book of Latin-American Verse*, E. Caracciolo-Trejo, 1971

PLJ: *Poetry of Living Japan*, D. J. Enright and T. Ninomiya, 1957

PP: Alfred French: *The Poets of Prague*, 1969

PPC: *Selected Poems of Paul Celau*, Michael Hamburger, 1972

PPPP: *Post-War Polish Poetry*, C. Milosz, 1965

PRP: Robert Pinget: *Plays*, 2 vols, S. Beckett, B. Bray, 1965–7
PRV: *Penguin Book of Russian Verse*, D. Obolensky, 1965
ps.: pseudonym of
PSAV: *Penguin Book of South-African Verse*, J. Cope and U. Krige, 1968
PSV: *Penguin Book of Spanish Verse*, J. M. Cohen, 1956
pt.: part
PTP: Luigi Pirandello: *Three Plays*, A. Livingstone, 1923
PWT: *Polish Writing Today*, C. Wieniewska, 1967
rev.: revised
RP: *Russian Poetry 1917–55*, J. Lindsay, 1956
RSP: Pierre Reverdy: *Poems*, A. Greet, 1968
SAWT: *South-African Writing Today*, N. Gordimer and L. Abraham, 1967
SCO: *Swan, Cygnets and Owl*, M. E. Johnson, 1956
sel.: selected by
SL: *Soviet Literature, an Anthology*, G. Reavey and M. Slonim, 1933
SP: Bert Brecht: *Seven Plays*, E. Bentley, 1961
SSP: *Six Soviet Plays*, E. Lyons, 1934
SSW: Jules Supervielle: *Selected Writings*, 1967
TC: Anton Chekhov: *The Tales*, 13 vols, C. Garnett, 1916–22
TCG: *Penguin Book of Twentieth Century German Verse*, P. Bridgwater, 1963
TCGV: *Twentieth Century German Verse*, H. Salinger, 1952
TCSP: *20th Century Scandinavian Poetry*, M. S. Allwood, 1950
TGBP: *Two Great Belgian Plays about Love*, 1966
TMCP: *Three Modern Czech Poets*, E. Osers and G. Theiner, 1971
TMP: *Twenty-five Modern Plays*, S. F. Tucker, 1931
TNM: *Two Novels of Mexico*, L. B. Simpson, 1964
TT: *Tellers of Tales*, W. S. Maugham, 1939
tr.: translated by
UP: *Ukrainian Poets*, W. Kirkconnell and C. H. Andrusyshen, 1963
VA: Andrey Voznesensky: *Antiworlds*, P. Blake and M. Hayward, 1967
VCW: Paul Valéry: *Collected Works*, J. Matthews, 1962
VSW: Paul Valéry: *Selected Writings*, 1950
VTT: Paul Éluard: *Thorns of Thunder*, G. Reavey, S. Beckett, 1936
WNC: *Writers in the New Cuba*, J. M. Cohen, 1967
ZS: Nikolay Zambolotsky: *Scrolls*, D. Weissbert, 1970

Dutch Literature

I

The literature of the Netherlands differs from that of the Flemish Belgians, which is treated in a separate section—though under the general heading of 'Dutch'. For the two languages are very similar. Flemish was a Frankish dialect which after the sixteenth century fell into disuse and was revived by Belgian writers in the nineteenth century; these drew, however, on literary Dutch as well. The spelling of Flemish is more archaic than that of Dutch. Dutch is gaining ground amongst Flemish speakers, but the University of Ghent continues to be a centre of Flemish learning and literature. The two literatures are gradually coalescing; but important differences are still manifest.

In the Netherlands many people speak English, German and French; the Dutchman's literary education is considerably higher than that of his British counterpart. But he tends to have a somewhat low regard for his own literature. This may account for Dutch literature's relative lack of self-confidence. The feeling is unjustified: the Netherlands in this century have produced two, perhaps even four, major novelists, and two major poets; and a host of important minor talents.

II

The Dutch literary revival of 1880, in the hands of the Eightiers (*Tachtigers*) as they called themselves, paralleled similar movements in other European countries; but it was—and had to be—more drastic. The way had been prepared by the novelist Multatuli (the pseudonym, meaning 'I have suffered much', of Eduard Douwes Dekker, 1820–87). The Eightiers, whose magazine was called *The New Guide*, attacked the effete remanticism, then too solidly established, for its sentimentality, conventional religiosity and unctousness. They changed the Dutch literary language by their insistence upon precision and eschewal of cliché.

The chief poet of this group was WILLEM KLOOS (1859–1938),

whose cult of beauty and art for art's sake now seems dated, but whose influence on Dutch poetry was great because of his originality of diction, his evocative rhythms, and the consistency of his critical thinking, which is basically Shelleyan. For him the function of art is the creation of beauty, and his position in Dutch poetry may fairly be described as similar to Shelley's in England. (The Keats of the Netherlands is certainly Jacques Perk, Kloos's close friend, who died in 1881 at the age of twenty-one. Perk was a better poet than Kloos: his sonnet-sequence to a Belgian girl he met briefly is one of the best things in the Dutch literature of the nineteenth century, and is far less lucubrated than anything by Kloos.) Kloos's first book, *Poems* (1894), is famous for its sonnets, which are, in their literary way, extremely beautiful. Kloos gradually declined into an emotionally lifeless perpetrator of philosophically pretentious verse; but his cult of worship of the elevated self was a necessary reaction to the complacency that had characterized Dutch literature before the Eighties. He is a vital figure in Dutch literature.

ALBERT VERWEY (1865–1937), like Kloos, was one of the early editors of *The New Guide*, but he severed his connection with Kloos in 1889, becoming critical of his worship of the irrational and his views about the non-political nature of literature. He was a friend (not a disciple) of George's (q.v.), and his manner is often reminiscent of the German poet's. He ended by seeing the function of poetry as a social binding of all peoples and times. Verwey was a skilful but largely artificial poet, at his best when he felt that his 'eternal self' was 'doomed to solitude'—a view against which he later reacted. Verwey underwent many changes of mind, and gives the impression of continually forming groups only to break away from them. But his progress was intelligent, and he, too, was an essential figure.

Dutch late nineteenth-century prose was directly influenced by Zola's naturalism (q.v.); but it also drew upon its own great pictorial tradition. There was a tendency to try to turn writing into a kind of painting, in which everything was to be described with minute and photographic accuracy. One is inevitably reminded of Holz (q.v.) and his search for an art that would exactly reproduce life. This is realism at its utmost limits; it sometimes even appears modernist because its syntax is stripped down until it resembles a diagram. LODEWIJK VAN DEYSSEL (ps. K. J. L. A. THIJM, 1864–1952), a friend of Kloos's and a fellow 'Eightier', began with an admiration of Zola, although his aestheticism led him to condemn Zola's moralism. His two early novels, *The Little Republic* (1888) and *A Love Story* (1887), are not really so much naturalist as defiantly realistic; they included some descriptions of sexual scenes which caused a twitter then, but which nowadays seem innocuous. His impressionistic prose poetry, attempts at making pictures with words (they are collected in *Apocalypse*, 1893), are failures. Until about this date he could profitably be compared to Holz (q.v.) in his tendencies; but soon afterwards he drifted into a whimsical mysticism on the pattern of Maeterlinck (q.v.). He was influential in Dutch literature, but left no really successful book except for his biographies.

The Dutch novel of this period seldom transcends national boundaries: the photographic accuracy of its portrayal of bourgeois society lacks psychological penetration, and the prose is clumsy. These novels are to literature precisely what sober, competent and unexperimental photography is to painting. 'Naturalist' should only really be used of this kind of fiction in its (in literature) misleading sense of 'like nature'.

There are exceptions amongst this generation of realists: the main one, LOUIS COUPERUS (1863–1923), is the only Dutch writer of this century to achieve a truly international reputation. He was a cosmopolitan character, of Javanese blood, who lived in Italy until the beginning of the First World War; he said of himself that although he loved the Netherlands he felt more Italian than Dutch. He began as a realist-naturalist under the influence of Flaubert, Zola and, to some extent, Tolstoi; but Zola did little more than provide him with a method. In *Footsteps of Fate* (1890; tr. 1890) the characters are the victims of inexorable fate in a manner typical of naturalism, but even here there is a hint that character is not destiny. For Couperus had an oriental bent in his make-up that led him to view man as unnecessarily concerned with his fate: he who resigns himself may find peace. The tetralogy *Small Souls* (1901–4; tr. 1914–18) gives a picture of Dutch family life on the scale of Galsworthy's *Forsyte Saga* (q.v. 1), but is infinitely more subtle and sensitive than that overrated work. Here Couperus compassionately traces the progress of a mentality from pettiness to desire, through suffering, for wisdom—and incidentally gives an incomparable picture of Dutch middle-class life. *Old People and the Things that Pass* (1908; tr. 1918; 1963), the story of the effect on two very old people and their ageing children of a murder committed sixty years back, in the colonies, shows him at his best. Although its impressionistic prose is sometimes unnecessarily hard to read it is masterly in its presentation of a present haunted by memories of the past. Couperus is a fascinating writer who only needs comprehensive republication in the English-speaking world to draw attention to his genius. Nearly all his work was translated into English. J. VAN OUDSHOORN (ps. J. K. FELYBRIEF, 1876–1951) is much more neglected. He is a mysterious, rewarding writer, whose *Alienation* (1914; tr. 1965), about a man who feels himself to have been ruined through masturbation, is a pioneer masterpiece. FRANS COENEN (1866–1936) was naturalistically inclined; his posthumous *The House on the Canal* (1937; tr. 1965) is, however, a tense psychological study.

P. C. BOUTENS (1870–1943), the best translator of his generation, was a poet similarly aloof from the Eightiers. He gradually withdrew into himself, but unlike Kloos he understood the nature of his intro-spection: rather than indulging in an egocentric programme he tempered his romanticism with thought. He was a natural symbolist, in that his poetry, essentially, seeks out a world beyond that of the senses. He was a classical scholar who achieved a mastery of form; but his poetry suffers from his lack of understanding of the sensual world, which seems to exert little pull on him. He was as good as an academic poet, trapped in thoughts of beauty but never ensnared in desire, can be—but no better.

The poet and novelist FREDERIK VAN EEDEN (1860–1932), a psy-chiatrist, was a co-founder of *The New Guide*, but soon reacted to Kloos's dedication to art for its own sake. More interestingly than Kloos or, indeed, Boutens, he oscillated between social conscience and individual realization, discovering—in so doing—a language of his own. But this tension between opposites, evident in his novel *The Deeps of Deliverance* (1900; tr. 1902) and in his poems of the late Nineties, did not last. To combat the anti-social villain in him, which produced his best work, he founded a semi-communist community, which (because of his admiration for Thoreau) he called Walden; this collapsed, as all such communities do, and eventually (1922) he fell into Roman Catholicism. *The Deeps of Deliverance*, a study of a young girl's development, is in bourgeois terms 'morbid', although it struggles out of such morasses into a false pleasantness before it finishes. Its best passages emphasize the difficulties of reconciling female sexuality with a male world, and are full of the kind of in-sight one might expect from a psychiatrist; when it rationalizes these into 'joy' it becomes programmatic and is as unconvincing as it is dated and boring. He wrote with humour and understanding of the failure of his Tolstoian community in *The Promised Land* (1909). He also wrote some of the best plays of his time, of which the most outstanding is *The Brothers' Feud* (1894).

The most important playwright of this generation, however, was HERMAN HEIJERMANS (1864–1924). Influenced in his technique mainly by Ibsen, he was a socialist who depicted, in a naturalist manner, the miseries of the poor. His most famous play, about oppressed North Sea fishermen, was *The Good Hope* (1900; tr. 1928), which was played all over the world. At the very end of his life he wrote a poignant novel, *The Little Dreaming King* (1924), about a boy's growing up in a slum. He was a Jew, and his comic sketches about Jewish life in Dutch cities, published under the name of Samuel Falkland, are unique in the language for their raciness and insight.

The writer who eventually most decisively broke with photographic realism was ARTHUR VAN SCHENDEL (1874–1946), who was born in Java. Van Schendel wrote of events in the external world, but described them through the eyes of a dreamer. He spent some years teaching in England and then in Holland before devoting himself entirely to writing. Curiously enough, although he was the first major novelist to break completely with the naturalist manner, one of the chief themes of all his fiction is man's impotence against his destiny. His first stories and novels, set in medieval times, were Pre-Raphaelite in mood. And yet the germ of his future work is contained in his first story, *Drogon* (1896): a dreamy, eccentric young man is 'fated' to seduce his brother's wife. *A Wanderer in Love* (1904) and *A Wanderer Lost* (1907) tell of a monk and his struggles against sexual desire. These have an irresistibly lush quality, somewhat reminiscent of Rossetti; but they are self-indulgent, and the pseudo-medieval background palls. Van Schendel continued in this vein, more or less unprofitably, until 1921, when he went to live in Italy. His Italian stories show signs of change. The period of his maturity begins in 1930, with *The 'Johanna Maria'* (tr. 1935), the biography (set in the nineteenth century) of a sailing vessel. This is written in the impassive style for which Van Schendel became famous: there is no dialogue, and the events described have an oneiric quality. There followed novels of high quality, in which Van Schendel more seriously explores his fatalistic theme: *The Waterman* (1933; tr. 1963), *The House in Haarlem* (1936; tr. 1940), *Grey Birds* (1937; tr. 1939). *Oberon and Madame* (1940) and other books of this period are actually gay in their romanticism. The posthumous *The Old House* (1946) is perhaps Van Schendel's finest work of all. Van Schendel was at his best when imposing a fierce restraint on his innate romanticism: when, as in *The Waterman*, he is showing how destiny—in the form of unobtrusive but stifling social pressure—overrides such romanticism. It was in *The Old House* that he brought this to near perfection. He is a difficult writer—as difficult to come to terms with as such Japanese as Toson and Soseki (qq.v. 4)—but an original and compelling one.

Poetry immediately before the First World War was represented mainly by Gorter, Holst and Leopold, as well as by Verwey. HERMAN GORTER (1864–1927) was a member of the Eighties movement, and up until *The School of Poetry* (1897) he indulged himself in an entirely subjective verse. This accorded with Kloos's prescription, but Gorter was in earnest in a way that Kloos could never have known: he flung himself into his own feelings and conducted an exploration of them so frenzied that he nearly lost his reason. The resultant poems were in freer verse than anything the Netherlands had seen. At this point Gorter really left the best of himself behind. After a study of philosophy he became a Marxist—but a curiously rigid one. His epic *Pan* (1916) is a grandiose work, highly doctrinaire—and hopelessly remote from ordinary experience, let alone that of the proletariat. Gorter's communism was characterized by so intense a degree of intellectual absolutism (his Marxist studies of Aeschylus, Dante and Shakespeare are unimpressive) that one must suspect that he clung to it as a man clings to a raft: for reasons of preserving his sanity.

The early work of HENRIETTE ROLAND HOLST (1869–1952) appeared in *The New Guide* (q.v.), but, in company with Gorter (of whom she wrote a biography, 1933) she became an adherent of William Morris socialism and then of communism. In the mid-Twenties she turned to a religious socialism. Her poetry suffers from lack of control. Probably her best work was in the realm of biography. She was married to the painter Richard Roland Holst.

The symbolist poetry of JAN HENDRIK LEOPOLD (1865–1925), whose output was small, resembles an island half-enveloped in haze: nothing is quite in focus or quite discernible. No doubt this remoteness (not at all like that of Gorter's epic) arose largely from the deafness from which he suffered. Like that of another deaf poet, David Wright (q.v. 1), his poetry has a sensuous musical quality. He made the best Dutch translation of Omar Khayyam. He was deeply influenced by the philosophy of his countryman, Spinoza, as well as by ancient Sufic poetry. During most of his lifetime he was not well known; now there is a revival of interest in his poetry. Verwey (q.v.) described his lyrics as 'like the swelling and fading of a wave that never breaks'. His world, particularly as expressed in the long poem *Cheops* (1915), is eminently worthy of investigation.

A. ROLAND HOLST (1888), one of the most lively literary members of the underground war against the occupying Nazis in the Second World War, is another important symbolist, who combines the Celtic esotericism of Yeats (q.v. 1) with the kind of pre-temporal paradises of which we catch so many glimpses in the French poetry of the first thirty or forty years of this century. Writing from the viewpoint of innocence (though not assuming it) he either celebrates the eternal lost world or, with perhaps more effect—and in a more hallucinated poetry—records visions of himself in the corrupted temporal world. His imagery is elemental, and in this and in his paganism he is reminiscent of Saint-John Perse. Some earlier collections are *The Confessions of Silence* (1913), *Beyond the Distances* (1920), *A Winter By the Sea* (1937); more recent is *In Danger* (1958). Dutch literature needs only to be better known for Roland Holst to have an international reputation. His language, like that of Saint-John Perse, matches his grand theme.

Dutch expressionism was imported from Germany and re-named 'vitalism' by its leader HENDRIK MARSMAN (1899–1940), who was supported by the humanist critic Dirk Coster (1887–1956). Marsman's vitalism differed very little from the second phase of German expressionism, which he had imbibed while in Germany as a young man; but he was one of the first outside Germany to perceive the genius of Trakl. His *Poems* (1923) and *Paradise Regained* (1927) contain explosive and implosive poetry, too experimental and programmatic to be effective, but suffused with undoubted energy. In 1930 he began to revise his ideas; the resultant collection of essays, *The Death of Vitalism* (1933), marks the beginning of his maturity. When the young Germans who had influenced Marsman in 1921 became Nazis, he looked into himself, rejecting the nihilistic and violent side of expressionism. His consistent self-consciousness saved him from his grandiose tendencies, but robbed most of his later poetry of spontaneity. In the Thirties he led a wandering life, searching for but not really finding a faith; always pursuing his idea of 'Gothic ardour'. His last poem, *Temple and Cross* (1939), on the theme of the conflict between Christ and Dionysus, comes down in favour of the pagan God. Perhaps the best of all his creative works is his novel *The Death of Angèle Degroux* (1933), the strange tale of a love affair between two 'superior' beings. The boat in which Marsman was escaping to England from France in 1940 was torpedoed, and all but his wife and one other passenger were lost.

EDDY DU PERRON (PS. CHARLES EDGAR DU PERRON, 1899–1940), Marsman's exact contemporary, was one of the liveliest and most valuable members of this generation. The son of rich parents, he came to Paris to work as a journalist when they lost their money. He was a close friend of Malraux (q.v.), who dedicated *The Human Condition* (q.v.) to him. He had an especial admiration for Stendhal, whom he physically resembled, for Multatuli (q.v.), whose work he helped to popularize, Larbaud (q.v.) and for Simenon (q.v.). Of the very best type of tough, intelligent, individualist left-wing intellectual, Du Perron exercised a strong influence on the generation that came after him; his death from heart disease at only forty-one was a tragedy. His poems are amusing, deliberately lightweight and in the intentionally matter-of-fact, colloquial '*parlando*' style that he and his *Forum* (q.v.) associates cultivated. But Du Perron wrote one classic, a book that demands to be better known outside Holland: *The Country of Origin* (1935). This autobiographical novel consists of descriptions of his life in Paris alternated with extraordinarily vivid memories of his Javanese childhood. There are few books as good on the East Indies; and few books recapture the mind of a child so exactly. Du Perron also wrote two other novels, some excellent short stories, and much fine informal critical prose.

Du Perron was the co-founder, with MENNO TER BRAAK (1902–40), of the *Forum* group, which was originally formed as a counter to Marsman's 'vitalism'. This group, which advocated lucidity, objectivity and quietude in place of expressionist rhetoric and noise, almost exactly parallels the German 'new objectivity' (q.v.), although it manifested itself rather later: it was in fact a modified expressionism, but wanted to shed the frenetic aspects while retaining the ground that had been won. The leading figure of the group was SIMON VESTDIJK (1898–1971), who became the Netherlands' most important writer after the death of Van Schendel (q.v.).

Vestdijk studied medicine, psychology and philosophy before he became a writer. He was among the most prolific: translator of Emily Dickinson, R. L. Stevenson and others, he found time to write thirty-eight novels, ten collections of short stories and twenty-two books of poetry—as well as twenty-eight non-fiction books. He wrote, it was said, 'faster than God can read'. He combines in his novels (his best work) a lust for life with a psychiatrist's objectivity. After the Second World War he was put forward as an exemplary writer by the Dutch existentialists (q.v.), whose leader was the poet and critic PAUL RODENKO (1920), a left-wing polemicist (who compiled the standard anthology of the work produced by the 'experimental' poets of the Fifties, q.v.). Vestdijk's outstanding work is the eight-novel autobiographical sequence *Anton Wachter* (1934–50). This has Proustian elements, but is generally characterized by Vestdijk's special, and at first off-putting, combination of vitalism and cerebral analysis. He has been unlucky in his translations: the only good novel of his that has appeared in English is *The Garden Where the Brass Band Played* (1950; tr. 1965). This is an account of how beauty and trust are destroyed in a small Dutch town at the beginning of the century. Nol, a judge's son, loves his piano-teacher's daughter, Trix; but trivial prejudices triumph. Vestdijk is more consistent in the shorter forms, however, when his ideas are most subordinated to his imagination, which gets free range. At one time put forward as the Netherlands' candidate for the Nobel Prize,

Vestidjk undoubtedly diffused his gift by too great a prolificity; but his best fiction will survive. He is an important essayist.

FERDINAND BORDEWIJK (1884–1965), a genial joker who took in earnest critics more than once, was an independent writer who successfully developed certain aspects of nineteenth-century Gothic. His *Fantastic Tales* (1919–24) combined the elements of Poe and the modern detective story. After this, becoming aware of surrealism, he turned to a more fantastic manner. *Groaning Beasts* (1928) is about a motor-race. *Bint* (1934) exposes the fascism latent in vitalism, and was itself accused of fascism. His finest novel, *Character* (1938), is written in a more conventional style. Grandly evocative of Rotterdam, the port of its setting, it tells of a father whose method of bringing up his (illegitimate) son is to oppose his every whim. Bordewijk was a versatile and eccentric writer the main function of whose work is to reveal the inadequacy of social structure and morality to human needs. He is notable as a recreator of the atmosphere of old places.

The figure of MARTINUS NIJHOFF (1894–1953) stands behind much of the Dutch poetry written since 1945, even though Achterberg (q.v.) is regarded as a more important poet. Nijhoff passed through a semi-expressionist phase, but by 1924, with *Forms*, had discovered the resigned and melancholy manner natural to him. He is a religious poet, searching for a means of redemption from adult corruption, which he sees in sexual terms: he postulates a Christ who is the equivalent of the child-in-the-man, through whom the man may gain salvation. Wise innocence may illuminate the adult's mundane and degenerate life. His language is deliberately sober and non-poetical. It is his awareness of the existence of an inner world rather than any specific poetic procedure that has made him important to the poets of a later generation.

GERRIT ACHTERBERG (1905–62) was the most gifted of the Dutch modernist poets. Words for him are in themselves magical, and his poetry is to be approached firstly for its necromantic qualities. He suffered from incapacitating mental illness, and wrote his poetry for therapeutic reasons; but he regarded it as therapeutic only because he thought of it as spiritually efficacious. He believed in the transmuting power of poetry, which he regarded as prayer. This belief gives his work a surrealist (q.v.) air. He eschews the ordinary materialistic meanings of words and tries to return to their true, primitive meanings—which centuries of corrupt usage have obscured and distorted. His central theme, expressed in various ways, is a version of the Orpheus myth: Orpheus does not want to bring Eurydice back to life, but to join her in death. This is Achterberg's response to the actual loss of his beloved. Inasmuch as a poet 'is', in a Sartrian (q.v.) sense, 'what he prefers', Achterberg is a poet of earth. He wryly contrasts the trivial nature of 'ordinary' life, with its little projects, with the depth of being itself. His verse became increasingly traditional in its forms. At his most eloquent he is a poet of purity and magic; but some of his work is spoiled by an eccentricity—arising from mental instability—that is irrelevant to his central vision. His poems were collected in 1963.

LUCEBERT (ps. L. J. SWAANSWIJK, 1924) tries, like Achterberg, to create an objective reality of language; but the process is less natural to him, the pressure to write less intense. He is an abstract painter and photographer as well as a poet, and since the Fifties has turned to drawing in preference to writing. He was then the most important representative of the 'experimental' school of poetry, with *The Triangle in the Jungle* (1951) and *Of the Abyss and Aerial Man* (1953). He is a cheerful rebel against all kinds of conformity, who writes a lightweight, playful neo-surrealist verse that mixes humour in equal proportion with social indignation. 'Atonal' (the author's term), it is full of neologisms, nonsense-propositions and startling juxta-positions—sometimes clothed in parodically solemn, hymn-like forms.

WILLEM FREDERIK HERMANS (1921) is the leading contemporary Dutch writer of experimental fiction. His initially sceptical approach may be compared to that of Robbe-Grillet (q.v.), from whom, however, he differs in other respects. Hermans began as a poet, but changed to fiction in 1949 with *The Tears of the Acacias*, a savagely cynical, scatological story set in occupied Amsterdam and in Brussels at the time of the liberation. Hermans, whose exasperated tone—in fiction and polemics—often recalls that of Céline (q.v.), has written in various experimental forms, but his main theme is the unavoida-bility of human chaos and individual anomie. With *The Dark Room of Damocles* (1958; tr. 1962) Hermans begins a new and less desperate approach: man's situation is the same, but the existence of values is obliquely conceded. *Memoirs of a Guardian Angel* (1971) reflects the same concerns.

After the war the individualist tradition of Du Perron was con-tinued in the magazine *Libertinage*, edited by the poet H. A. GOMPERTS (1915). This has steered a middle course between the socialism of *Podium* and the aesthetic *The Word*. The chief 'experimentalist' was Lucebert (q.v.); the most interesting poet of a more traditional bent is A. MARJA (ps. A. T. MOUJI, 1917), a 'committed' writer who calls his poetry 'anecdotic'.

JAN HENDRIK WOLKERS (1925), who is also well known as a sculptor, is a best-selling author—and a serious one. There is an element of sick meretriciousness in his work; but this is no more than incidental and irritating. He has a sense of wry and ironic humour that is genuine—and more understandable than his fiction as a whole, which is perhaps the reason for his wide appeal. Wolkers' novels that have been translated into English are characteristic work. *A Rose of Flesh* (1963; tr. 1967) is a study of a self-pitying, guilty man whose daughter has died in a scalding accident by his neglect (and that of his wife). He continually re-enacts this trauma, his own spirit scalded. *The Horrible Tango* (1964; tr. 1970) is also about a sick man. Wolkers' is one of the gifted of his generation; as yet he has not wholly realized it. *Turkish Delight* (1969; tr. 1974) is inferior.

GERARD KORNELIS VAN HET REVE (1923) wrote *Evenings* (1947), a description of a week in the life of an adolescent 'drop-out'. This compassionately traces the anguish that lies at the heart of his unease, and is one of the best studies of the younger generation written in the post-1945 period. HARRY MULISCH (1927) is self-consciously European. *The Stone Bridal Bed* (1959; tr. 1962) is a semi-surrealistic study of the post-war mentality of sometimes horrifying power.

III

The magazine *From Now On* was the vehicle for the Flemish revival, which closely paralleled those of the French-speaking Belgians and the Netherlands. The Flemish literature being insecure, the magazine was all the more fiercely assertive of its uniqueness. The father-figure for all Flemish writers at this time was the poet-priest Guido Gezelle (1830–99), who had almost alone re-created Flemish as a literary language. The poetry of Gezelle, a lovable man, persecuted for his love of Flemish by government and Church alike, is unlikely to survive except as a demonstration of linguistic skill and virtuosity. But as a whole it breathes warmth and simple faith in nature.

CYRIEL BUYSSE (1859–1932), a close friend of Maeterlinck (q.v.), was equally French in outlook. But unlike his associate he decided to write in Flemish in order to enrich and invigorate a literature he felt had become impoverished. He was a prolific author of short stories, travel books and essays; but did his best work in fiction and the drama. He published his first novel in the Dutch *New Guide* (q.v.) in 1890. Resembling Maupassant in lucidity, but influenced by Zola (q.v.) as a kindred spirit, he depicted farming and middle-class life without sentimentality. His most famous novel is the early *The Right of the*

Strongest (1893), a portrait of a coarse farmer who gets his way with his girl and everyone else; this is naturalist, but with the emphasis on the 'Darwinian' doctrine of the survival of the fittest. As a dramatist Buysse, who was made a Baron in the last year of his life, was influenced by Hauptmann and, closer to home, the Dutch Heijermans (qq.v.). He wrote neat comedies and, most notably, *The Paemel Family* (1903), about a farmer exploited by landowners and his struggle against them. Buysse had much contact with Dutch writers, including Louis Couperus (q.v.).

Gezelle's nephew STIJN STREUVELS (ps. FRANK LATEUR, 1871–1969), who rivalled Chiesa (q.v. 3) in longevity was for fifteen years a village baker. He read widely, and his natural countryman's fatalism was reinforced by Dostoevski, Hamsun, Zola (qq.v.) and Hardy (q.v. 1) and the other novelists he devoured. Ultimately, however, he eschewed literary influence and found that he could most effectively simply record the life he saw around him in Western Flanders. His early book of stories described life in the depressed flax-growing areas: *The Path of Life* (1899; tr. 1915). All the ingredients of his later work are apparent: fatalism, delicacy of observation of human aspirations, a poetic sense of inexorable, beautiful, cruel nature. He has in his succeeding fiction—short stories and short novels—no lesson to teach, only a fact to demonstrate; but, like Hardy, whom he somewhat resembles, he sees man as at the mercy of a blind destiny—in this case the natural cycle of the seasons; those who rebel suffer; it is better to be like Jan Vandeveughel in *Old Jan* (1902; tr. 1936), and endure. Although he does not have Hardy's massive sense of tragedy, and often takes refuge in an assumption that God's in his heaven and all's really right with the world (in which his shocked imagination does not believe), Streuvels deserves to be better known and more widely translated. There is an element of Flemish mysticism or fatalism running through his work that raises it above regionalism. *The Flax Field* (1907), for example, a drama of the conflict between father and son, is so intense and psychologically accurate that it transcends mere regionalism. Fortunately some of Streuvels' earlier work is available in a French collection, *August* (*L'Août*, 1928). *Life and Death in Den Ast* is available in an English translation.

HERMAN TEIRLINCK (1879–1967), son of ISIDOOR TEIRLINCK (1851–1934)—who with RAIMOND STIJNS (1850–1904) wrote *Poor Flanders*, a truthful picture of poverty and social injustice—expanded the horizons of the Flemish novel. He was first led to experimentalism by his failure to write with real effect about the peasants, whom he approached with urban preconceptions (he was born in Brussels). He became famous for *Mijnheer Serjanszoon* (1908), a tale of an eighteenth-century hedonist; this is witty and amusing, but is now as hopelessly dated as most of Anatole France's (q.v.) books; it is certainly not his best work, which it is too often claimed to be.

As a dramatist Teirlinck set himself the task of revitalizing, on broadly expressionistic lines, the Flemish theatre. His *Slow Motion Picture* (1922) is one of the most successful of all the later expressionist plays. Two lovers jump into a canal. As they drown they re-live their experiences together, including the birth of a now dead child; when the police rescue them they part as strangers—cured of love. This was one of the earliest plays to make effective use of cinema techniques, and Salacrou was clearly influenced by it in his *The Unknown Woman of Arras* (q.v.). *The Bodiless Man* (1935) employs the familiar expressionist technique of splitting one man into his component parts. *The Magpie on the Gallows* (1937), perhaps Teirlinck's best play, reveals the evils of puritanism.

The novel *Maria Speermalie* (1940) gives the history of a passionate and polyandrous woman who rises to the aristocracy. *The Man in the Mirror* (1955; tr. 1961) which addresses its old business-man hero in the second person throughout, is a tragi-comic masterpiece. The protagonist sees his past self, with its transgressions of bourgeois values, as someone elese. *The Struggle with the Angel* (1952), which ranges over six centuries, is less successful as a whole.

The leading Flemish poet, and perhaps the only other major twentieth-century poet in Dutch besides Achterberg (q.v.), was KAREL VAN DE WOESTIJNE (1878–1929). Van de Woestijne was initially influenced by the narcissistic decadence of Kloos, by George and Rilke (qq.v.), and, above all, by the ideas of Baudelaire. In his best poetry he achieves a manner entirely his own, compounded of nostalgia for childhood, sexual guilt and unrelieved bitterness. He died of tuberculosis. A robust, not to say lush, sensuality is challenged and penetrated by a cruel and almost metaphysical shrewdness. He was very much of his age, a typical tormented soul of the first quarter of the century; but he is particularly interesting because he felt his symbolist procedures, at which he grasped like a drowning man, to be continually threatened by his lack of faith in the Platonic assumptions underlying them; this explains much of the intensity of his bitterness and his supposed obscurity. He saw his own lust as a luxurious and hellish dissolver of the beauties of nature. He saw himself as a hazel-nut and, simultaneously, as the greedy worm within it; as it devours his robust centre he becomes 'an emptiness that does not speak or heed'; but, touched by a child's hand, he sings. His epic, systematizing poems of the Twenties are less successful than the early ones, but contain many fine passages. He wrote several volumes of literary criticism and prose, all of which are suffused with his own un-happy and melodious style.

No later Flemish poet of Van de Woestijne's stature has emerged. Elsschot (q.v.) wrote some good poems, but was primarily a novelist. PAUL VAN OSTAIJEN (1896–1928) was an expressionist and experi-mentalist who did not live long enough to entirely fulfil his gift. *Music Hall* (1916), however, was a really remarkable and original first collection of poems from a man of only twenty. The chief in-fluence was the unanimism (q.v.) of Romains and the *Abbaye* group (q.v.); but the poems in it, all evoking a great city, incorporate (and frequently anticipate) elements of the grotesque; van Ostaijen is never starry eyed as were some of the *Abbaye* group—on the contrary, he is deeply and naturally cynical in an extremely modern, specifically urban manner. After the surrealism of *The Signal* (1918) and *The Occupied City* (1921) van Ostaijen did in fact reach a more sombre and idealistic mood in *The First Book of Schmol* (1928), in which he essays a self-styled poetry of 'organic expressionism', which amounts to an attempt to combine words irrationally, in order to attain new meanings. He wrote a number of Kafkaesque prose works, such as *The Brothel of Ika Loch* (1925). Van Ostaijen exercised a strong in-fluence on the post-1945 Flemish poets.

RICHARD MINNE (1891) is the most intelligent representative of the traditionalist group, which strongly opposed the modernism of van Ostaijen. KAREL JONCK-HEERE (1896) began under the influence of Van de Woestijne, and although he reacted against him has re-tained his essentially expressionist attitude.

HERWIG HENSEN (ps. FLORENT MEILANTS, 1917) has also followed in this direction rather than in a modernist one. He began as an imita-tor of Van de Woestijne (q.v.), but later developed into an atheist-humanist poet of moderate though not great interest. He is a better playwright, especially in *Lady Godiva* (1946); in Hensen's version her sacrifice is wasted. Hensen's intelligent if not inspired plays are im-mensely popular with Flemish playgoers.

BERT DE DECORTE (1915) is the leading contemporary modernist poet, much influenced by Rimbaud as well as van Ostaijen. He is more interesting as a poet than Hensen, but does not seem to have decided what course to take. His best collection is *The Passage of Orpheus* (1940), in which Greek mythological themes are set off against a Flemish background. He is a learned poet, who writes in Latin and translates well from the Greek.

*

Until well after the First World War the regional fiction of Buysse and Streuvels—and that of their inferior imitators—was regarded as the only kind of effective fiction that Flanders could produce. Even Teirlinck did not come into his own until between the two wars, and Elsschot was shamefully neglected by all but a few.

WILLEM ELSSCHOT (ps. ALFONS DE RIDDER, 1882–1960) was for long better known in the Netherlands (he was 'discovered' by the *Forum* group) than in his native Belgium. At one point he remained silent for fifteen years. He is an unsensational, sophisticated, parodic, tender realist of genius; a delightful writer, and a major one. Elsschot is full of subtle feeling; and 'near sentimentality' (a term used by one critic) is less apt than saying that he always avoids it. His style is highly economical and lucid. Three of his novels have been translated by A. Brotherton (*Three Novels*, 1963); *Soft Soap* (1924), *The Leg* (1938) and *Will-o'-the-Wisp* (1946). *Soft Soap* is about the advertising world (Elsschot himself was the director of an advertising agency), and introduces his Chaplinesque character Laarmans—and the bourgeois crook Boorman, who can live with his conscience but sometimes comically tries to appease it. He appears again in *The Leg*, as does Laarmans, and in *The Tanker* (1942). *Cheese* (1933) is probably Elsschot's funniest book: an account of a man's dream of becoming a big cheese importer, which is very rudely shattered when he attempts to realize it. His best book, however, is his last: *Will-o'-the-Wisp*. A girl has given three Indian sailors a false address. Laarmans meets them and tries to help them find her, listening to their awed praises of her beauty until he wants her himself. Here Elsschot, in a novel of wide application, achieves a tenuous, sad sense of human brotherhood, of broken dreams, of sweetness. His poetry, all written about 1920, published in 1934 (*Yester Year*), has similar qualities: it is lucid, cynical, compassionate.

FELIX TIMMERMANS (1886–1947) is a minor figure by comparison, although he achieved an international success. He had skill, but his invention of the painter Breughel's environment is as swashbucklingly artificial in *Droll Peter* (1928; tr. 1930) as his Rabelaisian peasant in *Pallieter* (1918; tr. 1924). *Peasant Hymn* is available in English.

GERARD WALSCHAP (1898), an inspector of public libraries for much of his life, has written acerb novels of protest against the Flemish Catholic establishment. His heroes are amoral and instinctive men or women who obey nature and therefore find themselves ranged against society. His faith in a purely vitalistic approach to life, manifested in his best known novel, *Houtekiet* (1940), about a Utopian village community, seems naïve and inadequate; but the portrait of his hero has power and some depth. *Cure through Aspirin* (1943; tr.

1960) is more sophisticated and psychological in its approach. *Congo Insurrection* (1953) is a prophetic analysis of the shortcomings of Belgian colonialism. *Marriage* and *Ordeal* have been translated in one volume.

MAURICE ROELANTS (1895–1966) was a novelist and critic who tried to take Flemish letters in the direction of Dutch internationalism: away from provincialism and local elements. He wrote psychological novels in the French classical tradition: there are few characters, and nothing much happens except in their minds. The short story collection *The Jazz Player* (1928) contains his best work; but his few tense, intelligent novels are excellent studies of middleclass *angst*. They include *Come and Go* (1927), *Life as We Dreamed It* (1931) and *Prayer for a Good End* (1944).

LOUIS-PAUL BOON (1912) began as a vitalistic follower of Walschap, and he has remained a severe critic of society. But he is more modernistic in method, and his long novels are more reminiscent of Céline's (q.v.) than of Walschap's. He is concerned, without in the least disguising his own angry and exasperated feelings, to reveal the moral and physical corruption that underlies modern life. His novels are peopled with scores of characters, and in this at least seem to have been influenced by Dos Passos (q.v. 1); although his technique is modernistic, there is more than a trace of the old, pessimistic naturalist about him. His people are not usually intelligent or nice— and they are, of course, his choice. His finest books are the ironically entitled *My Little War* (1946), the vast *Chapel Road* (1953; tr. 1972) and *Summer in Ter-Muren* (1956), the moving story of a little working-class girl. Boon introduces himself into his own novels as a participant in the action and by holding conversations with his characters. Prolific and bursting with energy, Boon is Belgium's most gifted novelist writing in Flemish.

Boon's contemporary JOHAN DAISNE (PS. HERMAN THIERY, 1912) is a more cerebral writer. He describes himself as a 'magic realist' (q.v.), and this is useful inasmuch as he has the power to compel belief in his fantastic narrations. *The Stairway of Stone and Clouds* (1942) rather too sentimentally relates aspirations to reality: but the cinematic *The Man Who Had His Hair Cut Short* (1947), narrated by a man on the verge of madness, is more convincing. The long Joycean narration describes, at one point, the post-mortem of a girl whose body is rapidly rotting.

MARNIX GIJSEN (PS. JAN-ALBERT GORIS, 1899), a Belgian diplomat, has written a remarkable modern reinterpretation of the Susanna and the Elders story, *The Book of Joachim of Babylon* (1946; tr. 1951); like his near-contemporary Vestdijk (q.v.) Gijsen is Freudian in his approach and uses much autobiographical material. He is also bitterly anti-clerical, intellectual, sceptical and anti-nationalist. *Telemachus in the Village* (1948) is a vivid, shrewd, sad picture of life in a Belgian provincial town, *Lament for Agnes* (1951) a nostalgic story about an unhappy love-affair.

*

Teirlinck's contribution to the Flemish theatre has already been discussed; but certain other notable playwrights should be mentioned. GASTON MARTENS (1883) is a delightful minor playwright, whose *Birds of Paradise* (1944) enjoyed a huge success (in a French translation) in post-war France as play and movie. PAUL DE MONT (1895–1950), whose health was permanently impaired by his service in the First World War, was a notable satirist whose finest play, *The Trial of Our Lord* (1925), inspired Ghelderode's *Barabbas* (q.v.); it is an excellent play in its own right, and presents (better than in any of those well-made but *kitsch* 'courtroom dramas' of the period between the wars) all human justice as no better than a conspiracy. Johan Daisne (q.v.) has written effective, rather Teutonic plays illustrative of his Platonic and idealistic theses; none come up to the artistic level of *The Man Who Had His Hair Cut Short* (q.v.).

The leading figure of the younger generation of Flemish writers is the versatile poet, novelist and dramatist HUGO CLAUS (1929). A poet highly experimental and modern in style, he seeks to reinstate man in a context of pre-'civilized' innocence. His theatre is powerful and highly coloured: in particular *The Dawn Fiancée*, which enjoyed a success in a French version, is a robust treatment of a brother-sister incest theme, in which society's attitude to incest, rather than incest itself, is regarded as corrupt. His novel *Dog-Days* (1952) resolutely describes a young man's doomed quest for existential purity. *Shame* (1972) cleverly explores the emptiness of a Belgian TV team who are filming a passion play on a Pacific island.

Finnish Literature

Finnish, a Uralian language with nothing in common with Swedish, is now the vernacular of nine-tenths of the population of Finland. Modern Finnish literature proper dates from 1880, with the so-called Young Finland movement. The new native literature was of course influenced by both Swedish and Russian literatures, but also looked to the rest of Europe. Its main aim, however, was to create a genuinely Finnish culture. Probably the most important single influence, particularly on the novel, was Alexis Kivi (1834–72).

The leading writers of the Young Finland movement were: the brilliant woman writer Minna Canth (1844–97), playwright and author of short stories influenced by Ibsen, and still recognized for her ear for authentic dialogue; JUHANI AHO (ps. JUHANI BROFELDT, 1861–1921) and ARVID JÄRNEFELT (1861–1932). Aho, a parson's son, got to know Maupassant, Daudet and Zola (q.v.) in Paris in 1889. He was and remained a basically romantic writer; but his discovery of French realistic procedures did his work nothing but good. Prior to his visit to Paris he had written *The Railway* (1884) and *The Parson's Daughter* (1885). The former is a study of a primitive couple living in the backwoods; the latter deals with provincial middle-class life and touches on the question of the emancipation of women—a theme as common in Finnish as in Scandinavian literature. His first mature work, however, was the series of sketches he began to write while in Paris, *Shavings* (1891–1921), and which he continued to publish throughout his life. In these realism and romanticism are most attractively and effectively mixed; stylistically they influenced later writers. *The Parson's Wife* (1893) describes, in a fine detail not previously seen in Finnish, the misery of a woman tied to a partner she despises. *Panu* (1897) is a historical novel about Christianity's conquest of paganism. *Juha* (1911), a love story, studies the Finnish character; by this time Aho's romantic inclinations had fully emerged. But he always kept his realistic head, and, apart from the *Shavings*, *Juha* is his best novel. In his last phase he was influenced by Selma Lagerlöf (q.v.). Some of the *Shavings* have been translated into French; all that is available in English is a volume of selected short stories: *Squire Hellman* (tr. 1893).

Arvid Järnefelt was a lawyer who early came under the influence of Tolstoi. He gave up his legal career in favour of a writing life on a small farm. His novel *Fatherland* (1893) sensitively examines the difficulties experienced by a student, a peasant's son, in acclimatizing himself to bourgeois society. He finely described his Tolstoian change of heart in *My Conversion* (1894). Over the next thirty years he was regarded as an eccentric recluse, and was out of the main stream: even though some of his concerns (feminism, sexuality, the future of peasants) were Finnish, his Utopianism was out of place. Then, in 1925, he scored a major success with the religious novel *Greeta and his Lord*, which he followed with the three-part *Novel of my Parents* (1928–30). Järnefelt had a tendency to moralize, but his work is important for its psychological penetration and clear style.

The leading lyrical poet of this generation was EINO LEINO (ps. ARMAS EINO LEOPOLD LÖNNBOHM, 1878–1926), who became involved in the Young Finland movement while at university in the mid-Nineties. He was the first poet of real skill and flair since Runeberg, 'Finland's national poet' who died in 1877. But Runeberg wrote in Swedish, as did his important Swedo-Finnish near-contemporary Edith Södergran (q.v.). Leino did not clearly understand what could be done with the Finnish language in poetry, but his instinct told him that a change had to be made from a prosody ingeniously but unhappily based on German models. Leino began as a brilliant journalist and youthful national romantic; but his personal life became clouded when his marriage broke up towards the end of the first decade of the century, and he moved from a nationalist to a confused Nietzschean (q.v.) position. The brilliant lyrics of the young Leino, collected in *Songs of Man* (1896), represent the spearhead of the neo-romantic reaction to naturalism. His chief work, *Helka Songs* (1903–16), contains elements from folklore—particularly the great Finnish epic, the *Kalevala*—and combines patriotism with menacing undertones of a personal nature; here, drawing on the old oral tradition, he came near to creating truly Finnish rhythms. He wrote some twenty verse plays, fiction and criticism. The quality of Leino's purely patriotic verse is demonstrated in 'A Legend of Finland':

> In days of yore (or so the legends say)
> God and St. Peter passing on their way
> O'er land and sea, when night was near at hand
> Touched on the shore of this, our blessed land.
>
> They sat them down upon the sloping ground
> Where birch trees grow down to a quiet sound.

No sooner there, than Peter, who was wont
To argue, opened with this taunt:

'O Lord, what land is this we've come upon!
What people rudely poor and bent with brawn!
Soil rocky, rugged with but scanty yields
Of mushrooms and poor berries from the fields.'

But in His quiet strength the Good Lord smiled,
'The land may neither fruitful be, nor mild;
Cold and uninviting lies each farm,
But every heart is beautiful and warm.'

Thus saying, the Good Lord smiled silently
And lo! a splendor spread o'er all the sea.
The marshes dried, the wilderness was cowed,
And frozen fields soon yielded to the plow.

God and St. Peter then did take their leave,
But it is said, 'If on a summer eve
You sit beneath the birch, you still can see
God's smile move on the water—quietly.'

(TCSP)

The works of Leino's final years were tired, but it is still amusing to read that the 'second half of his short life was marred by bohemian debauchery'—and from the pen of a relatively modern critic.

The other poets of the turn of the century were not as naturally gifted. OTTO MANNINEN (1872–1950), a lecturer at Helsinki University and Finland's leading translator (Homer, Heine, Ibsen, Petöfi, Runeberg, etc.), wrote comparatively little. He began in patriotic and romantic vein; but later achieved a lyrical compression and elegance of form unique in at any rate conventional (i.e. based on Germanic metres) verse. His manner is often bitingly satirical. Although he did not achieve a personal rhythm, he did make interesting experiments within the stultifying tradition. His *Complete Poems* appeared in the year of his death.

VEIKKO ANTERO KOSKENNIEMI (1885–1962), another academic and scholar—he was an authority on Goethe—was even more traditional, as critic and poet, than Manninen, whose reputation was for a time rather unfairly obscured by his. Most of his poetry—such as *Spring Evening in the Latin Quarter* (1912)—has already begun to date. The early work is influenced by French Parnassian (q.v.) poetry and

Levertin and Fröding (qq.v.); later he turned to the poetry of classical antiquity. The most famous Finnish poet during his lifetime, his reputation is fading rapidly: it is not just that he refused modernism, but that he failed to understand it—and even resented it.

LARIN-KYÖSTI (ps. KYÖSTI LARSSON, 1873–1948), the son of a Swede living in Finland, was in the troubadour tradition; his first collection was called *The Spring Hummings of This Fellow* (1897). He wrote plays; and at one time turned unsuccessfully to symbolism (*Ad Astra*, 1907).

MARIA JOTUNI (1880–1943) was important as a novelist and a playwright. Her earliest short stories, influenced by Aho (q.v.), dealt with simple people and were written in a clipped, laconic style which combines humour, an acute feminine psychological insight and a sense of tragic destiny. She later turned from naturalism, but never lost her underlying sense of the tragic. Eventually she refined her techniques to a distinctly modernistic degree of concentratedness. Her use of dialogue is celebrated for its skill. Perhaps the finest of her work is to be found in *The Young Girl in the Rose Garden* (1927), a collection of short stories. However, *Everyday Life* (1909), a comedy describing one summer's day in the life of a rural community, is also a minor masterpiece.

Another distinguished prose writer of the earlier period is VOLTER KILPI (1874–1939), who began as a Pre-Raphaelite aesthete but graduated from this in a manner uncannily reminiscent of his exact contemporary, the Dutch novelist Arthur van Schendel (q.v.), whose work he could hardly have known. It must be added that Kilpi was more cosmopolitan from the start. His most substantial work is his epic trilogy, *In Alastalo's Room* (1933–7), about a patriarchal island community in the days of the decline of the sailing-ship. (Van Schendel, too, was interested in the sailing ship.) Kilpi used modernist techniques, including stream-of-consciousness, in this vigorous and often moving work.

KERSTI SOLVEIG BERGROTH (1886) wrote in Swedish until 1920, when she turned to Finnish. A highly prolific writer of stage comedies, journalism, girls' tales and novels, she lives in Rome. She is one of the relatively few writers (cf. Bely, q.v. 4) to have been influenced by Rudolf Steiner's anthroposophy.

The most eminent of modern Finnish novelists, however, has been FRANS EEMIL SILLANPÄÄ (1888–1964), Finland's only recipient of the Nobel Prize (1939). Sillanpää was at first influenced by Hamsun's (q.v.) vitalism. He had studied natural science at Helsinki, and his belief in the universe as a single living object dominates all his fiction. *Life and the Sun* (1916), his first novel, is a now somewhat dated piece of Finnish vitalism: it describes a summer in the life of two urban lovers, and represents them as but two aspects of nature coming together. It recalls Hamsun, Lawrence and Romains (qq.v.). Far superior is *Meek Heritage* (1919; tr. 1938), the best constructed of all Sillanpää's works; this deals with the events of the Finnish civil war of 1918 between Bolsheviks and 'Whites'. (Finland had taken advantage of the situation in Russia in 1917 to declare its independence; it gained this in 1918, and adopted a democratic and republican constitution in 1919.) The central figure of *Meek Heritage* is a tenant-farmer, a character who is resigned to his fate. Sillanpää's treatment is not profound; but it is humane. After this Sillanpää came under the influence of Maeterlinck (q.v.), and entered a more mystical period. He became famous with *Maid Silja or Fallen Asleep While Young* (1931; tr. 1933), his least satisfactory book. Sillanpää's short stories are possibly superior to his novels: better constructed and with a deeper psychological penetration. Here Sillanpää displays his genius for noting tiny inner movements of the mind and heart, and for suggesting unconscious motivation.

TOIVO PEKKANEN (1902–57) is in some ways a more interesting and enigmatic writer than Sillanpää. His work has been subjected to various interpretations. Is he a naturalist, a realist or a symbolist? The answer is that he has been all three. *My Childhood* (1953; tr. 1966) is a starkly objective account of the struggle of a working-class family. This came late in Pekkanen's surprisingly versatile writing career. Earlier had come the undoubtedly naturalistic *On the Shores of My Finland* (1937), describing a strike, and *Black Ecstasy* (1939), a psychological novel about love between peasants. His novel-cycle about his native port of Kotka (1957–8) employs the techniques of Dos Passos (q.v. 1), presenting its inhabitants in the dreary world in which they live, but also showing them in moments of true humanity, when their resignation changes to desire for a better life.

PENTTI HAANPÄÄ (1905–55), a self-taught writer, paid for his accurate savaging of the life of Finnish conscripts in the short-story collection *Field and Barracks* (1928) by being ostracized as every kind of insect; red, godless, enemy of security. These were the days of the rise of the fascist *Lapua* organization, which attempted *coups d'état*, and was a strong influence in the land. Haanpää's work later became accepted, but he compromised only to the (reasonable) extent of supporting his country against the Russians when they treacherously attacked it. *War in the White Desert* (1940) is the most vivid of all descriptions of the Russo-Finnish 'winter' war over whose fierce fifteen weeks the Red Army was humiliated—before using sheer extra might to force Finland to cede nearly 16,000 square miles of land. *War in the White Desert* was translated into French (*Guerre dans la désert blanc*, 1942). Thereafter Haanpää became a brutally powerful writer: ironic, uncompromising in his pessimistic view of life. After his accidental death by drowning there appeared *Magic Circle* (1957), perhaps his greatest achievement. Haanpää's view of life resembles that of Camus (q.v.); but he is not interested in solutions or protests. He relishes the comedy of human aspirations, played out against the wholly indifferent, and yet mockingly beautiful, background of nature. In this he recalls Bunin (q.v. 4).

Although not as gifted a writer, MIKA WALTARI (1908) has attracted much more attention outside Finland: with his skilful, well-written, intelligent but *kitsch* historical novels, most of which have been translated (*Sinuhe the Egyptian*, 1945, tr. and abridged 1949; *The Secret of the Kingdom*, 1959, tr. 1960; etc., etc.); but he has done his more serious work in the short story. Waltari was associated with the *Tulenkantajat* (*Torchbearer*) group when a very young man. The Torchbearers, 1924–9, were a left-wing, outwards-looking group: their motto was 'The large windows open onto Europe'. This group contained most of the Finnish writers influenced by expressionism, q.v., but it also belatedly incorporated some elements of futurism, q.v. It quickly dissolved, although an influential left-wing magazine bearing the same name continued until 1939.

Though Waltari caused something of a stir with his precocious first book, *The Great Illusion* (1928), about rebellious youth, he soon calmed down. His most interesting work is to be found in *Moonscape* (1953; tr. 1954), short stories. Here the cinemascope effect and relentlessly mindless piling up of historical detail are lacking, and there is some understanding of psychology. But essentially Waltari remains a good-natured purveyor of midcult fodder; his seriousness is continually swallowed by his reprehensible desire to fill the lounges of the West with pseudo-mystical consolation.

VÄINÖ LINNA (1920) caused one of the biggest recent sensations in Finnish letters with the publication of *The Unknown Soldier* (1954; tr. 1957), the story of a grousing soldier in the winter war. This sold half a million copies, which was unprecedented in a country of under five million. It is a vivid and vigorous book, making brilliant use of dialogue; polite society was shattered by its candour, but also fascinated. The trilogy *Under the Polar Star* (1959–62) deals with the Civil War of 1918, and again provoked controversy. Linna's views of the extremely complex issues behind the war are controversial, but they are undoubtedly more penetrating than those of the historians. He has been particularly anxious to dispel what he believes is the myth of a disinterested White army.

VEIJO MERI (1928) shares the post-war generation's disillusionment with war and bourgeois war-values (such as 'heroism', which he considers a mythical quality). *The Isolated* (1959) and *Events of 1918* (1960)—on the Civil War—portray individuals lost and isolated in the hell of war. *A Story of Rope* (1957; tr. in French 1962) is set in the First World War. Meri has also written about modern Helsinki ANTTI HYRY (1931) is an experimentalist, who cultivates a naïvely objective style that is interesting but apt to become monotonous. His best novel is *The Edge of the World* (1967).

*

Despite the genius of Leino, Finnish poetry has adapted slowly to this century. What the Finnish poet ANSELM HOLLO (1934)—he now writes in English and lives in Great Britain and America—has called 'Finnitude' grew up, and 'was liable to bog poetry down in either of two kinds of neo-romanticism: the "cosmic" . . . or the folkloristic. . . .' This was understandable in a new nation. But almost all poets until the Fifties tried to write Finnish poetry in predominantly German forms; since, as Hollo points out, Finnish is a Uralian and not an Indo-European tongue, the results were often 'somewhat repulsive'. The modernist poets of the Fifties therefore have less use for the Torchbearers (q.v.) as pioneers than they otherwise might. One cannot say that any of the Twenties poets discussed below really understood their reading of Nietzsche and French poetry. Like Ady (q.v. 4) in Hungary, they brought back something; but Finnish soil was less fertile than Hungarian.

Most of Finland's leading poets of the between-wars period were associated with the Torchbearers group (q.v.). UUNO KAILAS (ps. FRANS UUNO SALONEN, 1901–33), who died—like so many of his countrymen—from tuberculosis, was its leading spirit: he introduced the German expressionist poets into Finland in a volume of translations published in 1924. For a whole year (1928–9) he was seriously mentally ill. His earlier poetry is violent and tormented in a typically expressionist style; after his illness he reacted against this, to produce a more controlled—although not less disturbed—poetry. His first mature collection was *Sleep and Death* (1931) here for the first time his turbulent guilts, anguished self-scrutiny and hallucinations are subsumed under an iron discipline—representative of course, of Kailas' need for restraint and fear of mental collapse. His thinking about poetry was influenced by that of JUHANI SILJO (1888–1918), who was killed in the Civil War. Siljo believed in poetry as a means of self-revelation and of achieving a perfect life; Kailas clung to this without believing in it. (TCSP) P. MUSTAPÄÄ (ps.

M. HAAVIO, 1899–1973), a distinguished scholar, has drawn on Finland's early literature. The surface of his delightful poetry is deliberately light and easy; but this conceals a masterful adaptation of early manners to modern needs, and a profound humour:

> I am still far away.
>
> I will arrive tomorrow.
> Hey, my pack, my laughing pack!
> Hey, my friendly walking stick!
> Tomorrow we shall arrive.
>
> At a beautiful time.
> Just when the old sexton opens the loft of the belfry.
> Steam bath, Saturday steam bath.
> The music of the round
> Sounds in the village.
>
> I am still far away.
> A mist, a wild wizard's mist
> Seeks the hollows, mounds, shadows,
> Groups of aspen trees.
>
> Slippery rocks under foot,
> Stumps with staring eyes along the roadside.
> Welcome to you,
> Welcome, I am a bridegroom,
> The bridegroom of happiness.
>
> And so wildly in love.
>
> (TCSP)

LAURI VILJANEN (1900), another leading light in the Torchbearers group, is more important as an influence than as a poet. He is an intelligent conservative humanist, sometimes intolerant in his more recent criticism. He has kept Finns in touch with European developments for nearly fifty years. His own poetry is well-made but rather conventionally humanistic in content.

The leading woman poet of the Torchbearers was KATRI VALA (ps. ALICE WADENSTRÖM, 1901–44), who is often compared, for her intensity, to Edith Södergran (q.v.). Like the latter, Katri Vala died of tuberculosis. She introduced free verse to Finland. Her poetry of the late Twenties is her best—'I cycle my hunger's orbit/Bare and dreary as a prison yard./My senses and thoughts are rough from work'—because of its freshness, spontaneity and firmness of line. The later, more politically radical poetry is less important. Katri Vala died in Sweden; her *Collected Peoms* appeared in 1945.

AALA TYNNI (1913), Mustapää's (q.v.) wife, is an interesting poet, who has assembled an important anthology of European poetry—translated by herself—from A.D. 1000 to the present: *A Millennium of Song* (1957). Her most interesting original poetry explores the nature of human evil. LAURI VIITA (1916–65), who died prematurely in a car crash, was a predominantly urban poet (his first collection was called *Concreter*, 1947) who alternated between a grandiose 'cosmic' poetry—ineffective—and a simple, ballad-like style of great charm. He graduated into an impressive novelist; *Moraine* (1950), set in the Civil War, a study of urban life, is successful on sociological and psychological levels. HELVI JUVONEN (1919–59) was influenced by Emily Dickinson and, above all, Marianne Moore (q.v.): she projects herself into various animals in the same way, although her manner is considerably more personal. With Haavikko she was the leading Finnish modernist of the Fifties.

The most gifted Finnish post-war modernist is PAAVO HAAVIKKO (1931). A selection of his poems has been translated into English: *Selected Poems* (1968). Haavikko is an extreme modernist: his poetry combines hermeticism with a strong sense of, as he puts it (in the form of a question), 'How can we endure without falling silent when poems are shown to mean nothing?' He has indignantly repudiated the reactionary 'Finnitude' of his elders, and he shares his contemporary Meri's (q.v.) view of war. His poetry rejects any kind of easy way out, any neatness, and consequently often runs the risk of being found impenetrable. His poem-sequence 'The Winter Palace' is his most impressive work, and has attracted praise from Enzensberger (q.v) and other poets.

JUHA MANNERKORPI (1915), who was born in Ohio, is a more run-of-the-mill modernist, whose poetry, drama and short stories seldom transcend their influences (mainly Beckett); but he has made important translations from Beckett and other French writers into Finnish. TUOMAS ANHAVA (1927), a more original poet, has absorbed the influence of classical Chinese and Japanese poetry, which he has finely translated. A substantial retrospective selection appeared in 1967. MARJA-LIISA VARTIO (1924–66) began as a poet but then went on to write a series of highly poetic novels: essentially she was a poet. Her early death was a serious loss to Finnish letters. The posthumous *The Birds Were Hers* (1967) is her finest novel, the subtle and original story of a widow who, obsessed with birds, can relate to others only through her maid. With Haavikko at the forefront of the modernist movement is EEVA-LIISA MANNER (1921), who has graduated from the traditional to surrealist free verse; she has written fiction and drama.

*

Maria Jotuni (q.v.) was as distinguished in the theatre as in fiction. She began as an Ibsenian (q.v.) but soon branched out into comedy —her forte—with such plays as *Man's Rib* (1914). Her most powerful tragedy is her drama dealing with Saul, *I Am to Blame* (1929). Kersti Bergroth's (q.v.) comedies in the Karelian dialect have enjoyed a deserved success. LAURI HAARLA (1890–1944) wrote a number of successful dramas (and novels) on medieval subjects. A number of Finnish writers best known for their work in other fields—Waltari and Haavikko (qq.v.) among them—have written plays, but no major dramatist has emerged.

French and Belgian Literature

I

ÉMILE ZOLA (1840–1902), son of an Italian engineer (a naturalized Frenchman), is a logical point of departure in a survey of the modern French novel. The fiction that followed his may be described both as developing from and reacting to it. Just as modernism was a redefinition of romanticism rather than a return to classicism, so Zola's naturalism, with its pseudo-scientific programme and its over-simplified determinism, was essentially a necessary curbing of his own romantic extravagance. No true classicist would, for example, call a work of art 'a corner of creation seen through a temperament', as Zola did. His project as defined in *The Experimental Novel* (*Le Roman expérimental*, 1880; tr. 1894), though not privately believed in by him, is romantic in its grand excessiveness, and amounts to a romantic assertion of the authority of the artist. He claimed, for example, that mechanistic interpretations of the interplay of characters could guide government. As Jean-Albert Bédé has remarked, 'the *petite fleur bleue* will never fail to blossom in the corner of even his darkest novels'. Nor, he might have added, do the essentially romantic elements of horror and sexual decadence often fail to materialize: as in *Thérèse Raquin* (1867; tr. 1962), or in the lust and death scenes in *Nana* (1880; tr. 1922). For Zola 'science', really a constellation of pseudo-sciences in which he did not seriously believe, was among other things a means to romantic ends. But truth was always his aim, and his scientific aspirations are more important than his pseudo-science. One of his strengths lies in his depiction of various kinds of corruption. In the first instance corruption fascinated him as it fascinates almost all writers; but his scientific aims increased the powers and sharpness of his writing on the subject.

Zola, like Dreiser, is paramount in his account of individuality oppressed by social vastness. This illustrates the principle of determinism—man at the mercy of destiny; but just as surely it gathers the theme of alienation into its scope. Romanticism had concentrated on the uniqueness of individualities. Now positivism and scientific advance inevitably concentrated on the resemblances between individuals. Literature, in spite of itself, continued to concentrate on their uniqueness. ... And hence it became pessimistic (although Zola, in other respects a nervously inhibited man, relished escaping to his desk to dramatize his gloom).

However, the nature of Zola's creative imagination should not distract attention from his own conscious dedication to, or the widespread belief in, the salvation of mankind through the use of scientific method. The novels of Zola's middle period, the extensive Rougon-Macquart series, were considered by him to be a naturalist project; in this series he was the first to exploit the idea of hereditary determinism. Zola admitted that he did not believe in the bogus theory he used; but that he chose this instead of another framework is significant. He always employed a simple kind of symbolism to achieve his effects—in, for example, his study of the Parisian meat industry, *The Fat and the Thin* (*Le Ventre de Paris*, 1873; tr. 1895), the actual descriptions of piles of food are undoubtedly symbolic, as, more effectively, is the mine (= the birth of social revolt) in *Germinal* (1885; tr. 1894). In his last novels this element of symbolism became stronger.

Zola's novels, like Dreiser's, are a monument to the fact that literature can never become 'science'—any more than science alone can embrace truth. His way of writing, vigorous and crude, is impressionistic, not based on actual observation (although he uses a carefully gathered series of reported details). He reflects the true nature of nineteenth-century faith (or hope) in science; he anticipates modern sociology. It was Zola who forced the reading public to accept harrowing descriptions of poverty, disease and other largely industrial or urban phenomena in the place of insipid romantic fiction—or, at best, fiction containing characters with whom it could comfortably identify.

Naturalism originated in France with the documentary *Germinie Lacerteux* of the Brothers Goncourt, but did not gain acceptance until Zola's heyday and the record-breaking sales of *Nana*. Then the group around Zola, who now lived at Médan, published in 1880 a collection of supposedly 'naturalistic' short stories. It is interesting that the only stories here that accurately demonstrate the naturalist theory are by the least gifted members of the group. PAUL ALEXIS (1847–1901) remained a naturalist, many of whose works agreeably reflect his real distinction as champion whore-hunter of Paris; but there is not much in his novels (the best is *Madame Meuriot*, 1891) to remember. HENRI CÉARD (1851–1924) was another minor talent; the well-intentioned first of his two novels, *A Lovely Day* (*Une Belle Journée*, 1881), about a planned adultery that does not come off, has rightly been called 'a triumph of ... dullness'. The novels of the

Guadeloupean-born LÉON HENNIQUE (1851–1935) were not less dull.
Of the other two contributors to the 1880 volume—their stories, like
Zola's, quickly transcend naturalist doctrine—Maupassant (1850–
93) early developed out of naturalism, and Huysmans (q.v.) travelled
along one of the main channels of reaction to it: the reawakened
interest in religion.

Naturalism lasted for thirty years (1865–95), but its heyday
amounted to little more than a decade. The influential critic Ferdin-
and Brunetière (1849–1906) attacked it and inflicted serious damage
as early as 1883. The claims of science and positivism rapidly lost
their appeal. People became interested in psychology, philosophy
(such as Bergson's) and religion. The run-of-the-mill naturalist
novel, such as Céard's *A Lovely Day* (q.v.), was regarded by the public
as being as monotonous as it actually was. But while naturalism
proved inadequate, no really important new novelist emerged until
the end of the decade.

JORIS-KARL HUYSMANS (ps. GEORGES CHARLES HUYSMANS, 1848–
1907), born in Paris, began as a naturalist, at least in the sense that
his fiction was documented, but later extended his technique to
treat of more evidently subjective material. Huysmans, who was of
Dutch descent, was much admired by Oscar Wilde and other
English writers of the Nineties for his 'decadence'; but he soon
rejected the 'Satanism' of his most famous novel *Against Nature* (*A
rebours*, 1884; tr. 1959) and returned to Catholicism (1892), reflecting
the general revival of interest in religion.

There is not much to choose between his early short fictions.
Marthe (1876; tr. 1948), on prostitution, is meticulous and humanitarian; perhaps *The Vatard Sisters* (*Les Sœurs Vatard*, 1879), on Parisian
woman book-stitchers, contains the most clearly delineated characters. But in *Against Nature* he expressed for the first time his own sense
of frailty and preciosity; his elaborately constructed rococo defence of
aestheticism against coarseness, ugliness and boredom was what
appealed to Wilde. The behaviour of Des Esseintes, the hero, doubtless provided a programme for Huysmans himself to follow. The
tendencies were certainly already there in the Eighties: in what the
poet Jules Laforgue christened the decadent spirit (*l'esprit décadent*) of
that time: an anti-dogmatic and intensely anti-bourgeois hatred of
restraints, with a consequent seeking out of perversities that would
shatter *ennui*—but not too noisily because this was essentially a pseudo-
aristocratic, affected and enervated spirit. It goes without saying that
Des Esseintes is a worshipper of Baudelaire (q.v.). He is also a reader
of an unknown poet called Mallarmé (q.v.): this novel awakened
interest in the latter.

The rest of Huysmans' work describes the progress of his Catholicism. Now the hero, a later version of Des Esseintes, is called Durtal, and his experiences are largely Huysmans' own. In *Down There* (*Là-bas*, 1891; tr. 1924) he experiments with Satanism and occultism; but in the trilogy of novels *En Route* (1895: tr. 1896), *The Cathedral* (*La Cathédrale*, 1898; tr. 1898) and *Oblate* (*L'Oblat*, 1903; tr. 1924) Durtal finds the true, non-radical, Christian light. Huysmans was a gifted writer, in any of whose works characters are apt to leap to life; but his spiritual progress from exquisite dandy to monk-like devotee of God, while as sincere as his refusal at the end of his life to accept drugs for the painful cancer of which he died was courageous, is not altogether convincing. George Moore (q.v. 1) treated the same material with considerably more penetration. The interest of Huysmans' novels lies more in the light they cast upon the nature of the aesthetic reaction to positivism than in their account of religious experience. It is his style that betrays him: involute, mannered, as artificial at the end as at the beginning.

The Provençal ÉLÉMIR BOURGES (1852–1925), less talented, was another of those to react against naturalism and the climate from which it sprang. His attempt to elevate man above the gutter of naturalism was Teutonically inspired; but his abilities in the realm of the long novel, which he unfortunately favoured, did not match his erudition or give much scope to his miniaturist's capacity to evoke country scenes and customs. Consequently most of his novels fall grotesquely short of their intended effect. Bourges was less clear-minded than Huysmans, and his project was correspondingly vaguer. He disliked everyday reality, but blamed the naturalists for depicting it without beauty—which he offered as the only avenue of escape. Bourges, as a transcendentalist, was influenced by symbolism, though not very fruitfully. His philosophy is pretentious; but he does have a tiny niche in the French tradition of heroic exultation in the face of malign or indifferent fate (he admired the Greek tragic dramatists). His best novel, a first-class adventure story, is *Under the Axe* (*Sous la hache*, 1885), a story of the Chouannerie—the Royalist insurrections in Brittany and Normandy during the Revolution. This is more straightforward and less ambitious than the long, Wagnerian *The Twilight of the Gods* (*Le Crépuscule des Dieux*, 1884) and *The Birds Fly Away and the Leaves Fade* (*Les Oiseaux s'envolent et les feuilles tombent*, 1893), or the prose-poem on the Prometheus theme, *The Nave* (*La Nef*, 1904–22).

PAUL BOURGET (1852–1935), born at Amiens, was most gifted as a critic, but his novels are not quite negligible even today—and were once very widely read. Bourget, a friend of Henry James's (q.v. 1), ended as a Catholic fascist and supporter of *Action Française* (q.v.). The ultra-conservative moralist in him was in evidence from the outset; but until his conversion to Catholicism in 1901, and for some years after that, his intelligence remained in control. After some Parnassian (q.v.) verse of no account, Bourget published a series of essays in which he searched various leading literary figures (among them Baudelaire and Stendhal) for the flaw in them that had led to the pessimism he saw all around him. He derived his methods from his study of the critic H. Taine, but this led him to different conclusions from Zola. His first novel of consequence, *The Disciple* (*Le Disciple*, 1889; tr. 1898), condemns naturalism and decadence, and contains self-criticism (Bourget had been a member of the decadent café society called *Les Hydropathes* in the earlier part of the decade). This readable anti-positivist tract describes the malign influence, on a youth's morals, of a dear old determinist philosopher. Bourget is usually called a psychological novelist, and such indeed his approach seems to be; but he was really a conservative dogmatist, a smooth stylist with enough skill to dress his thesis, that France's sickness lay in the betrayal of her traditions, into respectable fictional clothes.

More attractive and more serious as an imaginative writer was RENÉ BAZIN (1853–1932), born at Angers. Bazin's staunch Catholic conservatism may have limited his range as a writer, but it was not tainted with the frenetic and viciously insensitive dogmatism (for all his long concealment of it) of Bourget. Shocked by naturalism, Bazin's sympathy with the humble and oppressed gives him more in common with Zola, for all their difference of approach, than he would have cared to acknowledge. His outstanding novel was not happily titled in its English translation: *Autumn Glory* (*La Terre qui meurt*, 1899; tr. 1899). This is a melancholy description of the exodus from the Vendée countryside of men tempted by the town; this might have been obscurantist, but, even if the peasants are unreal, it has instead the effect of a series of pictures by Millet, whom Bazin deeply admired. This and *The Children of Alsace* (*Les Oberlé*, 1901; tr. 1912), on the tragedy of an Alsatian family divided among itself between German and French claims, are certainly conventional; but in these examples of his fiction at least Bazin's eye is on the object and not on polemic.

More substantially gifted and complex was RENÉ BOYLESVE (ps. RENÉ TARDIVEAU, 1867–1926), born in Touraine. His youthful association with symbolists and experimentalists left little mark on his work. His best novel is *Daily Bread* (*La Becquée*, 1901; tr. 1929): a large Touraine household is seen through the eyes of a small boy. This contains a remarkably unsentimental portrait of a tough, dominating old woman. The sequel, *The Child at the Balustrade* (*L'Enfant à la balustrade*, 1903; tr. 1929), deals with the remarriage of the boy's father, and is more comic. Boylesve was one of the best of the provincial novelists, in whose best work there exists a tension between the restrained style and the lyrical content.

ÉDOUARD ESTAUNIÉ (1862–1943), born at Dijon and brought up by Jesuits, was a distinguished engineer as well as a novelist. He chose to put his vitality into his engineering and his melancholy into his fiction. Basically Estaunié resented the impression the Jesuits had left upon him; and in his most famous novel, *The Imprint* (*L'Empreinte*, 1896), he demonstrated with great psychological skill how the effects of such an education were indelible. But this was as far as he ever went in protest; later he even felt obliged to publish a novel—*Le Ferment* (1899)—exposing the dangers of a rationalist education. He was a timid but subtle soul, whose chief unhappiness—to a large extent hidden away in his subconscious—was that he could not be a free thinker. But the Jesuits, a good-looking, possessive and intelligent mother (widowed) and her rigid disciplinarian father standing in for his own, combined to instil into him, early on, a sense of inevitability. He stoically bore the burden of his inability to be free; but developed into an interesting analyst of unhappy men. His later books were not discussed as *The Imprint* was, and have been correspondingly undervalued. Estaunié was too sensitive and too honest to become a preacher of conservatism—and no doubt his engineering success (he became a Commander of the Legion of Honour and received the Belgian Order of Léopold) did his fiction good by relieving him of the burden of literary ambition. Estaunié's subject became secret unhappiness, and his later fiction—almost unknown abroad—will be read again, and reappraised; that of contemporaries more famous in the first decade of the century may not merit further attention. To read such novels as *The Secret Life* (*La Vie secrète*, 1909) or *The Ascension of Mr. Baslèvre* (*L'Ascension de Monsieur Baslèvre*, 1919) as biased towards Roman Catholicism is to miss their real subject: the tragedy of the paralyzed will. His last novel was *Madame Clapain* (1932). The meticulously observed fiction of this modest but distinguished writer is long overdue for rediscovery.

PAUL ADAM (1862–1920), who once had a wide reputation, possessed literary skill but little mind of his own. He began as a naturalist, soon became a symbolist (and 'decadent': he compiled a glossary to guide readers in the mysteries of 'auteurs décadents et symbolistes') and ended up as a middlebrow nationalist. To call him a forerunner of the unanimists (q.v.) is to exaggerate the powers of his mind: his accounts of collective emotions are more reactionary and sentimental than analytical. But his *The Mystery of Crowds* (*Le Mystère des foules*, 1895), which is about the Boulangist movement (q.v.), may have influenced Romains. Adam was a prolific author given to the production of cycles: the most famous series was called *Le Temps et la vie* (1899–1903), and consists of sixteen novels.

But better known as novelists at the beginning of the century were France, Barrès, Bourget (qq.v.) and Loti. The work of PIERRE LOTI (ps. LOUIS MARIE JULIEN VIAUD, 1850–1923), who was brought up in a Protestant household by a widowed mother and her sisters at Rochefort, will perhaps survive longer than that of Barrès, and as long as that of Anatole France. His fiction represents a reaction to naturalism in the form of regionalism and exoticism. Loti, for all his sentimentality and intellectually feeble vanity, has a residual charm that the socially genial and personally generous Barrès does not possess.

Viaud was a naval officer nicknamed Loti by the Tahitian heroine of his second novel; his first book, *Constantinople* (*Aziyadé*, 1879; tr. with sequel 1928), set in Turkey, was published anonymously. He then published the autobiographical *Rarahu: The Marriage of Loti* (*Le Mariage de Loti*, 1880; tr. 1890), an account of how he 'married' and then abandoned a Tahitian girl. This combined the exoticism of the far-away with a vague sensuality, all in a musical prose that was then new, but quickly cloyed. Readers liked the wrapped-up sexiness, made legitimate because the girl was a 'savage'. But the book, like nearly all Loti's work, is not quite awful: the melancholy nostalgia and expectation of death that pervade it are genuine emotions. *The Romance of a Spahi* (*Le Roman d'un Spahi*, 1881; tr. 1890) depicts a French soldier's sexual life amongst Senegalese women. Loti's best novels, however, were on Breton fishermen: *My Brother Yves* (*Mon Frère Yves*, 1883; tr. 1924), *An Iceland Fisherman* (*Pêcheur d'Islande*, 1886; tr. 1924). The second of these, brilliant in its impressionistic descriptions of the countryside of Brittany and of the sea, is a monument to 'pity and death' (as one of Loti's own travel books was called). Loti's best work was done by the time of his admission to the French Academy in 1891, but his subsequent travel books, notable for their ridicule of tourists, are readable. Loti's was an attenuated and egocentric talent at best; and as he became famous, which he did early, his style became too self-consciously *douce* and regretful of the passing of time. But his Debussy-like impressionism and his vision of nature as an agonizingly beautiful commentary on the ephemerality of existence cannot be ignored. At its very best his descriptive prose endows landscapes or the sea with the ecstatic transitoriness of orgasm, which is doubtless what he really—if un-consciously—meant.

The nationalist and anti-semitic MAURICE BARRÈS (1862–1923), who came from Lorraine and was responsible for the cult of it later so skilfully exploited by General de Gaulle, was always a gentleman, and one who charmed his opponents. For him literature was a sub-stitute for action; his self-imposed role was that of educator of his generation. But behind this lay what Gide (q.v.) shrewdly dis-cerned as a 'great anxiety about the figure he cuts'. He wrote, if one includes his posthumously published diaries, over a hundred books. An artificial writer, he had intelligence and even a kind of passion—but behind the charm was no heart, only vanity. His political position is even now somewhat ambiguous: one could make out a reasonable case for excluding him from the ranks of the French right. Essentially, perhaps, he was an aloof populist.

Barrès began, like Anatole France, as a detached ironist under the influence of Renan; he maintained this intellectual manner in his style for ever after. But his content is by no means always intellectual, and he quickly abandoned a non-partisan position for a political one: that of *Boulangisme*.

Général Georges Boulanger was regarded as the 'general of the revenge'—against Germany—and for a time he was the figurehead of a semi-populist, militarist and nationalist movement directed against the Third Republic; eventually his nerve failed, and his movement collapsed.

The Jewish Army Captain Alfred Dreyfus had been sent to Devil's Island for treason in 1894; by 1898 his cause had become that of the radicals, because it was discovered that he was innocent—and that forgery had been used in the case against him; and that, furthermore, since then facts had been suppressed. Dreyfus was not properly rehabilitated until 1906. Meanwhile the affair split France. Barrès had become Boulangist deputy for Nancy at the age of twenty-seven; in 1898, like most other Boulangists, he rallied to the anti-Dreyfusard cause: it did not matter whether Dreyfus was guilty or not: his supporters were international socialists, un-French, trying to cut themselves off from the living past.

Barrès the writer does not deserve the space he gets here; but his ideas, though less extreme than those of Maurras (q.v.), are im-portant to an understanding of modern French literature. He had begun as a kind of rationalist, and personally remained an unbeliever; but he came to elevate instinct above reason, and to regard national-ism as the fate, so to speak, of all men: men's attempts to uproot themselves can lead only to disaster. Barrès' well-written novels are no more than an illustration of this thesis (which was itself disastrous for France), and because of it they do not achieve, imaginatively, even as much as those of the humbler if equally conservative Bazin (q.v.).

The first trilogy of novels, entitled *The Cult of the Self* (*Le Culte du moi*, 1888–91), portrays Barrès as Philippe, a young man who cannot recognize any reality but that of self. The next trilogy, *The Romance of National Energy* (*Le Roman de l'énergie nationale*, 1897–1902), of which the most important is *The Uprooted* (*Les Déracinés*, 1897), is devoted to a demonstration of the necessity for the solipsistic individual to recognize his oneness with his race and region. Actually this, like all Barrès' subsequent novels, presents a rationalized version of the solipsism of the first trilogy. Barrès had seen his home occupied by the Germans in 1870, when he was eight, and the experience had been traumatic. In his books he either devises means of defence against such occupation (projecting them on to a national canvas) or escapes from the whole problem by going abroad (he was a restless traveller). In *The Sacred Hill* (*La Colline inspirée*, 1913; tr.1929) he advocates, although not without confusions, the Catholicism he did not believe in as the only solution for a unified and strong France, incorporating its past and assimilating its 'scientific' future. This, richly written, pulsating with the sort of 'sincerity' practised by statesmen, was almost convincing. At the very end, in the last novel, *A Garden on the Orontes* (*Un Jardin sur l'Oronte*, 1922), he advocated, in a style persuasively serene but faked, a sensuous 'inner' mysticism. Barrès was a bad influence and a bad writer, a polemicist concealing his cruel message under a sometimes bewitchingly 'magical style'. But it is hard not to sympathize with him: a spiritual guttersnipe, his actual books, like his famous courtesy, have a disarming effect. And at the heart of his racist malevolence there lurked the simple fear of the eight-year-old boy who had seen strange conquerors take over his own territory. As Gide said of him, a propos of his theories: 'This is the most touching, most moving thing about Barrès: his obstinate perseverance in the absurd'.

ANATOLE FRANCE (ps. ANATOLE-FRANÇOIS THIBAULT, 1844–1924), winner of the Nobel Prize (1921), son of a Paris bookseller, had until a few years after his death an international reputation far surpassing that of Barrès, and one out of proportion to his achievement; he is now, however, too summarily dismissed unread. There is nothing like as much to be said for him as for another neglected Nobel Prize winner, Hauptmann (q.v.); but there is something. What rightly militates against him, as against Bernard Shaw (q.v. 1), is his self-indulgent lack of critical rigour and his general air of dilettantism, in which seriousness gives way to elegance. But he was less superficial than Shaw, and more erudite and sensitive.

France began, like Barrès, as a disciple of Renan; he changed less in the course of his life. He retained his scepticism, combining it with a love of French pagan antiquity and a cynically irresponsible surface manner. His early Parnassian (q.v.) verse is important only for the clues it affords to the sensuality underlying this unconcerned persona. Under the influence of a literary mistress and of the socialist politician Jaurès, France developed into a socialist: he was a leading Dreyfusard, a pacifist (he tried to join up, at seventy, in 1914, but this was a temporary aberration in keeping with the spirit of that year) and, at the end of his life, a supporter of the Russian Revolution and the French communist party.

As well as personal reminiscences and *belles lettres* France wrote many novels. They are all marred by bookishness and contrived plots; he was always too much the literary man (his father had a passion for the eighteenth century) to survive in any important sense; but the reasonable enough reaction to him—Valéry, his successor in the Academy, failed to mention him in his traditional speech of praise —was surely really more to the inflated middlebrow reputation than to the inoffensive works themselves, which are amusing. *The Crime of Sylvestre Bonnard* (*Le Crime de Sylvestre Bonnard*, 1881; tr. 1891), the story of an old hedonist's capture for himself of the daughter of a former mistress, is pitched at exactly the right level, and can still give pleasure. *The Red Lily* (*Le Lys rouge*, 1894; tr. 1908) is a notable study of an enlightened woman, and contains a shrewd and valuable partial portrait, in the poet Choulette, of Verlaine. *The Amethyst Ring* (*L'Anneau d'améthyste*, 1899; tr. 1919) over-indulges France himself but contains memorable and telling caricatures of bishops and of anti-Dreyfusards more stupid than Barrès. *Penguin Island* (*L'Île des pingouins*, 1908; tr. 1909) contains some *longueurs*, but is representative of an intellectual's satirical view of emotion- or religion-driven man. France was frivolous, perhaps; but his genuine gift for conciseness should survive his overblown reputation.

Three other novelists, Philippe, Renard and Bloy, are exceptional. CHARLES-LOUIS PHILIPPE (1874–1909), a poor cobbler's son from Bourbonnais, has been curiously undervalued, in spite of the admiration and friendship of Barrès (who personally assisted him by getting him a civil service post), Renard and Gide. Philippe was neither a naturalist nor one who reacted against naturalism; he was instead influenced by Nietzsche (q.v.), Dostoevski and, in his own country, Renard. He was an original, a painstaking realist who wrote without much conscious artistry—but who achieved that marvellous art which results from the reportage of the innocent eye and the humble heart. It is a pity that he should have been preserved only through a minority cult. *Bubu of Montparnasse* (*Bubu de Montparnasse*, 1901; tr. 1932), his second novel, is one of the most exquisite of all the stories of young man and prostitute with whom he falls in love; it came from his own experience with a girl called Maria, whom he had tried—like his bank-clerk Pierre Hardy—to reclaim from her enslavement to a brutal pimp. It has been called sentimental; but this is a grotesquely unjust charge. One might just as well call the paintings of the Douanier Rousseau primitive . . . Philippe made no attempt to emulate the Tolstoy of *Resurrection* (q.v. 4) in Pierre's bid to redeem the girl, as has been suggested. He simply wants her for himself, away from the pimp Bubu; there is no high moral intention —after all, he first meets her when he hires her, and he never has moral thoughts about this. Philippe's fiction has the same rain-washed brightness as the painting of the Douanier Rousseau, and he sees life from a similar kind of perspective. Before this he had written *Mother and Child* (*La Mère et l'enfant*, 1899), the story of his mother and childhood. *Bubu* was followed by *Le Père Perdrix* (1903), *Marie Donadieu* (1904) and *Croquignole* (1906); *Charles Blanchard* (1913), per-haps his masterpiece, about his father's struggles in early life, was left unfinished when he died of meningitis.

Philippe was a 'natural', who complained of the tendency to make the novel 'the pretext for social and psychological studies': 'What is important', he said, 'is the creation of living characters'. Perhaps his greatest achievement, apart from his ability to evoke the pathos of poverty (leading to the aforesaid unfair and snobbish accusations of sentimentality), is the dateless quality of his prose. Despite 'science', life has not changed much since Philippe died in 1909, and *Bubu* could as well happen now as then—it reads like it.

JULES RENARD (1864–1910), born in Châlons-sur-Mayenne but brought up from the age of two in a remote part of Burgundy, was another original: a sharp, clever, sensitive countryman (and yet at home enough in the Paris literary world to be a co-founder of the magazine *Mercure de France*) quite out of key with his time. To try to relate his precise prose, which now has classic status, to any move-ment of the time is fruitless and misleading. His extreme bitterness reflected his rurally suspicious temperament and concern for creative as opposed to mundane values; but he did not lead or condone the bohemian life. He married in 1888 and from then divided his time between Paris and his old home town of Chitry, of which he was conscientious socialist mayor from 1904 until his death. He is most famous for *Carrots* (*Poil de Carotte*, 1894; tr. 1946), the story of how a

country boy bullied by his mother and ignored by his father learns
to put a shell around himself. His sourest and finest novel preceded
this: *The Sponger* (*L'Écornifleur*, 1892; tr. 1957) is about a man who
takes advantage of a couple's foolish admiration for his literary qualities. This, which is classic in its precision, is the book of an honest
man driven to despair by the nastiness and falsity of the bourgeois
attitude towards art. He wrote a number of successful plays of the
naturalist sort, of which *The Bigot* (*La Bigote*, 1909) is a bitter portrait of his own mother, whose treatment of him may have formed his
unhappy temperament. His most original writing is contained in
Hunting with the Fox (*Histoires naturelles*, 1896; tr. 1948), brilliantly
concentrated and poetic sketches of country phenomena, mostly
animals. Renard was for some time after his death seen as a too
affectedly pessimistic writer ('not a river but a distillery', com-
mented Gide); but the publication of his important *Journal* (1925-7)
demonstrated that he was a more complex personality than this im-
perceptive judgement allows for.

The frenetically destructive, impetuous LÉON BLOY (1846-1917)
was born in Périgueux in Dordogne of a republican anti-clerical
father and a mother of Spanish extraction. He became a Catholic at
eighteen, on his first visit to Paris, under the influence of the novelist
Barbey d'Aurevilly. From a free-thinker Bloy turned overnight into
a fervent and fierce mystic, a man from whom each one of his works—
essays, studies, novels and stories—was a confession extracted (he
said) by torture. Those who confuse the profession of Christianity
with the practice of charity will be more confused by Bloy: although
he believed that history was pre-ordained, 'a vast liturgical text',
expressing the will of God, he was none the less savagely unkind to
those instruments of it that God had predestined him to dislike. The
vituperative and scatological nature of his attacks was proverbial.
But Bloy's writing has a visionary quality; his are not simply the
ravings of a dissatisfied and vicious nature. He has unique (and carefully calculated) powers of invective. He was excessive, but possessed
absolute integrity. For most of his life he lived in dire poverty. When
the racist and proto-fascist Édouard Drumont wrote his attack on
French Jewry in 1886 Bloy replied, 'to the glory of Israel', six years
later, with a book claiming that the Jews above all provided a
testimony of the divine will. However, this may be construed as being
anti-semitic in effect, since for Bloy all degradation was glorious.
Much of the anger that Bloy directed at the complacency of his
times—as well as at naturalists, rationalists and Victor Hugo—
made people feel uncomfortable, and he was ignored and ostracized.
He castigated his co-religionists—particularly the putative father of

Apollinaire (q.v.), Pope Leo XIII, while he lay dying—as he did everyone else.

Bloy's first novel, *The Desperate One* (1886), glorifies Barbey d'Aurevilly, attacks the Establishment and presents Bloy the crusader as Caïn Marchenoir. The saga is continued in *The Woman who was Poor* (*La Femme pauvre*, 1897; tr. 1939). Bloy believed that the world was going to be ended and transformed, and that he had a special role in the transformation. *Pilgrim of the Absolute* (ed. R. Maritain; tr. 1947) contains much of his best writing.

One other odd man out, very different from Bloy, deserves to be mentioned: JULES VERNE (1828–1905), who was born at Nantes. Verne is frequently omitted from literary histories, but wrongly: although hardly a stylist, and certainly not a 'literary man', his impact on poets and writers has been considerable.

Indeed, the misanthropic and sinister Captain Nemo, and some other of his characters do possess a poetic appeal, even if this is of an adolescent nature. Verne began by writing opera libretti and plays in collaboration with Dumas *fils*, but discovered his métier in his early thirties with *Five Weeks in a Balloon* (*Cinq Semaines en ballon*; tr. 1870). The interest in Verne's stories, many of them set in the future, coincided with the rise of science; but even now, when science is in disrepute with the thoughtful, they are still read. Verne was—like Conan Doyle (q.v. 1), the creator of Sherlock Holmes—a boy at heart: but an ingenious and inspired boy.

ROMAIN ROLLAND (1866–1944), born at Clamecy in Burgundy, winner of the Nobel Prize (1915), was more important as a socialist and idealist than as a novelist. But he remains a significant figure in the late nineteenth-century reaction against determinism and gloom. He supported Dreyfus, was a pacifist in the First World War—he withdrew to Switzerland—and was a moderate partisan of the Bolshevik uprising. Later he protested against the Munich agreement. His inspiration came mostly from Beethoven—he was a musicologist—and Tolstoi (q.v. 4), whose condemnation of art he could not, however, entirely accept. Rolland was a fine biographer (Beethoven, Gandhi and others) and a competent playwright. *The Wolves* (1898; tr. 1937) is on the Dreyfus affair. The cycle of ten revolutionary dramas, *The Triumph of Reason*, incorporates the best of all his plays: *Danton* (1900) and *The Fourteenth of July* (1902; tr. 1918). Rolland's long novel *Jean-Christophe* (1904–12; tr. 1910–13), for which he was awarded the Nobel Prize, is now unreadable. It is the worthy study of a musician of genius (a kind of modern Beethoven), but it remains imaginatively sterile. Rolland failed to understand the problem of evil, and events have not justified his optimism;

but he possessed the kind of nobility of which the world is always in need.

II

Few of the so-called 'Parnassian' poets survived into the twentieth century; but it is necessary to begin this survey with the publication, in 1866, of Lemerre's anthology *Le Parnasse contemporain*. This was followed by two more volumes (1871, 1876), and contained poems by Verlaine and Mallarmé as well as by poets actually considered Parnassians. This school, of whom Leconte de Lisle was the acknowledged leader, in certain respects reflected the positivist spirit of the age; it reacted against romanticism and technical freedom, tended towards the art for art's sake (*l'art pour l'art*) that Gautier had advocated in 1836 in the introduction to his novel *Mademoiselle de Maupin*, and evoked exotic foreign cultures. The Parnassians were influenced by the development of archeological studies, by Buddhism (interpreted as a pessimistic religion of acceptance) and by Schopenhauer's philosophy, which is akin to Buddhism, that the phenomenal world is no more than a representation in man's mind. Above all, the ideal Parnassian poem was emotionally restrained, descriptive, often pictorial: in a word, it set out to achieve '*impassibilité*': impassiveness. It was therefore highly artificial. However, more important than any of this was the fact that behind this school of modified romanticism was the all-important figure of Charles-Pierre Baudelaire (1821–67). It is not possible to understand twentieth-century French poetry without knowing something of him and of two others who came after: Arthur Rimbaud (1854–91) and Stéphane Mallarmé (1842–98).

Baudelaire was the first poet of modern sensibility in these respects: he explored, rather than merely sympathized with, or 'excused', what in bourgeois terminology are the 'evil' elements in humanity; he pursued detailed investigations into sexual 'degradation' (his poems were called *Flowers of Evil, Les Fleurs du mal,* 1857); he was self-critical; he wrote of the city; he cast the poet in the role of 'dandy', a *persona* at once out of the common run and bizarrely artificial. In other respects Baudelaire was not so modern: his thought, judged simply as thought and not in the context of his poetry, is puerile; sometimes his language and assumptions retain many of the worst elements of romanticism. His essential modernity, however, is revealed in his famous sonnet 'Correspondances'. Here for the first time the poetic possibilities inherent in neo-Platonism were fully realized.

The Enlightenment of the previous century had been brought about in the first place by the apostles of reason, the *philiosophes*. But the irrational elements in humanity obstinately remained. Once people had looked to the Church to contain, control and interpret these elements. Now, more doubtfully, they were obliged to look to, among other things, art. The artist suddenly found himself a putatively responsible figure: he was either a priest who could interpret the will of the universe (God), or a prophet who could change the world—or both. Imaginative literature was no longer a commentary within an accepted system.

There was a definite *symboliste* movement in French poetry, dating from 1886. There were also reactions to it, such as the *École romane* and *naturisme* (qq.v.). But to look to the poets and practice of this particularly named *school* for the essence of symbolism is misleading; the school is long dead, whereas symbolism was with us before it and is still with us. Its essence is contained in Baudelaire's sonnet:

> Nature is a temple whose living pillars
> Sometimes give forth indistinct words;
> In it man passes through forests of symbols
> Which watch him with familiar glances.
>
> Like long echoes which from a distance fuse
> In a dark and profound unity,
> Vast as the night and as the radiance of day,
> Perfumes, colours, and sounds respond to one another.
>
> There are perfumes fresh as a child's skin,
> Sweet as oboes, green as meadows,
> And others, corrupt, rich, triumphant,
>
> Having the expansion of infinite things,
> Like amber, musk, balsam and frankincense,
> Which sing the raptures of the spirit and the senses.
>
> (FBS)

Here the poet is postulated, by implication, as a *seer*, as one who by use of his intuition may unravel the mysteries of the universe: penetrate to the hidden reality behind phenomena. There are 'correspondences' between different sense-impressions (synesthesia), and between *emotion* and *imagery*. This latter is very important, for it gets rid, at a stroke, of the necessity for a logically coherent surface in poetry: it introduces a new range for the responsible poet, even if it lets in charlatans and poeticules. Finally, there are correspondences between appearances (phenomena) and the reality which they conceal.

The view that modern French poetry stems from two aspects of Baudelaire: from the artist, via the Parnassians and Mallarmé to Valéry (qq.v.); and from the seer, via Rimbaud to the surrealists (q.v.)—is of course an over-simplification, but a useful one if not taken too seriously or literally. One line of development emphasizes intellect (Mallarmé, Valéry), the other emotion (Verlaine, Rimbaud, the surrealists).

Arthur Rimbaud (1854–91), the apotheosis of revolt, began as an imitator of the late (and still insufficiently appreciated) Hugo and of Baudelaire. The 'problem' of Rimbaud, who had renounced poetry by the age of nineteen, has not been solved, and will not be. It is enough to say here that it was Rimbaud who called Baudelaire 'the first seer, king of poets, a true God!' and that it was Rimbaud who considered the 'disorder of his senses' 'sacred' (this leads straight into surrealism).

Stéphane Mallarmé (1842–98) was very different. He, too, found Baudelaire as seer a springboard; but where Rimbaud concentrated on a disorder of the senses, he concentrated on the discovery—by means of a highly cerebral and hermetic poetry—of the world of appearances that lay behind phenomena. Baudelaire had defined the painter Delacroix as 'passionately in love with passion and coldly determined to find the means of expressing it'; as Marcel Raymond says in his classic account of modern French poetry, *From Baudelaire to Surrealism*, he 'defined himself at the same time'. And if Rimbaud followed his passion, Mallarmé followed his cold determination: his faith in artistry. Mallarmé's life, as an ineffective teacher of English, was uneventful, although he became increasingly well known after Huysmans' homage to him in *A rebours* (q.v.) in 1884. For Mallarmé poetry was sacred, and therefore an esoteric mystery ('Every holy thing wishing to remain holy surrounds itself with mystery'). He deliberately made his poems obscure, as a defence against vulgarity. It is a common criticism of him that he went too far in this. And yet he wrote 'Le sens trop précis rature / Ta vague littérature' ('Too much precision of sense destroys your vague literature'); the question of his obscurity is not easily settled. He believed that poetry was a sort of magic; his own poetry indisputably casts a spell. Like his successor Valéry, he resisted 'ordinary life'; in his case it filled him with a panic so intense that it may have been pathological. There is nothing as withering as the scorn of children, and Mallarmé's lack of success as a teacher must have influenced him considerably. Certainly he moved away from direct towards suggestive statement; from a 'Parnassian' poetry to one that has itself constituted, for many critics, a definition of symbolism.

Not many of the so-called Parnassian poets are read now. CATULLE MENDÈS (1842–1909), son of a Bordeaux Jewish banker, once a name to conjure with, is now only a part of literary history. Gide, who did not know him personally and was able to observe him closely at a theatre because of this called him a 'Moloch'. Novelist, playwright and poet, he was too metrically facile and too versatile to write anything worthy of survival. Larger claims are occasionally made for the Parisian SULLY-PRUDHOMME (ps. RENÉ-FRANÇOIS-ARMAND PRUD-HOMME, 1839–1907), and not only for the anthology-piece 'The Shattered Vase' ('Le Vase brisé') or because of the Nobel Prize he won in 1901. He made a sustained effort to transform his extensive knowledge of science and philosophy into poetry, in a series of optimistic epics, but ended by devoting himself to prose. His initial lyrical gift was in any case so slight that it would have vanished at any provocation. His cult of brotherhood through self-sacrifice, while well-intentioned and backed up by book-learning, was unrealistic.

The best of the Parnassians—better than their leader Leconte de Lisle—is the half-Spanish JOSÉ-MARIA DE HEREDIA (1842–1905), who was born in Cuba. It is true that his only original work, *The Trophies* (*Les Trophées*, 1893), a series of 118 Petrarchan sonnets, does not nearly constitute the history of civilization that he intended: but the sonnets are triumphs of sonorous artificial poetry, of pure artistry, and represent French frigidity and emotional superficiality at its rhetorically most gracious and magnificent. One might with some reason say that he was no poet; but he was a superb craftsman and his rhetoric influenced poets (arguably, Mallarmé).

One likes to, and is probably right to, think of FRANÇOIS COPPÉE (1842–1908), Parisian poet, dramatist and novelist, as a simple soul. In his day 'the poet of the poor' enjoyed enormous prestige; he is now only slightly less unreadable than the Victorian poetaster Martin Tupper. Beginning with sentimental pastiche of Parnassian poetry, he proceeded to a fluent 'plain style' in which he expressed specious pity for the poor. He ended as an anti-Dreyfusard and innocent anti-semite.

LOUIS MÉNARD (1822–1901), another Parisian, is a more interesting figure, since he influenced Leconte de Lisle and through him the whole Parnassian group and beyond, with his ideas of a 'mystical paganism'. His epic poetry is not important in itself; but his search for a humanistic and viable substitute for organized religion that would recognize the importance of the symbolic and the irrational, is intelligent as well as symptomatic of its time.

One of the main features of the symbolist school was a demand for a 'new prosody', that of free verse (*vers libre*), a term that embraces anything from prose to a verse that is only faintly irregular in a strictly metrical sense. The chief theorist of *vers libre* was GUSTAVE KAHN (1859–1936), poet and art critic born in Metz. In France *vers libre* developed from *vers libérés*, which had sought to do no more than free French verse from the strict classical conventions that the Parnassians had reimposed upon it. *Vers libre* sought to free poets from every restriction except a personal rhythm. Kahn made out a responsible and intelligently argued case for this at a time when it was needed. His own verse, in *Wandering Palaces* (*Palais nomades*, 1887), is striking but inchoate; nor, ironically, was he able to free himself as successfully as some other poets from formalistic inhibitions.

Here may be mentioned two Americans who (like the more notable Julien Green, q.v., a novelist, after them) came to regard themselves as French, and wrote French poetry of some technical mastery if not of genius. FRANCIS VIÉLÉ-GRIFFIN (1864–1937) was born in Norfolk, Virginia, but his parents were of French descentt and he was educated in France. He was one of the pioneers of free verse, and was a more successful practitioner of it than Kahn. His earlier poems (after a youthful period of 'decadence'), which are permeated with the spirit of the Touraine he loved so much, are his pleasantest; he is always at his best when writing of nature. He saw little evil in the world, but the optimism of his verbose later poems—for all their fluency—is simplistic rather than innocent in the manner of Thomas Traherne.

STUART MERRILL (1863–1915), born on Long Island, was of French descent on his mother's side. He was educated in France, but returned to America to study law and pursue socialism before finally settling in Versailles at the age of twenty-seven. Merrill was a gifted linguist, critic and translator, and he played a considerable part in the French symbolist movement; he was not a poetic genius, and his verse is not much read today except in the large anthologies representing his period. In these he has a rightful place. Like most of the symbolists, he was influenced by the music of Wagner; his poetry experiments not so much with *vers libre* as with 'orchestration' of sounds: assonance, alliteration, vowel-sounds in combination. This elegantly handled but too finely wrought style gave way to an emotionally more substantial one in the collections *The Four Seasons* (*Les Quatre*

Saisons, 1900) and *A Voice in the Crowd* (*Une Voix dans la foule*, 1909) which were inspired by socialism and influenced by naturism (q.v.).

The lush, mannered verses of ALBERT SAMAIN (1858–1900), born at Lille, were once the subject of a cult. They were little more than neatly turned Nineties notions of what poems ought to be: sweet, 'classical' (in the worst, artificial sense), and expressing vaguely melancholy longings for a 'romantic' life. Samain was a Dowson (q.v. 1) *manqué*. The 'sponger' who is taken up by the Vernets in Jules Renard's novel of that name (q.v.) would have been thought of by them as a kind of Samain: a defused poetaster.

The eccentric but unquestionably important SAINT-POL-ROUX (ps. PIERRE-PAUL ROUX, 1861–1940)—called the 'magnificent' because after inaugurating a new kind of poetry called 'l'idéoréalisme' he settled upon another, 'le magnificisme'—in his first poetry sometimes tended to obscure his considerable gifts in too great a welter of matter. He did not share the manner of the symbolists, but had their aim of animating and making apparent the world behind phenomena. Mallarmé referred to him as 'my son'. But before the turn of the century and the advent of Apollinaire, Reverdy, and Saint-Pol-Roux's close friend Max Jacob (qq.v.) he had anticipated the new developments, most particularly the notion—the faith—of the artist as God: as omnipotent creator of his own world. Saint-Pol-Roux is the so-to-speak missing link between the new and what preceded it. He never wrote with ponderousness or conceit, and the resultant, most eloquent mixture of Breton medieval myth and Baudelairian investigation is sweetly readable.

There is more than this to the matter of Saint-Pol-Roux, however, involving a most poignant history. Before he was fifty Saint-Pol-Roux retired to Brittany in disgust with the literary world and disappointed at his failure to achieve recognition. The surrealists organized a noble tribute in 1924, but this made little impression, and he remained in semi-oblivion. He was one of the first to protest, in *Supplication of Christ* (*Supplique du Christ*, 1933), at the Nazis' treatment of the Jews. In 1940 a drunken German soldier entered his house and tried to rape his daughter. Saint-Pol-Roux and his housekeeper went to her aid, whereupon the German began shooting: he badly wounded the daughter and killed the housekeeper. This was embarrassing for the German authorities, and while the old poet was recuperating with friends they ransacked his house and destroyed the work of thirty years: this included the second and third parts of a dramatic trilogy, the first part of which he had published in 1899. He was a legendary figure amongst the surrealists if not amongst the general readers; it is just possible that among what the Nazis destroyed were masterpieces. He was a gentle man, of absolute integrity, who ceased to try to please the literary world at about the turn of the century—hence the oblivion into which he fell. His competence as a commercial or merely fashionable writer is proved by the fact that (clandestinely) he wrote the 'book' for Gustave Carpentier's vastly successful *Louise*. What we have of Saint-Pol-Roux is never less than interesting; what the Nazis destroyed is likely to have been a mass of work at once more humane, humorous and enduring than that of Claudel. This was a true triumph of barbarism (PBFV4)

JEAN MORÉAS (ps. IANNIS PAPADIAMANTOPOULOS, 1856–1910), a Greek who became an adopted Frenchman, was successively a decadent and a symbolist before founding his own school. (It is his— extremely confused—'manifesto' in the newspaper *Le Figaro* of 18 September, 1886 that marks the launching of the actual symbolist movement.) However, he was never a symbolist in the Baudelairian sense, but rather a highly artificial poet whose search for a pro- gramme was more important to him than any programme itself: the process enabled him to conceal, from himself and others, the inclina- tions—chiefly the sexual inclinations, whatever these were—of his volatile nature. Moréas was a café-performer, a holder-forth, one who sought emotional stability in a 'position'; he was more publicist than poet. His earlier poetry is pastiche, but the cultivated work of his last years, *Stanzas* (*Les Stances*, 1899–1920), more austere, is more his own: it concentrates on the processes of avoidance of particular emotions, and is interesting though not appealing. It attempts to freeze an unbearable reality (but Moréas seems to have kept his secret) by imposing upon it a reason, a perfection, that does not exist; but its 'significance and humanity' suggest 'the disorder that preceded it' (Marcel Raymond).

Six months after being acclaimed as a symbolist, Moréas char- acteristically founded the neo-classical Romance School (*École romane*, 1891), with such fellow poets as CHARLES MAURRAS (1868– 1952) and RAYMOND DE LA TAILHÈDE (1867–1938). This was not important in itself, but it represented a certain over-idealistic, classical-Mediterranean element in French verse that has persisted. Romanticism was seen as the corrupting influence on French letters, whose fundamental principle was Graeco-Roman. (The classical principles advocated by these poets had little relation to antiquity.) Moréas hunted for archaic words and imitated Ronsard, but did not produce good poetry; in his own case the project was an attempt to model French literature on the history of Iannis Papadiamantopoulos' evasions of self-knowledge. ... Maurras became the rabid spokesman of this group, which he characteristically deluded himself into believing had great topical importance. Little need be said here of the Provençal Maurras as a writer; but his failure as a poet may well explain the fanatic rigour with which he pursued his nationalist and monarchist ideals. For most of his life he was stone deaf. In 1899 he founded, with others, *Action Française*; he saw much of its programme put into effect with the setting up of Vichy—which he appeared to imagine had true freedom of action, though he resented the German 'influence'. To Maurras all enemies of French glory and perfection (the Germans, the Jews, emotion) were anathema. Both claimants to the French throne, and the Pope himself, condemned him. He displayed little charity in the course of an unhappy and lonely life, only an aesthetic taste that might, in the absence of anti-romantic bias, have amounted to something. The French President released him from life imprisonment, to which he had been condemned in 1945, a few months before he died. Maurras was a mentally sick man, more obstinate than courageous, a monument to self-delusion whose self-confidence led even his 1945 prosecutor to a mistaken belief in his 'genius'. When he was condemned his comment was that Dreyfus had had his revenge. Maurras is unimportant, but the dream in which he lived—of classical restraint, of a glorious authoritarian France under a king, of the dross of life purified in the fire of the mind and turned to a finite beauty, of the blossom from 'the universal mud'—is an important theme in French literature. This was at once a reaction against romanticism and against the sense of loss it had brought with it, and a means of avoiding the anguish of personal experience—hence Maurras' lifelong admiration for Moréas. Not infrequently this limiting classicism was the result of an envy felt by the creatively feeble or sterile. Maurras, for example, could not express his love of and nostalgia for the ancient with real imaginative power; his skilfully achieved neatness of form is not enough to record this really passionate emotion. And so he erected it into a theoretical principle.

The most gifted poet, albeit a minor one, associated with the Romance School was probably Raymond de la Tailhède; he ceased to adhere strictly to its rules, and his poems became less mannered. He remained an artificial poet, but his later verse has the same kind of interest as Moréas'. (PBFV3) Some critics, however, regard MAURICE DU PLESSYS (1864–1924) as the most gifted of the group. Du Plessys, utterly dedicated to the idea of poetry, was a master of pastiche—in which he wasted much of his gift—whose pathetic life of poverty and sacrifice is almost too good to be true. But occasionally poignant lines shine forth from amongst his voluminous work.

The so-called 'naturist' protest was more immediately significant than that of the *École romane*, and was attended by poets less psychologically crippled. We may locate it most precisely in Charles-Louis Philippe's (q.v.) exclamation, from a letter of 1897: 'What we need now is barbarians. One ... must have a vision of natural life. ... Today begins the era of passion'. This was much later quoted with approval by Philippe's friend André Gide (q.v.), who had himself reacted against the inevitable preciosity into which symbolism had declined. Naturism's most important and representative figure, FRANCIS JAMMES (1868–1938), who came from the Hautes-Pyrénées, actually began by publishing a manifesto (one gets used to these in French literature) attacking it and substituting 'le Jammisme': a return to naturalness, truth—and God. The confused manifesto of the poetaster and playwright SAINT-GEORGES DE BOUHÉLIER (ps. STÉPHANE-GEORGES DE BOUHÉLIER-LEPELLETIER, 1876–1947), the initiator of naturism, was less well worked out and more artificial; but what Jammes and those he began by attacking had in common was a fervent desire to return to life itself, life as it is lived; they were ardent for 'real' and not mental experience. In other words, 'naturism' (never under any circumstances to be confused with naturalism) was nothing more than one of those returns of realism, those reassertions of common sense elements, that punctuate *avant garde* movements when they become diffused, or end them when they peter out. Jammes was a naïve (q.v.) writer *par excellence*. He began as a new, clean, instinctive poet, of charming clumsiness and simplicity; the poems of *From the Dawn Angelus to the Evening Angelus* (*De l'angélus de l'aube à l'angélus du soir*, 1898) are indubitably poems of adolescence but they have a remarkable freshness and earthiness after the life-starved preciosities of the minor symbolists. The following is an example, from that collection, of the poetry whose quality Jammes' friend Gide called 'aromatic'.

> I love the memory of Clara d'Ellébeuse,
> pupil in old boarding-schools,
> who on warm evenings used to sit beneath the may
> and read old magazines.
>
> I love no one but her; upon my heart I feel shining
> blue light from her snowy breast.
> Where is she now? Where was my joy then?
> Into her bright room the branches grow.

Maybe she's living still; maybe
we both were ghosts.
The cold wind of summers' ends
swept dry leaves through the manor yard.

Remember those peacock's feathers, in the big vase
By the ornaments made of shells? . . .
We heard there'd been a wreck
And we called Newfoundland: *the Bank*.

Come, come my darling Clara d'Ellébeuse,
let's love—if you are real.
In the old garden the old tulips sprout.
Oh come quite naked, Clara d'Ellébeuse.

This is certainly an original and evocative poetry of nostalgia; but Jammes, who went on to write many novels, and more poems, gently declined into a pious and self-indulgent bore. The values of his sorrowful, early novel, *Clara d'Ellébeuse* (1901 : she was one of his several passionate, excitingly chaste heroines) were as pagan as those of the poem quoted above; but Jammes, losing some of his initial energy, his fine innocence shattered by failures in love, drifted from the sphere of Gide's influence to that of the Catholic and morally rigid Claudel (q.v.). This surrender, even if in one sense a logical development and no sudden decision, slowly but surely sapped his creative energy, until little more was left than his delightful habits of observation, his lack of insipidity and his rhythmic prose. He contracted a respectable marriage (1906) and affected a dogmatic rigour that did not really suit him (his best work arose from a state of sexual tension, when he was priapically in pursuit but kept from consummation by being, so to speak, trapped in a frieze); worst of all, he himself subscribed to the legend of the simple, pious man living the village life close to God. People made pilgrimages to see him. And yet the poet in him, repressed, lingered on—just as the hare in his charming and prophetic book *The Story of the Hare* (*Le Roman du lièvre*, 1903) had sighed, in dull heaven, for the adventurousness of his existence on earth. But Jammes left enough behind him to ensure his survival as a poet of greater stature than nearly all his Catholic contemporaries, and as a lively prose writer. Jammes kept clearer too, of authoritarian right-wing politics, the 'Catholic Revival', than any other of his co-religionists.

Also usually classified with the so-called naturists was the overprolific PAUL FORT (1872–1960), the son of a Rheims miller. He numbered Gide, Moréas, Valéry (with whom he edited the review *Vers et Prose*) and Verlaine among his friends. In 1912 he was elected 'Prince of Poets' by some 400 of his contemporaries; he succeeded the inferior Parnassian Léon Dierx, who had succeeded Mallarmé. He founded the *Théatre d'Art*, later the *Théatre de l'Œuvre* (q.v.), in 1890, in opposition to the naturalist theatre. Fort regarded himself as a *trouvère* (the *trouvères* were the medieval poets of Northern France, influenced by the *troubadours* of the South, authors of the *Chansons de Geste*), a balladeer and modern folklorist. What links him with naturism is his treatment of 'ordinary' subjects. He wrote plays, and was much influenced in his poetry by the spoken word. His verse is free but strongly rhythmic; often he printed it as prose. Fort, as agreeable a poet as he was a man, was essentially another naïve writer; he wrote far too much, but his lyric gifts and sensitivity, combined with his transparent sincerity, saved him from triviality or pretentiousness.

ANNA ELIZABETH DE BRANCOVAN, COMTESSE MATHIEU DE NOAILLES (1876–1933), born in Paris of a Greek mother and the Rumanian Prince Bibesco, gained her title by marriage. 'Quite a great lady,' said the novelist and diarist PAUL LÉAUTAUD (1872–1956), 'but not quite simple enough.' As she grew older she cultivated an affected and fashionable hedonistic paganism, influenced by Nietzsche (q.v.); but her poetry is better than her 'philosophy', and is among the most technically outstanding written by French women. She is at her best in her earlier poems, which express sexual happiness and contain sensitive descriptions of landscape; the pessimism of her later poetry, despite sincerity and her fine rejection of Christian solace, tends to seem forced. She wrote three bad novels, but her autobiography (1932) is of great interest. The earlier work at least is due for reappraisal.

III

In Belgium two languages (Flemish, which is almost identical to Dutch, and French), two literatures, and two races, exist side by side. There is a separate section devoted to Flemish literature; the Walloons and those of Flemish and mixed blood who write in French are discussed here.

Modern Belgian literature begins with the launching of *La Jeune Belgique* (1881), edited by Max Waller, and *L'Art Moderne* (1880), edited by Edmond Picard. The groups, which had many members in common, around these magazines were dissatisfied, socialist-oriented young men: their main complaint was that Belgian literature had not received sufficient recognition in the general context of French letters, or established itself as an autonomous entity. Their chief mentor was the novelist and art critic Camille Lemonnier (q.v.), and the senior writer they most admired beside him was Albert de Coster, author of *Thyl Ulenspiegal*. As might be expected the main French influences upon them were naturalism and Baudelaire and his Parnassian followers (q.v.).

ALBERT GIRAUD (ps. ALBERT KAYENBERG, 1860–1929), not quite accurately described by one authority as a 'man of highly unpleasant nature', was born in Louvain, and was a member of the *Jeune Belgique* group. Like so many Belgian writers of his time, he began by studying law. Giraud, a shy rather than an unpleasant man, affected a haughty aloofness of manner and a coldly precise, colourful style in the manner of Heredia (q.v.). Like Moréas (q.v.), he emphasized style to the detriment of content: his poems are careful to avoid any personal intimacy, and in adhering to the Parnassian ideal of art for art's sake, he was trying to create an art that embraced only form.

The genius of ALBERT MOCKEL (1866–1945), from Liège, one of the most intelligent minds produced by modern Belgium and the most astute and witty critic of his generation, did not come out fully in his poetry. But he as much as any other one man was responsible for turning Belgian verse away from the Parnassian frigidity of Giraud to an intelligent practice of symbolism and relaxed form. He lived in Paris after 1890, returning to Brussels only when war began to threaten in 1937. Mockel was never over-doctrinaire, and his remain the most intelligent claims made for the symbolist movement in itself, even though he tends to overrate individual poets. He wrote the best critical accounts of Verhaeren (q.v.), a sensible book on Mallarmé, and a charming book of *Tales for Yesterday's Children* (*Contes pour les enfants d'hier*, 1908). His poetry is mainly musical, but never pretentious. It was this admirable man who, by the publication of his magazine *La Wallonie* (1886–92), ensured the acceptance of modern poetry in his country.

Vernon Mallinson, the excellent historian of modern Belgian literature, has pointed out that whereas in France the symbolist movement acted as, among other things, a channel of protest against Third Republic drabness and Parnassian perfection of trivia and bourgeois complacency, in Belgium it was both more vital and more native: the Belgian temperament is in itself, one might say, 'symbolist': 'artistic', mystical, aesthetic. One sees this quality to excess in Maeterlinck (q.v.).

CHARLES VAN LERBERGHE (1861–1907), born near Ghent, was at his best when his natural gaiety broke through his delicate, pre-Raphaelite timidity, as in his anti-clerical and anti-bourgeois *Pan* (1906). Otherwise he somewhat resembles his friend Maeterlinck in his vagueness. His most characteristic poetry, *Song of Ève* (*La Chanson d'Ève*, 1904), is a dreamy evocation, in a limpid verse, of woman from primal innocence to the renunciation of paradise. But it has poetic overtones. His play *The Scenters-Out* (*Les Flaireurs*, 1889), a morbid and tense drama of a girl doomed to death, is more power-ful; it reveals latent sadism and anti-feminine tendencies. When chased by an Italian girl the fascinated but horrified Van Lerberghe could not bring himself to marry her; unfortunately he never seriously explored the nature of his ambiguous view of women. Nevertheless, his poetry does not mean what it sets out to mean, and is interesting because of this. The tension between the conscious aim and the repressed emotion produces some memorable lines, such as 'All still neglects that we must die' ('Et tout ignore encor qu'il faut mourir'). (PBFV4)

GRÉGOIRE LE ROY (1862–1941) was a lesser poet, but is rightly re-membered for his power to evoke landscape—a tradition strong in a country so distinguished for its painters. His unconquerable despair and nostalgia came out pictorially; it is hardly surprising to learn that he tried to become a painter. For a time, exasperated by his 'artistic inactivity', he became a successful business man.

The Catholic MAX ELSKAMP (1862–1931), the wealthy son of a banker who remained for nearly all of his life (except for university studies at Brussels and youthful travels, and the years of the First World War, which he spent in Holland) in his native Antwerp, is a more fascinating poet than any of the preceding. An eccentric, and uninterested in fame, he published his earlier poetry in small privately printed editions illustrated by himself; only in 1898 did he collect them all into the volume *Praise of Life* (*La Louange de la Vie*). In youth he was a gifted athlete. His engravings have quality. Elskamp, a notable student of popular culture who founded an important Antwerp folklore society, is too often dismissed as a 'pious dilettante', an over-delicate Verlaine. It is an understandable judgement; but there is more in his poetry than that. His welding of sophisticated and often complex thought to simple, popular rhythms is not of merely academic interest. This kind of poetry is characteristic of him:

> I'm sad about my wooden heart
> And sadder still about my stones
> And those cold houses where

On wooden-hearted Sundays
The lamps eat light.

Elskamp combined the primitive with the metaphysically ingenious in a highly original and new way, and his successors outside Belgium (where he is regarded as a master) have not given his due. Although he would not travel, Elskamp was no recluse; nor was he a Parnassian perfectionist eager to escape from experience. On the contrary, he was a man of agonized sensibility; a little experience went a great way with him. Nostalgia made the end of his life almost intolerable; but the poems he then wrote, after a long silence, are his most powerful, combining Blakean simplicity with existential anguish in a poetry that yet remains to be fully recognized.

But the most important Belgian poet, the greatest Belgium has ever produced, is ÉMILE VERHAEREN (1855–1916), who was born near Antwerp. Whereas the Nobel Prize winner Maeterlinck is unlikely to be rehabilitated, the best of Verhaeren's poetry will certainly come back into favour. His vehement optimism is often condemned as facile and tiresome; but his detractors have not read him, and attack him for the least important although most strident aspect of his art. He possessed a force, a boldness and a robustness that his Belgian contemporaries lacked. His optimism, fostered in the years before the First World War, may seem over-idealistic to us; but it is a reflection of his enormous creative drive as well as of his guilt and regret at loss of belief in God. Verhaeren, too, was a lawyer. After extensive travel he produced his first collection, *The Flemish* (*Les Flamandes*, 1883). The exuberance of this celebration of modern pagan man produced guilt, a nervous breakdown and a subsequent celebration of monkish life 'as voluptuous as the joyousness of living illustrated in *Les Flamandes*' (Vernon Mallinson): *The Monks* (*Les Moines*, 1886). He now began to produce a more mature poetry, a savage attempt to reconcile his socialist faith in the future with his despair at the erosion of rural life by the growing cities. Verhaeren was in a sense the prophet of industrial doom; but with immense courage, which never modified the squalor revealed by his vision, he went forward to meet it. 'You command your heart's unease by indulging it', he said. This struggle reached its climax in his most ruggedly powerful book of poetry, the immensely influential *The Tentacular Cities* (*Les Villes tentaculaires*, 1895). Although this ends with a statement of faith in science, it is a deeply pessimistic collection, a thrilled and hallucinated account of the desecration of nature by machinery. Unlike his pessimism, Verhaeren's optimism is always, in fact, modified or ambiguous; at times it attains a true nobility.

Fatally run over by a railway train at Rouen in 1916, Verhaeren's last words were 'Ma patrie. . . . Ma femme!'; but he meant it, and in the light of his life the words are moving. In this poet lack of irony is a positive strength; and he is one of the very few upon whom Whitman's influence was not fatal. His real voice may be heard in his terrifyingly lucid description of 'The Peasants', whom he loved, in his first book: 'dark, coarse, bestial—they are like that . . . they remain slaves in the human struggle for fear of being crushed one day if they rebelled'. Verhaeren was Flemish, and in him we have perhaps the most powerful literary expression of the Flemish genius, which consists of an almost mystical capacity for redeeming a reality not quite believed in by an unparalleled fierceness of sensuality. (PBFV3).

By comparison, the poetry of FERNAND SÉVERIN (1867–1931), the lifelong friend of Van Lerberghe, is minor; but it is distinctly original in the context of the *Jeune Belgique* group. He shared the common Belgian inspiration of painting, but concentrated upon it exclusively, producing a classical poetry of landscape that is as serenely charming as it is limited.

The novelist CAMILLE LEMONNIER (1844–1913), who was born in Brussels, may reasonably be described as the father of the *Jeune Belgique*. In common with theirs, his inspiration was pictorial; thoughout his life he wrote art criticism. Lemonnier, now a too neglected novelist, began as a naturalist (Zola admired his work), but like all the other really gifted naturalists he soon found the theory constricting. He was a thoroughgoing romantic, in spite of his capacity for portraying the brutal and animal passions. He resembles Verhaeren in the loving truth with which he portrays peasants. He wrote nearly thirty novels, most of them eminently readable and intelligent, and many short stories. *A Stud* (*Un Mâle*, 1881), a non-moralistic account of country life in all its freedom, coarseness and pictorial beauty—the hero is a sexually well-endowed poacher—is more typical than the spate of, technically, more naturalist novels that followed it. The best of his other works of fiction are *Madame Lupar* (1888), a study of miserliness, *The End of the Bourgeois* (*La Fin des bourgeois*, 1893) and the mystery tales of *The Secret Life* (*La Vie secrète*, 1898). Few of his successors have been on a level with him.

Also from Brussels was the, at least by comparison, pallid EUGÈNE DEMOLDER (1862–1919), mainly an art critic but also author of three novels. One of these, *The Emerald Road* (*La Route d'émeraude*, 1899), a re-creation of the seventeenth century and the life of Rembrandt, deserves mention because it so aptly if tritely illustrates one of the chief characteristics of Belgian writing: competently executed, it tells its story in vignettes reminiscent of actual pictures.

GEORGES EEKHOUD (1854–1927), from Antwerp, is Lemonnier's only serious rival. At first associated with the *Jeune Belgique*, he broke away when it seemed that the group was tending to make a cult of objectivity. Eekhoud, although his attitudes are not without a nineteenth-century affectedness and tiresomely exaggerated pseudo-romanticism, was essentially genuine in his view of criminals and outcasts as saints. Anarchistic by temperament (his love for the lumpenproletariat ruled Marxism out for him), his lusty vitalism is too inchoate to have really sinister undertones; he has something in common with Gorki (q.v. 4), but had he lived to read Genêt (q.v.) one may guess that he might have done so with sympathy. His best novel, an uncompromisingly pessimistic tale of the destruction of Antwerp by well-meaning 'modernizers', *The New Carthage* (*La Nouvelle Carthage*, 1888; tr. 1917), could be called sociologically ir-responsible or prophetic—according to how the reader feels about urban progress towards the end of our own century.

LOUIS DELATTRE (1870–1938), a doctor from the province of Hainaut, wrote unpretentious, vivid short stories, dealing with incidents in the lives of patients and friends. These avoid senti-mentality by the careful exercise of the Belgian virtue of pictorial exactitude.

ANDRÉ BAILLON (1875–1932), born in Antwerp, is urgently due for rediscovery outside France: for all that he owes to Jules Renard and Charles-Louis Philippe (qq.v.), he was an original who projected his violent quest for himself, which ended in suicide in Paris, into a stream of autobiographical fiction that anticipated its time by some quarter of a century. Baillon had a full and eventful life. His parents died when he was six, and he was put in the care of a pious and cruel aunt. Then he was cheated of all his money by a confidence-man, and so tried to kill himself. After this he was, successively, café-proprietor, writer and chicken-breeder. He wrote his first novel, *Somewhere Myself* (*Moi, quelque part*, 1920), when he was over forty, during the war. It tells of the simple life he had led in a Flemish village earlier in the century, and of how he renounced the literary life. Soon afterwards he went to Paris, where he published the story of his long liaison with a pianist and prostitute called Marie, *History of a Mary* (*Histoire d'une Marie*, 1921). Other of his books describe life in the mental hospital at which he was twice a patient, and gave more of his autobiography. He killed himself when his mind seemed to be giving way completely. It is strange that Baillon, a profoundly original writer with a shrewd understanding of human nature, should still be unknown—and untranslated—in the English-speaking world.

The novelist, art critic and short story writer FRANZ HELLENS (ps. FRÉDÉRIC VAN ERMENGEM, 1881–1972), born in Ghent, is another writer neglected outside France. Whereas Baillon remained in a strictly realist tradition, Hellens is at least a fellow-traveller with the surrealists: but he cannot be classified as a surrealist because his prose, as distinct from the situations in his fiction, clings to a common-sense coherence—as an editor of poetry he resisted surrealism in the Twenties. Hellens conveys in his writing his sense of unreality as he passes through life; for him dreams are truer than life. This feeling of unreality stems partly from Hellens' feeling of uprootedness: he is a man of pure Flemish extraction who was educated entirely in the French tradition. His fiction describes the impingement of the medieval past of architecture and paintings, and the world of dreams, upon mundane modern reality. *Nocturnal* (1919), in which his mature technique first appears, is an account of a series of dreams. Hellens does not begin with a mystery and then proceed to explain it; he does just the opposite, taking delight in demonstrating the inexplicability of the apparently obvious. His most famous work, *Mélusine* (1920), which features Merlin and Charlie Chaplin (under the name of Locharlochi), was written in a trance that lasted several months. *Eye of God* (*Œil-de-Dieu*, 1925) is also about a Chaplin-like figure. This may remind us of another Belgian, Henri Michaux's (q.v.), obsession with Chaplin—and of his character Plume. Hellen's most characteristic title is the collection of short stories called *Fantastic Realities* (*Réalités fantastiques*, 1923). His strangest and most powerful, however, is *Moreldieu* (1946), in which he creates a repulsively fascinating and squalid criminal called Marcel Morel, and describes his project, which is to be equal to God. This is a highly original book, which in many respects anticipates and outdoes the *nouveau roman* that came just after it. Hellens was the moving-spirit of a group that in 1937 declared against the regionalism of Belgian writing on the grounds that this was keeping it out of the mainstream of European literature. His own work has certainly not been regional; and like Baillon's, it is hard to see why it is not better known outside Belgium. Mervyn Peake's fantastic novels have had great success in England since his death, but such a work as *Moreldieu* immediately exposes their dependence upon a rather undistinguished whimsicality. Hellens' work is important because it has seized upon that unmistakably Belgian quality of poetic awareness of the unknown that we find in Maeterlinck, and has tried to purge it of its vagueness. His influence on the development of Belgian poetry is discussed below.

CHARLES PLISNIER (1896–1952), from Hainaut, was another writer who began as a lawyer. He was at first a Trotskyite, but abandoned politics for literature in the early Thirties. The main theme of his fiction, however, remained destructive criticism of bourgeois institutions, particularly the family. His first novel, *Nothing to Chance* (*Mariages*, 1936; tr. 1938) is tendentious—but perhaps ironic; one of the faults is that this is not clear—in plot, but deadly accurate in its exposure of the hypocrisy of the religious and social sides of marriage. Plisnier's next novel, *Memoirs of a Secret Revolutionary* (*Faux-Passeports*, 1937; tr. 1938) won him the Prix Goncourt and led him to settle in Paris. Just as *Nothing to Chance* had anticipated the psychological novel of family life, so this anticipated the fiction of disillusioned communism. It consists of five separate narratives by five communists expelled from the Party for Trotskyist deviationism. The fervour with which they embrace their creed is religious in its intensity; and some of their sacrifices of outward appearance to attain inner grace remind one of those made in Graham Greene's (q.v. 1) novels. Plisnier next brought out a *roman-fleuve* in five volumes under the title of *Murders* (*Meurtres*, 1939–42); this is an intensive study of the effect of a capitalist economy on personal and family life. It contains much detailed description of bourgeois corruption, but is essentially a *roman à thèse* in that the hero and heroine are seen passing through various phases before achieving the state of Christian (Catholic) communism to which Plisnier now aspired. It was filmed with Fernandel and the young Jeanne Moreau in 1950. Plisnier failed to reconcile the aggressive anarchist and the pious lover of God in himself. His figure of the mediating, ever-loving mother, which appears in his fiction and his poetry, is mostly sentimental wishful thinking. But he will be remembered as an at times powerful chronicler of modern family life, and as an acute investigator of the effect of capitalist *mores* on the hearts of men. His style unfortunately became progressively more tedious.

Belgium has made a distinctive contribution to the French theatre through its special—and once again, pictorial—perspective of distortion and hallucination. The elements of the theatre of the absurd (q.v.) have always lain dormant in Belgian (and Flemish) drama; even its realism is so Gothic as to be distorted, its farce mirthless and grimly cruel. One of those seeking new forms in which to express the Belgian genius was Lemonnier (q.v.), with his 'tragic farce' and pantomime, *Death* (*Le Mort*, 1894). This tendency was finally established in Van Lerberghe's full-length *Pan* (q.v.) in 1906.

We must now consider the Belgian writer who achieved the widest

international fame (and the Nobel Prize in 1911): MAURICE
MAETERLINCK (1862–1949), born in Ghent. He was yet another who
gave up the law for literature. He began as a poet, with *Hothouses*
(*Serres chaudes*, 1889), but it was his never-performed play *La Princesse
Maleine* (1889; tr. 1892), hailed by the playwright, novelist (he wrote
the sharp, humane *Diary of a Chambermaid*, *Le Journal d'une femme de
chambre*, 1900; tr. 1966) and critic OCTAVE MIRBEAU (1850–1917) that
made his name. This was heralded as the break-away from naturalism that everyone had been awaiting; Maeterlinck was indeed
fortunate to have written it at the right time. He did not look back
for twenty years.

Maeterlinck's early poetry, much of it in free verse and much influenced by Whitman, came to be very influential—Yeats, (q.v. 1),
Rilke, Hofmannsthal (qq.v.), Edward Thomas and Eugene O'Neill
(qq.v. 1) were amongst his keen readers. Certainly these poems,
ultimately derivative like all Maeterlinck's work, now seem to us
sickly and affected: listless, falsely morbid, repetitive. But the free
verse is effective, and the emotions—derivative though they may be—
are genuine enough.

Maeterlinck's later successes include *Pelléas et Mélisande* (1892; tr.
1895), one of the most oppressive plays ever written, made by
Debussy into an opera that unlike its original has survived, and *The
Blue Bird* (*L'Oiseau bleu*, 1908; tr. 1909), an optimistic and charming
crib of Barrie's *Peter Pan* (q.v. 1) that won him the Nobel Prize and
was popular until the outbreak of the Second World War.

Maeterlinck began in fashionable (but true) fear and ended in
false (but sincere) peace. Like Macpherson with *Ossian*, Maeterlinck
with his plays struck a European mood. He was a modest and re-
tiring man, who would have been quite content to remain the minor
writer he in fact was. His death-haunted early work attracted and
pleasantly scared those who were exhausted by scientific materialism; the optimistic fake mysticism of his later phases, which embraced spiritualism and pseudo-scientific meditations on ants, bees
and aspects of nature, delighted middlebrows as 'deep', and con-
clusively demonstrated that Maeterlinck's responses to his age were
inadequate.

The early Maeterlinck did not have to affect a symbolist way of
looking at things, for this was the way he actually saw them. People
he believed, were at the mercy of a mysterious destiny, and this
destiny was their unknown life. Parallel to it was the 'ordinary' world
which in his early theatre he depicts as interpenetrated by this pagan
mystery. *The Sightless* (*Les Aveugles*, 1890; tr. 1895) is typical: the
guide of a group of blind people suddenly drops dead, and they

(humanity?) are left to grope in terror until they meet a stranger—death. It is certainly jejune; and yet its mood has not yet passed. The 'message' is the same as that of Beckett's *Waiting for Godot* (q.v.). Maeterlinck's best play, curiously enough, did not come until 1918, and was written out of his sense of rage at German atrocities in the First World War: the German brutality in *Le Bourgmestre de Stilemonde* (1919; tr. 1918) is fairly and truthfully portrayed, and the characters have psychological depth.

Maeterlinck was at his best when communicating an atmosphere of human terror at the true nature of destiny; when he essayed to explain this destiny in any detail he became a second-rate exploiter of silence, mystery and cheap *frisson*; when he tried to invent consolations he became third-rate. His voice will not speak to any succeeding generation, but it spoke strongly to his own.

Although some of the important modern Belgian playwrights—notably Crommelynck, Ghelderode and Soumagne (qq.v.) were born before 1900 and had work performed in the early years of the century their mature work does not date from before 1920, and they will accordingly be discussed in the later section devoted to more recent Belgian literature. There were several commercially successful dramatists as well as Maeterlinck; but probably no better play was written than Verhaeren's powerful though over-romantic and stylized *The Cloister* (*Le Cloître*, 1900; tr. 1915), the best of his five dramas; this strongly characterized and well-structured play is still effective to read, although it would probably not stand stage revival.

IV

The history of modern French drama begins with the actor André Antoine (1858–1943), originally a Paris gas clerk, the founder and director of the *Théâtre Libre*. It was Antoine who gave the predominantly naturalistic playwright Henri Becque (1837–99) his first chance, and later EUGÈNE BRIEUX (1858–1932), who was born in Paris. Brieux was a typical dramatist of the turn of the century, and enjoyed a vogue in Great Britain, where he was over-praised by Shaw (q.v.). He was a 'problem playwright', and his plays—of which *Damaged Goods* (*Les Avariés*, 1901; tr. in *Three Plays*, 1911), a competent crib of *Ghosts* (q.v.), on the ravages of hereditary venereal disease, is the most famous—became increasingly didactic. Less ambitious and more important was GEORGES COURTELINE (ps. GEORGES MOINEAUX, c. 1858–1929), born at Tours, many of whose later plays were put on by Antoine at the *Théâtre Libre* and its successor the *Théâtre Antoine*. Courteline's many farces have their origin in the popular music-hall sketch, many of whose later techniques, however, he actually anticipated and perhaps influenced; but there is an undercurrent of savagery and malice—always informed by intelligence—running through his work that gives it stature as literature. He is superior to another author of farces, much performed today, GEORGES FEYDEAU (1862–1921), whose manipulative technique is beyond question brilliantly elegant, but who has nothing whatever to say, and the resemblance of whose work—in its sheer craziness—to some modern drama is accidental. Nor is Courteline so far behind Alfred Jarry (q.v.) as the present vogue for the latter would suggest. Courteline's comic characters, although conceived as types, do achieve a life of their own; he is an accurate observer of manners, not content merely to raise a laugh, but intent on doing so by isolating and ridiculing a habit. He sees, within the strict and modest limits he set himself, as clearly as any writer, how conventions—from the loose ones of marriage to the rigidly enforced ones of military life— distort the human in people. Hence his brutality—which is not a whit too intense. *The Bureaucrats* (*Messieurs les ronds-de-cuir*, 1983; tr. 1928) are prose sketches worth reviving. His most famous plays are *Boubouroche* (1893), an archetypal cuckold figure comparable to Ben Jonson's Kitely in *Every Man in His Humour*, or Crommelynck's Bruno in *The Magnificent Cuckold* (q.v.), *Peace at Home* (*La Paix chez soi*, 1903; tr. 1933) and *Lidoire* (1892).

ALFRED JARRY (1873–1907), born at Laval in Mayenne, was one of those iconoclasts whose ideas, a generation or two after they fail with one public, are taken up by a new public—and even become commercially successful. He inherited his genius for the absurd from an unstable, brilliant mother. The germ of *Ubu Roi* (1896; tr. 1951) was a play written, mostly by Jarry at the age of fifteen, to ridicule a pompous schoolmaster. This master, Herbert, had been nicknamed Hébé by successive generations of boys—and this got transformed into Ubu. So Père Ubu, hero of *Ubu Roi* and other of Jarry's works, originated—like a good deal of anti-bourgeois humour—in the subversive fun of intelligent schoolboys. Although *Ubu Roi* ran for only two performances at the *Théâtre de l'Œuvre* (q.v.), it brought him notoriety—and the admiration of Yeats (reluctant: 'After us the Savage God'), Mallarmé, and Renard (qq.v.), who were present. When Jarry was not posturing in cafés he wrote more, and founded the College of Pataphysics (see below); but he ruined his health with absinthe-drinking, and died aged thirty-four.

Jarry's undoubted importance as a forerunner of dada (q.v.) and surrealism (q.v.)—and incidentally of such commercial phenomena as the profitable pseudo-surrealism of the Sixties—has led many critics to exaggerate his individual importance. Creatively he never grew up; his role is rather one of a culture-hero than an important author in his own right. He was rightly important to the surrealists; but need not be as important to us. He is not a hero of literature, but of the politics of literature—and of nonconformity. For most of Jarry's 'absurd' utterances are merely private, oblique expressions of his unhappy sadism, emotional inadequacy and misogyny. The fact that he made these utterances is more important than their intrinsic content, for ultimately we judge a writer's value by the quality, the integrity, of his attempt to come to terms with the existence of himself and others. Jarry's *Ubu Roi*, and its successors featuring the same gross hero, clever though they are, fail miserably by such standards. And Jarry himself took on the personality of his creation, adopting the pompous manner—until the mask became the face of the wearer. As far as *Ubu Roi* itself is concerned, one must accept David I. Grossvogel's judgement: 'the truth apparently lay in the revelation of a rather pathetic figure, a wizard of Oz amplifying his own fractious voice through the soundbox of what were to have been masks larger than life'.

Jarry spent the remaining eleven years of his life acting out his Ubu fantasy in private and in public (some of the successors to the first play are translated in *Selected Works*, 1965). But he did find time to write what is by far his best book, a brilliant short novel called *The Supermale* (*Le Surmâle*, 1902; tr. 1968). Enthusiasts taken up with Jarry's capacity for anticipating the future have failed to see that this cruel tale of a machine that falls in love with its creator is an indictment of his own loveless life and solipsism.

Another game of the absurd that Jarry lived out in his own life was his College of Pataphysics—whose members today include Queneau, Prévert and Ionesco (qq.v.). Pataphysics was originally what Ubu professed himself to be a doctor of; but Jarry took this over from him too. He defined pataphysics as 'the science of imaginary solutions, which symbolically attributes the properties of objects, described by their virtuality, to their lineaments' (cf. expressionism). It is only by a knowledge of pataphysics that Jarry's own transformation into Ubu, the personification of all the bourgeois vices which he loathed, may be explained—a tribute to its sense but not its warmth as he practised it. But Jarry is an important link between the old and the new.

The reaction to conventional or naturalist drama, and the skilful but lifeless 'well made' plays of VICTORIEN SARDOU (1831–1908), came, as we have seen, with Maeterlinck (q.v.). Another and rather different playwright was EDMOND ROSTAND (1868–1918), who was born in Marseille. Rostand intensified the reaction, but is a somewhat curious case: his *Cyrano de Bergerac* (1897; tr. 1937) is still a favourite, and is performed by reputable companies. But, like all his drama, it is anachronistic, a throw-back to late romanticism. Rostand, who was genuinely witty, was also unfortunately superficial, sentimental and often vulgar. His glitter is really his only true quality: fun for an evening, but embarrassing if not soon forgotten. It was apt that his Cyrano, the story of the huge-nosed, self-sacrificing, romantic swordsman, should have been translated by his English counterpart, the sickly-sentimental but skilful and witty poetaster (once immensely popular) Humbert Wolfe (q.v. 1). The play, his best, survives mainly because it provides a marvellous role for an actor. Rostand's other two notable plays are *The Young Eagle* (*L'Aiglon*, 1900; tr. 1927), on Napoleon's son, the so-called Duc de Reichstadt, who was played by Sarah Bernhardt, and *Chantecler* (1910; tr. 1921), which is his most ambitious attempt to break away from stultifying theatrical convention. Rostand's *kitsch* fluency and vulgar artifice are fatal to his better intentions.

However, the giant of the French theatre of this time, whose works have only become really well known in the last quarter of a century, is the diplomat, Catholic and poet PAUL CLAUDEL (1868–1955), who was born in a small village in the Tardenois, between Ile-de-France and Champagne. His recognition was delayed not only because his diplomatic career (he eventually became a French ambassador to Japan, America, and Belgium) isolated him from his country but also because he was unfashionable—and his dramas were desperately hard to produce. One problem of assessing Claudel lies in the fact that he has become identified with his religion: critics tend to like or dislike him according to whether they like or dislike Catholicism. Another is that he was in certain respects a repellently intolerant man, who remorselessly quarrelled with those who would not agree with him. His political opinions were unpleasant (though he was not an anti-semite or a supporter of Hitler); nor can he be cleared, for all his apparently intransigent rectitude, of charges of opportunism. In 1940 he wrote an atrocious ode welcoming Pétain ('Lift up your eyes and see something great and tricoloured in the heavens!') which reflected not only his warm approval of Vichy but also his desire to get Pétain's old job of Ambassador to Spain. In 1944 he wrote another equally effusive ode welcoming the arrival of Pétain's enemy de Gaulle. But there is more in his work than in the attitudes he revealed in his life. And even if his lack of humour and his pomposity ultimately keep him from the ranks of the most outstanding writers of the century, he can hardly be called a minor. As a playwright and poet sure of his Catholic mission his integrity was absolute. Inevitably, of course, it is to Catholics that he must appeal; that is as he would have wished. A Freudian interpretation would put the other side of the case—but this could not diminish the power of the work.

Claudel had a run-of-the-mill Catholic education, lost his faith, then regained it as the result of a mystical experience in Notre-Dame when he was eighteen. This was owed in large part to his reading Rimbaud's (q.v.) *Les Illuminations*, through which he claimed to have discovered the meaning of the supernatural. He learned from Mallarmé (q.v.); but for Claudel the mystery that poetry tried to decipher was always God's; to Rimbaud's and Mallarmé's teaching he added that of St. Thomas Aquinas. From this point, reached in his early thirties, he did not (unusually for a major writer) develop; he merely added. A large proportion of his creative work, especially poetry, was written before he was forty; he spent his last twenty-five years on biblical exegesis (whose value and validity only a minority, and this Catholic, will wish to establish).

Most of Claudel's plays were considerably revised; not so that they should succeed in the theatre, but so that they should express his meaning more clearly—this makes him, as a playwright, almost unique. In the end it was the stage that had to come to him . . . The success of his old age began with the production by Jean-Louis Barrault (q.v.) of his last epic play, written between 1919 and 1924, *The Satin Slipper* (*Le Soulier de Satin*, 1929; tr. 1931) at the *Comédie-Française* in late 1943. Previously he had scored theatrical hits abroad with *The Hostage* (*L'Otage*, 1911), and *The Tidings Brought to Mary* (*L'Annonce faite à Marie*, 1912; tr. 1927); the former had been produced at the *Comédie-Française* in 1934, and might be said to signal the beginning of his acceptance, though not his success, in his own country. His most personal and powerful play, *Noontide* (*Partage de midi*, 1906), 'written with my blood', was performed privately in 1916 but not publicly until 1948. This concerns a woman, Ysé, and her husband and two lovers—one of whom is Mesa, undoubtedly a representation of Claudel himself. This drama of violence and adultery, while it certainly advances Claudel's notion of woman as the cross man must bear, attains extraordinary psychological power in its own right: Ysé is unforgettable as a character, and only incidentally the illustration of a thesis.

As a poet Claudel regarded himself as 'called' by God to reveal the beauty and mystery of the universe. Quite early he abandoned the traditional alexandrine, for a 'verset' form of his own: this, based on 'the heart and lungs', has its main source in the Bible. Other French poets have used something like it: Péguy, Saint-Pol-Roux, Saint-John Perse, Blaise Cendrars, Valéry Larbaud, Patrice de la Tour du Pin, André Frénaud (qq.v.). Claudel regarded his poetry as a sort of re-creation, or re-presentation, of the universe, and as a sacred demonstration of the fact that life is senseless and meaningless without faith: the poet restores God to his place. One may well contrast and compare Claudel's ideas on breathing and form with those of the American 'Black Mountain' poets, who follow William Carlos Williams' and Charles Olson's (qq.v. 1) precepts: Claudel, too, believed that the rhythm of the poem should follow the poet's breathing. The result is very different from the American poetry: a mellifluous amalgam of chant, prayer, incantation and sensuous description. His best poetry is in *Five Great Odes* (*Cinq grandes odes*, 1910; tr. 1967), *Coronal* (*Corona benignitatis anni Dei*, 1914; tr. 1943) and those collected in *Poems and Words During the Thirty Years' War* (*Poèmes et paroles pendant la guerre de trente ans*, 1945). All these are essentially poems of praise although they praise a creation that demands the renunciation of personal happiness—including complete sexual happiness. It is a poetry in which joy in the stuff of life clashes with the spiritual rigour of the search for God. Written to aid the poet in his fierce battle against his sexuality, it sings like no other French poetry of this century; the question of whether it is to be considered, ultimately, as an elaborate rhetoric in which the author projects an invention of himself is one that critics will have to consider. Meanwhile, Claudel remains an exception to most of the rules of twentieth-century literature; he cannot be ignored. (PBFV4).

V

In the writings of ANDRÉ GIDE (1869–1951), born in Paris of strict Calvinist parents, a luminous intelligence is in varying degrees of control of a sensibility that continuously oscillates between two extremes: of spirituality (morality, belief in God, renunciation) and physicality (sensuality, atheism, freedom and 'authenticity') without there ever being a suggestion of a reconciliation. We see all this clearly from his *Journals 1889–1939* (1939, 1946, 1950; tr. 1953; sel. 1967), which some critics claim as his best work. Gide was a man of courage, a bisexual with a strong tendency towards homosexuality who determined both to pursue his pleasures and to make his delight in them as public a matter as was possible in his time (he upbraided Proust, q.v., for seeming to attack homosexuality, and for turning the men he had loved into women in his novels). The drama of his life was his marriage to his cousin, whose Christianity could not accept his paganism or his homosexuality. This union could not be consummated, partly owing to Gide's impotence; but he had a daughter by another woman. His wife Madeleine is portrayed in his novel *Strait is the Gate* (*La Porte étroite*, 1909; tr. 1924); it became clear, with the publication of the journal and of an early autobiographical essay *Et Nunc Manet in Te* (limited edition of thirteen copies 1947; 1951; tr. *Madeleine*, 1953), that she was the person he loved most in his life.

As well as fiction, Gide wrote essays, criticism, travel and political books, drama and such unclassifiable works as his *Fruits of the Earth* (*Les Nourritures terrestres*, 1897; tr. 1949), the pagan expression of his reaction to his strict Christian upbringing. Though his work is uneven, Gide was humorous and always tolerant; though he vacillated, his essential spirit was the nearest, in modern French literature, to that of Montaigne: cheerfully confessional, unselfishly hedonistic, sceptical, curious. The fate of the sceptic is never easy (he threatens too many spiritual functionaries' and philosophers' bread and butter), and it was not until the very end of his life that Gide was accepted. In 1947 he was awarded the Nobel Prize.

Gide did not have a powerful imagination, and his fiction therefore lacks body and sometimes even appears thin-blooded. And his intelligence was excessive in that it was irrepressible in the act of writing. There is a full understanding of passion in his fiction; but it is not conveyed in the fastidious texture of the writing—it is observed.

In *The Immoralist* (*L'Immoraliste*, 1902; tr. 1930) Gide presented a depraved hero, one of the (Calvinistically) damned. Michel takes his bride to North Africa, contracts and recovers from tuberculosis, and discovers his homosexuality and his hedonism. Eventually Marceline (cf. Madeleine), his wife, herself dies of tuberculosis. This is a better book than most critics have allowed it to be. Certainly it is concerned with ideas; it is also psychologically convincing. *The Pastoral Symphony* (*La Symphonie pastorale*, 1919; tr. 1931) is likewise convincing on a psychological level.

In the comic *The Vatican Cellars* (*Les Caves du Vatican*, 1914; tr. 1952) Gide concerns himself with the theme of 'the gratuitous act' by which (he experimentally postulates) a man may become free. This haunted and continues to haunt twentieth-century literature, from Gide through Pirandello, the surrealists, the existentialists (qq.v.) and beyond. Lafcadio, Gide's hero, commits an entirely disinterested murder; and the book ends ambiguously, teasing such readers as Claudel (who was sincerely upset by it) by not making it clear whether Lafcadio is going to give himself up to the police. *Corydon* (1924; tr. 1950), in the form of a dialogue, is a defence and exploration of homosexuality; possibly Gide's classical purity of style and structure here conceals a lack of depth. Gide affirmed his homosexuality as a part of his life—but he tells us curiously little, in his writings, about its motivations.

The Coiners (*Les Faux-Monnayeurs*, 1926; tr. 1950), Gide's only novel according to his own criteria (the others he called *récits*), is among other things a clever book—so clever that the majority dismiss Gide's own claim that it matches the untidiness of life, and accuse him of artificiality. Gide (a highly accomplished amateur pianist) was much influenced by musical structure in its composition. *The Coiners* consists of a number of themes but is mainly concerned with a group of young men around the novelist, Édouard, who is writing a novel called *The Coiners*. The plot is carefully and ironically melodramatic: one may interpret it, as one may interpret life, as having a complex pattern or having none at all. *The Coiners* is still a source book for novelists, and it anticipates many of the later developments in the novel. *The Coiners* lightly and good-manneredly demonstrates the consequences of living a forged life: not a popular message in an age when to be rated at all, in almost any field, is to be distorted into a puppet manipulated by publicists. . . . *The Coiners*, for all its fame, has not had its critical due; but one suspects that in this case the balance is restored by a continuing, wide and understanding readership.

The prolific Gide can be guilty of inflating the trivial by apeing the classically profound (in some of his drama, to some extent in *Corydon*, and in the *récit Thésée*, 1946). Other of his work is undernourished as the result of an excess of narcissism. But his best writing (and the *Journals* as well as *The Coiners* must be included among this) has a vitality and subtlety that still joyfully and teasingly eludes the solemn or censorious.

MARCEL PROUST (1871–1922), born at Auteuil, the son of a Jewish mother (the centre of his existence—though she died in 1905—from birth to death) and a distinguished doctor (who invented the phrase '*cordon sanitaire*'), is regarded by some as the greatest writer of the century, and by all as one of major importance. Proust suffered from chronic asthma from the age of nine, but he did a year's military service (1889–90) and was a well known society figure and entertainer until the early years of the century, when he withdrew from the world into the famous cork-lined room on Boulevard Haussmann (1907) to devote himself to his seven-volumed, unfinished novel, for which we now know—his contemporaries did not—he had been preparing since youth: in his translations from Ruskin, his elegant *Pleasures and Regrets* (*Les Plaisirs et les jours*, 1896; tr. 1950), with its preface by Anatole France (q.v.), in his unfinished novel *Jean Santeuil* (1952, tr. 1955) and in the critical and introspective studies of *By Way of Sainte-Beuve* (*Contre Sainte-Beuve*, 1954; tr. 1958). *Remembrance of Things Past* (*A la recherche du temps perdu*, 1913–27; tr. 1922–1970) is the collective title of his life's work. He published the first volume, *Swann's Way*, at his own expense in 1913, but it did not do well, largely owing to the war. But in 1919 *La Nouvelle Revue Française* brought out the second volume—Proust's reputation having gradually grown—and Léon Daudet, son of Alphonse Daudet and an anti-semite and, later, collaborator with the Nazis, saw to it that this ex-Dreyfusard half-Jew received the Prix Goncourt. For the last three years of his life Proust was famous. He would spend much of his time in bed, in a fur coat, writing, going out only at night, to gain material for his work. He was a genuinely sick man who used his sickness to protect himself and (as Gide observed) his writing. He was also a helpless victim of neurosis, caused largely by the homosexuality that dominated his nature but which he could never, although he indulged in it, accept. He was inordinately sensitive, often radiantly kind; but he could indulge in sadistic viciousness, as when he had rats beaten and stuck with hatpins, a procedure the viewing of which brought him to orgasm. However, there is comedy and robustness in his writing, which was the result of a determination not at all delicate, sickly or precious—but, on the contrary, remarkably tough. It was in art that Proust realized himself. Like Flaubert, and like many of his successors, he believed that art was the only real universe.

The narrator of *Remembrance of Things Past* is called Marcel: he resembles Proust in being neurotic, sensitive and asthmatic, but he is neither half-Jewish nor homosexual (a feature that leads to certain confusions and distortions, though some argue that these can be satisfactorily untangled). Almost everyone of importance or interest in the Paris society of Proust's time is involved in *Remembrance*; but no character 'is' a real person. Even the homosexual Baron de Charlus, besides being modelled on the poetaster Comte Robert de Montesquiou (who also served Huysmans for Des Esseintes, the hero of *Against Nature*, q.v.), combines traits exhibited by several other notables. Proust was well aware that he was creating an illusory world on paper, rather than providing a description of a real one. But he believed the fictional was superior to the real, since (as

Aristotle said of poetry) 'its statements are of the nature of universals'.

The discovery that *Remembrance* made for its author, and makes for its readers, is that all our pasts remain within us, capable of rediscovery. Proust's famous example is how the taste of a cake dipped into a cup of tea awakens an involuntary memory that expands like the ripples from a stone thrown into a pond. Like the important romantic philosopher Henri Bergson (q.v.), Proust returned to 'the immediate data of consciousness'—not for philosophical purposes but because he sought to perfect, through art, a life he found agonizing. Thus, as he lay dying he tried to perfect a passage in his novel describing the death of the novelist, Bergotte.

Had Proust not been a brilliant stylist he could hardly have prevented such a mass of analytical material from being boring; but although he is frequently abstruse, he is never abstract: all the processes he describes are the stuff of life. He can be criticized for some boring passages, especially those in which he dwells for too long on social rank. Again, it is likely that homosexual love is emphasized at the expense of (to avoid the tendentious term 'normal') heterosexual. Nevertheless, *Remembrance* is indisputably one of the world's paramount novels. It will be read long after Proust-worship, which is often tiresome, snobbish and uncritical, has passed.

The French produced surprisingly few distinguished war novels. An exception was provided by HENRI BARBUSSE (1873–1935), who was born near Paris, with *Under Fire* (*Le Feu*, 1916; tr. 1917). Barbusse had originally been an unsuccessful writer. He began as a fashionable and bad poet—a protégé of Catulle Mendès (q.v.), one of whose daughters he married. His fiction made so little impression that he had to earn his living as a journalist. At the outbreak of war, though ill, he joined up in an access of the patriotic feeling from which almost everyone else in France (and Great Britain and Germany) was suffering at the time. Like Sorley, Sassoon, Owen and other English writers, he quickly became disillusioned. *Under Fire* is the story of a doomed squad of men and their corporal in the perpetual winter of the trenches. The book convincingly shows men as exploited creatures fighting a war that can in no way benefit them. No French literature of the time so closely matched, in mood, the German left-wing and pacifist expressionism (q.v.). *Under Fire* was enthusiastically received in Geneva. After the success of this, Barbusse's earlier *Inferno* (*L'Enfer*, 1908; tr. 1932) was revived: this was a naturalist work, a series of Zolaesque *tranches de vie* that often display the lucid power with which Barbusse was to depict the filthy and squalid side of war in *Under Fire*. *Light* (*Clarté*, 1918; tr. 1919), an-

other war book, was militantly socialist; from this point Barbusse became a propagandist rather than a creative writer. *Under Fire* remains
the best direct account, in French, of the life of ordinary men in the
trenches; by comparison the war tetralogy of MAURICE GENEVOIX
(1890), collected in one volume under the title of *Those of Verdun*
(*Ceux de Verdun*, 1915)—good straight reportage though it is—is pale.
Genevoix, however, went on to write some good regional novels
(about the Nivernais), of which the best known is *Raboliot* (1925),
which won the Prix Goncourt. ROLAND DORGELÈS (ps. RENÉ LE-
CAVELÉ, 1886–1973), originally a humorous writer, wrote a highly
successful imitation of *Under Fire* in 1919, *The Wooden Crosses* (*Les
Croix de bois*; tr. 1921), but avoided Barbusse's impassioned grimness.

The Burgundian COLETTE (ps. SIDONIE GABRIELLE COLETTE, 1873–
1954) remains an essentially *fin de siècle* writer, but a versatile and
subtle original of undoubted stature. All her values and interests
stem from the Bohemian Paris of her youth: nostalgia, the cult of
youth and regret, a relaxed attitude towards morality. Colette was a
writer of more range than is usually acknowledged: she could subtly
trace the progress of moods in young people, evoke the urban life of
the *demi-monde* (she was herself a dancer and mime for some years
after her first divorce in 1906) and describe the countryside—landscape, animals, birds and flowers—with meticulous ease. Her first
books, the Claudine stories, were written under the direction of her
husband Willy, who signed them himself. *The Vagabond* (*La Vaga-
bonde*, 1911; tr. 1954) is basically her own story. *Chéri* (1920) and its
sequel (*La Fin de Chéri*, 1926; tr. 1960, 1963) form the exquisitely told
story of a young man's love for a woman of fifty, and of his gradual
decline. *Duo* (1934) is a study of a marriage destroyed and a man
self-destroyed by jealosy. *Gigi* (1944), impeccably observed and unsentimental, gained fame as a sentimental film.

The two chief criticisms of Colette have been that her identification
with nature is falsely sensuous, or even gushing, and that she is really
no more than a woman's magazine writer with a superior style. It is
true that when writing of her country childhood she occasionally
slipped into sentimentality, and equally true that the material of her
novels (which draw greatly on her own experience) is concerned with
sentimental and weakly 'romantic' people. But she herself is not
sentimental. Although no moral lens distorts her vision of them, her
tracery of her characters' moods and caprices and deeper longings
has the effect of sharp analysis. Although as a character in her novels
she may be sentimental, she is not so as writer. She brings instinctive
(not intellectual) female wisdom to the novel; with this she enchants
it (as in her autobiographical writings, dealing with nature and ani-

mals) or brings to it a glowing tolerance of the unchecked life of
instinct. Her exquisite libretto for Ravel's opera, *The Child and the
Spells* (*L'Enfant et les sortilèges*) is characteristic, and is one of the most
beautiful and tender children's stories ever written.

RAYMOND ROUSSEL (1877-1933), born in Paris, was a rich and
leisured eccentric who, because he anticipated them in so many ways,
was taken up by the surrealists (q.v.) in the late Twenties, and then
again by the exponents of the *nouveau roman* in the Fifties. After having
had initial ambitions, Roussel had no interest in fame or fashion,
and wrote for himself alone. He suffered from mental illness—his
case was described in print by his doctor, Pierre Janet, in 1926—and
spent his time travelling the world but not looking at it. Rather, he
laboured to construct his own world on paper. This world seems—on
the psychological level—to amount to an attempt to construct a denial of reality. The mechanics of Roussel's paranoia are of extreme
interest; but he is not always successful in holding the attention of the
reader. However, this is the kind of self-defeating process that attracted—and not foolishly—the surrealists and others; it makes him
important as an influence. Furthermore, an understanding of his
state of mind and intentions in his best works makes them more accessible. However, his procedures, some of them phonic, render him
well nigh untranslatable into English, although what has been done
has been done well. He was influenced by a host of diverse writers
(for example, Verne, Loti, qq.v., Dumas *père*) but exploited these
rather than viewed them critically.

Roussel wrote two novels in verse: *The Understudy* (*La Doublure*,
1896), a projection of himself as a failed actor making his masked
way through the Carnival of Nice (life), and *The View* (*La Vue*, 1901),
and several wildly anti-theatrical plays (which, though they were
derided, he could afford to put on with good casts): these would
perhaps lend themselves to modern productions, but are probably
best regarded as significant personal gestures.

Roussel's major works are *Impressions of Africa* (*Impressions d'Afrique*,
1910; tr. 1966) and *Locus Solus* (1914), which was adapted by the
prolific and skilful novelist PIERRE FRONDAIE (ps. RENÉ FRAUDET,
1884-1948) into a more viable play than he himself ever achieved.
Roussel had already, at nineteen, anticipated the method of his
later works, of combining precise description (of the Nice Carnival,
for example) with situational fantasy. Now he was concerned with
words themselves: he proceeded by pun and homophone, trying to
superimpose a purely verbal logic upon a (recondite) representational
one. *Impressions of Africa* is divided into two halves. The first presents
a series of isolated scenes involving a number of people shipwrecked

in Africa who are celebrating their captor King's coronation. The second begins at an earlier point of time and represents the whole action in the form of a parody (sometimes tedious) of conventional storytelling. Roussel's intention was not unlike Proust's: to recreate lost perceptions—but his method was linguistic. He anticipated not only *nouveau roman* but also, a critic has pointed out, that modern psychoanalysis (one of the chief British practitioners is Charles Rycroft) which defines its formulas as 'semantic ones . . . able to free the tongues of those for whom to be speechless is to suffer'. He left a key to his intentions, without which his most enthusiastic critics would be lost, in *How I Wrote Certain Books* (*Comment j'ai écrit certaines de mes livres*, 1935). He is a very important writer rather than a freak, as some have called him; but it should perhaps be pointed out that he failed to achieve a wholly satisfactory work. Attributing his mental illness to the 'violent shock' he experienced at the failure of *The Understudy*, he said that he vainly sought to recapture 'the sensation of mental sunlight' that he had experienced while he was writing it. He killed himself in Palermo.

VICTOR SÉGALEN (1878–1919), born in Brest, is a neglected writer. Novelist and poet, he was the friend and the influencer of Claudel, Perse and Jouve (qq.v.), who edited his poetry. He wrote *The Immemorial* (*Les Immémoriaux*, 1907) after visiting Tahiti—on the ship whose doctor he was—three months after Gauguin's death. This, one of the earliest books—half novel and half autobiography—to describe 'uncivilized' people accurately, sympathetically and unpatronizingly, and to lament the destruction of primitive wisdom, anticipates the work of the French anthropologist Claude Lévi-Strauss. Ségalen worked with Debussy on a lyrical drama, *King Orpheus* (*Orphée Roi*, 1921), travelled on an archaeological expedition to China, and visited Tibet. He absorbed much from the Orient, which he distilled into the highly original poetry of *Steles* (*Stèles*, 1912), *Paintings* (*Peintures*, 1916) and *Escapade* (*Équipée*, 1929). *René Lys* is a posthumous novel about China. He vanished when on an expedition in the forest of Hoelgoat.

CHARLES-FERDINAND RAMUZ (1878–1947), friend of the composer Stravinsky (for whom he wrote *The Soldier's Tale*), was born at Cully, a town on Lake Geneva, in Switzerland. He spent a number of years in Paris as a young man, but returned to Switzerland after 1914. Ramuz is a regional writer, who frequently employs the local Vaud dialect in his roughly told stories. Considering the fame of Giono (q.v.), to whom he is in some respects close, Ramuz is undeservedly neglected. True, several of his books have been translated into English, but he is seldom discussed; in his own country he was almost sixty before he gained popular recognition. His first novel, *Aline* (1905), on the wellworn theme of the village girl who is deserted by her seducer and kills her baby, is direct and deeply felt, but went unheeded. Critics told him to apply his gifts to a wider field than that of the Vaudois; the result was the semi-autobiographical *Aimé Pache, Vaudois Painter* (*Aimé Pache, peintre vaudois*, 1910), in which the artist-hero goes to Paris but discovers his roots in his native Vaud. Similar was *The Life of Samuel Belet* (*Vie de Samuel Belet*, 1913, tr. 1951). After 1919 followed—with the exception of the brilliant collaborative effort *The Soldier's Tale*—Ramuz's creatively least successful phase, in which he experimented with satire (*The Reign of the Evil One* (*Le Règne de l'esprit malin*, 1917; tr. 1922), in which the thinker destroys the novelist) and with modernist techniques unsuited to his genius. *Terror on the Mountain* (*La Grande Peur dans la montagne*, 1926; tr. 1966) marked the beginning of his maturity, in which he evolved an inimitable 'anti-literary', no-nonsense style (described by one critic as consisting of 'syntactical eccentricities . . . provincialisms, archaisms, neologisms, ellipses, missing verbs and Biblical echoes') perfect for his purposes, impossible for almost anyone else's. The most fully satisfying of his twenty-two novels is *When the Mountain Fell* (*Derborence*, 1935; tr. 1949). In this story of a young man who emerges from beneath the rocks of an avalanche some weeks after it has occurred Ramuz combines his brilliance of regional understanding with the more universal theme of self-discovery. To some critics Ramuz's style is monotonous; here at least, where the author creates the oral illusion of his own voice almost as remarkably as Céline (q.v.) does, this claim is difficult to sustain. Ramuz's *Journal* (1943; 1949) is of the utmost interest. This gruff writer, whose journey to self-fulfilment was as arduous and courageous as anyone's of his time, has not had his due.

LOUIS HÉMON (1880–1913) was born in Brest and emigrated to Canada in 1911. He was run over by a train while walking along a track in Ontario. Hémon, who worked as a journalist in England for eight years, published only one novel in his lifetime: *Lizzie Blakeston* (1908), about English life. *Maria Chapdelaine* (1916; tr. 1921), serialized in 1914 in Paris without attracting notice, brought him posthumous fame, and was immensely influential in French Canadian literature (q.v. 1), since it represented an enraptured treatment of the 'new Frenchness' in terms of the old France from which this sprang. An excellent novel by any standards, *Maria Chapdelaine* is one of those books that define the spirit and the aspirations of a whole community, in this case the *défricheurs* (clearers of and settlers in new land in forested Quebec) and their families. Maria's father Samuel

wrests a comfortable home from the forests, but must always move
further north to repeat his victory. A memorable section of the book
is devoted to the isolated family's joyous recognition of the signs of
spring. The man Maria loves is killed by the harshness of nature (he
is lost in the snow), and her mother dies; but, although offered a city
life in America, she decides to remain and to marry a neighbour—a
decision that is as moving as it is convincingly conveyed. Hémon was
always a devotee of sport and physical fitness, and one of the most
amusing of the short works that were issued after his death is *Battling
Malone* (1925). *Maria Chapdelaine* was filmed twice, memorably by
Duvivier with Madeleine Renaud and Jean Gabin (1934); René
Clément in 1953 filmed *Monsieur Ripois et la Némésis* (1926; tr. 1924).

The novelist and dramatist ROGER MARTIN DU GARD (1881–1958),
born in the Paris suburb of Neuilly, won the Nobel Prize in 1937. A
close personal friend of Gide's (q.v.), he spent his life in strict
seclusion and did not involve himself in literary affairs. Trained as
an archivist—this is significant in view of the massive build-ups of
detail in his fiction—he fought in the First World War and for a
while worked with Copeau (q.v.) at the Vieux-Colombier (q.v.). He
left behind him an immense novel called *The Journal of Colonel
Maumort*, on which he worked between 1940 and his death; this is so
far unpublished. It is possible, even likely, that it will prove a
masterpiece. Several other works have not yet been issued. It is
often suggested that the reticent Martin du Gard was not quite able
to compensate for his lack of genius, that his fiction is superbly
intelligent documentary, but more finely industrious than imaginative. This is certainly true of his second novel, *Jean Barois* (1913; tr.
1950) although it is an incomparable picture of France (in particular
the Dreyfus affair) in the thirty years before the First World War; it is
arguably so in the case of the *roman-fleuve* for which he was awarded
the Nobel Prize, *The World of the Thibaults* (*Les Thibault*, 1922–40; tr.
1939–40); but it is not true of his comic novel *The Postman* (*Vieille
France*, 1933; tr. 1955) which is surprisingly robust—and emphatically not true of the more seriously intended short novel about
incest, *African Confidence* (*Confidence africaine*, 1931). *The Journal of
Colonel Maumort* may surprise some critics. Martin du Gard has written two subtle farces and a technically more conventional but none
the less excellent realist drama, *A Silent One* (*Un Taciturne*, 1931), on
the subject of homosexuality (Gide wrote interestingly about it in his
Journal). Roger Martin du Gard was a versatile writer whose worth
has not yet been assessed.

The Thibaults concentrates on the relationships of the two Catholic
Thibault sons, Jacques and Antoine, with their father and with the

Protestant family of Fontenin. Jacques is an open rebel; Antoine, a doctor, is a moderate prepared to accept conventional ways if he can throw off Catholicism. Roger Martin du Gard saw clearly into the nature of French Catholicism. Both sons die as a result of the war, which the author pessimistically regarded as the end of the last tolerable chapter in human civilization. There is much remarkable detail: the slow death of Thibault senior from uremia (Antoine eventually puts him out of his misery); the actions of Antoine's love-rival Hirst, who kills his daughter, with whom he has been to bed, and her husband—and then takes Antoine's mistress back from him although she knows this. The detail in *The Thibaults* has been described as tending to dullness, and this cannot always be denied; but to take risks is necessary in this kind of novel—the slick, meretricious, unreal surface of C. P. Snow's sequence (q.v. 1), incidentally exposed by such a serious work as *Les Thibault* for the middlebrow journalism that it is, demonstrates the fact—and Martin du Gard is not often actually dull. Here the realist tradition, because it is sensibly used, lives effectively on. Roger Martin du Gard has been called a naturalist, but this is misleading; he is pessimistic about the nature of man, but has no special deterministic philosophy.

The Catholic FRANÇOIS MAURIAC (1885–1970), from Bordeaux, also received a Nobel Prize (1952). Mauriac's Catholicism is more attractive than Claudel's: less self-centred, more self-questioning, more merciful, more liberal-minded. Perhaps the human indignity reached by Claudel in his ode to Pétain is the automatic price of the pomposity of a too high self-regard; Mauriac could never, in any case, have erred in this respect. He attacked Franco, supported the Resistance (but denounced the savage witch-hunting of the years following the war) and was a critical and independent supporter of de Gaulle. In the latter half of his life Mauriac practised journalism, and became France's leading commentator on current affairs.

Mauriac writes on the same theme as Claudel—the meaningless misery of existence without God—but he finds less radiance in himself or the world. He was brought up strictly, in an atmosphere of Catholic puritanism, and has often been called a Jansenist. (The followers of the heretical Jansen 1585–1638, one of whom was Pascal, introduced a strongly pessimistic and puritanical streak into Catholicism; above all, they emphasized natural man's helpless inability to turn to God.) The gloomy novels of Mauriac's first and 'Jansenist' period, lasting until the early Thirties, are his most powerful. The change of heart he then experienced, which led to a softening of his general attitude—and, in particular, to a higher estimate of the spiritually regenerative powers of love—was totally sincere; but tension in him slackened, and his characters no longer make the same tragic impact. The attempted poisoner of her husband, *Thérèse Desqueyroux* (1927; all the Thérèse books tr. as *Thérèse: A Portrait in Four Parts*, 1947), is an absolutely typical Mauriac character, tempted by boredom with her deadly marriage into sin. In the later stories one can see the mellower and more orthodox Mauriac struggling with himself and her; it is less convincing, but he will do no more than bring her closer to official salvation. A priest did tell Mauriac (he said) how Thérèse might be saved. But the creative writer can hardly believe in such solutions.

Mauriac, who was encouraged by Barrès (q.v.), began with verse. His first mature novel was *A Kiss for the Leper* (*Le Baiser au lépreux,* 1922; tr. in *Collected Novels*, 1946 ff.), about an ugly man and his wife, who devotes herself piously to his memory after he dies. *Génitrix* (1923; tr. ibid), Mauriac's first undoubted masterpiece, is a bleakly pessimistic study of a murderously intense maternal possessiveness defeating itself in the moment of its apparent victory—and of the loneliness of a weak man to whom love has been nothing but a stultifying disaster. These novels, like most of Mauriac's others, are redolent of Bordeaux and the sandy, pine- and vine-filled country- side that surrounds it.

In *The Desert of Love* (*Le Désert de l'amour*, 1925; tr. ibid) Mauriac reached the height of his achievement. Masterly in technique, this book does end with a moment of love, as a hitherto estranged father and son—both doomed by their characters never to find fulfilment in love—briefly recognize each other and the desert of love in which each dwells. It is a bitter moment, but its lyricism is enough to clear Mauriac's earlier work of the charge of over-pessimism. *The Vipers' Tangle* (*Le Nœud de vipères*, 1932; tr. ibid) marks the stage when Mauriac was becoming dissatisfied with (and perhaps orthodoxly ashamed of) his own bleak pessimism. Most of the book is on a level with his best: Louis, a millionaire, keeps his family, whom he hates, in the vipers' tangle of the title. Spite is so strong in him that he even writes a diary in which he expresses his hatred of his wife. She is to read this on his death. Then she dies before him, and he turns—but not at all convincingly, psychologically—to Christ. However, the conversion is moving—its energy being gained from Mauriac's desire for change.

The fact is that Mauriac need never have chosen to portray this kind of character. There are people less depressing in life than the inhabitants of his fiction. ... While the tension in him, between dutiful love of God's human creation and despair at its vile helpless- ness, remained strong, Mauriac was a novelist of great power; but he cannot convincingly resolve such a tension (except temporarily, in the kind of momentarily non-solipsistic illumination provided at the end of *The Desert of Love*), because his imagination (unlike Claudel's) cannot fully believe in, record, the psychological detail of the amazing dynamics of such conversions as Louis', in *The Vipers' Tangle*, to Christ. The situation is further complicated by the fact that Mauriac has to equate a change of heart with a turning to Christ: he is not only religious but also Christian.

But Mauriac's fiction, though it deteriorated, never became less than interesting and intelligent. And in *A Woman of the Pharisees* (*La Pharisienne*, 1941; tr. ibid) at least, he returns to his old form. This deals with the sort of character with whom Mauriac has always been obsessed: the tyrannical *bien-pensant*. It is only at the end of the novel that Mauriac allows the sour and cruel monster he has created to glimpse the grace of inner sweetness; this cannot but be psychologically unconvincing. Sartre (q.v.) in fact accused this author of creating characters who were incapable of change (the strongest Calvinist element in Jansenism is its belief in predestination). This was damaging criticism, and angered the Catholic in Mauriac. It is true that doctrine finally caused him to manipulate his characters; but then his belief in doctrine, his faith, was the positive pole of the generator of his whole creative effort. . . . However, it must be conceded that the comparative serenity of the later fiction is, by the highest standards, false and morally imposed.

In his second phase Mauriac wrote some well-constructed plays, and continued until the very end to produce fiction of a high standard. His restrained style, of a classical purity, is universally praised.

VI

Although that extraordinarily fascinating and versatile writer JULES ROMAINS (ps. LOUIS FARIGOULE, 1885–1972), who was born in a village of the Cévennes, could claim to have invented 'unanimism', it was actually something—like all the contemporary philosophies worthy of note—that was very much in the air in the years before 1914, a French equivalent to the German 'O Mensch!' side of expressionism (q.v.). These were years of idealism more intense (and perhaps more complacent) than anything we have since witnessed. The men who started the First World War did not know what had happened; those who tried to make a settlement in 1919 were sentimental and pompous mediocrities without an elementary grasp of reality. The serious men of before 1914 may be forgiven for regarding politicians as human beings as responsible as themselves—and more gifted in action. No such mistake is made today except in the literature of *kitsch*: in the fantasies of Snow (q.v. 1) or Allen Drury. Hope for mankind was still not quite a drastic or startling emotion to hold—or an official's trick-cliché. Politicians had not yet fully emerged as the foci of the human sickness, as men behind whose comfortingly featureless masks the essence of criminality has been refined. This kind of idealism has tended to persist, if only as one element, in the work of Romains and of some of those others who began with him as unanimists and then went their different ways. We have seen it, too, in the influential poetry of Verhaeren (q.v.): it operates as an extreme cosmic excitement about mankind's new prospects. But here it is seriously challenged and undermined by knowledge of human nature: by guilt-inducing but irrepressible pessimism.

Unanimism—under any of its names, for its spirit was apparent in the work of men who had never heard of it—was also a response to the tendency of the world to contract (McLuhan's 'global village') owing to more and faster ships, railways, telegraph, etc. This group theory, by which collective emotions—of two people, of small rural communities, of cities, of countries, and finally of the whole world— transcend and are superior to individual ones, was also an attempt to rediscover the God who had given mankind a kind of unity, but who had vanished with the enlightenment of the eighteenth century. At a more scientific level, anthropologists and sociologists were examining the exact ways in which individuals are related to their groups. Émile Durkheim (1858–1917), one of the greatest of sociologists, a thinker of true profundity, had been led to postulate social facts as entities (not abstractions) in themselves. The supreme collective fact, he postulated, is religion. This was the field that Romains and others were to explore creatively: writers-as-scientists, but new scientists, uncertain of science's capacities. They extended rationalism.

It was in this spirit—the spirit not only of Verhaeren but of Whitman and the idealistic side of Zola—that Georges Duhamel, his brother-in-law Charles Vildrac (qq.v.) and others founded a Utopian community, *L'Abbaye*, at an old house at Créteil near Paris in the late summer of 1906. These men were making an experiment in living partly based on the idealistic prescriptions of the eighteenth-century sociologist François Marie Charles Fourier (to whom André Breton, q.v., wrote an ode). They were in effect repeating the nineteenth-century American Brook Farm venture, about which Nathaniel Hawthorne wrote his novel *The Blithedale Romance* (1852). One of Duhamel's *Pasquier Chronicles* (q.v.) similarly describes life at Créteil. Marinetti (q.v.) was a frequent visitor, as was Romains himself, and LUC DURTAIN (ps. ANDRÉ NEPVEU, 1881–1959), a doctor by profession, who wrote a novel, *The Necessary Step* (*L'Étape nécessaire*, 1907), which may be regarded as the group's manifesto. Durtain, who was a conscientious and humane man but not a gifted or profound writer, probably remained most faithful to the immediate ideals of *L'Abbaye*. The community remained in existence only until the autumn of 1907.

Romains began, as *L'Abbaye* group had, with mainly poetic aspirations. He published a book of poems at nineteen; in 1906, 'a muscular, blue-eyed cyclist', he turned up at Créteil with the manuscript of a collection called *The Unanimous Life* (*La Vie unanime*). As a student, while walking the streets, he had experienced a 'concept of a vast and elemental being, of whom the streets, the cars, the passersby formed the body', and of whom he (the writer-scientist in embryo) felt himself to be the consciousness. Romains' programme was (and to some extent always has been) concerned to employ the poet's intuition of the *Unanime* in aiding individuals to integrate themselves into it. The social and Utopian elements in this are obvious; it also lends itself to religious and mystical interpretations.

Romains' poetry, which is better than that of most novelists, and which he has continued to write, is spoiled by his didacticism; but it is still anthologized, read and studied, and has perhaps sufficient qualities to deserve this. The non-philosophical, lyrical poems in *Love Colour of Paris* (*Amour couleur de Paris*, 1921) are his best. His fine early novel *Death of a Nobody* (*Mort de quelqu'un*, 1911; tr. 1914), often rather misleadingly described as his masterpiece, quite transcends its author's didactic intentions. A retired employee, who has felt no collective radiance in his commonplace life, dies. His aged father comes to bury him. Gradually, in his death, he takes on 'collective' significance. This significance is his survival. Thus death gives meaning to his senseless life. Philosophically this book proves nothing. But it is highly original, establishes a not unimportant aspect of existence, and is above all authentic in its portrayal of people. In *The Boys in the Back Room* (*Les Copains*, 1913; tr. 1937) Romains allowed his gift of humour, often a saving one, to emerge. Seven young men, by a series of crazy jokes, awaken the bourgeois of two towns. This may instructively be compared to Frank's *The Robber Band* (q.v.), written seven years later. The subject matter of the trilogy *The Body's Rapture* (*Psyché*, 1922–9; tr. 1937) is erotic: Lucienne is awakened into love and lust by Pierre, whom she marries. The frankly sensual writing here is a great improvement on D. H. Lawrence's in *Lady Chatterley's Lover* (q.v.); the bisexual and puritanical Lawrence was ill at ease with his material, while Romains was more relaxedly trying to communicate his mystical sense of the pleasures of sexual love.

The twenty-seven volume *roman-fleuve, Men of Good Will* (*Les Hommes de bonne volonté*, 1932–47; tr. 1933–46), which has the longest list of characters of any novel, and covers the period 1908–33 in historical detail, as well as in terms of its characters' personal lives, is almost always described as a failure. Of course. The question is: how much does it actually achieve? And the answer is that it achieves more than is usually allowed. Romains put some of himself into one of the main characters, Jean Jerphanion; the writer he portrays in Pierre Jallez. If one reads *Men of Good Will* not as a bible of unanimism but simply as a survey (surely a heroic one) of elements of French society over twenty-five years, it is a rewarding experience. There are some thin and boring passages. But there are also some excellent volumes, mixing valuable records (of, for example, the fighting at Verdun, and of Soviet Russia), comedy (the pretentious writer Georges Allory), and psychological drama (the crime of the bookbinder Quinette, the gratuitous nature of which recalls that of Lafcadio in Gide's *The Vatican Cellars*, q.v.).

Romains' work raises some odd parodoxes. Why does *Men of Good Will*, by the apostle of unanimism, fail precisely in a 'unanimistic' way? How can one of the century's funniest writers produce work on current affairs so pompously absurd? Why in his drama does Romains seem to satirize the collective more than he advances it?

The answer is that he is a naïve (q.v.) writer, a lyricist who should follow his own imaginative bent and never try to philosophize or play a part in politics (this most unfascist of men even got himself called fascist by refusing to pursue his proper function of writer, and vainly meddling in public affairs). Had Romains confined himself to the creative exploration of his intuitions of the collective, instead of becoming a busybody in public matters—one book written in America at the beginning of the Second World War appears to discuss that catastrophe in terms of the author's own activities—he might have achieved the greatness he so narrowly misses.

Romains is an outstanding dramatist. His most famous play, *Knock* (1923; tr. 1935), which was directed and acted by Louis Jouvet, is a classic: a doctor sends a whole community to bed with an imaginary sickness. Other plays showed similar gullings of the populace by practical jokers or dictators, and Romains has been accused, by some, of admiring the jokers and showing contempt for the crowds. Actually the plays reveal Romains' creative misgivings about the over-simplifications inherent in this theories. But his public statements repudiating Hitler's kind of 'unanimism', while clearing him of fascist sympathies, lack imaginative conviction. Characteristically, Romains, who was gifted with a good grasp of the sciences, wrote an early and not foolish book on 'vision without sight'. He has always been interested in parapsychology.

GEORGES DUHAMEL (1884–1966), son of a muddling, lovable Paris chemist who qualified as a doctor at the age of fifty-one, began himself as a doctor. While at Créteil he wrote poetry and plays, but after war-service as a doctor he returned to fiction, and produced two *romans-fleuve, Salavin (Vie et aventures de Salavin,* 1920–32; tr. 1936) and the more famous but not superior *Pasquier Chronicle (Chronique des Pasquier,* 1933–45; tr. 1937–46). He began his literary career in earnest with two compassionate, ironic books about the sufferings he saw in the First World War: *The New Book of Martyrs (Vie des martyrs,* 1917; tr. 1918) and *Civilization* (1918; tr. 1919). These stories, as good as anything he wrote, are excellent examples of the writer fulfilling his proper function: they are committed to no more than humanity and compassion. *Salavin* is not an innovatory novel, nor a startling feat of imagination: it is nevertheless a lovely, often humorous, but ultimately sombre book. The hero is a failure and an idealist. He tries to be a saint, but fails comically—and terribly sadly for himself. His (gratuitous?) impulse to touch his boss's ear costs him his job; his vow of chastity costs his wife's happiness. Only as he dies, through an over-generous act, does he see that he has always lacked spontaneous love. Duhamel here performs the extraordinary feat of irradiating mediocrity, and demonstrating, with absolute honesty, how it may attain nobility. Of course it has been objected that Duhamel has spread out his material too thinly. But in this case the criticism has less force: the nature of the material is deliberately unmelodramatic, and yet it has an undoubted intensity. There is a trace of Futabatei's (q.v. 4) Bunzo in Salavin. To suggest, as one critic has done, that *Salavin* is modelled upon Dostoevski (simply because it has a 'negative' hero), and that by this standard it is 'thin', is misleading and unfair. It is more original than this. Its subtle and humane criticism of both kinds of Christianity makes it an interesting contrast to the work of Christian novelists.

The Pasquier Chronicle is delightfully written, but here Duhamel's humanity has become too diffused for completely successful fiction: the book really is too long, and lacks energy. The portrait of his own father, however, is loving and accurate; and there are other continuously interesting volumes. The whole is certainly superior to the middlebrow sham of, say, all but early fragments of Galsworthy's

Forsyte Saga (q.v. 1). However debilitated he is, Duhamel always has a radiant mind, and is ever anxious to avoid self-deceit. A post-war novel, *The Voyage of Patrice Périot* (*Le Voyage de Patrice Périot*, 1951) is certainly correct in representing scientists as naïve and politicians as vicious; nor is the human stuff of the story missing. Duhamel's critical works, essays and autobiographical volumes—*Light on my Days* (*Inventaire de l'abîme*, 1945, *Biographie de mes fantômes*; tr. in one vol., 1948)—are all of interest. During the Second World War he and his family stayed in France and suffered from the Nazis, though fortunately not drastically. Duhamel, in his war sketches and in *Salavin*, has left a literary testament to his radiant nature.

The idealism felt by Duhamel, Romains and so many others before the catastrophe of 1914 was modified or altered by events—but it was in most cases sharpened rather than destroyed. For most of those who came to manhood before 1914, and who then experienced the war, the future of the world was, and for reasons obvious enough, a major issue. Some writers, however, displayed their concern in a more oblique manner than the naïve Romains or the gently liberal Duhamel. For such as Claudel or Mauriac (qq.v.), of course, the answer lay with God. For those of the only temporarily weakened, mystical *Action Française* (q.v.) it lay in nationalism, new disciplines, and an acknowledgement of a Crown and Church (in which one did not necessarily have to believe as a private citizen). For unanimists and others it lay in new understandings, new hopes, new *rapprochements* (Romains wanted a Franco-German *rapprochement* in spite of Hitler). Some of those who had fought towards the end of the war, younger men, turned, as we shall see, to surrealism and to other allied movements of protest. One important aspect of all these movements was their antagonism, so profound as to amount to rejection rather than criticism, to the systems of living that had collapsed in war.

However, there is another group of writers, many of genius, who have at least these features in common: they do not share in nihilism or communism—or in the liberal humanism of such writers as Romains, Gide or Duhamel. They are (or have been called) 'right-wing' or 'fascist'. The category, like all categories, is a loose one. What characterizes all those included in it is not their 'right-wingedness', but rather the intensity of their repudiation of left-wing solutions. In Great Britain the category embraces a wide spectrum: from Belloc and Chesterton (qq.v. 1) to (an aspect of) Wyndham Lewis (q.v. 1); for its survivors—mostly deintellectualized, hysterical pseudo-writers or guttersnipe journalists—the Heath 1970 government was a Vichy, now, they feel, betrayed.

GEORGES BERNANOS (1888–1948), who was born and died in Paris, was a true spiritual son of Léon Bloy (q.v.). He undoubtedly belongs to the vituperative, enraged, frenetic wing of French Catholicism. But he is a subtler and more gifted novelist than Huysmans or Bloy, and even his fiercest detractors do not deny that he left behind him at least one masterpiece. The English writer one immediately thinks of in connection with him is Graham Greene (q.v. 1); but there are important differences, not the least among them being Greene's left-wing position. But if we speak of Dostoevski as Bernanos' conscious model, we shall not—as in the case of Duhamel—mislead.

Hate distorts and disfigures—in an almost 'expressionist' manner—the by no means ignoble passion of Bernanos' polemic (but he was considerably saner than Bloy, who must be described as to some extent unbalanced); yet his fiction is powerful and transcends its Christian terms of reference.

The young Bernanos was a supporter of *Action Française* and an admirer of the anti-semite Drumont. But he differed from most *Action Française* supporters in being obsessed (as Mauriac was) with the materialism of the bourgeois. This Bloy-like strain of spirituality runs through all his work, and is stronger than the other emotions which possessed him: royalism, hatred of atheists, patriotism. Basically Bernanos is a visionary, as he showed in no uncertain terms in his febrile and tormented first novel, *Star of Satan* (*Sous le soleil de Satan*, 1926; tr. 1940), in which a priest struggles with Satan (a horse trader) for his own soul and for that of a precocious village girl. There is melodrama here, but also power and a genuine apprehension of the mysterious and the supernatural. Bernanos' vision of life on earth, a theatre of struggle between God and Satan for the soul of man, is perhaps simplistic; but his view of human nature, although lurid, is neither unsubtle nor ignorant of the dynamics of lust and despair. His next two novels, *The Deception* (*L'Imposture*, 1927) and *Joy* (*La Joie*, 1929; tr. 1946), deal with a hypocrite priest. The second of these, whose main character is a saintly girl, introduces Bernanos' most Dostoevskian figure: a Russian chauffeur who murders the joyous girl, but then kills himself and thus brings the priest back to faith.

In 1931 Bernanos wrote the most savage of his diatribes, *The Great Fear of the Well-Disposed* (*La Grande Peur des bien-pensants*): this is an attack on those unbelievers who are merely Catholic out of tradition—and it amply demonstrates Bernanos' fundamental lack of sympathy with *Action Française*. He was a believer in God's kingdom; they were 'patriots'. Unfortunately the book is tainted with anti-semitism.

Diary of a Country Priest (*Journal d'un curé de campagne*, 1936; tr. 1937) is Bernanos' most famous book. It is another story of a saint: sick and unworldly, the priest of Ambricourt (in Northern France) tries to serve the poor. But the poor are vicious and abuse him. Finally, defeated in everything but his own sense of grace, absolved by an unfrocked priest, he dies. This, Bernanos' quietest and most carefully composed novel, is his most intensely moving.

Two books of Bernanos' that have been undervalued are *A Crime* (*Un Crime*, 1935; tr. 1936) and its extraordinary counterpart, written in 1935 but not published until 1950: *Night is Darkest* (*Un Mauvais Rêve*; tr. 1953).

In 1936 Bernanos was in Mallorca and saw the fascist atrocities committed there, blessed and encouraged by his own Church. In *Diary of My Times* (*Les Grands Cimetières sous la lune*, 1938; tr. 1938), one of the greatest of books of impassioned protest, he condemned what he saw. His *Action Française* friends, who had been taught by Barrès (q.v.) and others to regard the truth as the enemy of tradition, and therefore as something not to be uttered, condemned him in their turn. During the war he lived in Brazil, from which he periodically denounced the compromise of Vichy. However, Bernanos did not cease to oppose parliamentary democracy; but his resistance to it is based on his belief that it affords no protection from bourgeois greed for money and power. This makes him as anti-capitalist as any communist; but (unlike Greene) he will have no truck at all with godless communism. His hatred of fascism was inspired by human decency, not by any intellectual conversion to liberalism. He was an early supporter of de Gaulle—and while Gaullism was against the fact of Vichy, it remains in certain ways close to its conservative ideals.

One more novel of Bernanos' must be mentioned; it is regarded by many as the height of his achievement: *The Open Mind* (*Monsieur Ouine*, 1943, rev. 1946, correct text 1955; tr. 1945), which he had been working on since 1934, and first published in Buenos Aires. This concerns an utterly depraved populace, who are observed by the cynical Monsieur Ouine, who was in part a satirical caricature of the liberal, godless André Gide (q.v.) that is Bloy-like in its savagery, hysterically unjust in a personal sense, and yet full of meaning. The evil is depicted with gusto; but the note of grace is clearly sounded. Bernanos' technique here is almost *pointilliste*: the town is presented in a series of discrete episodes. However, this is a fragmented realism rather than an anticipation (as is sometimes claimed) of the *nouveau roman* (q.v.). *The Open Mind* is an important and powerful book, but not a better one than *The Diary of a Country Priest*. When he died, of cancer, Bernanos was working on a biography of Christ. His reputation was well served by the French composer Francis Poulenc, who turned his film-script *The Carmelites* (*Dialogues des Carmélites*, 1948; tr. 1961), based on Gertrud von Le Fort's novel *The Song at the Scaffold* (*Die Letzte am Schafott*, q.v.), into a successful opera.

In this writer we find French conservative Catholicism at its most honest and least unattractive—as well as a creative power that continually transcends the crudities and over-simplifications in which his convictions involved him. His best work represents a kind of justification of Bloy; and it is perhaps the most profound of all modern expositions of one of Bloy's chief themes, an extremely important one in French Catholicism: vicarious suffering. It is safe to say that the reader who remains emotionally immune to Bernanos at his most powerful is a remarkably insensitive one.

MARCEL JOUHANDEAU (PS. MARCEL PROVENCE, 1888) was born in Guéret, Creuse, which is some forty miles north-east of Limoges, and is the 'Chaminadour' of his books. Less widely known than Bernanos, he has a number of distinguished admirers (Gide, Claude Mauriac, Jean-Louis Curtis, qq.v. Thornton Wilder, q.v. 1, Havelock Ellis— and many more), and is clearly a writer of importance, a genuine eccentric (he has affinities, as a critic has shrewdly pointed out, with T. F. Powys, q.v. 1), a heretical Catholic who can only be ignored at the peril of missing strange and valuable insights. A schoolmaster in Paris from 1912 until 1949, he has written over seventy books, some of which are mere hack work, lives of saints and so on. He has been called a 'demented and ranting exhibitionist'; but this does not characterize him. His mysticism and pessimism are, perhaps, less offensive to his critics than the unique frankness of his *Marital Chronicles* (*Chroniques Maritales*, 1938, 1943), which tell of the difficulties (and pleasures) of his marriage, made in 1929, to a dancer and choreographer called Caryathis. His creative writing is tormented by an inchoate put powerful vision: of the world as the scene of Satan's winning battle with God for the soul of humanity; but when Jouhandeau tries to articulate this in his non-fiction it varies bewilderingly, and loses force. An anti-semite, public egoist, and bisexual, Jouhandeau fell victim to Nazi propaganda and visited Berlin during the occupation, a self-indulgence for which he was eventually forgiven.

Jouhandeau is a versatile and prolific writer. There are the novels of Chaminadour—including *Chaminadour* (1934–41) and *Mémorial* (1948–58)—comic and cruelly bitter accounts of the seamy side of life, but always bathed in the light of the supernatural. These works have something of the sensuous, thick-lined brutality of Rembrandt's drawings; occasionally Jouhandeau manipulates his situations to the benefit of this texture. His 'marriage' books, which include *Monsieur Godeau Married* (1933) and *Élise* (1933) and many others, as well as *Marital Chronicles* (he is Godeau; and Caryathis, who was recommended to him by Marie Laurencin, the painter and erstwhile mistress of Apollinaire, is the remarkable Élise), are lighter in tone, but still confessional in a unique manner; they contain much agonized self-appraisal. (*Marcel and Élise*, tr. 1953, is a selection from them.) Jouhandeau also published novels under his own name, including *The Germans in Provence* (*Les Allemands en Provence*, 1919), much more grimly naturalist in style than his later work; but here he had not found his true *métier*. Jouhandeau is above all a lucid chronicler of human secrecies, and in this sense a writer of great courage. He combines an extraordinary number of conflicting qualities; piety, impudence, sweetness, nastiness, affection, malice. . . . He will continue to be valued, but in rigorous selection.

PIERRE-EUGÈNE DRIEU LA ROCHELLE (1893–1945), born in Paris, is a less complex, less gifted conservative than the preceding writers. His is a tragic case. He invested his entire life with the heroic recklessness that Jouhandeau hoarded—for the most part—for use in his books; and Drieu La Rochelle's life was anguished and disgraced, his books mostly inferior. . . . Confusing creative exploration of his nearly demonic aggressiveness and driving need for women with politics in a peculiarly French manner, Drieu, who fought in the First World War and was spiritually lost after it, threw himself into almost every literary and political movement (communism, Catholic mysticism, surrealism, *Action Française* . . .) that came into existence during the inter-war years: this was both to escape from and yet, vainly, to discover some system that would accommodate him. His mystiques of sport and sex, however, remained consistent. Hysterically lacking in control though he was, it was an inner despair that impelled him—not an innate cruelty or even an urge to power. Like all Frenchmen, he had bad precedents to draw upon. (His Whitman-like war verse was hailed by Barrès, whom he reverenced, as the best to come out of the war.) As well as polemics, Drieu wrote novels and short stories in which he portrayed both his own and France's emptiness. Of these *The Fire Within* (*Le Feu follet*, 1931; tr. 1961) is representative. The writing is powerful; but the author fails to penetrate analytically the internal hell that he is describing. That was to come later. In the Thirties Drieu's aching pessimism found a haven in Doriot's shabby French Nazi party (*Parti Populaire Français*), and he wrote a book called *With Doriot* (*Avec Doriot*, 1937). His novel of 1939, *Gilles*, reaches his fictional nadir: the style is still powerful, reflecting its author's inner discontent, but the hero's involvement with Franco's fascists only pretends to solve his problem (it would be disturbing if it succeeded). With the occupation Drieu took over the *Nouvelle Revue Française* and turned it into a pro-Nazi paper. When he heard about this Aldous Huxley (q.v. 1) wrote to his brother: 'My old friend . . . has, alas, carried his pre-war infatuation with Doriot to its logical conclusion. . . . He is an outstanding example of the strange things that happen when a naturally weak man, whose talents are entirely literary, conceives a romantic desire for action and a romantic ambition for political power . . . there was something very nice about Drieu. . . .' When the game was up in 1944 Drieu tried to kill himself, failed, and went into hiding, where he wrote his best (unfinished) novel: *Mémoires de Dirk Raspe* (1966), in which he projected himself into a fictional figure inspired by Van Gogh. Here in full anticipation of his successful suicide of April 1945, he does not succeed in reconciling his concept of 'heroic energy' with his temperamental blackly cynical nihilism; but he does not try. He desperately relaxes, and invents the character he might better have been, scraping the bottom of the barrel of his memory for his old personal decencies. He is an important representative French writer, a genius crippled and destroyed by fervour.

HENRY DE MONTHERLANT (1896–1972), one of the most distinguished and versatile European writers of his generation, was born in Paris. He is very frequently described as a 'fascist', a 'collaborationist' and even as a 'soul kindred to Drieu La Rochelle'. All this is untrue. There may be things about Montherlant that are not palatable to everyone: he is aristocratic in attitude, he can perhaps be accused of *snobisme*, he does not believe in the Utopian capacities of mankind, he does not wear his heart on his sleeve, he has criticized romantic love, he has spoken uncomfortable truths at tactless times. . . . However, as one of his shrewdest critics has said, his worst political crime as a writer is to have a tendency 'to see moral problems in terms of aesthetics'. Some of the essays in *The June Solstice* (*Le Solstice de juin*, 1941), originally banned by the Nazis and only allowed to appear because a German official had translated some of Montherlant's work, suffer from this fault. However, they are also courageous essays: in them Montherlant was trying to maintain his independence as a writer. The suggestion that he was a collaborator has no foundation. Although more aloof from politics than most French writers, he has been unable to resist some involvement (partly to tease: it is not widely realized that he is a humorist who enjoys this aspect of the literary life); his 'record' is rather more 'left', or independent, than 'right'. For example, at the time of the Spanish Civil War he was unequivocally opposed to the fascists, and was known to be so. He refused an invitation to Barcelona in 1936 not only because he was ill but also because he felt he would be tempted to join in the fight against Franco. His apparently ambiguous political attitude recalls that of Wyndham Lewis (q.v. 1), who was more careless and less cautious, but is also widely misunderstood as politically reactionary. He shot himself when threatened with blindness.

Montherlant has made remarkable achievements as an essayist, a novelist, and, more recently, as a dramatist. Unlike Hemingway (q.v. 1), a writer almost infantile in comparison to him, he had some experience in fighting bulls, and in other sports, and he wrote much that is self-revealing on this subject (his best writing on bullfighting, which incidentally exposes Hemingway's *Death in the Afternoon* as naïve swagger, is in the novel *The Bullfighters, Les Bestiaires*, 1926, tr. 1927). He also wrote about his experiences as a soldier in the First World War in his first novel, *The Dream (Le Songe*, 1922; tr. 1962). This could be called 'hard', for it extols the Spartan virtues; but one has only to read Ernst Jünger (q.v.) to understand that it is not. Rather it reflects a romantic young man's determination to engage a bitterly hard world with honour and virtue. Although Montherlant has often chosen a generally Catholic as opposed to Protestant line, his 'Catholicism' is an essentially non-programmatic version of the specifically French brand of atheistic, external Catholicism: he is basically hostile to Christianity, not least because he believes it leads men to have false hopes and thus to be 'soft'. Not all critics have seen that *The Dream* is a shocked book, in which romanticism is brutally and deliberately deflated—but re-emerges in the rather self-conscious rhetoric of the style (and in the clumsiness with which the ideal of brotherhood is substituted for that of love).

His tetralogy *The Girls (Les Jeunes Filles*, 1936–9; tr. 1968) is one of his most celebrated and controversial works, but, although a superb *tour de force*, not (by his own high standards) his best. It has been widely misunderstood, taken for an anti-feminine tract where it is in fact a comic and ironic study of one aspect of its author. Its hero, Pierre Costals, is a brilliantly successful novelist who experiments with women. It is an error to try to extract a 'philosophy' from this novel, although one might well extract Montherlant's self-criticism. The worst mistake is to equate Montherlant with Costals. Montherlant, a public ironist, was always intelligently struggling to create non-subjective works; hence his post-war concentration on drama, in which he increasingly demonstrates unpalatable facts but remains stoically withdrawn from them. In this book, which is funny for those who are able to see Costals as simply a creation and not a vehicle for a philosophy, Montherlant did indulge an inclination; but he punished it. It is true that the girls who cling to Costals are seen by him as morally leprous, possessively draining the writer of his creative sap. But the Arab girl who does not cling is physically leprous. Embodied in *The Girls* is a close and rueful criticism of romantic love that, as a careful reading shows, involves Costals as closely as his women. The book is an exploration, not a statement. It is, after all, by a man who has said that most of the people around us who are capable of noble deeds are women.

The Bachelors (*Les Célibataires* 1934; tr. 1960) is one of Montherlant's most perfect and most moving novels. Here he was able to combine his regard for truth with his humour, tenderness for old age and fascination with the aristocracy. This is the story of two old penniless aristocrats, a baron and his sixty-four-year-old nephew; a senile madman and an obstinate, foolish old man who none the less achieves tragic grandeur in his unvictorious bid for both independence of his uncle and his aristocratic place in a society no longer constructed to accommodate him.

Montherlant finished a long novel about Africa called *The Black Rose* (*La Rose de Sable*) in 1932; so far only a part has been published, *Desert Love* (*L'Histoire d'amour de 'La Rose de sable'*, 1954; tr. 1957). On the strength of this (self-contained) section, the novel, a sympathetic study of a weak officer, serving in Africa, would seem to be one of his best. Certainly in *Chaos and Night* (*Le Chaos et la nuit*, 1963; tr. 1964) he achieves the depth and feeling of *The Bachelors*, and confirmed his position as France's leading living novelist. Here again the heroic spirit of a man triumphs over his own absurdity and failure: an old Spanish anarchist, grown near to madness after years of exile in Paris, returns to Madrid and an obscure and yet tragic and noble death. The theme is matched by the lucid beauty of the writing.

Montherlant had written for the stage before 1939; but it was not until the occupation that he turned seriously to it. *The Dead Queen* (*La Reine morte*, 1942; tr. 1951), played in occupied Paris, was a subtle gesture of the author's independence; but there can be no doubt of his anti-German sympathies. One of his most famous plays is *The Master of Santiago* (*Le Maître de Santiago*, 1947; tr. 1951), which portrays renunciation and adherence to principle at the expense of personal happiness. In *Those One Holds in One's Arms* (*Celles qu'on prend dans ses bras*, 1950), which was not a theatrical success, he contrasts a refined but involuntarily depraved old man with the noble girl who obsesses him. He has continued to produce excellent plays, including the vigorous *Malatesta* (1946), *Port Royal* (1954) and *The Cardinal of Spain* (1960). In early 1971 his moving play about a priest who loves one of his pupils (based on an experience of his own), *The Town Where the Prince is a Child* (*La Ville dont le Prince est un enfant*, 1951), was at last performed publicly and in its entirety. A long novel about the Roman Empire is scheduled for future publication.

Montherlant has been called a 'man of the Renaissance'. (It seems he lost his eye in the course of a nocturnal homosexual encounter with rough boys; he was as fond of girls.) It would be even truer to describe him as a writer profoundly concerned with the problem of how to re-introduce, into the universal guilt-culture of the 'civilized' world, the most life-enhancing elements of the shame-cultures of the past. Much of what his readers find unattractive in him may be thus explained. His essays and notebooks are essential to a proper understanding of him. *Selected Essays* (tr. 1960) is excellent in this respect, and contains a substantial selection from the note-books.

JEAN GIONO (1895–1970), who was born at Manosque near Aix, offers a complete contrast. His father was a protestant shoemaker born in France of Piedmontese parents, his mother a Parisian. He is a rich writer, combining the bleakness of Faulkner (q.v. 1), the ecstasy of Whitman, the relentlessness of the Greek tragedians, a Hardean love for his peasants and a crudely Melvillean *penchant* for 'big' symbols. He is a true naïve (q.v.) and he did not, on the whole, try to be a thinker. His experiences during the First World War were decisive, and led him to a lifelong pacificism. He was highly thought of during the Thirties, but his behaviour during the occupation lost him his popularity, which he only partly regained by his remarkable assumption of an entirely new style. Treatment as a sage advocating a return to the soil and an end of urbanism (pilgrimages were made to him, as they were to Jammes and Hauptmann (qq.v.), perhaps coarsened his sensitivity to people's individual sufferings and magnified his self-importance: he preached pacificism and then, in the defeat, gave every appearance of finding the Nazis no more repulsive than the French. He wrote for a collaborationist periodical, went to prison briefly (in 1939 and again in 1945), and eventually re-emerged in the new guise of historical novelist. His indifferent attitude to the Nazis was a compound of ignorance of the sophisticated nature of modern life and a sullen obstinacy rather akin to that of the British Mosleyite, also a lover of nature (though a trivial one when compared to Giono), Henry Williamson. The damage inflicted by war must ultimately be held responsible.

The novels of Giono's first and best period are nearly all set against Provençal rural backgrounds. He became famous with the trilogy *Pan: Hill of Destiny* (*Colline*, 1929; tr. 1929), *Lovers are Never Losers*

(*Un de Baumugnes*, 1929; tr. 1931) and *Harvest* (*Regain*, 1930; tr.
1939). The last two were made into successful and effective movies,
as was the comic short story *La Femme du Boulanger*, in which Raimu
appeared. All six of the films from Giono's books were made by
Marcel Pagnol (q.v.). One of the finest of all Giono's many novels is
The Song of the World (*Le Chant du monde*, 1934; tr. 1937). This, a tale
of violence and lust, and of a search (in Giono's native region) for a
pair of lovers, has an epic grandeur which clearly shows Homer as one
of the formative influences on the author. At his best Giono is unsurpassed in his communication of the rhythms of lives lived in ac-
cordance with nature's laws; unsurpassed, too, is his expression of
the simple happiness of simple people. However, when he is not
trying to be polemic, or to implement his programme for the abolition of industry (our possible sympathy for his point of view cannot,
alas, modify its naïvety), he can deal with more complex material.
His most powerful novel, *Joy of Man's Desiring* (*Que ma joie demeure*,
1935; tr. 1940), certainly expresses Giono's disillusion with and disbelief in the viability of the urban world; but this work of the imagination is very different from any of his works of prophecy. And
indeed, in the central figure of the book, a charlatan but a true
prophet, there are those elements of self-criticism that so often mark
the greatest literature.

After the war Giono wrote a series of historical 'Chronicles', including *The Hussar on the Roof* (*Le Hussard sur le toit*, 1951; tr. 1953)
and *The Straw Man* (*Le Bonheur fou*, 1957; tr. 1959), in which Angelo
Pardi, a Piedmontese officer, figures. These were a skilful new departure. In them he broke away from the dense, lurid, organic style
of the earlier books to a new simplicity. They are refreshing and full
of vitality. But, brilliant though they are, they have the status of pot-
boilers in comparison to the earlier work. The Second World War
had done something irreparable to Giono: for, whatever his errors,
the early books had been generated by hope as well as despair; their
sweeping lyricism had come from hope. In *Joy of Man's Desiring* Bobi
had given the community joy and brotherhood until sexual jealousy
intervened—was his death, stabbed by a flash of lightning as he
ascended a mountain in a storm, prophetic of the fate of Giono's
complex hope?

Giono's post-war rural comedies are pale parodies of what had
come thirty and forty years earlier. His best book of this period was
non-fiction: *The Dominici Affair* (*Notes sur l'affaire Dominici*, 1956; tr.
1956), in which he brought his understanding of his region to bear
upon the curious murder, by peasants, of an English touring family.
But in spite of the falling-off, Giono's achievement is a substantial

one. The earthy, impassioned style of the novels of his first period is not the least part of it.

There is as much confusion about the work of LOUIS-FERDINAND CÉLINE (ps. LOUIS-FERDINAND DESTOUCHES, 1894–1961), who was born and died in Paris, as about the facts of his life. What is certain is that, whether wittingly or willingly or not, he devised new procedures. Céline (he took his maternal grandmother's maiden name) was the son of the minor employee of an insurance company and a maker of antique lace. He enlisted in the Cavalry in 1912, was severely wounded in 1914, and awarded a seventy-five per cent disability pension. After a series of voyages and a sojourn in wartime London, Céline began to study medicine in 1918; in the following year he married the daughter of the director of his medical school. His writing career begins with his doctoral thesis on Semmelweiss (1924), the embittered discoverer of the cause of puerperal fever, who proved his point to his incredulous colleagues by slashing his fingers and plunging them into the putrescent corpse of a fever victim: he died soon after. This appealed to the then ambitious and bourgeois-oriented young doctor, and prophesied his own career; the misanthropist's suicidal gesture carried within it the seeds of a desperate humanitarianism. But Céline, whose self-infection began in earnest with *Journey to the End of the Night* (*Voyage au bout de la nuit*, 1932; tr. 1934), lived with his anguish and fever for nearly thirty more years. The hallucinated account of his spiritual adventures, in the guises of one Ferdinand Bardamu and his double Robinson, made him famous; but he continued to practise as a doctor among the poor. *Death on the Instalment Plan* (*Mort à crédit*, 1936; tr. 1938) tells of a nightmare childhood. It is not influenced by surrealism (q.v.), but partakes with huge greed of the blackness and despair, but not the hope, out of which the larger and inclusive movement of expressionism (q.v.) had come. Céline's own childhood had not been nightmarish; but his conscience, stimulated by the poor patients he treated, and by the misery and stupidity he saw around him—as well as the spite and envy that were a part of his character—compelled him to invent one. In those two books, the critic Roland Barthes has said, 'writing is not at the service of thought . . . it really represents the writer's descent into the sticky opacity of the condition which he is describing'. One thinks of Sartre's (q.v.) 'viscosity': that foul quality he ascribes to non-authentic experience, to all objects and persons who betray the individual's movement towards his freedom, to the self recalcitrantly clinging to its fear of existence. For Céline the world is in headlong decay. The physical voice of the self- and world-sickened physician, a kindly and humanitarian specialist in children's diseases, devotee of the music halls, dear and gay friend of such as the actress Arletty and the novelist Aymé (q.v.), gives the illusion of coming straight off the page: exasperated, always vigorous and spontaneous, enchanted, ribald, furious, eager, abandonedly vile, agonized. Céline called himself a classicist because he had worked hard to achieve this unique tone of voice. The bourgeois readership recoiled in horror, not wanting to listen to this ghost of their own internal monologue (but they bought his book); the patients came to the doctor.

Then Céline fell victim to the endemic French disease of anti-semitism. He may have been jealous of the number of successful Jewish refugees in the medical profession in Paris. At all events, his tone clearly reveals that he knew, all the time, that these emotions were vile. *Trifles for a Massacre* (*Bagatelles pour un massacre*, 1937) impressed Gide (q.v.) as a comic satire of a bestial Nazi blueprint for the destruction of European Jewry. Essentially, Gide was right. As a critic has pointed out, Céline's 'Jew' 'is a projection . . . of his own class's worst tendencies'. But his balance of judgement, always precarious, began to desert him. Like Jouhandeau (q.v.) he was a difficult and irascible man, an enemy to his literary friends, to all but his boon-companions. He became identified with the parodic *persona* of his anti-semitic pamphlets. Such madness, in a man of his sensibility, is not excusable at such a time. The first, characteristically, incorporates three of his magical 'Ballets', celebrations of all he loved in life. Then the war came. He volunteered but was rejected. During the occupation he called Hitler a Jew, predicted his defeat, repelled advances from the Germans on some occasions, incoherently approached them on others: put himself in an unnecessarily dangerous and foolish position. He associated with collaborators and practised madicine. He never denounced any individual. He later admitted to having been mixed up in doings, 'stuff connected with Jews', that were not 'my business'. In 1944, hearing himself condemned to death on the radio from London, he fled to Germany with the Vichy government, whom he served, with gleeful hatred, in a medical capacity. Then he escaped to Denmark, where he was imprisoned but not handed over to the French. Finally, sick with paralysis and pellagra, but cleared of all charges by a military tribunal, he returned to Paris (1951). Here he practised spasmodically, often for no fees, until his death. He had published *Guignol's Band* (*La Bande de Guignol;* tr. 1954), about his time in the London of the First World War, in 1944. His remaining books deal with his seventeen years of exile: they include the posthumous *Rigadon* and his hilarious account of Vichy in exile, *Castle to Castle* (*D'un Château l'autre*, 1957; tr. 1969). It is usually stated that the later Céline is a shadow of the one of the first two books. This is an exaggeration. The first two novels are undoubtedly epoch-making. But the later ones are remarkable, and have not had their due. There are no autobiographies like them. When the history books have been reduced to lists of whatever indisputable facts they contain, it is to Céline's accounts of twentieth-century life that the truly curious will turn.

Every novelist who survives is, of course, ultimately unclassifiable; but most may be usefully seen against the background of one tradition or another. An exception is BLAISE CENDRARS (ps. FRÉDÉRIC SAUSER, 1887–1961), who was entirely his own man even when temporarily involved with movements.

Although he claimed at various times to have been born in Paris, Egypt and Italy, Cendrars was in fact born in Switzerland, near Neuchâtel. He has been described, with justice, as 'one of the greatest liars of all time'. However, this likeable eccentric and continual traveller, who lost an arm fighting voluntarily for France in the First World War, certainly knew most of the French writers worth knowing during his lifetime; his lies were self-protective, strategic and humorous—not boastful, which they never needed to be. His father was Swiss, his mother a Scot. After several adventurous failures—as businessman, student and horticulturalist—he began to write seriously in about 1908. His poetry is impressionistic, formless, evocative; an Englishman would call it poetic prose; like all his work, it tends towards the journalistic, not troubling itself about aesthetic levels. His breathless, lyrical manner, anticipating itself, running on beyond itself and never catching up with itself—often highly effective—was influential, as was his philosophy: 'There is no truth other than absurd life shaking its ass's ears. Wait for it, lie in ambush for it, kill it'. *Easter in New York* (*Pâques à New York*, 1912) and *Panama* (1918; tr. 1931) contain some of his best poetic writing.

Cendrars' most conventional novel is *Sutter's Gold* (*L'Or*, 1925; tr. 1926). This tells the story of the Swiss General who discovered and created California, was ruined by the discovery of gold beneath his lands, but then made a new discovery of inner fortitude almost as resilient as that of any of Montherlant's (q.v.) characters. *Antarctic Fugue* (*Dan Yack*, 1927, 1929; tr. 1929) and *Moravagine* (1926; tr. 1969) complement one another: the first, constructive and optimistic, delineates the survival of a pragmatist, and is against creativity; the second is destructive (the name of the intensely anti-feminine hero means, of course, 'Death-to-the-vagina') but for creativity. Cendrars' work thus certainly touches on the matter of

Künstlerschuld (q.v.); but he is casual, and regards his creativity as a matter of survival as well as of morals. Cendrars, whose prose veers without unease or embarrassment between journalese and exquisite and inspired expression, was not primarily a writer; he was an adventurer highly suspicious of literature, but drawn to it as a con-man is drawn to a promising mark. He was gifted as a storyteller, and was much influenced and aided in this and other respects by an early visit to Russia. It is not easy to see his seriousness through the clouds of what many English-speaking readers would call his ir-responsibility, and he does share with his admirer Henry Miller (q.v. 1) a certain naïvety that leads him (like Miller) into foolish-ness as well as innocence. None the less, he is an important anti-literary writer, and one of whom a more detailed study should be made.

Two novelists who died young play an important part in French literature. ALAIN-FOURNIER (ps. HENRI-ALBAN FOURNIER, 1886–1914) was possibly the most severe loss French literature sustained during the First World War; he was killed in action during its first weeks. He left one novel, *The Lost Domain* (*Les Grandes Meaulnes*, 1913; tr. 1959), some short stories (*Miracles*, 1924), and a correspondence (1948) with the critic and editor Jacques Rivière (1886–1925) that is both fascinating in itself and wonderfully revealing of the feelings and aspirations of the literary young of that period. He came from the marshy and flat countryside around Bourges in Cher, and his fiction is redolent of its fenny, brooding atmosphere. His one finished work has irritated many critics because of what they take to be its immaturity and even 'nastiness'. The cult of childhood seems to these critics to be over-extended: the tragic ending, they maintain, is con-trived in its interests. Others see the book as the one successful novel to come out of symbolism. There is some truth in both views, al-though the severity of the first should be modified by the fact of the author's inability to demonstrate whether and how he would have developed. The story is one of a dream world, a manor, discovered and dreamingly enjoyed, abruptly lost, then rediscovered and de-stroyed. It is a classic of immaturity and adolescence, and possibly irritating for that. But it is told with lucidity, grace and even magic. Besides, what adolescent fantasy—and this is one—is not 'nasty' as well as lovely? Alain-Fournier showed, even within the limitations of this one book, that he was aware of the precarious nature of the lost paradise of childhood. What he could not quite cope with, except in the vaguest possible way, were the intimations of lust that bring it down upon its foundations. The 'love' in this book is unconvincing: the question is evaded. But Alain-Fournier might well, had he not disappeared (his body was never recovered), have developed the capacity to deal with this problem.

RAYMOND RADIGUET (1903–23), born in Paris, achieved success as an adolescent with some ambitious, precious, wicked, clever little *fantaisiste* poems (collected in *Cheeks on Fire, Les Joues en feu*, 1920), wrote two novels, and died of typhoid at twenty. He was introduced to Paris literary society by ANDRÉ SALMON (1881–1969), a minor poet and associate of the surrealists, Radiguet was greatly promising, but has been overvalued and turned into a cult; perhaps this has something to do with the fact that two of the men who first took him up, Cocteau and Jacob (qq.v.), were homosexuals with a tendency to sentimentality. His two novels do not fulfil their promise because they are emotionally immature. One does not expect every precocious adolescent to be a Rimbaud. But they are more than brilliant classical pastiche. *The Devil in the Flesh* (*Le Diable au corps*, 1923; tr. 1932), which is partly autobiographical, tells of a youth's love for an older married woman whose husband is at the war. The thoughtful austerity with which the tale is told is distinctly more concentrated than the feeling Radiguet put into it; but nothing is false or forced. *Count d'Orgel Opens the Ball* (*Le Bal du Comte d'Orgel*, 1924; tr. 1952) is closely modelled on Madame de La Fayette's *La Princesse de Clèves* (regarded as the first French psychological novel). The role of the epigrammatic sage was too much for Radiguet to manage: this novel does not escape affectation, although it is keenly intelligent. Radiguet was very much under the spell of Cocteau, and, in portraying women, possessed a similar sexually oblivious (pathic?) sensitivity, sympathy and gentleness. Radiguet did not have time to grow a heart, and the people of his novels are pale and a little too consciously classicized reflections of real people; but he had remarkable control over them, and might well have outgrown his dependence on the eighteenth century, to which he turned not because he understood it particularly well but because it offered him the artificiality and the stability he needed to fortify the legend of precocity that he was creating.

Mention should be made here of the so-called 'populism', an intelligent neo-realism that has persisted from the late Twenties until the present day. The prize for the best novel embodying 'populist' aims was instituted by Mme Antonine Coulet-Tessier in 1931, and is still awarded. No great novel has come out of this tradition, but many good ones have been written in it—and it could have its importance yet. There is no school; and from the outset the manifestos were sensible: in essence, no more was asserted than that a realist tradition (as well as middlebrow fiction) should exist by the side of

the *avant garde*. The novelists LÉON LEMONNIER (1890–1953) and
ANDRÉ THÉRIVE (ps. ROGER PUTHOSTE, 1891–1967) began by reacting
to the literature of *snobisme*, of 'those trivial sinners who have nothing
to do but put on rouge' of high society. They postulated an eclectic
realism, which would incorporate 'mysticism' (as an authentic
aspect of human experience) and which would guard itself against
'petty pessimism'. The movement was shortlived, but while it
lasted it was supported by such as Simenon, Duhamel, Romains,
Barbusse (qq.v.), Sinclair Lewis (q.v. 1), Heinrich Mann and
Aragon (qq.v.). The original populist group is often called 'neo-
naturalist', but this is misleading and arises from a semantic confusion. What Thérive and Lemonnier were trying to establish was
simply a fluid, adaptable realism—but Lemonnier called it a 'true
and indispensable naturalism': a vehicle, he meant, for the honest
and loving depiction of the ever-changing reality of the world: 'we
are sure to prolong the great tradition of the French novel, which
always disdains pretentious acrobatics in favour of writing simply
and truthfully.' But perhaps the term naturalist was partially
justified: in the sense that the original populists did intend 'to
depict the people'. There was, in their pronouncements, a hopeful
and even a socialist note. In many of their actual novels, however,
there existed more than a trace of gloom. We find pessimism in
Thérive's own early *Without Soul* (*Sans âme*, 1928), as in his later
Voices of Blood (*Les Voix du sang*, 1955). But it is materialism
that arouses his gloom. His portrait of weak, life-battered eccent-
rics are effective, but his style is in general too elegant for his
material. Lemonnier's *Woman without Sin* (*Femme sans péché*,
1931), not a pessimistic book, is a psychological study of a proletarian woman.

The most considerable 'populist' novelist, however, was EUGÈNE
DABIT (1898–1936), son of a Paris Labourer. Dabit worked at menial
jobs, joined up and served at the front, and then began to educate
himself. He discovered the angry nineteenth-century writer Jules
Vallès (one of the generous, hate-impelled ancestors of Céline), the
gentle Charles-Louis Philippe (q.v.), and others, and he conceived
the ambition to illuminate the lives of the humble of Paris as they
had not been illuminated before. He did not succeed in this; but
his novels, and especially the first, are today unduly neglected.
Hôtel du Nord (1929; tr. 1931), based on some of what he had seen in
the hotel his parents now managed, was awarded the first populist
prize. He wrote several more novels, including *Villa Oasis* (1932) and
A Brand New Death (*Un Mort tout neuf*, 1934). Dabit was a depressed
personality whose experience had taught him that the world was a

place without consolations. He died of scarlet fever while in Russia, where he had gone (with Gide, q.v.) to attend Gorki's (q.v. 4) funeral. *Hôtel du Nord* was made into a good movie by Marcel Carné; the script is by Prévert (q.v.).

Dabit had a deep suspicion of the 'populist' label. This was reasonable. No one likes to be labelled—and thus put away. But his work is in fact firmly in the realist tradition Lemonnier and Thérive so undogmatically tried to consolidate. The populist movement was certainly ephemeral; it is quite often dismissed. I have chosen to give it space because so many realists, in no way attempting to fulfil its programme, in fact do so.

Thus the Breton LOUIS GUILLOUX (1899), who was with Dabit on his final trip to Russia, wrote in this tradition until he was past fifty, though, as Malraux (q.v.) said of him, he has 'an eternal grudge against reality' so powerful that it compels him to express himself, not lyrically, but 'through this same reality': his characters, observed in a minute detail reminiscent of the heyday of naturalism, 'give the impression of being seen in a kind of phosphorescent light. . . .' His early novel *The House of the People* (*La Maison du peuple*, 1927), a close study of poverty, received praise from Camus (q.v.). His masterpiece, a remarkable novel that finds a perfect objective correlative for the conflict in the author between his poetic and his political inclinations, is *Bitter Victory* (*Sang noir,* 1935; tr. 1938). This is set in 1917, in Brittany, and concerns the last day of Merlin, a schoolmaster who indulges his nihilism and hatred of the bourgeois, and yet meanly clings on to his bank securities. And since he cannot attain inner freedom, and believes in nothing, he kills himself. Since the war, during most of which he was in hiding in Toulouse, Guilloux has become more disillusioned, but has retained his passion for delineating all aspects of urban life in meticulous detail: *The Game of Patience* (*Le Jeu de patience*, 1949), immensely long, analyses the life of a Breton town over fifty years. Much more interesting and more like *Bitter Victory* is *Parpagnacco* (1954), in which the author entirely (as if heeding Malraux's remarks, made in the Thirties) abandons his usual method. This strange book tells of a search for a girl in Italy undertaken by two Swedes, who remain possessed by an icy Northern evil. *The Confrontation* (*La Confrontation*, 1968) is also a successful novel, combining the old realism with procedures well assimilated from more recent novelists: an old man recreates the life of a stranger, in a town between Paris and Brest, in a quest to discover his 'worthiness' (if he is 'worthy', he will be given money by a mysterious rich man). Guilloux, if he has never quite repeated the achievement of *Bitter Victory*, with its stiflingly accurate account of an acute intelligence trapped in 'viscosity' (q.v.), is none the less a considerable and, in England, too easily ignored novelist.

JULIEN GREEN (1900), who was born in Paris of American parents, has in common with Guilloux a concern with the inner world of his characters. Apart from the years 1939–45 he has lived in France. He is bilingual, and writes his novels in French. *Memories of Happy Days* (1942), a moving autobiography, is in English. His *Journals*, which have been appearing since 1928, give a full account of his Jansenist anguish (pt. tr. as *Personal Record, 1928–39*, 1940; tr. as *Diary 1928–57*, 1962). No Roman Catholic writer has a more tortured soul than Green, but it is misleading to call him a 'Catholic novelist': until *Moïra* his novels do not deal with problems of faith, but with problems of anguish and illusion—particularly with the false promises held out by sexual release and physical love. Green's technique is Victorian-Gothic—his novels are highly melodramatic— but he is a modernist because his subject is the Nietzschean one of 'man without God'; for Green godlessness is epitomized in man's condition of lustfulness and panic. He has perhaps learned more from Balzac than anyone else, although when he was young he read Dickens, Hawthorne and others with rapt attention.

Green, says a critic, is 'incapable of the exhibitionism which delights other Catholics also dwelling in Sodom'. He has always been a restrained writer, but has never concealed the fact that he was 'crucified in sex'. *Avarice House* (*Mont-Cinère*, 1926; tr. 1927) was a Gothic tale of a miserly woman trapped in a hate relationship with her daughter. *The Dark Journey* (*Léviathan*, 1929; tr. 1929), equally Gothic, comes nearer to the bone of Green's concerns: a man, in raping a servant girl, scars her face by lashing her with a branch; she falls in love with him and flees with him. *The Dreamer* (*Le Visionnaire*, 1934; tr. 1934) shows the other side of the penny: the ecstatic hero realizes that life is anguish but that there really does exist another and perfect world.

However, Green's best work lay in front of him, and belongs to the post-war period. One of his three plays, *South* (*Sud*, 1953; tr. 1955), set in the American South, has power; but the two novels *Moïra* (1950; tr. 1951) and *Each in His Darkness* (*Chaque Homme dans sa nuit*, 1960; tr. 1961) represent the peak of his achievement. In the first a puritanical young student at an American university murders a girl with whom he has been to bed. Here faith does have some say, if only obliquely, for without it Green could not have achieved the serenity of his characterization of the people whose sexuality so violently disturbs them. *Each in His Darkness* approaches the problem of Catholicism more openly. Wilfred Ingram, target of many homosexual approaches, is a draper's assistant who wants to live a good Catholic life but whose sensuality torments him. Ingram's 'Catholicism' as contrasted with his sexually disturbed life makes sense whether the reader is Roman Catholic or not. It might be objected that Green's idea of erotic pleasure is an unrealistic one; the answer is the question, Who's is not? He is a frenetic writer— but no novelist has exploited modern Gothic to such effect.

*

Before considering Saint-Exupéry and Malraux, two novelists of action, it would be wrong to leave unmentioned the eccentric, versatile armchair adventurer PIERRE MAC ORLAN (ps. PAUL DUMARCHAIS, 1883–1970), born at Péronne, in Picardy. Before the First World War, in which he fought, he was a cartoonist, and assumed his Scottish pseudonym. His early novels were fantasies, the best known of which is *Yellow Laughter* (*La Rire jaune*, 1914), a parody of H. G. Wells (q.v. 1) in which the earth is invaded and overcome by the yellow laughter of the title. Mac Orlan, who was an outer member of Picasso's circle, flirted with a poetry that never, as a critic has said, became more than prose: *Complete Poems* (*Poésies documentaires complètes*, 1954). However, it is a pleasantly readable prose. But his adventure stories at their best are at least reminiscent of Conrad or Stephenson; and in his tough studies of port life he reaches the peak of his achievement. Marcel Carné captured the exact taste of it all in his 1938 movie (with Jean Gabin, Michèle Morgan and Pierre Brasseur all playing magnificently) of *Quay of Shadows* (*Le Quai des brumes*, 1927). Mac Orlan, also an art critic and essayist, was a thoroughly competent professional writer. He has written novels about magic and the supernatural, of which he has an extensive knowledge. The excitement and action in his tales spring from a philosophy that prefers the stable adventures of the mind to the cruel and dangerous ones of actuality.

ANTOINE DE SAINT-EXUPÉRY (1900–44), however, could not live happily without facing the actual challenge of death. He belongs to the long line of literary men of action, which includes figures as diverse as d'Annunzio (q.v. 3), T. E. Lawrence, Ernst Jünger and Malraux (qq.v.). It is likely that the legend (he had, like T. E. Lawrence, a genius for 'backing into the limelight') and the man himself—much loved, mysterious and heroic—have become confused with the worth of his actual books. Born at Lyon, he had a radiantly happy childhood: this was the paradise that he fell back upon when his search in dangerous action—flying—for release from inner tensions and for human brotherhood exercised intolerable strains. His first book, *Southern Mail* (*Courrier-Sud*, 1928; tr. 1933) is a relatively crude adventure story, based on Saint-Exupéry's experiences as a pioneer of commercial flying; but it does contain some of the descriptions of flying for which Saint-Exupéry is famous. *Night Flight* (*Vol de nuit*, 1931; tr. 1932) is a great improvement. It contains two well drawn characters: the externally ruthless but inwardly tender head of a newly established South American airline, and his mystical chief pilot. This essentially simple and well constructed book may well be Saint-Exupéry's best, although it does not contain all his best writing, which is distributed between the two non-fiction books, *Wind, Sand and Stars* (*Terre des hommes*, 1939; tr. 1939), on being a flier in the Thirties, and *Flight to Arras* (*Pilote de guerre*, 1942; tr. 1942), on his experiences as a reconnaissance pilot at the time of the defeat of France. He left a charming children's book, *The Little Prince* (*Le Petit Prince*, 1945; tr. 1945) and anon the whole inferior posthumous collection of aphorisms and meditation slung together under the title of *The Wisdom of the Sands* (*Citadelle*, 1948; tr. 1950). One must not look for more in Saint-Exupéry than he can truly give; when he tries to be metaphysical he can be portentous and even pretentious—but when he sticks to the task in hand, as he did in *Night Flight*, and simply projects his feelings and sensations and his accurate memories (he had been in South America operating an airline), then, as Gide observed, he is truly metaphysical. Furthermore, he still has no rival in the literature of flight.

The spectacular ANDRÉ MALRAUX (1901), born in Paris, is another who writes from experience of various kinds of action. But he is more effective as an intellectual than Saint-Exupéry; and when, after his pro-communism (he was never a Marxist) of the Thirties, he became Minister of Propaganda and then Culture in de Gaulle's governments (he departed when the General did), he dried up as a novelist, and has concentrated on the history of art. In his youth he was an archaeologist and an adventurer, and became involved, in the Twenties in Indo-China, with the smuggling of statues. He was also involved in revolutionary activities in China. In the Second World War he was in the tank corps and was taken prisoner. He escaped and became a guerilla leader, was recaptured; and then set free when his comrades raided Toulouse Prison where he was held. During the Spanish Civil War Malraux fought against the fascists as an airman.

Malraux is important among modern writers as one who, despite his (self-styled) Dostoevskian imagination, has always wanted to do something, to be 'engaged'. Not for him the notion of the writer committed to no more than his function as writer. A consistent theme throughout his fiction has been a Spenglerian notion of the decline of the West, in which he has perhaps continued depressedly to believe: thus the post-novelist elevates only graphic art above fatal history; the Minister, instead of pursuing fiction, has the historic buildings of Paris cleaned and restored—and, alas, vulgarized. Malraux's 'swing to the right' after the war should be regarded not as political but as springing from a conviction that the Russian form of communism is more of a threat to Western freedom than the corruptions of capitalism; doubtless there was an element of personal ambition. There was enough 'leftism' in de Gaulle to satisfy him; his complacency about the system that the General would leave behind him on his departure (the uneasy France of Pompidou) is more criticizable. In any case, the choice of so shrewd and sensitive a man cannot be ignored. The key to his behaviour is to be found in *The Voices of Silence* (*Les Voix du silence*, 1951; tr. 1953), the book on art in which he reveals himself as pessimistic determinist arguing for the deliberate assertion of art over history: because art is the only permanent expression of man's will over fate. The inevitable corollary is that forms of society (even the General's) are not in this way permanent. However, Malraux does, at times thrillingly, put forward art as the only common denominator of mankind. It would be *logical* for a man holding such views to be Minister of Culture in any government.

Malraux established himself as an important writer with his third novel, *Man's Estate* (*La Condition humaine*, 1933; tr. 1948), the background of which is Chiang Kai-Shek's coup against the communists of 1927. This is a novel without a 'plot' in the conventional sense: it consists of a series of scenes, cinematic in technique, throughout which a lurid drama of deceit and murder is played out. This was one of the earliest serious novels to have many of the features of a thriller, and in this way led on from Conrad (q.v.), by whom Malraux must have been influenced. It was perhaps the first book to reveal the true nature of twentieth-century politics in action; those who read it and then accused Malraux, twelve years later, of betraying the left were far off the mark: he had never, as a writer, pledged himself to them (nor, of course, has he ever repudiated some measure of communism, at some appropriate time, as a necessary form of change). After a more straightforward novel, *Days of Contempt* (*Le Temps du mépris*, 1935; tr. 1938), the unequivocally anti-fascist story of a communist imprisoned by the Nazis and freed by a comrade's stratagem so that he may continue the fight, Malraux produced what is probably the best of all his books: *Days of Hope* (*L'Espoir*, 1937), on the tragic prelude to the Second World War, the Civil War in Spain. This employs the same highly effective cinematic technique as *Man's Estate*, and contains a classic account of the heroic defence of Madrid. It reflects the Spanish Civil War more fairly than any other book (Barea's, q.v. 3, reporting was from the inside), in its desperate untidiness, its marvellous hopes, and in its irony—men of intellect riddling one another with bullets. It is frequently, and rightly, compared with Hemingway's sentimental but best-selling *For Whom the Bell Tolls* (q.v. 1) to the detriment of the latter. There was only one more novel to come. While in prison Malraux began a long novel, much of which the Germans destroyed. The surviving part of *The Struggle with the Angel* (*La Lutte avec l'ange*) is *The Walnuts of Altenburg* (*Les Noyers de l'Altenburg*, 1943, 1945; tr. 1952), a 'dialogue novel' of great interest, but a failure as fiction. The story offers a framework for discussions of Malraux's ideas; freed from the pressures of his imagination, he becomes (as all human beings do) more philosophical, rhetorical, consciously noble; it represents a diffusion of imagination. But there are memorable passages, in particular an extraordinary re-creation of the madness of Nietzsche (q.v.).

It seems that Malraux, when he was driven by his imagination, sought in action some kind of reification of his ideals; driven by his (considerable) intellect, he has postulated art as man's eternal escape in books that may well be bad art-history, but which are none the less important. He and Saint-Exupéry served as models for many writers. Of his involvement with politics we may at least say that his shame is his own business. How must he have felt as he 'briefed' Nixon for his Chinese adventure (1972)?

The novelist, geographer, historian and art-historian ANDRÉ CHAMSON (1900), who was born at Nîmes, resembles his wartime comrade and friend André Malraux in a number of ways: he is concerned with personal courage as a way of life; he, too, was associated with left-wing activities in the Thirties, and was actually in politics; again, a qualified archivist, he became director of the art gallery of the Petit Palais, in Paris, after the war; he wrote on the Spanish Civil War. Chamson, who has written poems in Provençal and is an admirer of Mistral (q.v.), is essentially a regionalist, although not a militant one like Giono. On the whole his social concerns have emerged most fruitfully in his regional rather than in his metropolitan novels; an exception is *The Year of the Vanquished* (*L'Année des vaincus*, 1935), on Nazi Germany and its blighting of Franco-German proletarian friendship. This was in the same international spirit as Pabst's movie, *Comradeship* (*Kameradschaft*, 1931), which showed German miners coming to the aid of French in a disaster.

Unfortunately the imagination of Chamson, who is an admirably humane and intelligent man, is not sufficiently powerful to give his fiction as a whole much colour or conviction. In that respect he has written little better than his first novel, *Roux the Bandit* (*Roux le bandit*, 1925; tr. 1929), about a tough peasant who refuses to join up, and is sought by *gendarmerie* while the locals fête him and turn him into a hero—and its successor, *The Road* (*Les Hommes de la route*, 1927; tr. 1929), a vivid and sympathetic depiction of nineteenth-century Provençal peasants leaving the country to live in the town. *The Sum of Our Days* (*Le Chiffre de nos jours*, 1954) is a lucid re-creation, in fictional form, of Chamson's Cévanole childhood. Chamson has always been obsessed by Catholic cruelty to his Protestant ancestors, and in *The Superb* (*La Superbe*, 1967) he traces the history of the persecuted *camisards*, the Huguenots who eventually rose up in the early eighteenth century. This is often an effectively dispassionate picture of persecution, though the struggle for objectivity is a painful and over-lengthy one. Chamson is important for his understanding of his region and as a representative of the minority Protestant tradition.

VII

PAUL VALÉRY (1871–1945), born at Sète on France's Mediterranean coast near Montpellier, represents an end-development of nineteenth-century symbolism as much as a beginning to twentieth-century modernism. Universally considered to be France's greatest poet of the century, he has had little direct influence. He was austere but also smilingly humorous; indeed, his sense of fun was probably the chief factor in the stability he maintained in despite of a mind stretched in many directions. Valéry's coldness, for all his natural reticence, was only apparent; otherwise the surface of his poetry would merely look like a picture of the sea—and not resemble the sea itself: glitteringly delicate, richly suggesting its hidden depths.

Valéry's external life was uneventful. He studied law, did military service, worked as a civil servant and then for a news agency for over twenty years until 1922, when he retired. He married in 1900. To begin to approach his highly abstruse but beautiful poetry—perhaps the most sheerly 'beautiful' of the century—it is necessary to consider his hermetic beginnings under the influence of Mallarmé, whom he knew well; and to understand that he desperately desired not to be a poet—or a writer at all—but just a thinker.

Thus, after some prolific early poetry in the manner of the symbolists and Mallarmé, Valéry gave up writing poetry—in an access, one may guess, of sceptical despair, as well as because of an unhappy love affair—and invented the cruelly impossible Monsieur Teste, master of thought, who only lacks the 'weakness of character' that is necessary to become a universally acclaimed genius. But of course Monsieur Teste—*Monsieur Teste* (*La Soirée avec Monsieur Teste*, 1896, 1919, 1946; tr. 1947)—was only one side of Valéry. In 1912 he took up work on some of his early poems, including 'The Young Fate' (La Jeune Parque' 1917), which he expanded into one of his major works, and in 1922 brought out a further volume, *Enchantments* (*Charmes*, 1922). All his life he worked on his *Notebooks* (*Cahiers*, 1957–61; pt. VCW), which since their publication in twenty-nine volumes have been seen to form an essential part of his prose work. He combined within himself, perhaps more successfully than any other modern writer, the roles of scientist and poet. No philosopher will ever regard him as a philosopher; but the work he did in the 257 *Notebooks*, lucid dawn research (he favoured the early rather than the late hours) on the mental origins of his poems and other writings —should eventually be considered as far more important than any twentieth-century philosophy; they suggest, indeed, that philosophy (in at least the British sense) is now an exhausted vein. The conscious basis of his poetic art had been anti-romanticism; but in 1912 he became involved in a struggle to push back to the utmost the limits of irrationality. The result, especially in 'The Pythoness' ('La Pythie'), 'The Cemetery by the Sea' ('Le Cimetière Marin') and 'The Young Fate' is a poetry of weight, sonorous beauty and, above all, extraordinary Mediterrean wildness and robust sensibility. During the twenty years of his poetic silence Valéry had pondered on the problem of creativity, and had discovered that, in the words of his most famous single line, 'Le vent se lève! . . . il faut tenter de vivre!' ('The wind rises! . . . We must try to live!'). He set out to investigate the unconscious origins of his early poetry; to examine the method by which the irrational is made significant. The project grew; the campaign against romanticism became a reluctant definition of it, its iron surface redolent of its secret beauties and mysteries. Valéry's finest poetry has an emotional substance that his original master Mallarmé's usually lacks: at its core is an educated Latin sensuality, even at times a smiling hedonist ('the astonishing spring laughs, violates. . . .'). The theory-bound French critics who accused him of turning poetry into an intellectual exercise (this was a mid-century phase of reaction, and has now been dropped) ignored all but the strict classicism of form that his temperament required. That first great rediscovery of his poetic power, 'La Jeune Parque', makes this clear: 'without doubt the most perfect and the most difficult poem in the French language', an enraptured account of a young girl's apprehension of spring and desire, of the poet's own abandonment of the shadowless death of thought for the disturbing uncertainties of life:

> Were purpose clear, all would seem vain to you.
> Your ennui would haunt a shadowless world
> Of neutral life and untransforming souls.
> Something of disquiet is a holy gift:
> Hope, which in your eyes lights up dark alleyways,
> Does not arise from a more settled earth;
> All your splendours spring from mysteries.
> The most profound, not self-understood,
> From certain night derive their riches
> And the pure objects of their noble loves.
> The treasure that irradiates your life
> Is dark; from misty silence poems arise.

T. S. Eliot (q.v. 1) was right when he asserted that it is Valéry who will be, for posterity, 'the representative poet' of the first half of our century. This is not to say that he was 'better' than, for example, Rilke; but he does represent the absolutely sentimentive (q.v.) artist. He is the major poet who is also the major critic, in the most accutely self-conscious, the most 'sentimentive' century. What he wrote about the composition of his poetry is among the most searching of all criticism; doubtless it is significant that it is by a poet, and that it is self-criticism.

As one may gather from reading Gide's *Journals*, Valéry (whom Gide loved none the less) seemed in certain respects to be a cold, irritating and even an ungenerous man. He was, Léautaud says, 'violently anti-Dreyfus'—but not too seriously. Unable to reach in conversation the precision he achieved in writing, he tended to substitute for it a sweepingly superior condemnation of everything. However, he was also gay and vivacious, 'the depths of his soul broken open by laughter', said Cocteau. But the oft-repeated charge of 'cerebral narcissism' must stand—indeed, a cerebral narcissism was essential to this poetry. Valéry carries one aspect of the French poetic genius to a point of richness that no one without passion could have done; no one will deny him his place as one of the four or five of France's supreme poets.

*

While Valéry was going his own independent way, much was happening in French poetry. The First World War did not produce the quality of poetry from France that it produced from Great Britain and Germany: against Sorley, Owen, Sassoon, Rosenberg (qq.v. 1) in Britain, and Stadler, Stramm and Trakl (qq.v.) and others in Germany, France can really only offer Apollinaire.

Some would class CHARLES PÉGUY (1873–1914), who was born at Orléans and died at the head of his troops on the Marne in the first weeks of the war, as a war poet. He had anticipated and ardently desired the war since 1905. But the lines 'Happy are the dead, for they have gone back to / The first clay fed by their bodies . . .' ('Heureux sont ce morts, car ils sont retournés / Dans ce terre au nourris de leur dépouille . . .'), too famous outside their context in the long poem *Éve*, while they reflect the universally keen war-spirit of 1914, are not about the realities of war itself (which Apollinaire's poems, for all their ironic playfulness, are), and were in any case written before it. Judged by the poetic standards of the war poetry of Owen and others, these lines are as specious, although less egocentric, than Rupert Brooke's (q.v. 1) popular 'war' sonnets. Péguy was a playwright and poet, but owes his high, possibly too high, position in French literary history to his essays and to his foundation and editorship of the influential *Cahiers de la Quinzaine* (1900–14), the files of which provide an indispensable guide to the France of its period. Péguy began as a socialist and an agnostic, but ended as a right-wing Catholic crusader. A supporter of Dreyfus, he quarrelled with the manner of the Dreyfusards' exploitation of their victory. Péguy was always high-minded, a man of passionate integrity and sincerity; it may well be that the legend (hagiography is not too strong a word) of the man has seemed to invest his visionary verse with qualities that it does not possess. It is interesting to speculate upon what the always just Péguy, who loved his country and its army, would have felt about the glory of the war by 1917. One can be sure that he would not have pretended.

The historical importance of the indisputably noble Péguy and of his changing convictions, from intellectual agnostic international socialist to unorthodox Catholic patriot and Bergsonian anti-intellectual, is evident. But how will he be judged as a poet? He stands outside the mainstream of twentieth-century European poetry because he speaks absolutely directly and offers no linguistic difficulties whatever. His poems, long and repetitive, can only (and then remotely) be compared to those of Claudel—to no one else's. Péguy is even more anachronistic, and writes, with a countryman's simplicity, of the 'supernatural' itself as 'carnal'. The main poems are a recast of his earlier play, *The Mystery of the Charity of Joan of Arc* (*Le Mystère de la charité de Jeanne d'Arc*, 1909; tr. 1950), the poem of his 1908 re-conversion, *Ève* (1913)—10,000 lines—and *The Mystery of the Holy Innocents* (*Le Mystère des Saints Innocents*, 1912; tr. with other poems 1956). Passionate, incantatory, diffuse, this poetry compels attention by its sheer force of conviction; it rings true; but it cannot come to the point ('like a cunning peasant', said a critic, remembering Péguy's peasant origins of which he was so proud), and little in it com-pensates for the monotony of the repetitions. It should perhaps be judged not as poetry but as a rhythmical prose of the same kind as that of Ramuz (q.v.), to whose fictional style it has been compared: 'full of knots and slag ... harsh and strong ... primitive ... con-crete and spoken ...' (PBFV4; FBS).

Most of the other twentieth-century French poets (few of whom approach Valéry in seriousness or importance) may be considered in relation to, or at least seen against, the background of that exceed-ingly Gallic phenomenon, surrealism—which critics take too seri-ously at grave risk. Dada (q.v.), which manifested itself in Switzer-land during and as a protest against the First World War, was the movement out of which it sprang; and dada, of course, was one of the outcomes of expressionism (q.v.). The co-founder of dada, TRISTAN TZARA (1896–1963), originally a Rumanian, collaborated with the surrealists from 1929–34. Previously Breton had supplanted him as leader of the Paris dada group (1919). Dada was necessary to literature, although in its extremity of romanticism it could ulti-mately only laugh at itself ('true dadas are against dada'): by being at all, it contradicted itself, was pacifist and yet nihilist, totally destructive and yet hoped (Tzara's words) for 'a purified humanity'. Dada , picked out at a very apt random by Tzara from a *Larousse* with a paper-knife, means 'hobby horse', 'obsession'; it also, of course, mocked at the bourgeois God, the authoritative father (cf. expres-sionism)—rather as Blake more than a century before had with his 'Nobodaddy'.

Predictably, Tzara abandoned nihilism and became more politic-ally committed. His long poem *Approximate Man* (*L'Homme approxi-matif*, 1931) tries to express his revolutionary hopes, but most of it is bogged down in an obsessional verbalism. After the Second World War, during which Tzara had engaged in anti-Nazi activities in the South of France, he moved to a more conventional and lyrical poetry. Important as a literary symptom, his own work is moving in the context of his struggles—but scarcely effective in its own right.

Surrealism was, in basic literary terms, a revolution against *all* kinds of formal literary expression (but with literary antecedents: including de Sade, Nerval, Isidore Ducasse, self-styled Comte de Lautréamont, 1846–70—the overrated sick adolescent who wrote *The Songs of Maldoror, Les Chants de Maldoror*, 1868; tr. 1944—the more gifted and important Charles Cros, 1842–88, Jarry, q.v., and, with reservations, Baudelaire, q.v.). The surrealists proper, those who lived for the movement—officially promulgated in 1922—and never broke away, were not over-gifted writers, but confused romantic theoreticians. One cannot take André Breton, the chief surrealist, at times a veritable Stalin with his purges, wholly seriously as a creative writer: his confusions require to be studied; he is a symptom of twentieth-century unease. The history of surrealism proper is no doubt the history of Breton (its custodian). Nihilistically humorous though it often is, surrealism, in broadest terms, is an attempted answer to 'the absurd', a desperate appeal to the unconscious, to dreams, to the irrational, to establish 'a new declaration of the rights of man'. The movement eventually split up into political activists (such as Aragon) and 'explorers of the marvellous' (such as Breton).

For the truly gifted writers, on the other hand, surrealism provided a new beginning, a break with conventions; they went on to new pastures. The surrealists proper either busied themselves, like Breton, with coercion and polemic (*Manifeste du Surréalisme*, 1924; *Qu'est-ce que le Surréalisme?*, tr. 1936, etc., etc.) or, unable to discover any commitment, killed themselves. JACQUES VACHÉ (1896–1919), the chief influence on Breton, killed himself in 1919. JACQUES RIGAUT (1899–1929), after breaking with literature (logically enough) and trying marriage with an American girl, killed himself in 1929; he had condemned himself to die, at the precise date and time he did die, in 1919. Surrealism naturally attracted such war-victims. In it, nihilism was engaged in a continuous struggle with hope; Breton, Éluard and other lesser poets tried to reconcile these in the figure of a mysterious woman; later some, but not Breton, substituted for her the communist party. God (meaning) was pitted desperately against death (meaninglessness, the 'absurd'). But now the conflict resolved itself as a battle between *signs* and *chance*. You pursued the meaningful mystery, the strange woman, and waited for the revelation; or you killed yourself; or you joined the proletariat.

ANDRÉ BRETON (1896–1966), born in Tinchebray in Normandy, wrote poems, but these are mostly of documentary interest: nine-tenths of his energy went into his concern for the movement he had been foremost in creating. In seeking to save dada from its self-destructiveness, he turned it into surrealism (the actual word was coined by Apollinaire), the concept of which, for the rest of his life, he strove to promote as a key to self-knowledge and human freedom.

Breton began as a disciple of Valéry; then, as an army psychiatrist in the First World War, he became interested in the ideas of Freud, to which he remained loyal. His strongly anti-literary bent came from Vaché, who was not a surrealist on paper but in life; this loyalty was reinforced by his 'comic' suicide. *The Magnetic Fields* (*Les Champs magnétiques*, 1921), Breton's experiments in automatic writing in collaboration with PHILIPPE SOUPAULT (1897), was the only technical innovation introduced by surrealism. It was an important one, because it opened the way not only to unconscious writing (if in fact that can be achieved) but also to the operations of chance—and to the establishment of those significant coincidences that Jung called synchronicity. All subsequent surrealist experiments can be traced back to this, as can every one of the antics of the pseudo-*avant garde* of the Sixties—and, indeed, every one of the experiments of writers such as William Burroughs (q.v. 1).

Breton, 'the glass of water in the storm' (the surrealists gave themselves and each other such names), continued to defend surrealism against subordination to any ideology, even to specifically anti-bourgeois ones such as Marxism. This amounted to a defence of literature, if only a certain kind of literature, against commitment; as such it is important.

Breton's actual poetry (PBFV4; FBS; BSP) suffers from a certain rigidity; one feels that he needs a visual medium, so that rather than strain for highly emotional or dramatic effects he cannot achieve, he could attain the sort of casual charm of a Dali composition—second-rate art at its best, but unpretentious. However, in what is his most important creative work, the prose *Nadja* (1928; tr. 1963), he comes close to the definition of the mad, psychic, liberating woman whom he sought, and who haunted his imagination. The long surrealist prologue is irrelevant; but the part dealing with the strange Nadja, written in more coherent form, is one of the more memorable of modern attempts to penetrate the mechanical face of the everyday and inhabit the mysterious reality behind it. Nadja's unpredictable nature is presented as emanating from this super-reality.

Many writers and poets who never joined the movement as such were 'fellow travellers'—or genuine ancestors. Saint-Pol-Roux (q.v.), though a survivor from symbolism, is clearly one of them, and was recognized as such. But no predecessor was closer to surrealism than the half-Polish, half-Italian GUILLAUME APOLLINAIRE (ps. GUIL-LAUME-ALBERT-VLADIMIR-ALEXANDRE-APOLLINAIRE DE KOSTROWIT-SKY, 1880–1918). Apollinaire was a bastard: his mother Angelica, a 'demoniacal coquette' and gambler who brought him and his younger brother up in Monte Carlo, had worked in the Vatican.

Apollinaire may never have known who his father, most often assumed to have been an Italian army officer, was, but he never denied that it had been Pope Leo XIII, and would have liked nothing more than for posterity to thus settle the matter. Another story, which he did not discourage, has it that he was descended from Napoleon.

Apollinaire, a quintessentially inquisitive spirit, loved by his friends, a legend in his own lifetime, was a characteristic early twentieth-century man: he was everything at once: scholar and vagabond, traditionalist and innovator, aesthete and pornographer, atheist, agnostic and religious man. When the Mona Lisa was stolen the police put him in prison. He was that kind of person. Close friend of Picasso and Braque, he was fascinated by painting, and wrote about it; he was, one might say, in on the discovery of cubism, although he did not fully understand it until the very eve of the publication of his *The Cubist Painters* (*Méditations esthétiques: Les Peintres Cubistes*, 1913; tr. 1949), whose sub-title he added at the last moment. In art cubism, which originated in the practice of Cézanne, was an attempt to give more than merely a representation of objects: to give a full account of their structure, and their positions in space. Several views of an object, including geometrical ones, would be superimposed on one another. Literary cubism is necessarily a somewhat vaguer term; its tendency, however, may be summed up in Apollinaire's own invention of the term 'Orphic Cubism', which he used to describe the painting of Robert Delaunay: 'the art of painting new structures out of elements that have not been borrowed from the visual sphere but have been created entirely by the artist himself, and have been endowed by him with the fullness of reality'. Substitute 'writing' for painting and add a substantial quantity of salt and we know as much about the programme of literary cubism as is good for us. What it actually *is* may most clearly be seen in the poetry of Reverdy (q.v.). Apollinaire went from -ism to -ism, continually being reproached for betrayal; after two years on the front and a serious head-wound he became more sympathetic to traditional procedures, but continued until the end (weakened, he died of influenza on 10 November, the day before the Armistice), to preach the spirit of the new. He coined the word surrealism in one of his programme notes for the Cocteau-Picasso-Massine-Satie ballet *Parade,* and used it to describe his play *The Breasts of Tiresias* (*Les Mamelles de Tirésias*, 1918; tr. in *Odyssey*, December, 1961). This is chaotic and impudent, but not really at all like the *Ubu Roi* of that egocentric precursor of surrealism, Jarry (q.v.); it can be variously interpreted, but its high spirits undoubtedly conceal a self-disquiet and a dissatisfaction with the role of *avant garde* clown and travelling king of all the -isms. After all, Apollinaire was no poetaster searching in theories for the substance of a genius he lacked: he was a lyric poet of genius, but one who in 1898 had found the scented perfectionism of the symbolists totally inadequate.

Most of Apollinaire's poetry is in *Spirits* (*Alcools*, 1913; tr. 1964; 1965) and *Calligrammes* (1918); it is collected, with the theatre, in *The Poetic Works* (*Œuvres Poétiques*, 1956). The so-called calligrammes follow on from earlier poets who wrote their verses in the shapes of hour-glasses, diamonds, and so on: Apollinaire shapes a poem on rain like rain, on a car like a car, and so on. He had been doing it since the early years of the century. In these charming poems, inevitably slighter than some of his others, he took 'concrete poetry' (q.v.) as far, poetically (but not graphically), as it could go. Other poems read rather uneasily: like a mixture of the crude Italian, Marinetti (q.v. 3), Whitman and Verhaeren (q.v.). But the best, 'Zone', 'Song of the Badly Loved' ('Chanson du mal aimé') and many others, combine a melancholy lyricism, eroticism, sweetness, out-of-the way knowledge, cosmopolitanism and passionate feeling. Apollinaire removed the punctuation of *Alcools* at the proof stage: 'I cut it out . . . for the rhythm itself and the division of the lines are the real punctuation'. But in technique he was less anti-traditional than he appeared and felt. When he is most moved his rhythms are usually regular.

Apollinaire's war poetry, much of which was published posthumously, eroticizes, and, at its most effective—when nervousness becomes power—transcends violence. There will always be readers ready to accuse such poems as 'The Horseman's Farewell' of 'bad taste' or 'lack of feeling'; but it is not less serious in quality than anything by Sassoon or Owen:

> Oh God how pretty war is
>   With its songs and long rests
> I have polished this ring
>   I hear your sighs in the wind
>
> Goodbye! Here is his gear
>   He vanished from sight
> And died over there while she
>   Laughed at fate's surprises

War for Apollinaire represented the emptiness within himself, which in the later poems becomes a secret grief. This secret grief is, as has been pointed out, fear of poetic inadequacy; it is also fear of the restless 'incertitude' (his own word) that had kept him on the move, from -ism to -ism, for the whole of his life. A poet of genius, the proto-surrealist who died before surrealism, he already lived at the heart of two of surrealism's profoundest paradoxes, in one of which hope wrestles with despair; the other is summed up in Valéry's laconic statement that 'the ideal of the new is contrary to the requirements of form'.

Apart from his amusing and efficient pornography, done for money, Apollinaire wrote two novels: *The Assassinated Poet* (*Le Poète assassiné*, 1916; tr. 1923) and *The Seated Woman* (*La Femme assise*, 1920). These are indispensable to a study of him, but neither succeeds as a whole. Much more successful are the delightful short stories of *The Wandering Jew* (*L'Hérésiarque et Cie*, 1910; tr. 1965), in which Apollinaire shows his scholarly and Slavic side, and revels in mystery, colour and magic with the natural facility of an Isaac Bashevis Singer (q.v. 1) and the confidence of a poet. (ASW; ASP; PBFV4; FBS; MEP; PI; Selected Writings tr. 1950).

The Parisian LÉON-PAUL FARGUE (1876–1947) might be described as a prince of minor poets. In certain respects, especially in his sense of humour, he resembles his friend Erik Satie, the composer whose loveliness and importance (suppressed by music journalists, fearfully oblivious to him, for fifty years) is just becoming apparent—Satie set some of his poems. Fargue was never a surrealist, but Breton pronounced him 'surrealist in atmosphere': and, like Saint-Pol-Roux, he is a link between symbolism and surrealism. He was as famous, in literary Paris, for his bohemian personality, conversation and inveterate telephoning of friends from far-flung bars as for his poetry. He has been solemnly criticized for 'wasting himself' on trivial literary activity, but the roots of his poetry, which has more substance than is immediately apparent—and little more whim-sicality than Satie's massively strict music—needed the nourishment of this kind of life. The solitary Fargue is the poet of Paris and of its streets, and to evoke it accurately and vividly he frequently and increasingly used prose forms. His earlier poetry, written while he was a disciple of Mallarmé (also his schoolmaster at the Collège Rollin), groped to define small nostalgias:

> Charitable hand that chastely
> Warms the other, frozen hand.
> Straw that a bit of sun kisses
> Before the door of a dying man.
> A woman held out but not embraced
> Like a bird or a sword.

A mouth smiling far off
To make certain that you die well.

(FBS)

Later he relied on Paris itself to make these definitions, training his
apprehension of it to become ever sharper: 'poetry is the only dream
in which one must not dream'. Much of Paris and Parisian bohemian
and literary life died with him. He is wrongly described as an escapist:
one does not 'escape' into one's own loneliness and nostalgia. Like
Satie, Fargue mistrusted 'greatness', and his unpretentiousness too
easily encourages his neglect. His occasional reminiscences, such as
the contrast between Mallarmé as schoolmaster and teacher of
'Twinkle, twinkle, little star', and Mallarmé as poetic sage (included
in *Refuges*, 1942), are charming and wise. His most famous book,
whose title describes him so well, is *The Paris Pedestrian* (*Le Piéton de
Paris*, 1939); much of his work appears in *Poésies* (1963), which was
introduced by Saint-John Perse. *Lanterne Magique* (1944) was translated in 1946. (FBS; PBFV4)

MAX JACOB (1876–1944) was born of Jewish parents at Quimper in
Brittany. He too was a legendary personality: friend of Picasso and
Apollinaire, painter, homosexual, Catholic, recluse, one-time
astrologer, humorist. He was taken by the Gestapo to the concentration camp at Drancy, where he died, not long before the liberation
of Paris. He even made a pun about that (in a message to a friend he
wrote: 'Pris par la Gestapo. Prononcez "J'ai ta peau"'). Jacob was
above all a gentle and good man, whose existence was one long
striving to keep at bay and yet to understand the keen misery of his
childhood, when he had three times tried to kill himself. No one
could penetrate the various masks—clown, martyr, saint—beneath
which he lived. His refusal or inability to be himself weakens his
work, which none the less has enormous charm and wholesomeness.
His life, which in one of his relatively few serious moments he called
'a hell', was most unfortunately complicated by a homosexuality
which he could not accept. He made no attempt to deal with this
anguish in his work, which consisted of poems, prose poems, short
stories and surrealist texts. He had visions of Christ in 1909 and in
1914—this one in a cinema, 'in the one-and-threes'—and in 1915
he was finally received into the Roman Catholic Church. Like most
surrealists, Jacob believed in signs, and waited for them. From 1921,
just as he had become famous, he retired to an Abbey at Saint-
Benoît-sur-Loire. It seems that his homosexual tendencies played a
great part in his decision. He did not finally settle there until 1936,
after which he is said to have succeeded in leading the life of humility

and prayer he so desired. He did not, however, cut himself off from poetry, painting or his friends (who visited him regularly until the war).

Jacob's most enduring writing is probably to be found in his letters; although that judgement might be shown to be unfair by a really rigorous selection from all his humorous poems, including those written in Breton. *The Dice Box* (*Le Cornet à dés*, 1917), prose poems, his most influential collection, contains the sharpest expressions of his mental crisis: he reluctantly discovers his anguish in a series of casual apprehensions, anecdotes, 'cubist' visions of 'ordinary' objects. But Jacob did not in his work achieve the serenity he may have found towards the end of his life. He was himself a work of art, a mystifier whose holiness some of his closest friends regarded as just one more joke. (JDP; FBS; PBFV4)

VALÉRY-NICOLAS LARBAUD (1881–1957) was born of rich parents in Vichy, and never entirely shrugged off the burden of the fortune he inherited. A friend of Gide's and of most of the other writers of his generation, he was never affiliated to any movement. A traveller and scholar, he did much for English literature in France, translating Coleridge and, later, some of James Joyce's *Ulysses* (q.v.). In his *Poems of A. O. Barnabooth* (*Poèmes d'A. O. Barnabooth*, 1923; first issued 1908 as *Poems of a Rich Amateur, Poèmes d'un riche amateur*; tr. *Poems of a Multimillionaire*, 1955) and in the prose *Intimate Journal of A. O. Barnabooth* (*Journal intime d'A. O. Barnabooth*, 1913) he projects himself into a cynical young South American who searches for his true identity while fervently responding to twentieth-century mechanization. His best work is probably the faintly sinister short novel *Fermina Marquez* (1911), describing the havoc played in an exclusive boys' school by the advent of two beautiful girls. Larbaud was intelligent, civilized and super-cultivated, but his vein of creativity was a thin one (PBFV4)

JULES SUPERVIELLE (1884–1960), born of French-Basque parents in Montevideo, is an influential poet, a pantheist whose gentle meditations offer an interesting contrast to the more explosive surrealists. Supervielle has introduced into French poetry the South American traditions of acceptance of the harshness of existence, and of playfulness. He is a tragic poet, but not a pessimistic one:

> When the horses of time stop at my door
> I always hesitate a little to watch them drink
> Since it is with my own blood that they quench their thirst.
> They turn toward me with grateful eyes
> While their long draughts fill me with weakness

And leave me so weary, so alone and uncertain
That a passing night invades my eyelids
And suddenly I feel the need to rebuild my strength
So that one day when the team comes to drink
I may live again and slake my thirst.

(FBS)

Supervielle's most frequent theme is death: as the inevitable end of life (although he lived to a good age, he had a serious heart condition), as the thief of life, and as the goal of life. In his quiet and technically highly accomplished poems we do not see him (and ourselves) protesting, but rather hiding from a threat we ought to but cannot accept. A good part of his mature poetry, which begins with the collection *Gravitations* (1925) may be seen as a series of rueful, graceful strategies for spiritual or physical survival:

> Presences, speak low,
> Someone might hear us
> And sell me to death
> Hide my face
> Behind the branches
> And let me be indistinguishable
> From the shadow of the world.
>
> (FBS)

In Supervielle, as Laura Riding (q.v. 1) once said of another poet, 'fear is golden'. An unusually accessible poet who is yet truly 'modern' in spirit, he offers an excellent introduction to contemporary French poetry and its concerns. He has also written drama, novels, fine short stories—*Souls of the Soulless* (*L'Enfant de la haute mer*, 1931; tr. 1933)—and children's stories, of which *The Colonel's Children* (*Le Voleur d'enfants*, tr. 1950) is the most enchanting. (SSW; PBFV4; FBS; MEP)

Recently rediscovered and reassessed, the work of the scholar and diplomat OSCAR VENCESLAS DE LUBICZ MILOSZ (1877–1939) contains, buried within a mass of gorgeous reconditeness, some poems of quite astonishing beauty. Milosz was a Lithuanian who learned French as a child and early chose it as his language of literary expression. A linguist and expert in philosophy and physics (it has been claimed that he evolved the theory of relativity at the same time as Einstein), he travelled in the East and wrote fairly conventional symbolist poetry. After the war he represented his country in Paris; in 1926 he retired to Fontainebleau, to a home he filled with birds. He became a French citizen (1930). His metaphysics have been described as 'an exotic blend of Catholicism, Swedenborg, Böhme, Eastern traditions and modern physics'—a mixture heady enough to enrapture any symbolist. His best poems sense the Platonic world of perfect objects as a pre-human paradise through the window of his mundane existence:

> Go down on your knees, orphan life,
> Feign prayer, while I count and count again
> Those patterns of flowers that have no sad and grimed
> Suburban garden counterparts
>
> Such as are seen hanging on doomed walls through rain.
> Later you will lift your gaze from the blank book:
> I shall see moored barges, barrels, sleeping coal
> And the wind blowing through the sailors' stiff linen. . . .

Milosz's collected works, in eleven volumes, were published 1960–3. He wrote plays—*Miguel Manara* (1912; tr. 1919)—and philosophical explications. (MSP; PBFV4; FBS)

Recognition abroad came late for PIERRE-JEAN JOUVE (1887), who was born at Arras; he has been influential among poets in France, but until recently not much read by the general public. As well as a poet, he is a novelist, music- and art-critic, essayist and translator of Shakespeare. Never a poet easy of access, it is best to approach him in terms of his influences: unanimism (soon repudiated by him, however, as *'néfaste'*: ill-omented, unfortunate; but it is symptomatic of his high serious honesty); Romain Rolland (q.v.); Freud (decisively); Roman Catholicism; Blake; Mozart (he has written well on *Don Giovanni*: *Le Don Juan de Mozart*, tr. 1957); the English metaphysical poets; the composer Alban Berg (on whom he has also written illuminatingly).

Jouve began as a 'unanimist' poet; but he has proscribed all his work before the 1929 collection, *The Lost Paradise* (*Le Paradis perdu*). After emerging from the influence of Romain Rolland he underwent what he describes as a 'moral, aesthetic, spiritual crisis'; be became a Catholic and a Freudian; and at about this time he married a psychoanalyst. As he puts it, 'I have two fixed objectives: . . . to work out a poetic language that would hold its own entirely as song; to find in the poetic act a *religious* perspective—the only answer to the void of time'. Jouve, like Claudel, but from the standpoint of an entirely different temperament, saw God's kingdom of the world threatened by an engulfing Eros, the twin of death. He found no pleasure in a world from which God appeared to have withdrawn himself, and his poetry until the war (and his Swiss exile) seems, as one critic has expressed it, 'repellent and grandiose'. But acquaintance with his later work makes the earlier, which appeared in such books as *Nuptials* (*Les Noces*, 1928) and *Blood Sweat* (*Sueur de sang*, 1933), more accessible because more understandable. The poetry of the first and disturbed period is highly original, an example of a poet obstinately going his own way and finding ultimate acceptance. It is not always successful in holding its own as 'song' ('*chant*'), and its theological themes are often obscure; but Jouve does convey, urgently, his sense of the ambiguities of an eroticism whose irresistibly holy-seeming exaltations divorce him from God. These poems describe the impossibility of a physical renunciation that is nevertheless seen as necessary to salvation. They are not like Milosz's symbolist poems: Jouve's God is 'dead' (in the sense of the recent theological controversy). The predicament is summed up in 'The Death Tree': if man is 'saved from the sun' (of desire) by the death tree, it is the absence of the 'Angel'—but this saving tree's roots are 'convulsed in desire', and the tree 'shuts', trying to kill the man. Then the Angel returns, and 'The dark uncertain fight took place in confusion'.

War jerked Jouve from what threatened to become an obsession, and he began to write

> for god and fire
> For a love of place
> Let the void be rid of man
> Frozen by a flame.
>
> (IN)

His resistance poems, collected in *The Virgin of Paris* (*La Vierge de Paris*, 1946), discovered new concerns; the collection contained his most famous poem, 'Tapestry of Apple-trees', welcoming the 'iron beasts of love', the invading armies of the allies, into Normandy in 1944.

Jouve's novels, the best known of which is *Paulina 1880* (1925), all belong to the Twenties and Thirties, and describe people who are, like himself, simultaneously obsessed by the erotic and the mystical. (IN; PBFV4; FBS)

The premier 'poet's poet' of our time, SAINT-JOHN PERSE (ps. MARIE-RENÉ ALEXIS SAINT-LÉGER LÉGER, 1887), who was born on a small coral island his family owned near Gaudeloupe, chose to earn his living in the diplomatic service. He was General Secretary of the Ministry of Foreign Affairs from 1933 until the fall of France, when he went into exile in America. He lived in Washington for some years, but finally returned to France. Only Saint-John Perse's first collection, *Eulogies* (*Éloges*, 1910; tr. 1956), was published under his own name. In 1960 he was awarded the Nobel Prize. He is a modest and self-effacing man, who has stated that his name 'does not belong to literature'. His admirers and translators include many of the illustrious names of the twentieth century: Rilke, Eliot (q.v. 1), Hofmannsthal (q.v.), Ungaretti (q.v. 3) and others.

Saint-John Perse was influenced by Claudel in his use of form: he writes in long, incantatory lines. His poetry is rooted in the early twentieth-century rediscovery of the past, most famously represented in Stravinsky's *Rite of Spring* and Eliot's *Waste Land*. He is encyclo-paedic, technical, concrete, cryptic—but only as cryptic as the history of the earth as recreated in the mind of the poet. His descrip-tions of the world follow, it has been suggested, not recognized roads or currents, but 'isobars or isotherms, hitherto unsuspected but real paths'. He wishes to recapture the lost language, not of God—for Saint-John Perse, too, that particular God is dead—but of the Gods: the manifold voices of nature. He explores the universe historically, geologically, above all anthropologically, in his irresistibly epic terms—and in doing so discovers himself; he is a kind of Lévi-Strauss who is also a *chanteur*. His language is stately, ceremonious; he is an atheistic priest, conducting rites of nature. He has all the ecstasy of a Claudel, but sees no horror or tragedy or senselessness in a creation without Christianity. *Eulogies* contains his most personal poems, inspired by his marvellous childhood on the coral island, with a nurse, who was, secretly, a pagan priestess, and by his blissful dis-covery of the world in those surroundings.

Anabasis (*Anabase*, 1924; tr. 1930) is perhaps the most optimistic major work of the century. The sweeps of conquering armies of which it is full, the establishment of a town by nomads that it cele-brates—these show the poet conquering the word, discovering language: 'Saint language', which contains all the Gods and is man's profoundest experience. With this poem Saint-John Perse con-fidently took up the mantle of Orphic poet. *Exile* (*Exil*, 1942; tr. 1954), his unhappiest volume, but not a pessimistic one, describes the hero-poet cut off from his quest. *Winds* (*Vents*, 1946) both enhance and disturb life; *Rains* (*Pluies*, 1943) wash it clean; in these poems and in *Snows* (*Neiges*, 1944) Saint-John Perse literally de-scribes the elements, at the same time as integrating them into his huge single metaphor. *Seamarks* (*Amers*, 1957; tr. 1958) similarly describes the sea, but in treating it as loving the earth he also (for the first time) deals with the erotic. *Chronique* (1960) welcomes old age; *Birds* (*Oiseaux*, 1963; tr. 1966) traces the same mystery in the ways of the birds.

Saint-John Perse is a consistent Platonist: he seeks the true order of things in the entire universe; he also seeks to return to his enchanted childhood. His work shows no development. Except for its affinities with Claudel—himself an anachronism—it is detached from modern literature; it employs figures of medieval and Renaissance rhetoric hardly remembered today; yet it has, for those who have read it, a nearly Biblical value. Saint-John Perse's vision of paradise has not reached many readers directly—but in a diffused manner: through the many poets whose work it has nourished. (PBFV4; PI)

PIERRE REVERDY (1889–1960) was the son of a Narbonne winegrower ruined in the disaster of 1907; always something of a recluse, he was associated with the group around Apollinaire, and then with the surrealists, but never entered wholeheartedly into any *avant garde* activities. He was only in his mid-thirties when he retired to the Abbaye de Solesmes, where he lived for most of the time until his death. Although he did not have so acute a personal problem as the homosexuality of his friend Max Jacob, he was afflicted with religious doubt, which arose from his anguish at his inability to penetrate the mystery of the universe—a failure he attributed to his own inability to apprehend God. He did not find the peace he hoped for in the ascetic life he chose. He is rightly described as 'the' 'cubist' poet: he continually tries to understand, and in doing so superimposes one view (one image) of his subject-matter onto another. But what Reverdy most distrusted was the ordinary perception of his senses. His strangely fragmented and difficult poetry, arranged geometrically on the page, is like that of a man who insists to another: 'I know that our words agree on what we see, but I do not believe that we see in the same way'. His effort, which remained consistent and unchanging all his life, was to express his own sense of the real behind the perceived. His desolate poems might be those of a frustrated painter (he wrote commentaries on paintings); certainly, to be approached at all, they must first be approached as cubist paintings:

> Someone has just gone by
> And in the room
>   has left a sigh
> Life deserted
>   The street
>   An open window pane
> A ray of sunshine
> On the green plain
>   (MEP)

Reverdy is trapped (as he often said) between reality and dream: between (in fact) the agonizedly perceived, and the intangible and elusive emotions that it conjures up—those, for Reverdy, are intimations of the existence of a true world. Poems are 'crystals precipitated after the effervescent contact of the mind with reality'. His is possibly a too remote, difficult poetry ever to have much general appeal; but he is important to other poets. For a time, in Paris during the First World War, he came under the influence of—or perhaps initiated—Huidobro's 'creationism' (q.v. 3): 'whatever the eye looks at, let it be created'. But the eventual difference was that while creationist poets subscribed to the notion of the poet as 'a little God' 'bringing the rose to flower in the poem' itself, Reverdy remained in a position of humility, regarding his poetry as a means of apprehension of the world—not as a way of becoming independent of it, and of compensating for godlessness by becoming god. *The Sackcloth Glove* (*Le Gant de crin*, 1927) is his intensely fascinating poetics. (RSP; PBFV4; MEP; CFP)

PAUL ÉLUARD (ps. EUGÈNE GRINDEL, 1895–1952), one of the surrealists ('the nurse of the stars') who became a communist, has achieved the widest popular fame of any of his generation as a love poet. Éluard was born and died in Paris, and was always an essentially urban poet. He was a surrealist, generously searching for the elusive purity of the erotic and for a human brotherhood that his high sophistication—rather than his intelligence—kept warning him was inaccessible. Intimately associated with Breton in the surrealist movement, Éluard possessed the poetic genius Breton lacked; like Breton, he was obsessed with the feminine figure in which all conflicts would come to rest and be reconciled. It was his broad human sympathies rather than any intellectual Marxist conviction that caused him to break with Breton and surrealism, and to join the communist party (to which, characteristically, he remained faithful until his death). His political poetry is forced and embarrassing—especially in the light of the (now more evident) betrayal of communism by those who have acted in its name; but his innocence preserved him from falsity. The fact is that while Éluard needed the liberation from convention that surrealism offered him, and the anti-bourgeois and humanitarian ideals that communism seemed to offer him, he was not convincing either as a surrealist or a communist: he was a naïve (q.v.) writer moved by the notion of human freedom, and made indignant by poverty. His poetry has a touch of folk-song about it, which makes it accessible to a non-literary public; indeed, he is an anti-literary poet, but not a proletarian one—he is too sophisticated, and has too many moments of loneliness. Until 1936

Éluard's subject was, almost invariably, the relationship between men and women. With the Spanish Civil War he came to believe that a poet's duty was to be 'profoundly involved in the lives of other men'. During the war he became, with Aragon, the leading poet of the resistance, in which he was active. At one point he had to hide in a lunatic asylum, about which he wrote one of his most moving prose works, *Memories of the Asylum* (*Souvenirs de la maison des fous*, 1946); this experience may have reminded him of his 1930 experiment in collaboration with Breton, when they tried to simulate various kinds of mental disorder: *The Immaculate Conception* (*L'Immaculée Conception*). After the war he became increasingly active as a cultural ambassador, and his poetry lost its intensity. No better tribute to him could be devised than the fact that his best poetry is loved and intuitively grasped by the intelligent young. (ESW; VTT; PBFV4; FBS; MEP)

LOUIS ARAGON (1897), born in Paris, was successively dadaist, surrealist and communist. An *enfant terrible* when young, surrealism for him, too, was a liberating phase rather than a matter of conviction. His own lyricism is usually more important than the various surrealist experiments in which he is supposed to be participating. He visited Russia in 1930 and was so impressed with what he saw that he broke with surrealism and became a realist. Breton could never have written: 'If by following a surrealist method you write wretched stupidities, they are wretched stupidities. And inexcusable'. 'We have no talent', said Breton at the time of their inevitable quarrel. 'Under pretext that this is all surrealism', replied Aragon, 'the next cur who happens along thinks himself authorized to equate his slobberings with true poetry, a marvellous comfort for vanity and stupidity.' Aragon had written a hallucinatory, surrealist novel about Paris, *The Peasant of Paris* (*Le Paysan de Paris*, 1926). Now he turned to solid novels of socialist realism, beginning with *The Bells of Basel* (*Les Cloches de Bâle*, 1933; tr. 1937); this was followed by many others, under the general title of 'The Real World'. These are readable and competent rather than inspired; *Aurélien* (1945; tr. 1946) is perhaps the best of them.

Aragon's best moment came with the war. Not only was he one of the leaders of the literary resistance, but also, through his poetry, he became the spokesman of France. The poems of *Heartbreak* (*Le Crève-cœur*, 1941) and *The Eyes of Elsa* (*Les Yeux d'Elsa*, 1942) celebrated both France and his love for his wife, the writer Elsa Triolet. *The French Diana* (*La Diane française*, 1944) contained dramatic ballads, some of them among Aragon's best poetry, to keep up morale against the Nazis and their French collaborators. In the Elsa poems

Aragon used traditional techniques with great skill; they were as appropriate for the times as poetry can be. But they were written only for those times, and have not worn well. Much that was moving in the heat of the moment now appears as sentimental cliché, however effectively exploited. Literature is no more, to Aragon, than a weapon in the service of social revolution; he remains an exceptional author of this kind of writing. In the post-war years his fiction has been less crudely propagandist than his verse. (PBFV4; MEP; PI)

The Parisian ROBERT DESNOS (1900–45) did not, alas, live to take up the important place in French post-war poetry he would undoubtedly have had: he died of typhus soon after the war as a result of ill treatment in a Nazi concentration camp. An early surrealist, who used to deliver long 'automatic' monologues, he broke with the surrealists in 1929—one of the victims of Breton's overzealousness. Surrealism helped him, but, like Éluard, he was a natural lyric poet and his best work is not composed only with the subconscious, however it may have seemed at the time. Desnos wrote in the belief that a poet in his lifetime produces one poem, but is only capable of bringing parts of it to the surface. His surrealist poems, some of them produced in a trance-like state, were collected in 1930, and they —together with some charming nonsense poetry—remain his best. Much of the poetry of his latter years was rather too self-conscious. However, the famous 'Last Poem', written to his wife not long before he died (he had been taken for resistance activity), is a good example of his gift, poetically slight but pure and sincere:

I have so fiercely dreamed of you
And walked so far and spoken of you so,
Loved a shade of you so hard
That now I've no more left of you.
I'm left to be a shade among the shades
A hundred times more shade than shade
To be shade cast time and time again into your sun-transfigured
    life.

(MEP; see also PBFV4; FBS)

VIII

JEAN-PAUL SARTRE (1905), born in Paris, dominated French literature for a quarter of a century. He is a philosopher (but in the French, not the British sense: professional British philosophers shudder at his

name and think of bedrooms, spit and semen; they only read him on
holiday), political activist, refuser of the Nobel Prize (1964), critic
and playwright as well as novelist. His existentialist philosophy
derives from Heidegger, Kierkegaard, the phenomenologist Husserl
and (indirectly) from Nietzsche (qq.v.). Very briefly, Sartre sees
man in an absurd and godless universe, but capable of achieving
meaning if he will only make the choice to exist as himself. However,
his activity (bourgeois, and in 'bad faith') consists in a perpetual
attempt to alienate both himself and his neighbours from the freedom involved in choice. Sartre was attracted by phenomenology
because (again briefly) this is a philosophy that seizes upon phenomena as they present themselves to consciousness—rather than
debating upon their nature. Sartre sees man as trapped in 'viscosity':
his first semi-autobiographical novel *Nausea* (*La Nausée*, 1938; tr.
1965) describes the nauseousness of this state with brilliant conviction, and is on a level with his greatest achievements. It contains
most of the essential matter of his metaphysical *Being and Nothingness*
(*L'Être et le Néant*, 1943; tr. 1957): this, partly written while Sartre
was a German prisoner of war, is often shrugged off as bad philosophy. So much the worse, perhaps, for the philosophy that can thus
shrug it off. Sartre is and always has been quasi-Marxist, a 'fellow
traveller'; it is certainly possible to re-interpret his philosophy, to
adapt it to Christianity or to an attitude not involving support for
any political party; but his restatement of the situation of human
authenticity in an atheist century is too important to be ignored. It
is only when he turns Marxist, advocating violent revolution in
place of individualism, that he becomes seriously contentious; but
this Marxist role is not one with which he himself has been wholly
happy. From the time he thus committed himself he ceased to write
fiction, undoubtedly the form in which he has most distinguished
himself.

His short stories, collected in *Intimacy* (*Le Mur*, 1939; tr. 1956),
are essentially sympathetic but gloomy accounts of the various
mechanisms by which people remain trapped in boredom, abstraction, essence (as opposed to existence; being as opposed to becoming).
Nausea analyses the psychology of the condition at greater length and
with detailed imaginative penetration. The trilogy *The Roads to
Freedom* (*Les Chemins de la liberté*: *The Age of Reason, L'Âge de raison*,
1945; tr. 1947; *The Reprieve, Le Sursis*, 1945; tr. 1947; *Iron in the Soul,
La Mort dans l'âme*, 1949, tr. 1950), which is unfinished, is an ambitious and full-scale treatment—and one of the most outstanding
works of fiction of the century. The writing of it caught Sartre in full
indecision between individualism and collectivism. His hero,

Mathieu, goes in the direction of commitment, following the direction of his creator's intellect; but his impulses towards individualism are as energetically and sympathetically described as are those towards political cohesion. As a true representation of intellectuals of Sartre's generation (Mathieu, like Sartre, has studied philosophy and is a teacher), the novel transcends its thesis. It is also a demonstration of the fact that a masterpiece need not be innovatory in form. Sartre drew on what suited his imaginative convenience: the 'simultaneism' of Romains and Dos Passos, the epic structure of Zola, the demotic language of Céline (qq.v.). Mathieu's personal drama of freedom, culminating in what is usually taken to be his death in action (although Sartre has stated that Mathieu was not in fact killed), is played against that of many other characters, which is in turn related to France's descent into the self-disgrace of Vichy and defeat—in its turn seen against international events: the abject selling of Czechoslovakia to the Nazis, symbol of man's desperate need to imprison himself.

Sartre is also an expert dramatist. Nearly all his plays have been written from the intellectual standpoint of a man who is prepared to dirty his hands in the interests of the future of society (compare Brecht's carefully ironic and ambiguous verdict on Stalin: 'a useful man'). But they frequently betray individualist sympathies; and it is to the credit of their author that this should be allowed to be so. Doubtless he, too, has observed the case of Brecht. The human drama is often more absorbing than the thesis. (It is surely significant that Sartre has never joined the communist party, and is a critic of such Russian actions as the invasions of Hungary and Czechoslovakia.) No play he has written actually succeeds in showing how it is possible to remain 'authentic' and at the same time 'dirty one's hands' in the cause of the future, and this is Sartre's chief problem— one which he preferred, however, not to solve in his friend Camus' manner. His best play is the one in which it is not touched upon: *In Camera* (*Huis-Clos*, 1945; tr. 1946). Here three people, each of whom has been guilty of 'bad faith' (refusing the choice of an authentic existence) find themselves shut up, after death, in a drawing-room in hell. They discuss their lives, and become trapped in an eternal vicious circle: the coward man loves the lesbian who loves the infanticide girl who loves the coward. . . . 'Hell is other people' ('L'enfer, c'est les autres'), says one of the characters, thus crystallizing Sartre's view of bad faith: the failure to define oneself by reference to other people. This brilliant and grim comedy is as likely to survive in the theatre as any post-war play; there are few modern plays on its level.

Other plays by Sartre include *Crime Passionnel* (*Les Mains sales*, 1948; tr. 1949), his most moving play, and in effect an attack on the inhumanity of communist tactics—but it can, of course, be looked at in another way. *Nekrassov* (1955; tr. 1956), a satire on anti-communism, is his funniest play; but it irritated most theatre critics by scoring unforgivable points against the press and therefore against their way of life. *Loser Wins* (*Les Séquestrés d'Altona*, 1959; tr. 1960) deals with the theme of personal responsibility by way of German war-guilt; it is a highly effective drama, which seems (to me) to contain some self-criticism in the figure of the Nazi recluse, Frantz, who justifies himself to a jury of crabs in a secret upstairs room (Sartre has experienced hallucinations of marine crabs).

Sartre's drama has consistently tended to humanize his Marxist ideology, which is made vulnerable by the actual behaviour of Russia, the 'Marxist state'. His debate with Camus is absolutely central to the concerns of our time, and therefore to its literature.

ALBERT CAMUS (1913–60) was born in Algeria of an Alsatian father (killed in the First World War) and a Spanish mother; he grew up poor, but his childhood was not an unhappy one. He had a brief period (1934) in the communist party, but left at that time because he disliked its attitude towards the Arabs. He studied philosophy at the University of Algiers, became a journalist there and was in-volved—as actor, writer and director—in left-wing theatrical acti-vities. His early essays, collected in *The Wrong Side and the Right Side* (*L'Envers et l'endroit*, 1937) and *Nuptials* (*Noces*, 1938) lay the founda-tions of his later work: they oppose the sensual pagan values of the sun-drenched Mediterranean to those of the gloomy, intellectual North. He went to Paris, worked for a while on the newspaper *Paris Soir*, and then returned to Algeria to teach. His first two important books, *The Outsider* (*L'Étranger*, 1942; tr. 1946), and the long essay, *The Myth of Sisyphus* (*Le Mythe de Sisyphe*, 1942; tr. 1955), were pub-lished when he returned to Paris. He joined the resistance and edited and contributed to the resistance journal *Combat*. Until he was over thirty Camus suffered from recurrent bouts of tuberculosis. After the war he was an editor at the leading publishing house of Gallimard. He received the Nobel Prize in 1957; less than three years later he was killed (he was not driving) in a car smash resulting from an, apparently, 'absurd' bout of speed not unusual on French roads.

Camus' first novel, *The Outsider*, is about Patrice Meursault ('the only Christ we deserve', Camus said later), who kills an Arab on a beach in apparent self-defence, 'because of the sun'; through his indifference and his incompetent lawyer he is condemned to death.

Superbly effective in its psychological presentation of the protagonist and in evoking the atmosphere of Algiers, it deals on another, more symbolic, level with the problem of 'sun-drenched' pagan values versus those of a more northern and 'serious' society; with hedonism and the search for happiness within a framework of meaninglessness. The novel is relentless, too, in its demonstration of how remote the relationship of Meursault's trial is to his act: it exposes, often satirically, the hideous inadequacy of public versions of private events. Meursault reaches a state of happiness because he has refused to subscribe to meaningless social rituals, to mourn at his mother's funeral, to plead 'innocent' or 'guilty', to act as a 'concerned' person when accused of a crime. He rejects society's values, but cannot discover his own until the point at which he is suspended between life and death; then he understands his existence as itself a happiness.

The essays in *The Myth of Sisyphus* represent man as like Sisyphus in his absurd task, but happy in his losing battle. It is necessary, he argues, to go through two stages: to accept that you live in an absurd universe, and then to fight against this acceptance. 'This *malaise* in front of man's own inhumanity', he wrote there, 'this incalculable let-down when faced with the image of what we are, this "nausea" as a contemporary writer [Sartre] calls it, also is the Absurd'. The key word is *malaise*: Camus insists, as Sartre insists, on man's duty to attain a 'good faith'. But their solutions differed.

His play *Caligula* (CTP) had been drafted in 1938 and was performed in 1945. It is interesting to compare this treatment of the notion of the 'absurd' with that of the dramatists of the absurd: Camus demonstrates the absurdity of such a life as Caligula's (or Hitler's); the dramatists of the absurd present is *as such*.

Camus soon developed his sense of the mad logic of nihilism (which in his work is always equated with the madness of a Caligula, or a Hitler) into a humanist defiance of it, which he spent his life in trying to formulate. 'Every negation contains a flowering of *yes*.' In the novel *The Plague* (*La Peste*, 1947; tr. 1960), whose occasion is a plague that afflicted Oran in the Forties, the rat-carried virus is despair, total acceptance of absurdity. It is easy to see why Camus should have been associated with Sartre as an existentialist. Both, in their different ways, were saying the same thing about man's condition. The German expressionists had sensed it, but in general they over-reacted and became lost in abstractions; these were statements as lucid as the century's literature had seen.

The disagreement between Camus and Sartre arose from a review, in Sartre's paper *Les Temps Modernes*, of Camus' book *The Rebel* (*L'Homme révolté*, 1951; tr. 1953). This book was a refutation of communism, an attack on some aspects of Marx—particularly his historical determinism—and a condemnation of the Russian concentration camps, on the grounds that no ends could justify unjust means. He drew unwelcome attention to the 'fascism' that came in the wake of the French and Russian revolutions, to the 'Caesarism' that 'Promethean' revolutionary endeavour invariably seemed to flounder into. In effect Camus was postulating a non-violent liberal, democratic, multi-party alternative to communism. He was in no way, of course, condoning capitalism; and no serious person suggests that he was. But he was putting forward the notion of a state of 'ethically pure' revolt, which could continuously humanize all tendencies to revolutionary absolutism. The book was reviewed in Sartre's paper by Francis Jeanson, who objected to it on the grounds that while Russia was imperfect it was none the less the only Marxist state and therefore in a privileged position. Camus replied arrogantly and injudiciously, ignoring Jeanson and addressing himself to Sartre. Sartre's own reply was excellent to the extent that he attacked Camus' tactics. And he was right in pointing out that anti-communists rejoiced in the sufferings inflicted on anyone by the enemies of their convenience—rather than deplored them because they were actually cruel. But on the question of the existence of concentration camps in Soviet Russia—and the lack of human freedom in that country—he was plainly embarrassed. Defending Marx, whom Camus had attacked, he was careful to describe himself as 'not a Marxist'; he pointed out that his own paper had not ignored the question of the camps; he was effective in drawing attention to a certain arrogance and egocentricity in Camus' character. . . . But he was uneasy on the central question. And he paid Camus a magnificent (subconscious?) compliment, born of profound respect, when he told him that his attitude left him nowhere to go but the Galapagos Islands: these are remote and hardly populated, true; but another who had gone there and been stimulated to extraordinary activity was Charles Darwin. . . . The debate, of course, continues—and is central to modern literature, which is, predominantly, a literature of the thus divided left.

Camus had shortcomings as an arguer. The criticism that his proposals lacked a sociology is not without point; but nor is his reply: that authoritarian Marxism puts sociology above humanity. Again, there is some substance in the description of Camus as one with the mentality of a 'poor white', no more than—on the Algerian question—a 'conscience-stricken paternalist liberal'. His sense of absurdity is then explained as arising from the dilemma of one who feels moral responsibility for Arab society, but can never belong to it.

Useful criticism; but it assumes enormous moral superiority in its maker—who, freer in the first place, can truly 'belong' to alien, oppressed societies?; and it ignores the possibility of psychic ('Freudian') imperatives turning into ethical ones.

Camus wrote several more plays and a series of stage adaptations of prose works; his version of Dostoevski's *The Possessed* (*Les Possédés*, 1959; tr. 1960) is perhaps the most dramatically effective of his theatre. *The State of Siege* (*L'État de siège*, 1948; CTP) was a fiasco when Barrault (q.v.) put it on in 1948; *The Just* (*Les Justes*, 1950; CTP), about the assassination of a Grand duke in Russia at the beginning of the century, was more skilful but still over-didactic. In his adaptation of Dostoevski Camus concentrated more on character and achieved greater dramatic success.

In *The Rebel* and in other works such as *The Just* Camus had come out in favour of individual integrity against 'party solidarity'; in his novel *The Fall* (*La Chute*, 1956; tr. 1957) he made a defiant gesture in favour of the unpredictable, mysterious, autonomous creative imagination; it is also a savage, but not altogether unsympathetic, gloss on Sartrian existentialism. Camus here pitted creative subversiveness against intellectual social conscience. His anti-hero, Jean-Baptiste Clamance, is a caricature of the artist as God: a Gallic Felix Krull (q.v.), a con-man, a disembodied voice 'confessing', a 'judge-penitent' in a Dutch bar, a Paris lawyer abdicated from 'business' to the Amsterdam waterfront because he 'fell' when he failed to rescue a girl from drowning. But Camus makes Clamance enjoy his 'fall'. And in *The Fall* the guilty and famous artist Camus expatiates upon, but enjoys, his guilt and fame; he comes to rest in a diabolical scepticism, gleefully and slyly—as Germaine Brée has remarked—presenting a 'penitent' who will not make the existentialist 'choice' to 'leap' into authenticity. Certain sentimental or puzzled journalists attributed a 'conversion' to Christianity to Camus on the strength of *The Fall*; but he quickly disposed of any such notion.

Exile and the Kingdom (*L'Exil et le royaume*, 1957; tr. 1958) contained six short stories, each employing a different technical approach. It seems as though Camus was trying to escape from 'morality' into the not so certainly responsible area of the imagination; from philosophy, or his approximation to it, into the more alarming and (possibly) more reprehensible reality of creativity; from the idea of freedom into the dangerously unknown element of freedom itself. His posthumously published *Notebooks* (*Carnets*, *1935–1942*, 1962; tr. 1963; *1942–1951*, 1964; tr. 1966) tend to confirm this.

It is unfortunate that Camus was taken up by the American and French right-wing as a hero. He is, most emphatically, a writer of the left—but not of the 'committed' left. Thus he was able to condemn Stalin's Russia along with Franco's Spain, and to urge the Algerians to work out a union with France. This last proposition was a politically naïve one. But if politics is never to be more than 'the art of the possible' then it may well become a humanly worse activity than it already is. . . . One can pay no greater tribute to Camus than Sartre did in his obituary notice: 'Camus could never cease to be one of the principal forces in our cultural domain, nor to represent, in his own way, the history of France and of this century'.

*

The approach of the novelist, poet and pataphysicist (q.v.) RAYMOND QUENEAU (1903), born at Le Havre, offers a striking contrast; but if his emotional intensity is less, his awareness is not. Queneau is an erudite encyclopaedia editor, grammarian, philosopher and historian of mathematics as well as creative writer. Since 1936 he has been an associate of the publishing firm of Gallimard. He was a surrealist until 1930, when he broke with Breton.

Queneau's poetry and song is ingenious, and some of it has been successful in cafés and cabaret. But, the pleasant—and never offensive—pop element apart, it is more experimental than substantial. The do-it-yourself sonnet kit, *Hundred Thousand Billion Poems* (*Cent mille milliards de poèmes*, 1961) is an amusing way of expressing distrust of the efficacy of 'sonnets', but cannot stand the strain of being solemnly hailed as a major *avant garde* piece—as, alas, it is in some quarters. The best poems are in *Les Ziaux* (1943), Queneau's first collection.

Queneau's deep knowledge of mathematics, linguistics, science and philosophy must be accounted one major influence upon him. The others are: Céline (q.v.), who caused him to continue (in his very different way) to try to reintroduce the colloquial into the literary language; surrealism, which taught him disrespect for established values but respect for the irrational; the sheer clownishness of Charlie Chaplin (cf. Henri Michaux, Franz Hellens, qq.v.); and the linguistic games of James Joyce in *Finnegans Wake* (q.v. 1). He has a sappy good humour that makes the best of his work delightful, clever and influential where influence matters; but his distrust of passion or passionate commitment, intellectually decent though it is, robs it of the ripe wisdom that one feels its author possesses. Despite the amount of subtle material crammed in, much of it over the reader's head, there is always also a sense of something emotional being held back.

Queneau's first novels *The Bark Tree* (*Le Chiendent*, 1933; tr. 1968), 'the *nouveau roman* [q.v.] twenty years before its time' (Robbe-Grillet, q.v.), is one of his best: written in his inimitable brand of demotic French, it gives meaning to an abstract philosophical meditation on 'I think therefore I am' by transforming it into a 'story' about a bank clerk. In *The Sunday of Life* (*Le Dimanche de la vie*, 1952) Queneau achieves his most perfect balance between humour (which does not here degenerate into whimsy) and humanity; an amiable young man opens a shop and passes on the confidences of customers to his wife, who has enormous success as a fortune-teller; when she is ill he disguises himself and replaces her. *Zazie* (*Zazie dans le métro*, 1959; tr. 1960) sympathetically and feelingly recounts the adventures of a little girl who, by her innocence and because of their corruption, creates havoc among adults. The ultra-sceptical *Exercises in Style* (*Exercises de style* 1947; tr. 1958), a *tour de force*, describes the same trivial—but is it?—incident on a bus in ninety-nine different styles.

Few writers have succeeded better than Queneau, who found what he wanted in Céline and made it into a thoroughgoing technique, in reproducing the spoken language; he uses phonetic spelling, incorrect grammar and any other aid in order to capture it. If anything in Queneau's work comes near to being sacred, then it is certainly the language as it is spoken. In his humour Queneau recalls his fellow-pataphysicist Boris Vian (q.v.) and the Irish humorist Flann O'Brien (q.v. 1).

The anthropologist, novelist, poet and autobiographer MICHEL LEIRIS (1901), who was born in Paris, was until recently one of the most neglected of living writers. He too began as a surrealist, and has written surrealist poetry, the most recent of which is collected in *Nights without Night* (*Nuits sans nuit*, 1946). His anthropological works, including *Race and Culture* (*Race et civilisation*, 1951; tr. 1951), are of importance; he specializes in Africa. But his greatest achievement is in his autobiography, consisting of *Manhood* (*L'Âge d'homme*, 1939; tr. 1963) and the books, *Erasures* (*Biffures*, 1948), *Gear* (*Fourbis*, 1955) and *Fibrils* (*Fibrilles*, 1966) that makes up *The Rule of the Game* (*La Régle du jeu*). These are not 'novels'; but in the ambience of Leiris' subtle considerations such distinctions become pointless: he does not doubt that all writing is in a sense 'fiction'. And he immediately acknowledges that the writer's subject is himself: his project is to write a book that is an act: 'the danger to which I expose myself by publishing my confession differs radically, on the level of *quality*, from that which the matador constantly assumes in performing his role'—but none the less, because by confession he exposes and maltreats his extreme timidity he does endanger himself, and because in language he commits himself to the rule of his game with as much courage as the *torero*, so he sees the project as parallel to his. Leiris' honesty is not merely conventional candour: in his autobiography he faces (as the *torero* faces the bull) that horror of death, of annihilation, that has always prevented him from pursuing physical life whole-heartedly. Such a project could be wholly pretentious, the work of a concealed journalist or, more tiresome, of one anxious to please journalists; the quality and sincerity of Leiris' self-examination ensure that the opposite is true. Furthermore Leiris rejects—and no doubt this is one of the reasons for which his fellow anthropologist Lévi-Strauss admires him—chronology as dull and rational: he chooses to examine his life as a synchronous phenomenon, analysing it as one block, in terms of the formation of his own language.

Leiris broke with surrealism, perhaps mainly because it changed the field of the unknown in so assiduously searching for the unknown; but he remained steeped in it (as he admits); his thoroughgoing Freudianism assured his receptivity to everything given, most particularly dreams—and his hostility to selective procedures. *The Rule of the Game* is a tragic work in the sense that its author could not tell himself, or us, that he had been able to find meaning, pattern, in his lived—as opposed to his written—life. However, he tried to kill himself because of it. His life was saved by a tracheotomy. The scar from this he calls his *fibule*. At this point the man becomes the writer, the writer becomes the man. Although still not known well in English-speaking countries, Leiris has had increasing influence in France.

MARCEL AYMÉ (1902–67), born at Joigny in central France, an uncommitted and ostensibly metaphysical satirist of all human manifestations, comedian, friend of Céline's, offers a complete contrast. A prolific and popular writer, he has been described as an unacknowledged genius by some and as a facile waster of comic gifts by others. The truth, as so often, lies between the two extremes. He does have comic power, but in his novels he does squander it—in monotonous repetitiousness, wild fantasy or gratuitous and insensitive cruelty. His first great success, *The Green Mare* (*La Jument verte*, 1933; tr. 1955), contains the same mixture as its numerous successors: a robustly Rabelaisian approach to a provincial community, every aspect of whose affairs is satirically surveyed within the limits of a cleverly tailored plot. Aymé is always highly professional—sometimes too much so. His plays, with which he was also successful, are on the same pattern; but here the professionalism is too obtrusive, and they do not rise above the level of entertainment. Aymé's best work is in the short story: two volumes in English draw on several collections: *Across Paris* (1958) and *The Proverb* (1961). Here the fantastic element is not drawn thinly out, or over-elaborated, but is concentrated into something that is usually pointed. In 'The Walker through Walls' a clerk discovers that he has the power to acquire wealth dishonestly (by walking through walls), but is destroyed by sex. This has real point, which is satisfyingly presented in terms of an entirely logical tale.

Aymé is merely Rabelaisian, something that even the most repressive male communities have been able to excuse (they set up a delicately etherealized image of women and then, presumably, relieve the strain of its unreality by unkindly upsetting the obliging ladies themselves). Other twentieth-century writers, usually following on de Sade, have evolved a literary pornography. The three most important of these are GEORGES BATAILLE (1897–1962), PIERRE KLOSSOWSKI (1905) and 'PAULINE RÉAGE', whose identity is unknown. Bataille (to whom Leiris' *Manhood* is dedicated) was always cheerfully surrealist in spirit, in that he never took his literary project as anything but a game. His erotic novels, the best of which are *Story of the Eye* (*Historie de l'œil*, n.d.) and *L'Abbé C* (1950), parody eighteenth- and nineteenth-century pornography, including its deliberate intention to arouse sexually; but, discovering in this way a means of circumventing the conventional reticence about sex, they reveal hidden ('shocking') facts about its sado-masochistic component. *L'Abbé C* deals with a prostitute and a priest whom she tempts, seduces and destroys—the psychological relationship between these two is delineated with an ironic subtlety of originality and brilliance. Bataille is a writer of importance. Klossowski is a scholar, translator of Virgil, Catholic, essayist and exegetist of de Sade, whose approach is quite different: he treats his highly erotic material in a frigidly aloof, philosophical style. The most important of his novels is the trilogy *The Laws of Hospitality* (*Les Lios de l'hospitalité*, 1953–60) whose hero—a theologian, 'K'—prostitutes his wife, Roberte, to other men, in order to know her better; she also prostitutes herself. Roberte, however, is a politician—and bans a book by her husband. All this is presented in a theological framework, stemming from the 'discovery' of the point of view that Roberte may prostitute herself to her nephew because the body is only a vessel for the spirit. . . . There are three novels: *Roberte, This Evening* (*Roberte, ce soir*, 1953; tr. 1969), *The Revocation of the Edict of Nantes* (*La Révocation de l'Édit de Nantes*, 1959), *The Prompter, or Theatre of Society* (*Le Souffleur, ou le théâtre de société*, 1960). This was followed by *So Fatal a Desire* (*Un si funeste désir*, 1963) and *Baphomet* (1965). Klossowski's chief awareness is that, like de Sade, he is creating erotic fantasy in the form of words; his abstruse fiction probes the relationship between actual fulfilled lusts and verbal fantasy. He is a most interesting, although difficult writer.

'Pauline Réage's' *The Story of O* (*Histoire d'O*, 1954; tr. 1970) is the virtuoso classic of female 'masochism', and demonstrates the limits of pornography as an art. It is an intelligent, humorous, distressing book; no one has 'revealed' its author. This is a novel to ignore or to come to terms with; but not to condemn. It is cleverly truthful to a sexual mood. When a trade edition appeared in Great Britain during 1970 it quickly flushed out those whose highest sexual satisfaction comes from moralizing.

It is not perhaps so great a jump from 'Pauline Réage' to PAULE RÉGNIER (1890–1950), who has become famous, since her suicide, for her journal and her letters. Badly deformed by a childhood illness, she was a devout Catholic and a recluse, who loved unhappily in youth and lived on, miserable and poor, for over thirty years. Her novel *L'Abbaye d'Évolayne* (1933) is a classic of its kind, for in its simple plot she was able to project her own situation, in which she felt emotionally rejected (the poet she loved, killed in the war, had liked but not loved her, as she discovered after his death), sexually frustrated, devoutly Catholic. A passionate girl's husband decides, owing to his war experiences, to become a monk; she agrees to become a nun, but suffers from jealousy and finally kills herself in front of him. Beneath the surface of this moving book there is a good deal of raging sexuality. Paule Régnier wrote several other novels, but none approaching this one.

A good number of French men and women did not deserve their fates at the hands of the over-jubilant and revengeful anti-Vichyssois who gained power in 1945, but LUCIEN REBATET (1903) is hardly one of them. His book *The Rubbish* (*Les Décombres*, 1943) was one of the more repulsive to be written under the German occupation. His guttersnipe fascism and racism would not now be remembered had the sentence of death passed on him after the war been carried out. Fortunately and rightly he was reprieved, and in prison wrote a very long novel, *The Two Flags* (*Les Deux Étendards*, 1951), which, although unduly long, is nevertheless, a remarkable and powerful work. There are no politics in it. It resembles *L'Abbaye d'Évolayne* inasmuch as it portrays a young couple who agree to indulge their religious and not their sexual vocation: as a Jesuit and a nun respectively. In *The Ripe Corn* (*Les Epis mûrs*, 1954) he traces the defeat and ultimate death in battle of a composer. He convinces the reader of his hero's genius and the obstacles to it. Here Rebatet actually succeeds in transforming into a valid criticism of society the nihilism that had previously led him into fascism. Rebatet is a little overpowering, but there can be no doubt of his gifts.

SIMONE DE BEAUVOIR (1908), born in Paris, the lifelong companion of Sartre, has made vital contributions to existentialism, but is also an important novelist. *She Came to Stay* (*L'Invitée*, 1943; tr. 1949) is an acute analysis, in existentialist terms, of a *ménage à trois* that ends in murder. *The Blood of Others* (*Le Sang des autres*, 1944; tr. 1948) is set in the Thirties and early Forties, and is a study of a girl who discovers through love her ability to die for freedom: at first accepting Nazi doctrine, she ends by fighting in the maquis. These two novels are distinguished by their characterization and convincing action. The next, *All Men are Mortal* (*Tous les hommes sont mortels*, 1946; tr. 1955), is an experiment that fails. By tracing, from the fourteenth century to the present day, the existence of an Italian who drinks an immortality potion it tries to prove that immortality is meaningless, because any individual would see his own projects ruined; it is ingenious and often amusing, but remains a thesis novel. The partly autobiographical *The Mandarins* (*Les Mandarins*, 1954; tr. 1957) is a shrewd *roman à clef*, with portraits of Sartre, Camus, the sociologist Raymond Aron, and Nelson Algren (q.v. 1)—with whom Simone de Beauvoir herself was involved somewhat as she describes her psychiatrist protagonist as being involved here.

Nothing Simone de Beauvoir writes, from fiction to sociology (*The Second Sex*, *Le Deuxième Sexe*, 1949; tr. 1960) is less than absorbing and of the highest intelligence, but none of her later fiction has equalled her first two novels—better have been her volumes of autobiography: *Memoirs of a Dutiful Daughter* (*Memoirés d'une fille rangée*, 1958; tr. 1959), *The Prime of life* (*La Force de l'âge*, 1960; tr. 1962) and *The Force of Circumstance* (*La Force des choses*, 1963; tr. 1965). These are vivid, exact and in certain respects—as in the passages about adolescence—unsurpassed in modern French literature.

VERCORS (ps. JEAN BRULLER, 1902), born in Paris, was before the Second World War a well-known illustrator and etcher. After the war he invented a highly effective technique for reproducing paintings. He founded, with friends, the clandestine publishers Les Éditions de Minuit, whose first book was his own *The Silence of the Sea* (*Le Silence de la mer*, 1942; tr. 1944), the story of a 'good' German, who loves music—and of silent resistance to the enemy. When the book appeared in England and America many famous French writers—Mauriac, Gide, Aragon (qq.v.)—were suggested as its author. It is a simple, moving tale, which had a profound effect on the oppressed Frenchmen of the time. Vercors did not equal it until 1961, with *Sylva* (tr. 1962), the charming story of a vixen turned woman and 'tamed'—but not completely—by an English squire.

ROBERT MERLE (1908), a Frenchman born in Algeria and a professor at the University of Toulouse, spent some time before the

Second World War in America. Later he was at Dunkirk. *Weekend at Dunkirk* (*Week-end à Zuydcoote*, 1949; tr. 1950) reflects both experiences. It is too self-consciously 'tough' (where it need not have been) and too obviously destined to become a 'screen epic' (1965); but the descriptions of action are excellent. The historical and anti-racist *The Island* (*L'Île*, 1962; tr. 1964) is probably his best: Merle has the unusual gift of being able to write 'adventure' without distorting or over-simplifying character. His radicalism is doubtless a crude element, but it is only reactionaries who find it—in the unpretentious context of such a book as *The Island*—offensive. *Behind the Glass* (*Derrière le vitre*, 1970) resorts, honourably and usefully, to the 'simultaneism' of Romains and Dos Passos, to make a sincere and objective examination of the day of 22 March, 1968, when the students rose in revolt at Nanterre. Merle is a competent and honest writer whose work always repays reading.

The Parisian ROGER VAILLAND (1907–65) was one of the surrealists who turned Marxist—and in 1952 joined the communist party, only to break away from it within a few years. Vailland was a fine writer and an elegant stylist who succeeded only once in producing a work that reconciled the disparate elements in himself. The conflict in him is not so much between erotic hedonism and humanitarian concern as between erotic hedonism and a guilty conscience posing as humanitarian concern. His best novel was his first: *Playing with Fire* (*Drôle de jeu*, 1945; tr. 1948), a study of life in the underground (in which Vailland played a part). Marat is a hero, but for him the risks and the adventure are an exciting game that symbolizes life as a whole. Vailland here both resolves his own problems and gives a memorably acute and amusing portrait in depth of the kind of man for whom war and its concomitants are a heaven-sent opportunity for self-realization. But Vailland was a naïve (q.v.) writer; the attempt to be a 'social realist' distorts, in varying degrees, the true intentions of all his other books—none of which, however, lacks vivid or comic passages. The cynical, stylish egoist was very much uppermost in Vailland's fiction; the communism is unconvincing. Unhappily he never, after *Playing with Fire*, found a suitable objective correlative. The predominant influence on him was the eighteenth-century writer Choderlos de Laclos, author of *Dangerous Acquaintances* (*Les Liaisons dangereuses*, 1782; tr. 1924), a detached and aristocratic analysis of sexual relationships in the years before the Revolution.

SAMUEL BECKETT (1906), born of a Protestant family in Dublin, usually writes in French and often translates his work into English himself. He went to Paris as an exchange lecturer in English at the École Normale in 1928, and had soon become a member of the literary circle around James Joyce (q.v. 1)—and had written on him. In 1937, after a period of travel, he settled permanently in Paris. He was quite close to Joyce, and occasionally took down passages of *Finnegans Wake*—but he never, as is often stated, acted as his 'secretary'. As a writer Beckett is not as comic as Joyce; but it seems that he is less gloomy as a man, although when young he suffered from a legendary apathy. Where he resembles Joyce is in his close knowledge of philosophical meditation, of the metaphysical and theological speculations of such thinkers as Aquinas, Vico and Descartes—and in his preoccupation with languages. He was a keen athlete at school; soon afterwards all the energy he spent on this went into lie-abed 'metaphysical games'. During the war he was a member of the resistance; finally he had to flee to unoccupied France. His great creative period occurred in the five or six years after the war. He gained universal recognition with the play *Waiting for Godot* (*En attendant Godot*, 1952; tr. 1956). In 1969 he was awarded the Nobel Prize. He is a cricket enthusiast.

Beckett writes in French as a discipline: to protect himself from lapsing into rhetoric, from which his concentration on composing in a language not his own deflects him. His manner and material are almost exclusively Irish, and the chief influence upon him is certainly Swift, the Englishman who returned to the Ireland of his birth to experience the quintessence of its despair. The rigour of Beckett's investigations into existence, often functioning as a bleak parody of the precise trivializings of linguistic philosophers, probably derives from his Protestant ('almost Quaker') upbringing. His work embodies all the anguish and anxiety of theological speculation, but icily transfers this from its 'safe' context of the Christian system to one of utter meaninglessness. This is familiar—the world of the modern writer. But Beckett's account of it is made peculiarly desolate by his concentration on the solipsist isolation of his characters, who meditate ceaselessly upon their coming extinction, continuing the while to contemplate language, their only weapon—a useless one.

Beckett's first excursions, in English (*Poems in English*, 1961), were poor verse but may now be seen to contain—in the way the early poetry of prose writers so often does—the germs of his later concerns. His first novel, *Murphy* (1938), written in English, also contains all upon which the later work would elaborate. Murphy's world is South London. He is for a time kept by a prostitute (the only tender portrait in the whole of Beckett), but eventually becomes an assistant male nurse in a lunatic asylum. He is happy here, but dies in a fire caused (accidentally) by himself. His ashes are scattered, also accidentally, on the floor of a Dublin pub. The influence of Joyce is more apparent in this early book than anywhere else in Beckett.

Beckett's 'trilogy', consisting of *Molloy* (1951; tr. 1955), *Malone Dies* (*Malone meurt*, 1951; tr. 1956) and *The Unnameable* (*L'Innommable*, 1953; tr. 1958), has been published as a single volume (*Three Novels*, 1959). These reverse the Cartesian *cogito ergo sum* by reducing existence to pure thought. They are not philosophy, however, but a violently negative parody of philosophy. They define 'Irishness'—hopelessness, helplessness, perennial passionate despair at pointless passion—perhaps as precisely as it has ever been defined, but hardly transcend it. (There is no hint to be found, in Beckett's writings, of why he should have loathed and fought against Nazism; whereas such concern is actually one of the characteristics of the work of that other proponent of man's absurd conditions, Camus.) Molloy, crippled, sets off on a bicycle to find his mother, in which archetypal project he fails. Malone characterizes the artist: he writes confused and absurd tales in a room of whose location he is ignorant. There is no *Künstlerschuld* (q.v.) here, it seems—but is there? Beckett's books are certainly on the theme of the absurdity of existence; they gain their strength from being about, more particularly, the absurdity of his (writer's?) existence. The Irish are always desperately repentant of their nihilistic violence; one feels that Beckett entertains similar feelings about the results of his own examination of existence: in enjoyably reducing it to a squalid, mad game he omits to give an account of the fine, hopeful, unsqualid detail. . . .

The Unnameable is a monologue in a void, as potent of philosophical misery as an Irish hangover. In *How It Is* (*Comment c'est*, 1961; tr. 1964) Bom and Pim crawl belly down in the primeval slime with their sacks containing tinned fish—and their tin openers. It is this syntaxless book, above all, that shows Beckett to be, not a pointer forward to new literary ways, but the last parodic naturalist: his fiction has stripped life of such 'illusory' details as provided the realist and naturalist novelist with all his matter, and concentrated upon the naturalist thesis. In quest of reason, and finding none, he has elevated purposelessness itself into a reason.

His plays are theatrically effective presentations of the same themes, and because their mood coincided with that of Europe they achieved enormous commercial success. He has since revenged himself for being thus taken up by 'writing' plays in which nothing happens at all—much praised by reviewers of plays, for many of whom 'the void' may be a comforting thought. *Waiting for Godot* was widely misinterpreted as a 'statement' with a 'meaning'; critics searched in it for meanings. But it is no more than a brilliant (quintessentially Irish) portrait of human uncertainty. It 'says' nothing whatever about God(ot), only that when he is expected he does not come. It says more about (God)ot—i.e., as has been pointed out, Charlot, the French name for Charlie Chaplin—God's little victim enmeshed in life and, amazingly, laughing. Hence the vaudeville energy of Beckett's play, and its gaiety. The enjoyment of the play itself, and the enjoyment Beckett got from writing it, provide some answer to the inevitable charge of pessimism. *Endgame* (*Fin de partie*, 1957; tr. 1958) is a dramatic parallel to *How It Is*. In *Krapp's Last Tape* (1959), written in English, which undoubtedly deserves the status of a stage masterpiece, an old man plays back, on his tape recorder, some of the tapes upon which he has kept records of his experiences. Here we see most clearly the Beckett who was influenced by Proust (q.v.), and who wrote a book on him (1931). His last substantial work, *Play* (1963), pushes nearer to stillness, silence and death, and points to a further withdrawal of Beckett's art from life. The short *Lessness* (1970) neither play nor novel, neither poetry nor prose, tries to record, using language itself, the final failure of language to provide a secure refuge. Beckett, always a writer of great integrity, has finally pared away everything sensual and sensuous; it seems that there can be nothing left now but silence.

'The absurd' is an important but minor literary genre; Beckett, however, is not a minor writer: he has never been content simply to accept, and thus present, the apparent absurdity of the human condition. His work is ultimately ambiguous, for while it is obviously pessimistic about the human chances of achieving metaphysical happiness, it does not promote (as Sartre and Camus do) atheism: Beckett is too sceptical to do this, whatever his mood or expectations. His importance is undoubted; but he is pre-eminently a historian of mental anguish: his art has increasingly rejected quotidian detail, and inevitably it lacks richness.

Thief, pimp, professional masturbator, betrayer, queer, JEAN GENÊT (1910) was born in Paris but abandoned by his mother to the Public Assistance—a gesture that has taken him his life to answer. Branded by his foster-parents as a thief, Genêt between the ages of ten and thirty-eight conscientiously sought out trouble. In 1948 he was let off a sentence of life-imprisonment because of his literary achievements. For Jean-Paul Sartre, who with others made this sensible and humane act of clemency possible, Genêt is a modern existentialist hero, as he explains at length in his fascinating *Saint-Genêt* (*Saint-Genêt, comédien et martyr*, 1952; tr. 1964). For Sartre Genêt is exemplary because of his choice to become the image (thief, criminal) that his foster-parents—and then society—thrust upon him. This view of him has validity, but only the validity of an abstraction. Until

Genêt gained a literary reputation, just after the end of the Second World War, his project was an essentially bourgeois one. It is a testament to his genius that, especially as a playwright, he then proceeded to develop. For the author of the novel *Our Lady of the Flowers* (*Notre-Dame des fleurs*, 1944; tr. 1964), written clandestinely in pencil on brown paper in prison in 1943, and of the autobiography *Thief's Journal* (*Journal du voleur*, 1948; tr. 1964), the nadir of existence lies in an elaborate—and itself ritual—denial of bourgeois rituals, an antithesis of the French version of the British public school 'code': to be filthy, to steal, to be a coward, to masturbate, to fart sensuously and enjoy the smell, to betray, to be a studiedly conventional 'enemy of society'. The 'nastiness' of Genêt's content, which deals with the degraded underbelly of society, is directly contradicted by the stylistic beauty of his prose: the kind of prose taught mindlessly in the 'best' schools, a kind of prose at which Genêt happens to excel. There is, then, an irony in *Our Lady of the Flowers*: the 'rotten', 'perverse' criminal uses a highly academic, 'proper' style to relentlessly record petty vilenesses, which range from how to produce an especially satisfying type of fart ('a pearl') to tossing off into a murdered man's mouth: all to offend and affront the beloved, repudiating mother into a gesture of attention that will cancel the original abandonment—Genêt's notion of this unknown real mother quite clearly being derived from the petit-bourgeois figure of his foster-mother. More inventive is *Querelle of Brest* (*Querelle de Brest*, 1947; tr. 1966), Genêt's best novel: here, in a terser prose, the author seems to have taken thought (but not too much) and set himself to examine the nature of 'immorality' from a more general standpoint. The sailor Querelle is an autonomous creation, into which a hero-worshipping, sexually thrilled author has breathed real power.

Genêt's theatre explores the sociological implications of the project he pursued before President Auriol (who invited him to dinner) pardoned him and thus rehabilitated him, in his own eyes, by acting as his mother (who was a whore) ought to have acted. His main theme, although approached in a totally different way, is the same as that of Max Frisch (q.v.): that society (and other people) impose an image upon the individual by which he is deprived of his freedom. In his life as thief, beggar, homosexual prostitute and convict, Genêt's writing was all fantasy (and masturbation fantasy at that); his theatre represents the act of breaking free. *The Maids* (*Les Bonnes*, 1947; tr. 1954), a powerful play (fuelled, perhaps, by misogyny) shows how fatal decisions may be made in illusory situations. His best play, *The Balcony* (*Le Balcon*, 1956;), shows false dignitaries acting out their erotic fantasies in a brothel while a revolution goes on outside; finally the makebelieve events within the brothel become interwoven with the 'real' facts outside—but political power is brilliantly postulated as having its origins in erotic fantasy. This is obviously a limited view, and the play is too subjective to have universal validity; but it demonstrates Genêt's progress from rhapsodic narcissist to skilful satirist.

MARGUERITE DURAS (1914) was born in Indochina and did not come to Paris until she was eighteen. She has dispensed with some of the trappings of the conventional novel, but her greatest debt is to those who have tried to extend the resources of realism rather than to those who have made radical alterations in technique. She became famous through her script for Alain Resnais' lushly middlebrow film *Hiroshima mon amour* (1959), which uses new techniques without real urgency. She is a skilful, ingenious and intelligent writer, but she is prone to create characters who seem unusual but are in fact no more interesting than any shallow follower of fashion. Anna, the heroine of *The Sailor from Gibraltar* (*Le Marin de Gibraltar*, 1952), hunts for a love once casually tasted, but eventually accepts what is to hand. This remains curiously unconvincing, almost as if the boring Anna were being invested by the author with the virtues of a spurious 'modernity'. *The Square* (*Le Square*, 1955; tr. 1959) is an ordinary and even sentimental story of a young housemaid who falls into conversation with a salesman; it is tricked out with such devices as repetition, and 'explanation' is withdrawn pretentiously: the content is highly suitable for ladies' hairdressing saloons. Marguerite Duras' novels are, indeed, most voraciously devoured by women who do not read the romantic magazine serials only because they are ashamed to, and because they would like to feel capable of reading 'something deep': their discussions of their reading are keyed to remarks made by newspaper reviewers of novels. Iris Murdoch (q.v. 1) is an appropriate translator here, since her own interminable series of novels fulfils a similar function in Great Britain. But *Moderato Cantabile* (1958) and *Ten-Thirty on a Summer Night* (10.30 *du soir en été*, 1960; tr. 1962) are superior, and the latter in particular contains some writing finely evocative of a small Spanish town on a rainy summer evening. And yet both (unnecessarily) promise more than they deliver: they would be better literature if they did not pose as 'literature', every other page or so asking to be 'the latest Duras'. It is not that Marguerite Duras is stylistically insincere or an 'opportunist', as has been alleged; but it seems that she could not accept that her gifts were largely those of a realist; this feeling led her, honourably enough, to experiment. . . . Her attitude towards and use of time in her fiction is seriously discussed by some critics; but it amounts to no more than an often ponderous emphasis on the fact that it passes.

HERVÉ BAZIN (1917), a grand-nephew of René Bazin (q.v.), made a stir with his first novel, *Viper in the Fist* (*Vipère au poing*, 1947; tr. 1951). He came from a Catholic and conservative family, and violently rebelled against it by writing his account of a boy's psychological conflict with his detestable mother. *Viper in the Fist* is powerful although the character of the woman is too unrelievedly evil; excellent, too, is the indignant documentary realism of *Head Against the Walls* (*La Tête contre les murs*, 1949; tr. 1952), an exposure of the conditions in French mental hospitals. But Bazin thereafter failed to develop his gifts, and instead fell back upon a sensationalism that soon began to seem artificial.

JULIEN GRACQ (ps. LOUIS POIRIER, 1910), the friend of Breton (q.v.) and author of the best book on him, translator of Kleist and satirist of the literary establishment (he declined the Prix Goncourt) is a history teacher, as well as a novelist and essayist. He was profoundly influenced by surrealism—and by Breton more particularly—but has never been a surrealist or practised aleatory or 'automatic' techniques. When his first novel, *The Castle of Argol* (*Au Château d'Argol*, 1939; tr. 1951) appeared Breton saw in it the 'flowering' of surrealism, which 'doubtless for the first time . . . freely turns around to confront the great experiments in sensibility of the past and to evaluate . . . the extent of its achievement'. Gracq is a highly studied, 'exquisite' writer, whose prose often reads like a surrealized parody of eighteenth-century Gothic; he has also been much (perhaps over-) influenced by Lautréamont (q.v.). He is steeped in the world of the German *Märchen* and of all the later versions of the Grail legend. He made his reputation with *A Dark Stranger* (*Un Beau ténébreux*, 1945; tr. 1951), a novel of the same kind. That a real and infernal place of the spirit exists in Gracq's books is undeniable, as is his integrity (the charge of 'fake', which has been levelled, is wrong); but he does not often do much more than evoke the atmosphere of this place. Only in *A Balcony in the Forest* (*Un Balcon en forêt*, 1958; tr. 1960) has Gracq chosen a modern setting: his literary Lieutenant Grange commands a small post on the Belgian frontier during the autumn of 1939. He and his three men are lulled into an enchantment by the thickly forested Ardennes countryside and by the women they find. Then the Germans come. This has magnificent passages, but is none the less over-written; even here, the magical revelation promised by the rich prose does not come. Gracq's work is too like a wonderful sauce—for meat but served without it.

JEAN-LOUIS CURTIS (ps. LOUIS LAFFITTE, 1917) was born in Orthez.

He is one of the very best of the 'conventional' novelists now writing in France: he is not worried about originality of technique and prefers to concentrate upon what he can do well, which is to anatomize bourgeois societies and 'artistic' communities. His second and so far most successful novel was *The Forests of the Night* (*Les Forêts de la nuit*, 1947; tr. 1950): this, set in Curtis' native region, was the first book to portray France as much of it really was under fascism. Satirically, but always sympathetically where it matters, Curtis shows how, in a little town on the borderline between Vichy and the occupied zone, present attitudes to the Nazis and the collaborators have their origins in the past. Sociologically this is a more adult book than Vailland's *The Rule of the Game* (q.v.). Curtis has not equalled it, but has continued to write intelligent fiction: *Lucifer's Dream* (*Gibier de Potence*, 1949; tr. 1952) is an acid picture of post-war Paris, but always a sensible one. *The Side of the Angels* (*Les Justes Causes*, 1954; tr. 1956) is a distinguished *roman à clef*.

FÉLICIEN MARCEAU (originally ALBERT CARETTE, 1913) was born in Belgium and worked for the Nazi-controlled radio during the occupation; he was imprisoned, exiled from Belgium, changed his name and became a French citizen. He achieved fame with a finely made comedy, *The Egg* (*L'Œuf*, 1956; tr. 1958), on the theme of the hypocrisy of society, which execrates crime but admires criminals. Marceau is not an innovator, but is a highly original stylist. When his elegant, fanciful idiom does not dissolve into preciosity he achieves subtle and sometimes moving effects. *The China Shepherdess* (*Bergère légère*, 1953; tr. 1957) is a fantasy that is actually not tiresome. But Marceau's best novel is *The Flutterings of the Heart* (*Les Élans du cœur*, 1955; tr. 1957), a study of a provincial family on the decline which combines wit, compassion and freshness of observation. He has written well on Casanova and what is perhaps the best of all the many books on his favourite, Balzac: *Balzac and His World* (*Balzac et son monde*, 1955; tr. 1967).

ROGER NIMIER (1925–64), who was killed in a car crash, was a kind of Gallic equivalent of the middle-aged Kingsley Amis (q.v. 1): slick, heartless, sly, antiprogressive but brilliant, talented and puzzled—and ambitiously curious about human feeling. *The Blue Hussar* (*Le Hussard bleu*, 1950; tr. 1953) gives a sharp picture of a French regiment in the Germany of 1945; it is an unpleasant and even a shallow book, but it accurately reflects the attitude of a generation which was in 1945 terrified of its cruel emptiness but which formed, a quarter of a century later, the 'backbone' of Pompidou's France. Nimier wrote nothing else of interest, and faded out some ten years before his premature death. His essays are on a level with those of the reactionary British Catholic journalist and popular romancer John Braine; but he possesses a better education, a better intellect and a better style.

ANDRÉ GORZ (1926) was born in Austria of a Jewish family that emigrated to Switzerland. He became a naturalized Frenchman, and deserved the enthusiastic preface Sartre wrote for his autobiographical *The Traitor* (*Le Traître*, 1958; tr. 1959): the important thing about this book was that Gorz literally 'redefined' himself— and created an authenticity—by writing it. Sartre's claims for it as 'an invitation to life' after the great slaughter of the twentieth century are justified.

MICHEL DEL CASTILLO (1933), who is wholly Spanish, was born in Madrid; at six, as a refugee from Franco, he was taken to France, where he was interned in a concentration camp; he was then sent to another camp, in Germany—then to a Jesuit school in Spain, from which he ran away, at the age of sixteen, in order to return to France and his mother. He tells this story in his first and best novel, *A Child of Our Time* (*Tanguy*, 1957; tr. 1958). In *The Guitar* (*La Guitare*, 1957; tr. 1959) he tried a more inventive kind of fiction. A dwarf seeks to melt the hearts of his fellow men by the magic of his guitar, but they regard this as witchcraft, and stone him. Del Castillo called this 'a book of utter despair'. The successors to his powerful tale, which is set in Galicia, have proved disappointing.

FRANÇOISE SAGAN (PS. FRANÇOISE QUOIREZ, 1935) has one distinction: her lucid style. She writes of bored, shallow, boring, spoiled people seeking relief in brief sexual contacts. Her great successes have been *Bonjour Tristesse* (1954; tr. 1957) and *Aimez-vous Brahms?* (1959; tr. 1960), both of which have been enshrined in *kitsch* celluloid. Françoise Sagan's 'sophisticated' manner is as effective a cover for mental vacuousness as money is an effective substitute for intelligence—we may judge of this from her devoted readers as well as her characters.

IX

The Fifties in France was the decade of the emergence of 'antiliterature', '*chosisme*', the 'anti-novel', the 'new wave', the 'new novel'; the phenomenon as a whole is important, but its many components should not be taken too seriously. With two or three exceptions no exponent of the 'new novel' has shown signs of possessing more than a minor talent. Like all blanket terms, *nouveau roman*, which was invented by journalists—mainly hostile—to describe the work of Ollier, Pinget, Robbe-Grillet and others, can be misleading; but it is none the less more useful than most such terms.

In 1948 NATHALIE SARRAUTE (1902), who was born in Russia of Russian-Jewish parents who separated soon after her birth, published her first novel, *Portrait of a Man Unknown* (*Portrait d'un inconnu*, 1947; tr. 1959). Her *Tropisms* (*Tropismes*, 1939, rev., add., 1957; tr. with essays, 1964), short sketches contrasting the exiguousness of bourgeois habits with their rich subconscious origins, had passed unnoticed. Sartre wrote a famous preface to her novel, in which he hailed the arrival of the *anti-roman* (a term used by the seventeenth-century writer Charles Sorel to describe the reprint of a novel in which he had mocked the pastoral artificialities of his day). What Sartre—whose own *Nausea* (q.v.) is, although in a different way, itself clearly an anti-novel—meant was that Nathalie Sarraute's fiction questioned its own validity: its writer questioned the moral propriety of writing fiction, and the effectiveness of fiction itself. 'Where is the invented story that could compete with that of the . . . Battle of Stalingrad?' she asked. '. . . The character as conceived of in the old-style novel (along with the entire old-style mechanism that was used to make him stand out) does not succeed in containing the psychological reality of today . . . the whole problem is here: to dispossess the reader and entice him, at all costs, into the author's territory.'

The nineteenth-century novel, with its characters and plots, had the confidence of a society that was successfully expanding. Nineteenth-century criticism liked to insist upon 'consistency of character', 'soundness of plot'. The programme of the new novel rejects this: it is morally reprehensible to lead the reader to expect to see consistent characters and 'plots' around him. Again, it is false to present characters whose lives are determined by 'clock time': we do not recollect experience in terms of clock time. The new novel deliberately returns to what Henri Bergson (who, perhaps because his ideas became vulgarized by Shaw, q.v., himself and others, seldom gets his due in discussions of the new novel) called 'the immediate data of consciousness'. The new novelist is a phenomenologist: a subjective realist.

The average British reader remains cut off from the developments of continental philosophy, whereas the French are aware of the phenomenology of Edmund Husserl (1859–1938) through the work not only of Sartre but also of his friend Maurice Merleau-Ponty. Phenomenology played an essential part in the formulation of the existential position; it is not too much to say that its world is the world of the new novelists (and, although less deliberately, of many more writers in many countries). Husserl began by relating states of mind to objects: all states of mind, he pointed out, are directed to real or imaginary objects. The new novel reinstates the object-for-its-own-sake, elevates it (Robbe-Grillet) to the status of an independent world. Like Butor (q.v.), Husserl was interested in the difference between states of mind towards the same object: the man who led the Free French is different from the man whose daughter died young, and *he* is different from the man who resigned power in 1969. Husserl was not, as a philosopher, interested in the actual: his investigations were 'eidetic' (conceptual); he is concerned not with what is perceived but with the mechanics of perception. Anything can be discussed in Husserl's philosophy because anything can be 'constituted' in the mind; hell-fire, then (one could argue), may be 'reinstated'. Husserl is not troubled by the 'ridiculousness' of the notion of a flat earth: it may be studied as a phenomenon in consciousness. The later Husserl increasingly tended to interpret commonsense reality (it gets reasserted in philosophy every so often) as mere 'data for consciousness'—once again, his relevance to literature is obvious. This development in his philosophy may be linked to one of the gravest objections that has been made to the new novelists: that the horrors of Viet Nam or Czechoslovakia are no more than data for their consciousness. . . .

And so the new novelist takes you inside his laboratory, shows you what he is doing and how he is doing it, and frankly admits that what he is giving you is not susceptible of verification. Like a 'new cook' he dispenses with the opaque wall and substitutes one of glass (it makes his cooking cleaner, but it also turns him into a more narcissistic exhibitionist—one who has to turn his back with an elegant gesture and a pretence of pinching in a subtle flavouring as he pisses into your soup). The new novelist is not likely to be a Christian, since he does not believe in order: his fiction does not demonstrate the existence of a concealed order (as does, say, Saint-John Perse's poetry), but draws attention to the fact that his own selective procedures and patternings are false impositions of order on the chaos of life; he admits that it is only his consciousness which imposes duration on a discontinuous series—but, unlike the essentially romantic Bergson, prefers to leave the matter at that. However, the new novelist is likely to be 'left-wing'—at least to the extent that he rejects the essentially right-wing (and authoritarian) myths of social stability and order in the best of all possible worlds.

This thinking is of great importance, and its impact upon other literatures (such as that of Great Britain) will (or would) undoubtedly prove fruitful. But it is critical and philosophical thinking. The imagination is relegated to a secondary position; in the case of the sly behaviourist Robbe-Grillet it is actually discredited as wholly mythical, in favour of the 'geometry'—the hard measurable facts of the external world—that he naïvely sees as 'factual' (though science, considered in the terms employed by Robbe-Grillet, is actually as mythical as anything else). The phenomenon of the new novel is ambivalent: it seeks to recharge the batteries of creativity, but it also jealously seeks to destroy the intuitive richness of creation by cerebralizing it.

All *avant garde* notions eventually fragment, and 'common sense' reasserts itself—but it can be an enriched common sense, because it has absorbed the essential revolutionary elements. This will be the fate of the new novel, at least as it is exemplified in the work of most of those now called new novelists, which uniformly lacks robustness. To achieve robustness, to avoid the boring effect created by detailed —and inevitably narcissistic—mental self-exploration, at the same time avoiding the error of false objectivity: this is what novelists should now be trying to do, and they should be doing it through the writing of fiction rather than of criticism, or criticism disguised as fiction. But they will certainly in one way or another have taken account of the new novel, will have absorbed it. Familiar disparagement of it is, alas, based on ignorance—or a preference for the erection of dream-yarns.

*

'Tropism' is a biological term for the automatic, i.e. the instinctive, turning of an organism in a certain direction in reaction to a stimulus; this is, for Nathalie Sarraute, who must certainly be regarded as one of the chief pioneers and anticipators of the new novel (although she is less programmatic than her successors), a description of instinctive human authenticity that is concealed by the clichés of speech and the (bourgeois) rituals of society. Tropisms are 'inner movements . . . hidden under the commonplace . . . they . . . seem to me to constitute the secret source of our existence . . . veritable dramatic actions . . . constantly emerging up to the surface of the appearances that both conceal and reveal them'. Her technique must not be confused with that stream-of-consciousness (q.v.) which is a pushing-out of the frontiers of realism; Sarraute tries to describe, by means of metaphor, or what she calls 'images', the 'tropisms' that 'glide quickly round the border of our consciousness'.

The anonymous narrator of *Portrait of a Man Unknown* describes selected details of the suspicion between a miser (or one 'the others' call a miser) and his daughter. *Martereau* (1954; tr. 1964) is narrated by a sick, indeterminate young man playing at art, living in the spacious home of relatives, fascinated by the character of Martereau, whom he suspects to be a crook. The narrator (who is as much a representative and critique of the novelist as any of Kafka's central characters) is seen as himself creating the other characters; but he cannot create—'fix', deal with in his mind—Martereau, whom he has idealized. There is much suspicion, here, on the part of the creator, of what she is creating. In *The Planetarium* (*Le Planétarium*, 1959; tr. 1961), her best novel, the egocentric savagery hidden by the social behaviour of shallow, 'polite' people is depressingly revealed. The hero of *The Golden Fruits* (*Les Fruits d'or*, 1963; tr. 1965), her most comic novel, is itself, a 'worthless' book called *The Golden Fruits* (or is this not, perhaps *The Golden Fruits* we are reading?): its rise and fall. A savage work doubtless drawing on experience of the long period in which the author was entirely neglected (her first book got only one review), *The Golden Fruits* formidably exposes the mindlessness of a certain section of the 'reading public'. Since this novel Nathalie Sarraute has published two radio plays, *Silence* and *The Lie* (*Le Silence* suivi de *Le Mensonge*, 1967), commissioned and broadcast by West German radio (Stuttgart), where she has been received with great interest.

ALAIN ROBBE-GRILLET (1922), born in Brest, was trained as an agronomist and then worked as a statistician and in research on tropical fruits. He is as clever as any French writer of his time; but frigidity and a childishly brash over-confidence rob his fiction of imaginative significance. He is ingenious to a degree; a brilliant publicist; but never wise or mellow: a scientist come into literature in order to show its inferiority, indeed, its meaningless; not merely a philosopher disguising himself as a novelist, but a bad philosopher— adhering to the discredited and simplistic theory of behaviourism— disguising himself as an advanced novelist. What he writes is of undoubted interest; but it has the quality of the production of a computer that has somehow been endowed with the orientations of a statistician on heat in a shop full of dirty pics and girlie magazines. In Robbe-Grillet we have the purest possible case of the artist-as-solipsist, although he rationalizes his solipsism into a complaint (irrelevant to literature) that only Robbe-Grillet of all mankind is capable of taking the geometrical world as-it-is. Robbe-Grillet sees the world of objects and wants to accept it without anthropomorphizing it; of human beings who have the habit of anthropomorphization—the whole human race, including his unwitting self—or of human beings who discern purpose in the universe, or who are sceptical, he can tell us nothing. The mean little grid he clamps on to phenomena is simply his own: phenomenology here is transformed into a sullen, bored (*In the Labyrinth*) or smutty (*The House of Assignation*) assertion of self. It is a fascinating and repellent enterprise. But it is an odd and ambiguous one, so that Robbe-Grillet—who is the centre of a cult—has been credited with a number of high-minded intentions. For example, he has been presented as the pioneer revealer of the world as-it-is: indifferent, unconnected with man, incapable of being 'humanized' into a sentimental system on a theological model. This was Robbe-Grillet as *chosiste*: presenter of things as simply there. Since Roland Barthes put forward this Robbe-Grillet, others have postulated other Robbe-Grillets—the most ambitious one following the author's own evaluation of himself as in 'the Stendhal-Balzac-Flaubert-Proust-Gide tradition': 'as a result [of his work], man is enabled to enter uncharted domains of fiction in search of a new reality which he can only attain through works of art . . . [he] appears to stand at the most advanced point of evolution of the twentieth-century novel and film' (Bruce Morrissette). This is from an intelligent and illuminating study, and I quote it as contrast to the view I have put forward. The fact is that only those who 'like' Robbe-Grillet's cerebral behaviourism will 'like' his fiction. His importance as an influence and as a stimulus is undeniable. But if the literary value of his work depends on the truth of his philosophy, as it surely does, then his admirers are in the position of dogmatists.

The Erasers (*Les Gommes*, 1953; tr. 1964) is a diabolically ingenious, perhaps parodic, adaptation of the Oedipus theme. It is full of tricks: duplicated events, symbols, contradictions, 'clues', scenes that are 'imagined' and therefore do not really take place in the novel, and so on. The 'plot' is simple: a detective, Wallas, kills the supposed victim (his father) of a murder that he is sent to investigate. The novelist desperately tried to 'erase' the notion that the Oedipus myth has any relevance to modern man: this is his way of saying that it ought not to. There is a good deal of *chosiste* description —of a tomato, the rubber (eraser) that Wallas seeks throughout the book, the paper-weight that the supposedly murdered man keeps on his desk. Each of these objects does in fact have a significance outside itself: the rubber is an erotic object, the segment of tomato is 'perfect' but for an 'accident': 'a corner of the skin, detached from the flesh over the space of one or two millimetres, sticks up imperceptibly'. This accident, for Robbe-Grillet a horrifying wrecker of symmetry, with the force of an emotion spoiling a thought, is the novel itself. This book has everything, one might say, except feeling; its successors are elaborations of it: *The Voyeur* (*Le Voyeur*, 1955; tr. 1958), *Jealousy* (*La Jalousie*, 1957; tr. 1959), *In the Labyrinth* (*Dans le labyrinthe*, 1959; tr. 1960), *The House of Assignation* (*La Maison de rendez-vous*, 1965; tr. 1970) and the 'film-novels', including *Last Year at Marienbad* (*L'Année dernière à Marienbad*, 1961; tr. 1962), partly a successful middlebrow hoax (it had its audiences busily discussing its 'meaning') and partly a sincere visual exploration. *The House of Assignation* is a largely sadistic pornography played against the 'Hong Kong' of the popular cinema; once again, it is ingenious and even humorous, but the only accessible feeling is the 'eroticism' offered by dirty booksellers. Robbe-Grillet's frenzy is directed at his inability to be a machine; if the world of *The House of Assignation* is the one in which he feels himself trapped then one can understand his aspiration and his error in treating the scientific view as an absolute. He is a fascinating and undoubtedly important critic, using the form of fiction to discredit fiction itself. A real novelist will benefit from his speculations—which is hardly what this icy playboy himself, desperately trying to disembarrass himself of the furtive eroticism that is the surface of his romanticism, can have intended.

The theories of the new novelists do not agree, and they lead to very different results. The 'new' novels have only one thing in common: they are conscious and critical of themselves. Thus MICHEL BUTOR (1926), who was born in Lille, does not share Robbe-Grillet's overriding desire to divest himself of humanity and merge himself into the geometrical neutral world; on the contrary, although as intellectually subtle as Robbe-Grillet, he is clearly in full possession of his emotional faculties. Whereas Robbe-Grillet has exploited surrealism, Butor has been influenced by it. His early poetry he himself characterizes as irrational and demonstrative of his confusion at the time. Butor studied philosophy at the Sorbonne; one of the only two of his teachers for whom he felt respect was Gaston Bachelard, by whose thought he has been profoundly influenced. His novel, *Passage of Kites* (*Passage de milan*, 1954) tries to study the corporate as well as the individual life of the inhabitants of a block of flats throughout one evening and night; in certain respects it represents a highly sophisticated excursion in, and extension of, unanimism (q.v.). The intricate *Passing Time* (*L'Emploi du temps*, 1957; tr. 1961) gives an account of a young Frenchman, Jacques Revel, as he tries to find his bearings in the British industrial city of Bleston. Butor had spent two years as a lecturer in Manchester, and Bleston—the 'hero' or anti-hero of the book—is not unlike it. Like so many novels of its kind, *Passing Time* incorporates elements of the detective story: the Bleston murder mystery Revel reads becomes 'real' to him, and its author becomes himself involved in a murder mystery similar to the one he has invented. ... The whole thing is mysterious, but the mystery is something like that of real life—and the search for 'mean-ing' and 'solution' has a resemblance to any person's bewildered desire for 'a place' when he suddenly becomes conscious—when he breaks or is awoken out of habitude.

In *Second Thoughts* (*La Modification*, 1957; tr. 1958) the narrator addresses himself throughout in the second person. It traces the decision, made on a rail journey, of a typewriter salesman (i.e. writer) to leave his wife for his mistress. Really, it is a study of a man who pretends to himself that external actions can achieve inner freedom; *Second Thoughts* is a novel in which one can aptly trace the shift from a moral to an existential viewpoint: Léon is not judged, but presented as incapable of escaping from his own 'bad faith', his failure to respect the freedom of himself or others. *Degrees* (*Degrés*, 1960; tr. 1962) projects Butor the moralist as Pierre Vernier, teacher in a lycée, agonizedly attempting to preserve the detailed truth of life at the lycée for the sake of his nephew—so that he should have understanding of it. It is Butor's most ambitious, fearsomely com-plex and painstakingly honest novel—the teacher has to hand over his job of recorder to others, but it becomes apparent that until nearly the end he is only pretending to allow them to speak—and it illustrates his dilemma. Butor believes that the function of the writer is to improve the world; but he is not prepared to compromise by oversimplification. In an oblique way, he rejects Sartre's (not happily held) theory that it is necessary to have 'dirty hands'. He is highly intellectual: he has been accused of using 'tricks' when in fact he has been intellectually scrupulous. His difficulty is to hold the atten-tion of the reader without sacrificing the subtleties and sophistica-tions that he feels necessary to describe the truth. One might put it in this way: a wholly 'sentimentive' (q.v.) writer, he is in danger of cutting himself off altogether from nature—and what matters most of all to him. He has tried to resolve his difficulties by writing books that cannot be classified as novels, such as *Mobile* (1963), a 'struc-tural' presentation of American society, and by his 'serial opera', with music by Henri Pousseur, *Votre Faust*. *Mobile* builds up a picture of its subject from advertisements, quotations, the author's own descriptions and other elements, all presented in a complex typo-graphical scheme. Unfortunately some degree of self-satisfaction has obtruded here: this is a book that requires another book to explicate it, and that has attracted an undesirable cult. Butor, a sensitive instrument and originally a writer of imaginative power, is declining into a fragmenting intellectual, an explicator of explications; thus, much of his recent work consists of increasingly complex essays explaining the development of his fictions. Ironically, as he vanishes into what amounts to hermeticism, he preaches the necessity of hermeneutics; but this becomes a passion directed only at himself.

CLAUDE MAURIAC (1914), the son of François Mauriac, is a pole-micist for 'the new literature', on which he wrote an influential book, as well as a novelist himself. All his novels, including *The Dinner Party* (*Le Dîner en ville*, 1959; tr. 1960) and *The Marquise Went out at Five* (*La Marquise sortit à cinq heures*, 1963; tr. 1965), deal with Bertrand Carnéjoux, a successful novelist and womanizer. Mauriac has faithfully and intelligently followed those precepts of the new novel that militate against traditional realism, but (unlike Butor) he does not really believe in his characters, and the reader becomes aware that this fiction is a conscientious critical exercise.

CLAUDE SIMON (1913), born of French parents in Tananarive in Madagascar, looked at first towards Camus (q.v.) and Faulkner (q.v. 1); his novels themselves have perhaps looked towards rather than been influenced by the new novel, although his imagination has been fertilized by its eruption. Butor's is a formidable intellect, but Simon may emerge as the finer and more natural novelist. One can extract a philosophy from Simon: the notion of everything as in flux and unstable—which is once again a feature of Bachelard's thinking. But what are more important are his portraits of human beings: these, not the abstractions, came first. Simon does not set out to abolish the 'story' of the traditional novel, but rather seeks to trace it in the unconscious and painful making: he is the fascinated chronicler of what must happen in life before fictions can be made, and is much less conscious of himself as writer than Robbe-Grillet or Butor. His first novel, *The Trickster* (*Le Tricheur*, 1945) was con-ventional; its themes, and those of his next two novels, were not to find adequate expression until *Wind* (*Le Vent*, 1957; tr. 1959). This is the story, in dense prose, of a man who cannot but bring disaster to all he touches. Antoine Montès, a sailor, comes to south-eastern France to recover some vineyeards he has inherited: everything, his human relationships and his vines, collapses before the wind. Of Simon's other novels, all impressive, *The Flanders Road* (*La Route des Flandres*, 1960; tr. 1962) is the best. Like Karl in Frank's much inferior *Karl and Anna* (q.v.), Georges has heard throughout his war (the Second World War) of a woman; after it is over he has an affair with her. She is Corinne, for whom Georges' Captain probably com-mitted suicide: she had been unfaithful to him with his batman. The character of the dead Captain is reconstituted, too, in Georges' and his companions' minds as they spend their aimless war. He 'comes to life' in their memory as meaningfully to them as when he was in fact alive. And so the Corinne of Georges' invention is as real to him as the true Corinne he seduces after the war. Simon shows everything as changing, and individuals therefore falling back into themselves and superimposing their images of reality upon reality itself. Robbe-Grillet preaches the perniciousness of this; Simon sees the acceptance of it as salvation. He shows order as perpetually destroyed by chance, life as having significance only in the mind, death as having significance only in the memories of the undead. For him, it seems, the tragedy is not that life is 'tragic', but that people do not accept it. He therefore presents his characters as tragic because their consciousness is directed upon their experience in such a way that their hopes of order actually create disorder. Like Faulkner, to whom he owes so much, he seems to gloat over man's helplessness in confused flux. *The Palace* (*Le Palace*, 1962; tr. 1964) contrasts his realization of this situation with his revolutionary aspirations, in a powerfully evocative story of the Spanish Civil War, of the assassination of a revolutionary leader by other revolutionaries. In Simon we see the determinist gloom of naturalism replaced by a conviction that chaos must supervene: he is the novelist of entropy, of running down. When C. P. Snow (q.v. 1) launched his 'Two Cultures' he postulated the literary man as one who did not understand the Second Law of Thermodynamics; he forgot (or was ignorant of?) Simon, who is its laureate.

CLAUDE OLLIER (1922) met Robbe-Grillet in Germany during the war when they were both working in Nuremburg as deported labourers; it is said that much of the latter's system originated in Ollier's mind. There may even be some injustice in describing him as the disciple of Robbe-Grillet. His first novel, *The Setting* (*La Mise en scène*, 1958) is about an engineer mapping a road across the African desert; he is puzzled by traces of someone who has been there before him. *The Maintenance of Order* (*Le Maintien de l'ordre*, 1961) describes, again in an African setting, two assassins stalking their intended victim. The second of these novels builds up a considerable tension of curiosity; the first, which is open to the unique interpretation of each of its readers, is less penetrable than anything of Robbe-Grillet's. (Nothing, incidentally, could be more 'anthropomorphized' than the desert in this book.) Ollier has said that he is interested in creating other worlds, not in order to 'counterweigh' 'this' one, but to compare with it. He is that rare phenomenon: a genuinely experimental writer, a pioneer, who works intelligently in strange territory in order to discover the results.

An important if difficult writer is MAURICE BLANCHOT (1907), a distinguished critic as well as novelist, who unites in himself almost every modernist tendency. Although his fiction is read by few,

Blanchot is highly respected in France as a thinker and writer of unimpeachable integrity. In Great Britain he would be a laughing-stock, although perhaps recognized by journalists in his declining years; in America he would perhaps live in a community that had contracted out. France, by respecting him, allows such a man to attain to his full seriousness; Great Britain would torment him into personal eccentricity—and then pity him.

Paul West aptly quotes Blanchot's question:

> what can this thing be, with its eternal immutability which is nothing but a semblance, a thing which speaks truth and yet with nothing but a void behind it, so that in it the truth has nothing with which to confirm itself, appears without support, is only a scandalous semblance of truth, an image, and by its imagery and seeming withdrawals from truth into depths where there is neither truth nor meaning, not even error?

This should be compared to what Broch (q.v.) said on the same subject; it is one of the questions at the heart of *Künstlerschuld* (q.v.). Blanchot, however, has an affirmative attitude towards creation: man may recreate himself as he writes; the creation of the great definitive 'fiction' of all time may change the world because in the writing of it man may change himself. Literature is the expression of man's progress from silence to silence, and 'above all the domain of the "as if" ' (Maurice Nadeau).

In *Thomas the Obscure* (*Thomas l'obscur*, 1940, rev. 1950) Thomas seeks himself in various settings, some or even all of which may be hallucinatory. This is much less easily readable than Gracq (q.v.), but less playful: the writer is seeking to purge himself of the 'ordin-ary', which poisons his perception. The effect is somewhat akin to that created by Kafka's work, but, as has been pointed out, Blan-chot's real ancestor is Mallarmé. However, Blanchot's novels con-siderably outdo Mallarmé's poems in obscurity; they may even qualify for the title of the most recondite in the world. And yet time, one feels, will make them more accessible.

The Swiss ROBERT PINGET (1919) was born in Geneva; he is a collaborator of Beckett's, and has an undoubted kinship with him in metaphysical direction although less in style. His novels are less individual and interesting than his plays, although the writing of novels has been important to him in releasing his full creative poten-tial; and some of his best plays have been dramatized from novels. *No Answer* (*Le Fiston*, 1959; tr. 1961) is an unsent letter written by a father to his prodigal son, of whose whereabouts he has no idea. His reports on events in his town, which are repeated in different forms, get mixed in with his observations on his feelings; it all seems the work of a fumbling and drunken old fool, until one realizes that the writer is trying to abolish the reality of his grief—just as a new novelist softens the anguish of living by writing novels that try to abolish reality. When he put this on the stage in *Dead Letter* (*Lettre morte*, 1960; PP) Pinget made the old man speak his helpless piece to a post-office clerk (whom he asks vainly for a letter from his son) and a bartender, both of whom are played by the same actor. Then some strolling players come into the bar and idly repeat passages from their current farce, about the return of a prodigal son. ... Becket has brilliantly transferred a radio play of Pinget's, *The Old Tune* (*Le Manivelle*, 1960), in which two old men chatter crazily together, from a French into an Irish idiom. Pinget's themes are exceedingly close to Beckett's, and he will inevitably suffer by comparison. But this is so because of a real affinity; and Pinget's genuine Frenchness contrasts strangely and interestingly with Beckett's Irishness. *Baga* (1958; tr. 1967), a fantasy, is more original but less confident and substantial.

J. M. G. LE CLÉZIO (1940) was born in Nice of a Mauritian family (his father's forbears emigrated from England in the eighteenth century), and is English by nationality. He studied at the Universities of Bristol and London, and, like Van Gogh and other unfortunates, has taught in an English school. Le Clézio is brilliantly accomplished—perhaps almost too much so. His first novel, *The Interrogation* (*Le Procès-verbal*, 1963; tr. 1964), is his most powerful and convincing. Adam Pollo, a student who has lost his memory, goes mad in the solitude of a seaside villa into which he has broken. He goes into the town and addresses a crowd, whereupon he is put into a mental hospital. This may be read as a study in madness and as 'philosophy' in the manner of the new novelists; but there is at present more imagination and interest in psychology than philosophy in Le Clézio. His second novel, *The Flood* (*Le Déluge*, 1966) appeared in English in 1967.

PHILIPPE SOLLERS (1936), editor of the influential magazine *Tel Quel* and a highly intelligent critic (he has written on Francis Ponge, q.v.), is less successful as a novelist. *The Park* (*Le Parc*, 1961; tr. 1967), in which a man invents or recalls (which?) three other characters, in an orange exercise book, never achieves a more than philosophic interest. Character has an extraordinary and mysterious way of 'taking over'. Philosophically this is reprehensible—perhaps too reprehensible for it to happen here.

X

With new producers active, the French theatre after the end of the First World War became as lively as and considerably more interesting than the German. AURÉLIEN MARIE LUGNÉ POË (1869–1940), who had put on Jarry's *Ubu Roi* (q.v.) in 1896, was still active at the Théâtre de l'Œuvre. JACQUES COPEAU (1879–1949) carried on with the experimental Théâtre du Vieux-Colombier, which he had started in 1913, until 1924—when he went to Burgundy to train a new generation of actors. This band eventually became his nephew Michel Saint-Denis' Compagnie des Quinze. One of Copeau's actors was the director and actor LOUIS JOUVET (1887–1951), who established his own theatres soon after the war. Jouvet was closely associated with Giraudoux (q.v.), and he lived to stage a play by Genêt. Jouvet also found time to star in a number of memorable movies. The Russians George and Ludmilla Pitoëff produced many Russian and Scandinavian plays. Not long before the outbreak of the Second World War Jouvet was invited to produce at the Comédie-Française, and Copeau's work was recognized when he was appointed a director. Another of Copeau's pupils had been CHARLES DULLIN (1885–1949), who had founded his own *avant garde* Théâtre de l'Atelier in 1921; his pupil JEAN-LOUIS BARRAULT (1910) has been one of the chief forces in the French theatre since the occupation, during which he put on Claudel (q.v.).

JEAN COCTEAU (1889–1963), poet, novelist, illustrator, film-maker, was one of the most versatile of all modern writers; but his greatest achievement is undoubtedly in the theatre; he was a successful playwright in both *avant garde* and traditional forms. And yet it is unlikely that anything by Cocteau will survive the century; nor was he influential except as a personality. Homosexual, drug-addict, socialite, Cocteau's desire was to astonish and surprise; he did astonish and surprise people, but never for long. His genius was for talent. The friend of Proust, Radiguet, Picasso, Cendrars, Apollinaire, Max Jacob, Poulenc—of everyone who mattered—he understood them and surprised even them; yet it is hard now to see even his best plays as possessing real substance. He was ultimately more interested in the topical, in the cleverest possible exploitation of the very best fashion, of the very best people, of the immediate moment. He did it all in the name of the poetic, the eternal, the anti-fashionable. He understood this; and we believe him. Yet there was at his heart some

kind of tragic emptiness—perhaps to do with his disturbed sexuality
—that seems to have prevented him from achieving emotional
solidity in his life or in his work.

So runs one judgement. But as soon as we agree with it we want to
question it. For the worth of this man is as elusive as was his emotional centre of gravity. We have to look again. Perhaps he will survive. . . .

His verse is fantastic, precious, virtuosic, charming, modish; never
more than poesy at best, but it can be touching even while it is
stylish. What characterizes it most is Cocteau's fancifulness. His
fiction is less rarefied. *The Potomak* (*Le Potomak*, 1919) was a mixture
of texts and drawings, not a novel; but *The Grand Ecart* (*Le Grand
Écart*, 1923; tr. 1925) is a conventional, and charming, 'education
novel'. *The Impostor* (*Thomas l'Imposteur*, 1923; tr. 1957) is a hymn to
the cult of youth of which Cocteau was the supreme embodiment; if
it does not survive as reading matter it will, like its author, be an
essential part of literary and sociological history. Cocteau's best
novel followed in 1929: *Children of the Game* (*Les Enfants terribles*, 1929;
tr. 1955), a sinister study of four young bourgeois who create their
own world with disastrous results. In 1950 Cocteau made a memorable film of this novel.

Some of Cocteau's earliest ventures were in ballet; he wrote the
sketch for *Parade* (1917), Satie's masterly score for which evokes its
time, complete with Cocteau and all the others, with haunting perfection; and he went on creating ballets until the Fifties. His first
major play, and still the one by which he will live in the theatre if he
lives at all, was *Orpheus* (*Orphée*, 1926; tr. 1962); this was on a theme
that obsessed him for the whole of his life. It was produced by
Georges and Ludmilla Pitoëff. In Cocteau's version of the myth,
which is comic and ironic but never flippant, the lovers are not happy
until their departure to the next world. *Orphée* depends on an ingenious director and many props; but its reconciliation of the mythical with the modern is no more certainly a confidence trick than it is
a *tour de force*. . . . The dying Rilke (q.v.) began to translate it, and
sent a telegram: 'Tell Jean Cocteau I love him, for he alone has access
to the world of myth. . . .' *The Human Voice* (*La Voix humaine*, 1930;
tr. 1951), in which a woman tries to get her lover back, on the tele-
phone, shows two Cocteaus: the homosexual Cocteau revenging
himself on women by showing one in a humiliating position, and the
showman Cocteau manufacturing a piece of impeccable middlebrow
theatre in order to do it. Even *The Eagle with Two Heads* (*L'Aigle à
deux têtes*, 1946; tr. 1962), his most pretentious play, a romantic
Ruritanian melodrama, has a residue of poetry.

Opinion is nowhere more sharply divided than on the subject of Cocteau. Certainly much of his work lacks spontaneity; certainly the rebel was also a socialite. But he was a magician: real magic or sleight of hand? It is hard to say, because Cocteau's case may resemble that of a genuine medium who, in terror of failure, arranges to cheat. . . . There is a unique quality in his work, an elusive quality like the true personality of its creator: alarmed, secret: the pale face of the showman caught in an accidental beam of light is seen, for a fleeting moment, at some private task. . . . If the secret comes out anywhere, it comes out in *Orphée*, and in the film (1949) of the same title. Cocteau will continue to fascinate.

JEAN GIRAUDOUX (1882–1944), born at the Limousin town of Bellac, was a professional diplomat and Germanophile whose first literary successes were with a series of clever, bright novels about adolescence. The best of these and Giraudoux's best single work, was *Simon the Pathetic* (*Simon le pathétique*, 1918, rev. 1926), the most famous *My Friend from Limousin* (*Siegfried et le Limousin*, 1922; tr. 1923), which became *Siegfried* (1928; tr. 1930) in the theatre. This was an attempted resolution of Giraudoux's own problem: the pellucidity of his fanciful world was threatened by the fogginess of German 'thought'. In *Siegfried* Jacques, the hero, is a Frenchman who loses his memory in the war, and consequently becomes a leading figure in German politics; he is rescued and returned to his proper Frenchness by one of Giraudoux's many delightful, undefined women—but he is still 'German-minded'. In fact Giraudoux never did resolve the conflict; but Jouvet (q.v.) saw what he could make from Giraudoux's scripts, and the fundamental crack was skilfully papered over to yield a quarter of a century of solidly successful theatre. The first international hit was *Amphitryon 38* (1929; ad. 1938); revivals suggest that this rhetorical, meretricious, beautifully made farce about the Gods depended largely upon the right actors (Jouvet, Michel Simon in Paris; Lunt and Fontanne in New York) at the right time. *Tiger at the Gates* (*La Guerre de Troie n'aura pas lieu*, 1935; tr. 1963) found the perfect translator in Christopher Fry (q.v. 1), another sentimental fantasticator, though on a smaller scale. This anti-war play is one of his best.

Giraudoux tried to fuse seriousness with comedy and delight; but his seriousness consisted too much of a soft-centredly Teutonic romanticism and woman-worship, and he was too tempted by the opportunity of middlebrow dramatic success, to which his great skill and elegance gave him relatively easy access. At the very end of his life he wrote *The Madwoman of Chaillot* (*La Folle de Chaillot*, 1945; ad. 1949), an uncomplicated satire on greed: this has no intellectual distinction but is inspired by a passion for decency. In it Giraudoux may have found his true, modest level.

JEAN ANOUILH (1910), from Bordeaux, is yet a third playwright who has been accused of a basic superficiality; he is perhaps fortunate to have had so much critical attention lavished upon him; but he has been a major figure in the French theatre since the Second World War because he has maintained consistently high standards despite a remarkable prolificity—and, above all, because his mastery of his craft is assured. If in the last decades he has degenerated from bitter critic of society into entertainer, he must nevertheless be the finest entertainer in the modern theatre. Although Anouilh's early plays (the first was *The Ermine, L'Hermine*, 1932; tr. 1955) were produced by such as Jouvet and Lugné-Poë (q.v.), it took him some ten years to attain to a stable position in the theatre. The earlier plays reflect the poverty in which Anouilh lived: individuals obsessed by purity reject the corruptness of society and lead private existences. But even in the best of this period Anouilh reveals a certain fundamental paucity of thought. One of the first of his plays to achieve a success, *Traveller without Luggage* (*Voyageur sans bagage*, 1936; tr. 1959), deals with an amnesic ex-soldier who returns home to discover from his family, who are not sure of his identity, that he has been a vicious and cruel character. He chooses, as circumstances allow him to, not to re-become himself, but to assume the identity of one who was a pleasanter person. The play is gripping and, in terms of technique, formidable; but as has been well said: 'the hero has made no effort to understand his past, he has simply dismissed it'. This is the fatal flaw that Anouilh's consummate theatricality and sure sense of atmosphere conceal: his bleak pessimism is the bleaker for being, beneath the flashing froth of skill and gaiety, shallow and incapable of self-examination. None the less, his stage people, unlike Giraudoux's, have a reality in their 'all-too-humanness', so that his plays remain interesting spectacles. *Ring Round the Moon* (*L'Invitation au château*, 1947; tr. 1950), among other plays by Anouilh, attracted that master of the scented epigram—the 'sheer verbal magic' of suburban dramatic clubs—Christopher Fry, who incidentally removed its 'French' beastliness by excising the impurity of the heroine; in this form it provided a feast for London theatregoers. Anouilh has produced two impressive updated versions of myth: *Point of Departure* (*Eurydice*, 1942; tr. 1951) and *Antigone* (1942; tr. 1946), which played during the occupation to audiences who slowly realized that the plausibly presented Creon represented Vichy compromise, whereas the pure and idealistic Antigone represented unsullied France. Anouilh has divided his production into 'Pièces roses', 'Pièces noires' and, more recently, 'Pièces grinçantes' (grinding). Both these are 'black' pieces. Characteristically, Anouilh's version of the Orpheus myth revolves around the question of Eurydice's purity; she is killed in a car-crash, but returns to tell Orpheus of her corrupt past—he chooses to join her in death. In *Waltz of the Toreadors* (*La Valse des toréadors*, 1952; tr. 1956) Anouilh concentrates, with success, on the sexual atmosphere generated by his unhappy pseudo-philosophy: General Saint-Pé (who appeared in the earlier *Ardèle*, 1948, tr. 1951), tormented by his crazy, nagging wife, tries vainly to escape from his lonely eroticism by re-idealizing the object of each new sexual episode, and ends as he began. *Becket, or the Honour of God* (*Becket ou l'honneur de Dieu*, 1959; tr. 1961), successfully filmed, is dramatically effective, but the brilliant *coups de théâtre* hardly conceal that no more is stated, in psychological terms, about the reasons for Becket's change of heart than was explained about the amnesic Gaston's choice of a 'good image' in *Traveller without Luggage*. The best one gets from this consummate master of the theatre is sharp characterization and a despair at the glib falsity of life—and at the inefficacy of the theatre-as-life.

ARMAND SALACROU (1899), born at Rouen, also took some ten years to establish himself; during this time he was supported and encouraged by Jouvet. His very early plays were produced by Lugné-Poë. A man of great intellectual mobility, Salacrou has been influenced by, and has sometimes anticipated, all the *avant garde* movements of the century, from socialism to the theatre of the absurd. But his most substantial plays are essentially realistic in form; the stronger his feelings in them, the more realistic they are likely to be; even where the situation is not realistic the treatment tends to be. Unfortunately his dramatic skill, in all but a few of his many plays, is such that he seems to resolve his genuinely complex themes too glibly. But in a handful of plays he rises above this. One of them, *Time Confounded* (*Sens interdit*, 1953), is a remarkably successful experiment, as theatrically clever as almost anything by Anouilh, and with more genuine intellectual content. It postulates a world in which time is reversed and life is lived backwards: people eagerly await their youth, their innocence—and their illusions. *No Laughing Matter* (*Histoire de rire*, 1939; tr. 1957), by contrast, shows Salacrou in his role as author of Boulevard plays; it was filmed in 1941, with Fernand Gravey. Even here there is a caustic sting in the tail for alert members of the audience. His best play is often taken to be *Men of Darkness* (*Les Nuits de la colère*, 1946; ad. 1948), a resistance drama, set in Chartres; after the action, which involves betrayal and murder, the characters defend their own positions. *The Earth is Round* (*La*

Terre est ronde, 1938) anatomizes fascism, in the religious fanaticism of Savonarola, with fairness and intelligent sensitivity. In *The Unknown Woman of Arras* (*L'Inconnue d'Arras*, 1935) a man sees his whole life in flashback in the minute before he dies, a suicide because of his wife's unfaithfulness. Here this is no mere device: the events are presented as though observed in a final moment. Salacrou's drama, which frequently illuminates those depths of human anguish upon which Anouilh's more sparkling theatrical edifice only floats, deserves to be introduced more generally into the English-speaking world.

CHARLES VILDRAC (ps. CHARLES MESSAGER, 1882–1971) began as a poet, and was one of the Abbaye group (q.v.). His early poetry expressed Whitmanesque ideals of camaraderie and human goodness; but his optimism found its most effective outlet in the drama. *S.S. Tenacity* (*Le Paquebot Tenacity*, 1920; tr. 1922), a good popular play which was put on by Copeau at the Vieux-Colombier, showed two comrades after the same girl while the boat that is to take them to a new life in Canada is held up in dry-dock. The go-ahead one gives it all up, marries and settles for a bourgeois existence in France; the shy dreamer goes ahead to adventure. This provides an excellent example of the conventional play that does not owe its success to pretentiousness or to the advancement of offensive philosophies. Vildrac's usual procedure is to take 'humble', 'insignificant' people (such as workmen or factory workers), put them in situations of stress, and then depict the true structure of both their characters and their humanity. In *The Misunderstanding* (*La Brouille*, 1930), about a realist and an idealist who quarrel over business methods, he shows a fine awareness of his own idealism. *Three Months of Prison* (*Trois mois de prison*, 1943) was written while Vildrac was playing an active part in resisting the Nazis. He has written notable children's books.

JEAN-JACQUES BERNARD (1888–1972), a Frenchman born at Enghien in Belgium, was the son of TRISTAN BERNARD (1866–1947), who wrote ingenious moralistic comedies. Bernard's theatre is essentially a development out of Maeterlinck's (q.v.), but with more emphasis on psychology and unconscious motivations. His earlier plays formed a series called 'the theatre of silence' (tr. *Five Plays*, 1939): characters are put into miserable love-situations, and their speech either feebly tries to contradict or brokenly hints at the mysterious morass of feeling into which missed opportunity has plunged them. *The Sulky Fire* (*Le Feu qui reprend mal*, 1921), the first of the 'theatre of silence' series, broods for its three acts over a returned soldier's suspicions of his wife's fidelity. Effective within his extreme limits,

Bernard failed in his later attempts to broaden the horizons of his theatre.

MARCEL PAGNOL (1895–1974) born near Marseilles, is an even better example than Vildrac of the naïve (q.v.) writer who is aware of, or simply keeps within, his limitations, and entirely avoids distortion or offence. All who have seen his earthy films, on his own and other writer's scenarios, have been grateful. His occasional vulgarities and sentimentalities are unimportant, and may even be enjoyed. *Topaze* (1928; tr. 1963) is about a schoolmaster who is dismissed for conscientiousness. He is taken up by a racketeer for use as an innocent front-man; but he learns about life and outdoes his exploiter. Pagnol's other important work is his trilogy about the Marseilles waterfront: *Marius* (1929), *Fanny* (1931), *César* (1937). This, some of which has been filmed in Italian and German as well as French (with the incomparable Raimu), is simple fare—but its comedies and tragedies are faithful to the simple lives it depicts. If not taken more seriously than intended, it is delightful.

JEAN SARMENT (ps. JEAN BELLEMÈRE, 1897), born at Nantes, was an actor with Copeau and Lungé-Poë; he evolved into a writer of minor, but delicately melancholy plays involving characters who prefer to escape from life by way of dreams or impostures. His first and best play, *The Cardboard Crown* (*La Couronne de carton*, 1920), shows the self-defeat of a young romantic who can only win his girl when he is acting a part; this knowledge causes him to cease to love her. *Fishing for Shadows* (*Le Pêcheur d'ombres*, 1921; tr. 1940) deals with illusion and identity: a poet kills himself because he cannot prevent himself from conjecture about the identity of a girl who drove him mad and who returns to him. Marcel Pagnol directed the excellent movie version (1934) of *Leopold the Well-Beloved* (*Léopold le bien-aimé*, 1927), which starred Sarment himself, and Michel Simon. This is a sad comedy about an ageing failure with women who is persuaded that he is, after all, a roaring success with them. His youthful autobiographical novel, *Jean-Jacques of Nantes* (*Jean-Jacques de Nantes*, 1922) has interest and charm.

*

The notion of man as in an absurd situation in the universe is not new in literature; as one aspect of his feeling towards his existence it is implied in Greek tragedy. But for the twentieth century perhaps the aptest expression of it was made by Albert Camus in *The Myth of Sisyphus* (q.v.): man is seen as Sisyphus trying to push a stone to the top of a hill in the full knowledge he will never, can never, succeed.

The so-called theatre—or literature—of the absurd was never a school; it was a term applied to certain writers, nearly all of them playwrights, who shared this attitude. Argument about whether one or two of them—such as Beckett and Genêt (qq.v.)—really or completely 'belong' to the theatre of the absurd is fruitless. What distinguishes the playwrights of the absurd from predecessors and successors who share their philosophical attitude is that in their case the attitude shapes the actual form of the play. This is why the movement had spent itself by the early Sixties: no matter how philosophically desirable, it is difficult to write a full-length play on these principles that will hold the attention of an audience. Paris, the headquarters of the *avant garde*, was also the headquarters of this kind of theatre; but the movement had influence in America (Albee, Kopit, qq.v. 1), England (Pinter, Simpson, qq.v. 1), Italy (Buzzati, q.v. 3), Germany (Grass, Hildesheimer, qq.v.), Czechoslovakia (Havel, Mrozek, qq.v. 4), Switzerland (Frisch), Poland and Spain. It is a movement of sociological importance; but no dramatist who has not clearly transcended its boundaries can be called more than a minor talent.

Although one of the roots of the theatre of the absurd is in the ridiculous, 'absurd' here means more than this: it has its original meaning of 'out of harmony with reason or purpose'. This drama tries to express the notion through its structure. Other important roots of the theatre of the absurd are: the literature of nonsense (Morgenstern, Ringelnatz, even Busch, qq.v., and Edward Lear and Lewis Carroll); the world of vaudeville and the circus; the early silent comedy movies, notably those made by Mack Sennett; Valle-Inclán (q.v. 3).

Martin Esslin, the excellent historian of the theatre of the absurd, has distinguished from it a theatre of the 'poetic *avant garde*', which 'relies on fantasy and dream reality' to the same degree as the theatre of the absurd; but 'basically . . . represents a different mood . . . more lyrical, and far less violent and grotesque . . . [it] relies to a far greater extent on consciously "poetic" speech . . .'. Esslin is probably right to class the plays of Audiberti, Ghelderode (qq.v.) and of the delicate but exceedingly slight HENRI PICHETTE (1924), who is half-American, among this 'poetic *avant garde*'.

EUGÈNE IONESCO (1912) was born in Slatina in Rumania, of a Rumanian father and French mother. He was educated in France, and has lived there except for a dozen or so years spent in Rumania between 1925 and 1938. He did not start writing plays—although he published Rumanian poetry and criticism—until 1948, when he was suddenly stimulated into it by the 'absurd' world conjured up to him by the phrases contained in an English manual. The result was *The*

Bald Prima-Donna (*La Cantatrice chauve*, 1950; IPI), in which the text-book clichés of two bourgeois families are exploited for far too long. It was a highly amusing event, but not a very exciting beginning. Ionesco is not in fact a writer of great importance, although one feels impelled to say this only because he has had too much solemn attention; within his essentially pataphysical (q.v.) limitations, Ionesco is a good playwright. But he has little emotional substance, and his work rests on the philosophical tenets of absurdity and linguistic futility. He has written many plays, and is an amusing though not always unconfused controversialist. One of the best of the plays is *Rhinoceros* (*Le Rinocéros*, 1960; IP4): there is feeling and real bitterness in this ferocious fable about the progressive transformation of humanity into rhinoceroses (fascist conformists; worshippers of nature); Béranger, Ionesco's 'average citizen', whom he first introduced in another of his better plays, *The Killer* (*Tueur sans gages*; IP3), does not resist the 'mastification' because he wants to, but because he must: at the end it is 'too late' to become one of them. He does not care enough. . . . In this bitter twist we catch a glimpse of a profounder Ionesco. *The Killer* cleverly depicts death as a pointless and cheap giggler. Ionesco is an expert and intelligent critic of bourgeois conformity; but so far he has had little of significance to add to what other writers have said about the particular area he inhabits. It is in one sense excellent that Ionesco should enrage conformists of the political left and right; but he himself does appear to suffer from Béranger's clownish indifference: its nature could provide him with the theme of a more satisfying drama.

ARTHUR ADAMOV (1908–70) was born in the Caucasus. His father, a rich oil man of Armenian extraction, educated him in French, and French is his main language. At the age of sixteen Adamov was associating with surrealists. Later he edited a magazine and became a friend of Éluard's (q.v.). He then underwent a crisis, which he described in his autobiographical *The Confession* (*L'Aveu*, 1946; pt. tr. *Evergreen Review*, 8, 1959). Martin Esslin isolates from it the following quotation, which he rightly calls the 'basis' of both existentialist literature and of the theatre of the absurd:

'What is there? I know first of all that I am. But who am I? All I know of myself is that I suffer. And if I suffer it is because at the origin of myself there is mutilation, separation.

I am separated. What I am separated from—I cannot name it. But I am separated.'

Adamov's first plays were influenced by expressionism (q.v.) inasmuch as they reacted against the presentation of named characters, and reverted to types. This work is a clear demonstration of the fact that all *avant garde* movements are but facets or developments of the original expressionism; it was even partly inspired by one of the founding fathers of expressionism, August Strindberg (q.v.).

It is interesting that Adamov, although always sympathetic to communism, should gradually have shifted from a primarily 'metaphysical' centre of gravity to an unquestionably Marxist one, closely allied to Brecht's idea of an 'epic theatre' (q.v.): it seems that too rigid adherence to the theory of the absurd leads to sterility. But Adamov's plays have always had more substance, mystery and passion about them than Ionesco's. Although he intends to present Alienated Man rather than alienated men, a realistic sense of the latter pervades most of his plays. He is interested in individuals as well as in abstractions. Adamov sees man's alienation from the unnameable ('Formerly it was called God. Today it no longer has any name') as mutilating him, and in one of his plays he shows this literally: in *The Large and the Small Manœuvre* (*La Grande et la petite manœuvre*, 1950) the victim of opposing political factions is cut down to a useless trunk in a wheelchair—but the activists are depicted as just as helpless. *The Invasion* (*L'Invasion*, 1950) is about Pierre's quest for what his brother-in-law's eminent literary work meant. Jean has bequeathed all his immense mass of papers to him; but they are in an appalling physical state and cannot be reduced to order. Pierre finally destroys the papers, which have by this time destroyed him.

Professor Taranne (*Le Professeur Taranne*, 1953; MFC; AD) is based on a dream of the author's. Professor Taranne is accused of obscenity and plagiarism, and finds himself in a situation that can only be described as Kafkaesque; he ends by exposing himself, the act of which he had originally been (falsely) accused. Once again we have the theme of the artist exposed as a fraud. Soon after this Adamov came to his best play, and the best produced by the theatre of the absurd: *Le Ping-Pong* (1955; tr. 1962), in which, far more horribly, subtly and effectively than in Elmer Rice's *Adding Machine*, a machine (a machine, it should be noted, that is a game of chance) is shown as gaining control over human affairs. Two young men who play on a pinball machine in a café come to regard it as both a work of art and a good business investment. They become slaves to the pinball machine, and are at the last seen as two foolish old men playing pingpong—one of them drops dead, the other is left alone. This, as may easily be seen, is open to a Marxist as well as to an 'absurd' interpretation; and with his next play *Paolo Paoli* (1957; tr. 1959) he turned his back on the absurd and embraced the activist theatre of Brecht—but not in any simplistic manner. *Paolo Paoli* deals with the years

1900–14, during which the First World War was brewed. Paoli lives by killing rare butterfies, his friend deals in ostrich feathers: beauty is destroyed by the profit-motive. In this intricate play Adamov's skill is almost the equal of Brecht's; but a writer ought not, perhaps, to be so certain of where he is going. *Sainte Europe* (1966), a satire on General de Gaulle (who seemed to obsess him), is an almost disastrous failure.

JEAN TARDIEU (1903) was before the Second World War a poet somewhat in the vein of Ponge (q.v.); he translated Hölderlin with conspicuous success. After 1945 he seemed to find a new and stronger confidence, and in 1947 began to produce short experimental plays and sketches for radio and cabaret. These are slight, but have often anticipated the larger-scale works of better known dramatists. Tardieu is unambitious and playful, and his work carries little weight; but it is delightful and makes no large claims.

BORIS VIAN (1920–59) trained as an engineer but abandoned this career to play jazz and to write. If anyone could be described as the French Flann O'Brien then it would certainly be Vian, who was full of the same kind of lore; but his activities were wider, and included pornography, singing, acting, drinking, translating, inventing gadgets—and, alas, dying young. He wrote an opera to music by one of France's foremost composers, Darius Milhaud (once Claudel's secretary in South America), four tough thrillers, one of which was banned (Vian was an adept at enraging 'public moralists'), five novels rather disappointing as wholes but containing passages of great power, two of which have been translated, short stories—and plays. Vian's remarkable gift, which ought however not to be exaggerated as it occasionally has been (for example in Great Britain), may have been weakened by its wide application; in the drama it found its proper outlet. Cocteau was excited by his first play, *The Knacker's ABC* (*Équarrissage pour tous*, 1950; tr. 1968), a 'paramilitary vaudeville' which finely mocks patriotic and other pompous pretensions; it caused great offence. *The Empire Builders* (*Les Bâtisseurs d'empire ou le Schmürz*, 1959; tr. 1967), a theatrical success, was put on after Vian's death from the painful heart disease from which he had been suffering for some time. This is a superior production, and is almost certainly the best thing Vian ever did. A family runs away from a terrible noise, going to higher and higher floors and smaller and smaller flats in the same building. Ultimately the father is cut off from his family and dies in terror. The *Schmürz* is a bleeding, bandaged figure, silent, struck continually by the characters and yet never noticed by them. In this personal statement about his doomed flight upwards from death Vian succeeded in making a universal one: we grandiosely build higher and higher, and our world gets smaller and smaller, we ignore and ill-treat our authentic selves (our *Schmürzes*), which represent both our freedom and the possibility of accepting death without fear. Just before the father succumbs to terror and dies his *Schmürz* (*Schmerz*: pain) dies: his chances of freedom have vanished. But after his death other *Schmürzes* enter; a reminder of the possibilities for man. If one must classify, this impressive play is surely more 'existentialist' than 'absurd'.

FERNANDO ARRABAL (1932) was born in Melilla in what was then Spanish Morocco; he studied law in Madrid, but left Spain for France in 1954. He writes in French. Arrabal, a minor playwright with a resourceful technique who owes most of all to Beckett, cruelly contrasts innocence with reality, as in his first play *Picnic on the Battlefield* (*Pique-nique en campagne*, 1958; tr. *Evergreen Review*, 15, 1960), in which a mother and father come to join their son in the front line for a picnic; they are all wiped out. His most savage play is *The Two Executioners* (*Les Deux Bourreaux*, 1958; AD), an exposure of conventional morality—most particularly, perhaps, of the type of brutal obscurantism practised in fascist Spain. Here 'justice' is revealed as hatred and torture, and 'duty' is to condone it (there is an analogy here with Franco's establishment of tyranny in Spain). Arrabal has more recently, and disappointingly, been experimenting with abstract spectacles—less with texts than with the theatre itself.

*

The influence of ANTONIN ARTAUD (1896–1948), who was born at Marseille, is by no means exhausted. In fact, except in France, where he has profoundly influenced Barrault and the leading director associated with the Theatre of the Absurd, Roger Blin, his views have so far been mostly misapplied—by such as the British director Peter Brook, who has modified his demands for a revolutionary theatre into something eminently acceptable to pseudo-radical audiences, and therefore commercially viable. Artaud, 'the magic cudgel', began as a symbolist poet and leading light of the surrealists; 'expelled' by Breton, he, Robert Aron and Roger Vitrac (q.v.) founded in 1927 the *Théâtre Alfred Jarry* and put on Strindberg's *Dream Play* (a performance that Breton was prevented by the police from disrupting), the last act of Claudel's *Partage de Midi* (q.v.) produced as farce, and plays by Vitrac himself. Artaud had already acted in films (including the role of the young monk in Carl Dreyer's *La Passion de Jeanne d'Arc*) and with Lugné-Poë, Dullin and Pitoëff: he knew the practical and theoretical theatre intimately. Artaud's impassioned theory of the theatre, which may yet prove to be the main force in taking it out of the middlebrow domain, is set forth in the collection of essays called *The Theatre and its Double* (*Le Théâtre et son double*, 1938; tr. 1958); in this are republished his manifestos of 1932 and 1933, both called *The Theatre of Cruelty* (*Le Théâtre de la cruauté*). In 1935 he was able to find funds to form his own theatre of cruelty, and with the help of Barrault and Blin he put on a performance of his own play, *Les Cenci* (in *Complete Works*, *Œuvres Complètes*, 1957–67). This failed, and Artaud's capacity to conduct everyday life began to collapse. He had suffered from mental instability since childhood. After a visit to Mexico and a session on drugs (with which he had been experimenting for many years), he had to be given electric-shock treatment and hospitalized at Rodez (1937), where he stayed for nine years. He had many devoted friends, including Barrault and Adamov; but his condition would not allow of his release until two years before his death, of cancer.

Artaud's thinking was most profoundly influenced by his own experiments with himself, which went farther than those of any surrealist (with the exception of RENÉ DAUMAL, 1908–44, a consumptive surrealist novelist and disciple of Gurdjieff's who allowed himself to die in the interests of self-exploration); drugs were merely incidental, for Artaud's entire life was dedicated to the realization of his ideal. Outside influences on Artaud included (predictably) vaudeville and comic films—and particularly, a performance by a troupe of Balinese dancers that he witnessed in 1931.

Artaud's ideas are important and revolutionary: they faithfully represent the spirit of modernism, demonstrating its essential romanticism—and, incidentally, once again, the extent to which the expressionist movement contains this. Hofmannsthal's 'Chandos letter' (q.v.) and Artaud's *Theatre and its Double* are not as far apart as might be imagined. A *Sprachkrise* (q.v.) is at the heart of both. Artaud was tormented personally (not just intellectually) by the collapse of the illusions about words in their relation to the things they denote. His is an anti-language as well as an anti-psychological theatre. He wanted a return of myth, a ritualized theatre of movement and gesture, shapes and lights; a theatre that would confront the audience's problems so extremely, so 'cruelly', that it would liberate from the chains of rationality. Actors and audiences should be 'victims burnt at the stake, signalling through the flames'. The terror of the plagues of history, Artaud said, released men from the restraints of rationality and morality, and purified them, giving them a primitive power (cf. Camus' *The Plague*, q.v.). Thus the stage must surround the audience, and terrify it. But no account of Artaud's theatre can convey the brilliance of his detail and the subtle passion of his language.

Artaud's own *The Cenci* does not fulfil its author's programme; his most powerful work is contained in his correspondence (1923) with Jacques Rivière (q.v.), his letters to Jean-Louis Barrault (1952), and some of his poems and short plays. Such a theatre as his must doubtless be modified—but not by the values of the drawing-room, the beauty saloon or the theatre critic's local. In this sense much of the lip-service paid to his ideas, especially in Great Britain, is not always of much more value than the genteel opposition that vague notions of it arouse. Artaud will be even more important to the theatre than he has already been.

His friend ROGER VITRAC (1899–1952), born at Pinsac, was one of the best playwrights to come out of surrealism. His plays lightly mock the bourgeois and their idols; had he emerged at the same time as Ionesco he would have been regarded as his equal. *The Mysteries of Love* (*Les Mystères de l'amour*, 1927) is quite as 'absurd' as anything of Ionesco's, and has passages of greater linguistic suggestion. *The Werewolf* (*Le Loup-garou*, 1939), set in an expensive madhouse, is masterly in its capture of the speech of the mentally ill.

XI

GEORGES SIMENON (PS. GEORGES SIM, 1903), born at Liège of a French father and Dutch mother, has on occasion been over-praised—as when a critic adjudged him superior to Balzac. But Simenon is one of the very few writers (others are Kenneth Fearing, Julian Symons) who have consistently raised the thriller to a literary level. Simenon can evoke the exact atmosphere of a place, of a kind of day, as acutely as any of his contemporaries. A true 'naïve' (q.v.), he is admired by almost every 'intellectual' in the world. His technique is to take a character and then—he works very quickly—go along with him in a situation that takes him to the end of his tether. His great strengths are his natural sense of poetry and his freedom from distorting moral preconceptions about conduct, which he is able to present with a remarkable empathy. The objectivity of his treatment of ruthlessness, greed and murderousness provides an example of a sort of compassion that contrasts oddly with the psychologically limited charity of orthodox morality. As a faithful entertainer of the best minds, Simenon is indeed a strange case: how should such as Ford, Eliot, Montale, Graves, all admirers, avidly read one who gives them such honest fare, fare they could not themselves provide? In 1931 Simenon invented his famous detective, Maigret, the only credible fictional detective of the century. But much of his best work has not featured Maigret. *The Stain on the Snow* (*La Neige était sale*, 1948; tr. 1953) is about life under Nazi domination, and traces the motives and fate of a man who kills a German. *Pedigree* (1948; tr. 1965) is autobiographical, telling of his Liège childhood. In *The Little Saint* (*Le Petit Saint*, 1965) Simenon successfully tells the story of a dwarf who becomes a painter. Simenon's detractors, often puzzled academics for whom his *tranches de vie* are too frighteningly raw, accuse him of lacking intellect; this is to miss the point—we should send such critics back to Schiller. Here is an author the legitimate enjoyment of whom may be seriously interfered with by the frequently egregious urge to evaluate.

One other modern Belgian novelist of some distinction is FRANÇOISE MALLET-JORIS (1930), who was born in Antwerp and is the daughter of the writer Suzanne Lilar (q.v.). Her father is a lawyer and politician, who has served in the Belgian government. She studied in America and Paris and made an immediate impression with what remains her best novel: *Into the Labyrinth* (*Le Rempart des Béguines*, 1950; tr. 1953), a story of the narrator's lesbian affair with her father's mistress. This was a well deserved success. The novels that succeeded it have all been competent and intelligent; she has not yet written again as coolly and as effectively.

*

The Belgian contribution to the French theatre has been considerable; most of it has been on the part of Flemings, such as Maeterlinck, who wrote in French. This Belgian vein, of other-worldliness paradoxically combined with immediate sensual grasp of phenomena—and most characteristically emerging as a type of comedy or farce—is in fact a vital component of French-speaking theatre. Drama, it seems, is a form in which Belgian genius naturally manifests itself.

FERNAND CROMMELYNCK (1885–1970), another Fleming, was born in Brussels, but early established himself in Paris as a precocious young actor and playwright. His mother was French, his father an actor from whom he learnt much. Between the wars Crommelynck had a high reputation; he has published nothing since a play on Shakespeare's Falstaff in 1954, and outside France at least the reputation has rather unfairly faded. He wrote some fairly successful plays as a very young man, but he was thirty-five when he had his first international hit, *The Magnificent Cuckold* (*Le Cocu magnifique*, 1920; TGBP), produced in Paris by Lugné-Poë. He then moved back to Paris, and he and his family shared a house with Verhaeren's widow. In their distortedness and grotesqueness Crommelynck's plays are undoubtedly expressionist (in the sense of expressionism that includes Grünewald and other artists of the past, and is as much a part of the Flemish as of the German genius); Sternheim (q.v.), who lived in Belgium, must at least have read Crommelynck with pleasure. *The Magnificent Cuckold*, at first mounted by producers as a farce, but more recently presented as tragedy, is undoubtedly a black (though not a 'sick') play. It shows the destruction of a happy marriage by the demon jealousy. Bruno, the village scribe and poet, is in effect played by two actors, one of whom—his secretary Estrugo (an Iago)—represents the jealous and curious element in him that must know what it is that possesses him. Bruno has affinities with the jealous Kitely of Ben Jonson's *Every Man in his Humour*—as Crommelynck himself shares something of Jonson's truculent, subtle approach. Bruno looses his wife Stella to every male in the village, in order to discover the nature of the sexual hold she has on him. (As in the case of Kitely, there are hints of voyeurism.) Even when he finally loses her, to a foolish suitor, he cannot believe it, and jokes about it: this is a trick. In other words, Bruno becomes more interested in the mechanism of his sexuality than in its object; the sentimentive, one might say, undermines and destroys the naïve component of his personality. There is an underlying theme, here, of criticism of the artist, for whom love is less important than its analysis; the result is that Stella is doomed to a commonplace existence at the hands of an utterly commonplace man—but the moral is obvious. This play, whose language is unusually beautiful and poetic—in this respect it outruns anything by Giraudoux or Anouilh—is one of the century's highest dramatic achievements. De Meyst's 1946 Belgian movie, of the same title, with Jean-Louis Barrault and Maria Mauban, is a classic.

Golden Guts (*Tripes d'or*, 1925) has been compared to Molière's *The Miser* (*L'Avare*), but is closer to Jonson's *The Alchemist*; Crommelynck makes it clear by the name of one of the characters, Muscar (reminiscent of Mosca, Volpone's 'parasite'), that he is aware of Jonson—whose mantle, indeed, he is more entitled to wear than any other contemporary playwright. In this, produced by Jouvet in 1930, a miser is persuaded by his doctor to cure himself of his avarice—for this interferes with the course of his love—by swallowing his gold. After a month of constipation he dies in voiding himself of it. Although painstakingly realistic on the surface, this is essentially symbolist, brilliantly exploiting the age-old equation between excrement and gold (tormentedly apprehended by Luther and made explicit by Freud). Outside the action, haunting it and at one moment desperately seeking entrance to the stage, is Azelle, the beloved of the miser.

Another notable play by Crommelynck, whose output is small, is *Hot and Cold* (*Chaud et froid*, 1934), in which an unfaithful wife becomes a faithful widow. He is one of the century's half a dozen most distinguished dramatists. He has also written two amusing novels, both of which deserve translation: *That is the Question* (*Là est la question*, 1947) and *Is Mr. Larose the Killer?* (*Monsieur Larose, est-il-l'assassin?* 1950).

MICHEL DE GHELDERODE (1898–1962), another Fleming, and a devout Catholic, was born in Ixelles in Brabant. An eccentric recluse who lived in a room full of puppets, armour and seashells, Ghelderode was another natural expressionist; one cannot understand his work without recognizing its roots in the art of Brueghel and Bosch—and its affinities with the pre-expressionist Belgian painter (whose father was English), his friend James Ensor. He is the most Flemish of all Belgians using the French language, but the closest in spirit to the Elizabethan farce of Marlowe (*The Jew of Malta*) and Middleton or Tourneur (*The Revenger's Tragedy*). Much of what seems unfamiliar in his drama—deformed puppets, cruelty accepted as inevitable, tormented medieval characters—is a part of Flemish folk-lore, and, especially, of the tradition of the Belgian puppet-theatre. For Ghelderode, as for Bernanos (q.v.), life is a perpetual struggle between good and evil, and the devil is real. But Ghelderode's Catholic faith keeps him happier than Bernanos': he does not feel himself to be the centre of the drama, and instead concentrates on recreating a world where this drama may be seen more clearly: medieval Flanders. Ghelderode seems as strange in this century as his French language must have seemed to him in his authentic Flemish world. Yet he is steeped in the theatre—in the kind of theatre that hardly exists any longer in Great Britain: the folk theatre that has no eyes whatever on, not even an awareness of, the 'rewards' of stardom, or notoriety in a cultural capital; a theatre that concentrates on what it is. From 1927 until 1930 he was closely associated with the Flemish Popular Theatre, and many of his plays (some of which are for puppets) were first given in Flemish translation. The world of Ghelderode's plays might remind one of that of Gracq (q.v.); but it is in sharper focus, it is natural to Ghelderode, and its novelty does not fatally engage his intellect. No mists obscure its darkness. It is a world that has fairly been called 'putrid'; but, unlike the equally putrid world of bourgeois reality, it has the beauty of the Flemish masters. Almost every one of his many plays has at its centre a surrogate for a lonely, psychically mutilated—impotent or crazily sadistic—creator. In *The School for Jesters* (*L'École des bouffons*, 1942) it is Folial who, ennobled (the playwright 'taken up' by the public?), has to tell his disciples the secret of his art ('cruelty'). In *Hop Signor!* (1935) a married virgin lusts in 'an old, forgotten cemetery' for a virgin executioner, who finally beheads her. This was put on by Barrault in Paris in 1947, and gave Ghelderode fame—his *Chronicles of Hell* (*Fastes d'enfer*, 1929; GSP) caused a scandal in 1949, to which he was quite indifferent. He attended no performances.

Barabbas (1928; GSP), still performed in Holy Week in Flanders, is the most vivid and moving of all modern versions of the drama of the crucifixion, the agony of which is set against a Brueghelian funfair. In *Pantagleize* (1929; GSP) a revolution is started when the saintly innocent, Pantagleize, says 'It's a lovely day'. No 'civilized' theatre can afford to ignore Ghelderode, any more than in the long run it can neglect Artaud—and it is a hopeful sign that both have made a considerable impact on the American theatre. Ghelderode wrote several short novels, of which *The Comic History of Klizer Karel* (*L'Histoire comique de Klizer Karel*, 1923) is typical.

HENRI SOUMAGNE (ps. HENRI WAGENER, 1891–1951), who was born in Brussels, has been shamefully neglected outside France—especially when one considers that not even the best British dramatist of the past half-century has produced anything remotely on a level with the masterpiece that made him famous in the Twenties: *The Other Messiah* (*L'Autre Messie*, 1923). Soumagne, like many other Belgian writers, was a lawyer. (Whereas in Great Britain the majority of solicitors and barristers are, from the first, arch-conservatives and careerists, in Belgium as elsewhere many more young men enter the law from a sense of idealism.)

The Other Messiah deals with Kellerstein, a rich Jew who returns one Christmas Eve to one of the scenes of his early struggles, a Warsaw bar with 'that characteristic smell of fried onions, sweat and intelligence that so often permeates places where Jews hang out'. Kellerstein does not believe in God because he has failed to find a firm-breasted woman. Another character bets him that God exists, and the matter is settled by a 'boxing match': a series of arguments that register as 'punches', under which the characters reel. This is one of the most brilliantly and subtly handled scenes in the whole of modern theatre. Kellerstein loses (unfairly), and has to admit that God does, after all, exist: hasn't the landlord's daughter got firm breasts? Who is he, then? By now the characters are all drunk, and it becomes clear that Kellerstein himself is God: his father was a carpenter. ... When will he proclaim the new laws? 'Soon. ... But right at this moment God's as pissed as a newt. ... And he can't preach a Sermon on the Mount from under a table.' This, which provoked riots in Prague, is neither a religious nor an anti-religious, but a sceptical play, an oblique attack on argumentativeness. Soumagne's later plays were, with one partial exception, ingenious and provocative, but did not have the feeling or the really audacious brilliance that distinguished *The Other Messiah*. The exception, *Madame Marie* (1928), gives a version of the Christ story in which Jesus is ironically postulated as being so divine—sympathetic, understanding, comforting, strengthening—that he is embarrassed by being turned into a legend: he does not wish to be burdened with religion. Matthew, the villain, is seen as 'arranging' for the divinity of Christ, in which he does not believe; but finally he is forced to believe in what he has devised. Soumagne wrote little more for the theatre after this, but turned instead to the reconstruction of actual crimes, including *The Strange Mr. Courtois* (*L'Étrange Monsieur Courtois*, 1943), about a policeman who was also a thief and killer.

HERMAN CLOSSON (1901) resembles Soumagne in that he sees the historical image of heroes or saviours as false; but where Soumagne sceptically seeks a true basis for feeling Closson is. more narrowly cynical and aggressive. His first play, which is unpublished, consists of the monologue of an old woman sitting on a lavatory. He is a technically accomplished dramatist, but in none of his plays has he been able to surpass his cynicism or even to point out, with total effect, the contrast between history and the reality it purports to depict. His best play is *False Light* (*Faux-jour*, 1941), about three men, long resident in the tropics, who invite a cover-girl to spend a holiday with them. She does so—and nothing happens. This is on the familiar Belgian theme of men searching for the identity of the emotion or desire that impels them (cf. the motive for Bruno's self-destructive jealousy in *The Magnificent Cuckold*). Can it be that Belgian writers seek for a visual representation of their emotions? The native genius is for making such representations. . . .

SUZANNE LILAR (1901), the mother of Françoise Mallet-Joris, wrote a clever variation on the Don Juan theme in *Burlador* (*Le Burlador*, 1947; TGBP): her Don Juan is pure and a self-deceiver, who really loves all his women. The philosophy behind this approach is outlined in an interesting book (we do not often find the wife of a minister of Justice vaunting a theory of *l'amour fou*): *Aspects of Love* (*Le Couple*, 1963; tr. 1965).

*

The leading spirit in the foundation of the magazine *The Green Disk* (*Le Disque Vert*, 1922) was Franz Hellens (q.v.), the most advanced of the Belgian *avant garde*. But the programme sensibly proposed by Hellens was so eclectic as to amount to no programme: he wanted the poet to do no more than to discover and to adhere to his own vision of life. Closely associated with *The Green Disk* was ODILON-JEAN PÉRIER (1901–28), who died of heart disease. Piérier found a clear and lucid style, and much of his poetry is touching in its brave intimations of early death; but he never found a language in which to describe the difference between his own anti-romantic austerity and the puritanism he loathed; when he offers justifications of his position they are too obviously second-hand. And one feels that by so resolutely denying himself any romantic self-indulgence he failed to discover his own mind. Perhaps his best work, in which he came nearer to this than in his poetry, was the novel *Passage of Angels* (*Le Passage des anges*, 1926).

ERIC DE HAULLEVILLE (1900–41), born in Brussels, who married the sister of Aldous Huxley's first wife, was yet another victim of the Nazis: he died after fleeing from them, when ill, to the South of France. His earliest poetry, uncertain of direction and heavily influenced by surrealism, is his most vital.

The leading Belgian poet of modern times is HENRI MICHAUX (1899), who was born at Namur and who describes himself in an autobiographical note as 'Belgian, of Paris'. Michaux, who is also an artist, is a writer of international stature. He had already established himself as such when Gide (q.v.) devoted a pleasant and chatty little book to him in 1941; since then his reputation has been assured. Michaux, although a very different kind of writer, resembles the Argentinian Borges (q.v. 3) in that he gladly forgoes the world of the flesh for that of the mind. For Michaux, therefore, to write a poem is in a sense to 'kill' it: once the word is made flesh it goes the way of all flesh. But a certain robustness, evident in his sense of humour and satirical bent, rescues Michaux from any tendency to preciosity or solipsistic over-obscurity. There is, especially in *A Certain Plume* (*Un Certain Plume*, 1930; pt. MSW) a distinctly engaging quality to his work. Everything he writes bears the stamp of authentic experience. He has frequently experimented with drugs, since hallucinations and similar experiences are as interesting to him as external affairs are to others. Like Borges, he is important because his concern with inwardness is not a pose or a game. He has been put forward as a surrealist; but this is misleading, because his poetry and prose arise from a deliberate intensity of self-exploration rather than from a wilder rummaging of the unconscious or a total yielding to impulse. It was Supervielle (q.v.) rather than any surrealist who first encouraged him. His early work appeared in *The Green Disk*.

Michaux, a poet who has never sought to hide his anguish, writes to 'exorcize': to keep at bay, really, the irrational demons of desire or impulse that lead men into action—and to neutralize 'the surrounding powers of the hostile world'. He is too tempted, too human, to be able to live inside himself except in the act of writing, by which he forces himself to do so. What he clings on to is the magic of words, which are like spells against the madness that he continually invites by his almost fanatic refusal to become 'engaged' or committed. When Michaux ran away from home as a young man, to become a widely faring sailor, he was literally trying to disengage himself from the whole accumulation of individual 'facts' that comprised Henri Michaux. The impulse behind his quest was ambivalent: to withdraw in horror, to refuse; but also to wash clean and recreate a rational—in the Swiftian sense—being. He meticulously described South America and Asia in his travel books *Ecuador* (1929) and *A Barbarian in Asia* (*Un Barbare en Asie*, 1932; tr. 1949), but excluded accounts of history or culture.

A remote and impossibly difficult writer? On the contrary, a remarkably accessible one. Michaux wears his fine seriousness with an agreeable and unconceited humour; the poet of inner space remains—the point can hardly be over-emphasized—human. His Monsieur Plume is his own apotheosis of Charlie Chaplin: defenceless, a creature whose lack of offence releases the vilest impulses of perversion and tyranny in others—but a poet, different. If he goes into a restaurant it will be to order something not on the menu; his request will strike the management as sinister, his excuses will fail to convince, the place will become a turmoil, the police will be involved. . . . On another occasion he wakes up to find that his house has been stolen. Tried and condemned for allowing his wife to be run over by a train (which rushed at where their house had been, and damaged him) he tells the judge that he has not been following the case. The early Chaplin could have made movie versions of each of the fifteen episodes in this book without taking thought. In the satirical fantasies of *Elsewhere* (*Ailleurs*, 1948), which collects earlier works, the influences of Swift and Voltaire are apparent. His poetry has about it an elegiac quality that X. J. Kennedy catches well in this first stanza from 'Nausea or This is Death Coming On?':

> Give yourself up, heart.
> We've struggled long enough.
> Let my life draw halt.

> Cowards we were not.
> Whatever we could we did.
>   (MP)

In a prose poem Michaux introduces camels into Honfleur (which changes the place), and flees on the fourth day. . . . Since the accidental death of his wife in a fire in 1948 (he wrote *We Two, Nous deux encore*, 1948, about their life together) Michaux has concentrated more exclusively on his painting—a retrospective exhibition was held in 1965—and on writing careful accounts of his experiments with drugs. He has actually spoken of renouncing literature, and certainly he finds his paintings more self-expressive. Posterity, however, will value him most as a writer. Gide has been sneered at for not understanding Michaux; but he could recognize a delightful and important writer—and this is, perhaps, understanding enough. (MEP; PBFV4; CFP; FWT)

In Belgium itself one of the most highly regarded of the poets and critics born within this century is ROGER BODART (1910). He, too, trained as a lawyer. He is an authoritative, generous and sympathetic critic of his Belgian contemporaries. As a poet he is strictly traditional —as traditional as his unquestioning religious belief. But the poems are finely made and their classicism serves a purpose, because its very rigidity produces an effect of great suggestiveness. Bodart seeks to manipulate his tendency to sentimentality into a valid warmth, and he sometimes succeeds. His optimism rests on assumptions too easily made for him to be an important poet, but when he writes of his love for nature, specifically the landscape of his native land, he achieves a touching authenticity.

EDMOND VANDERCAMMEN (1901) is more distinctly Belgian, and has been more influenced by Flemish literature. He has been related to unanimism (q.v.), already introduced into Belgian literature by the Flemish poet Paul van Ostayen; but he is really more concerned with the primitive mystery of being. His poems express a pantheism that is commonplace but deeply felt; their strength lies in the details he gives of his attitude rather than in the attitude itself. He has been much influenced by Spanish poetry. Some of his best poetry is collected in *September Bees* (*Les Abeilles de septembre*, 1959).

Leaving aside the unique Michaux—a genuinely 'denationalized' author?—the chief contribution of French-speaking Belgian literature has been to the theatre; this has been considerable. The younger Belgian poets, aware of this, seem to be turning theatrewards. CHARLES BERTIN (1919), author of *Black Song* (*Chant noir*, 1949), has written a number of interesting plays. The poet JEAN MOGIN (ps.

JEAN NORGE, 1921) wrote a play of remarkable power and psychological penetration in *To Each According to His Hunger* (*A chacun selon sa faim*, 1950), which is a portrait of a religious fanatic.

XII

France has always been the home of -isms as well as of good writers. One or two, such as unanimism, naturalism and, particularly, surrealism (qq.v.), were important, although of course less so than the individual writer. Among other trivial -isms of this century, we may note intimism, synthesism, integralism, musicism, floralism, aristocratism, druidism, totalism and lettrism. This last movement was inaugurated by ISIDORE ISOU (ps. JEAN-ISIDORE GOLDMANN, 1925) in the years immediately following the end of the Second World War. Isou was a Rumanian who came to Paris in 1945. It did not change the course of French poetry, and it was not important; but it does usefully illustrate the manner in which Paris remains the head-quarters of the *avant garde*—'the *avant garde* of the *avant garde*' as the faintly megalomaniac Isou puts it. No doubt there is in France, as has more than once been suggested, a somewhat dull 'conformity to non-conformity'; but because such creatively ungifted writers as Isou, the novelist MARC SAPORTA (1923), or the 'concrete' poet PIERRE GARNIER (1928), editor of *Les Lettres*, are not insincere or even pretentious, but simply an orthodox and agreeable part of the French scene and honourable and dedicated men, they do act as a stimulus to literature everywhere. Lettrism was a fearsome theory involving typography and phonetics, and is really connected with concrete poetry, though it is more intellectual than most concrete poets (as apart from their specially appointed critics) are prepared to be. Since the radical breaking down of language that lettrism involved was supposed to lead to the annihilation of the difference between the letter and the spirit, it is not surprising that reports of its success have not yet filtered through, nor that it has passed out of fashion; nevertheless, it was not quite contemptible, and in certain intellectual respects it reflects the preoccupations of the age.

However, the mainstream of French poetry since the war may be seen to parallel—if only very approximately—the developments in philosophy (not of course as non- or anti-literary as in the Anglo-Saxon countries) and fiction. Thus it is no accident that Philippe Sollers (q.v.) has devoted a book to FRANCIS PONGE (1899), who was born at Montpellier. Ponge, along with Michaux, is now one of the 'old masters' of French poetry. He has been a teacher, a journalist and a publisher; from the late Thirties until the end of the Second World War he was a committed communist. He did not begin to attract attention until 1942 with *The Set Purpose of Things* (*Le Parti pris des choses*). Paul Bowles was translating him by 1945. He had had some association with the surrealists, but had apparently no serious literary ambitions. He did not achieve real fame, however, until he was nearly sixty. Ponge himself repudiates the label poet; and if from the very broad Gallic interpretation of that term he is a poet, few British critics would think of applying it to him. But he is a writer of interest to poets—of this there can be no doubt. Ponge might most appropriately be described as a practising phenomenologist: instead of philosophizing, however, like Husserl (q.v.) and his successors, he describes his approach to and mental involvement with objects. These descriptions are frequently lyrical and humorous. (*Dix cours sur la méthode*, 1946, is a characteristic title: it irreverently recalls one of Descartes' masterworks, *Discours de la méthode*.) Ponge is no more concerned with the inner life than Robbe-Grillet (q.v.); but his art does not attempt to erect a philosophy; ineffably modest, it simply describes a certain way of looking at the world, which in the prose poems presents itself as a number of isolated fragments. There is no behaviourism here—unless the reader wishes to infer it. Furthermore, his world of objects is humanized by what only some Frenchmen might not recognize as the most preposterous romantic-isms, ironies and suggestive metaphors: a cigarette has passion as it is smoked, it's 'rough work' opening an oyster, as 'the prying fingers get sliced, the fingernails are snapped off', of a match 'Only the head can burst into flames, in contact with a harsh reality'. Prob-ably *Soap* (*Le Savon*, 1967; tr. 1969) is his most famous poem: it is a long meditation, begun in 1942 when soap was a valuable com-modity, on every aspect of this 'stone-like object with its marvel-lous powers of dissolution and rebirth'. He collected much of his work—essays on his procedures and poems—together with new material in the three volumes of his *Great Miscellany* (*Le Grand Recueil*, 1961). He is certainly an important ancestor of the *nouveau roman*, but this is because of his method which has classical but, as I have pointed out, not behaviourist implications. Ponge can be and has been overrated; but he is a genial and thoughtful writer. (PBFV4; CEP; FWT)

The Parisian JACQUES PRÉVERT (1900), once a surrealist and then a Marxist, is a casual and cheerful anarchist. He did notable work in films, writing the scripts of a number of Carné's best films, including *Le Jour se lève* and *Les Enfants du paradis*. Prévert is a true cabaret poet, a gleeman, a professional, whose technical skill is very considerable. His themes are often sentimental, but never offensively so—although the best setting for such work is usually the authentic (not the slick or pretentious) night-club for which it was created. Prévert's work, however thin—and much of it is this—always possesses vigour and the authority of tough experience. He has achieved the genuinely popular poetry that has eluded nearly every poet who has tried it; and yet at the same time he demonstrates, so to speak, that popular poetry has its limitations. For although he is an effective poet, he is inevitably a superficial one. His simplicities ring true, but their reverberations are strictly limited. The finest feature of his work is its lucid onslaught on the 'official', the pompous and the dehumanized. Although the magazine *Commerce* had published the long comic satire, *A Try at a Description of a Dinner of Disguised Guests in Paris, France* (*Tentative de descriptions d'un dîner de têtes à Paris-France*, 1931) which is one of his best and most characteristic works, and other poems and stories, Prévert did not become really well known until in 1946 a friend—René Bertelé, author of a study of Michaux—collected together, from newspapers and even from the tablecloths on which they had been written down, all the poems he could find and brought them together in *Words* (*Paroles*, 1946; pt. tr. 1966), which was a phenomenal and deserved success. Several collections have followed, and it is hardly to be wondered at if some of the poems in them are exceedingly slight. But they are slight rather than self-parodic or factitious. Prévert's poetry justifies the claim made for it by one critic: it is 'both public and innocent'. (MEP; PBFV4)

One of the most fascinating and original poets of Prévert's generation is JACQUES AUDIBERTI (1899–1965), who was born in Antibes, the son of a master mason. He was a journalist who did not start serious writing until he was almost thirty. After that he wrote plays, novels and criticism as well as his extraordinarily dense, rich poetry. In all his work Audiberti combines wide erudition and verbal exaltation with an unobtrusive psychological sensitivity. His many novels, such as *Abraxas* (1938), *Urujac* (1941), *Gardens and Rivers* (*Les Jardins et les fleuves*, 1954) are virtuoso performances, treating fantasy, pagan story and myth in a remarkable variety of styles. They reflect his view of life more chaotically than his other work, although they contain superb passages. The drama form concentrated his mind, and his parodic procedures gained in signficance. *Quoat-Quoat* (1946) combined his favourite theme of paganism asserting itself through a veneer of pretence with a parody of nineteenth-century melodrama. The effect is that of a kind of modern hilarody. The passengers on a ship bound for Mexico become prey to the savage and primitive forces of the stone of the ancient Mexican God Quoat-Quoat. *The Transient Evil* (*Le Mal court*, 1947), which was a commercial success, is set in the eighteenth century; it shows an innocent princess shrouded in the inevitable evil of experience. In the superb *Natives of the Bordeaux Country* (*Les Naturels du Bordelais*, 1953) Audiberti presents one of the most vital charlatans of modern drama: La Becquilleus, poet, aphrodisiac-seller and top-fuzz. The entire cast is transformed—into critics and into beasts. *Pucelle* (1950) is his subtle adaptation of the Joan of Arc story. Audiberti was affected by surrealism, and found it liberating; but he early saw that its eventual outcome could be to destroy literature by denying it the pole of tension offered by form. Even his first collection (1929), the poems in which were about Napoleon, was by no means surrealist. He drew upon the entire tradition of French poetry, particularly upon Hugo, to produce a highly intricate, rhetorical poetry. This is as versatile as the prose fiction, but every so often is precipitated a poem of quite astonishing metaphysical brilliance compounded with passion:

> People suffer. As for suffering, suffering does not consider it.
> She demands everything, except herself on the gallows.
> Absent from the star where you named her. . . .
>
> (CFP)

Rampart (*Rempart*, 1953) is devoted to his native Antibes. The whole body of Audiberti's poetry, with its self-styled 'abhumanism', involving a re-thinking of life, a literal re-making of it on paper, is already overdue for review; it seems to have important implications for the difficult future of poetry everywhere.

RENÉ CHAR (1907), born in the province of Vaucluse in the South of France, where he now lives, was a fully-fledged member of the surrealist movement and a close friend of Éluard's (q.v.); but his heart was never fully in it and his style cannot be called surrealist. Surrealism was for him no more than a liberating force: although his collected poems in the manner of surrealism, *The Masterless Hammer* (*Le Marteau sans maître*, 1934), are classics of the genre, he was still looking for his own style. He was a brave resistance leader in the Second World War, and was described by his friend Camus (q.v.), whose assumption that modern man needs to recreate his moral world he shared, as the greatest of modern French poets. Char is a hermetic (q.v. 3) poet in that he seeks to substitute poetry, for him a celebration of eternal truths in a language that entirely transcends that of the everyday, for the 'religious' that he has rejected for reasons identical to those of Camus; furthermore, he uses, or tries to use, words divorced from their traditional associations. His pre-war work consisted of a search for the meaning and function of poetry; since he was involved, as a freedom fighter, in a reassertion of a straightforward humanism, it has become a communication of his inner apprehensions about truth. One might compare him to Saint-John Perse, but the older poet began with and has retained a sense of the friendliness of the natural world that René Char does not possess. He loves his native Midi, and his poetry is soaked in its atmosphere; but the simple celebration of its mysteries is not enough. His poetry, which has tended increasingly to freer forms and thence to prose, seeks to recreate its often fleeting occasions. His style is as oracular as that of the fragments of Heraclitus, the pre-Socratic philosopher whom he profoundly admires; but he is not a mystic: his poems are offered as revelations, and the external world is very much present to him. What he calls 'fascinators', common events that may suddenly illuminate or reveal, are really poetic 'epiphanies': thus 'The Lark':

> Last cinder of sky and first ardour of day,
> She remains mounted in dawn and sings perturbed earth,
> Carillon master of her breath and free of her route.

> A fascinator, she's killed by being dazzled.
>
>   (CEP)

It is easy to misconstrue this as surrealist, for surrealism has so clearly been a part of its author's apprenticeship. But it is aphoristic, gnomic, in a way no truly surrealist poem can be: it seeks, like all Char's poems, to capture an aspect of the eternal in the instant. There is an effort here to create a poetic language that recalls the intentions of Stefan George (q.v.); but Char does not reject life as the German poet did. On the contrary, he affirms it, with, as one of his critics (Alexander Aspel) has well said, 'an exasperated serenity'. In the lark Char sees not only the lark itself but also creatively free man, capable of exercising his possibilities. The last line is illuminated by his famous statement, made apropos of his *Leaves of Hypnos* (*Feuillets d'Hypnos*, 1946; pt. tr. *Botteghe Oscure*, XIV, 1954), that he practised a 'humanism aware of its duties, discreet about its virtues, wishing to keep in reserve the inaccessible as a free field for the fantasy of its suns, and resolved to pay the price for this'. The main difficulty encountered in reading Char's work is that words do in fact have traditional associations; even if a poet can intimate processes of actually becoming—as Char does—the ghost of old poetic techniques lingers and to some extent interferes with communication. The creation of this kind of hermetic poetry does not perhaps lie within the English language; but it is worth attending to Char, whose integrity is beyond question: all foreign example, properly understood, acts invigoratingly. (HW; PBFV4; PI; FWT; CFP; MEP)

Such a poet was bound to attract gifted followers, and three leading poets who have thoroughly assimilated his influence are YVES BONNEFOY (1923), born in Tours, the Parisian ANDRÉ DU BOUCHET (1924) and JACQUES DUPIN (1927), born at Privas in Ardèche. Bonnefoy, who is distinguished as translator of Shakespeare and as a critic, is the most highly regarded French poet of his generation. Like Char, Bonnefoy is a hermetic poet; but he has read Valéry (q.v.) and learned much from his grave and sonorous manner, and Jouve (q.v.), and is both more urban (or less rural) and more literary than Char. His philosophical ambitions are not, like Char's, unobtrusive. The basis of his outlook is that death illuminates and makes sense of life, and he prefaced his first sequence of poems, *Of the Movement and Immobility of Douve* (*Du mouvement et de l'immobolité de Douve*, 1953; pt. tr. in *Selected Poems*, 1968) with Hegel's dictum that 'the life of the spirit . . . is the life which endures death and in death maintains itself'. What symbolized the truly sacred has now become meaningless to men, who have therefore lost the sense of the sacred altogether; now death must be the sacred. He sees his poems as a series of intuitive approximations to this sacred reality—which is, so to speak by definition, indefinable. Douve is the beloved ('at each moment I see you born, Douve, / At each moment die') who is glimpsed as herself and as various aspects of nature or landscape. Although Bonnefoy's poetry has a certain magnificence, and brilliantly succeeds in creating a new style that sedulously avoids perfection of form (as an artificiality), there is a certain monotony and lack of warmth about it; with the warm and gentle Char we feel that the poet has to speak as he does, and we seek to penetrate his utterance; with Bonnefoy there is often a feeling that the poet's intellect has played a much greater part in the poem's creation than its pretentions acknowledge. None the less, as the impressive—and in this case moving —poem 'Threats of the Witness' (CFP) demonstrates, this is a poetry of authority. (PBFV4; MEP; CFP; FWT)

Du Bouchet is less ambitious, or less philosophical, than Bonnefoy. Like Ponge's, his poetry is one of things; but in this work only an austere world is presented. Aside from Char, the chief influence on du Bouchet has been Pierre Reverdy (q.v.). Like Reverdy, he agonizedly searches for moments of communion with a nature stripped of all lushness or sensual pleasure: a nature bleak, galvanic, elemental.

This is a convincingly honest poetry, but one whose terms of reference are so far limited. (PBFV4; CFP; FWT)

In the post-surrealism of Jacques Dupin, who is a publisher and art-critic, there is greater positiveness of feeling, and more humanly satisfying imagery. Such poems as 'The Mineral Kingdom' (CFP) which recreate an experience of hope ('The fire will never be cured of us, / The fire that speaks our language'), rely more upon words themselves than upon the lay-out of the poem on the page (as in du Bouchet). His seeing of all experience in elemental terms—stone, minerals, mountains—is rendered in harsh and demanding imagery; and his world is more limited than Char's full-blooded, sun drenched one—but his apprehensions have been wrung out of him, as in 'Air':

> The body and the dreams of the lady
> For whom the hammers whirled
> Are lost together, and return
> Retrieving from the storm clouds
> Only the tattered rags of the lightning
> With the dew to come.
>
> (CFP)

This is a highly elliptical account of a love-encounter, from which the 'essence' has been extracted, in the manner of Char. The second line transforms 'lust', 'feelings of love', into an image that is redolent both of pagan mystery (Jupiter or Thor making thunder) and of quarrymen's techniques. The decrease of interest in this love-figure, a romanticized and archetypal one, since she is 'la dame', 'comes back' to the poet as a storm's end, with dew of the succeeding morning to come. The anthropomorphism is so intense that the experience itself is eliminated from the account of it. .... (PBFV4; FWT)

GUILLEVIC (ps. EUGÈNE GUILLEVIC, 1907) who was born at Carnac in Brittany, the son of a policeman, is in a sense a less ambitious poet. A civil servant for most of his life, he joined the (clandestine) communists in 1943. He was a friend of the ill-fated Drieu La Rochelle's, and of Éluard's (qq.v.). Guillevic, too, is concerned with matter, and in the uniquely French manner of this century wishes to abolish his personal identity (hence his abandonment of his Christian name). But no philosophical programme can be inferred from this. Once he committed himself to the Marxist task of analysing society in terms of exploiters and exploited he lost much of his original power—particularly since, a naïve (q.v.) poet *par excellence*, he tried to use his earlier procedures to achieve this.

He is essentially a 'poet of elementary matter' (Alexander Aspel): a namer of the nameless origins of humanity: the mud, the slime, the water, the foul depths of caves. But after his first two collections he became more self-conscious, and most of the startling effects of his later poetry may be traced to genuine insights in the earlier ones. (CEP; FWT) *Selected Poems* (1968; tr. 1974).

JEAN FOLLAIN (1903–1971), born at Canisy in Normandy, is more casual—partaking of the manner of Fargue (q.v.)—but not necessarily less significant. He describes his moments of illumination without fuss, cheerfully, charmingly; he is frank in his nostalgia, recalls his childhood openly. He is one of those delightful minor writers the effect of whose modest vignettes is that of a fresh, beautifully observed impressionist painting: an improvement upon life, thus adding to our and his life—without metaphysics. (CFP; MEP)

ANDRÉ FRÉNAUD (1907), born in a small town in Saône-et-Loire, Burgundy, wrote quieter but ultimately more deeply felt and illuminating poetry about the German occupation than Aragon's (q.v.)- in *The Magi* (*Les Rois mages*, 1943). Frénaud has rightly been referred to as an existentialist poet. He is concerned with a quest for self, and his best poems express, beautifully and simply, moments of authenticity and freedom won from misery, or recognitions of loveliness in things that had become sordid. He is a lyrical, affirming poet, who combines something of the tenderness of Éluard with a good-tempered ruefulness that is all his own. (CFP; FWT; PBFV4)

The poet and novelist ANDRÉ PIEYRE DE MANDIARGUES (1909), born in Paris, is undoubtedly an important writer. He was associated with the post-war surrealists, and is often called a surrealist, but once again, the function of surrealism for him has been no more than a liberating one. His novels, of which *The Motorcycle* (*La Motocyclette*, 1963; tr. 1965) is famous as a film (a poor one), are certainly as realist as they are surrealist. Pieyre de Mandiargues brilliantly and accurately shows people behaving in what psychiatrists call 'fugues'. In *The Motorcycle* a girl bored with her husband speeds off, fatally, to meet her lover. She is doomed by her attachment to speed and lust; the erotic detail is described with a redoubtable psychological accuracy. This same precision applies to his poetry and prose poems, which often begin on surreal premises but soon concentrate into careful, uninhibited description. Pieyre de Mandiargues' greatest achievements are probably his novels; but in these he is a poet in the power of his description of the actions of people in despair (CFP; FWT)

PATRICE DE LA TOUR DU PIN (1911), born in Paris, educated in Sologne (which is the background of his poetry), offers a contrast to all the foregoing: he is one of the few poets of merit to have been honoured as 'an answer to surrealism'. He has given force to this interpretation by declaring, misguidedly, that his work is 'absolutdly independent of the modern spirit'. And, in mistaken emulation of Claudel (q.v.) and with high Christian zeal, he has embarked on an enormous project (patently beyond his powers) of assembling a *A Summa of Poetry* (*Une Somme de poésie*, 1946, 1959, 1963), which he is still continuing. In fact, and against his orthodox wishes, his poetry is rightly described as 'hermetic and personal': he is the Gallic equivalent of a Wilson Knight crossed with J. C. Powys and T. H. White: violently eccentric, obstinate, conceited, medieval, foolish to ignore. *The Quest for Joy* (*La Quête de joie*, 1933), which was acclaimed, was extraordinary: a kind of grail poem, in traditional form, incorporating ghosts of the medieval past as reinterpreted by the Victorians. But the question was whether the young poet would or could eventually achieve the precision lacking in the poem. He did not. A prisoner of the Germans for much of the Second World War, he returned and inflated himself into a poet-philosopher: his lyrical gift departed. His ideas about poetry are summed up in *The Dedicated Life in Poetry* (*La Vie recluse en poésie*, 1938; tr. 1948). (PBFV4)

PIERRE EMMANUEL (ps. NOËL MATHIEU, 1916), born at Gan in the Pyrenees and educated partly in America, is another Christian traditionalist, but of a very different kind; he is a disciple and a friend of Jouve (q.v.), but his amiable and superficial fluency, which functions as a kind of inoffensively optimistic journalism, has prevented him from ever attaining Jouve's eminence. He has a slick, pleasant and sincere style, but has failed to develop it into anything serious.

PHILIPPE JACCOTTET (1925) was born at Moudon in Vaud, in Switzerland, but settled in France in 1946. He shares the same concerns as his contemporaries, but is less austere and more conversational, less hermetic, seeming to address the reader more directly and in a more friendly way. He writes gently and subtly of death—

> Don't worry, it will come! You're drawing near, you're getting warm! For the word which is to end the poem more than the first word will be near your death. . . .

—addressing lovers, equating their 'coming' with the intimation of death and with the end of his poem. He has translated Musil (q.v.) into French. Jaccottet has written what are perhaps the most satisfying and substantial poems of any poet of his generation who has absorbed and understood modernism. Others of this age group, such as MICHEL DEGUY (1930) have demonstrated both intellectual agility and feeling, but have not yet—as Jaccottet has—found the means to combine them. (PBFV4; FWT; CFP)

German Literature

I

There was a German literary renaissance between 1880 and 1900. In 1880 literature was debilitated; by 1900 there was a host of new talent. Poetry was in 1880 represented at its worse by a multitude of mediocre narrative romances, but at its better only by the monotonous and self-consciously 'beautiful' verses of PAUL HEYSE (1830–1914), the first German to win a Nobel Prize (1910). Heyse did good work as a collector of German short stories, and some of his own, particularly *L'Arrabbiata* (1855; tr. 1855) and the English collection *The Dead Lake* (1867; tr. 1870) deserve to survive; his poetry, plays and novels are now unreadable. The better poets, among them von Eichendorff, Mörike and above all Heine, were dead. The Swiss C. F. Meyer (1825–98) wrote lyrics that sometimes anticipate later poetry in their tentative symbolism; significantly, this poetry originated in a pathological melancholia. But such an excellent example of his best work as 'Lethe' (PGV) has its roots firmly in romanticism. These writers influenced such twentieth-century poets and novelists as Ricarda Huch (q.v.), but did not impel them towards modernism.

It is unnecessary to speak of the theatregoers' average diet in the early Eighties: this consisted of farces or ponderous imitations of Schiller's historical plays.

In fiction there were a few exceptions to the general rule of sentimental family tales and massively erudite but poor historical novels in imitation of Scott. Some memorable novellas were written. The Swiss Gottfried Keller published the final revision of his major novel, *Green Henry* (*Der grüne Heinrich*, 1880 tr. 1960), in 1880. The most shining exception was Theodore Fontane, who did not begin to write novels until he was in his middle fifties. Fontane was claimed by, and encouraged, the naturalists. But he was a non-romantic realist, not a naturalist; his work in any case transcends that of the programmatists whose admiration he gained. Two other forerunners of the naturalist movement that was so soon to erupt do, in terms of lifespan, belong to this century. The novels of FRIEDRICH SPIELHAGEN (1829–1911) were once admired. He was a socialist who advocated social realism in his criticism, but who could not achieve it in fiction because he had neither grasp of character nor conception of a prose style appropriate to his material. His best book is *Faustulus* (1898), a satire on what he took to be the Nietzschean idea of the superman.

WILHELM RAABE (1931–1910) is, by contrast, a major figure. A genuine humorist, influenced by Dickens and Sterne, he combined a temperamental pessimism with decency, detachment and a sharp intelligence. His best work, *Stopfkuchen* (1891), belongs to his final period. *Abu Telfan: Return from the Mountains of the Moon* (*Abu Telfan, oder Die Heimkehr vom Mondgebirge,* 1868; tr. 1881) is a shrewd criticism of his Germany.

Six more nineteenth-century figures are relevant. Four are poets and two are thinkers, the influence of whose ideas cannot be ignored. WILHELM BUSCH (1832–1908), caricaturist as well as poet, is as famous in Germany for his *Max and Maurice* (*Max und Moritz,* 1865; tr. 1913) as Edward Lear is in the English-speaking world for his nonsense verses; but he was not as poetically gifted as Lear, and his 'nonsense' is not true nonsense, as Morgenstern's (q.v.) is. But Busch was a genuinely comic poet. There is rather more, in fact, of Hilaire Belloc (as comic poet) in him than of Lear or Carroll; he has Belloc's stolidity and cheerful sincere dismay. Of a pious girl burned to death he says:

> Here we see her smoking ruins.
> The rest is of no further use.

Busch had to satisfy a large and indiscriminate audience (from 1884 onwards he produced an annual); his aggressiveness and contempt for bourgeois religion do not always save his work from mediocrity. But he never entirely lost his gift.

PAUL SCHEERBART (PS. BRUNO KÜFER, 1863–1915), novelist and poet born in Danzig and a friend of Dehmel's (q.v.) and Przybyszewski's (q.v. 4), was possibly more important than Busch. Certainly he was carefully read by Ringelnatz and Hans Arp (qq.v.), to mention only two. He wrote fantastic 'cosmic' novels (adventures in space in a bottle, dancing planets, and so on) that may be considered, although they are so whimsical, as early prototypes of Science Fiction. His nonsense poetry (*Katerpoesie,* 1909), which was republished in Germany in 1963, should be more widely known. Like Fritz von Hermanovsky-Orlando (q.v.) Scheerbart was a friend of the Prague painter and writer Alfred Kubin.

DETLOV VON LILIENCRON (1844–1909), impoverished Baron, soldier, perpetual debtor, adventurer, wag, good fellow, wrote plays and fiction, but is now remembered for his poetry. Like Roy Campbell (q.v. 1), another not altogether convincing laureate of the soldier's life, Liliencron was a stylist rather than a thinker; his modest innovations—the abolition of some archaisms, the introduction of a few everyday (but not colloquial) words—were accidental, a result of his military forthrightness. Wounded in the two wars of 1866 and 1870, Liliencron was forced to resign his commission in 1875 because of debts; he spent two 'lost' years in America (house-painting, horse-breaking: the usual), and then took a job in Germany as a bailiff and, finally, parish-overseer. He was a scamp (this is, surprisingly, the right word): he had suffered too much, said his friend Richard Dehmel, not to be beyond dignity and honour. Liliencron was best when most subdued, although in his sporting-voluptuous vein ('With a plume in my helmet in sport or in daring, Halli! / Life gave me no lessons on fasting or sparing, Hallo! / No wench so unwilling but yields her to me. . . .' and so on) he has undoubted verve even when he prompts a smile. But while he was the best of the so-called 'impressionist' poets, it is going much too far to claim, as one critic does, that his technique is a precursor of expressionism (q.v.) because, it is claimed, 'he gives a series of realistic impressions (rather in the Japanese style) from which everything unnecessary has been eliminated'. 'Day in March' is characteristic. Beginning with pure description of cloud-masses, cranes, larks, it concludes: 'brief fortune dreams its way across wide lands. / Brief fortune swam away with the cloud-masses; / I wished to hold on to it, had to let it swim away' (TCG; see also PGV, CGP). The description here is for the sake of the observation about 'brief fortune'; and even in his poems where the essentially late romantic observations are absent, they are implied. Liliencron is a late nineteenth-century poet, not a proto-expressionist.

The poet RICHARD DEHMEL (1863–1920) was until his death rated far too highly; he is hardly read now. His historical importance, as one influenced both by Nietzsche (q.v.) and socialism, is undoubted; his inconsistency—militarism, worship of ruthlessness, socialistic sympathy—is symptomatic. Dehmel's development as a poet is illusory; his ideas are as uninteresting as his over-sexed brand of vitalism, leading to a transparently spurious programme for 'spiritualizing' sex.

But when he was not intellectualizing, Dehmel was better as a poet. He translated Verlaine well, and learnt from him. The handful of satisfactory poems he left are evocations of landscape. To him this was doubtless an exercise in creating 'atmosphere' rather than in the more important matter of expressing his thoughts. But it was then that he came closest to expressing himself: 'The pond is resting and/

The meadow glistening. / Its shadows glimmer / In the pond's tide, and / The mind weeps in the trees. / We dream—dream-. . .' (TCG; see also PGV, CGP).

FRIEDRICH NIETZSCHE (1844–1900) was insane (the diagnosis is 'atypical general puresis') for the last eleven years of his life, so that his work was all done well within the limits of the nineteenth century. But no discussion of modern Western literature can avoid referring to him: his influence upon our century has been decisive. His creative work consisted only of poetry: the long prose poem *Thus Spake Zarathustra* (*Also sprach Zarathustra*, 1883–5; tr. 1961) and the shorter lyrical poems *Dionysus-Dithyrambs* (*Dionysos-Dithyramben*, 1884–8).

Nietzsche, until 1889 one of the most lucid of nineteenth-century German prose writers, has been interpreted in a variety of conflicting ways; as proto-Nazi, as proto-communist, and as existentialist prophet of human freedom. He was not himself consistent, but his complete (syphilitic?) breakdown at the age of forty-five prevented him from reconciling some of the most glaring contradictions in his work.

First and foremost, Nietzsche consistently attacked the *status quo*. His work was unheeded until the Dane Georg Brandes (q.v.) began to lecture on it in 1888; there had been no such forceful denunciation of bourgeois complacency in the century. Nietzsche rediscovered the Dionysian and anti-intellectual principle that life is tragic: he hailed the Greek tragedy of Aeschylus and Sophocles as the supreme achievement of art ('We have art in order not to perish of truth') because it emphasized that man must suffer to know joy ('All joy wants the eternity of all things, wants honey, wants dregs, wants intoxicated midnight, wants graves, wants the consolation of graveside tears, wants gilded sunsets'), and celebrated the irrationality of the instincts that he believed had been weakened by Socrates, by Euripides and, then, finally and fatally, by Christianity.

Nietzsche's advocacy of a 'superman' ('Übermensch'), now perhaps better rendered as 'overman' if only because of its unfortunate associations, was used by fascist ideologists; but they certainly misunderstood it. His appeal to the youth of his day to reject knowledge for its own sake, and to live by instinct, was not as crude as the Prussian militarists, and then the Nazis, liked to pretend. (When he attacked the acquisition of knowledge for its own sake he was, if only in part, reacting against the German educational system, which undoubtedly crammed its victims with accumulations of meaningless facts to a dangerous degree.) Nietzsche's overman gives his life meaning by learning to create, to love his enemies, to be virtuous; he would have seen the Nazi, as Nietzsche himself saw Bismarck, as a failed overman—a mere crude pursuer of power.

Unfortunately Nietzsche's descriptions of his 'new man' are themselves partly responsible for later misinterpretations (some would put it more strongly than that); and he certainly had a sinister side to him, as may be seen in his hysterical glorifications of force, war and the military. Nietzsche was a formative influence on expressionism (q.v.). His message 'God is dead', and consequent exhortation to man to turn against his narcissistic, death-resisting intellect, profoundly affected the succeeding generation of expressionist (and then surrealist) poets, who put all the emphasis upon intuition rather than upon rational perception.

Nietszche's idea of 'the eternal recurrence of the same', another of his rediscoveries, was part and parcel of his demand that literature should revitalize itself by means of myth (myth naturally being preferred to debilitating 'morality' and rationalism); it had a profound effect, as may be seen in the fact that well over half the major works of this century have employed or drawn upon myth.

Freud said of Nietzsche that he probably had more knowledge of himself than any other human being. Certainly no pre-Freudian writer, with the possible exception of Coleridge, formulated so many 'Freudian' concepts. Thus, he said: 'One's own self is well hidden from oneself: of all mines of treasure one's own is the last to be dug up'. His use of a new psychology was all-pervasive in its influence, not only upon writers who did not hear of Freud until during or after the First World War, but on Freud himself. Nietzsche could be strident, even horrisonous; but he is a key figure. The difficulties raised by his overman exactly parallel the difficulties that lie at the heart of expressionism: both raise the urgent question, When does a nihilism become a barbarism?

The philosopher WILHELM DILTHEY (1833–1911) is important for the emphasis he put on psychic as distinct from materialistic manifestation, and for his confidence in the capacity of poets to make meaningful statements about the mysteriousness of life, which can thereafter be intellectually analyzed. For Dilthey, too, intuition is primary. His poetics, the most important to be published in Germany in his lifetime, concentrated upon the creative process and the experience of the creator—and thus played a part in the genesis of expressionism. His frequent insistence that 'the origin of all genuine poetry is in experience' has been of importance both to poets and to some critics, as has his subtle treatment of the nature of the experience that can lead to poetry: something actively and intensely felt, and subsequently transformed; something that is processed by the poet in his totality—by 'the whole man'. Later Dilthey saw certain short-comings in his formulation of the problem; his criticism of individual poets is sometimes theory-bound; but the value of his always sober insistence upon the primacy of experience and intuition, and his account of the imaginative process, is undoubted, and helped greatly to prepare the atmosphere for the eruption of genuine poetry that began at the time of his death. (One might say the same of the English 'pre-romantic' poet and critic Edward Young, who influenced Dilthey and was hailed by the surrealists.) His work is ably summarized by H. A. Hodges in *The Philosophy of Wilhelm Dilthey* (1952).

II

The most indefatigably polemical of the German naturalists (q.v.) was ARNO HOLZ (1863–1929). He was no more than a competent writer at best but he has importance as one of the leading figures, with his friend and collaborator JOHANNES SCHLAF (1862–1941), of German naturalism; above all he was generous in his encouragement of writers better than himself. In his treatise *Art: Its Nature and Its Laws* (*Die Kunst: ihr Wesen und ihre Gesetze*, 1890–2) he gave an almost fanatic definition of naturalism, in which he went so far as to assert that art is different from nature only in its means. He formulated the 'law' that 'art has the tendency to return to nature'. The problem was a scientific one: art was photographic, and its only limitations were its means. Earlier (1885) he had written a book of lyrics conventional in form but decidedly 'modern' in that it dealt with social and sexual themes: this was *The Book of the Age* (*Das Buch der Zeit*, 1885). At the turn of the century, he began, under the influence of Whitman, to advocate free verse rhythms: metrical form is 'smashed', and its place is taken by rhythmical form. There are to be no rhymes or stanzas, and the poem turns on an invisible central pivot: that is to say, each line is centred on the page—making Holz's own examples look rather like some concrete poetry (q.v. 3). The basic notion behind this, that of an 'inner rhythm', is by no means silly: it characterizes all literature. But Holz, although his ideas are of interest as an extreme development of French naturalist theory, was overconfident and over-theoretical; and his creative powers were limited. The truth is, he and nearly all the other early German naturalists were critics at heart: they recognized that the romanticism of their day was outdated, that Goethe had exhausted its soil; and that the political progress of their country had been retarded.

But they had no inner creative urge, such as characterized almost all of the writers associated with the first phase of expressionism. Holz's creative sterility is well shown in 'Its roof almost brushed the stars. . . .', ostensibly a 'naturalist lyric' about a starving young man in a garret who could only stammer 'O Muse! and knew nothing of his destitution' (TCG; see also PGV). This succeeds only in achieving the banal and outworn romanticism against which the naturalists were reacting.

Other naturalists of historical interest who should be mentioned are the critic and novelist MICHAEL GEORG CONRAD (1846–1927), who made personal contact with Zola, the brothers HEINRICH (1855–1906) and JULIUS HART (1859–1930), critics, dramatists and poets, and the Scottish-born poet, novelist and anarchist JOHN HENRY MACKAY (1864–1933): these championed Zola intelligently and not un-critically, but could not convincingly emulate him in their own creative work. All were members, with Holz and others such as the critic and novelist WILHELM BÖLSCHE (1861–1939) and Gerhart Hauptmann (q.v.), of an *avant garde* literary club called *Durch*. The heroes of *Durch* were Ibsen (q.v.) and Tolstoi (q.v. 4). The Free Stage (Die freie Bühne), modelled on Antoine's Théâtre Libre (q.v.) in Paris, lasted from 1889 until 1891 (but later if special performances are counted), and put on plays by Ibsen and Zola as well as Holz and Hauptmann. The heyday of German naturalism may be measured by its duration.

Holz and Schlaf scored a success with a volume of three stories called *Papa Hamlet* (1889), which they published under the name of Bjarne P. Holmsen (chosen because of the esteem in which Scandinavian writers were then held). These tales are an attempt to be totally objective and photographic; but the subject-matter is sensational (thus betraying subjectivity) and the disjointed style—called 'Sekundenstil' (i.e. style that tries to reproduce the passing of seconds) an early forerunner of 'stream of consciousness' (q.v.) technique—produces an effect of dullness. This, with its short scenes, came close to drama, and Holz's and Schlaf's next effort was a play, *The Family Selicke* (*Die Familie Selicke*, 1890), which followed the same technique and had the same sensational, sordid subject-matter.

MAX KRETZER (1854–1941) is the most typical of all the German naturalist novelists, and although he sold well until 1939, he is today forgotten. Here is an example of a writer with the same kind of impulses as Theodore Dreiser (q.v. 1), but without the genius or sensibility. Much of his work stems from painstaking imitations of individual novels by Zola or Dickens, but he is at his unimpressive best when writing of his own experiences, as in his most famous novel, *Meister Timpe* (1888), where he traces a family's decline from the middle to the lower classes, or in *The Signwriter* (*Der Fassaden-raphael*, 1911). He pretended not to have read Zola.

HERMANN SUDERMANN (1857–1928), like Kretzer an East Prussian, achieved enormous success as playwright and novelist. A clever if not wholly honest craftsman, he gave the middle classes just the kind of pseudo-controversial material they wanted: he was readable, and seemed to have a social conscience. Sudermann's play *Honour* (*Die Ehre*, 1889; tr. 1915) set him up for a quarter of a century as Germany's leading popular playwright. In it he combined a bow towards the 'new' ideas with a masterly grasp of old-fashioned stage technique. Like Sardou's (q.v.), his plays are mechanically 'well made', and thoroughly deserved Shaw's (q.v. 1) epithet of 'Sardoodledom'. An archmiddlebrow, Sudermann exploited naturalism for commercial ends—not, doubtless, because he so planned it, but because, along with his undoubted skill, he had a commonplace mind. His literary reputation was eventually destroyed by the implacable opposition of the critic and poet ALFRED KERR (ps. ALFRED KEMPNER, 1868–1948), who understood true naturalism as it was exemplified in Ibsen and Hauptmann (qq.v.). Sudermann also wrote novels: regional (his best), historical and sensationalist. *The Song of Songs* (*Das hohe Lied*, 1908; tr. 1909), about a loathsome aristocratic General and the girl he 'corrupts', was a *cause célèbre* in Germany and England. Its moral, that a high society which does not work must be 'rotten', was peculiarly edifying to its bourgeois audience. All Sudermann's work was directed at the public, who devoured him avidly; he is today unreadable, for he wrote from no inner compulsion.

MAX HALBE (1865–1944), another of those whose intense natural-ism is now outdated, came from near Danzig. Influenced first by both Ibsen and Gerhart Hauptmann (qq.v.), he later became friendly with Wedekind (q.v.). *The Breaking of the Ice* (*Der Eisgang*, 1892), in which rivalry between two brothers is depicted against the background of the gradually unfreezing Vistula, draws from Ibsen for its symbolism (socialism flooding forth) and Hauptmann for its psychology. Halbe's great success was the play *When Love is Young* (*Jugend*, 1893; tr. 1916). This is his best work because it stems from the conflicts of his own youth; however, its language, once admired, now seems more poetical than poetic, and its machinery creaks. As a tragedy of adolescent love it is a genuine predecessor of Wedekind's *Spring's Awakening* (q.v.); but the latter unkindly exposes its short-comings. Halbe did try to participate in some proto-expressionist theatrical activities, but these were short-lived experiments. His autobiography *Turn of the Century* (*Jahrhundertwende*, 1935), telling of his years of association with Wedekind and others between 1893 and 1914, is valuable for the background of German naturalism and of the group around Wedekind.

PAUL ERNST (1866–1933), novelist, poet, critic, playwright, developed through theological, naturalistic and Marxist phases to his own abstract position, which involved a crude, neo-classical cult of a super-hero, the lifeless star of 'meta-tragedies', of which Ernst left a number. By means of his theories he was able to condemn *King Lear*. He ended up as a kind of transcendental Christian, praised by the Nazis. His output is as enormous (one verse epic extends to 100,000 stanzas) as it is undistinguished.

The poet, novelist, critic and historian RICARDA HUCH (1864–1947), more interesting, and for long acclaimed as modern Germany's outstanding writer ('Germany's first lady', said Thomas Mann), allowed herself to be by-passed by naturalism and the movements that succeeded it. Her high-bred loftiness would not have allowed her to dabble in anything that dealt in detail with such crude material as the lives of the poor. She did not lack concern, but it was aristocratic. Instead she drew her inspiration from C. F. Meyer, Heyse, Keller (qq.v.), and earlier writers. She lacked a sense of humour, and was unable to see the shortcomings of nineteenth-century German bourgeois respectability—she signally failed to take a critical view of it in her smooth, lush first novel, *Unconquered Love* (*Erinnerungen von Ludolf Ursleu dem Jüngeren*, 1893; tr. 1931). Her verse is sentimental and wooden. In retrospect a rather stupidly grand old lady, perhaps—but one who was a scholar, who proudly refused Nazi honours and secretly opposed their regime, and who, in her small way, developed. Her only work of interest now is the detective story, *The Deruga Trial* (*Der Fall Deruga*, 1917; tr. 1929): superior and intelligent detective fiction, this stands up today: it displays most of Ricarda Huch's virtues and powers in a, for once, congenial and creatively modest framework.

Finally we come to the man within whose work the imaginatively sterile German naturalist movement became transformed. GERHART HAUPTMANN (1862–1946), dramatist, novelist and poet, was once a literary giant, and his 1912 Nobel Prize surprised no one. Now he is little read outside his own country, except by academics; yet critics accord him more than mouth-honour, and it seems certain that a substantial amount will remain to be rescued and rehabilitated from the vast mass of his drama and fiction, though not from his verse. New and improved English versions of his works continue to be made, and his plays are still being performed. His importance is more than historical.

His elder brother CARL HAUPTMANN (1858–1921), gifted, but not as a writer of fiction, was a rather embarrassing imitator of Gerhart—even to the reading of his plays to devoted disciples and the acceptance of the title 'Master'. However, his play *War* (*Krieg*, 1914; tr. in *Vision and Aftermath, Four Expressionist War Plays*, 1969), the last and best of a trilogy, is exceptional. It prophesied with remarkable accuracy the real nature of what, at the end of 1914 (the play was written in 1913), was still felt by the vast majority to be a noble and holy war, and in doing so partook of the spirit of expressionism. Hauptmann's gloom here was generated not by the cast of events suiting a dark temperament—as often happened with expressionist writers—but by a keen and early understanding of what the cataclysm would really mean. *War* still reads remarkably well. Unfortunately nothing else Hauptmann wrote matches it.

Gerhart Hauptmann was born in Silesia, and at first intended to be a sculptor. After a Byronic poem (later withdrawn) and some fiction, he took the German-speaking world by storm with his drama *Before Dawn* (*Vor Sonnenaufgang*, 1889; tr. 1909. All Hauptmann's dramas before 1925 were collected and tr. L. Lewisohn and others in *Dramatic Works*, 1913–29). Here he was influenced by Holz: there can be no doubt of the 'consistency' of his determinism here. A family of Silesian farmers become drunks when coal is discovered on their land. An idealist who believes in 'scientific determinism' comes amongst them and falls in love with the one alcoholically uncorrupted member of the family, the daughter Helene. The reformer, Alfred Loth, rejects her on the grounds of her heredity, and she kills herself. Very much a young man's play, and delightfully close to naturalist theory for Holz. . . . But it had real dramatic impact: one could already have discerned, from the depiction of the main characters, both Alfred Kerr's much later tribute, 'this is not accuracy; this is intuition', and Thomas Mann's even more remarkable one, 'He did not speak in his own guise, but let life itself talk'.

However, these tributes were to, and are really only applicable to, the plays of Hauptmann's earlier period: it is for these that he will be remembered. *The Weavers* (*Die Weber*, 1892; tr. in *Five Plays by Gerhart Hauptmann*, 1961), about the 1844 revolt of Silesian weavers (his grandfather had been one of them), was one of the first plays in which the hero was the crowd. This transcends both politics and naturalist theory by, to adapt Mann's remark, 'letting the weavers themselves talk'. This, along with *The Assumption of Hannele* (*Hanneles Himmelfahrt*, 1893; ibid.), in which a poor, dying girl has visions of her ascent to paradise, was banned. In revenge Hauptmann wrote one of the best and liveliest of all German comedies, *The Beaver Coat*

(*Der Biberpelz*, 1893; ibid.). Authority has seldom been more accurately caricatured. The thieving, cunning washerwoman Wolffen is done with a vitality that acts as a perfect contrast to the absurd official Wehrhahn. This will play almost anywhere and in almost any language with success. Two other plays of Hauptmann's early period that will also continue to survive are the tragedies *Drayman Henschel* and *Rose Bernd* (*Fuhrmann Henschel*, 1898; *Rose Bernd*, 1903; ibid.).

Gerhart Hauptmann was—in the terms of Schiller's distinction between 'naïve' and 'sentimentive' (q.v.)—a 'naïve' writer. The playwright who was translated by James Joyce (q.v. 1) and admired by pretty well every important writer in the world, became, as Michael Hamburger has well said, 'defeated by the tension of the age'. In deep sympathy with humanity, he failed to understand the changes that were taking place around him. Hauptmann the old mage, who modelled himself on Goethe and imagined that he had improved Shakespear's *Hamlet*, is a figure of little interest. His enormous dull epics, in monotonous verse, are of no value; his final tetralogy, again in verse, on the subject of the House of Atreus is inadequate because its turgid language fails to function except as an outmoded notion of grandeur. The bright, empathic young playwright becomes 'a great man', and so his work declines: instead of positive achievements, he produces nothing that is more than 'interesting'—such as his treatment of *The Tempest* theme in *Indipondi* (1920), in which he celebrates incest. He accepted the Nazis, but never actively collaborated; later he published attacks on them.

Hauptmann's intentions oscillated between naturalism and what may be called a kind of neo-romantic symbolism, seldom free from sentimentality. At his best, naturalism functioned as a matrix for his intuitions. In fiction, too, Hauptmann vacillated between two extremes: an erotic paganism and a pious Christianity. In *The Fool in Christ, Emanuel Quint* (*Der Narr in Christo*, 1910; tr. 1912) he shows a modern misunderstood Christ coming to grief; but in *The Heretic of Soana* (*Der Ketzer von Soana*, 1819; tr. 1960) his subject is a priest converted to sensuality and neo-paganism.

Hauptmann was a true naïve, who would have done better work throughout his life if he had observed reality more calmly and been content simply to celebrate nature—as he always did in his heart.

His attempt to synthesize his inner and outer worlds was a conspicuous failure: an object lesson in how not to approach the twentieth century.

III

It is customary to associate three poets of the turn of the century: the Hessian Stefan George, the Austrian Hugo von Hofmannsthal, and the German-Czech Rainer Maria Rilke. At this time a number of 'isms' were in currency: impressionism, symbolism, even a 'beyond naturalism'. But, as a critic has written, 'the dark horse with the staying power will be found wearing the dun colours of *Sprachkrise* [crisis in language]'. The question being asked by the important poets was, Can language communicate?

The work of STEFAN GEORGE (1868–1933) is the least enduring and important. However, despite his limitations and ridiculosities, he was one of the men who helped to bring into Germany a viable poetry; and he did write a handful of fine poems. Authorities appear to differ on the subject of his influence. One critic calls it 'profound and extensive'; another says he 'has had comparatively little influence in Germany, and none outside'. This last is an incautious remark: George's influence on Rilke and Hofmannsthal was certainly extensive; he had followers outside Germany, especially in Holland. His undoubted genius was too often vitiated, first by the self-consciousness of his decadent-symbolist pose, and later by his assumption of a mantic role.

He went to France as a young man, became friendly with both Mallarmé and Verlaine (qq.v.), and returned to Germany full of certainties: 'A poem is not the reproduction of a thought but of a mood', he wrote. 'We do not desire the invention of stories but the reproduction of moods.' As he grew older he became increasingly dogmatic. He had a vein of real poetry in him, as such individual poems as 'The Master of the Island' (PI) clearly show; but he wrapped this around and eventually concealed it with rhetorical and critical paraphernalia: a bizarre pomposity, that can, retrospectively, easily be seen as psychologically defensive. He was a master of conventional form—his typographical eccentricities are acutely fastidious but not innovatory—and over his life he succeeded in imposing a rigid discipline. He is not a likeable poet, but to call him a proto-Nazi is misleading. The Nazis were far too vulgar for him: when they came to power he went into voluntary exile in Switzerland, and refused all the honours they offered him. The imperious George did, however, attract proto-Nazis, and he himself did envisage a 'new Reich' (*The New Reich, Das neue Reich*, 1928, is the title of his last book); but his was a cerebral vision of the future.

George began and ended as a symbolist and preacher of 'art for art's sake'; but he was less original than his first master Mallarmé (q.v.). Some of his best poems are in *The Year of the Soul* (*Das Jahr der Seele*, 1897), and owe much to Verlaine. From its most famous poem, and George's, we can see that for all his 'hardness' George was essentially a neo-romantic: for all his dogmatic pronouncements his real gift lay in an unspectacular but exquisite capacity to reflect his inner states in landscapes:

Come into the park they say is dead and look: the gleam of distant smiling shores, the unhoped-for blue of the pure clouds shed a light on the ponds and the variegated paths.

Gather the deep yellow, the soft grey of birches and of box—the breeze is mild—the late roses have not yet quite withered; choose them, kiss them, and wind the garland,

And do not forget these last asters either; twine in with gentle hands the purple round the tendrils of the wild vine and, with the autumn scene before you, whatever there is left of the green life.

(PGV)

This is a self-portrait: the heart of this homosexual only seems dead: a little 'green life' remains. The behest to gather and kiss the roses is excessive but pathetic because so sentimental and unrealistic.

George's 'philosophy', which is hardly worth taking seriously, but which did not seem so ridiculous at the time it was propounded, derived immediately from Nietzsche, but was severely limited by its furtive homosexual orientation. It was a philosophy of the spirit. The poet (George himself) is priestly reconciler of nature and the intelligence: an unmistakable, if idiosyncratic, version of Nietzsche's 'overman' (q.v.). The poem, static, sculptured, perfect, is literally holy: transcendent of all the experiences that occasioned it; and the poet (*qua* poet) is no single personality but a cosmic ego: in short, a priest-God owing allegiance to nothing and no one beyond himself (except, if he is not George, to George). Hence the mathematical nature of the forms imposed upon his poetry, and the involved structure of his sequences. No concession is to be made to the reader, who either possesses the magic key to the system or—more likely—does not. The attitude to language is resolutely anti-demotic: a poem is profaned if it employs words 'conversationally' or even simply prosaically. The idea is Greek antiquity (or George's idea of it), by the example of which the new Germany—in reality a renewal of the old hero cult—is to be created and Europe saved.

Of more consequence is George's actual poetic method. He achieved a certain austerity of diction by dropping unnecessary words (yet another rejection of ordinary idiom), and by reducing punctuation to a minimum. He employed a 'centred' full-stop or period, in which he has been imitated by, among others, the rough-neck American poet James Dickey. Since he considered his poetry to be the apotheosis of beauty and truth, it required special typography; from 1897 this was provided by Melchior Lechter, 'the William Morris of Germany'.

George's 'system' finally lost what claim to respect it had possessed when, at the beginning of the century, he met and fell in love with a very young, good-looking poet called Maximilian Kronberger ('Maximin'), who died at sixteen. George's worship of this young man was excessively, perhaps wholly, narcissistic—'I, the creature of my own son, am attaining the power of the throne', he wrote—but none the less became a cult. *The Seventh Ring* (*Der siebente Ring*, 1907–11) sublimates his lust for the boy into a massive, mathematically systematized cycle of poems.

George's ideas about poetic language reappear in much more viable and convincing form in Rilke, who wrote: '*No* word in a poem . . . is *identical* with the pure-sounding word in ordinary usage and conversation; the purer legitimacy, the large relationship, the constellation which receives it in verse or in artistic prose alters it to the very kernel of its nature, makes it useless, unfit for mere intercourse, inviolable and lasting'. George lacked the sensibility to write like this; but he must be given credit for his insight.

His best will emerge more clearly when more critics are willing to examine his work in the light of his homosexual state of mind, and consequently to locate those moments when his landscapes most faithfully reflect his despair. His image was that of a poet-priest, a master who read his poems by candlelight in darkened rooms; but the real George is a man in love with men-in-his-own-image—and afraid of the consequences. He introduced new poetic methods into Germany; but his own answer to the 'crisis of speech' was negative. (The fullest translated selections from George are in *Poems*, tr. 1944; *More Poems*, tr. 1945; and *The Works of Stefan George*, tr. 1949. See also PI, TCG, TCGV, PGV, CGP, CGPD.)

Most of George's disciples were talented cranks; others were brilliant but not creative. The chief exceptions were Borchardt, Wolfskehl and Schaeffer. Not one of them was wholly committed to George.

The most interesting of the three was KARL WOLFSKEHL (1869–1948), born at Darmstadt, who was Jewish. He died in New Zealand, where he found refuge from the Nazis. His was a less doctrinaire, more attractive and friendly personality than that of George. Author of dramas and epics as well as poems (in freer forms than those of George), Wolfskehl is most likely to survive in his posthumous collection of letters from New Zealand, *Ten Year Exile: Letters from New Zealand 1938–1948* (*Zehn Jahre Exil: Briefe aus Neu Seeland*, 1959). These are warm, intelligent and generous; above all, they demonstrate the predicament of a German Jew who had lost a Germany in which he was once at home (MGP).

RUDOLF BORCHARDT (1877–1945), another Jew (he fled to Italy before 1933) was independent-minded, erudite and almost self-destructively eccentric. He was predominantly a critic, but some of his poetry—if not his translated epics in his own brand of Middle High German—is due for re-examination. He also wrote a number of short stories, novels, and a play. Borchardt is almost impossibly ponderous; but his intentions may be compared to those of Doughty (attempts to revivify the present language by use of the archaic), Pound ('creative' translation) and, less happily, Swinburne. His brilliance finds it difficult to struggle free of his laboured style, but it is interesting trying to rescue it.

ALBRECHT SCHAEFFER (1885–1950) came from West Prussia. He, too, left Germany on account of the Nazis: he lived in the U.S.A., and died in the year of his return to Germany. He was poet, critic, dramatist and essayist; but his best work is in his fiction. His first mentor was George, and it was under George's influence that he formulated his lifelong view of the world as 'Spirit', whose medium is the poet. None of this is of account, nor are Schaeffer's 'lyrical epics'; but his short fiction, in which his intellectual preoccupations are sometimes swallowed up by other and more pressing concerns, is more substantial. He dealt with prostitution in *Elli, or the Seven Steps* (*Elli oder Sieben Treppen*, 1920) and incest in *The Lattice* (*Das Gitter*, 1923). In the first of these he satirized both Wolfskehl and the cult of George.

A writer who had contact, but no more, with Stefan George, as well as with Dehmel (q.v.), was MAX[IMILIAN] DAUTHENDEY (1867–1918), born in Bavaria of a Russian mother and a German father of French ancestry. He was painter, novelist, short-story writer, dramatist, and, above all, poet. As a painter he was, like the contemporary Englishman Charles Tomlinson (q.v. 1), frustrated; his poems, often captivatingly, try to paint impossible pictures. Doubtless he formed his passion for colour when serving a seven years' apprenticeship in his father's black-and-white photography business. He gained some success as a novelist (for which he was denounced by George, who regarded the novel as mere reportage), but his poetry remained little read until after his death. For Dauthendey nature is suffused with living atoms: stones and mountains have feelings. Life is tragic, but must be lived as a sensitive orgy. His position resembles that of Edith Sitwell (q.v. 1), another gifted but dead-end experimenter with synaesthesia (the concurrent use of several senses or types of sensation; or the description of one sensory experience in terms of another: air sings, taste sounds, sounds or colours taste, and so on). Dauthendey spent his last years in the Far East, where he wrote two volumes of markedly German 'oriental' short stories, full of transcendent sexuality. He also wrote travel books and humour in the vein of Wilhelm Busch (q.v.).

The Viennese HUGO VON HOFMANNSTHAL (1874–1929), who had Jewish and Italian blood, is one of the most astonishing poets of the turn of the century. If the humourless George is representative of a certain morbid and proselytizing streak in the German temperament, then Hofmannsthal, altogether more attractive, represents the best of Vienna in its palmy days—before the collapse of the Austro-Hungarian empire in 1918. All his writing could be said to be about this heady disintegration and collapse. Taken up by George when a precocious and attractive young poet, he was rejected when he gained success through drama. Yet the young poet Hofmannsthal had something in common with George: poetry is the language of inner life; the words it employs must *belong* to the inner life; each prose word has a poetic 'brother-word': itself, used in a different, purer, truer sense. But the theorizing was an afterthought: the young poet was in the throes of creation. Hofmannsthal was a creative and critical genius: what happened to him, and his account of it, is of immense importance for a fuller understanding of what the term 'modern' in literature means.

The boy Hofmannsthal, almost as precocious as Rimbaud, began by writing lyrical poetry of an exquisite quality; in those few years, his confidence was unbounded. He was 'anti-naturalistic', because naturalism, as he saw it, tried to expunge or at best distort the mystery of life; but this poetry transcends theory. Two examples will demonstrate his lyrical mastery. The first, 'The Two' (*Die Beiden*), is a love poem, a perfect expression of the violence that lurks behind tenderness and passion:

> Like the full wine-cup in her hand
> Her smiling mouth was round;
> Her steadfast tread was light and sure,
> No drop spilled on the ground.

> The horse that carried him was young;
> As firm as hers the hand
> That with a careless movement made
> His horse beside her stand.
>
> But when he reached to take the cup,
> Their fingers trembled so,
> They saw between them on the ground
> The red wine darkly flow.
> (tr. James Reeves)

This is effective on a purely realistic level. It also expresses the inevitably brutal side of love: the spilt wine represents (i) the spilt blood of virginity, (ii) the 'wounds' of that discord which romantic love precedes, and (iii) lust's waste of 'holiness'; the communion wine, Christ's blood, flowing on the ground (Hofmannsthal began and ended as a Roman Catholic).

The other poem, 'Ballad of External Life' ('Ballade des äusseren Lebens') may be (and has been) too easily misunderstood as wholly pessimistic:

> And children grown up with deep eyes that know of nothing, grow up and die, and all men go their ways.
>
> And sweet fruits grow from the bitter ones and drop down at night like dead birds and lie there a few days and rot.
>
> And always the wind blows, and again and again we hear and speak many words and feel the joy and weariness of our limbs.
>
> And streets run through the grass, and places are here and there, full of torches, trees, ponds and threatening and deadly withered . . .
>
> Why were these constructed? and never resemble one another? and are innumerable? Why do life, weeping, and death alternate?
>
> What does all this profit us and these games, we who are grown up and eternally alone and wandering never seek any goal?
>
> What does it profit to have seen many such things? And yet

he says much who says 'evening', a word from which profound
meaning and sadness run

like thick honey from hollow honeycombs.

(TCG)

The critic who has stated that here Hofmannsthal 'reflects the
emptiness of human existence' and 'has ... no answer to all his
questionings' has not considered the Platonic world that almost gaily
haunts this vision of despair. This functions as what we call 'beauty'
—a 'beautiful' melancholy—and as the poet's own sheer energy:
his joy in extracting the non-materialistic truth from the gloomy
life-situation. As a critic has pointed out, while the poem does say
that 'Outer life is futile', 'this outer life as reflected in poetry is
"much"' ['he says much who says "evening"']: 'the reader should
remind himself that, according to Hofmannsthal, words used
referentially [i.e. in an "everyday" way: to "get" things: for materialistic, and finally futile purposes] must be distinguished fundamentally for the same words used poetically'. His poem 'can be
called dreary and decadent only if the words that compose it are
understood as being carriers of a life content'.

Hofmannsthal's score or so of youthful lyrical poems, cast in
traditional forms, adumbrate his later, tragic predicament. Hofmannsthal is a poet of 'the romantic agony', who sees the lover, the
lunatic and the poet as intuitive, helpless, passive possessors of the
secret of a lost and yet, paradoxically, attainable world: the Platonic
realm of perfection, of which this world is but an imperfect and
distorted copy.

However, Hofmannsthal—increasingly erudite, a student of cultures foreign to him—had a tough streak of intellectual scepticism:
very early he condemned the aesthete (an aspect of himself) as a
dreamer who must die without ever having lived. And in the poems,
incomparably the best things he ever did, he continually hints at the
necessity for 'engagement' (but not political), for life—for the very
thing that the autocratic George guarded himself against. He was,
as he put it in the prologue to one of his short plays: 'Full of precocious wisdom, early doubt,/And yet with a deep, questioning
longing'.

Hofmannsthal's poetry depicted a precarious unity (implied partly
in the wholeness of the poem itself), precarious because—like the
fatih of ages, like the Austro-Hungarian Empire, like European culture, like the poet's own inspiration—threatened with final disintegration. This explains the baroque element in Hofmannsthal: he

was fascinated by the sugary putrescence of the expiring body, as his librettos for the lush Richard Strauss show; this led him to an admiration for the 'decadent', and for such comparatively inferior writers as Swinburne (q.v. 1), a delirious and metrically gifted but ultimately superficial poet. Little of this rococo extravagance leaked into his early lyric poetry.

Why did Hofmannsthal abandon lyrical poetry? He answers himself in one of the most prophetic of modern literary documents: *The Letter of Lord Chandos to Francis Bacon* (*Ein Brief des Lord Chandos an Francis Bacon*, 1902; tr. in *Selected Prose*, 1952).

The 'Chandos letter', as it is usually called, is an expression of a personal psychological crisis; it was also prophetic of an international cultural cataclysm. In it Hofmannsthal takes on the *persona* of a fictitious Elizabethan, a 'younger son of the Earl of Bath', who writes to Bacon to apologize for (and in one way justify) his 'complete abandonment of literary activity'. In a sense Hofmannsthal solves his problem. But the solution is temporary. The crisis here related was repeated every time Hofmannsthal attempted a creative work (i.e. perpetually); it was seldom resolved. The subject of the letter is really that *Sprachkrise* of which George was aware but with which he failed to deal.

Suddenly, for Hofmannsthal, the world appeared as without meaning or coherence; he lost his faith in the customary modes of thought. As a consequence language itself, and his faith in it, failed: 'Words fell to pieces in my mouth like mouldy mushrooms'. Chandos-Hofmannsthal is 'forced to see everything . . . in uncanny close-up'; he can no longer approach men or their actions 'with the simplifying eye of custom and habit'. In other words, *scepticism* and *curiosity*—those qualities so dangerous to Catholicism, and for so long resisted by it—have entered into his soul. Words 'turn and twist unceasingly', and at the end they reveal 'only emptiness'. There can be no more lyrical poetry because the author has lost confidence in the magic of words; the successful young poet had maintained the tension between love of death and resistance of it, between a cynical, sceptical solipsism and an outward-looking love. Such maintenances are little short of miraculous.

In such early playlets as *Death and the Fool* (*Der Tor und der Tod*, 1893; tr. 1914; *The Fool and Death*, 1930; and in *Poems and Verse Plays*, 1961), as well as in the poems, the urge to create takes precedence over intellectual anxieties. The protagonist of *Death and the Fool* is Claudio, an aesthete—cynical, impressionist (everything, for him, 'passes'), sexually selfish—who is confronted by death in the guise of an elegant violinist. Certainly, the play may be said to have a 'moral': the young nobleman, named after the condemned man in *Measure for Measure* who is not ready for death, finally discovers, to his horror, that he has not lived. But *Death and the Fool* is not an 'explicit . . . warning against aestheticism', although it has been described as such: there is too much vitality in Claudio's monologue, too much ambiguity of approach. What still fascinates Hofmanns-thal—although he clearly sees the sterility of his hero's life—is de-cadence, the mystery of death, the denial of conventional morality.

Michael Hamburger has implied that Hofmannsthal's work did not lose power: that he 'reversed' the well-established German pro-cess of turning from prose to (over-dignified) verse, and moved from the lyrical dramas of his youth to 'the poetic prose' of his 'last and greatest tragedy, *Der Turm*; a prose both highly colloquial and con-densed'. (Another critic describes it as 'creeping'.) Hofmannsthal did remain intelligent and aware; but the large-scaled *Der Turm* does not equal, let alone develop from, his early lyrics. . . . Even if the 'greatness' of his latter years was more intellectually viable and less empty than that of, say, Hauptmann—still, he had, in his way, been forced to abdicate as poet. This is not discreditable: many poets have refused to abdicate. . . .

We may trace through Hofmannsthal's dramas the fate of his desperate attempt to preserve and reinvigorate the traditions of the nineteenth century. After 1902 he was essentially a progressive con-servative (never a reactionary). He shunned expressionist techniques, and cultivated a symbolist realism which he regarded as 'conser-vatively revolutionary'. He tried in a public capacity to preserve European culture (he founded, with Max Reinhardt, the Salzburg Festival). His comments on individual writers were penetrating, but his programmatic criticism is rightly described as 'cloudily in-effectual'. Hofmannsthal remained true to himself: a 'modern', an expressionist or surrealist Hofmannsthal, would have been wholly factitious. But most of his later work, judged in the light of the earliest, lacks, for all its admirable qualities, inner strength, originality and conviction of language. Hofmannsthal was a traditionalist, but one who saw into the abyss, that 'emptiness' or 'void' of which he had written in 1902. It is ironic, to say the least, that he had to pay such a price for his sensitivity, intelligence and social conscientiousness. His youthful phase he called a 'pre-existence'.

After 1902, creatively 'blocked', he began to adapt and recast plays of the past (he had done this before, but in a different spirit, with Euripides' *Alcestis*, 1893): *Electra* (*Elektra*, 1903; tr. in *Chief Contem-porary Dramatists*, 1930; *Selected Plays and Libretti*, 1964), *Oedipus and the Sphinx* (*Oedipus und die Sphinx*, 1905), three of Molière's plays, *The*

Play of Everyman (*Jedermann*, 1911; tr. 1917). This last was highly successful. For his final play, *The Tower* (*Der Turm*, 1925, rev. 1927; tr. in *Selected Plays and Libretti*, 1964), he drew on Calderon's *Life is a Dream* (*La Vida es Sueño*): a prince is imprisoned in a tower by his father, who fears that he will supersede him before the time falls due. Sigismund, the prince, represents the spiritual authority by which a country needs (Hofmannsthal implies) to be ruled; he becomes the leader of a non-Marxist proletarian revolution, but is poisoned by the proto-Fascist Olivier. In the 1925 version his deathbed is visited by an orphan who pledges to carry on his peaceful and purifying work. But in 1927 there is only Sigismund's last despairing remark: 'Witness that I was here, though none has recognized me'. Soon afterwards Hofmannsthal, shattered by his son's suicide, died.

In *The Tale of 672. Night* (*Das Märchen der 672. Nacht*, 1904), a novella, Hofmannsthal tried to do justice to the theme of *Death and the Fool*. A late, and posthumously published, fragment—begun, however, before 1914—was yet another attempt to solve the problem of 'aesthetic sterility': *Andreas, or the United Ones* (*Andreas, oder Die Vereinigten*, 1930; tr. 1936) deals with temptation in Venice (like Mann's *Death in Venice*, q.v.); the hero has, significantly, almost the same name as that of the seventeen-year-old Hofmannsthal's first play, *Yesterday* (*Gestern*, 1891). But none of his late fiction equals his few 'pre-Chandos' short stories, notably 'Cavalry Patrol' ('Reiter-geschichte', 1899). There was cruel justice in Hermann Bahr's (q.v.) remarks that 'I cannot forgive him for not having died at twenty [twenty-eight would have been nearer the mark]; if he had, he would have been the most beautiful figure in world literature', and that he had mistaken, in Hofmannsthal, 'the smiling death of Austria for a holy spring tide'.

RAINER MARIA RILKE (1875–1926), christened René, was born in Prague, of German descent, and Austrian nationality; in 1918 he found himself a Czech. His story of an aristocratic ancestry may have been invented: actually Rilke was descended from Sudeten trades-men and peasants, and received a middleclass upbringing ordinary in everything save his peculiar mother, who pretended until he was five that he was a girl called Sophie, with long hair and dolls. Rilke was one of this century's great originals, and for this reason it would be misleading to call him an 'expressionist': he incorporated what expressionism stood for in his work, but much more as well. He was not associated with the expressionist or with any other movement. The crisis he suffered before the First World War, out of which the *Duino Elegies* came, coincided with the expressionist movement. (All Rilke's important poetry has been tr., some many times, into

English, most devotedly but not always successfully by J. B. Leishman, who sentimentally lamented Rilke's fundamental hatred of Christianity. The best complete tr. of his masterpiece, *The Duinese Elegies, Duineser Elegien*, 1912–22, is by Ruth Spiers: this has not yet been published in book form owing to copyright difficulties. *Duino Elegies*, tr. J. B. Leishman and S. Spender, 1939; *Poems 1906–1926*, tr. J. B. Leishman, 1959; *New Poems, Neue Gedichte*, 1907, 1908, tr. J. B. Leishman, 1964; *Sonnets to Orpheus, Sonette an Orpheus*, 1923, tr. J. B. Leishman, 1936; *The Book of Hours, Das Stundenbuch*, 1905, tr. A. L. Peck, 1961; *Poems from The Book of Hours*, tr. sel. Babette Deutsch; *Selected Letters*, tr. R. F. C. Hull, 1946. See also MEP, PGV, CGP, CGPD, MGP, TCG, TCGV, PI.)

Rilke wrote poetry in Italian, French and Russian, as well as German; he also wrote fiction and drama (between 1895 and 1901). (His early autobiographical novel, *Ewald Tragy*, c. 1898, published in German, 1944, has not been tr.; but *The Notebook of Malte Laurids Brigge, Die Aufzeichnungen des Malte Laurids Brigge*, 1910, tr. 1930, and the earlier *The Tale of the Love and Death of Cornet Christopher Rilke, Die Weise von Liebe und Tod des Cornets Christoph Rilke*, 1906, tr. 1932, are available.)

Rilke, who rightly called himself 'a bungler of life', tried to behave responsibly, but remained in certain respects innocent, childlike—and selfish. He was, if it were an adequate term (which it is not), a 'womanizer'. His being was dedicated to his poetry; essentially the facts of his life interested him only inasmuch as they affected this. The Russian-born German novelist and critic LOU ANDREAS SALOMÉ (1861–1937), to whom Nietzsche had proposed and who was later to become a valued associate of Freud, became his mistress when he was twenty-two, and throughout his life he turned to her as a confessor and (almost) a muse. 'She moves fearlessly midst the most burning mysteries', he wrote, 'which do nothing to her. . . .' But he could not live even with her, and their physical relationship ended when he married the sculptress Clara Westhoff in 1901. However, he could not live with Clara either, and before long he was alone in Paris. Until his death he pursued a number of relationships with women younger than himself; these always stopped short, not of sexual contact, but of permanent domestic cohabitation, which he would not endure.

Once in Paris, Rilke became secretary to the sculptor Rodin. He had had important enthusiasms before: Italy (where he met Stefan George, whom he continued to admire); the Danish novelist Jens Per Jacobsen (1847–85), a sensuous realist who made an ideal of flawless work (as distinct from life) and who celebrated an autonomous nature; Russia; monkhood; and then the painters' community near Bremen to which his wife belonged. But this new admiration was the most intense of all: Rodin, like Rilke himself, insulated his work from 'ordinary life'; it was (Rilke said) 'isolated from the spectator as though by a non-conducting vacuum'. Rilke told his wife in 1902, possibly tactlessly, that Rodin had told him that he had married 'parce qu'il faut avoir une femme': another bond between them. He had chosen not bourgeois—or even bohemian—happiness, but art. 'Rodin has lived nothing that is not in his work.' However, Rodin overworked him, and he left his household abruptly; but later there was a reconciliation.

Rilke's first notable poetic work was *The Book of Hours*, divided into 'The Book of Monkish Life', 'The Book of Pilgrimage' and 'The Book of Poverty and Death'. He called these poems 'prayers'; but the God he invokes in them is not God the Creator—or any Christian God. Rilke consistently maintained his animosity to all forms of Christianity, and to Jesus Christ in particular, all his life; on his death-bed he refused to see a priest. His God has 'no use for the Christians': he is a figure existing only in the future, utterly meaningless, in fact non-existent, without humanity, and above all *living truly*: he is a partly Nietzschean God who will be perfected by artists, and of course in particular by Rilke himself.

The later Rilke may be discerned in some of the poems in *The Book of Hours*, but in general fluency, in the form of technique, takes over and submerges the sense. The author is still a thoroughgoing romantic.

It was in some of the *New Poems* published in 1907 and 1908 that Rilke first succeeded in translating external phenomena into 'inwardness'. Since at least 1899 it had been his ambition to express the 'thingness of things' by understanding their spirit and then expressing this in new forms of words: to destroy the killing material necessity of making *definitions*. It is significant that at about this time Hofmannsthal, in 'Chandos', was worrying about exactly the same problem: how can we be sure, he asked, what the word 'apple' really 'means'? It means one thing to one person in one context, and so on. . . . Rilke distrusted language, too; but eventually, unlike Hofmannsthal, he found confidence in himself as a worthy sounding-board for nature. Hofmannsthal declined material irresponsibility: he felt impelled to care for the future, to be a guardian of what was best in the tradition; to found a Salzburg Festival. Rilke, seeing with cruel shrewdness that 'ordinary life', political or merely humanitarian activism, required *definitions*, over-simplifications, rejected that kind of life: he deliberately cultivated what he called 'the child's wise incapacity to understand'.

The very first of the so-called *New Poems* to be written, in the winter of 1902–3, was the famous 'Panther', which he saw in the Jardin des Plantes in Paris. This poem, whose method Rilke was not to adopt fully until about 1906, is self-descriptive, but only by dint of extreme concentration upon the object itself.

> His gaze those bars keep passing is so misted
> with tiredness, it can take in nothing more.
> He feels as though a thousand bars existed,
> and no more world beyond them than before.
>
> Those supply-powerful paddings, turning there
> in tiniest of circles, well might be
> the dance of forces round a centre where
> some mighty will stands paralyticly.
>
> Just now and then the pupil's noiseless shutter
> is lifted.—Then an image will indart,
> down through the limbs' intensive stillness flutter,
> and end its being in the heart.
>
> (tr. J. B. Leishman)

This deals, despairingly, with the poet's own problem of 'images': the panther, imprisoned by bars, lives in a world of bars. His will, and his enormous energy, are stupefied. He does sometimes experience a picture, an image, of the real world beyond the bars; but this is then 'killed' by his trapped, disappointed and frustrated heart. Rilke had written in an earlier poem: 'You are murdering what you define, what *I* love to hear singing'. The bars stand for both the habit of constricting reality by defining it, and the materialism that leads to this habit; thus truth 'ends its being in the heart'. Almost a quarter of a century after writing this, Rilke said in a letter: 'A house, in the American sense, an American apple or one of the vines of that country has *nothing* in common with the house, the fruit, the grape into which have entered the hope and meditation of our forefathers. The lived and living things that share our thought, these are on the decline and can no more be replaced. *We are perhaps the last to have known such things*'. Rilke always had a true love for things— the objects, persons, situations of his poems; and 'The Panther' was his first poem to successfully express the anguished discrepancy that he felt between his inner vision and the destructive external world.

But the *New Poems* were also influenced by the formal, anti-romantic elegance and concentration achieved by such French poets as Verlaine and Mallarmé as well as by Stefan George and Hof-mannsthal: his interest in Parnassian poetry helped Rilke to struggle against the fluency that, because it becomes so facile, spoils *The Book of Hours*. These new poems may be seen as a reconciliation of the aims of different schools: of the 'romantic', with its insistence on the importance of the poet, with the more 'classical' views of poets such as Mallarmé, who wished to achieve an autonomous poetry that was divorced from the life of the poet; a reconciliation, indeed, of feeling and thought.

It was by submitting himself to the strict discipline necessary for the composition of the *New Poems* that Rilke was later able to complete *The Duinese Elegies* and their successors, *Sonnets to Orpheus*. But before he could write this last work he endured a mental and physical crisis, during which he questioned the value of poetry itself. It is because Rilke fought to dedicate himself to poetry, because he so fiercely questioned the validity of what he had chosen to do with his life—to absorb it into art—that we cannot call him a facile or super-ficial devotee of 'art for art's sake'. 'Art', he said in the years im-mediately before the writing of the first elegies, 'is superfluous. . . . Can art heal wounds, can it take away the bitterness of death?' And he would have liked, he said, to be a country doctor. Yet he miserably and increasingly succumbed to erotic temptation—temptation because in every case he reached a point at which he felt that he had to dissociate himself, thus causing unhappinesses which deeply distressed him. He could not resist sex, although he desired to; but he could not accept its human consequences. He went some way towards resolving this dilemma in his poetry, which is more than most of his kind can do, and he thus gave a valuable account of the manner in which the creative imagination threatens personal virtue. Whether that account is worth his transgression of virtue (by causing unhappiness) is an unanswered question—but one he never hesitated fearlessly to ask himself. The main theme of *The Duinese Elegies* is 'the virtually anti-human or extra-human lot of the poet' (Eudo C. Mason).

Rilke's crisis was partly precipitated by the writing, in Paris, of *The Notebook of Malte Laurids Brigge* (begun in 1904). This consists of a series of notebook-jottings by a Danish poet who has come to Paris. It has been said that Malte 'was' Rilke, but Rilke denied it. Of course he was not Rilke: no fictional character can 'be' a real one, whether this is intended or not. Malte was, however, a picture of the 'human' Rilke: a mixture of the man as he was in his 'non-poetic' existence, the man he wished to be, and the man of whose life and death (Malte perishes in a terrible unspecified way) he was mortally afraid. The story is of one who has, like the prodigal son, fled from love—as Rilke always did when it seemed that he might be caught and trapped by it. Malte was made Danish both because Rilke could thus distance himself from him, and because the writings of J. P. Jacobsen (q.v.), particularly the reminiscences of childhood in the novel *Niels Lyhne* (1880; tr. 1919), and other Scandinavian writers such as Herman Bang (q.v.), had always excited and moved him. The re-creation of Malte's childhood is based on an idealization of Rilke's own childhood (Malte is, of course, of aristocratic descent) and on his thrilled response to Jacobsen, from whom he also took over and developed the notion of 'authentic death' (*der eigene Tod*): a dignified, profoundly sceptical and anti-Christian desire to accept death as a part of life. (Sartre, q.v., spoke, in his moving obituary of Camus, q.v., of the 'pure . . . endeavour of a man to recover each instant of his existence from his future death'.) Malte's city is a nightmare; his contact with urban life is continuously horrifying.

It is often suggested, especially by those who wish to claim Rilke as a potential Christian, that this novel is representative of a cult of decadence and 'disease' found in the work of Maeterlinck and Verhaeren (qq.v.). Rilke read both these poets, but the judgement is altogether misleading. For *Malte* may fairly be looked upon as both a negation and a culmination of the *Künstlerroman* (q.v.): the artist's true education is death: 'everyone carries within him', he wrote, 'his own death'.

Rilke, then, underwent the most serious crisis of his life in these years of the composition of *Malte*: his faith in language, in his own capacity to achieve a dedicated poetic life, in art itself, was threatened. He solved—or partially solved—the problem, which had affected his delicate health, by the sporadic achievement of a trance-like state in which he was able to write poetry. In May 1911 he wrote to his rich, intelligent friend and patron Princess Marie von Thurn und Taxis-Hohenlohe: '. . . this long drought is gradually reducing my soul to starvation. . . . as if I had completely lost the ability to bring about the conditions that might help me . . .'. The Princess invited him to her castle at Duino, on the Adriatic coast, and after Christmas left him there alone. In a letter to Lou Andreas-Salomé, to whom he nearly always addressed himself in moments of crisis, he pointed out that psychoanalysis 'was too fundamental a help' for him: he did not want to be 'cleared up'. And he spoke of his life as 'a long convalescence'. A few days later, in another letter to Lou, he astonishingly diagnosed the 'inward' aspect of the disease (leukaemia) that was to kill him in fourteen years' time: 'It may be that the continual distraughtness in which I live has bodily causes in part, is a thinness of the blood'. This indeed is an apt characterization of Rilke the human being. He has been called 'cold'; but that epithet does not accurately describe him. His poetry is anything but cold. However, his relationships can legitimately be called 'thin-blooded', and with just the sinister overtone that our retrospective knowledge of his death adds to the passage in the letter: Rilke was well aware of how sinister poetry itself was. But now in the castle of Duino he waited for his anguish to awaken his creative powers in the dangerous process he called 'reversal', in which he received his poetry almost, as it were, by dictation. One day he did 'hear' a voice calling the words with which the first elegy begins: 'Who, if I shrieked out in pain, would hear me from amongst / The orders of angels?' He wrote the whole of the first two elegies; then, in three short spells—oases in a decade of silence—he wrote three more. The rest were written in early 1922.

Rilke has frequently and wrongly been approached as a thinker or philosopher rather than as the poet he was. His poems must be read as accounts of the destiny of a dedicated poet tormented by the need for religious certainties in a godless universe. Rilke's angels represent many things, but chiefly the terrible and beautiful heart of a universe that can offer no hope of immortality. They are neither Christian nor 'real'. To call them symbols, however, is to oversimplify. They are poetic destiny, hard truth, apostles of 'inwardness'; whereas ordinary perception simply sees, the poet, in Rilke's term, '*in*-sees': discerns the *thingness* of things. Again, these angels call upon the amorous poet to put aside his sexual curiosity. In his life Rilke was morally humiliated, selfish and disingenuous in his tiresome search for a woman who, having been enjoyed by him, would 'withdraw': become an 'Eloisa' (i.e. Heloise). In his poetry he ceases to be disingenuous. Rilke's elegies trace the course of his engagement with his angels, from despair to rejoicing, back to despair, and finally to a kind of acceptance of himself.

The first lines of the first elegy ask the question, 'How can we endure beauty in a godless universe?':

Who, if I shrieked out in pain, would hear me from amongst
The orders of angels? Even if one would take me
To his breast, I should be overwhelmed and die in his
Stronger existence: for the beautiful is nothing
But the first apprehension of the terrible,
Which we can still just endure: we respect the cool scorn
Of its refusal to destroy us. Each angel is terrible.

And so I swallow down the signal-note of black sobs.
Alas, with whom can we share our solitude?
Not with angels and not with men; but even
The percipient animals well understand
That we are lost in the interpreted world.
Perhaps there is just one tree on a hillside
Daily to reassure, or yesterday's street,
Or a trivial habit enduring for its own sake. . . .

For a gloss, in English poetry, on the difficulties of the phrase 'the interpreted world', one cannot do better than turn to Robert Graves' (q.v. 1) poem 'The Cool Web' with its evocative line, 'There's a cool web of language winds us in'.

After Rilke had finally completed all the elegies—they were at least partly delayed by erotic complications of his own making—he wrote, very rapidly, the sequence of fifty-five free sonnets called *Sonnets to Orpheus*, who is addressed as the God of poetry (and as an idealized Rilke). This is a more modest sequence than the elegies, but it in some ways equals it. It is important to recognize that Orpheus here is not the 'angel' of the elegies, but 'the exact opposite. . . . Whereas the Angel had been the apotheosis of self-sufficient Narcissism . . . Orpheus is convinced of as freely giving himself . . . to all things . . .' (Eudo C. Mason). In this sequence Rilke went a long way towards redeeming the human side of himself from the charge of coldness and remoteness; and he himself became, in his last years, more approachable.

Rilke, a pagan poet, possessed as much scope and linguistic capacity as any poet of the century. To regard him as primarily a thinker or mystic is a serious mistake; but his attitude towards death may have something to teach his readers, inasmuch as it can help them (Christian or not) to overcome the disastrous complacency of official Christianity, with its promise of an earth-like heaven. In his repudiation of bourgeois pseudo-certitude he showed much courage; as much as other more politically orientated writers who exposed other failings of the bourgeois life. Although Rilke transcends all the theoretical aspects of the modern movement, he is essential to an understanding of it.

IV

Most of the clear-cut forerunners of expressionism were dramatists. The most important was the Swedish August Strindberg (q.v.), but the others were mostly Austrians and Germans, social satirists and critics among them. Expressionism as a phenomenon in poetry and fiction is best approached via the drama, where it takes its simplest form—as the externalization of internal events. This was preceded by the deliberate depiction of unreality, or the baffling mixture of it with reality.

The most famous play of the Austrian HERMANN BAHR (1863–1934), *The Concert* (*Das Konzert*, 1909; CCD), a farce about a wife's clever plot to recover her pianist husband's errant affections by making him jealous, foreshadows expressionism in no way at all; but its author, primarily a critic and publicist but a novelist as well as dramatist (about eighty plays) and theatrical producer, eventually became a spokesman of expressionism; his book *Expressionism* (*Expressionismus*, 1914; tr. 1925) was not a merely opportunistically late one.

Bahr was an intelligent although never profound man, genuinely sensitive to literary movements and to the impulses behind them. First an Ibsenian naturalist and an associate of Holz (q.v.) and his circle, he soon fell under the influence of French symbolism, and became the leading spirit (as he claimed, the founder) of the *Jungwien* (Young Viennese) group, which included Hofmannsthal and Schnitzler (qq.v.). He understood naturalism better than any of its leading proponents, and brilliantly prophesied that it would be succeeded by 'a mysticism of the nerves'. His novel *The Good School* (*Die gute Schule*, 1890), a polemic in favour of sexual experience (the 'good school' of the title), tried to put decadent 'nervousness' into effect, but is not more than a patchwork of French influences. Eventually Bahr returned to the Roman Catholic Church and to repentant championship of the baroque that he now considered to be the cradle of all Austrian genius.

PETER ALTENBERG (ps. RICHARD ENGLÄNDER, 1859–1919), who was born and died in Vienna, has been amusingly described as 'a bizarre character frequenting literary cafés' who fervently 'loved ladies noble and very ignoble'. A friend of Bahr's, Altenberg was a poseur most of whose energy went into his café life—'a presidential poet with his halo of harlots'—but his impressionistic prose sketches, when not too studied, have sharpness and charm. Hedonistic but hypochondriacal advocate of a healthy open-air life and frequent baths, Altenberg was more a man of his time than he or most of his friends realized, but his fragmented method of writing had some influence, especially in Russia—he was certainly read, for example, by Elena Guro (q.v. 4). There was something pathetic and insubstantial about the semi-invalid Altenberg with his insistence on physiological perfection as the basis of all other perfection and his hymns to his own health; but Hofmannsthal (q.v.) paid him just tribute when he said that his books 'were as full of dear little stories as a basket of fruit'.

The Viennese Jew ARTHUR SCHNITZLER (1862–1931), novelist and dramatist, trained as a doctor, was much influenced by Freud, with whom he conducted a correspondence from 1906. He did not begin writing creatively until his late twenties, when he began contributing to Viennese periodicals under the name of 'Anatol', the name he selected for the hero of his first series of playlets.

Schnitzler accomplished much in spite of limited technical resources. He combined an understanding love-terror of his disintegrating milieu, a Don Juanism rather resembling Rilke's (q.v.), and, most importantly, an intuition of subconscious sexual motivation. When Freud read his play *Paracelsus* (1897; tr. 1913) he remarked that he had not thought an author could know so much. . . . He is most famous for the sexually cynical, meticulous but essentially light-weight *Merry-go-round* (*Reigen*, 1900; tr. 1953; filmed as *La Ronde*, 1950); but Schnitzler's best full-length play is probably *Professor Bernhardi* (1912; tr. 1936). This is a subtle and objective study of the position of the Jew in pre-war Vienna. A Jewish doctor refuses a priest access to a girl who is dying of an abortion: she is in a state of euphoria, and will spend a happier last hour in ignorance of her fate. (Actually, she is informed of it by the ward-sister, so the Professor's gesture is useless.) After much unpleasant intrigue, Bernhardi goes to prison—from whence, however, he is triumphantly released when a Prince requires his services. The priest calls on Bernhardi to tell him that he has agreed with him in this case—but could not say so in public.

In *Anatol* (tr. 1933–4), and other plays on the autobiographical theme of philandering, Schnitzler has many keen insights into the sadistic, masochistic and other nerve-strains of romantic love, but does not always succeed in rising above his own personal difficulties. Further, his account of the love-process (his own), its rapture always declining into pathological jealousy, boredom or disgust, is too specifically decadent-Viennese: Schnitzler, whose psychiatric knowledge caused him to question the scientific efficacy of naturalism, is always the analyst of the decadent culture; but he was humanly very much of it, for all his capacity for detachment. When, as in *Playing with Love* (*Liebelei*, 1895; tr. 1914), he succeeds in presenting a woman whose substantial and wholesome emotions genuinely expose the shallowness of a philanderer, he ultimately collapses into rhetoric, facile moralization and sentimentality.

He is at his best when he avoids too much heady, decadent elegance on the one hand, and guilty morality on the other. Then he does adumbrate a non-naturalistic method of describing internal reality adequate to his needs. The interior dialogue (an early example) of the short story 'None but the Brave' ('Leutnant Gustl', 1901; tr. 1926) is less an ambitious extension of naturalism than a genuine foreshadowing of modern techniques: the human deficiencies of the horrible Leutnant as he contemplates suicide are unerringly revealed. Even subtler is the later novella, 'Fräulein Else' (1924; tr. 1930): a financier names as price for the redemption of a girl's father that she strip for him in her hotel room at midnight; she does strip, but in the lobby of the hotel—and then kills herself.

The first and best of Schnitzler's two novels, *The Road to the Open* (*Der Weg ins Freie*, 1908; tr. 1923) portrays a vast social canvas with a success surprising to those who think of the author only as a miniaturist: once again, the author is at his best in his remarkably objective treatment of his fellow Jews.

Schnitzler is a pioneer in interior monologue and invented, out of his technical inability to create dramatic action, a new kind of 'cyclic' play. Most likely of all to survive are some dozen or more of his novellas. Ten representative ones are collected, in an excellent translation by Eric Sutton, in *Little Novels* (1929); also notable for its foreshadowings of methods to come is 'Bertha Garlan' ('Frau Bertha Garlan', 1901; tr. 1913), a meticulous tracing of different kinds of sexual processes.

The poet, novelist and playwright RICHARD BEER-HOFMANN (1866–1945), another Viennese Jew, and a close friend of Hofmannsthal (q.v.), was not as gifted as Schnitzler, though in the earlier *Jungwien* period he was more prominent. Beer-Hofmann, who was a talented theatrical producer, began as a typical neo-romantic and ended as an unequivocal upholder of the Jewish tradition. He was a more lush and flamboyant writer than Schnitzler, and had none of his consulting-room dryness—for which he substituted a lyrical, quasi-religious element. His first play was *The Count of Charolais* (*Der Graf von Charolais*, 1904; pt. tr. *This Quarter* [Paris], II, 3, 1931), an adaptation of the English Elizabethan play *The Fatal Dowry* by John Ford and Philip Massinger. This is decidedly decadent—a very proper little lady is turned into a lustful tart by a professional seducer—but naturalistic at least inasmuch as all its characters are represented as driven by an uncontrollable destiny. The most successful character is a senile judge who gives his daughter away to a 'noble' man who will presumably spare her the horrors of sex. He never completed his intended trilogy on the life of King David, but the frankly Zionist

Jacob's Dream (*Jaakobs Traum*, 1918; tr. 1946), the prelude, proved popular on the stage; the first and only one of the cycle itself to be completed was *Young David* (*Der junge David*, 1933). One of his poems, 'Lullaby for Miriam', written in 1898, was once famous, but has not survived the test of time. The death-ridden novel *The Death of George* (*Der Tod Georges*, 1900), about the premature death of a gifted man and the terminal illness of an imaginary woman is as a whole oppressive and even affected; but it is not without psychological merit. The narrator, Paul, may fairly be described as a 'nerve mystic': the presentation of his state of mind is more interesting than a bald account of the plot suggests. Like his creator, Paul eventually escapes from his mystical longings into a not ignoble but unfortunately creatively sterile Jewishness.

OTTO JULIUS BIERBAUM (1865–1910) has been referred to as a 'gifted university scholar' who took 'to light literature much as a prostitute takes to her trade'; but this is to misunderstand him. He was a sort of German Alfred Jarry (q.v.) without the dedication to self-destruction. He was a co-founder of two important periodicals, *Pan* and *Die Insel*, which later became the famous publishing house Insel-Verlag. Neither his poems nor his novels have depth, because they were conceived in self-satisfaction; but his consciously Wildean flippancy, irreverence and hatred of sexual hypocrisy were genuine qualities. His cabaret verse and his initiation of the 'Literary Cabaret' movement ('Überbrettl'), conventional in form but truly gay, indirectly influenced Brecht (q.v.). His various novels are deliberately decadent fantasies after the manner of Wilde (q.v. 1) and Huysmans (q.v.).

The poet and translator RUDOLF ALEXANDER SCHRÖDER (1878–1962), who was born in Bremen, helped Bierbaum to found *Die Insel*. Versatile and talented, he was a modest man, with, as the saying goes (creatively speaking), much to be modest about. His conservative protestantism was too rigid to allow of much originality, as may be seen in his too formal poetry, which is full of orthodoxly Christian platitudes.

He wrote a number of hymns. Much of what little creative energy he had was vitiated by his pious dogmatism; but then it might well be said that the latter was but a reflection of the former. A fine classicist, his best work is undoubtedly his translation from Greek and Latin poetry—Homer, Virgil, Horace. During the years of the Third Reich he maintained a dignified neutrality; some of his poems circulated secretly. Despite his undoubtedly blinkered vision, Schröder possessed personal nobility and courage.

The playwright FRANK WEDEKIND (1864–1918), born in Hanover

but brought up in Switzerland, was a less fortuitous anticipator of expressionism and surrealism. Wedekind was successively secretary to a Danish confidence-man (whom he portrayed in *The Marquis von Keith*), circus-worker and cabaret-entertainer (he sang Überbrettl songs to his own guitar) before he took to writing plays. Cripple (he was lame) and showman (he liked to present and act in his own plays), Wedekind fought all his life against the censors; it is important to realize that he achieved his present reputation only at the end of his life. He sang many of his famous ballads at 'The Eleven Hangmen' ('Die elf Scharfrichter'), the literary cabaret in Munich. He was for most of his life regarded as a clown. It is said that even as he died (of acute appendicitis) he sang his own song 'Search fearlessly for every sin/For out of sin comes joy. . . .' And he himself was surely, in some way, author of the final hilarious scene: the speaker of the graveside eulogy read from his paper: 'Frank Wedekind, we loved you. Your spirit is with us. Here falter, tears. . . .'

It is sometimes said that Wedekind is a 'naturalist-expressionist', But although his plays incorporate some realism, his main impulse, besides gaiety (that should not be forgotten, and only will be in petit-bourgeois disgust), is indignation rather than a sense of an inexorable fate. Wedekind was a solitary figure, best regarded—as has been suggested—as a bridge between the *Sturm und Drang* period (the 'Storm and Stress' movement of the German 1770s, characterized by a reaction against reason, and by reliance upon inspiration), particularly its doomed prodigy, the brilliantly gifted dramatist Georg Büchner (1813–37), and expressionism.

Wedekind's first important play *Spring's Awakening* ('*Frühlings Erwachen*, 1891; FTS) is his most lyrical and human. Hideous adults—caricature schoolmasters and 'respectable' parents, all representative of the tyrannical and repressive father—penalize and attempt to destroy adolescents who have discovered the powers of sex. A boy impregnates a girl, who dies of the abortion her parents force upon her. He, expelled from school, is tempted to commit suicide by the ghost of a fellow-pupil (carrying his head under his arm) who has shot himself for failing an examination; but he is saved from this by a moralist in evening dress (Wedekind). The mechanisms of the adults' antihuman behaviour are brilliantly revealed; and there is more feeling in the depiction of the young people than Wedekind ever again displayed.

Earth Spirit and its sequel *Pandora's Box* (*Der Erdgeist*, 1895; *Die Büchse der Pandora*, 1904; FTS) combine social satire with a morbid but always energetic dissection of femininity. Alban Berg made his unfinished opera, *Lulu*, out of them. Wedekind wrote the play as a whole, but was forced by censorship troubles to divide it. *Lulu* certainly had some effect on Brecht. The stage is peopled by crooks, whores and perverts; their centre is the destructive Lulu, whom Wedekind regarded as the archetypal woman. But he had two sides to him: the moralist-prophet of the joys of sex; and a more personal fear of women, perhaps originally connected with his deformity. In the final scene Lulu is murdered by Jack the Ripper. We see an aspect of Wedekind himself in the role of Lulu's discoverer, Dr. Schön (Dr. Beautiful), an absolute hedonist. He is destroyed by Lulu, since he understands her and is therefore a hindrance to her own total triumph. Clearly Wedekind feared the consequences of his own view of life. He was not a profound thinker, but his work reflects admirably the beginnings of our nerve-shot age. He picked up much of his attitude towards women from Strindberg (q.v.), whose second wife was for a time his mistress.

The *Marquis von Keith* (1901; FMR 2) celebrates a confidence-trickster: cynical, it is also gay. *Such is Life* (*König Nicolo oder So ist das Leben*, 1902; tr. 1916) is one of Wedekind's most interesting plays, and his most lucid spiritual autobiography. A king (Wedekind, the artist) is dethroned by a butcher (the common herd). He takes on various humiliating jobs, and finally becomes an actor. The butcher-king is entertained (like the herd) by his acting, and offers to make him court jester (Wedekind as clown entertaining the bourgeois). He dies, and is buried in the royal tomb. This perfectly embodies Wedekind's view of himself as tragic and trapped clown.

Wedekind also wrote some notable short stories in the Nineties, of which 'The Fire of Egliswyl' (in *Fireworks, Feuerwerk*, 1905) is the most outstanding. A promiscuous village boy falls in love with a frigid servant-girl; when at last he climbs into her bedroom he finds that her coldness and that of the weather, combined, have made him impotent. He then sets fire to all the houses in which his previous victims live, and returns triumphantly to his servant-girl. But she, cheated of her own satisfaction, denounces him. In another delightful tale a husband calls on a friend. This friend has his wife in bed with him. He covers her face, thus exposing her body: the husband, not recognizing her, congratulates him on his good taste.

Another important pre-expressionist was CARL STERNHEIM (1878–1942). The son of a Jewish banker, Sternheim was born in Leipzig, but spent the latter part of his life in Brussels. His third wife was Wedekind's daughter, Pamela.

Sternheim, who was prey to increasing depression and restlessness, is one of the few successful twentieth-century German comic playwrights; his humour is savage, stemming from his Jewishness and

consequent sense of belonging to an isolated minority, and it lacks
Wedekind's sexual morbidity. He was the creator, in his dialogue,
of what is often called a 'telegraphic style': a parodically staccato
series of epigrammatic exchanges which at least hint at the 'alienation effect' (q.v.) later to be created by Brecht. His best plays move
very fast, and their characters are clearly conceived of as 'stage
people'. Sternheim punished the bourgeois, in fact, by exploiting an
exaggeration of their own clipped speech—a speech-style in which,
as Walter Sokel has said, 'they aped the Prussian ruling caste'.

Sternheim's most famous work is the eleven-play collection *From
the Heroic Life of the Bourgeoisie* (published 1922); the best are the first
two of a trilogy consisting of *The Knickers*, *A Place in the World* and
1913 (*Die Hose*, 1911; MT6; *Der Snob*, 1913; tr. in *Eight European
Plays*, 1927; *1913*, 1914), and *Bürger Schippel* (1913), which the Hungarian composer Ernst von Dohnanyi turned into an opera.

The trilogy tells the story of the Maske family. *The Knickers* begins
with Theobald Maske, a Prussian petty official, beating his wife for
threatening his position: watching the passing of the Kaiser in the
Zoological Gardens, her knickers have fallen to her ankles and halted
the royal progress. . . . In fact, the mishap has attracted two male
witnesses of it to apply for lodgings in Maske's house: a pseudo-
romantic poet and an awkwardly sentimental, Wagnerite barber.
The young wife, a sentimental dreamer, imagines herself in love with
the poet—but he, like her, is a day-dreamer, and at the crucial point
he chooses to lock himself up and write bad verse rather than seduce
her. The barber, when given his chance, prefers a night in his own
bed. Meanwhile Theobald has been overcharging these two lovers
for their rooms, and generally exploiting them. Here, with suitable
irony, we see the ignorant bourgeois as the invincible superman—
the poet, Scarron, is no match for him—and trickster. The next two
plays trace the vicious history of the Maskes' son, Christian. Sternheim's attitude is ambiguous, for while he reveals the Maskes and his
other bourgeois characters as absurd, he nevertheless presents them
as heroes; because they ruthlessly exploit society, they are more admirable than the people they crush and trick. Sternheim hates and
intellectually despises them; but there is an element of admiration in
his attitude. This stems from his essentially cynical view of society:
everyone wants only to achieve respectability, as the comedy *Bürger
Schippel* demonstrates.

Sternheim's plays (with some unimportant exceptions) are mainly
satirical: he does not examine or scrutinize his ambiguously vitalist
attitudes towards basic drives. They resemble Wedekind's in that the
characters are dehumanized, stripped of such characteristics as might

soften the harsh outlines of their biologically predetermined ambitiousness; this was the foot, so to speak, that Sternheim had in naturalism, and it prevented him from ever becoming a fully-fledged expressionist. In his unduly neglected fiction Sternheim made more effort to express and examine the consequences of his pessimistic view of human nature. There was, after all, a frustrated man of warmth— if not a lyricist—in Sternheim: he had wanted to be the German Molière, but failed because of his flat, cold characters. Some of his best stories are collected in *Annals of the Origin of the Twentieth Century* (*Chronik von des zwanzigsten Jahrhunderts Beginn*, 1918) Several are ironic parables, like Wedekind's *Such is Life*, of the artist's plight In 'Schuhlin the Musician' ('Schuhlin', 1913; tr. in *Best Continental Stories of 1927*, 1928) the eponymous hero lives off a rich pupil and his wife, whose whole lives are devoted only to serving him. The chef of 'Napoleon' (1915), clearly a representation of the artist, achieves understanding of (and conceives scorn for) society by learning how to provide them with superior food. The comparison of the writer with the chef was prophetic. Sternheim's highly concentrated and fragmentary methods of prose technique (he wrote it out 'ordinarily' and then 'treated' it) were carried to their logical fulfilment in Robert Musil's *The Man without Qualities* (q.v.). An important and competent writer, Sternheim never quite achieved his great potential. But his prose does not today get the attention it deserves, even if its experimentation is ultimately more suggestive than creatively successful. He would be amused to hear that in the Sixties he was still being accused by journalists of 'wilful' experimentalism and (in *The Knickers*) of bad taste. . . .

Pessimism, tempered by a strong religious sense, replaces the urge to satire in the work of ERNST BÁRLACH (1870–1938). Born in Holstein, Barlach began as sculptor and only took to the serious writing of plays when he was over forty, by which time he had withdrawn into the virtual seclusion, in Mecklenburg, of his last twenty-eight years. Barlach's sculpture, which is nearly all in wood; is 'modern [i.e. purposefully distorted] Late Gothic', and has great power; the Nazis destroyed some of his work as 'decadent', but a good many of his single figures survive. He was probably lucky not to have been sent to a concentration camp. He illustrated his plays with his own engravings. He was a genuinely isolated figure who has some affinities with Blake, and who may be compared to similar eccentric, non-urbanized semi-recluses such as David Jones, in at least the fact that he combines a strong folk-element with a sort of 'rough', untrained but formidable intellectualism, an obstinately persevering drive towards precise self-expression that looks, as one approaches it, first wilfully recondite or 'mad' (cf. Blake), then odd, then unexpectedly sophisticated and, finally, self-fulfilling. Barlach came from a region of dark clouds and murk near the North Sea; a certain Scandinavian gloom pervades all his work, and a genuine sense of the comic can do little to dispel it; but of his power and sensibility there is no doubt. He visited Russia for two months in 1906, and the suffering human beings he saw there, sharply etched against grey infinities of space, strongly affected him, and taught him humility.

What links Barlach to expressionism is his concern with 'inwardness': the exterior of his carved figures is patently expressive of their inner natures In fact, he is more truly expressionist in his sculpture than in his writing, for he always tended towards establishing a realistic basis in the latter, and criticized his closest friend, the poet Theodor Däubler (q.v.), for trying to express himself in incomprehensible ciphers.

Barlach was a happy pessimist, in that his enjoyment of his transcendentally loving struggle with inevitable human imperfection came to be greater than his *angst*; thus his best work is saved by a refreshingly unmystical earthiness.

Barlach's first completed play, *The Dead Day* (*Der tote Tag*, 1912) ought to have remained on the realistic plane of its beginning. Barlach should have concentrated on expressing his theme at this level. Despite its power, the play is overridden by a windy abstractness. Mother and son live together in a vast hall, in perpetual twilight; the 'spiritual' son tries to break away from the 'physical' mother, who plots continually to keep him in immaturity. His father is pure spirit—he turns up with only a stone, which symbolizes sorrow. He has sent a magic steed to take the boy into bliss, but the mother murders it, and all ends in the 'dead day' of stifling physicality, not very happily symbolized here by Barlach as mother-love. It is interesting that while he wrote this play he was bringing up his four-year-old bastard son, Klaus: he had spent the years 1906–9 in legal battles to get him away from the (stifling?) mother. (The less precise and more divine the afflatus, the more strictly earthy, perhaps, its occasion.)

The best scenes in *Blue Boll* (*Der blaue Boll*, 1926) depict Boll's lusty self-confidence, and amount to a convincing realistic portrait of a certain kind of guilty, lively upstart; but Boll's transfiguration is more doubtful.

Barlach's best work is in parts of his posthumous autobiographical novel *Seespeck* (1948), where the style is precise and the self-examination continually revealing. Here the grotesque sometimes becomes prophetic, and Barlach achieves the quality of his best figures: man, his mind in the configurations of his body, reaches desperately out to 'God', to powers outside himself—and we are spared the transcendental definitions. There was much that was superfluously mystical in Barlach, but there is a validity in his view of life as a struggle between non-materialistic aspiration and physicality—though none in his 'philosophical' solution, described by one critic as a 'profounder cosmic emotion'. When, as in his carvings and in parts of his plays and novels, he is content to describe the plight of modern man as a believer who has lost his belief he is a moving writer.

V

Most of the expressionists proper, as well as Brecht and Rilke, admired [LUIZ] HEINRICH MANN (1871–1950) more than his younger brother THOMAS MANN (1875–1955); now this is rightly regarded as having been because Heinrich was cruder, less complex and more sensational. But, ultimately superior though Thomas is, it is problematical whether full justice is now done to Heinrich Mann's best work.

Born in Lübeck, son of a wealthy Senator and a partly Brazilian mother, Heinrich was at least as prolific as his brother, and published more than fifty books in his lifetime, mostly fiction, but also plays, essays, memoirs, and an anthology. The obvious difference between him and his brother is that he early decided that literature should be politically committed, which the more conservative Thomas always denied.

The Mann brothers have a theme in common: the creative artist's relationship to society. But the early Heinrich can be classified with Wedekind and Sternheim as an unequivocal castigator of the Wilhelmine bourgeoisie; his brother cannot. He soon made up his mind that the artist represented, or ought to represent, revolutionary progress. Practically all Heinrich Mann's literary inspiration came from outside Germany: from Stendhal, Maupassant, Zola and D'Annunzio (qq.v.) in particular. Even before he was forced out of Germany by the Nazis he had spent much of his time in Italy. In his work the conflict between southern and northern blood is more unevenly fought out than in that of his brother: the south is the victor.

His first book of consequence was *Berlin, the Land of Cockaigne* (*Im Schlaraffenland*, 1901; tr. 1929), in which the unbridled but vital sexuality of the hero, Andreas Zumsee (a German version of Maupassant's womanizer, Bel Ami), is contrasted with the debilitated and worthless society of Berlin, whose rottenness is portrayed with memorable savagery. The trilogy *The Goddesses, Diana, Minerva, Venus* (*Die Göttinnen*, 1902–3; *Diana*, tr. 1929) has affinities with Wedekind's *Lulu* (qq.v.), but is more caclulatingly frenzied. Like Mann, Violante d'Assy, the *femme fatale* heroine, has mixed northern and southern blood; a Nietzschean superwoman (rich, emancipated), she nevertheless feels herself to be artificial. This is a historically interesting novel, but quite unreadable today: Mann's own concerns are too inexorably submerged in a neo-romantic programme.

It was in the novella 'Pippo Spano' (TT), included in his collection *Flutes and Daggers* (*Flöten und Dolche*, 1904–5) that Mann came closest to his brother and anticipated expressionism. Here and in the famous *The Blue Angel* (*Professor Unrat*, 1905; tr. 1932 and, as *Small Town Tyrant*, 1944) of the following year Mann first expressed his deeper as opposed to his more superficial and programmatic self: for there was a distraughtness and nervousness in him which undermined his over-confident polemics, but which gave his best fiction its cutting edge.

In 'Pippo Spano' Heinrich Mann is frightened about himself. Mario Malvolto, a poet, uses his art as a means of preserving his narcissism intact. He feels himself, like Violante, to be *artificial*—this is Heinrich Mann's great theme—but he cannot accept reality because he fears and despises it. (Thus the Mann of *Berlin, the Land of Cockaigne* had tried to pretend that reality consisted solely of swinish and contemptible bourgeoisie.) But he keeps a portrait of one Pippo Spano, a strong and passionate *condottiere*, in his study: here, he feels, is an authentic, not an artificial, man. Such characters fill his books. A girl, Gemma, falls in love with him on the strength of his work. He determines to respond—at last—as Pippo Spano would. Then scandal supervenes, and the 'authentic' thing to do is for the lovers to enter into a suicide pact. They do: but having stabbed Gemma, Mario cannot kill himself; he will create a masterpiece from his experience. Dying, she calls him 'murderer!' but his agreement is 'comic': his masterpiece is a comedy, and 'one does not kill oneself really at the end of a comedy'.

The original Josef von Sternberg movie of *The Blue Angel*, with Jannings and Dietrich, and with an admirable script by Carl Zuckmayer (q.v.), was a work of genius, but in some ways, perhaps inevitably, misrepresented the novel. In the film the schoolmaster is finally seen as an object of pity; in the novel there is no such compassion. Ostracized by the community because he has fallen for the singer Rosa Fröhlich, at the Blue Angel, Professor Unrat ('Filth') revenges himself by using her as bait to lead his judges into the same humiliating situation; previously he had been the most rigid of all of them, a stifler of youthful love and life like the adults in Wedekind's *Spring's Awakening* (q.v.). The downfall of the tyrant Filth is in a sense the downfall of the whole community, which beneath its respectable and placid exterior is seething with lust and anarchy.

The conflicts of 'Pippo Spano' are partially resolved, but painfully and artificially, in *Without a Country* (*Zwischen den Rassen*, 1907): the protagonist, Arnold Acton, a spokesman for Mann, preaches thoughtful action: the intellectual must learn to defascinate himself of the strong man, the Pippo Spano, and to act for himself; thus Arnold is at first fascinated by his politically reactionary rival in love—but is regenerated when he realizes that he must fight. As he triumphs, and his mistress returns to him, there is a victory of Social Democracy: it is the dawn of a new age. . . . This is a very bad book; indeed, Heinrich's lapses were always more drastic than his brother's.

In *The Little Town* (*Die kleine Stadt*, 1909; tr. 1930), however, this optimism receives more convincing treatment. The inhabitants of an Italian town are affected by the arrival of an operatic troupe in just the way that those of the German town of *The Blue Angel* were by Rosa Fröhlich; but his time, in a novel of charm and comedy, they are led to discover their own natures and to attain a degree of harmony. However, a pair of lovers from the troupe die tragically. Is this a sacrifice of art to the common good?

The trilogy *The Kaiserreich*, *The Patrioteer* (*Der Untertan*, 1918; tr. 1921; and as *Man of Straw*, 1947), *The Poor* (*Die Armen*, 1917; tr. 1917) and *The Chief* (*Der Kopf*, 1925; tr. 1925), deteriorates as it proceeds; but the first part, with *Henri IV* (q.v.), is undoubtedly his best work. Diederich Hessling is the first large-scale proto-Nazi in German literature, and he was created before 1914 (the novel waited until 1918 for publication). No one saw what could happen in Germany more clearly than Heinrich Mann. His brother supported the 'decent war', and there was public controversy between them; but Thomas later came to criticize his own attitude. Thomas was the subtler writer, but at this stage his innate conservatism prevented him from attaining the insight of *The Patrioteer*, in which Heinrich Mann provides the first psychological dissection of the fear, stupidity and ruthlessness that went to make up a mentality which, within a year or two of the end of the war, was to be the property of an average Nazi. *The Poor* is more polemical—in *The Patrioteer* satire provides most of the creative energy—and *The Chief* (which does not continue the story) is a failed experiment in documentary fiction.

Heinrich Mann's creative powers subsequently became submerged in his political programme. But they were to erupt once more in his two historical novels about Henry IV of France, the enlightened and tolerant ruler whom he set up as his ideal: *King Wren: the Youth of Henry of Navarre* and *Henry, King of France* (*Die Jugend des Königs Henri Quatre*, 1935; *Die Vollendung des Königs Henri Quatre*, 1937; tr. 1937, 1939). Unlike Thomas, Heinrich always wanted to repudiate his German origins. Here he pays unequivocal tribute to Mediterranean blood: Henry, in Mann's idealized version of him, combines the reason of Mario Malvolto with the ability to act of Pippo Spano, but on a suitably grand scale. This Henry retains emotional innocence (from which his sexuality benefits, in manifold love-affairs), but his intellect is subtle. And in this characterization Mann was able, perhaps disingenuously, to resolve his doubts about the intellectual artist being an *actor*: Henry acts the part of regal splendour because it is good for his people. This, Mann's last important book, can be shown to avoid the complex moral problems that his brother faced. For Thomas, shrewd and often opportunistic irony; for Heinrich, political commitment. But *Henry IV* is none the less a major work of the second rank—and is easier to read than any of the more massively complicated works of Thomas. As an imaginative writer, Heinrich Mann's best is usually to be found in satire; when reasoning takes over, he is less convincing. But in *Henry IV* he managed a non-satirical monument to his beliefs.

In Thomas Mann we find the *Zeitgeist*, in all its violence, concentrated within the stolid limits of a phenomenally intelligent, though not intellectually original, conservative. No wonder that Mann, whose external life was uneventful, struggled for years with guilt at abandoning his family role of 'Bürger'; being a writer made his inner life a continuously hard one. He was always reticent and careful—even cunning—about where his sympathies lay, and he retained to the end the mercantile acumen of his forebears. Heinrich was the opposite: 'right' about the kind of war the 1914–18 one was going to be, where his brother was patently wrong (and later admitted it), he has less to offer. The Hungarian Marxist critic Georg Lukács has posited Mann as a realistic bourgeois writer who clearly saw that time for his class had run out; and his sympathy for Mann is so great that, since as a Marxist he could not honestly claim him as a 'revolutionary' he calls him a 'naïve' (q.v.) writer, in Schiller's sense. But Mann is a 'sentimentive' writer *par excellence*, whose strictly 'non-confessional' methods conceal more subjective expression. There is more of Thomas in his work than of Heinrich in his. Thomas was an artfully, almost deceitfully, sophisticated manipulator of his audience: he conserved the cultivated merchant in himself, survived as an old-fashioned bourgeois, secretly tried to achieve within himself a compromise between a solid decent commercialism and spirituality, between optimism and pessimism, throughout his writing career of almost sixty years. He was not a dishonest or an inhumane man; but he became, perhaps inevitably, pompous—although no doubt parodically and comically so. One of the most revealing stories he ever wrote, 'Tonio Kröger' (1903; tr. in *Stories of a Lifetime*, 1961), contains this paragraph, in which he sees himself with absolute clarity (the fourteen-year-old Tonio is, like Mann, the son of a rich grain merchant and a Latin mother):

> The fact that he had a note-book full of such things [poems], written by himself, leaked out through his own carelessness and injured him no little with the masters as well as among his fellows. One the one hand, Consul Kröger's son found their attitude cheap and silly, and despised his schoolmates and his masters as well, and in his turn (with extraordinary penetration) saw through and disliked their personal weaknesses and bad breeding. But then, on the other hand, he himself felt his versemaking extravagant and out of place and to a certain extent agreed with those who considered it an unpleasing occupation. But that did not enable him to leave off.

Later, when a young man, Tonio realizes that 'knowledge of the soul would unfailingly make us melancholy if the pleasures of expression did not keep us alert and of good cheer'. This was something that Rilke understood; and it is evident from this story and his other early work that Mann's problem, too, was the nature of the relationship between art and human virtue: is it necessary to 'die to life in order to be utterly a creator'? This is what Tonio soon tells himself, as, successful in his work, he cuts himself off from 'the small fry' who do not understand the nature of the difficulty. He knows that 'Nobody but a beginner imagines that he who creates must feel. . . . If you care too much about what you have to say, if your heart is too much in it, you can be pretty sure of making a mess'. We can see from this that Mann was no more a straightforward romantic than he was a 'naïve' writer. But he is not simply attacking imaginative writing here; he is criticizing it from the inside (as an imaginative writer); drawing attention to an aspect of its nature. And yet, like Tonio, the twenty-eight-year-old Mann was 'sick to death of depicting humanity without having any part or lot in it. . . ' It was the observing *coldness* (his own, as a writer), too, that shocked him: 'To see things clear, if even through your tears, to recognize, notice, observe—and have to put it all down with a smile, at the very moment when hands are clinging, and lips meeting, and the human gaze is blinded with feeling—it is infamous . . . indecent, outrageous. . . .' Tonio makes this declaration to a sensible girl, and when he ends by saying that he loves life none the less, she tells him that he is 'a bourgeois *manqué*'. When, after thirteen years in the south, he visits his home town, he finds that his parents' house has become a public library; he is also mistaken for a 'swindler'—the artist as swindler was to be one of Mann's chief themes. Finally Tonio resigns himself to the fate of being a writer, but affirms his faith in 'the human, the living and usual. It is the source of all warmth, goodness, and humour. . . .'

This was an advance, in Mann's terms, from the novel that brought him phenomenal success at the age of twenty-six: *Buddenbrooks* (1901; tr. 1930). This superficially resembled Galsworthy's *Forsyte Saga* (q.v. 1); but in fact it embodied a profound pessimism, and was, as has been well said, 'a novel of death, resignation and extinction'. In it the heir of the great nineteenth-century mercantile family dies simply because he has not the will to survive. Mann himself did survive, respectable and 'happy' with his good marriage; but there was always a reluctance to do so. He is one of the most anti-creative creators of his century: trapped in nostalgia for nineteenth-century stolidity, whose faults he sees clearly, he opts for a bourgeois democracy and a bourgeois solution. Humane culture, the public man continuously pronounces after his post 1914–18 War conversion to democracy, can provide the answer. He posits an artist who will combine self-discipline with the necessary 'licence' to perform his function; but this is artificial. Mann the creative writer horrifies himself with visions of the sick creative writer; Mann the publicist seeks refuge in what, compared with his novels, are sonorous pomposities. He fails to solve his problem, because he can never be committed; but he provides priceless insights. It is interesting that as early as *Buddenbrooks* Mann sees the decline of the great bourgeois family as the result of the lack of a will to live; and this weakening of the will he sees as being in its turn the result of 'artistic' blood and sexual licence. Mann made a fiction both effectively popular and genuinely 'highbrow' (an unusual achievement) out of the change of heart indicated in 'Tonio Kröger'; but of his 'message' he never really convinces either himself or the astute reader. Throughout his life he refused to adopt a philosophy; but it is necessary to regard him not as a sceptic but as an ironic comedian: a comic exploitation of his own indecision characterizes his work.

It is probably heresy to suggest that Mann's great works, the full-scale novels, are less good than one short work he wrote in 1912; but here the story entirely transcends the moral. In *Death in Venice* (*Der Tod in Venedig*; tr. in *Stories of a Lifetime*, 1961) the forces of perversely apprehended beauty function with as much power as the novelist's implied judgement. One of Mann's chief poses was as poet of the process of regeneration and redemption; but this pose is the least convincing aspect of his fiction—and the 'bigger' it is the less convincing. In this novella he describes with uncanny accuracy how being a writer affected him. When the great writer Aschenbach, hitherto a self-disciplined character, falls in love with the beautiful Polish boy Tadzio (to whom he does not even speak), and gives way to fantasies of passion, he realizes that the moral order has collapsed: 'the moral law' has fallen in ruins and only the monstrous and perverse hold out a hope. Thus, and most memorably, the alarmed (not didactic) Mann exorcized the spectre of moral licentiousness in himself. He said that Aschenbach was suggested by the composer Mahler as well as by a passage in the diary of the homosexual poet Platen—but he was at least as much suggested by himself. His passion has the authenticity of Rilke's lines, quoted above: 'For the beautiful is nothing/But the first apprehension of the terrible. . . .'

The Magic Mountain (*Der Zauberberg*, 1924; tr. 1927) most ambitiously expands on this; but its heart, for all the brilliant comedy—and, indeed, the subtle majesty of its structure—is sterile. An engineer Hans Castorp, goes to a Swiss sanatorium for a visit of three weeks; he stays seven years, during which he is 'educated' (*The Magic Mountain* is, as Mann himself often said, 'a queer, ironical, almost parodic' version of the *Bildungsroman*) out of his obsession with death. But his regeneration is comic rather than tragic in spirit, for he is ridiculous. In a sense, Mann is on the side of the devil. The sickness of the world in which Castorp compulsively moves is what he enjoys; the thesis of sickness as a sign of distinction, to be overcome and replaced by a 'life'-enhanced health, is, for all the apparent profundity with which it was advanced, academic in Mann: this does not act upon him as a creative but as a pseudo-philosophical yeast. Mann was a realist in most of *Buddenbrooks*, but elsewhere only by fits and starts; as a conscientious humanitarian made intelligently aware of the *national* consequences of Schopenhauer, Nietzsche and Wagner, his problem was to evolve a fiction that at least appeared to be positive. So Castorp is a comic caricature, a 'representative' rather than (in a realist sense) a man at all; the time (1907–14) is the past; the structure is fashionably based on myth (that of the hero in quest of adventure): the whole huge apparatus looks impressively positive. And once this is seen, *The Magic Mountain* is even funnier in its sly cunning. It is significant that Mann never, here or elsewhere, can define or communicate the nature of the 'love' by which 'death' may be outwitted. The only love he can communicate with true power is that of Gustav von Aschenbach for Tadzio; and this is a love of death. All Mann can do at the end of the novel, when Castorp finally leaves the death-enchanted mountain in order to enlist as a soldier, is to hope that 'Out of this universal feast of death, out of this extremity of fever, kindling the rain-washed evening sky to a fiery glow, may it be that love one day shall mount?' This is the rhetoric of a liberal activist, not the insight of a creative writer.

In the novella 'Mario and the Magician' ('Mario und der Zauberer', 1930; tr. in *Stories of a Lifetime*, 1961) Mann presents a Hitler or Mussolini type figure as, significantly, an evil artist: a hypnotist who fascinates his audiences. The 'wholesome' Mario's defeat of this charlatan is unconvincing. Mann was wrong, too, in his wishful public belief that the Germans would repudiate Hitler.

The Biblical tetralogy *Joseph and his Brothers* (*Joseph und seine Brüder*, 1933–43; tr. 1948) builds up, with an immense panoply of learning, the figure of a 'chosen one', a suffering, regenerated, redeemed con-man who reconciles simplicity with sophistication, superstition with scepticism, *Geist* with *Leben* ('spirit' with 'life'; an opposition fundamental in the German temperament), to achieve an enlightened society: a democratic Germany. In exile in America, Mann could relax enough to fantasize this Joseph, an artist turned successful business-man, and a society that could exorcise its demons. The cheerfulness of the ending has been as brilliantly stage-managed by Mann as, in the novel, Joseph has stage-managed the scene of his 'recognition'; it is only in the light of reflection that it strikes the reader as incongruous.

In *Doctor Faustus* (1947; tr. 1949) Mann attacked what he so reluctantly and secretly was: an 'expressionist' artist; but his composer Adrian Leverkühn (born 1885) went the whole hog, which Mann himself did not. Mann here regards music as specifically 'devilish': Germanic (Hitlerian). Leverkühn comes to realize, with the help of the devil, that creativity has been bought at the price of syphilis: his manic-depressive personality is, literally, devilish. Mann saw that 'expressionism' run riot had led to fascism; but he did not see the other side of the picture, and in portraying a *non*-charlatan as positively evil—he emphasized that the humanly successful artist must be a confidence man: himself.

In *The Holy Sinner* (*Der Erwählte*, 1951; tr. 1951) the protagonist is born in incest, marries his 'sister' who is his mother, and becomes Pope (so that his mother can call him 'father'): its nihilism is decked out in a mannerist prose that makes the vicious message look noble and even positive—at least to the middlebrow audience whom Mann delighted in hoodwinking.

The Black Swan (*Die Betrogene*, 1953; tr. in *Stories of a Lifetime*, 1961) is undeniably 'sick'; and Mann, who was getting old and tired, is for once slick and facile in his execution. *The Holy Sinner* looks like a 'regeneration' story, but in fact the author is splitting his sides; *The Black Swan* is a solemn (and pitiless) rehash of the old theme that it is bad for society when people go against nature. The 'characters' are garishly unreal. A widow of fifty falls for a young American. She becomes unduly sensitive to scents, only to trace one to a compost-heap. She experiences a return of menstruation: but this is cancer of the womb (described in repulsive detail), and she dies.

Then Mann had a last renewal of energy, and—appropriately— decided to tell the truth. *The Confessions of Felix Krull, Confidence Man* (*Bekenntnisse des Hochstaplers Felix Krull*, 1954; tr. 1955) is supposed to be unfinished—but it was finished by Mann's death. His zest in this picaresque novel is greater than it had been for forty years. Certainly the relaxed story of yet another 'chosen being', a gay criminal amorist, is his best novel since the first, *Buddenbrooks*.

Mann was a black pessimist trapped in the Germanism he so vigorously resisted. The author who wrote an early story in which a man dances himself to death in women's clothes, to music composed and played by his wife and her lover, may well have felt he had something to live down (and he, unlike many decadents, had meant it). He distrusted 'inwardness', but ignored or failed to discern the fact that such poetry of 'inwardness' as *The Duino Elegies* (q.v.), wrung out of a tortured selfishness (not hedonism), does have a glow of love towards others—because it is not meretricious, does not cheat the easily cheated audience, does insist on communicating its uncompromising message. Mann does not achieve this degree of poetry: in terror of his inwardness, he tried to turn it into a kind of outwardness. But he remained humorously aware of this, and at the end, in *Felix Krull*, he openly and amusingly confessed his inadequacy.

VI

Expressionism—the literary movement of approximately 1910–1925 —was the first, and the most violent and explicit, manifestation of modernism. The term—an early application of it was made by German art critics to an exhibition of French paintings by Picasso and others held in Berlin in 1911—was not liked in literary circles until after the outbreak of the First World War, when the movement became increasingly political, and was taken up by more or less polemic critics such as Hermann Bahr (q.v.). Marinetti (q.v. 3) and his futurist manifesto were welcomed in Berlin in 1912, and there was a widespread movement by then, exemplified in the founding of two (rival) magazines, *Die Aktion* and *Der Sturm*, and of literary clubs and cabarets. A good many untalented poeticules and criticasters could and did jump on the bandwagon. The impact had first come from the visual arts, and the German visual expressionist movement (e.g. *die Brücke*, the Bridge group founded in Dresden in 1905, and incorporated into *Der blaue Reiter*, the Blue Rider group, in 1911) predates the literary. It was Bahr who said that the chief characteristic of the movement was the shriek, an expression of inner agony—aptly depicted, in a famous and hysterical painting, by the Norwegian Edvard Munch, a friend of Strindberg's (q.v.).

The German reaction to the disintegration of the old culture and to the impending catastrophe of the war, to the growing notion that man was alone in a hostile universe, was the most anguished of all; frequently it took violent or gruesome forms. Equivalents of expressionism arose elsewhere, but there is an expressionism that is a peculiarly German phenomenon: apart from its intensity, its most notable feature is the hostility of the younger towards the elder generation, often manifesting itself as hatred of the father or father-figure. Expressionism 'is part of the great international movement of modernism in art and literature; on the other hand, it is a turbulent and vital chapter in the catastrophic history of modern Germany': 'the antithesis (and chief victim of) Nazism as well as its forerunner and kin' (Walter H. Sokel). The imagists (q.v. 1) in England—whose actual work is less drastically 'modern' than that of the German expressionists—concentrated upon the formal, stylistic aspects of poetry; the Germans were from the beginning as concerned, however vaguely, with wider implications: being Germans, they were more philosophical in their approach. But their initial failure to make satisfactory aesthetic formulations testifies to their initial creative strength: theoretical programmes inevitably sap creativity. And, of course, the more considerable the gifts of those poets or writers now usually called expressionist, the more isolated or remote from the movement they tended to be. Neither Trakl nor Kafka (qq.v.) had anything seriously to do with any programme, and the work of both transcends programmatic concerns.

The first nominally expressionist poem appeared in the periodical *Die Aktion* in 1911. It was called 'World's End':

The bourgeois' hat flies off his pointed head,
the air re-echoes with a screaming sound.
Tilers plunge from roofs and hit the ground,
and seas are rising round the coasts (you read).

The storm is here, crushed dams no longer hold,
the savage seas come inland with a hop.
The greater part of people have a cold.
Off bridges everywhere the railroads drop.

(MGP; see also TCG)

This was by JAKOB VAN HODDIS (ps. HANS DAVIDSOHN, 1887–1942),
who went mad in 1914 and was, after nearly thirty years in an
asylum, murdered ('deported') by the Nazis. His poem was 'expressionist' because, as well as satirizing bourgeois complacency and
ironically predicting disaster, it presented what Michael Hamburger
has called 'an arbitrary concatenation of images derived from contemporary life . . . a picture, but not a realistic one'. Van Hoddis
was a comparatively crude poet; more gifted was ALFRED LICHTEN-
STEIN (1889–1914), who was killed in action in Belgium at the beginning of the war. His poem 'Twilight' (whether dawn or dusk is not
specified) was admittedly modelled on van Hoddis' 'World's End',
but as Hamburger has pointed out, he allows 'the images to speak
for themselves'. 'Twilight' is less contrived than 'World's End', for
while Lichtenstein was a genuine poet, van Hoddis was probably not
more than a gifted and zestful perpetrator of sardonic *montage*. In
Lichtenstein's poetry there is a wholeness of vision: integrity of surface is preserved even while the familiar world is cruelly, gaily or
sadly dislocated:

A fat boy is playing with a pond. The wind has got caught in a
tree. The sky looks wasted and pale, as though it had run out of
make-up.

Bent crookedly on long crutches and chattering two lame
men creep across the field. Maybe a blond poet is going mad.
A pony stumbles over a lady.

A fat man is sticking to a window. A youth is on his way to
visit a soft-hearted woman. A grey clown is pulling on his boots.
A pram screams and dogs curse.

(TCG; see also MGP)

Lichtenstein, as is now often pointed out (following Hamburger), paralleled Eliot and Pound in a number of ways: in his use of *collage*, his introduction of an ironic *persona* (called Kuno Kohn) and his mocking and deprecatory tone. He also wrote a children's book.

AUGUST STRAMM (1874–1915), a poet and dramatist who was killed on the Russian front, combined a respectable life in the Central Postal Ministry with study at university and some of the most violent experiments yet seen. He is a crude writer, but one of exceptional integrity. For many years he could not get his work published at all; but Herwarth Walden's *Der Sturm* took his play *Sancta Susanna* (1914; tr. in *Poet Lore*, XXV, 1914), and he soon became its co-editor. Stramm's work, like that of E. E. Cummings (q.v. 1), is less radical than it immediately suggests; he owes much to Arno Holz (q.v.) and to the shrill Marinetti (q.v. 3). But he sought for self-expression, not sensationalism, in his war-poems. It is misleading to describe him as an expressionist or a pre-expressionist, although he was hailed as such when his work became widely known after the war: in the typical expressionist poem the external scene expresses the poet's inner state. In Stramm there is no external scene: there are no images, and conventional logic, syntax and all description are eschewed. The weakness of his poetry is lack of feeling; but this arises not from coldness but from undue concentration upon technique. Under the pressure of war, however, Stramm wrote to greater effect.

Stramm's plays are less successful. Intended for intimate theatres, they exploit gesture, pause and (even the intimate theatre not then being quite what it is now, only verbal) ejaculation. Doubtless *Powers* (*Kräfte*, 1915) seemed effective in Max Reinhardt's production; but the text left it all to him.

Before passing to others who died in the war, it is necessary to consider a poet who had nothing to do with the expressionist movement, and yet can only be classified as an expressionist (if he can be classified as anything)—and one whose most earnest work falls lamentably short of his ostensibly least serious. CHRISTIAN MORGENSTERN (1871–1914), a consumptive, was lucky to live as long as forty-three years, and it is unlikely that he would have had he not been so devotedly cared for by his mistress Margarete Gosebruch; certainly he lived, from his early teens onwards, in the shadow of a premature death.

Morgenstern knew Ibsen and translated both his and Strindberg's plays into German. He was influenced first by Nietzsche, then by mysticism both Eastern and Western, and finally by the 'anthroposophy' of Rudolf Steiner, a partly mystical and partly practical system that embraced the whole of life; it still survives. Morgenstern believed that his philosophical poetry was his most important contribution to literature. It is in fact, as Leonard Forster has written, *innig*: 'sincere-fervent', linguistically uninspired and over-intense. His 'nonsense-verse', however, which he began writing (relaxedly: this is the clue to its achievement) in his twenties, puts him on a level with, and possibly even above, Lear and Carroll. His earnestness as a serious poet is pathetic; but it allowed him to relax in officially non-intense off-moments, and thus, in his ostensibly 'light' verse, to comment more pungently on his problems than he ever could when he was trying.

One of his chief problems was the way in which words are related to the things they denote. Morgenstern's approach is one of laughter; but he created his own autonomous poetry. The world of Baron von Korf and Professor Palmström is even more self-contained than that of Lewis Carroll. Morgenstern the mystic struggled hard and with humourless solemnity with the universe: everything was at stake. As soon as he played with it, with nothing at stake, he became a major poet: probably the most successful 'nonsense' poet in the history of literature. Man is a linguistically endowed animal. Morgenstern played with his language as few had played with it before; he demonstrated both its inadequacies and its capacity to create a world of its own. Although he himself saw no essential difference between his 'serious' and his 'nonsense' poetry, in the latter he unobtrusively mocks his mystical pretensions,

> Palmström's grown nervous; henceforth
> He will sleep only to the North. . . .

without really undermining them. In 'The Dreamer' he sees himsel even more lucidly:

> Palmström sets a bunch of candles
> on the table by his bedside
> and observes them slowly melting.

> Wondrously they fashion mountains
> out of downward-dripping lava,
> fashion tongues, and toads, and tassels.
> Swaying o'er the guttering candles
> stand the wicks with flames aspiring,
> each one like a golden cypress.

On the pearly fairy boulders
soon the dreamer's eyes see hosts of
dauntless pilgrims of the sun.

(MGP)

At rock bottom Morgenstern was a sceptic, who dissolved his kindly immortal longing in metaphysical laughter:

There was a fence with spaces you
Could look through if you wanted to.

An architect who saw this thing
Stood there one summer evening,

Took out the spaces with great care
And built a castle in the air.

The fence was utterly dumbfounded:
Each post stood there with nothing round it. . . .

(tr. R. F. C. Hull)

His inimitable and still by no means widely enough known poetry has been much translated. (Notably by Max Knight, *The Gallows Songs*, 1963, and by W. D. Snodgrass and Lore Segal, *Gallows Songs*, 1968. See also MGP, TCG, TCGV, PGV.)

GEORG HEYM (1887–1912), poet and short-story writer, escaped the war only because he was drowned while trying (vainly) to rescue a friend with whom he was skating on the River Havel. Heym was influenced by Baudelaire and, above all, Rimbaud; he was also another of those Germans who were fascinated by the early poetry of Maeterlinck; he must have owed much, too, to the poems of Émile Verhaeren (q.v.), with their visions of the encroaching cities, for one of the main themes of his talented, death-intoxicated poetry is 'the God of the City', with his 'slaughterer's fist' shaking as devouring fire rages along a street. Yet Heym, who was physically a giant, had a side to him as conventional as his verse-forms: he wanted to be a soldier or a consul, and was quite as full of zest for life as he was fascinated by death. His joy in horror, which parallels that of Benn's (q.v.) poems of almost exactly the same time, may have stemmed, like Wilfred Owen's (q.v. 1), from a repressed homosexual streak; but the athletic Heym would have recoiled from this in more terror than Owen did. He had extraordinary difficulties with women. As has often been repeated—it was first stated by Ernst Stadler (q.v.)—his poems achieve such tension because he contained the turbulence of their emotions in strict verse forms. There is some truth in the judgement that 'the general impression of Heym's poetry is that of a boyish elaboration of the macabre', but it fails to do justice either to the authenticity that lay at the heart of expressionism or to Heym's poetic confidence. It is true that he made a fetish of a schoolmate's suicide—as a courageous act—and had a skull decorated with vine leaves on his desk; but he was an equally intense sports lover. Shame (as he recorded in a diary) at his 'delicacy' was the reason for this. The truly lived-out dichotomy produced the tension from which the poems arose.

> They tramp around the prison yard.
> Their glances sweep its emptiness
> Searching for some meadow or some tree,
> Sickened by the blankness of the walls.
>
> Like a mill-wheel turning, their black tracks
> Go round and round and round.
> And like a monk's shaved head
> The middle of the yard is bright.

There is social indignation here; but more than that. The prisoners are trapped bourgeois who march pointlessly—de-sexed like monks —on the periphery of the 'brightness' that is their birthright. Heym could achieve a deeper and more mysterious, personal note, as this opening stanza from 'Why Do You Visit Me, White Moths, So Often?' shows:

> Why do you visit me, white moths, so often?
> You dead souls, why should you often flutter
> Down to my hand, so that a little
> Ash from your wings is often left there?
>   (MGP; see also TCG, PGV)

The Alsatian ERNST STADLER (1883–1914), who was killed early in the war, was a notable scholar (he studied at Oxford 1906–8) as well as an influential poet. He had founded a periodical, *Der Stürmer* (*The Assailant*) as early as 1902, together with his friend René Schickele (q.v.); its object was to accomplish a cultural *rapprochement* between France and Germany. Stadler was influenced by French poets, notably Jammes and Péguy (qq.v.), both of whom he translated, Verhaeren, Hofmannsthal and George (qq.v.) as well as by Whitman. He was one of the most considered, quiet and intellectual of the early modernists. Of the gifted young poets—French, British, and German—who were slaughtered in the First World War, he is the most likely one, had he lived, to have developed procedures that would have enabled him to fulfil his undoubtedly major potentialities. He was one of the most intelligent critics of his generation.

Stadler has been described as a 'semi-modernist', and with some justification. His optimism and idealism led him to have hopes for the real world, so that his repudiation of conventional reality—his 'expressionism'—was less absolute than that of Trakl or even Heym (q.v.). He belongs mainly to the functionalist, sober, 'responsible' side of expressionism, and he anticipated by some years the so-called New Objectivity (*Neue Sachlichkeit*).

His first book was derivative, even 'decadent'—and some poems in his second (and only important) collection, *Decampment* (*Der Aufbruch*, 1914), are marred by an immature voluptuousness. Stadler was wholeheartedly against the disintegrating, rotten-ripe society of this time; but unlike Trakl, Benn (qq.v.) and others, he believed in the future and maintained that 'true art' existed to serve it. He often used a long, rhyming line to evoke what Michael Hamburger calls 'an elemental vision that is religious and erotic'. Probably just as years of war would have shattered his idealism, so they would have shattered this only occasionally convincing technique. He summed up his dilemma most acutely in 'Form is Joy'; and this can be taken, too, as a prophecy of the direction in which he might have gone:

> First mould and bolt had to burst, and world press through opened conduits: form is joy, peace, heavenly content, but my urge is to plough up the clods of the field. Form seeks to strangle and to cramp me, but I desire to force my being into all distances—form is clear hardness without pity, but I am driven to the dull, the poor, and as I give myself limitlessly away life will quench my thirst with fulfilment.
>
> (PGV; see also TCG, MGP.)

GEORG TRAKL (1887–1914) was an Austrian poet who managed, despite an almost completely deranged life, to achieve a body of poetry of absolute integrity—which incidentally fulfilled the expressionist programme of 'visionary poet' and anticipated certain aspects of surrealism. Trakl was born in Salzburg, the son of an ironmonger. He did badly at school, and before he had left was sniffing chloroform and drinking heavily. He decided to become a pharmacist—

probably because of the opportunities it would and did give him to indulge in the drugs of his choice—trained in Vienna, did a year of military service, and then returned to Salzburg. His sister, Margarete, who was a concert pianist, committed suicide. A sister figures in Trakl's poetry, as does the theme of incest; no reliable biographical conclusion can, however, be drawn. Only one book of poems appeared in his lifetime, in 1913; this was a selection made by Franz Werfel (q.v.).

Trakl's letters show that he had as deep a seriousness about his poetic vocation as Rilke, whom he influenced and who was one of his first understanding readers; but unlike Rilke, who never touched any drug or stimulant, Trakl could not endure his existence without their help. Fortunately he was physically very strong, although his way of life would inevitably have destroyed him had he not destroyed himself. The philosopher Ludwig Wittgenstein, recognizing Trakl's genius although admitting that he could not understand his poetry, made a considerable sum of money available to him through his patron—Ludwig von Ficker, who published most of his later poetry in his magazine *Der Brenner*—but even this upset his delicate sensibility.

When the war came Trakl was called up as a lieutenant in the Austrian Medical Corps. After the battle of Grodek, the title of one of his last poems, he was given the task of caring for ninety seriously wounded men: he had neither the skill nor supplies, and broke down. He was put under observation as a possible case of what used to be called *dementia praecox* (schizophrenia), an unlikely diagnosis. He developed a delusion that he would be executed as a deserter (he had seen the hanged bodies of deserters at Grodek), there was no intelligent person within reach, and he died of an overdose of cocaine, probably unintentionally.

Trakl, while he is one of the most individual poets of the century, typifies not only the 'visionary poet', as has been mentioned, but also the 'alienated artist'. He is an early case of a man driven deep into himself by a world he finds intolerable. The process was at least helped along by his family's ridicule of him for writing poetry, their equation of 'poetry' and 'failure'. Poetry was his only real therapy—for his 'anti-therapy' was the alcohol and drugs which he used simultaneously to protect and destroy himself. His life paralleled that of a fictional expressionist hero, well defined by W. H. Sokel as one whose 'superiority is the bane of his life . . . [and] . . . casts him into outer darkness. His nature is unique; his words find no echo.' Not for nothing did Trakl poetically identify himself with the 'righteous' Caspar Hauser (q.v.), who 'truly adored the sun, as, crimson, it sank from the hilltop . . . and the joy of green', and into whose heart God had spoken 'a gentle flame': 'O man!'—but who was pursued by 'bush and beast' and sought by his murderer, and who at the end

> Saw snow falling through bare branches.
> And in the dusking hall his murderer's shadow.

> Silver it fell, the head of the not-yet born.

(tr. D. Luke in *Selected Poems*, 1968, the best and most representative English collection; see also MGP, TCG, PGV, MEP and R. Bly and J. Wright, *Twenty Poems*, 1961. *Decline*, tr. M. Hamburger, 1952, contains one version not subsequently republished.)

The expressionist 'message' is well concealed in Trakl's poetry—it is never advanced polemically; but those who think of him as predominantly morbid should be reminded that his gloom arose from a consciousness of joy rather than from decadent self-indulgence. He is an absolutely ambiguous poet, and it is as wrong to speak of pure ugliness in his work as it is of pure beauty: they go together. He used colour more than any poet before or since. The philosopher Martin Heidegger tried to show, in a controversial essay, how his use of colour implies two opposed qualities. Thus 'green' (which appears as frequently in his poetry as it does in that of Lorca, q.v. 3 or Hagiwara, q.v. 4) is both spring-like, pristine—and decay. But Michael Hamburger has challenged this view as an oversimplification. The world of Trakl's poetry, his inner world, is built up, like a dream-picture, from disparate images of the external world. Much has been written attempting to explicate this world, for all sensitive readers intuit that it is meaningful, if in no familiar manner.

Trakl was first influenced by Rimbaud, the French symbolists and Nietzsche; the chief influence on his later and more doom-ridden poetry was the Swabian poet Friedrich Hölderlin (1770–1843), a prophetic and visionary figure who—mad for the last thirty-seven years of his life, anti-orthodox but profoundly religious, above all the expressor of a sense of hopeless isolation—was gratefully rediscovered in this century. As Trakl grew older and progressively failed to make satisfactory contact with his environment, or to fulfil his conviction that (as he said in a letter to von Ficker) 'all human beings are worthy of love', or to find anything to contradict his sense of impending doom, his guilt assumed gigantic proportions. His poetry is impenetrable because, as Walter Sokel has pointed out, 'withdrawal and disguise' were the keynotes of his existence: he could not face himself any more than he could face the world. And yet his poetic integrity, even in a disintegrating culture (the Austrian decay was the most immediately evident and poignant of all), was such that it forced him to face himself; and so, in Sokel's words, 'Upon the visionary screen a carefully masked biography of the poet's essential existence is projected in fragments'. Trakl haunts his own poetry, a ghost possessed by already tainted joy, and then by guilt and death. His theme is of decline into death; a recurrent, and often final, image is of the falling head: 'Fading, the head bows in the dark of the olive tree', '. . . the wine-drunk head sinks down to the gutter', '. . . O how softly / Into black fever his face sank down,' 'From the stony wall / A yellow head bowed down', 'Silver it fell, the head of the not-yet born', '. . . he bows his head in purple sleep'. This, doubtless prompted by his own drug- or alcohol-induced sinkings-into-trance, suggests the resignation of the intellect to extinction. In Trakl's poetry everything sinks unhappily but intoxicatedly downwards, through a Nature seen as through the eyes of a painter (Rilke shrewdly pointed out in a letter that 'a Trakl [one thinks] . . . could have exercised his painting and music instead of poetry'—Rilke could not), into oblivion. He is the mythical youth Elis, whose own 'decline' is when the blackbird calls in the black wood, and who is dead, or at any rate not yet born. Death implies innocence, perhaps even ignorance, of human corruption. Trakl's poetry does not so much refer, however, to the state of innocence itself as to the anguish or corruption that modern life (particularly the city) thrusts upon the individual. One of the functions of poetry, for Trakl as for certain other expressionists, was the creation of a separate world—this one being too painful. But the poet's own 'autonomous', subjective world is shot through with intimations of the 'real' world: there is a tension between the 'real' and the 'unreal', between the world of pure imagination and the world upon which it depends. Thus Trakl the man is involuntarily haunted by guilt about his sexual desire for, or possibly relationship with, his sister; but Trakl the poet, even while expressing this guilt, questions its validity—if only by implication. Trakl's last poem is called 'Grodek', and one may see in it—dramatically—how the poet was related to, dependent upon, the man. For it was at Grodek that Trakl endured the experiences that led him to attempt suicide, to be removed to a military hospital, and there to die of an overdose of cocaine:

At nightfall the autumn woods cry out
With deadly weapons and the golden plains,
The deep blue lakes, above which more darkly
Rolls the sun; the night embraces
Dying warriors, the wild lament
Of their broken mouths.
But quietly there in the pastureland
Red clouds in which angry god resides,
The shed blood gathers lunar coolness.
All the roads lead to blackest carrion.
Under golden twigs of the night and stars
The sister's shade now sways through the silent copse
To greet the ghosts of the heroes, the bleeding heads;
And softly the dark flutes of autumn sound in the reeds.
O prouder grief! You brazen altars,
Today a great pain feeds the hot flame of the spirit,
The grandsons yet unborn.

(MGP)

The 'world' of this poem is not more incoherent than a dream is incoherent; but it needs as much effort of understanding as a dream —and the means of its interpretation are as various and as uncertain. ... However, the figure of the sister is here, a ghost ambiguously 'greeting' ghosts. And this last of Trakl's poems most poignantly illustrates the dilemma common to all would-be denizens of autonomous worlds. ...

It is his most sensitive translator, Michael Hamburger, who has pointed out that the many mythical figures in Trakl's poetry frequently stand, not merely for childlike innocence, but for actual exemption from original sin: feeling trapped by his own narcissism (with, it should be added, a sensitivity more intense and articulated than the normal), the poet postulates the impossible, or at least the unknown—the unknown of which he yet has a vague premonition, which he catches, ghost-like, haunting that terrified consciousness of decline.

It is tempting to try to interpret Trakl's poetry in symbolist terms; but while this may sometimes indicate his own conscious intentions, it does not, I think, lead to the richest response. For example, Hamburger has interpreted him as 'a Christian poet', and by this he presumably means a poet who believed—in the core of his being—in Christ as redeemer. I can find no evidence of this; his use of Christian material seems to me a pagan use. The way to read him is intuitively; his poems must be seen as paintings, but also as desperate attempts to visualize his inner landscape. This is an enigmatic poetry that has no trace of pretentiousness in it. Unlike Dylan Thomas (q.v. 1), Trakl did not become increasingly submerged in beery rhetoric—for all the alcohol and drugs he took. His poetry is about himself, and if we want to discover the universal in it we must, I think, approach it—first—in that way. He 'perished', Rilke said, 'under the too great weight of his creation and the darkness which it brought upon him'.

VII

There were other expressionist poets, or poets intimately associated with the expressionist movement. When expressionism went into its second and inferior phase in about 1914, and became strident, sociological, political and programmatic, these multiplied to such an extent that only a directory—and that in small type—could deal with them all. Time has in any case extinguished most of the reputations. However, a number of more important poets were either on the fringes of the movement, or claimed by it.

ELSE LASKER-SCHÜLER (1869–1945), as well known for bohemianism as for poetry, was friendly with Dehmel, Kraus, Kokoschka, Däubler, Werfel and Benn (qq.v.). Her first liaison was with the not conspicuously talented vagabond poet and novelist PETER HILLE (1854–1904), whom she commemorated in *The Peter Hille Book* (*Das Peter Hille Buch*, 1906–7). Trakl (q.v.) met her briefly and dedicated a poem to her. She was for a time married to Herwarth Walden (ps. Georg Levin), the editor of the expressionist magazine *Der Sturm*. But even though she was an enthusiastic propagandist for expressionism, she was a true eccentric original, and could never have belonged to any movement. Her remark 'I die for life and breathe again in the image' is marvellously evocative of expressionism; but her inner world was largely a product of fancy (rather than imagination), and had been formed from her Westphalian childhood and (mainly) from her Jewish background.

She lived for the last eight years of her life in Jerusalem, where she was regarded as a national Jewish poet: a fitting apotheosis, for Judaism—both religious and secular—had been her chief inspiration. She wrote novels and a play, but her important work is in poetry. At their best, her poems have the colourful, grotesque, humorous quality of the paintings of Chagall; apparently surrealistic, they are actually rooted in a warm primitivism. The expressionists

welcomed her because of this primitivism, but her alliance with the
movement harmed her art by making her take thought—which was
not her strong point. Her 'mysticism' is deliberate, an attempt at
thinking, not felt at all; her impersonations of oriental princesses
are merely tiresome. When she is at her weakest, which she often is,
she is not evoking an inner world but merely seeking an escape from
reality. Too many of her fabulous inventions are of this character.
Her romanticism is often profoundly bourgeois in type, for all her
detestation of the species: it is, after all, a bourgeois habit to 'hate
love among the common plebs' as she did, adding 'love is for Tristan
and Isolde, Romeo and Juliet. . . .' She is at her best in those short
poems where she is least obsessed with the intellectual nature of her
symbols—colour, the East in general, the search for God—and
more impelled by powerful emotion into the creation of an uncalcu-
lated language. (The grotesque and sometimes nightmarish humour
of her autobiographical *My Heart* [*Mein Herz*, 1912] is appealing
but relatively trivial.)

Over Shining Shingle

O to go home at last—
The lights fade fast—
Their final greeting gone.

Where lay my head?
Mother, say soon.
Our garden, too, is dead.

A bunch of grey carnations lies
In some lost corner of the house.
Every ounce it took of all our care,

It wreathed the welcome at the door,
And gave itself, in color generous,
O mother dear.

It spread the sunset gold,
And in the morning soft desires,
Before this downfall of the world.

None of my sisters live now and no brothers live.
Winter has played with death in every nest
And frozen cold our every song of love.

(MGP)

This poem, beautiful in its simplicity, was written in the Forties, under the strain of knowledge of the fate of so many of her race, and included in the collection *My Blue Piano* (*Mein blaues Klavier*, 1943), in which for the first time she recaptured the purity of her poems of thirty years before that (these were collected in the book she most prized: *Hebrew Ballads, Hebräische Balladen*, 1913). She illustrated most of her own books. (MGP, TCG, CGP, CGDP).

A less influential but equally enthusiastic proponent of expressionism was the 'bearded Oceanus' THEODOR DÄUBLER (1876–1934), who was born, of German parents (he had an Irish grandmother), in Trieste. He evolved a tiresome mystical system—sun is father, earth mother, and the earth is perpetually struggling to join the sun—and wrote an epic, *The North Light* (*Das Nordlicht*, 1910, rev. 1921) of over 30,000 lines to illustrate it. He had connections with the semi-expressionist group *Charon*, founded by the poet OTTO ZUR LINDE (1873–1938), which aimed to penetrate to the ultimate meaning in sound. Out of this came his famous synaesthetic poem 'I hear a million nightingales singing', which is something of a *tour de force*. He knew Yeats (q.v. 1), who was doubtless sympathetic to his astral claptrap; he was also a close friend of the proto-Nazi critic Moeller van den Bruck. But Däubler, novelist and critic as well as poet, was no Nazi. His fate, it seems, is to be represented in anthologies by short poems that are described as 'uncharacteristic'. Much of his best work is in *The Way of the Stars* (*Der sternhelle Weg*, 1915). In such a poem as 'Cats' (MGP) he writes a characteristically 'expressionist poem' of high quality. (TCG, CGPD.)

ALFRED MOMBERT (1872–1942), a Jew from Karlsruhe, was not as involved in expressionism as Lasker-Schüler and Däubler, but was nevertheless included in some anthologies. Mombert's inoffensively grandiose work is now largely forgotten, but in his time he was regarded by a few as the outstanding genius of his generation. Benn (q.v.) names him and Däubler as pioneers of expressionism. Mombert began by writing shorter poems, but about 1905 began a lifelong attempt to base a 'modern myth' on his spiritual life. Mombert's virtues of nobility and courage were personal rather than literary; his best writing is contained in the posthumous collections of his letters made in 1956 and 1961. The later works, of which the most notable are *Aeon* (1907–11) and *Sfaira der Alte* (1936–42), are cast in the form of 'symphonic dramas'. They were not intended for the contemporary stage, but for the 'new humanity' of ages hence. The lovely and wise old poet who figures in the latter of these 'symphonic dramas', who holds converse with trees, parks and other inanimate things, is a curiously appealing figure—but the work is none the less a penance to read. At the end of his life Mombert was sent to a conentration camp, but a friend ransomed him and he was able to go to die in Switzerland. The man, in this case, is better than the work.

Neither WILHELM LEHMANN (1882–1968) nor his friend OSKAR LOERKE (1884–1941) was involved in any programme; but both have enough in common with early expressionism to be considered here. Both are more important poets than Däubler or Mombert, and both continue to exercise a powerful influence on post-war German writing. Lehmann, who was born in Venezuela, began with a volume of stories in 1912 and a novel four years later. His first book of poetry did not appear until 1935, when he was well over fifty. His life, with the exception of a spell of captivity as a prisoner-of-war in England in the First World War, was uneventful. He was a teacher until 1947, when he retired. He was perhaps the most serene of all modern poets, and one of a very few who did not lose the faculty of lyricism.

Lehmann is an esoteric, not a hermetic (q.v. 3) poet: the reader needs information, but this is available from books on natural history; and the best poems stand on their own. Lehmann has a passion for 'nature'—flowers and animals—and is a 'nature poet' of comparable stature with, but very different from, Robert Frost and Andrew Young (qq.v. 1). 'The true poet can be singled out by his close connection with natural phenomena', he has written, 'and his belief in the power of language'. Lehmann's poems are ' "deeds" ', he says, 'of my eyes'. 'God and the world only appear to the summons of mysteriously definite planned syllables.' For Lehmann, exact description of the world in minute particulars is a magical act; the English might respond more readily and fully to the poetry of an Andrew Young in the light of this. This is really the limit of Lehmann's 'mysticism', which is refreshingly less ponderous and complex than that of, say, Däubler (q.v.). He is passive, rather than prosily inventive of vast schemes, in the face of what the natural world does to him. Thus two of the chief features of his poetry are exactitude of detail and a dislike of abstraction. . . . When the wind seemed to be 'moved to pity' by the horror of post-war starvation and desolation, in 1947, he watched spring return: 'It is nothing. Abortive magic? It worked. I am nourished. I hear song'. Lehmann's fiction is autobiographical and essential to an understanding of his poetry, although not on the same high creative level. His criticism illuminates his own practice more than that of his subjects. The integrity of his faith in Nature and its power to survive even the 'second flood' of the Second World War are most apparent in his poetry, much of the best of which was written in old age. (MGP, TCGV, PGV.)

His close friend Oskar Loerke worked for most of his life in Berlin as a reader for the important publishing firm of S. Fischer Verlag. Like Lehmann's, his work has come to the forefront only since the war; neither writer was taken much account of before, and both were frowned upon—though not proscribed—by the Nazis. Loerke wrote book reviews, two novels, and some musical studies as well as poems. His attitude (the last of his seven volumes of poetry appeared in 1934, a year before Lehmann's first) has much in common with Lehmann's, but he is more incantatory, and more melancholy. Lehmann would never have written that 'The mountain of care stands . . . glassily in front of every goal, and everyone who seeks happier regions finds it barring his way to the world' ('Summer Night over the Country', PGV). He much resembles Heym and Lichtenstein (qq.v.) in that he writes 'modernist' poems in strict forms. His poems often dramatize his spiritual adventures in a series of vivid and violent metaphors; they are both more personal and more mythographically ambitious than those of Lehmann. (MGP, PGV, TCG.)

ELISABETH LANGGÄSSER (ps. ELISABETH HOFFMANN, 1899–1950), born in the Rhineland, was partly Jewish; she became a Roman Catholic. She established a modest reputation as a poet and novelist before 1933, but it was the novel *The Indelible Seal* (*Das unauslöschliche Siegel*, 1946) that brought her fame. The persecution she suffered at the hands of the Nazis, including forced labour, brought about her early death. Her daughter was imprisoned in Auschwitz Concentration Camp, but survived.

As a novelist Langgässer was perfervid and humourless, but undoubtedly gifted and original. Her Catholicism is remorseless and would be tiresome even to fellow converts; but in her poetry and shorter fiction her imagination takes precedence over her religious obsessions, with happier results. And yet so discerning a critic as Broch (q.v.) suggested that *The Indelible Seal* might be the first genuinely distinguished surrealistic novel. Certainly the crudity of Langgässer's lifelong view of existence as a battleground for Satan and God is in direct contrast to the complexity of other aspects of her work. Perhaps, like Graham Greene (q.v. 1), she should be treated as one of those who are Roman Catholics in order, so to speak, to be novelists. . . .

As a poet Langgässer made no secret of her debt to Wilhelm Lehmann (q.v.), whose view of nature she consciously Christianized. She is not as distinguished a poet because her dogmatic ardour, not necessarily in tune with her imagination, imparts a sense of strain to her language; her devotion never strikes one (as does, say, George Herbert's) as being 'natural'. But she has insight as well as dignity and beauty of feeling, and can at her best find an appropriate language. Her terms of reference, even in moments of extreme emotional stress—as exemplified in 'Spring 1946' (TCG) when she was reunited with her eldest daughter after the latter's imprisonment— are mythical or Christian, or both. One of her obsessive themes was the reconciliation of the pagan with the Christian world—in other words with the effective Christianization of herself. The poem 'Rose in October' (TCG) perfectly illustrates both this and her usually recondite general methods. If Langgässer lacks simplicity, she does at her best convey an ecstatic sense of nature. (See also PGV.)

Her first novel, *Proserpina* (1932), reflects her concerns: the techniques are varied and sophisticated, but the content—the struggle between good and evil for the soul of a small child—is crude in the extreme. *The Indelible Seal*, which reminds one as much of J. C. Powys (q.v. 1) as of Greene (q.v. 1), Bernanos (q.v.) and Faulkner (q.v. 1) with whom she is so often compared, is concerned with the soul of Lazarus Belfontaine, a Jew converted to Roman Catholicism for extra-religious reasons. 'Enlightenment' is here unequivocally pictured as hideously evil: the result of Belfontaine's lapse is spiritual emptiness and moral foulness. But his baptism, fraudulent or not, is literally an 'indelible seal', and after the murder of his second wife he is redeemed, and finally appears during the war as a saintly beggar. Langgässer's rather puritanical but none the less fanatically anti-Lutheran Catholicism was as dogmatic as her vision was wild; here Belfontaine is saved from hell by a miraculous 'grace'. But it is the hell, not the grace, in which Langgässer is really interested. The grandly pious structure of the novel is not really of literary interest. In this author the complexities of narrative and style reflect extra-Catholic fascinations, which are consequently consigned to hell. Thus Belfontaine's unbelieving hell is surreal.

The Quest (*Märkische Argonautenfahrt*, 1950; tr. 1953) is the story of a pilgrimage, made in 1945 by seven people, in search of just such a vague, radiant grail as the author depicts in the poem, 'Rose in October', already referred to: 'Deep in the azure—Condwiramurs [wife of the Grail-questing hero Parzival] and Grail at once—the rose, red in blue, not spirit, not flesh, carries its structure high over field and lea into the ether'.

Langgässer's earlier books, such as *The Way Through the Marshland* (*Der Gang durch das Ried*, 1936), about a butcher's son who runs away and joins the Foreign Legion, are less complex but not less mannered. Her best work is to be found in *The Torso* (*Der Torso*, 1947), a collection of short stories mostly about war-time Germany. Here she is less ornate and spiritually ambitious. However, even at her most convoluted, she remains an engrossing novelist. The dogma she professed only appeared to resolve her violent confusions; but of the quality of her feeling, when not exacerbated by theological rationalizations, there can be no doubt.

The Silesian MAX HERRMANN-NEISSE (1886–1941) was a distinguished poet who associated with and was influenced by individual expressionist poets (for example, Loerke and Schickele, qq.v.) and the expressionist movement, but was never of the movement. His sense of his own doomed hideousness—he was huge-headed, his face that of an aged man, his body tiny and hunchbacked—was modified by his inherent sweetness and his grateful love for his wife Leni. He began as a more or less strident ironist, in the spirit of the times; but his irony became muted and more effective as he grew older. Herrmann-Neisse is still underrated today: he is a more individual poet than he has been given credit for. Expressionism gave him the courage to follow his own instincts, but while his usually traditional form does not function, like that of Heym or Loerke, as a pole of tension, his practice has nothing in common with 'neo-romanticism'. His mood of ironically tinged melancholy, perfectly poised in his best poems, is unique. After 1933 Herrmann-Neisse left Germany as a voluntary exile; he died in 1941 in London, where his last collection of poems had just appeared. He wrote several entertaining farces, and novels, notably *The Dying Man* (*Der Todeskandidat*, 1927). (MGP TCG, CGPD.)

GOOTFRIED BENN (1886–1956) was both an expressionist and (later) a historian of expressionism. He was also the only German poet of indisputable genius who (for a short time) embraced Nazism. He is certainly, in his way, a seminal twentieth-century figure, whether the praise of his poetry since 1945 has (as has been claimed) been 'largely uncritical' or not.

Benn, son of a Prussian Lutheran pastor and a French-Swiss mother, was a doctor. He served in the Medical Corps during 1914–18 and 1935–45; otherwise he practised in Berlin as a specialist in skin and venereal diseases until his retirement in 1954. He had been 'non-political' until 1933, and therefore profoundly shocked his friends when he gave support to Hitler—though he never joined the Nazi Party. When his work came under attack from the Nazis, he withdrew into 'inner exile' (his own term, widely adopted), saw his works banned, and sweated it unhappily out until 1945—when the Allies once again banned him (for his former Nazi sympathies). His subsequent response to fame and adulation was privately exultant, but publicly cynical, sardonic and dignified. He had never been lovable, and was not going to be now. But the old man, while continuously resisting emotion as he always had, was moved: he would even have liked to make a full, positive public gesture. Death, however, saved him from such an indignity, although he did give some lectures and interviews; probably death was right.

Two things may be said about Benn; each has an element of truth. On the one hand, he was hailed as 'one of the grand old men of literary Europe'; on the other, he was 'a highbrow charlatan ["It is not a bad word", he wrote. "There are worse."] and a lavish stylist' who 'in spite of his nihilism and his voluptuary's fingering of futility ... makes a sharp verbal impact' (Paul West). His readers are repelled at the insensitivity that led him to support Hitler, that led the exquisite master of cerebration to fail to discern the nature of Nazism, and yet they are compelled to admit that he spoke 'from the innermost core of our time' (Wilhelm Grenzmann). Unlike another and more committed Nazi supporter, the Austrian poet Weinheber, Benn always had taste; yet this collapsed, if temporarily, when Hitler came to power. Reluctant to do more than impertinently and shockingly examine the body of life, Benn at his best is impelled to probe deeply into its unanaesthetized body; the explanation of the disturbing effect he has must be, at least in part, that he, too, is this body.

The first book was a collection of poems, *Morgue* (1912). The surgeon plays at enjoying the horrors (the aster someone had stuck between the truck-driver's teeth, which he 'packed into the chest' during the post-mortem; the dead girl's body harbouring a nest of rats; the morticians' mate who stole a dead whore's gold filling because 'Earth alone should return to earth'), but his pity, too, is evident. In *Sons* (*Söhne*, 1913) and *Flesh* (*Fleisch*, 1917) the poems are less sensational, on the whole subtler. But not many of the poems in these first collections are memorable. However, Benn never wrote more effectively than in the two early 'Songs' of 1913, the first of which states an attitude he strove to hold all his life:

> Oh that we were our primal ancestors,
> A little lump of slime in tepid swamps,
> Our life and death, mating and giving birth
> A gliding forth out of our silent sap.
>
> An alga leaf or hillock on the dunes,
> Shaped by the wind and weighted towards earth

A dragonfly's small head, a seagull's wing
Would be too far advanced in suffering.
                    (tr. Michael Hamburger)

After a short period in the early Twenties when he did not write at all, Benn's work began to reflect his reaction against the optimism and the hope inherent in the expressionist movement (if not always in certain of the best poets associated with it). Always influenced by the nihilist side of Nietzsche, he now read Oswald Spengler's *The Decline of the West*, with which he agreed, and which caused him more pleasure than despair. There was a strange moral and emotional obtuseness about this undoubtedly gifted man—or was it an obstinate bloody-mindedness? In any case, it amounts to the same thing: a crass, monstrously egoistic insensitivity, a moral stupidity not unakin to that sometimes displayed by the Scottish poet Hugh MacDiarmid (q.v. 1). Benn, who had never previously subscribed to a view more optimistic than that the sole way of transcending the absurdity of life was by means of an autonomous art, now spoke of a 'bestial transcendence'. His transition to a support of Nazism is thus easily explicable on merely intellectual grounds. And yet his 'Answer to the Political Emigrants', written in reply to a thoughtful, shocked letter from Thomas Mann's son, the playwright Klaus Mann (q.v.), makes sickening reading; Goebbels had it featured prominently in the press. Suddenly the non-political, fastidious Benn was moved to speak of Hitler as 'magical'—and to state that 'all thinking persons' must recognize his true function. Alas, one cannot doubt Benn's sincerity. It is likely that he was surprised when in the following year he found he had to 'defend himself' against the charge of Jewish ancestry; one would give a great deal to know exactly how he felt as he sat down to perform his task. He had never been an anti-semite. His early prose writings now also brought him trouble: they were 'degenerate'. Indeed, if Benn had really shared in the Nazi brand of vitalism, then he should have been the first to condemn them. For the Dr. Rönne—justifiably referred to by critics as Rönne-Benn—of the short stories collected in *Brains* (*Gehirne*, 1916) is undoubtedly 'degenerate', not only by the Nazis' but by any 'civilized' standards.

Rönne can only affirm consciousness of himself: this is all he makes of 'reality'. He cannot 'bear' or 'grasp' reality, knows only 'the opening and closing of the ego'; 'confronted with the experience of the deep, unbounded, mythically ancient strangeness between man and the world, [he] believed completely in the myth and its images'. Rönne's is an apathetic personality because, disbelieving in the possibility of communication, he does not try to achieve any. Rönne, who also figures in some dramatic sketches, is a frigidly theoretical creation—but a very remarkable one.

Benn was forbidden, by the Nazis in 1937 and by the Allies in 1945, to publish; but in 1948 the ban was lifted (it was an anti-Nazi who arranged this). He now emerged as one who championed aestheticism rather than any other form of transcendentalism. Thus his new poems were called *Static Poems* (*Statische Gedichte*, 1948): they manufactured a sense of order, a purposefulness, which was to be set against the absurdity of life, especially the absurdity of change—or so Benn intended, and so most of his critics have followed him. Benn's only novel, *The Ptolemean* (*Der Ptolemäer*, 1949; pt. tr. in E. B. Ashton, ed., *Primal Vision*, Selected Writings, 1961: this contains much prose and poetry), about a beauty-specialist, makes the same point: his Ptolemean is a transparent if ironic symbol for the poet, Benn, who creates beauty in a pointless world: 'From foreign papers I see a single *maison* offers sixty-seven different brands of hair lotions and cosmetic waters, so *that* is not dying out—but when it is all up, they'll find something else, oils for robots or salves for corpses'. Meanwhile, the only sense you can make out of life—Benn says—is what you do, literally, *make*: in that way you can decide.

Benn was convinced, from early on, that the only possible intellectual attitude to adopt in the face of the twentieth century was a nihilistic one. And he was always ready to evolve theories with this notion as a basis. But he did not tell the whole story in his theoretical writings, which have none the less caused almost all his critics to call him a 'wholly cerebral', or an 'Apollonian' poet. Actually, Benn was here perpetrating a fraud: he was an intelligent man, blessed with a lucid style, posing as an original thinker; and he was a poet of romantic impulses posing as a voluptuous, clinical hedonist. What people have taken as theorizing in good faith is in fact a series of brilliant self-protective devices. Michael Hamburger has well exposed the tawdriness and moral dubiousness of Benn as a public thinker; and we know that the consequences of his public attitudes resulted in his disgraceful public endorsement of the Third Reich. But of the private man we seem to know nothing.

We need not here indulge ourselves in the so-called 'biographical fallacy'. It is sufficient to say that critics, hypnotized by Benn's brilliant, disgusting or shocking public performance, choose mainly to relate this to his poetry. Other facts, however, are equally public, if not—so to say—equally performed: Benn had a private life, he practised as a doctor (attended to the sick, whether in civilian or military life), had women and wives, deplored Hitler but continued ('objectively', as someone has said) to help him. Benn never said why he chose to heal the sick—surely mercy to venerealees is a pointless activity in a pointless world? Neither, although appearances may suggest the contrary, did he ever adequately explain his poetic impulse. His 'theory of poetry', most carefully set out in *Problems of the Lyric* (*Probleme der Lyrik*, 1951), is a coruscating artifact, designed to portray his own poems as coruscating artifacts—and as nothing else. Benn's criticism and self-explication is a cunning affair, because it sets out to conceal as much as to reveal.

It is probably a mistake to call any poet 'purely cerebral' or 'purely Apollonian'; certainly it is so in the case of Benn. What his best poetry is about, what it describes the act of, is the strangling at birth of romantic or sentimental or (sometimes) aesthetic impulses. Thus, he juxtaposes a warm, ecstatic not always devulgarized 'South' with a harsh, no-nonsense Nordic nihilism. This he systematizes into a sort of negative 'philosophy of life'; but it is not really a philosophy at all, and it will not stand up to serious examination. One of Benn's 'philosophical' tenets was that 'change' was 'absurd'; this was merely a screen for his acute nostalgia. Loving the stable past, represented by among other things a God-loving father, and yet wanting—often slickly—to be up with the times, Benn marred even his finest set of poems, those of the mid-twenties, with extraordinary neologisms: clevered-up technical and scientific jargon. As Hamburger has rightly objected, these 'have no business to be there'. Benn's poetry is seminal because in it he is recording the disturbances of an intelligent modern sensibility; but it is as though he doubts his own modernity, and feels obliged to assert it in this strident manner.

Benn was embarrassed by beauty and tenderness and delight and tried to turn his affirmations of these qualities into hedonistic negatives. Consequently, his poetry is crippled: faces that wear masks for too long must themselves come to resemble them. But his poetry, despite its faults, does have its element of integrity, and it does contain a secret history of what this clever century does, in its agony, to simplicity—to delight, love, affirmation. Even the distortions in Benn's work, stylistic and mental, are ultimately an affirmation, an attempt to create the communication and love he denies, to make beauty. He preaches a selfhood as unavoidable, but loathes it and wants to return to the ancient unity of the original slime. The dense blocks of language of which some of his poems of the Twenties consist, in which the verb and sometimes even syntax itself are eliminated, are primeval in just this way: they seem to point to a regression to a more archaic utterance, and they provided Benn himself with a means of escape from his terror of death by dissolution into absolute cerebration. Analyse how Benn's poetry actually works, ignore what he says, and sometimes even what the poetry seems to try to say, and you come closer to the heart of the poet.

We can seldom ignore in Benn's work the cruel obtuseness of the self-styled hedonist; but nor can we always ignore the tenderness of the doctor who preserved life while officially not believing in it. It is significant that in a late poem (1948), characteristically a mixture of self-love and tender idealism (here for once not distorted out of recognition), Benn should have postulated himself as Chopin ('he for his part was unable/to explicate his nocturnes'): a 'minor' composer, exquisite, 'romantic', loved by the vulgar as by the discriminating—and full of 'emotion': not a 'mathematical' or 'scientific' type; and that one of the very last poems should end:

> Often I have asked myself, but found no answer,
> Where gentleness and goodness can possibly come from;
> Even today I can't tell, and it's time to be gone.
>
> (MGP)

Perhaps Hofmannsthal should have the last word: like many readers of Benn's poems, he saw him (in an essay) as the 'man lurking beneath the bridge over which every man passes, the unknown beggar at his own hearth'.

(As well as in the comprehensive *Primal Vision*, see TCG, PGV, CGVD, MGP, MEP.)

VIII

Expressionism proper, the self-conscious movement permeating all spheres of thought and activity, flourished in the theatre as nowhere else (except, perhaps, in the cafés). There was, significantly, no single outstanding dramatist. The typical expressionist play might combine features of the drama of Strindberg (the supernatural) and of Wedekind and Sternheim (satire on the bourgeois); it would probably be more strident, more obviously experimental. As well as in the dramatic fragments or sketches that nearly all the expressionists wrote (e.g. Benn, Stramm, qq.v.), it is in the drama proper that we hear most loudly the ecstatic or agonized cry that is so characteristic of the movement.

The Austro-Czech OSCAR KOKOSCHKA (1886) is an important figure and a great painter, but not a major writer. However, his first play, *Murder, Hope of the Women* (1907; GED) has been called the first expressionist drama—and certainly it is an early and pure example. In Vienna, in the summer of 1908, it created an outrage, as did *Sphinx and Strawman* (*Sphinx und Strohmann*, 1907), which was performed with it—neither is more than a few hundred lines long. The characters have no names, and much of the dialogue consists of exclamation and disjointed sentences. The very violence of the conception, and the lack of an element of reality, anticipate dada and surrealism (qq.v.) as much as expressionism. Later came *The Burning Bush* (*Der brennende Dornbusch*, 1911); once again, the subject is man and woman, their love and hate for each other, and their eventual regeneration. These first plays reflect Kokoschka's sexual turbulence at the time; but in typical expressionist fashion he exploits this to present—or attempt to present—a frenetic picture of the situation between the sexes. Later *Sphinx and Strawman* was expanded into the three-act *Job* (*Hiob*, 1917; GED), the nearest Kokoschka came to writing a 'normal' play: it has some relaxed sparkle and wit, in the Viennese manner. *Orpheus and Eurydice* (1919) reflects the author's sufferings in the war, when he was very seriously wounded, and his consequent pacifism, as well as his continuing obsession with the conflict between man and woman.

Kokoschka's plays have intrinsic worth as well as historical importance (Thornton Wilder, q.v. 1, is an unexpected acknowledger of their influence on him); but because his gift is not for language their excesses seem melodramatic; they are mainly to be regarded as an essential part of his development. Kokoschka drew most of the illustrations for Walden's *Der Sturm* (q.v.). (A volume of Kokoschka's short stories has been translated: *A Sea Ringed With Visions*, *Spur im Treibsand*, 1962).

REINHARD SORGE (1892–1916) was first influenced by Nietzsche; then, just after his only work of importance had been performed, he discovered Christ and tried to give publicity to his repudiation of Nietzsche's overman. He can hardly be said to have repudiated his expressionism, however, because his mood was continuously fervent in the expressionist manner; his conversion to Catholicism merely anticipated by a few years the conversion of scores of minuscule expressionists either to some form of Christianity or to communism. Yet his verse-play *The Beggar* (*Der Bettler*, 1912; tr. Acts 1–3 only, GED), while of little literary value, anticipates many innovations and notions, including that of the 'theatre as hospital' (if, indeed, this can really be said to be new at all, in view of Aristotle's *Poetics*). A beggar-poet is presented as in conflict with his insanely materialistic engineer-father. The play now seems intensely puerile, but it does give a clear notion of what expressionism as a movement was about: the spiritual poet feels compelled to regenerate the people, rather than to entertain them; and in doing so he has to destroy his father, whose 'insanity' takes the form of wanting to aid the world from without (by utilizing the canals on Mars). The beggar-poet-son wants to regenerate it from within. After writing some grandiose mystical dramas and verse, Sorge was killed on the Somme. His impassioned attitude had been carried over into his life: he and his wife spent the first nine months of their marriage in mutual prayer so intense that they forgot to consummate their union.

PAUL KORNFELD (1889–1942), who later successfully turned to bizarre comedy before he was murdered by the Nazis in a Polish concentration camp, wrote two scarcely more dramatically effective expressionist plays, one bleakly pessimistic, the other ecstatically optimistic: *The Seduction* (*Die Verführung*, 1913) and *Heaven and Hell* (*Himmel und Hölle*, 1919). Kornfeld eschewed all characterization, and sought to portray his heroes as lonely souls embattled with bourgeois authority and heartlessness. His hero performs a 'gratuitous act', the murder of a bourgeois he dislikes on first sight, and is sent to prison, where he is surrounded by grotesque functionaries. Persuaded to escape for love, he is himself destroyed. The second play is even more nakedly programmatic, and contains less satire and more sentimentality: the redeemer is a repulsive lesbian tart who, after sacrificial execution, rises—with others—to heaven on a cloud to divine choruses. Kornfeld, whose later less ambitious comedies show more of his gift, exhorted actors to ignore the objective (which did not exist), and represent only abstract ideas.

Of more account than these was WALTER HASENCLEVER (1890–1940), who was another victim of the Nazis: he committed suicide in an internment camp in France, having emigrated there in 1933. Hasenclever, a friend of Werfel's and Kokoschka's, began as a 'shocking poet' (confessing his sexual adventures), and became a highly successful writer of film-scripts and musical comedies after the heyday of expressionism; but he was best known for *The Son* (*Der Sohn*, 1914, produced 1916), the best of all the many parricidal plays produced in Germany during this period. The plot is crude—the son, esctasy-possessed, is eventually forestalled from shooting his father only by the latter's fatal stroke—but the language is more convincing; and by casting his play in a traditional form Hasenclever maintains dramatic tension. The expressionist theatre owed much to its producers—mainly Erwin Piscator and Leopold Jessner; but Hasenclever's particular friend was the more conservative Max Reinhardt (q.v.), which may possibly account for the comparatively more conventional form of *The Son*.

This doubtless helped the Viennese ARNOLT BRONNEN (ps. ARNOLD BRONNER, 1895–1959) to write the most publicly shocking of all the plays on this popular subject: *Parricide* (*Vatermord*, 1915, produced 1922), in which the son, about to be seduced by his naked mother, despatches his father (Herr Fessel = fetter) with a coal shovel as he breaks into the bedroom. Bronnen went to East Germany after the defeat of 1945. But for a time he had been in charge of Nazi radio drama. His latter-day confessions, though produced for communist consumption, are of interest.

Three other expressionist playwrights contributed drama of more permanent value. ERNST TOLLER (1893–1939), a political activist who took part in the worker's November revolution of 1918 and went to prison for five years (1919–24) as a consequence of his Chairmanship of the Bavarian Soviet Republican party, killed himself in New York after six years of exile. Toller's abundant dramatic genius was to some extent vitiated by his political passions—although he would not have accepted the charge. His first play was *Transfiguration* (*Die Wandlung*, 1919; tr. *Seven Plays*, 1935), in which for perhaps the first time the established expressionistic technique of alternating reality with dream is presented with real dramatic effectiveness. But although it is expressionist in technique, this play could also be regarded as symbolist. The pacifist hero is portrayed in realistic scenes, which alternate with dream ones that contrast with his idealism: there is no 'inwardness', only a beckoning towards Utopian socialism. Toller was an agonized Utopian (some of his most moving work consists of lyrics written in prison) but, despite his skill and passion, his language does not really measure up to his convictions. He feels impelled to write of man the frustrated socialist animal, rather than to record the details of his own suffering: the lack of selfishness spoils or at least vitiates, his art. His most famous play is *Masses and Man* (*Masse Mensch*, 1921; tr. *Seven Plays*), in which the characters are anonymous. Dramatically this is one of the most effective of all expressionist plays, but from its realistic scenes one infers how much more powerful it might have been if Toller, instead of concentrating on a 'message', had concentrated on finding an objective correlative for his emotions in a human situation. Almost always in his plays the human situation in which the imaginative writer is interested gives way to a programme that has to be 'expressionistically' realized. The exception is *The Machine-Wreckers* (*Die Maschinenstürmer*, 1922; tr. *Seven Plays*; 1923), his finest achievement. Doubtless this is because it is his most realistic play, and realism happened in fact to be where he excelled. This is based on the 1815 Luddite revolt in England, and is largely historical. Although this has a 'message'—man's enslavement by machinery, and all the capitalistic consequences—it grips the spectator and the reader because of its dramatic situation: its irony (the hero is murdered by the men he works to free) goes beyond any programme: Toller had become temporarily fascinated by reality rather than theory. None of his many other plays reaches this standard except *Hinkemann* (1923; tr. *Seven Plays*), on the not uncommon theme of the soldier who has been emasculated through war injury (compare Ernest Hemingway's *The Sun also Rises*, later *Fiesta*, (q.v. 1). Here Toller does become interested again in his character as a character, rather than a symbol: Hinkemann could not be happy even in a socialist Utopia, and this tragic fact is what fascinates Toller.

Such is Life (*Hoppla, wir leben!*, 1927; tr. *Seven Plays*), produced by Piscator (who with characteristic ruthlessness added some fifty minutes of his own business, mostly consisting of filmed material), deals with the emergence from isolation in a mental hospital of a revolutionary, Karl Thomas. His betrayer, also a former revolutionary, is now a minister in the capitalist government. Thomas plots to kill him, but is forestalled by a fanatic; however, he is arrested for the crime, and in prison (prophetically) commits suicide: here Toller projected his own sense of ineffectuality. His later plays could only demonstrate his sense of hopelessness and frustration. If he could have examined his disillusion in non-political terms, he might have found creative satisfaction; as it was, the events of 1933 in Germany broke him both as man and playwright. He could never examine in enough depth his disappointment that 'mankind' rejected 'the poet'; 'Men make them suffer', he wrote in prison. 'Men they love/With inextinguishable ardour,/They, who are brothers to the stars and stones and storms/More than to this humanity'.

FRITZ VON UNRUH (1885–1970), who was born at Coblenz, is a forgotten man of German letters. Unruh was the son of a general who insisted—against advice—on his son's taking up a military career. The whole of his writing may be seen as a protest against this. Unruh left the Imperial Guard in 1912 in order to devote his life to literature, but was recalled in 1914. After the war Unruh became a political activist, and was a member of the Reichstag. He left Germany in 1932. He was not successful in re-establishing his reputation there on his return, although he continued to write.

Unruh's first, pre-1914 plays are on the theme of duty and aristocratic revolt, and led to his being compared with the Prussian dramatist Heinrich von Kleist (1777–1811), who had also resigned from the army to devote himself to literature. On the surface the early plays are aristocratic in sympathy; actually they foreshadow

Unruh's expressionist future: the heroes are vitalists in love with death, although they call their nihilism relief from tedium and the achievement of glory. Unruh's change of heart, which led him to recognize nationalism as a symptom of the death-wish, came within a month or two of the beginning of the war: it was a logical step. The now somewhat embarrassingly hysterical dramatic poem *Before the Decision* (*Vor der Entscheidung*, 1919) was written in October 1914, but not published until five years later. This is a record of Unruh's 'transfiguration'; it ends as the soldier hero, Ulan, calls his troops to battle—against their own masters. But it was his one-act *A Family* (*Ein Geschlecht*, 1917) that turned him into a leading expressionist dramatist overnight; this remains his best play. The verse in which it is written is not poetry, but is effective in the theatre. This, too, ends in an army's revolutionary march on its masters. The Eldest Son, who denounces the Mother for carrying both life and therefore death in her 'moisted womb', has committed rape, as a soldier, and is condemned to die. (His brother has just been killed in battle.) His behaviour incidentally exposes the hypocrisy of this judgement, but it goes further: his aggression towards everything (except his sister, for whom he lusts) is prompted by his sense of the absurd—and thus, as W. H. Sokel has pointed out, foreshadows an 'existential' attitude. He kills himself. The Mother, who is executed as the leader of the rebellious soldiery, represents the life-force—she figures in other expressionist works, particularly those of Werfel (q.v.), and is ultimately derived from the anthropologically incorrect postulation of an ancient matriarchy in *Das Mutterrecht* (1841) of the Swiss J. J. Bachofen (1815–87), which has been no less uncritically accepted in our own time by the English poet Robert Graves (q.v. 1). However, the Youngest Son, who was also condemned to death for cowardice and desertion, takes her place as leader, and the soldiers march off: he lacks the father's hardness, and has heeded his mother's last call for the creation of a new race. *Square* (*Platz*, 1920), the sequel, lacks the fierce passion that lifted its predecessor out of the commonplace. The Youngest Son (now called Dietrich) resigns his leadership, chooses a spiritual lover rather than a sensual one, and looks forward, from amongst the ruins of his political dreams, to the creation of 'a new man', the stock-figure of 'Phase II' expressionism. *Bonaparte* (1927; tr. E. Björkman, 1928), the only one of Unruh's plays to be translated, prophesied the rise of the Nazis.

Unruh continued to write plays, the most recent being the comedy *Bismarck* (1955), and he achieved fame in this form; but his best work has been in prose. His best book, written while at the front at Verdun in 1916, has been translated: *Way of Sacrifice* (*Opfergang*,

1918; tr. 1928). If this is not a classic of description of war itself, it is a classic of description of man's mind when he is at war. *The End is Not Yet* (1947, in English; German version: *Der nie verlor*, 1949) is about Nazism. Unruh had a grotesque, unusual sense of humour, which has more often been seen since the war in his comedies and novels. *The Saint* (1950, in English; *Die Heilige*, 1951) is about Catherine of Siena. Unruh has believed throughout his life in the primacy of 'ideas' over 'facts'; his work, however, has been at its best when the facts rather than the ideas pressed themselves upon him.

GEORG KAISER (1978–1945) is certainly the paramount dramatist of expressionism; whether he was more than that is doubtful. His enormous output has now dated, and it remains to be seen whether his greatest successes, such as the *Gas* trilogy, could stand revival. Besides some seventy dramatic works, he wrote two novels and over one hundred poems. His vision was the one common to most expressionists: the regeneration of man. Kaiser was a brilliant theatrical craftsman, but like every one of the expressionist dramatists his language is scarcely adequate to sustain the explosive content of his plays. He has been revived on the post-war German stage and occasionally elsewhere, but usually in his capacity as a satirist rather than as a pioneer of expressionism.

Kaiser's theories of dramatic presentation, like his personality as a whole, were violently forthright—and crude. His plays are shorn of 'facts' so that the ideas' may emerge the more forcefully. His chief models were Plato's dialogues (in his consideration 'the greatest plays'). When his landlord prosecuted him for selling some of the furnishings of the villa he rented him, Kaiser's defence was that he was an artist who had needed the money; he was sent to prison (only in France might he have got away with this line of defence). There is no distinction between thinking and feeling; 'the intellect is a wound'. His earliest plays owed much to Wedekind (q.v.), although Kaiser went further with caricature. In *Headmaster Kleist* (*Rektor Kleist*, 1905) a boy commits suicide because of his teachers' tyranny. This is farcical satire, full of hate for the school system. He first attracted attention with *From Morn to Midnight* (*Von Morgens bis Mitternachts*, 1912; tr. 1920), about a bank clerk's embezzlement of a large sum and his discovery that it is of no use to him. He is finally betrayed by a Salvation Army girl (for the reward) after attending a gigantic bicycle race—an impressive scene, for Kaiser was a master of the theatre—and kills himself. Kaiser achieved real fame, however, with a play written in 1914 but not performed until 1917; *The Burghers of Calais* (*Die Bürger von Calais*), based on the famous story, but with an additional hero: a successfully activist intellectual who sacrifices himself in order to achieve a universal rebirth.

Kaiser's most famous play was the trilogy *Gas*: *The Coral*, *Gas I*, *Gas II* (*Die Koralle*, 1917, *Gas I*, 1918, *Gas II*, 1920; tr. in TMP). In the first the Billionaire gains self-identity and (expressionist) freedom by murdering his secretary and double, and is executed. In *Gas I* his son continues the management of his gas producing factory, giving the workers a share of the profits. It explodes, and the son tries to deliver his workmen from their enslavement to the machine, but they oppose him (cf. Toller, q.v.) and stone him to death; he expires as he affirms a vision of regenerated man. In *Gas II* the workers have already become slaves, and an entirely impersonal war is in progress. However, the war is lost and the workers gain control of the factory from the state. The end is cataclysmic. Not only did Kaiser thus prophesy the atom bomb, but also his faceless and nameless villains truly resemble the horrifyingly dehumanized politicians of today.

The true dramatic situation did not interest Kaiser, and his plays, for all their passion, have no more warmth or humanity than Shaw's (q.v. 1); but Shaw was witty, and Kaiser was not. Although his later plays are more realistic in style, they continue to explore the world of ideas rather than that of situation, of psychology: Kaiser never even succeeded in depicting the kind of personality (like his own) that is driven by a vision from an objective viewpoint. He himself gradually withdrew from reality, since—as for so many of the expressionists—it proved so unaccommodating to his ideas. (One of his two novels, *Villa Aurea*, 1940, appeared first in English tr.: *Vera, or a Villa in Sicily*, 1939.)

One other of the many expressionists deserves notice. HANNS JOHST (1890) may be treated as symptomatic of the 'evil wing' of expressionism, and of its totalitarian tendencies: his plays, novels and verse are derivative, and whatever small promise they had is easily discountable in his later commitment of 'unchanging loyalty' to Hitler. *The Lonely One* (*Der Einsame*, 1917) is about the nineteenth-century poet Christian Grabbe, one of those hailed by the expressionists as a precursor. Johst, an opportunistic anti-semite who was showered with honours by the Nazis, reached his nadir with *Schlageter* (1933), in which a saboteur executed by the French in the Ruhr in 1923 is made into a hero. One can see the future Nazi and honorary SS man foreshadowed even in the earliest of Johst's plays and novels.

IX

The major novelists, apart from Mann, are Kafka, Musil, Hesse, Broch—and, I would add, the over-neglected Döblin (qq.v.). These are discussed in the following section. Here I deal with a selection from the vast number of other novelists, beginning with those usually classed as expressionists.

The Prague-born FRANZ WERFEL (1890–1945) was an ecstatic sensitive who almost inevitably lapsed into best-selling middlebrowdom. He began as an expressionist poet, continued as an expressionist dramatist, and ended as a progressively inferior 'epic' novelist. As has been well observed, the 'rhetorical plush and pathos of his verse have not worn well', and it is necessary to select rigorously. The single poem Hamburger and Middleton choose to represent him by in their *Modern German Poetry* is an excellent example of his touchingly ecstatic—and typically expressionistic—manner, and his stylistic brilliance:

> Tell me, what brought you safely
> Through all the nightseas of sand?
>
> In my hair shone unfailing
> A nest a nest of blue light.
> (MGP)

This is more attractive than the injunction to us all, in *Veni Creator Spiritus*, to 'rise from our stricken lowlands' and 'storm into one another like flames'. Werfel's early poetry, which contains his best work, possesses the skill and charm that never left him. In the Twenties, when his verse had lost its early fervour, he wrote a revealing little poem about himself as conductor, reproving 'applause as he acknowledges it' and showing the 'harassed features of a saviour'. This has been called ironic; but is perhaps more appropriately regarded as revealing a charming and decent awareness of his essential vulgarity. W. H. Sokel is correct when he says that in his final works Werfel achieved 'a happy and profitable blend of commercialism and Judaeo-Christian sentiments', and his accusation that Werfel achieved 'communion with the masses' by over-simplifying and sentimentalizing his fiction is a fair one—but he was not exactly a charlatan. It was simply that his original creative gift, a lyrical one, was very small and delicately balanced; but his skill was disproportionately high, and he fell an easy victim to self-inflation. His sweetness turned syrupy, and he fell in love with his own religiose image. His 'spiritual quest', inspired by Gustav Mahler's widow, whom he married, might easily have been filmed in technicolour: its culmination is all too easily understandable. His nauseous *The Song of Bernadette* (*Das Lied von Bernadette*, 1941; tr. 1958), turned into an even more nauseous film, made (as Sokel rightly says) 'millions of shopgirls weep and rejoice'. The vulgarizing tendency appears at least as early as the novel *Verdi: a Novel of the Opera* (*Verdi: Roman der Oper*, 1924; tr. 1924). Werfel genuinely loved Verdi's music, and edited an important edition of his letters as well as adapting two of his operas into German; but the Verdi of the novel, a kind of Werfel, bears no resemblance to the historical Verdi. Here is a *Wandlung* indeed.

Werfel was an important figure in the expressionist theatre from the time of his adaptation of Euripides' *The Trojan Women* (*Die Troerinnen*, 1915), with its religio-pacifist message. In *Goat Song* (*Bocksgesang*, 1921; tr. 1936), peasants in rebellion worship a monster only half-human; destroyed, this beast leaves his legacy in the form of a child. This is typically ambivalent: it can be taken as a condemnation of the bestial in man, or as a vitalistic affirmation—or, confusedly, both. Perhaps Werfel, having lost the poetic faculty of his youth, found himself most truly and least offensively in the comedy *Jacobowsky and the Colonel* (*Jakobowsky und der Oberst*, 1944; tr. 1944), in which a clever Jewish refugee gets an anti-semitic Polish colonel through the enemy lines. Here a more than usually relaxed Werfel disguises mockery of his own pretensions as a tribute to Jewish ingenuity. (There are translations of Werfel's poems in MGP, PGV, TCG; and in *Poems*, tr. 1945; most of his novels appeared in English.)

Werfel, as a Jew, could not but have chosen exile—nor, doubtless, would he have wished to do so. JOHANNES R. BECHER (1891–1958), who would have been a minor figure without the existence of the expressionist movement, unlike his almost exact contemporary Johst (q.v.), chose the way of the left. A communist in 1918–19, he spent 1935–45 in Russia, and then became Minister of Culture in East Germany. His prolific verse is in the frenzied 'poster' style of Mayakovsky (q.v.), but, like that of the English pseudo-satirist Christopher Logue's lacks underlying genius. He began by expressing the sense of loneliness felt by the individual in large cities, but soon found a facile way of merging himself with these masses, only miserable when divided. His best work is the novel *Parting* (*Abschied*, 1948): in so far as it is polemic it fails (the boy-hero solves his problems too easily, by becoming a revolutionary and refusing to join up in 1914); but the effects of stultifying bourgeois existence on the young before the First World War are often sharply recollected.

LEONHARD FRANK (1882–1961), novelist and dramatist, was accused of being a vulgarizer of expressionism, and this would be true if the movement could have been vulgarized. But he was a genial, humorous, unpretentious writer who increasingly tended towards crudity and the (inoffensively) middlebrow; his best work, based in experience, had real substance; the disjointed techniques of expressionism added nothing essential to it: at heart, Frank was an optimistic naturalist. His sympathy with the proletariat was by no means theoretical: the son of a carpenter, he had known poverty and had been a worker. His best novel was certainly his first, *The Robber Band* (*Die Räuberbande*, 1914; tr. 1928), which must have influenced Erich Kästner (q.v.). Frank offers what Sokel calls the 'best example of the Expressionist's *Wandlung* from self-abasement to human dignity through revolt, and thereby shows us the genesis of the activist attitude'—but the novel's energy comes, too, from the element of sheer fun of the plot, which involves a gang of boys who form themselves into a secret society and have various anti-social adventures. It should be compared with Jules Romains' nearly contemporaneous *Les Copains* (q.v.). However, *The Robber Band* is also a sour variation of the *Künstlerroman* (q.v.), since its hero (ironically named Old Shatterhand, after the fantasy-German—noble, tough, and so on—created by the Wild West Adventure author KARL MAY, 1842–1912, Hitler's favourite writer), a painter, utterly lacks self-conviction or the will to live, and eventually kills himself. In *The Singers* (*Das Ochsenfurter Männerquartett*, 1927; tr. 1932) Frank shows his 'robber band' turned into timid bourgeois. In his next novel, *The Cause of the Crime* (*Die Ursache*, 1915; tr. 1928) Frank turned rather ostentatiously to Freud. The hero, a masochist like Old Shatterhand, discovers through self-analysis (of, among other material, his dreams) that his inferiority is the result of humiliation which Mager, a sadistic teacher who figures in *The Robber Band*, forced upon him. He decides to visit him to discuss the matter, but when they meet finds that Mager is still a sadist—and so strangles him. Again, expressionist though it was in style and message, this novel had such a wide appeal because of its realism and the suspense that Frank built up. The murderer, Anton Seiler, uses his trial as an opportunity to broadcast his message—just as Kaiser (q.v.) had in real life.

Man is Good (*Der Mensch ist gut*, 1917), the most explicitly expressionist of all his works, written in Zurich—where he had joined

Schickele (q.v.) and other German pacifists—was notorious for the picture it gave of the suffering caused by war and for its possibly deleterious effect on the German home front. Frank was a writer of international stature by the time the Nazis came to power in 1933—when he found it necessary to flee. His *Carl and Anna* (*Carl und Anna*, 1926; tr. 1929) shows him at his most sentimental; it was taken as seriously all over the world as Muriel Spark (q.v. 1) is now. *Heart on the Left* (*Links wo das Herz ist*, 1952; tr. 1954), an autobiographical novel, is the best of his later books, doubtless because, in the words of one literary historian, it displays 'scant regard for elementary decency'.

JAKOB WASSERMANN (1873–1934), a German Jew who spent most of his life in Austria, had sincerely grandiose pretensions not unlike those of Charles Morgan or Lawrence Durrell (qq.v. 1), and these led middlebrow critics to regard him—in the Twenties—as an equal of Dostoevski and Thomas Mann (q.v.); none the less, unlike at least Morgan, he deserves rescue from the total oblivion into which he has now fallen. His best book is his autobiography, *My Life as German and Jew* (*Mein Weg als Deutscher und Jude*, 1921; tr. 1933), but his novels are not entirely negligible. Wassermann was a public figure in much demand as a Jewish liberal—a kind of 'exposed nerve of humanity', like the more substantial Arthur Koestler (q.v. 1). His friends, who included the composer Busoni and the writers Döblin, Schnitzler, Mann and Hofmannsthal (qq.v.), were mostly of superior creative calibre to himself. His later novels are well-meaningly pretentious; they ape profundity but are not rooted in his own German experience. Hence his popularity amongst a wide middle-brow readership in the English-speaking world. But even if he could not adequately reveal the reasons for human cruelty, he was a true humanitarian. His best novels are *The Dark Pilgrimage* (*Die Juden von Zirndorf*, 1897; tr. 1933), in substance an attack on Jewish religiosity, and *The Maurizius Case* (*Der Fall Maurizius*, 1928; tr. 1929), about an old case reopened. This latter novel often falls into pastiche of Dostoevski, but remains an effective crime story. *Caspar Hauser* (*Caspar Hauser oder Die Trägheit des Herzens*, 1908; tr. 1928) is mannered and laboured, but the passion of its message does come through: on the familiar motif of the imprisoned prince, used by Hofmannsthal in *The Tower* (qq.v.), the real theme is the destruction of innocence by the 'system'. (Caspar Hauser, 'the wild boy', had appeared on the streets of Nuremberg in May 1828. He was like an animal, yet able to give an account of himself: he said he had been kept in a hole by 'the man'. After becoming transformed into a handsome youth, in 1833 he was found shot in the breast. Probably he was a hysterical impostor; but the story naturally attracted many German novelists and poets, especially those of the expressionist generation. George Trakl, q.v., was obsessed with it.) *The Goose Man* (*Das Gänsemännchen*, 1915; tr. 1922) is an over-ambitious attempt to improve upon Heinrich Mann's *The Little Town* (q.v.) in that it tries to portray the artist reconciled with society; its shortcomings may be seen by comparing it to Heinrich Mann's earlier book.

Sometimes described as the initiator of expressionism (because of an occasion in 1910 on which he publicly read a poem of his Austro-Czech compatriot Werfel in Berlin), MAX BROD (1884–1968) is certainly best known as the friend of Franz Kafka (q.v.), preserver (against his instructions) of his works, and editor and interpreter of them. Inevitably his views on Kafka have been violently challenged, although all are grateful that he disobeyed the instructions. However, he has been a prolific author on his own account. A good deal of his work has been translated into English, but not the most outstanding: *The Great Risk* (*Das grosse Wagnis*, 1919). This subtle dystopian novel anticipated many aspects of *Brave New World* and *1984* (qq.v. 1), and is in some respects superior to Zamyatin's *We* (q.v. 4), a much more widely acknowledged prototype. Here a society that was started on idealistic but intelligently realistic principles turns into a nightmare totalitarian state. *The Great Risk* dissects and condemns expressionist activism; but Brod continued to believe in Israel as a possible Utopia, and lived there from 1939 and was the director of the Habima Theatre in Tel Aviv. Brod was a passionate Zionist from when he came under the influence of the philosopher Martin Buber, soon after 1908.

Brod's novels have not been very successful in English, largely because his style is cumbersome and turgid; he lacks his friend Kafka's narrative facility, and this even applies to *The Great Risk*. *The Redemption of Tycho Brahe* (*Tycho Brahes Weg zu Gott*, 1916; tr. 1928) sets the mystical Danish astronomer against the 'scientific' Kepler in a Bohemian castle; an account of it, alas, is more inspiring than its text. This is more straightforwardly expressionist than *The Great Risk*, since it unashamedly uses an unhistorical version of the past (cf. Werfel's *Verdi*, q.v.) in order to explore the problems of the present. Brod wrote many plays, including dramatizations of Kafka's *The Castle* and *America* (qq.v.), some volumes of verse, and critical books, including *The Kingdom of Love* (*Zauberreich der Liebe*, 1928; tr. 1930), which, as well as being autobiographical, is about Kafka, who is seen as an expressionist saint. *Mira* (1958) is about Hofmannsthal (q.v.).

Although KARL KRAUS (1874–1936) was one of Robert Musil's

(q.v.) pet hates—'There are two things against which one can't fight because they are too long, too fat, and have neither head nor foot: Karl Kraus and psychoanalysis'—perhaps partly owing to the latter's jealousy, he was none the less one of the most notable of all modern satirists. Success never made him complacent or less critical of his audience. For well over half his life he ran and wrote most of his own satirical paper, *The Torch* (*Die Fackel*, 1889–1936). A Jew, he was born in what is now Czechoslovakia and was then a part of the Austro-Hungarian Empire: at Jičin in north-eastern Bohemia. However, he became to all intents and purposes a Viennese. Kraus was a writer who understood and accepted the fact of the disintegration of the Empire—and its implications—and (the fun apart) his life may be seen as dedicated to an intelligent and just reappraisal. If his themes—the corrupting effects of commerce, the enslavement of men by machinery, sexual hypocrisy—seem familiar, then he was one of those who helped to make our century aware of them. He fought the press and what it represented—lack of values, hypocrisy, vulgarity—all his life; in turn journalists suppressed mention of him whenever possible. His support of the Catholic-fascist Dollfuss, towards the end of his life, was an unfortunate miscalculation, not a change of heart: he believed that Dollfus could save Austria from annexation by the Nazis. The other side of the picture, which the socialist friends he lost never saw—it did not appear until sixteen years after his death—is to be seen in his attacks on the Third Reich, *The Third Walpurgis Night* (*Die dritte Walpurgisnacht*, 1952).

Kraus's finest work, however, is an enormous play that has never, in fact, been performed in full: *The Last Days of Mankind* (*Die letzten Tage der Menschheit*, 1922). This is partly documentary, with a cast of hundreds—it anticipates the methods of Brecht and Weiss (qq.v.) and makes some use of expressionist technique. When performed, it was necessarily condensed. With adjustments, it would make—were the terms not almost a contradiction—intelligent television. *The Last Days of Mankind* is an attack on war and on the press, which Kraus saw as representing and maintaining the forces that cause war. He was fifty years ahead of the irresponsible Canadian arch-popster McLuhan in pointing out that 'printed words have enabled depraved humanity to commit atrocities they can no longer imagine. . . . Everything that happens happens only for those who describe it and for those who do not experience it'. In *The Last Days of Mankind* the continuation of selfish life, with the people still on their diet of cliché, is contrasted with the horrors of war. At the end the Voice of God speaks the ghastly words attributed to the aged Franz Josef in 1914: 'I didn't want this to happen'. Kraus also wrote some pungent criticism and poetry (*Poems*, tr. 1930, including sel. from *The Last Days of Mankind*). He still has not had his full due because modern literary journalists who do investigate him prefer hastily to redraw the curtains they have unwittingly opened: his work is a mirror of smallness and irresponsibility. Only at times of crisis or international despair is he reprinted and praised. He is important, too, for his colloquial style and his shrewd concern for the German language. He was a man who foresaw almost all the excesses of our post-1945 age, and to that unhappy extent would have been at home in it; it desperately needs, moreover, a man of his integrity, imagination and ability.

The early death from consumption of KLABUND (ps. ALFRED HENSCHKE, 1890–1928) moved his friend Gottfried Benn (q.v.) to the least restrained peroration of his life. Klabund was a poet, free adapter from other languages (notably oriental), short-story writer, dramatist and novelist. His historical novels such as *Rasputin* (1929), *The Incredible Borgias* (*Borgia*, 1928; tr. 1929) and *Peter the Czar* (*Pjotr*, 1923; tr. 1925) are tedious, though they enjoyed some middlebrow success (as the title of the Borgias one amply shows). His oriental adaptations, though often too deliberately and voluptuously concinnous, brilliantly construct exquisite alien worlds. Klabund was undoubtedly gifted; he was as undoubtedly capable of crass vulgarity. Although he was never nominally one of the group, he may be regarded as a typical expressionist; his undoubted talents never quite lifted him out of the rut of a mere category, unless in a few of his adaptations and short stories, and in the play *Circle of Chalk* (*Der Kreidekreis*, 1924; tr. 1928), on a theme also used by Brecht (q.v.). Sokel mentions a story of Klabund's as exemplifying the 'crassest example of the vampire-personality in Expressionism': in 'The Man with the Mark' the protagonist becomes a writer only when his face is disfigured by a disease. Now he wears a mask and waits in the café for people from whom to gain material for his writings; he has none of his own (cf. Musil's infinitely subtler study of a 'man without qualities', q.v.). A girl falls in love with him, asks to see what is behind his mask, and when she is shown kills herself. He writes a story about this. As Sokel points out, this is a crudely naïve attack on the concept of 'art' and on the artist as a user of a mask, a 'romantic fraud', to hide the horror of his empty self. . . . (Cf. Thomas Mann, q.v.)

More substantial, but formidable and bewildering, was the eccentric organ-builder, music-publisher and horse-breeder HANS HENNY JAHNN (1894–1959). Jahnn made his reputation as a playwright, with such plays as *Pastor Ephraim Magnus*, which caused an uproar when staged by Brecht and Bronnen (qq.v.) in 1919. In his play *Die Krönung Richards III* (1921) the deformed King, decidedly a sick 'expressionist artist', kills because of his ugliness. But posterity will be more interested in his strange, genuinely original but not uniformly readable novels *Perrudja* (1929) and the trilogy *Shoreless River* (*Fluss ohne Ufer*, 1949–50: I. *The Ship*, tr. 1961). This latter work occupied him for the sixteen years before its publication. Jahnn is the kind of writer who is excessively praised by a very small minority; universal recognition never came to him, although his reputation is now slowly growing.

Jahnn is generally spoken of as having been influenced by Joyce and Freud, which he was; but Kafka was a more potent and first-hand influence than either. His obsessive emphasis on sexual violence springs naturally from an expressionist background, but is in its context entirely his own. It was the Pole Witold Gombrowicz (q.v. 4) who suggested that when approaching 'difficult books' we should in the first instance 'dance with' them; it is obvious what is meant by this excellent advice. Unfortunately it is not easy to 'dance' with Jahnn's prose for very long at a time, so that his monumental trilogy presents almost insuperable obstacles to the reader. *Shoreless River* is based on theoretical musical principles; but sometimes these vitiate literary effectiveness. Jahnn's dark mysticism endows his work with power—especially when retrospectively contemplated—but it detracts from its actual viability. However, there can be no doubt that he is an important writer.

The central figure of *Shoreless River* is Gustav Anais Horn, who sets out on a voyage on a ship, 'Lais', with a mysterious cargo. His fiancée is murdered, but it is not until the second volume that we discover by whom. Horn enters into a friendship with her murderer, and lives first among South Americans and then (as the pacifist Jahnn did during the 1914–18 war) in isolation in Norway. He remains haunted by the fate of the *Lais*, and by the injustice meted out by the 'civilized' minority to their more or less primitive fellow-humans. But while living by his own laws, he discovers his musical potentialities. Jahnn, whatever his shortcomings, remains an intensely fascinating writer, although one never perhaps in complete control of his material. Is the 'river' of the trilogy an 'inward' or an 'outward' stream? There is controversy on the point; we should not ignore the possibility that Jahnn failed fully to resolve his confusions.

LION FEUCHTWANGER (1884–1958) was born in Munich. Another immensely popular middlebrow novelist, he was not as gifted as Werfel (q.v.), although he had talent; but he never wrote as offensively. A good and honest man, Feuchtwanger is one of those prolific

creative writers whose most distinctive work is to be found in autobiography: *Moscow 1937* (*Moskau*, 1937; tr. 1937) and *The Devil in
France* (*Der Teufel in Frankreich*, 1941; tr. 1941). He collaborated
with Brecht (q.v.) on three plays. The most famous of his many
novels is *Jew Süss* (*Jud Süss*, 1925; tr. 1926), which plagiarises a novel
by the early nineteenth-century German imitator of Walter Scott,
Wilhelm Hauff. Others treat historical subjects such as Elizabeth I,
Nero and the French Revolution. Feuchtwanger's knack was to
make 'modern' treatments; associated with left-wing expressionism,
his method of exploiting history proved exceedingly popular. The
results are profoundly vulgar and strictly unhistorical, but never
unintelligent.

The attempt of the noble-minded Bavarian doctor HANS CAROSSA
(1878–1956), poet and autobiographical novelist, to reconcile science
with poetry is intellectually unconvincing, and, like his poetry, has
dated badly; but his effort had style, character and dignity. Carossa
has a niche as a minor writer. His chief inspiration was Goethe.
One of Carossa's most beautiful books, which will survive as a
classic of childhood, is *A Childhood* (*Eine Kindheit*, 1922; tr. 1930),
the first and best of an autobiographical sequence which includes
A Rumanian Diary (*Rumänisches Tagebuch*, 1924; tr. 1929), *Boyhood
and Youth* (*Verwandlung einer Jugend*, 1928; tr. 1931) and, finally,
The Young Doctor's Day (*Der Tag des jungen Arztes*, 1955). Carossa's
solution to the problems of evil is mystical, over-dependent on
Goethe and therefore inappropriate to his century; but in his refusal
to deny evil, and in his own life-style (which his literary style well
reflects) he achieves quality.

GERTRUD VON LE FORT (1876–1971), daughter of a Prussian officer,
is a more notable and original, and less pompous, traditionalist
and conservative than Huch (q.v.). While some German writers
claimed after the event to have practised an 'inner emigration'—so
that the term became discredited—Gertrud von Le Fort's withdrawal
was absolute in its dignity and integrity. She fled to Switzerland after
her books had been banned and her family estate confiscated. She
had become converted to Roman Catholicism in Rome in her late
forties, but being of Protestant stock—and studiously tolerant—she
maintained an ecumenical bent. All her more important work follows
her conversion. Like so many German writers, she chose to use history
as a means of illuminating the present. She is not as readable as Bergengruen (q.v.)—not, that is to say, as energetic and in love with life
and its colour—but her intellect is more potent: she has even
prompted Carl Zuckmayer (q.v.) to remark that she is 'the greatest
metaphysical writer of the twentieth century', which would not be

an exaggeration if modified to 'woman writer'. Although in no sense 'modern', Gertrud von Le Fort has been consistently intelligent; her work is still much studied and read, and since the war many of her books have been translated into Eastern languages, especially into Japanese.

For all her over-heavy emphasis on the spiritual, Gertrud von Le Fort's fiction is cast in a realistic form. It hardly does justice to her to declare (as is often done) that her three great subjects are the (German) Empire; woman as virgin, bride and mother; and the Church. Her fiction is, so to speak, better than this, although it is unlikely that further interest will be taken in her ponderous poetry. *The Song of the Scaffold* (*Die Letzte am Schafott*, 1931; tr. 1953), a novella, the basis for Bernanos' (q.v.) libretto for Poulenc's opera *Dialogue des Carmélites* (1956), is probably her most intense and effective work. Although religious faith is shown as the only answer to the nihilism and despair felt by the expressionist generation, this story of a nun faced with execution during the French Revolution gives as accurate a portrayal of *non*-Catholic anguish as most fiction of its time.

Another converted Roman Catholic novelist is WERNER BERGEN-GRUEN (1892–1962); he fell foul of the Nazis, and was forced to retreat to the Tyrol, where he spent the war years until he was smuggled into Switzerland by friends a few months before the unconditional surrender. Like Le Fort, he did not become a Catholic until he was nearly fifty. Born in what was then Russia, of a noble family, Bergengruen is representative of the right-wing, aristocratic opposition to Hitler, who banned his works. He is at his best as a short-story writer; but his novels have the virtue (not as common in Germany as in some other countries) of being eminently readable without ever being ponderous, vulgar or slick. *The Last Captain of Horse* (*Der letzte Rittmeister*, 1952; tr. 1953) is a series of connected tales told by an old Czarist Captain-of-horse, who reappears in other volumes in his capacity as story-teller.

Bergengruen is better in the shorter forms, in which he was influenced by E. T. A. Hoffmann (of whom he wrote a study), because his natural vitality and his delight in story-telling are nearer to the essence of his creative imagination than his conservative 'philosophy'; but this is not negligible, and *A Matter of Conscience* (*Der Grosstyrann und das Gericht*, 1935; tr. 1952), in which Nazidom is transferred to a small Italian Renaissance state, is one of the most successful of modern German historical allegories. Here moralizing and psychological analysis are excluded in favour of dialogue, a technique that works well. *On Earth as it is in Heaven* (*Am Himmel wie auf Erden*, 1940), personally banned by Goebbels (himself once the author of a pitiful 'Dostoevskian' 'novel', *Michael*) is set in sixteenth-century Berlin, and once again treats history with more success and less vulgarity than most German novelists. Bergengruen is also an attractive minor poet in traditional modes, being best known for his lyrical 'resistance poems', *Dies Irae* (1945).

RENÉ SCHICKELE (1883–1940), like the Manns, Arp, and Benn (qq.v.), was divided from birth: he was an Alsatian, his mother being French and his father German. All his life he worked to heal the split between the two countries, and he deserves to be regarded as one of the fathers of whatever cultural residue there may remain in the notion of the E.E.C. . . . He wrote poetry, fiction, criticism and drama. His poetry gained him the reputation of an expressionist, but he was never committed to the movement, and his fiction is mainly conventional in form: he believed too firmly in the concrete ever to be seriously influenced by the movement. Of his many novels the large trilogy *The Rhineland Heritage* (*Das Erbe am Rhein*, 1925–7; *Maria Capponi*, 1925; *Heart of Alsace*, 1929; the third part, *The Wolf in the Fold* [*Der Wolf in der Hürde*] has not yet been translated) is probably the most outstanding, although his earlier and more obviously 'expressionist' novel *Benkal the Consoler of Women* (*Benkal der Frauentröster*, 1914) is interesting because of its unusual emphasis on character delineation. The sculptor Benkal is a typical expressionist 'artist as his own victim' figure. Feeling incapable of love, this narcissist destroys his masterpieces and drinks a toast to life.

Not one of the Nazi exponents of 'Blood and Soil' belongs in this book, which deals with literature. The East Prussian poet and novelist ERNST WIECHERT (1887–1950), who wrote novels protesting against technology and intellectualism, and preached the virtues of a life close to the soil, does; that he was in no way akin to the Nazis is surely proved by the fact that they imprisoned him for a time in 1938. His account of this, *The Forest of the Dead* (*Der Totenwald*, 1945; tr. 1947), is his best book. His fiction is evocative of the East Prussian landscape, but traces less convincingly (and with a too obvious indebtedness to Knut Hamsun, q.v.) his attempts to escape from misery and his slow acceptance of a Christian feeling. The best novel is probably *The Baroness* (*Die Marjorin*, 1934; tr. 1936), about a woman's fight to reconcile an embittered soldier to life.

ARNOLD ZWEIG (1887–1968), a Silesian Jew, became a pacifist and socialist after the First World War. *Claudia* (*Novellen um Claudia*, 1912; tr. 1930), a psychologically accurate but saccharine series of accounts of 'artistic' people, in particular of a fragile girl and her timid academic lover, showed the influence of Thomas Mann rather than any politically left-wing or expressionist influences. His *The*

Case of Sergeant Grischa (*Der Streit um den Sergeanen Grischa*, 1927; tr. 1927) was not, as J. B. Priestley (q.v. 1) pronounced, 'the greatest' of the war novels; but it was among the first half-dozen. Certainly it was Zweig's own best book. Few modern authors have traced the pitiless nature of bureaucracy more truthfully than Zweig in this tale of a Russian prisoner murdered ('executed') because, although he is not guilty, the system demands a victim. Also remarkable was the thoroughness and fairness of Zweig's picture of the German army. Here was a novel that *demonstrated* the human monstrousness, the inevitable injustice, of war.

In 1933 Zweig, who had become a Zionist in the Twenties, went to Palestine; but he returned to East Germany in 1948, and became identified with the regime to the extent of becoming President of the Academy of Arts. The novels that Zweig intended to stand with *Grischa* in a series, as exposures of bourgeois hypocrisy, are comptent but more doctrinaire: the best is *Young Woman of 1914* (*Junge Frau von 1914*, 1931; tr. 1932), in which the criticism of the pre-war society, although justified, is too angry to be altogether good for the fiction. His later work is of little interest. He was blind for the last forty years of his life.

It is extraordinary, on the face of it, that HANS FALLADA (ps. RUDOLF DITZEN, 1893–1947) wrote any novels at all; yet his output, considering his relatively short life, was large—and he has yet, perhaps, to receive his proper due. His subject was most often and certainly most famously 'the little man', the innocent victim; but he was not much like a 'little man', and was anything but an innocent victim. A novel that told the story of his life would be criticized as straining the reader's credulity. Son of an eminent Prussian judge, he ran away from home, tried to kill himself, was accused of writing obscene letters to the daughter of one of his father's colleagues, and shot and killed a young friend in a suicide pact whose terms he did not honour. He escaped trial for this, and war service, on the grounds of insanity. During the war he became addicted both to drink and morphine; at the same time he displayed his lifelong flair for survival against high odds by becoming a successful farmer. Finally he went to prison for stealing in order to maintain his drug supply.

At this point writing came to his rescue. Ernest Rowohlt, publisher of so many of the best writers of the time (Kafka, q.v., among them), gave him a part-time job in his Hamburg firm so that he could write.

He obliged with what, although it is early work, is most probably his best novel: *Peasants, Bosses and Bombs* (*Bauern, Bonzen und*

Bomben, 1930). He had been working at it intermittently throughout the Twenties. It remains one of the most vivid and sympathetic accounts of a local revolt (of farmers, in Holstein, a town where he had worked selling advertisement space for a paper) ever written: 'marvellously accurate', the verdict of a critic writing as late as 1968, is no exaggeration. His enormous success of 1932, *Little Man What Now?* (*Kleiner Mann—was nun*; tr. 1933) is not quite as good only because its range is smaller. It remains one of those few world best-sellers that merit attention to this day. Fallada—the name came from Falada, the cut-off horse's head, in the Grimm tale, that told the truth despite the uncomprehending world—could tell a story; in this respect he was perhaps no more remarkable than Feuchtwanger (q.v.) or half-a-dozen others; but his very psychopathic disabilities enabled him to achieve a naked sympathy with all the oppressed. This gives his work a special quality. He did not seriously deteriorate as a writer: his own personal troubles saw to that. When Hitler came, he stayed in Germany—perhaps too drunk and indecisive to get out—and wrote whimsical tripe that nevertheless has in it a yearning for better things. In *Wolf Among Wolves* (*Wolf unter Wölfen*, 1937; tr. 1938) he could get away with it as far as the Nazis were concerned because he was dealing with the inflation and allied problems they 'solved'. *Iron Gustav* (*Der eiserne Gustav*, 1938; tr. 1940) is a less easy compromise: the protagonist becomes a Nazi; but there is muted criticism, and the sensation of being up against it is vividly conveyed. Fallada suffered anguish under the Nazis, but his wildness did not allow him to make more than a token protest. He got rid of his first (helpful, teetotal) wife, and married a fellow-alcoholic. Then he shot and wounded his first wife, and was once again imprisoned. The Red Army happened to appear at this somewhat crucial time, and he found himself 'elected' Mayor of Feldburg in Mecklenburg. It is probably a pity that he was not an ironist. But his case is remarkable enough, and why the Nazis did not do away with him is a mystery. After he died there appeared *The Drinker* (*Der Trinker*, 1950; tr. 1952), which explains something of his own predicament—but not enough. As one who felt the anguish of his times quite as strongly as any more 'committed' writer, and whose own private hell strangely failed to vitiate his achievement, Fallada demands critical attention. His real theme was his own weakness of will—and its concomitant eruptions of violence; for this he found an occasionally perfect objective correlative in victims of fate, in men who were as 'ordinary' as he was extraordinary. He was one of those writers who will be looked at again in depth.

LUDWIG RENN (ps. A. F. VIETH VON GOLSSENAU, 1889–1968) who

lived in East Germany, is famous for one book, his first: *War (Krieg,* 1928; tr. 1929). This utterly matter-of-fact, non-judging, terse account of war is probably the best book on the subject to be written in the century. It has, above all, what one critic has called 'the severity of objective eloquence'. It moves at great speed, and perfectly conveys men's necessarily dehumanized habits of mind in the trenches. *War* might seem 'hard', insensitive, easy to write; but the perspective is continuously human: recording this is one who is patently not dehumanized. Renn came from an old and noble family, and had begun life as a soldier (1911). The war changed everything for him, and eventually turned him into a lifelong communist. He himself dates the change in his outlook to when, on the front, he 'ceased to drink'; indeed, *War* does read exactly like the narrative of a man who has suddenly ceased to drink, and who awakens, starkly, to what is going on around him. It has that profoundly moral awareness that never goes with what Renn here so studiously avoids: moral judgement. It is above politics; it is scrupulously fair and attaches 'blame' to no one. Instead it portrays human weakness and human misery. The difference between its compassion and that of *All Quiet on the Western Front* (q.v.) is just the difference between matter-of-fact, practical aid, and effusive sympathy. Renn's account of the final collapse of the Germans is perhaps the most remarkable part of a remarkable book—undoubtedly one of the greatest on war of our time.

It is ironic that the chief formative influence on the future communist Renn's deservedly much admired style was the Swedish geographer, explorer and travel writer Sven Hedin (1865–1952): Hedin, gifted but personally repellent, was an unrepentant Nazi sympathizer, who was decorated by a grateful Hitler in 1940. Renn was never able to write another book like *War*. In its sequel *After War (Nachkrieg,* 1930; tr. 1931) he tried to portray the confusion of the Weimar Republic, but failed to grasp the material. After twice being made a prisoner by the Nazis, he escaped to Switzerland, and then took an active part in the Spanish Civil War. From then his history is one of increasing intellectual commitment to communism. He went to East Germany in 1947, and there wrote run-of-the-mill novels, autobiographies, travel books and children's books.

ANNA SEGHERS (PS. NETTY RADVANYI, 1900), who also now lives in East Germany, won the Kleist prize with her first novel, *The Revolt of the Fishermen (Der Aufstand der Fischer von St. Barbara,* 1928; tr. 1929); it is a concise and psychologically accurate account of the revolt of Breton fishermen against their grasping employers. She wrote nothing less tendentious except her famous *The Seventh Cross (Das siebte Kreuz,*

1941; tr. 1945), which was filmed; this meticulously documented description of Nazi Germany remains the best book she has written. It tells of the escape of seven victims from a concentration camp, only one of whom avoids the cross set up for him by the camp commandant. Some of her later books contain vivid passages, but have become increasingly propagandist.

ERICH MARIA REMARQUE (PS. ERICH PAUL REMARK, 1898–1970), who was born at Osnabrück, in Hanover near the Dutch border, was a soldier in the First World War and then, before the phenomenal success of *All Quiet on the Western Front* (*Im Westen nichts Neues*, 1929; tr. 1929), a teacher, businessman and sports reporter. This novel of the war seen through the eyes of an ordinary soldier is not in the same class as Renn's *War* (q.v.), which it nevertheless eclipsed: characterization is lacking, and the claim that it 'speaks for its generation' is false—in certain respects it said, as Renn's book reveals by contrast, just what this generation wanted to hear. However, it is a vastly overrated rather than a bad book: within the author's fairly narrow limits it is truthful; it does show war as being unheroic, and the point of view of the 'cannon fodder' is faithfully adhered to. But the horrors are crudely piled on. *All Quiet on the Western Front* is not in fact better than a book that helped to prepare the way for its success, the fictionalized war-diary *Private Suhren* (*Soldat Suhren*, 1927; tr. 1928) by the poet, painter, translator and dramatist GEORG VON DER VRING (1889–1968). Remarque afterwards became the popular recorder of human heroism in the face of horrors economic and personal—as in what is his best novel, *Three Comrades* (*Drei Kameraden*, 1937; tr. 1937)—or racial. His heart was as big as his truly literary skill was small. He left Germany in 1933, became an American citizen in 1947, and a film star in 1956, when he played in the movie of his own *A Time to Live and a Time to Die* (*Zeit zu leben und Zeit zu sterben*, 1954; tr. 1954).

ERNST JÜNGER (1895), brother of the poet F. G. Jünger (q.v.), is another writer—an interesting, but rather repugnant one—whose primary inspiration was derived from war. In Jünger an impulse towards violent and dangerous action—he ran away at seventeen to join the Foreign Legion, saw four years' almost continuous warfare between 1914 and 1918, and was then again a soldier in the Second World War, at the beginning of which he performed an act of conspicuous and suicidal heroism—is contradicted, rather than balanced by, its exact opposite: a need for static contemplation, reflected in his botanical and naturalistic studies. Jünger has been mistakenly revered since 1945, by injudicious critics and by himself, as a 'great' writer; his combination of aristocratic nihilism and soldierly virtue conceals the frigidity of an intrinsic behaviourism and even, perhaps, a streak of plain middlebrow vulgarity: a tawdry ideology posing as a profound one. The effectiveness of his prose depends to a surprisingly high degree upon frigid abstractions that are either meaningless or, worse still, heartlessly insensitive. But he is a fascinating writer.

Jünger's first book, *The Storm of Steel* (*In Stahlgewittern*, 1920; tr. 1929), which he has continually revised, might be said to be the earliest of all the 'anti-war books', except that, realistic though its descriptions of the horrors are, it does not reflect a hatred of war. These are ecstatic, depersonalized etchings, achieved through participation in violence. A bombardment of shells is 'the spectacle of a greatness that no human feeling can match', and it thus quells fear. This is the key to Jünger's earlier work: he sought God in war. He found danger an anaesthetic. After the First World War he busied himself with botany and allied sciences: ever in pursuit of the static, the rigid, the ordered, the hard. There is no sweetness in his botany, and little feeling for beauty.

Jünger's most interesting, original and probably best book is the collection *The Adventurous Heart* (*Das abenteuerliche Herz*, 1929, withdrawn, curtailed, revised and reissued 1936), which anticipates Robbe-Grillet's (q.v.) behaviourism by a quarter of a century. Like Robbe-Grillet, although more gifted, Jünger's only passion is for the world-as-it-is: he has hardly an inkling that his 'detached', 'reasonable', 'scientific' objections to anthropomorphism provide an excuse to participate in a process of dehumanization, of denying love.

Jünger was politically involved, at least until 1933, with a totalitarian 'National Bolshevist' group; but all that was 'Bolshevist' about it was that it favoured a *rapprochement* with Russia against the West. In the psychologically inept *The Worker* (*Der Arbeiter*, 1932) Jünger advocated a semi-mystical workers' revolution—but by 'workers' he only meant 'technocrats'. The Nazis themselves did not suit him, and he withdrew from their scene; but they made liberal use of his ideas— and he could not complain. His system had little more concern with people than the Nazis; in his desire for a political situation in which everyone would 'unite' with everyone else to win a 'war', Jünger was—and is—indulging himself. In Paris as a German officer in the Second World War he enjoyed being a 'cultivated' member of the master-race, and the 'sympathy' he shows for French and other suffering in his war-diaries is intellectual rather than emotional. He possesses conscience as a pedigree dog possesses breeding, and this is petrified like a flower plucked and under botanical observation— not like a growing flower. His breeding, this cerebral notion of decency, prevented him from being bad-mannered enough to join the Nazis, and even led him, in his first novel, *On the Marble Cliffs* (*Auf den Marmorklippen*, 1939; tr. 1947) to perpetrate a work that they eventually, after it had sold well over a quarter of a million copies, banned—but without reprisals against himself. The term 'magic realism', often associated with the works of Hermann Hesse (q.v.), has been applied to this work: a fantastic situation is realistically treated. The narrator and another man settle, in isolation, just as Jünger did, to botany and meditation after fighting in a long war. But a pillaging, plundering Despot lives in the forest surrounding them, and they are forced to join battle with him (though they were once in his band). It has not been doubted that this was a thinly disguised attack on Nazidom; actually, in creative terms, it was a rationalization of Jünger's own predicament: the meditative life is portrayed with spurious mysticism, and Jünger's fascination with the Despot's lust and cruelty is hardly concealed. *The Peace* (*Der Friede*, 1943, 1945; tr. 1948), written in 1943 and circulated in typescript, reflected the views held by the participants in the June 1944 *putsch* against Hitler; but Jünger managed to remain 'uninvolved'. His friend and protector in Paris and after the war was General Speidel, who was arrested by Himmler in 1944—and thus managed to rise to a high position in the Nato hierarchy. It should be emphasized that Jünger was never an anti-semite or a member of the Nazi party, and that he has never lacked courage; but he contributed through his human coldness and insensitivity to the nihilism that made Nazidom possible. It is significant that *The Peace*, the nearest he came to protest, was written just after his eighteen-year-old son Ernestel was killed in action in Italy; but its philosophy is exactly the same as that of *The Worker*.

In the long futuristic novel *Heliopolis* (1949) Lucius de Geer (Jünger) sees human conflict as inevitable. Now this may be so. But it is all too obvious that Jünger, for his part, sees it only because he draws his nourishment from it. He has no despair. This implies that, however fascinating his work may be, it is inevitably second-rate. *Visit to Godenholm* (*Besuch auf Godenholm*, 1952) once again explores the military frustrations of ex-soldiers: here two of them go to a magician to regain the power they have lost. *The Glass Bees* (*Gläserne Bienen*, 1957; tr. 1961) is shorter, lighter and more overtly satirical: a more attractive note has crept in. But still there is coldness rather than wisdom, or even warmth, at its heart. Jünger is at fault not because his view of life is nihilistic, but because this view does not go further than an ingenious self-indulgence. He has not neutralized the demonic element in his militarism, and we must shudderingly agree with H. W. Waidson that 'one need have no regrets that he has never been let loose to operate on the patient' of modern man. It is all very well so say that 'when he deals with objects, forces, intellectual perceptions, he is unapproached by any German writer of this century'; but when the same critic adds, 'it is precisely with human beings that he breaks down', he is adding a very great deal.

The lifelong left-wing commitment of THEODOR PLIEVIER (1892–1955) led him to settle in East Germany in 1945, where he had an official position in the cultural hierarchy; but, soon disillusioned, he fled in 1947 to Bavaria, and died in Switzerland. Plievier, whose name is sometimes spelt 'Plivier', was a journalistic novelist, more concerned with politics than with literature. The son of a poor Berlin tile-cutter, Plievier was a sailor from an early age, and was one of the leaders of the sailors' revolt at Wilhelmshaven. *The Kaiser's Coolies* (*Des Kaisers Kulis*, 1929; tr. 1931) made him famous; it is written in a deliberately flat, non-literary style, and while not as effective as Renn's *War* (q.v.), is nevertheless a powerful book, containing the most vivid of all descriptions of the Battle of Jutland. Before Plievier fled to Russia in 1933 he wrote *The Kaiser Went, the Generals Remained* (*Der Kaiser ging, die Generäle blieben*, 1932; tr. 1933), which is more tendentious. Plievier became disillusioned with the Russians in 1936, but could not get away until nine years later. The book that put his name before a world-wide public, *Stalingrad* (1945; tr. 1948), is a massively effective piece of journalism: crude, clumsy and lacking in characterization, it yet conveys a convincing picture of the collapse of the German military machine in Russia. This is documentary, but Plievier rightly gives himself the freedom of fiction. *Moscow* (*Moskau*, 1952; tr. 1953) and *Berlin* (1954; tr. 1956; reissued as *The Rape of a City*, 1962) are the sequels. Throughout this vast work the viewpoint changes from avidly pro-Russian to anti-Russian (but not anti-communist). The finest of Plievier's writing is to be found in *Berlin*, in the section that describes the final destruction of the city.

HERMANN KESTEN (1900), born in Nuremberg, fled to Amsterdam in 1933, and then in 1940 to New York. He now lives in Rome. He was always radical but not communist. His earlier novels, such as *Joseph Breaks Free* (*Joseph sucht die Freiheit*, 1927; tr. 1930) were rebellious in theme in a rather conventional manner, but psychologically they were solid enough. In *The Charlatan* (*Der Scharlatan*, 1932) he characterized Hitler. His Spanish trilogy, the middle part of which, *I, the King* (*König Philipp II*, 1938; tr. 1939), has been translated, studied the present in terms of the past, in the German fashion. *The Children of Guernica* (*Die Kinder von Guernica*, 1939; tr. 1939) is set in Northern Spain at the time of the Civil War. His best novel, in which his sense of irony at least equals his indignation, is *The Twins of Nuremberg* (*Die Zwillinge von Nürnberg*, 1947; tr. 1946). One twin, Primula, marries a Nazi; the other Uli, marries a writer who, like Kesten, has to emigrate. The time span is 1918–45, and the account of a Germany that the author had not known is in its way as remarkable as that of Carl Zuckmayer in *The Devil's General* (q.v.). It is in this remarkably un-Teutonic and lucid book that Kesten's usually somewhat too crude, or at any rate unsubtle, notion of the tyrannical dogmatic enemy is most effectively modified, and it deserves to be better known.

The melancholic STEFAN ZWEIG (1881–1942), an almost over-gifted Viennese Jew, was the archetypal casualty of the collapse of the Austro-Hungarian Empire; that he killed himself in 1942 (he and his wife committed suicide in Brazil) rather than a quarter of a century before sometimes seems like an accident. Zweig had an acute sense of historical crisis, but could not respond adequately to it in creative terms; so it was his vulgarity that came to the fore, in a series of worked up biographies, brilliant and intelligent, but lurid, over-simplified and ultimately little more than autobiographical in significance. He wrote on, among others, Verhaeren, Romain Rolland (qq.v.), Masaryk, Hölderlin, Kleist, Nietzsche (q.v.), Casanova, Freud (who considerably influenced him in his approach to biography), Stendhal, Tolstoy (q.v. 4), Marie Antoinette, Queen Elizabeth and Mary Queen of Scots. ... Nine of the shorter of these 'analyses', as he called them, may be found collected in *Adepts in Self-Portraiture* (*Drei Dichter ihres Lebens*, 1928; tr. 1929), *Three Masters* (*Drei Meister*, 1920; tr. 1930) and *Master Builders* (*Baumeister der Welt*, 1925; tr. 1939). These amount to little more than superb journalism. Zweig had a wide circle of artistic friends (Verhaeren, Rolland, the composer Richard Strauss and hosts of others), and it may be that most of his genius came out in sympathetic friendship. Certainly the promising *Jungwien* (q.v.) poet and dramatist was destroyed by the disintegration of his world. He was at his best in the short story, and if he is to be remembered it will be for such examples as *Amok* (1922; tr. in *The Royal Game*, 1944). His posthumous autobiography, characteristically entitled *The World of Yesterday* (*Die Welt von Gestern*, 1943; tr. 1943), is a moving work.

Life struck from the very beginning at the Austrian novelist JOSEPH ROTH (1894–1939), a half-Jew: before he was born his father left his mother; he died in a lunatic asylum in Holland without Roth's ever seeing him. Roth was only forty-four when, an alcoholic, he died in a Paris hospital, down on his own luck and agonized by events in Vienna. He was basically conservative—he wrote in 1939 that he 'desired the return of the Empire'—but his sufferings prevented his becoming a reactionary. His theme is invariably, directly or indirectly, the results of the dissolution of the Austro-Hungarian Empire. He cannot see, as Hofmannsthal (q.v.) saw, the broader implications of this event, but records its effects on himself realistically and self-critically. An officer in the First World War, he was accidentally involved in the Russian Revolution; his wife went mad soon afterwards, and he was forced to take jobs such as cinema-usher to survive. His greatest success was *Radetzkymarsch* (1932; tr. 1974), which nostalgically but unsentimentally depicts the Austria of Franz Josef. It is a memorable and indubitably major book, as are *Job* (*Hiob*, 1930; tr. 1931) and his last novella, *The Legend of the Holy Drinker* (*Die Legende vom heiligen Trinker*, 1939; HE). *Hiob*, the story of a wandering Jew, is as autobiographical as *The Holy Drinker*, a bittersweet picture of Roth's final demoralized years in Paris, drinking and living on despair and chance.

About the Viennese novelist HEIMITO VON DODERER (1896–1966) there is some controversy. Like Stefan Zweig's his point of departure was the collapse of the Austrian monarchy (and of the Russian Czardom, which he saw as a prisoner-of-war in Siberia during the Revolution); but, although a monumentalist, Doderer's Austrian sense of the comic saved him from Zweig's anguish and sense of permanent exile. Is his reputation, however, grossly inflated, or is he really one of the outstanding writers of the century, as is sometimes claimed? The question can best be answered by comparing his work to that of the novelists who most influenced him: Dickens, Proust and Musil (qq.v.). By the side of this, his novels may seem to lack an inner core of vision, to reflect no very profound response to the disintegration of European life. His major novel is *The Demons* (*Die Dämonen*, 1956; tr. 1961), a continuation of *The Strudlhof Steps* (*Die Strudlhofstiege*, 1951) and *The Illuminating Window* (*Die erleuchteten Fenster*, 1951). The message of this large-scale portrait of Vienna is that concrete actuality is the only reliable touchstone; that all our 'demons' arise from imagination. Doderer utilizes the techniques of Proust and Musil, only to deny the validity of their vision. And this seems to stem not from conviction but from creative inferiority. But there is some fine and humorous writing, and when Doderer forgets his message in his enthusiasm for his characters he is lively and amusing. But the problem of length defeated him. His monumentalism is pretentious, because attended by no inner compulsion: the pattern he tries to create is artificial. Broch, Musil (qq.v.), and others, did not overcome the especially Teutonic problem of length; but for them it was a genuine problem; Doderer could better have written realistic short novels. Doderer is a writer well aware of the impulses inherent in literary modernism, but he is, in his own words, a 'naturalist ; it is a pity that his fiction does not behave as though this were more straightforwardly so. A contrary critical view, eminently worthy of attention, represents Doderer as a neglected master. The chief objection—apart from the fact that so many of Doderer's tricks, particularly his punning, have an element of charlatanism—is the crudity of his 'naturalism', in which even character itself is subordinated to luck or chance. Furthermore, the dependence on *The Man without Qualities* (q.v.) and the desire to outstrip it are too much in evidence. But Doderer, it must be admitted, often *looks* very like the major novelist he aspired to be. Such a perceptive critic as Paul West would clearly like to prefer him to Broch or Musil; but when he says that Doderer is 'in favour of such an ostentatious sensibleness as that recommended by C. P. Snow' (q.v. 1) then some of us will not be tempted to go further.

In contrast to Doderer, the Swiss ROBERT WALSER (1878–1956) was a miniaturist with a fastidious conscience. A humble and diffident man, he was the younger brother of a fairly well known decorative painter, Karl. Before going to Berlin in 1905 he was a banker and clerk. There he wrote his three published novels (at least one other, most probably more, were destroyed). He became mentally ill in 1913 and returned to Switzerland, where he struggled vainly to live as a writer. In 1929 he gave up and entered hospital. Four years later he transferred to another hospital at Herisau, where he remained for the last twenty-three years of his life.

Walser's gift was delicate and fragilely held, but quite as considerable as that of most 'monumentalists'. Christopher Middleton has pointed out—in the introduction to his translations of Walser's short stories: *The Walk* (*Der Spaziergang*, 1917; tr. 1957)—that behind Walser's charm and clarity lies a sense of nightmare, and that his stark simplicity influenced Kafka (q.v.). In Walser's shorter sketches men move through a dreamlike world. For example, in the sketch 'The Walk' a young writer goes to a town to lunch with a patroness, visit a tailor—and convince a tax-man that he deserves special consideration. But the subtlety of style gives this work several levels, of which one is humour and another nightmare. What is unusual in Walser is his ability to transform the commonplace into the remarkable. His freshness and his lyrical quality are evident even in his first immature collection of sketches, *Fritz Kocher's Compositions* (*Fritz Kochers Aufsätze*, 1904), which are represented as posthumous schoolboy essays. The device was characteristic and apt: there was always a strong element of the child-like in Walser, but there was also an ironic playfulness about him. which he could perfectly express through a schoolboy *persona*. This, with its deceptively simple descriptions of his home town and so on, is a lovely book, and enables us to see at once that Middleton is right when he describes Walser's 'archetype' as 'the Holy Fool'.

Walser's three novels are extraordinary, and all the more so for being, not consciously experimental or 'modern', but rather intensely his own. 'Not caring about artistic propriety, I simply fired away', he told Carl Seelig regretfully in 1937; but we are grateful that he didn't care, even if later, when his mental state was too precarious for him to leave hospital, he wished he had. *The Tanner Family* (*Die Geschwister Tanner*, 1907) was hardly a novel by the standards of its time, since it consists of a series of relatively brief sections: letters, monologues and narrative passages. *The Assistant* (*Der Gehülfe*, 1908) is a (mainly) comic treatment of what we may call 'the man without qualities' (cf. Musil) theme: the restless Joseph Marti would like, so to say, to realize himself without ever committing himself. He is a gentle and quiet man in conflict with a loud, coarse and yet not wholly unlovable one—his employer, the engineer Tobler, a portrait that only needs wider currency to be acknowledged as a comic classic.

Jakob von Gunten (1909; tr. C. Middleton, 1970), which influenced Kafka perhaps as much as any single book, is another novel that demands to be better known. Jakob attends the Institut Benjamenta, where there is only one, indefinitely repeated, lesson, given by the principal's sister. Instruction consists of learning the school rules by heart, and tasks are limited to sweeping and scrubbing. Like the pupils in ostensibly more conventional establishments, most are cheerful—but since their destiny is to be valets they entertain no hope. Ironically, Jakob's presence here is an act of rebellion against his family. ... But although he begins by hating the principal Benjamenta and his sister, later, by reaching an understanding that even these two are human in their need for love and sympathy, he comes to love and eventually to identify himself with them. When the school breaks up with the death of Benjamenta's sister, Jakob sets off with Benjamenta—satisfying the latter's craving—on an aimless journey. In certain respects this beautiful and subtle book is equal to Kafka's unfinished novels: though haunted by mystery, it is none the less not so starkly non-realistic: humanity does not even have to keep breaking in, for it is there all the time. Walser was a major writer who has yet to be fully discovered in the English-speaking world.

FRIEDO LAMPE (1899–1945), born in Bremen, accidentally shot by Russian troops, remained almost unknown until ten years after his death, when his work was republished. Like Walser's, his stories employ ostensibly realistic methods to achieve far from naturalistic effects. *On the Edge of Night* (*Am Rande der Nacht*, 1933) gives an account of various people's activities at twilight in autumn in Bremen; the matter-of-fact, almost lyrical realism has a sinister quality, which also characterized the novella *September Storm* (*Septembergewitter*, 1937).

Carl Zuckmayer (q.v.) described the Viennese ALEXANDER LERNET-HOLENIA (1897) as the most distinguished Austrian writer after Hofmannsthal; he is his close friend, but this does approximate to Lernet-Holenia's reputation just before the war. He is not a good poet or a lasting dramatist, but his novels are superior to the better known ones of Werfel (q.v.). Outstanding is *The Standard* (*Die Standarte*, 1934), an exciting and intelligent story of the decadence of the Austro-Hungarian monarchy. *Mars in Aries* (*Mars im Widder*, 1941) counterpoints an ironic account of the mobilization of 1939 with the personal experiences of an Austrian officer, and was in its necessarily ultra-subtle way an anti-war and anti-Hitler novel.

We all know of ERICH KÄSTNER (1899–1974) from his *Emil and the Detectives* (*Emil und die Detektive*, 1929; tr. 1930; 1960). This is a charming children's book, in which the author avoids sentimentality, and is able to portray the innocence that forms the basis of his more important work, his satirical poetry. He began as a conscious exponent of the 'new objectivity' (q.v.), but his irreverent sense of humour puts him out of reach of any theory. He has remained very much his own man, and has failed only when he has tried to bear too earnest witness to the horrors of his time (as in the drama *The School of the Dictators*, *Die Schule der Diktatoren*, 1956). He is one of the outstanding children's writers of the century, because—whatever he may intend—his poker-faced moralism appeals to the child (and to the child in the adult mind) as a mask just teetering on the edge of collapse into total and uncontrollable laughter.

Kästner's ideal style is laconic. When he lapses into other styles, as in his novel *Fabian, The Story of a Moralist* (*Fabian, die Geschichte eines Moralisten*, 1932; tr. 1932) the results are embarrassing. His children's fiction is charming; his poetry (the largest selection is in *Let's Face It*, 1963; also TCG, MGP), for all its surface humour and even whimsy, is more serious and substantial. As a poet Kästner was from the beginning a self-styled 'workaday poet' (*Gebrauchslyriker*), one who deliberately set out to be functional, to be useful. His achievement is to have written such simple and yet penetrating poems. Not many modern poets have succeeded in preserving lucidity at so little cost to integrity of content. 'Evolution of Mankind' (TCGV) is typical:

once 'these characters used to squat in trees . . . then they were lured
out of the primeval forest and the world was asphalted . . .'. Then
follows an account of what men do: 'tele-phone . . . tele-view . . .
breathe in the modern way . . . split atoms . . . cure incest. . . . Thus
with head and mouth they have brought about the progress of
mankind. But apart from this and taking a wide view they are still
basically the same old apes'.

HERMANN KASACK (1996–1966), who was born in Potsdam, regarded himself primarily as a poet, but is more celebrated as a
novelist and usually classed as one. He was a doctor's son, and for
most of his life worked in publishing. He was a friend of Oskar
Loerke (q.v.), edited his diaries, and was much influenced by him
in his poetry, for which he was well known in the Thirties. During
the years of the Third Reich he lay low, but he did publish a retrospective selection of his poems in 1943: *Life Everlasting* (*Das ewige
Dasein*). As a young man Kasack wrote plays—one of them about
Van Gogh—without much success. His present reputation is almost
entirely based on his novel *The City Beyond the River* (*Die Stadt hinter
dem Strom*, 1947; tr. 1953), which was written during and immediately after the war years.

Kasack's ultimate literary origins may fairly be described as expressionist. In an article on him W. F. Mainland has quoted a piece
of his early poetry that makes this abundantly clear: 'The horror,
Night, destroys the evening walk. Emptiness of talk ungulfs gesture
with a sob. Mouth's dark chasm holds the cry—so take me. Street
tears apart, men silhouette. I fall, rubble weighs on my head. Hands
flutter apart with the hat raised in greeting, and still in dream this
hovering lingers; its moan dies away at the sight of mask; hair makes
strand of face. Horrified, hunted, body lashes drifting space'. As
Mainland says: '. . . this was the fibre from which grew the admired
economy of Kasack's style; he found the significance of gesture, discovered the motif of the mask which was to recur with the deeper
significance in his post-war novels'.

The first part of *City Beyond the River* is a genuinely imaginative and
complex response to the nightmare conditions of the defeated Germany of the immediate post-war years. Robert Lindhoff, an oriental-
ist, crosses a bridge into a strange city. The book remains on a high
creative level until about half-way, when Lindhoff discovers that he
is in a city of the dead, of ghosts awaiting final dissolution. Then,
although still interesting, the narrative becomes abstract; creative
pressure yields to cerebration. Kasack's pantheistic-Buddhist solutions are not convincing; but his diagnosis of human illness, including the hideous misuse of technological advance, is brilliant and

edged; his subtlety and integrity are not in question. *The Big Net* (*Das grosse Netz*, 1952) has good passages, but is a failure as a whole. The satirical intelligence with which it exposes human stupidity in dependence upon press, statistics and 'images' put across is worthy of Kraus (q.v.), or Wyndham Lewis (q.v. 1), and those of its episodes that are imaginatively charged are powerful (and often comic); but too much of the novel is contrived. Nevertheless, *The Big Net* has been underrated: lack of integration should not blind us to the quality of the intelligence that underlies it.

Forgeries (*Fälschungen*, 1953), although it lacks the scope of the two earlier books, is rightly regarded as Kasack's best-integrated work. A collector comes to prefer his antiques to his wife or his mistress; when he sees his mistake he has to destroy all he loves—both the fakes and the genuine articles. This is a psychologically convincing story which raises questions of truth and falsity (and of the righteous kind of self-deception that may be practised by those who are dedicated to beauty and to the past.

X

The Czech FRANZ KAFKA (1883–1924), born, like Rilke, in Prague, has been both more widely influential and more widely interpreted than any other single modern writer. Known during his life by only a select few, he wanted his three unfinished novels to be burned after his death, but his friend Max Brod (q.v.) published them. Research into his life has shown him to have been a painful neurotic, especially in his relationships with women; but he could be gay and happy, and the popular portrait of him as 'the sick artist' is too one-sided. Kafka's father, a self-made Jewish haberdashery merchant, was a dominating personality, and profoundly affected his son's attitude to life. On the one hand, Kafka wanted to win his approval; on the other, he despised his materialism and the respect for bureaucratic procedures that naturally went with it. If he is not ultimately, for all his enormous influence and his unerring finger on the pulse of his century, a supreme writer, then this is because he lacks human warmth—and that, in turn, is because he could never reconcile his emotional desire for patriarchal approval (and all that this implies) with his sophisticated rejection of it. Kafka worked as an insurance clerk until tuberculosis forced him to retire. He published six collections of stories, fragments and aphorisms in his lifetime, and was not as obscure as it sometimes supposed; but it was not until Brod issued *The Trial* (*Der Prozess*, 1925; tr. 1955), *The Castle* (*Das Schloss*, 1926; tr. 1953) and *America* (*Amerika*, 1927; tr. 1938) that he achieved world-wide fame. These three unfinished novels are his most famous but not his best—or at least not his most fulfilled—work, which is to be found amongst the short stories. Also published and in translation are his diaries and some of his letters.

Kafka is not interested in character: he is a writer of fables, but of fables in the intrinsically ironical style of the tales of the Hasidim and other traditional Jewish writings. A man seldom serene in himself, his narrative calm—especially in such a tale as *Metamorphosis* (*Die Verwandlung*, 1912; tr. 1961)—can be appallingly serene. This is partly because his work is oneiric in quality—and dreams speak in the 'pictorial language speech once was'.

Kafka, I repeat, is not interested in character: he is a writer of fables, but of fables that evoke the bewildered, humiliated or defensive states of mind of a single protagonist. He read widely, and was influenced by such diverse writers as Dickens and the Freud of *The Interpretation of Dreams*. Indeed, his fiction is most usefully approached as dream. He is still one of the most consistently 'modern' of twentieth-century writers: attempts to interpret him in terms of any modes that preceded him—even of those practised by writers who influenced him—are doomed to failure.

One of Kafka's most characteristic short stories is *Metamorphosis*. Gregor Samsa's life is dedicated to supporting his parents; his father has had a business failure. He wants to send his sister to music school, where she may develop her talent for violin playing. He works as traveller for a warehouse. It becomes clear in the course of the narrative that Gregor is the kind of man most other men would call 'an insect': he has no 'backbone'. It is into an insect, in fact, that he finds himself turned: 'As Gregor Samsa awoke one morning from uneasy dreams he found himself transformed in his bed into a gigantic insect', the tale begins. His first thought is that he will not be able to go to work. And throughout he feels no self-pity, no surprise that he has been thus transformed (is it not natural?)—only a rather mild instinct for survival, which quite soon subsides into an acceptance of death; as soon, in fact, as he sees himself unable to resume his job. He ends up 'quite flat and dry', expiring without complaint. Gregor is Kafka's most passive hero: he has no defence against his family's loathing of him. He could bite, but does not. Literally, he turns into what he is: a repulsive and filthy insect. All his hatred and resentment of his father are submerged in guilty approval-seeking; he feels himself obliged to compensate for the business failure to the extent that he does not even think about it: his whole wretched existence, humiliated and criticized by his employers, has been dedicated to serving his family. And so, of course, his involuntary metamorphosis is a final and definitive coming-to-the-surface of his hatred, a distortedly and exaggeratedly cruel revenge; this insect that cannot even assert itself enough to acquire a personality revenges itself by *turning into itself*. There is no escape from guilt and sin and wretchedness. This is what the insurance clerk Kafka thought of himself for giving in to what he interpreted as 'his father's wishes', instead of devoting himself to writing. Gregor is certainly a self-portrait. But he is more than this. He is, too, like almost every other of Kafka's protagonists, the imaginative artist, the creator. For this 'insect' has had at least this power: the strength, as secret from himself as from others, to become what he is: to make metaphor reality. In that situation he is entirely alienated, since although he at first imagines he is speaking he soon discovers that what comes out is a series of insect squeaks (the public's 'understanding' of writers?). When he wants to express good intentions, he hisses horribly, and his father throws fruit at him.

Metamorphosis belongs to Kafka's early maturity, and originates in self-punitive fantasy. Gregor's punishment for not being his true self is to become the untrue self he was. His function as 'artist' is only to confer power and horror; Kafka was as yet unconscious of this aspect of his work, and his guilt at being a creator is at this stage swamped by a more subjective and neurotic guilt. But that the repulsive insect-form did already represent the creator is evident from the very early sketch 'Wedding Preparations in the Country'. The hero Raban's fantasy is of splitting himself into two: an image would perform 'duties', while the true self would stay in bed—a giant beetle.

Walter Sokel's division of Kafka's maturity into three phases is useful and not too arbitrary: 'In the first phase of his maturity (1912–1914) the protagonist represses his inner truth, but his truth erupts in a catastrophe—accuses, judges, and annihilates him. This is the phase of . . . the powerful tales of punishment and death which are Kafka's most . . . popular. . . . The second phase (1914–1917) begins with *The Penal Colony* and continues with the short parabolic pieces of the *Country Doctor* volume. . . . In this phase a detached perspective views and contemplates a paradoxical discrepancy between self and truth. The final phase (1920–1924) is Kafka's . . . most profound. It comprises the four stories of the *Hunger Artist* volume . . . "Investigations of a Dog" and "The Burrow" and . . . *The Castle*. In . . . that phase . . . Kafka presents the protagonists' deception of the world, perpetrated by his desperate need to create and fulfil his existence'. (*America* was written 1911–14, *The Trial* 1914–15 and *The Castle* 1921–2).

America, although apparently more realistic than anything else Kafka preserved (he destroyed some novels in manuscript), is essentially of the same pattern with the rest: the protagonist is accused, judged and condemned. Sent to America by his family for, he thinks, *being seduced*, he enters a similar situation and is similarly exiled—and so on. In *The Trial* the hero is arrested for an unknown crime of which he nevertheless feels guilty—and is eventually 'executed'. The basis of the states of mind of nearly all Kafka's heroes is their sense of alienation and, further, their agonies of guilt because of this.

Max Brod, and his translator Edwin Muir (q.v. 1), thought of Kafka as a religious novelist. His victims, they assert, represent Mankind in a state of original sin or truth-seeking. A fabulist, Kafka can perhaps be so interpreted. But the trouble with this view is that it posits a Kafka who at heart believed in a purposeful universe; and one of the essential features of his work, taken as a whole, seems to lie in its agonized doubts on this very point. His anguished protagonists have, precisely, no certainty of anything. The Divine, which Brod and Muir postulate as being symbolically or allegorically omnipresent in his work, actually remains undefined in it; the nature and quality of the sinister threat, functioning externally as bureaucratic menace to life and freedom, and internally as *angst*, remain unknown. Kafka is, as Günther Anders has said in the most provocative of all the studies of him (*Kafka: Pro et Contra*, 1951; tr. as *Kafka*, 1960), a sceptic who doubts his own scepticism—and, one may add, doubts that doubt to the point where he asks that his work be destroyed.

This request of Kafka's that such of his works as were not published should be destroyed was not simply neurotic. In his writings he had got beyond neurosis, and he knew it: he could not have perpetrated the bad taste, the personal ambitiousness, the ignorance, or the stylistic confusion of Hitler's *Mein Kampf*—but he could have invented its spirit. And he had come to see that those who invent, in words, may be responsible for more than words. His decision may have been right or wrong; but it must be respected as essentially beyond private neurosis.

One of Kafka's last fragments was *The Castle*, the best of the novels. Whereas the hero of *The Trial* was Josef K., the hero of this is simply K. The connections with Kafka himself are obvious and, of course, have not been overlooked. 'A Hunger Artist' (published in 1922), which was written in the same period, is a more successful treatment of the same theme. As Sokel has noted, 'The perspective of the punitive fantasies, seeing the protagonists as victims of external injustice and outrageous fortune, tends to prevent us from noting the sub-merged inner force that drives them to their catastrophes'. This applies equally to the works of Kafka's last phase: the hunger artist, like K, is so put upon as a victim that we do not notice what Sokel rightly calls 'the crucial fact': that he is a fraud. The difference between the punitive fantasies and these later works is that now Kafka's protagonists (all unequivocally himself) 'oppose a unified self to truth'.

I agree with Sokel and other commentators in seeing K's claim to an appointment of Land Surveyor as a colossal confidence-trick—a confidence-trick from which the reader's attention is distracted by K's blandly righteous and urgent attitude. In fact K has no more right to the position than any other person. Were the claim legitimate, this would be made clear. Of course, we may see K as confidence-man or the unhappy victim of a delusion that involves an unwitting confidence-trick—as we wish. But indisputably he is guilty of deception. His degree of guilt is ambiguous—sickeningly so. Kafka lived in a world, as we all do, in which blame is no longer precisely measurable (and therefore no longer precisely expiable) and in which no authority can go unquestioned.

While Kafka may legitimately be regarded both as a spokesman for the Jews (as a German-speaking Jew in Prague he was doubly alienated; but he also felt alienated from his own race because of his lack of instinctive sympathy with Zionism) and as an ambiguous but revealing commentator upon the loss of religious certainty in his century, he is most directly to be considered as the most potent of all modern doubters of the human sufficiency of art. As Günther Anders writes, he considered his work suspect and ordered it to be destroyed because 'his writing possessed *only* artistic perfection'. (Here he may be linked with at least two others, also Jewish, who arrived at similar although more overtly stated conclusions by different paths: Broch q.v., and the American poet Laura Riding, q.v. 1.) The reasons for Kafka's wish to destroy his work are most evident in *The Castle*. Kafka's intended ending to this book (he told Brod) was to be that as K lay dying, exhausted by his struggles, word was to come from the Castle that although his legal claim is not recognized, 'taking certain auxiliary circumstances into account' he will be allowed to 'live and work in the village'. Such a fate doubtless seemed appropriate and even merciful for so persuasive a charlatan. But when Kafka postulated the artist as a charlatan he drew attention to an issue wider than that of the artist in society: for the predicament of the writer, with his egotistic concern to achieve 'artistic perfection', may not be so different from that of any other human being, also non-altruistically concerned with the establishment of mere perfection of an external *persona*. However, the creative predicament, not a whit mitigated by its universality, is in the godless twentieth century paradigmatic of this state. Kafka, with his acute sensitivity, exemplified it both as man and writer.

GUSTAV MEYRINK (ps. GUSTAV MEYER, 1868–1932) was born in Vienna but spent much of his life in Prague. His early short stories combine Jewish grotesqueness with more conventional satire against the bourgeois. Sometimes mentioned as having an affinity with Kafka (but this is far-fetched) even his best work—e.g. *The Golem* (*Der Golem*, 1915; tr. 1938)—suffers from superficiality, as though he could never quite develop confidence in himself. His conversion to Buddhism had a charlatan element in it. The Golem is a robot-figure—from Jewish lore—who accidentally gets out of his rabbi-owner's control, and starts to smash up the city. This has great energy and colour, but little depth.

Another, less well-known, author occasionally mentioned as akin to Kafka is FRITZ VON HERZMANOVSKY-ORLANDO (1877–1954), who was born in Vienna. His collected works did not appear until after his death (1957–63), and he published only one novel in his lifetime. Herzmanovsky-Orlando's fiction is in the mainly Czech-Jewish tradition of grotesquerie, and he was friendly with Kubin and Scheerbart (qq.v.). But it is not really 'kafkaesque' to any greater degree than Kafka's own work partakes of this particular half-whimsical, half-Jewish tradition. Herzmanovsky-Orlando's fiction is less whimsical and rather more serious than either Meyrink's or Kubin's, and at the same time more wildly grotesque.

HERMANN BROCH (1886–1951) has aptly been called 'the reluctant poet' ('poet' being used more in the sense of 'artist'). English-speaking writers have found his fiction difficult of approach. Not even his German readers have found him easy. A novelist of unquestionable importance, altiloquent but not pretentious, Broch could be obscure, prolix, humourless and plain boring. But he was a pioneer, and is as important in literature as he was heroically virtuous in his life—especially in his American years.

Broch was born in Vienna, the son of a Jewish textile manufacturer. Until the age of forty-two he ran the family's mills, and became a well-known conciliatory figure in Austrian industrial relations. As well as gaining a theoretical and practical mastery of the techniques of milling, Broch studied philosophy, mathematics, logic and physics at the University of Vienna, and knew many of the leading writers, who did not consider him one of them. Broch became a convert to Roman Catholicism well before he was thirty, but this was never much more than a gesture to the solidarity of the Catholic middle ages. Although he made efforts to disembarrass himself of the connection in the last years of his life, his thinking had always been 'post-Christian'.

In 1928 Broch sold the mills and returned to the University of Vienna in order to obtain a doctorate in philosophy and mathematics. His sense of the approaching economic depression probably made this a less difficult decision. After a year he left the University. He discovered that neither philosophy nor mathematics was adequate to express his ideas: he was forced to turn to literature. He then produced *The Sleepwalkers* (*Die Schlafwandler*, 1931–2; tr. 1932), *The Unknown Quantity* (*Die unbekannte Grösse*, 1933; tr. 1935), and began the novel now known as *The Tempter* (*Der Versucher*, 1953), upon a drastic revision of which he had not finished working at the time of his sudden death of a heart-attack. It was also in the Thirties that Broch wrote his famous essay on James Joyce (q.v. 1). After the *Anschluss* he was put into prison by the Gestapo; when released, he managed to escape from Austria, and eventually went to America. While in prison and literally facing death, he began to elaborate on an eighteen-page story he had read—by invitation—on Viennese radio in 1936, 'Virgil's Homecoming'. This had been an expression of his scepticism about literature. By 1940 what is by some regarded as his masterpiece, *The Death of Virgil* (*Der Tod des Vergil*, 1945; tr. 1946) was completed—but he worked at details for five more years. After this publication he once again renounced literature, teaching and devoting himself (effectively but at high personal cost) to helping individual refugees; but when a publisher desired to reprint five of his earlier stories he found himself unable to resist the temptation to change these into a 'novel in eleven stories': *The Innocents* (*Die Schuldlosen*, 1950). Much loved by many friends, Broch none the less died poor and alone—in a New York 'cold water' flat.

Broch saw history dialectically, as a process of cycles of two millennia (cf. Yeats, q.v. 1). The Christian era arose from the ruins of the pagan, but is now—having achieved its fullness in the Catholic middle ages—itself in ruins. Our era, like Virgil's, is one of 'no longer, not yet'. There are now 'partial systems': war, business, literature— all these are examples. Literature is as inadequate as, but more noble than, the other systems. The result of combining several of these partial, inevitably secular systems is by no means a valid syncretism, but increasing chaos. Broch's solution, in so far as he successfully formulated one, is for the individual to eschew all frenzies of eroticism and religiosity—as well as all partial systems—and to behave 'realistically'. Those who feel tempted to look to the nominally

Catholic Broch for support for a 'new Christianity' should note that his system cuts God out altogether.

His first novel, which is the first of the trilogy *The Sleepwalkers*, is taken to be his most successful by perhaps the majority of critics. It is decidedly easier to read than *The Death of Virgil*. The trilogy as a whole reveals Broch's dialectic theory: *Pasenow the Romantic* is contrasted with *Esch the Anarchist*; both are found wanting. The 'new' man is to be seen in *Huguenau the Realist*. The triad is: Romanticism—Anarchy—Actuality. However, Broch was by no means simple enough, or lacking in subtlety, to try to portray Huguenau as a 'nice' or a 'good' man: he is, however, for a time, a truly 'objective' man (we may compare him, perhaps, to what Brecht called Stalin: 'a useful man'), and Broch admitted that in him he saw his own 'super-ego'. This notwithstanding that he is an army deserter, rapist, swindler and murderer. In technique *The Sleepwalkers* is influenced by Dos Passos, Joyce (qq.v. 1), Gide (of *The Counterfeiters*, q.v.) and Huxley (q.v. 1), but the overriding design is unquestionably Broch's own. He had no hesitation in making use of any technique that might help him to achieve his complex purpose.

Broch found philosophy inadequate: it could not consider the irrational. But when he turned to fiction he incorporated all of the philosophy he knew (he had studied under distinguished philosophers) into it. Scrupulous to the last degree, Broch saw that everything in fiction must be conditioned by the personality of the writer, and he therefore took care to present the personality of the 'author' of his first novel: this Dr. Bertrand Müller is the author of both an essay and a lyrical ballad that are incorporated into the work. He is not Broch; but he probably 'is' Broch self-observed.

The Tempter (*Der Versucher*), which Broch finally proposed to call *The Wanderer*, is a study of the rise of Nazism. Marius Ratti comes to the mountain village of Kuppron and corrupts it. The novel as it was posthumously published is the result of extensive revision at the end of Broch's life; in respect of readability, which is not unimportant (when a basic intelligence in the reader is granted), it is his best novel. Marius, a false prophet, exploits the people of Kuppron. But the central character is the doctor who narrates the story.

The Death of Virgil, which deals with the last eighteen hours of Virgil's life, has been too confidently disposed of. Broch will be remembered, it is asserted, for *The Sleepwalkers* alone. The later novel certainly contains some of the longest sentences in literature, which have been characterized as 'page-long sentences with their cottonwoolly thump of pointless repetition'; but explained thus: 'Undoubtedly this prolixity is meant to indicate the endlessly trivial nature of human experience. . . . These sentences roll on because in nature there is no full stop'. And so, even if repetitions are boring or 'cottonwoolly', they are not 'pointless': the over-confident dismissal of *The Death of Virgil* is insensitive, if only to Broch's intentions. He himself described the book as 'a poem . . . that extends in a single breath over more than five hundred pages'. This novel is a monumental literary account of the insufficiency of literature. The dying Virgil comes ashore at Brindisi in the train of the Emperor Augustus, and is borne to the palace. He spends the final night of his life in regret. Then he speaks to his friends, and finally to Augustus, who persuades him to hand over his manuscript rather than destroy it (Virgil in return is given the right to free his slaves). The last part is a description of Virgil's transition from life into death.

Must we condemn *The Death of Virgil* because, as Aldous Huxley complained to the author, it is unreadable? (Huxley put it politely, saying that 'quantity destroys quality', and that Broch had imposed too great a 'strain' on the reader to guarantee obtaining 'an adequate response'.) No: for however strongly we may feel about Broch's portentousness, his failure to incorporate into his work the sense of humour he undoubtedly possessed, his ponderousness—in two words, his Teutonic heaviness—to dismiss *The Death of Virgil* is in itself an inadequate response. It may fail, but its treatment of the two themes of the reconciliation of life and death, and the insufficiency of art, is heroic; it is also radiant with intelligence. So few have persevered with the formidably difficult prose of *The Death of Virgil*, especially that of the long second section in which Virgil goes over his past life and its wastefulness in denying the truth of ugliness for the sake of artistic beauty, that we require further reports of the experience of concentrating upon it. Like his Virgil, Broch sought for 'a potency of expression . . . beyond all earthly linguistics . . . a speech which would help the eyes to perceive, heartbreakingly and quick as a heartbeat, the unity of all existence . . .' and he believed that 'the effort to approach such a language with paltry verses was rash, a fruitless effort and a blasphemous presumption'. Even a sceptic, who cannot believe that such a 'potency of expression' is humanly accessible, cannot but be impressed.

Although HERMANN HESSE (1877–1962), critic, poet, short-story writer, water colourist and—above all—novelist, lived in Switzerland from 1911, and became a Swiss citizen in 1923, he was born in Swabia. He won the Nobel Prize in 1946. Although Hesse was not as ambitious in his aims as Broch, he had much in common with him, chiefly an overriding desire to reconcile such opposites as death and life; but he was more drawn towards the East, and to such thinkers as Jung, than Broch. He has been more heeded in the East than in the West; there have been two editions of his complete works in Japan alone.

The novel with which Hesse made his reputation, *Peter Camenzind* (1904; tr. 1961) is nearer to Keller than to anyone else: it is a charming, idealistic, derivative novel, soaked in neo-romanticism but partially redeemed from this by integrity. A Swiss peasant becomes a famous writer, but renounces the decadent city and goes back to his native countryside. It was self-prophetic. In *The Prodigy* (*Unterm Rad*, 1905; tr. 1957) he relived his early years, when he ran away from theological school, but showed the hero, Klein, collapsing under the strain and drowning himself. Married to a woman nine years older than himself, and with three sons, Hesse was a prolific success. But he was unhappy. Yearnings very like those that stirred Broch prompted him to travel, first to Italy and around the continent, and then, in 1911, to India. This made a deep impression upon him, but one which he could not assimilate. He felt it ought to be his spiritual home, but could not make it so. In fact he was not ready for India; he was tired of his 'happy' marriage, and wanted to find good 'artistic' reasons to cast it off. He tried to rationalize these impulses in *Rosshalde* (1914; tr. 1971), the story of a dedicated painter with a similar problem; it is the least honest of his books.

With the war Hesse turned pacifist, and although he worked to relieve the sufferings of German prisoners-of-war he became unpopular and lost many friends. He went through the familiar crisis in which art can offer no solace: it seems insufficient. He left his wife (whose mental health had broken down) and underwent Jungian analysis. The result was his first major novel, *Demian* (1919; tr. 1965), which made him an entirely new (and wider) reputation.

This is the first-person narrative of Emil Sinclair (the pseudonym under which Hesse published it). Sometimes described as an expressionist novel, it is certainly so in that Emil's exploration of a 'dark' world is undertaken in defiance of his bourgeois parents, for whom such things do not even exist: it is an 'anti-father' novel. Otherwise it is an original synthesis of lyricism and symbolism both Christian and Jungian, whose theme is a quest for individual values. But Emil's young friend Demian is a kind of expressionist 'new man': he performs miracles, has followers, and is sacrificed in the war. His mother Eva is a 'wife-mother figure', a fount of the life-instinct, who makes herself available to Sinclair whenever required. Everything that takes place is 'real' enough, and yet the overall effect is 'magical'; hence the term 'magic realism'. The quest for personal values is seen as essentially a magical one. As Hesse picks up each influence—

Nietzsche, Christianity, Jung—he transcends it in favour of his own semi-mystical synthesis: for him the solution must always be in individual terms, and must therefore be unique. *Demian* is a fascinating and readable novel—much more easily readable than anything by Broch—and has the glow of genius. But its glow is suspect, as though poisonous feverishness were concealed by flushed sweetness: Hesse was anticipating an achievement he had not yet reached. But from this time he was increasingly regarded as a mage, and he prided himself on acting as what he described as a 'counsellor' to many young people. T. S. Eliot was so impressed by the non-fiction *In Sight of Chaos* (*Blick ins Chaos*, 1920, tr. 1923)—no doubt his close friend Sydney Schiff, who wrote under the name Stephen Hudson (q.v. 1) and who translated it, drew his attention to it—that he paid the author a personal visit (and quoted from him in the notes to *The Waste Land*).

In *Siddharta* (1922; tr. 1957) the increasingly antinomian Hesse drew on his Indian experiences. The hero, son of a Brahman, is first an ascetic then a sensual materialist, but does not learn anything until he becomes the assistant of a ferryman-mage who plies between the two worlds of spirit and flesh. . . .

Der Steppenwolf (1927; tr. 1965) shows Hesse both at his strongest and weakest. Of all the considerable pioneers in fiction of his time, Hesse was perhaps the most conservative: unlike Broch, he liked to rely as far as possible on traditional forms, and often he would take a specific nineteenth-century model. Here he drew on the realistic fairy stories of E. T. A. Hoffmann, the pioneer of 'magic realism'. Harry Haller, who is Hesse projected, is forty-eight and has decided upon suicide at fifty; but he finds a more meaningful solution in the 'MAGIC THEATRE. ENTRANCE NOT FOR EVERYBODY: FOR MADMEN ONLY'. The German conflict between Nature and Spirit is age-old, and to outsiders it can become wearisomely oversimplified and tiresome. It does so in the inferior works of late expressionism. But it has seldom been so charmingly presented (if not resolved) as in Hesse's *Steppenwolf*. The agonized Haller has devoted himself to pure spirit; now he finds himself entranced by the world of the flesh—and yet feels himself to be a half-wolf, and only half-man. At the end, when his prostitute Hermine has been shrunk 'to the dimensions of a toy figure' and put into the pocket of the musician Pablo, the proprietor of the 'magic theatre', he determines to 'begin the game afresh', although he knows he will 'shudder again at its senselessness': 'One day I would be a better hand at the game'. Unlike Broch, Hesse was learning to go in a more relaxed direction: to modify his Germanic philosophical certainties with humour and forbearance. In the fifteenth-century *Narziss and Goldmund* (1930; tr. 1932) he presents the same conflict, but in a less imaginative and more self-indulgently symbolic manner.

Hesse's most successful novel, *The Glass Bead Game* (*Das Glasperlenspiel*, 1943; tr. as *Magister Ludi*, 1949; tr. 1970), took him eleven years to write. The glass bead game is Hesse's own 'game' (the irony is characteristic): the quest for perfection, for the possibility of stating what Klein had only been able to feel as he drowned. The protagonist is Joseph Knecht, the imagined country Castalia, an idealized society that is nevertheless disintegrating because of its commitment to the spirit. We read of Knecht's education in Castalia, his two years in a monastery outside Castalia, and his eight years as Magister Ludi. Finally, like Ibsen (q.v.), who gave up esotericism in order 'to build houses for ordinary people', he decides to try to introduce life into the impoverished and abstract world of his country. The book ends ambiguously with his death by drowning. This could suggest despair of ever achieving a reconciliation; but since Knecht leaps into the water in order to leave an example of sacrifice for the young man to whom he has been tutor, some kind of hope remains. Knecht's suicide is one of those acts that go entirely beyond their author's intentions, and pose a meaningful question. The narration is made after Knecht's death, and subtly implies a Castalia that is no longer impoverished (or de-culturized).

The Glass Bead Game creates its own convincing world, and works its problems out entirely within that context. Hesse retained the gift of pure lyricism: the ability to find simplicity and sweetness at the heart of complexity.

With the Austrian ROBERT MUSIL (1880–1942) we come to an absolute scepticism. Born in Klagenfurt, Musil gave up military school in order to qualify as an engineer. Later he studied philosophy and psychology. He had a distinguished record as an officer in the First World War. After this he worked for a while as a civil servant and a magazine critic; then he tried to settle down as a playwright and freelance writer, but his small private fortune was lost in the inflation. A society was formed to help him financially, but with the *Anschluss* Musil left for Switzerland. The last four years of his life were poverty-stricken, and doubtless contributed to his early death.

Musil wrote two novels, *The Confusions of Young Törless* (*Die Verwirrungen des Jünglings Törless*, 1906; tr. 1955) and the unfinished *The Man without Qualities* (*Der Mann ohne Eigenschaften*, 1930–43; rev. ed. 1952–7; tr. 1953–60), some short stories, collected in English in *Tonka* (tr. 1965), a drama, *The Visionaries* (*Die Schwärmer*, 1921), a farce, *Vinzenz and the Girl Friend of Important Men* (*Vinzenz und die*

Freundin bedeutender Männer, 1924)—characterized by Brecht and Zuckmayer, when submitted to them as playreaders for the Deutsches Theatre in Berlin, as being, in Brecht's words, 'shit'—and many essays and reviews.

It should first be stated that the German edition of Musil's major novel, edited by Dr. Adolf Frisé, has come under very heavy fire from his English translators, Mr. and Mrs. Ernst Kaiser: they argue that after the fourteenth chapter of Part III—Musil had revised only as far as this when he died—Frisé has presented no more than an unwarranted and arbitrary construction, based on early and sometimes rejected drafts. Their case seems to be proven.

Young Törless is certainly a masterpiece. Its ostensible subject is homosexuality and sadism at just such a military academy as Musil himself had attended; indeed, a meticulously realistic account of this is given, one quite good enough to satisfy the most demanding realist. However, the true subject is the 'growing up' of Törless, his shift from pure (innocent) subjectivity to an awareness of objectivity, and his consequent sense of the gap between 'experience' and 'reason'. True, there seems to be something almost monstrously cold about him, in his capacity for analysis; but we feel repelled as though by a real young man. Musil had been tough enough to survive life at a military academy, and no doubt it hardened him; but, as Mr. and Mrs. Kaiser have pointed out, 'no adult Törless ever came into existence'—either as Ulrich in *The Man without Qualities* or as Musil himself.

Musil's few short stories are exquisitely written and realized. If anyone has doubts about either his psychological or his imaginative grasp, then these will be quickly dispelled by the first of his stories 'The Perfecting of a Love' ('Die Vollendung der Liebe', 1911), Musil's own favourite, in which a woman achieves a sense of love for her husband by allowing herself to be seduced by a ridiculous stranger. 'The Temptation of Silent Veronika' ('Die Versuchung der stillen Veronika', 1911), a study of a psychotic woman who has been buggered by a dog, is even more unusual for its time, although not perhaps as successful. It has been compared to both the Rilke of *Malte Laurids Brigge* and Trakl (qq.v.), with the proviso that whereas these writers' methods were 'an organic part of their subjects and of themselves . . . the garment Musil wears in his story was put on for the occasion'.

Musil's other stories, really better considered as novellas, collected in a volume entitled *Three Women* (*Drei Frauen*, 1924), are as subtle and original, but possess somewhat more of the surface realism that characterizes *The Man Without Qualities*. They are better than his

302 GUIDE TO MODERN WORLD LITERATURE 2

two plays, neither of which is good theatre, although both are interesting to read in the light of the novel that followed them. *Vinzenz* had a short-lived success.

The Man Without Qualities is one of the longest novels ever written, but its action is confined to a single year, that of 1913–14. It has been called a 'great novel' but 'an unsuccessful work of art' because it is unfinished. However, if one were required to define its form in one word, then this would be 'unfinishable'. Its hero Ulrich, 'not godless but God-free', has withdrawn from life, paralysed by uncertainty. In view of Broch's (q.v.) explanation of our age as one of 'no longer, not yet', it is interesting to compare Ulrich's reaction: 'His view was that in this century we and all humanity are on an expedition, that pride requires that all useless questionings should be met with a "not yet", and that life should be conducted on interim principles. . . .' Again, one is reminded of Broch's 'partial systems' by Musil's view that any individual quality becomes useless when it is independently propagated for its own sake. But Musil is temperamentally more Swiftian than Utopian, although he does not deny the possibility of a solution. One of his basic concerns is what might be called 'the solipsist problem': the problem of the dichotomy between each man, enclosed in his own private world, and all men, somehow (how?) concerned in 'society'. Musil's approach is comic and ironic. One of the main themes of *The Man without Qualities*, which is a plotless although realistic novel, is the so-called 'Collateral Campaign'. This is a project by 'important' people to celebrate 1918, the seventieth anniversary of the ancient Emperor's accession to the throne. It is 'collateral' because the Germans have similar plans for their Emperor. Ulrich becomes honorary secretary of this campaign: a campaign that the reader knows, retrospectively, could not come off. That year, 1918, in fact saw the end of the Austro-Hungarian Empire. Musil's novel exists deliberately on the edge of the precipice of 1914, but does not really ever dive headlong over it: the novel teeters; but Austro-Hungary (the Kakania of the novel) did fall.

Another major theme is the affair of the sex-murderer Moosbrugger, with whose fate Ulrich feels strangely linked. 'If mankind could dream collectively', Ulrich thinks, 'it would dream Moosbrugger'. Austria and German did, of course, dream the psychopath Hitler collectively. . . . This theme is indeed, as the Kaisers have remarked, 'the sombre reflection' of the Collateral Campaign.

Musil shared with Rilke a realization of how the impersonality of modern technology strangles the inner life of man. But unlike Rilke he remained an uncommitted sceptic: for him and for his hero Ulrich, any choice, any action, is only one out of a number of possibilities, and has no more validity than its alternatives. Thus life, like Hardy's (q.v. 1) 'fate', is for Musil indifferent, open-ended; it is inferior, unrealistic to be attached to single causes (again, we recall Broch's 'partial systems'). Man, reckoned Musil, is tempted by life as a fly is to a fly-paper; the fate of the committed is to perish in its stickiness. And yet, paradoxically, in *The Man without Qualities* he is searching for a total reality, even though it eludes him. Scepticism is stretched to its utmost limit, and ironically tested as the only intelligent basis upon which to conduct life. Musil's Ulrich is, in one important aspect, the artist; but he is paralysed rather than sick—and, because of Musil's view of the nature of 'engagement', he is not seen as evil. *The Man without Qualities* was the latest of the great novels of the first half of this century to gain recognition; it will throw up more and richer interpretations.

The prolific ALFRED DÖBLIN (1878–1957) did not achieve as much as any of the preceding writers dealt with in this section. He is nevertheless unduly neglected, and his best fiction will come back into its own. Döblin is often classified as an expressionist, and with some justification; but his position was an unusual and original one. He came from the seaport Stettin in Pomerania (now Polish), and qualified as a doctor in 1905; after an interlude as a newspaper correspondent he settled down as a psychiatrist in the working-class Alexanderplatz of Berlin in 1911. He had written the novel *The Black Curtain* (*Der schwarze Vorhang*, 1912) by 1903, although he did not publish it until he had made contact with literary, particularly expressionist, circles. He became a contributor to Walden's *Der Sturm* (q.v.), and his novel *The Three Leaps of Wang-Lun* (*Die drei Sprünge des Wang-Lun*, 1915) made him famous. As a Jew Döblin could not have lived in Germany after 1933, but as a socialist he would not have done so anyway. He went to Russia, Palestine, France and, finally, America, where in 1941–2 he became a Roman Catholic. After the war he returned to West Germany, where he edited a magazine and continued to write.

Döblin's work always contained a strongly religious element. The stories and sketches in his collection *Murder of a Buttercup* (*Die Ermordung einer Butterblume*, 1913), which are linguistically as interesting as anything he ever wrote, are mainly expressionistic and socialistic—in the title-story, as a business man decapitates a butterfly, the nature of the profit-motive is revealed. But *The Three Leaps of Wang-Lun* (these 'leaps' are vital decisions in his life) is religio-political rather than merely political. Wang-Lun is a fisherman's son who founds the sect of 'truly weak ones', intelligent hippies, who are destroyed by the Chinese establishment. This novel incidentally reminds one of how meticulously some sections of modern youth are now fulfilling an expressionist programme.

Wadzek's Struggle with the Steam-Machine (*Wadzeks Kampf mit der Dampfturbine*, 1918) is more satirical and grotesque, and foreshadows *Mountains, Seas, and Giants* (q.v.) in its posing of the problem of man and machinery. *Wallenstein* (1920) is a long, intelligent and subtle historical novel in which Wallenstein, the man of action, is set against the passive man, the Emperor Ferdinand; it is also, in the fashion of the time, a comment on the current situation.

The distinctly Wellsean dystopia *Mountains, Sea and Giants* (*Berge, Meere und Giganten*, 1924; rev. as *Giganten*, 1931) is the culmination of four years of frenzied satirical and attempted dramatic activity. Under the pseudonym of 'Linke-Poot' Döblin wrote a series of political satires, which he collected into a volume in 1921; his plays of the same period were not successful. *Mountains, Seas and Giants*, which has, surprisingly, been misinterpreted as a Utopia, is set in the period A.D. 2700–3000. Man has mastered machinery to the extent of making Greenland free from ice (by use of Iceland's volcanoes); but nature takes is revenge.

Berlin Alexanderplatz (1929; tr. 1931) is often, but misleadingly, compared with Joyce's *Ulysses*. Its genius—it is very nearly a great novel—is not comic. Technically Döblin borrowed from Dos Passos' *Manhattan Transfer* (q.v. 1), and also used every device of *montage, collage* and interior monologue: advertisements, popular songs, radio announcements, mythological parallels. There are two heroes: Franz Biberkopf, a simple-minded proletarian, a victim of 'the system'; and the teeming life of Berlin.

When the novel opens Franz Biberkopf has just been released from a four-year sentence for the manslaughter, in a rage, of the girl with whom he has been living. He cannot understand his freedom, which has a traumatic effect on him, but he manages to find a job as a street-vendor. He can only solve his problems by drink; but even this very simple man is able, through suffering, to learn in the end. He gets in with criminals, and in particular with a vicious but shrewd gangster called Reinhold, by whom he is thrown from a car. He loses an arm. He flirts with the Nazi movement. Old friends help him, and he begins a happy association with a prostitute. However, she is murdered by Reinhold when she will not yield to his demands. This drives Biberkopf mad, and he spends a long time in a mental hospital in a semi-catatonic state. We leave him working as a hospital porter; he is not prosperous, and never will be; but he has learned, despite his simple and over-trusting nature, to try to steer a decent course: he had earned an identity.

The most remarkable element in *Berlin Alexanderplatz* is the success with which it depicts the mental processes that motivate the behaviour of a man so simple and unsophisticated as to be almost (but not quite) 'wanting'. Döblin portrays this distinctly non-literary figure with no patronage at all, and is able to invest him with the humanity that is his due. Döblin deserves a higher status than he has been accorded: he achieved something here that no other German achieved. I doubt if there is any more convincting, accurate and sympathetic portrait of a proletarian in twentieth-century literature. Faulkner (q.v.) was of course a masterly presenter of idiots and primitives; but Franz is neither idiotic nor primitive.

Berlin Alexanderplatz lacks greatness only because it lacks cohesion: in the very last analysis, teutonic nobility of purpose, a didacticism, is seen to stand in place of compassion; and the poor effects can be traced to an attempt to conceal elements of a detached clinicism that is disingenuously not self-acknowledged. And yet it is the experience of a number of readers that when the novel is considered in retrospect, these shortcomings seem less vitiating.

Men Without Mercy (*Pardon wird nicht gegeben*, 1935; tr. 1937) is the only novel besides *Berlin Alexanderplatz* by Döblin to have been translated into English (pt. *November 1918*, q.v., is in HE); one would not have chosen it, although it usefully illustrates his concerns. Set in an anonymous, totalitarian country, it traces a lifelong process of self-destruction originating in an adolescent moment of self-betrayal—this, however, being almost forced upon the hero by his bitter, ambitious mother. In this book Döblin hovers uneasily between realism and fable, between a Marxist-Freudian and a religious attitude. The hero's mother prevents his joining a revolutionary comrade, and he becomes a highly successful capitalist and, indeed, an enemy of the revolution to which his young heart had been pledged. Eventually he is killed during a riot. In his younger brother we see, although in a somewhat ambiguous and unsatisfactory portrayal, a passive semi-religious revolutionary. *Men Without Mercy* is an interesting but not fully resolved novel, in which shrewd socio-political analysis is unfortunately not supported by a convincing or consistent psychology.

This was followed by a long work about South America, *Land Without Death* (*Das Land ohne Tod, Der blaue Tiger*, 1936–8), and by the trilogy *November 1918*, begun in 1939 and finished in 1950: *The Betrayed People* (*Verratenes Volk*, 1948), *Return from the Front* (*Heimkehr der Fronttruppen*, 1949) and *Karl and Rosa* (*Karl und Rosa*, 1950); this dealt with the Spartacus League and the events in Berlin between November 1918 and January 1919 leading up to the murder of Rosa

Luxemburg and Karl Liebknecht. This work is shrewd, mature and politically balanced; the reasons for the failure of the revolution—misplaced idealism—are made manifest.

Döblin was a versatile writer of short stories and novellas, and the absence of a comprehensive selection in English translation is a matter for regret. As in *Berlin Alexanderplatz*, he adopted every kind of technique or form—from the expressionistic and the fantastic through the realistic to the detective story—that would suit his purpose.

His last novel, *Hamlet* (*Hamlet oder Die lange Nacht nimmt ein Ende*, 1957) shows no falling off in power, and is one of his most interesting. It is about an Englishman, shattered by the war, returning home to find his marriage in as great a state of ruin as his mind. Again, Döblin combines a remarkable number of different techniques—flashback, interior monologue, reference to myths—in a lucid narrative.

Döblin is a difficult writer, but this cannot account for the comparative neglect into which he has fallen. Germany has not produced more than half a dozen better ones in the course of the century.

XI

The movement known as dada was founded in 1916 in Zürich, which was, significantly, the headquarters of German pacifism; it was there that René Schickele (q.v.) edited his pacifist *Die weissen Blätter*, in whose pages Hans Arp's poetry appeared. It was not a specifically German, but rather a European pacifist movement. It may be regarded as an offshoot of, or as originating in, German expressionism because its form was a protest against the war—this had existed in Germany from before 1914, whereas its first expression in, for example, English is probably seen in the poetry of Charles Sorley (q.v. 1)—and because it was clearly an evolution of cabaret-literature. By 1924 the initiative had passed to Paris; the surrealism into which dada developed is a French movement.

'The eel of the dunes', HANS ARP (1887–1966) sometimes referred to as Jean Arp, was born in Strasbourg, of parents who favoured a French Alsace-Lorraine, only a few years after its annexation by the Germans. He was tri-lingual, having a fluent command of French, German and Alsatian (in which his first poem was written). Arp was a sculptor and graphic artist of international stature; and although he made no creative distinction between the visual and verbal aspects of his work, regarding them as complementary, he has always been very much better known as an artist than as a writer. However, his were the only literary contributions to dada that are likely to survive. In this respect he differs from his fellow German MAX ERNST (1891), 'Loplop, the Superior of the Birds' (the surrealists, q.v., gave themselves or each other such names), who engaged in literary activity—such as the production of collage novels, and some poetry—but never of a more than peripheral sort. For Arp poetry was a necessary means of expressing his essentially surrealistic response to existence: childlike, spontaneous, cheerfully and mockingly aleatory in the face of a supremely confident assumption of the total absurdity of everything.

Arp's poetry provides a clear illustration of the close relationship of surrealism to expressionism (of which it was one development). Arp was himself associated with *Der blaue Reiter* and the magazine *Der Sturm*. One of his most characteristic poems, of which he made several versions because of the importance to him of its theme, mourns the death of that expressionist saint, Caspar Hauser (q.v.) (TCG, MGP). His poetry at its best, being cast in the form most natural to his temperament, incidentally reveals the sterility of almost all 'concrete' poetry (q.v. 3)—at its worst in the cleverly neat, frigid, devitalized experiments of the Scot Edwin 'bloodless magpie' Morgan—for verbal dexterity and rearrangement are two of Arp's chief means. When he searches for himself amidst the light he finds himself thus: 'L-ich-t'. This characteristic makes his poetry all but untranslatable. Arp is not a casual poet: his regret at the loss of the innocence of childhood, as in the 'Caspar' poem, is deeply felt and expressed with a simple, sweet lyricism rare in its time:

> woe our good Caspar is dead
> who's going to hide the burning flag in the cloud-tail now and play a black trick every day.
> who's going to grind the coffee-mill now in the age-old barrel.
> who's going to charm the idyllic roe now from out of the petrified paper-bag. . . .
> woe woe woe our good Caspar is dead. holy ding dong Caspar is dead. . . .
> his bust will grace the fireplaces of all truly noble men but that is small consolation and snuff for a death's head.
>
> (tr. R. W. Last, *Hans Arp*, 1969)

The charm and lightness of tone only mute the poet's sense of loss. Arp plays, but not for relaxation. He made many versions of his poems, and there is as yet no satisfactory edition; the nearest approach is in the two-volume *Collected Poems* (1963–4). Arp fully deserves the title given to him by R. W. Last, his leading British interpreter: 'the poet of dadaism'. His poetry is a genuine and never calculated response to experience.

Arp's friend HUGO BALL (1886–1927) was born not far from him, at Pirmasens near the French border. He was always a fierce critic of all things German, and for the latter half of his short life lived in Switzerland. A student of philosophy and a very influential figure, he left little of creative value: his poetry (MGP) compared with Arp's is merely programmatic. His best-known poems invent new words— 'Ensúdio tres a sudio mischumi' and so on; but Morgenstern (q.v.) had anticipated him: 'Kroklowafzi? Sememeil!/Seiokrontoprafriplo. . . .' He worked with Max Reinhardt (q.v.) before the war, then went to Zürich as a pacifist, and in 1916 was the leading spirit in the founding of dada; he played the piano at the Café Voltaire, the home of dada cabaret. Within little more than a year he had repudiated all this activity on the grounds that dadaism was not, in reality, a revolt against war and its allied demons (as it was supposed to be) but a dangerous and egotistic endorsement of it. In other words, he saw in this extreme manifestation of expressionism negative, totalitarian and demonic symptoms. His small creative capacity did not survive this shock, and he fell into a pious Roman Catholicism; his last book was about saints. He also wrote an acute study of Hermann Hesse (q.v.), whom he knew well. Ball's letters (*Briefe 1911–1927*, 1958) are an invaluable source. His wife Emmy Hennings (1885–1948) was among the performers on the first evening of dadaist entertainment on 2 February 1916.

Another German who helped to found dada in 1916 was the poet RICHARD HUELSENBECK (ps. CHARLES R. HULBECK, 1892–1973). Huelsenbeck, a psychiatrist, went to the U.S.A. in 1936. His poetry, which was collected in *The Answer of the Deep* (*Die Antwort der Tiefe*, 1954), is slight; his contribution to dada was mainly personal. His autobiographical *With Wit, Light and Guts* (*Mit Witz, Licht und Grütze*, 1957) is a valuable source.

KURT SCHWITTERS (1887–1948), born in Hanover, was another sculptor and painter who was also a poet and member of the dadaist circle. He called his own form of dada, 'abstract collages' that made up poems and paintings, *Merz* because of a fortuitious piece of advertisement, *Commerz und Privatbank*, on an early one. In art he was chiefly influenced by the abstract painter Wassily Kandinsky, in poetry by Arp. His poetry is more merely eccentric, slight and less poised than Arp's; but it is not aleatory junk. The best known poem is 'To Anna Blume', 'beloved of my twenty-seven senses. . . . Anna, a-n-n-a I trickle your name. Your name drips like soft beef-dripping. . . . Beef dripping trickles over my back. Anna, you dripping creature, I love you' (TCG). Schwitters emigrated to Norway in 1937, and escaped from there to Britain, where he was treated shamefully, in 1943. He died at Ambleside, after having worked as a portrait-painter. Only one of his three immense (as big as a house) *collages*, *Merzbau* as he called them, survives, and this is unfinished; it was moved from Ambleside to Newcastle University in 1965.

The Saxon JOACHIM RINGELNATZ (ps. HANS BÖTTICHER, 1883–1934) is one of the few 'functionalists' whose verse is still printed in antho-logies. 'Ringelnatz' means 'watersnake', 'ringed adder' or 'little sea-horse'. He was a clown and vagabond by choice; during the First World War he efficiently commanded a minesweeper. Previously he had been, among other things, a seaman, newspaper-boy, librarian and bar-poet. He devoted most of his life to successfully performing his grotesque and comic cabaret poetry, especially in Berlin and Munich. His two novels about his war experiences show his other side. He was also a talented painter.

Ringelnatz's clowning was a conscious and intelligent form of reaxation, with an undertone of savagery. His most famous pose in his cabaret acts was that of an experienced ordinary seaman. He wrote, charmingly, that his '*Ideal*' was to have, after his death

> A little street . . . given my name,
> A narrow twisty street with low down doors,
> Steep stairways and cheap little whores,
> Shadows and sloping windows I want.
> It would be my haunt.
>
> (MGP)

Even his trivial songs have charm and quality (two tr. in TCG). . . . *liner Roma* . . . (1924), prose poetry, is often mentioned as having some affinities with dada, as has Ringelnatz's choice of the cabaret as as his main medium.

Surrealism (q.v.) was predominantly a French movement; dada, its earliest group manifestation, cannot be described as German, although it was certainly expressionist. The one really gifted dada writer, Arp, was as French as he was German. German writers have had a greater awareness of surrealism than, for example, British and American writers; but not one besides Arp and the relatively minor figure of Schwitters can usefully or accurately be described as a surrealist. There are no English or even American novelists as surrealist as Kasack or Langgässer (qq.v.); but even these owe as much to Kafka, who was not surrealist, as they do to surrealism.

XII

The so-called *neue Sachlichkeit*, the new 'reality'/'objectivity'/'sobriety'/ 'matter-of-factness', was not a reactionary or anti-modernist movement: though pessimistic and down to earth, it was neither a return to the naturalism of thirty years before nor to the Ibsenian realism from which that sprang. It was a move away from the violent extremes and abstractions of what Michael Hamburger calls 'Phase II' expressionism. Again, more stable forms, more concrete situations, reflected the comparative stability of the Weimar Republic between 1923 and the 1929 economic slump that brought about its downfall. But the new objectivity, as we view it retrospectively, did not repudiate the basic methods of expressionism; it repudiated only the empty (and almost wholly unimaginative) idealism into which it had turned. Thus, such a clear-cut practitioner of the new objectivity as Erich Kästner had no desire to return to the literary situation of 1900—only to correct the false optimism (largely dispelled by the failure of the 1918 revolution to usher in a new Utopia) of the later expressionists. The degree of pessimism in the new objectivity varied considerably; it is delicately balanced by optimism in the most notable of all the novels, *Berlin Alexanderplatz* (q.v.). Rather than pessimistic, the approach was *matter-of-fact*; but perhaps such an attitude is bound to tend towards pessimism—in the absence of just that fervency which the new objectivity above all eschewed.

The movement manifested itself most explicitly in drama. Language remained concentrated and terse, new ideas continued to flow, but the visionary element vanished. For the time being there was no background of disquietude and agitation. Most of the expressionist dramatists felt that they had 'grown out' of their former ecstatic beliefs, although their best work lay behind them. Only a few, such as Johst (q.v.), flung themselves into the new barbarism of Hitler. Some, such as Hasenclever and Kornfeld (qq.v.), wrote cynical comedies.

There developed, alongside this, a brand of 'idealistic' realism, usually nationalistic; but it was crude and consistently unsophisticated, and attracted no writer of real merit. None of the many *Heimatkunst* (literally, 'native-land-art') novels, the most successful of which was *Winter* (1927; tr. 1929), by FRIEDRICH GRIESE (1890), came up to the level of Wiechert's or Carossa's (qq.v.) fiction. But while Wiechert went to Buchenwald for a time, many of those classed as 'idealistic' realists became Nazis or fellow-travellers.

HANS GRIMM (1875–1959) was not a Nazi, but he was a racist, and was a favourite in the Third Reich. As recently as 1947 he was described as 'indisputably the greatest living master' of the longer short story, which ought perhaps to go on record as one of the dozen silliest judgements ever attempted. The not ill-intentioned Grimm, a Kipling without genius, wrote an enormously long and now un-readable novel called *People Without Room* (*Volk ohne Raum*, 1926). It sold in millions. The style is modelled on that of the Icelandic sagas; the content, whether the result of an inner viciousness or mere foolishness, is nauseous. It relates, at insufferable length, the ordeals of Germans both in their own overcrowded country and in South Africa. Thus literature at its best under Hitler.

The Berliner HANS JOSÉ REHFISCH (1891–1960), who sometimes used the names GEORG TURNER and RENÉ KESTNER, was a prolific and facile but not unintelligent writer. His best and most successful play was *Who Weeps for Juckenack?* (*Wer weint um Juckenack?*, 1924). Reh-fisch had, as H. F. Garten says, 'a remarkable talent for presenting vital topics of the day in a somewhat conventional form'. *Chauffeur Martin* (1920) was expressionist—the hero accidentally knocks a man over, rebels against God and is spiritually reborn. *Who Weeps for Juckenack?* is firmly in the spirit of the 'new objectivity': the hero's project for rebirth, in putting him outside the pale of the law, results in his madness and death.

More substantial if not more representative of the new mood were Ernst Toller's *Hinkemann* (q.v.), Frank's dramatization of his novel *Karl and Anna* (q.v.) and the strongly anti-war *Miracle at Verdun* (*Wunder um Verdun*, 1930; tr. 1932) by the Viennese HANS CHUMBLERG (1897–1930), in which the dead of the First World War arise to pre-vent another war. Chumblerg, who died in an accident at the dress-rehearsal, enclosed this action in the framework of a dream. Ironic-ally, the play is set in the late summer of 1939.

It was natural that in this period the war should be viewed more dispassionately and calmly. The spate of 'war books' began in Germany, as elsewhere, at the end of the Twenties. People found that they were now able to write soberly about their war experiences. The retrospective sobriety and precision of Remarque's journalistic-ally effective *All Quiet on the Western Front* or Renn's profounder *War* (qq.v.) would have found little or no response at the beginning of the Twenties.

Other popular topical themes were no newer, but were given new treatment. As controls became less hysterical and rigid so works dealing with the theme of adolescence versus parental or educational authority tended to become less critical of the establishment. Thomas Mann's son KLAUS MANN (1906–49) wrote, at the age of nineteen, a play called *Anja and Esther* (1925) in which the younger generation are portrayed as fostering a sickly cult of eurhythmics, decadent romanticism and homosexuality; Sternheim's last important play, *The School of Uznach*, subtitled 'the new objectivity', satirized this. Other works dealt with law-cases and incidents from history. Two playwrights, Brecht and Zuckmayer, were markedly superior; but several others were distinguished craftsmen who wrote intelligent plays.

FERDINAND BRUCKNER (PS. THEODOR TAGGER, 1891–1958), a Viennese, began as a violently expressionist poet in the 'telegram style' initiated in the theatre by Sternheim and in poetry by Stramm (qq.v.); his poetry in this vein was wholly derivative. Then he emerged as a differently named, cynical and shocking realist, creating a sensation with his first, skilfully constructed play *The Malady of Youth* (*Krankheit der Jugend*, 1926), in which youth sees itself as a disease. If you grow up, you die spiritually; the only solution is suicide. The atmosphere here is expressionist—but drained of all ecstasy or even hope. The play ends with death, and no other solution is offered. *The Criminals* (*Die Verbrecher*, 1928) exposes, again with great technical skill, the processes of law as neither just nor humane. Both these plays are realistic in form but thoroughly expressionist in temper: the one depicts a cult of death, the other takes pleasure in revealing the law, beloved of the bourgeois mentality, as an institution set up to insulate behaviour from conscience. But this, of course, is the sober (*sachlich*), deromanticized expressionism of the new objectivity. The techniques employed in Bruckner's next, historical play, *Elizabeth of England* (*Elizabeth von England*, 1930; tr. 1931), which made him world famous, were again expressionist: as in *The Criminals*, Bruckner used the device of 'simultaneous action', in which the stage is divided into two sections (to depict the Spanish and English side by side). Lytton Strachey's *Elizabeth and Essex*, the least convincing and psychologically most lurid of his books, had appeared in 1928, and Bruckner drew on this to provide a 'love interest'. It was his worst, most successful play. *Timon* (1931), based on Shakespeare's play, was expressionist self-criticism, its ostensible moral being that the individual must fulfil the needs of the community; but most of *Timon*'s energy derives from Bruckner's non-programmatic fascination with his hero's misanthropy. The theme continued to interest Bruckner: he made two more versions, the last one *Timon and the Gold* (*Timon und das Gold*) in 1956, two years before his death. *Races* (*Die Rassen*, 1933; tr. 1934), about an Aryan who loves a Jewish girl, was written after Bruckner had left Germany. Apart from Brecht, Zuckmayer and Wolf (qq.v.), Bruckner was the only playwright able to re-establish himself in the post-war German theatre. He had written two historical anti-Hitler plays in exile, and made a successful comeback in 1946 with the second of these: *Heroic Comedy* (*Heroische Komödie*, 1942–6). *Fruit of Nothing* (*Früchte des Nichts*, 1952) returns to the theme of *The Malady of Youth*, this time treating of the young at the end of Hitler's war. *Death of a Doll* (*Der Tod einer Puppe*, 1956) is in verse and is influenced by Greek classical models. Bruckner was a good working dramatist: he never achieved a major work, but seldom fell below a certain level of competence and integrity.

Bruckner's only serious rival for the position of leading dramatist after Brecht and Zuckmayer is FRIEDRICH WOLF (1888–1953), who was born at Neuwied in the Rhineland. Wolf was a member of the communist party who returned to East Germany after the war and was there held in an esteem second only to Brecht's. Like Bruckner, Wolf began as an expressionist. Although his 'message' was unequivocally Marxist, he had a gift for vivid if not deep characterization, and his plays still grip. *Kolonne Hund* (1927), about a land reclamation scheme in which he had taken part, was his first effective play. His great success was *Cyanide* (*Cyankali*, 1929), an exposure of the inhumanity of the law forbidding abortion. *The Sailors of Cattaro* (*Die Matrosen von Cattaro*, 1930; tr. 1935) is a documentary play about a mutiny in the Austro-Hungarian navy in 1918. *Professor Mamlock* (1933), on the subject of the Nazi persecution of the Jews, is his most famous play because of the widely shown Russian film. His best, and certainly most interesting, play, however, is *Beaumarchais* (1940), in which he portrays his own dilemma: an emotional revolutionary who cannot accept the revolution himself. He was unhappy in East Germany, where he wrote only light comedies and reproached himself for not more openly criticising the regime.

The modern theatrical giant of Germany is BERTOLT BRECHT (1898–1956), who was born in Augsburg, Bavaria. Essentially Brecht was a poet (and a legendary performer of songs to his own guitar accompaniment); and although his poetry, previously underrated, has begun in recent years to receive its due, his chief fame is as a playwright. Yet while his plays will certainly survive, his poetry will survive longer.

Brecht served as a medical orderly in the last year of the First World War; the experience was decisive, inasmuch as it left him with no illusions about what man could so easily be ordered to do to man. It seems that he had already reacted against the chauvinism, militarism and economic greed that characterized the German society of his adolescence. The most studiously anti-literary of all twentieth-century writers, Brecht certainly first conceived his scorn for bourgeois '*Kultur*' when he observed the hypocritical nature of pre-war Augsburg society's devotion to it. By the age of twenty he had started to write poetry and drama. In 1922 his *Drums in the Night* (*Trommeln in der Nacht*, 1923) was produced in Munich, and soon afterwards awarded the Kleist Prize. Although wholly individual, this also managed to be a typical (and early) product of the new and more sober mood. But Brecht added a poetic tang to the sobriety. Andreas Kragler comes back from prisoner-of-war camp to discover that his girl has been sleeping with a black-marketeer. He becomes involved with the revolution of 1919, but eventually decisively rejects it in favour of taking up again with his faithless girl. Here perhaps we see the cynical Brecht, the one who will on no account 'rot in the gutter' so that a mere (communist) 'idea may triumph'; but we also see a Brecht who was already fascinated by communism. At the end of this play Kragler abuses the audience and hurls his drum at the Chinese lantern that serves as a stage moon, which falls into the waterless river: Brecht's concern to do away with stage illusion, later to be developed into the theory of 'alienation effect' and 'epic theatre' (qq.v.), was thus apparent in his second play.

The eponymous hero of his first play, *Baal* (1922; GED), written in 1918 and produced in Leipsig in 1923, is illustrative of the same side of himself; but here his nihilism and antinomian zest for life emerge rather more strongly. Brecht's Baal is a coarse, kindly criminal—tramp, drunkard, poet, homosexual, murderer, joker, honest and disillusioned man. He enjoys his life. *Baal* was an anti-sentimental comedy. Its amorality, whether or not the result of youthful excess, was dramatically justified: it presented the late expressionists with the reality of their dream, and ironically created a character morally no worse—but decidedly less pompous, idealistic or acceptably fragrant—than the heroes of the still militaristic bourgeois.

The greatest individual success Brecht ever had was with *The Threepenny Opera* (*Die Dreigroschenoper*, 1929; MT; BP); this is based on John Gay's *Begger's Opera*, and has music by Busoni's brilliant pupil Kurt Weill. The criminal gang whose exploits everyone so much enjoyed, were supposed, by Brecht, to be bourgeois capitalists. But however ingeniously he directed the piece to be produced, this is not quite how it can be taken. Once more, it is essentially nihilistic, and may be taken as a satire on communist revolutionaries as well as on capitalists. Its real mood is one of gay cynicism: nobody in authority is respected, and who is going to stand up (at any rate to be counted) to deny that such authorial aggressiveness as is contained in Macheath's incitement to the audience to 'smash the faces of the police with heavy iron hammers' is directed at *all* police, and not merely at capitalist police?

At this time, when National Socialism was making headway in Germany, Brecht had been studying Marxist communism, including *Das Kapital*, very carefully. How well he grasped it, in an intellectual sense, is not clear; but he has been accused of treating the twentieth century as though it were the nineteenth, and of a general lack of sophistication. 'In his theoretical efforts', writes Peter Demetz, 'Brecht is like an eagle whose eyes triumphantly and sharply view the future of the arts—but the eagle's feet drag the rusty chains of Marxist iron and lead'. His next short plays—after one more satirical opera, again done with Weill, *The Rise and Fall of the Town of Mahagonny* (*Aufstieg und Fall der Stadt Mahagonny*, 1929)—were 'theoretical efforts', *Lehrstücke*, 'teaching pieces', in the sense that they were consciously didactic pieces, designed to bring their audience to an awareness of the inevitability of the historical process as envisaged in Marxist theory. These are by no means bad playlets; but because they are theory-bound, they are Brecht's weakest. They include *Baden-Baden Cantata of Acquiescence* (*Das Badener Lehrstück vom Einverständnis*, 1930; tr. *Harvard Advocate*, CXXXIV, 4, 1951; *Tulane Drama Review*, IV, 4, 1960) and *He Who Said Yes/He Who Said No* (*Der Jasager/Der Neinsager*, 1930; *Der Jasager*, tr. *Accent* VII, 2, 1946). These short plays were followed by longer ones of the same kind: *St. Joan of the Stockyards* (*Die heilige Johanna der Schlachthöfe*, 1932; FMR) and *The Measures Taken* (*Die Massnahme*, 1931; MT). The thesis of each play is that it is necessary to renounce individual, incidental compassion—and even to be cruel—in order to create a better world, in order, that is to say, to follow the party line. For by now Brecht was, or believed himself to be, a convert to communism. *St. Joan of the Stockyards*, loosely adapted from, or suggested by, Shaw's (q.v. 1) Salvation Army play *Major Barbara*, is set in Chicago. Johanna begins by preaching the Gospel to and helping the oppressed workers; having caused a general strike to fail, she ends, by attacking all religion (he who asserts the claims of spirituality, she says, must 'have his head beaten on the pavement till he croaks') and by affirming that 'nothing should be called honourable but what/ Finally changes the world'. In *The Measures Taken*, based on a Japanese No play, four communist infiltrators are sent into China. One of them gives way to his immediate humanitarian impulses, with the result that no long-term progress is achieved, and the mission itself is threatened. The 'emotional socialist' then emerges as an individual —he tears off his anonymous mask—and agrees to be liquidated. The lesson, of course, is that the aims of the party come before any manifestation of individuality—even pity.

Compared to the plays of Brecht's later period, these polemics of the Thirties are crude works; and they are crude because they are dogmatic. *Fear and Misery in the Third Reich* (*Furcht und Elend des dritten Reiches*, 1941; tr. 1942; as *The Private Life of the Master Race*, 1944) is superb on the realistic level, but sickeningly disingenuous when it toes the communist line. *Round Heads and Pointed Heads* (*Die Rundköpfe und die Spitzköpfe*, 1938; tr. *International Literature*, May, 1937), a satire on Nazi anti-semitism, is a total failure, and even appears to be itself anti-semitic. The earlier *The Mother* (*Die Mutter*, 1933), an adaptation from Maxim Gorki's (q.v.) novel, is perhaps the best of all the Thirties plays: it is frankly party propaganda, but in the cunning and vitality of the leading character we already get a hint of Mother Courage (q.v.). Something goes on despite, or as well as, the call to come to the aid of the party. *Señora Carrar's Rifles* (*Die Gewehre der Frau Carrar*, 1937; tr. *Theatre Workshop*, II, 1938), based on a play by Synge (q.v. 1) and set in Spain, is in Brecht's most realistic vein.

Brecht went to Denmark when Hitler gained power; when this was overrun he escaped through Sweden, Finland and Russia (he had been there before in 1935, and apparently did not wish to stay— perhaps because Russia was then in alliance with the Third Reich, perhaps because he did not savour the prospect of living there) to America, where he lived in California until 1947. He was then brought before the notorious Committee on Un-American Activities, whose chairman praised him for his 'co-operation'; yet he left America and waited for nearly two years, in Zürich, to get into Western Germany; but the occupying powers refused him permission. The East Germans, by contrast, offered him a theatre. He settled in Berlin in 1949, and ran the Berliner Ensemble from then until his death of a coronary thrombosis in 1956. It is now run by the actress Hilda Weigel (whom he had married in 1928 after divorcing his first wife). He retained Austrian citizenship and a Swiss bank account. The workers' riots of 1953 upset him, and he suggested in a poem that the government dissolve the people and elect another one;

but he made no open protest. However, the charge that he wrote a regulation 'ode' or 'odes' to Stalin, made by Hannah Arendt as though she had read them (she calls them 'thin'), has not been substantiated: no 'odes to Stalin' have been produced or quoted, and Miss Arendt's silence when courteously challenged on this point has been puzzling to her admirers. Nothing Brecht said about Stalin is less than highly ambiguous. When he came back from Moscow in the Thirties and was asked why he had not stayed there, he said that he had not been able to get enough sugar for his tea and coffee (did not find enough sweetness?).

Mother Courage (*Mutter Courage und ihre Kinder*, 1949; tr. in *New Directions*, 1941; MT; SP), a chronicle of the Thirty Years' War based on a story by Grimmelshausen, the seventeenth-century German author of *Simplicissimus*, portrays the indomitable lust for life of a greedy, mean, malicious, amoral, uncharitable, cunning and yet vital canteen-woman. Brecht's intentions here were as Marxist as ever: war is commercially motivated and destructive, and those who live off it, like the sutler woman who loses all her family, cannot see what they do to themselves. But his imagination and his own love of life created a work that transcends any thesis. After the first performance in Zürich in 1941, when the audience responded sympathetically to Mother Courage, Brecht tried to emphasize her inhumanity by rewriting parts of the text, and as director (of his wife, who presumably played the part as he required it). But it was as though he were trying to rewrite and re-direct the part of his own anti-virtuous, opportunist, cynical Baal—with the aim of demonstrating his essentially bourgeois character and motivations. He could not take away Mother Courage's humanity; even rigidly Marxist critics still saw her as human. Brecht was not a man who would not conform: he could not.

Brecht's other major plays are: *The Life of Galileo* (*Leben des Galilei*, 1955; FMR; SP; BP), which was translated into English by Brecht himself with the help of Charles Laughton, who played the main role in America; *The Good Woman of Setzuan* (*Der gute Mensch von Sezuan*, 1953; SP); *The Caucasian Chalk Circle*; and some would add the more straightforwardly comic *Herr Puntila and his Man Matti* (*Herr Puntila und sein Knecht Matti*, 1948). *The Life of Galileo* portrays the scientist as a man avid and voracious for life (Laughton's 1947 performance, in which he returned to the stage after eleven years in films, is legendary) and for truth; but not one prepared to sacrifice his life for a principle. Like the real Galileo, who is supposed to have muttered '*Eppur si muove!*' (And yet it moves) after recanting, he gives way out of fear; but a copy of his work is smuggled abroad. Brecht's Galileo is, significantly, a mixture of his own Baal and Švejk (q.v. 4). But Brecht lets us know that had he behaved boldly, he would not have been tortured. . . .

The detail of *The Good Woman of Setzuan* and of *The Caucasian Chalk Circle*, Brecht's tenderest play, again seems to challenge the comparative crudity of their 'message'.

Brecht's dramatic theories, although criticized by himself as abstract, if not actually disowned ('I developed—oh calamity!—a theory of the epic theatre', he once said), and inconsistent, are very important for the enormous influence they have wielded since the end of the Second World War.

Brecht's theorizing was not consistent, but the notion basic to it was that the audience at a play should be made to *think* rather than to become emotionally identified with the characters. Aristotle had said in his *Poetics* that 'tragedy . . . is a representation of an action that is worth serious attention . . . presented in the form of action, not narration; by means of pity and fear bringing about the catharsis [untranslated] of such emotions'. Now until recently *catharsis* had been understood by nearly everyone, including Brecht, to mean 'purgation' (the best guess is probably more like 'a healthy emotional balance'). Brecht thought of the theatre that had preceded him as an 'Aristotelian' theatre in which the spectator was 'purged' of his fear and pity—fear and pity aroused, for example, by portrayal of tragic injustice—and therefore rendered a harmless member of society. Brecht, in the words of his Russian friend Sergei Tretiakov, wanted an 'intelligent theatre . . . not [one that left] the spectator purged by a cathartic but [that left] him a changed man . . . to sow within him the seeds of the changes which must be completed outside the theatre'. These changes, needless to say, were revolutionary in nature. 'The performance must not be a closed circle where the heroes and villains balance, where all accounts are settled. . . . it must be spiral in form . . . the spectator must be brought out of equilibrium'. Brecht called the 'Aristotelian' theatre 'dramatic', his own 'epic'. His type of theatre is calculated to make the spectator observe (not become involved); to awaken him to action (not to accept tragedy but to join the communist revolution in order ultimately to remove tragedy from the face of the earth); to argue (not state); to present man not as already known and unalterable but as an evolving object of investigation; to cause the spectator not to feel but to reason; to present theatre in tableaux (montage), not as 'organic' ('well made').

H. F. Garten has said that Brecht's 'conversion to communism was not actuated by any genuine sympathy for the poor. . . . It was born from a deep-rooted hatred of the bourgeois class from which he himself had sprung; and it was a desperate effort to escape from the total nihilism of his earlier years . . .'.

This is partly true; but the matter is more complicated, and the first statement is as unjust as it is incorrect. Brecht's poetry—in which is embodied his most substantial achievement—leaves no doubt whatever of his sympathy for and intuitive understanding of other human beings. These lines of verse occur in the play, *The Good Woman of Setzuan*; the poet who wrote them sympathized with his fellow creatures—and possessed that faculty so rare in male writers, understanding of women:

> I saw him at night puffing out his cheeks in his sleep: they were
> evil.
> And in the morning I held his coat up to the light: I could see
> the wall through it.
> When I saw his cunning laughter I was afraid, but
> When I saw the holes in his shoes, I loved him very much.
>
> (SP)

That Villon was always a strong influence on Brecht is no accident. Villon presents himself in his poetry as a damned soul. Brecht is progressively less explicit, but is always something more than a mere polisson. He likes delinquents. Like Villon, he feels at home with criminals. However didactic *The Threepenny Opera* is supposed to be, there can be no doubt that its vitality is derived from Brecht's sheer pleasure in the refreshingly sincere vitality of the criminal classes. He preferred, as many do, their kind of criminality to the version of it practised by 'respectable' society in its pursuit of business, war and the maintenance of 'law and order'. But he knew that it was not socially preferable; and Garten is right in saying that Brecht wanted to escape from his nihilism. This nihilism he saw as identified with the values of the individual, and he was deliberately hard on the claims of the individual in his early communist plays. But he was fundamentally 'Švejkian' in the face of all authority; and not even his strong sense of guilt at his instinctive nihilism (it almost amounted, in communistic terms, to a sense of identification with the *Lumpenproletariat*) could scotch his sly and yet lusty sense of humour—or his undoctrinaire sympathy with all human creatures. Brecht was in fact so fascinated by Švejk (q.v. 4.) that he devoted a whole dramatic sequence to him, *Švejk in the Second World War* (*Schweik im zweiten Weltkrieg*, 1957).

Brecht felt guilty because in pursuing this vein of poetry he thought he might be renouncing the happiness not only of himself but also of the whole species. We have encountered the problem of what may be called *Künstlerschuld* (artist-guilt) before: in Rilke, in Mann, and, most particularly, in Broch; Brecht was not immune to it His solution is not to his discredit, nor does it reflect a lack of sympathy with the poor—as Garten suggests. Communism advocated what seemed like an anti-bourgeois solution, and entailed a discipline of the intellect over the emotions; this was what Brecht required, and he felt himself 'converted' to it. After persecution by the Western authorities, who first impertinently hauled him in front of a committee to question him on his beliefs and then prevented him from entering his own country, he went to East Germany, who had offered him the theatre he wanted. After the workers' riots of 1953 he wrote 'A Bad Morning':

> The silver poplar, a beauty of local fame
> An old hag today. The lake .
> A puddle of dirty suds—do not touch:
> The fuchsia among the snapgragons cheap and vain
> But why?
> Last night in a dream I saw fingers pointing at me
> As at a leper. They were callous, stained with work and
> They were broken.
>
> You don't know! I cried,
> Conscious of guilt.

(MGP)

Brecht's first commercially issued book of poetry, *Manual of Piety* (*Die Hauspostille*, 1927) has been translated by Eric Bentley; a selection is in *Selected Poems* (1947). (See also MGP, TCG, PGV, MEP, PI.) He is one of the foremost lyrical poets of his time, and is unsurpassed in the modern ballad form. In German his collected poems comprise seven volumes; and now that his achievement is becoming better known the claim that he is 'a great and major lyricist' no longer strains credulity. A subtle and sensitive manipulator of tone, he has a remarkable variety of modes, ranging from the ironic, lugubrious ballad through the autobiographical disguised as folk-poetry to the pellucid nature lyric—very often nature is as seen by cynical urban man. His gravelly, world-weary tone does not conceal his power and depths of feeling. More perhaps than any other writer of his times he 'touches the ordinary human heart' without recourse to sentimentality. Adherence to communist dogma led Brecht to compromise his creative freedom—but not more seriously, perhaps, than (say) T. S. Eliot's adoption of Christian dogma led him to compromise his.

CARL ZUCKMAYER (1896), who was born in Nachenheim in Rheinhessen, is Germany's leading living playwright of the elder generation. He has found less favour with reviewers in the past decade because he has not tried to keep up with fashion. But critics have become increasingly aware of him and of his achievement, not only as a dramatist, but as poet and writer of fiction and outstanding autobiography. Zuckmayer, who has always worked within the traditions of the realistic theatre, is not an innovator; nor does he see as much as Brecht saw. But within his limitations he is a considerable writer. His genius is best characterized, perhaps, in terms of an instinctive moral decency. When we read his remarkable autobiography. *A Part of Myself* (*Als wärs ein Stück von mir*, 1966; tr. 1970—it must be added that this translation, without declaring it, abridges Zuckmayer's text in an unsatisfactory manner), we feel grateful to the life out of which his work has sprung.

Zuckmayer fought throughout the First World War, and then went to study law at Heidelberg. His first two plays were in the expressionist vein, entirely foreign to him, and they flopped. He was obliged to take many menial jobs before he found success with his comedy *The Merry Vineyard* (*Der fröhliche Weinberg*, 1925). This, set in the Hessian Rhineland, yoked splendid mockery of a pompous young pseudo-patriot and proto-Nazi with broad rustic humour. It was the result of real *joie de vivre*, not of a calculated attempt to give the public what it wanted. And its cheerfulness caught the German public at just the time when it was least distressed and most relaxed.

The best of the early comedies is *The Captain of Köpenick* (*Der Hauptmann von Köpenick*, 1931; tr. 1932), which was a success but earned Zuckmayer the permanent hostility of the Nazi party. It is set in Berlin in the early part of the century; its target is militarism. The hero, a cobbler called Voigt, is forced into the position of rebel by the heartlessness and injustice of bureaucracy. The system will not allow him to get a pass without a job, or a job without a pass. Had he been in the army he could have obtained either. . . . Eventually he masquerades as a captain in order to get his way. In the end he fails; but the point of his human superiority has been established. Zuckmayer rightly felt himself to be the successor of the Gerhart Hauptmann who wrote such comedies as *The Beaver Coat* (q.v.), and Hauptmann himself praised him.

Soon after this success Hitler came to power, and Zuckmayer went to Austria. Here he wrote two historical plays, *The Rogue of Bergen* (*Der Schelm von Bergen*, 1934) and *Bellman* (1938; rev. 1953 as *Ulla Winblad*). The first is little more than a potboiler; the second, on the life of Carl Michael Bellman, the eighteenth-century Swedish poet, is a gay and delicate *tour de force*.

After the *Anschluss* Zuckmayer moved to America, went briefly to Hollywood, and then became a farmer in Vermont. Here he wrote his most famous play, *The Devil's General* (*Des Teufels General*, 1946), which is known throughout the English-speaking world as play and film. Suggested by the suicide by aircrash of the First World War fighter-ace Ernst Udet when, as a quartermaster-general in the German air-ministry, he fell foul of the Gestapo, *The Devil's General* captured the atmosphere of Germany under the Nazis with uncanny accuracy. Alexander Lernet-Holenia (q.v.) exclaimed to the author, 'You never left!' Like Udet, Zuckmayer's Luftwaffe General Harras hates Nazidom, but does no more about it than make risky, sarcastic jokes. Harras discovers that his chief engineer, Oderbruch, has done more about his own anti-Nazi convictions: he has been sabotaging aircraft production. Harras finally takes to the air in one of the sabotaged machines.

Zuckmayer, as he has become older, has tended towards conservatism and a sympathy for Catholicism; in two more recent plays the desire to make a moral point to a certain extent spoils their psychological credibility. *The Cold Light* (*Das kalte Licht*, 1956) is flased on the case of Klaus Fuchs, the atom spy, although there seems to have been no attempt to represent Fuchs' character. Kristof Wolters, a German refugee, is shipped off to Canada but released as a useful scientist. Wolters is not presented as a dedicated communist but as one embittered by his experiences. Northon, a British security agent, causes him to confess by 'converting' him—but from exactly what? This is a confused play, for Zuckmayer has tried to solve his problem—of how validly to temper a wild and anti-social disposition—in too crude terms. Northon is presented as a 'saved character' but he is unconvincing.

The Clock Struck One (*Die Uhr schlägt eins*, 1961), in nine scenes, tries to deal with too many problems at once, but possesses a more authentically human hero than Wolters. It has been well said that the theme of all Zuckmayer's later plays has been, in one way or another, 'the guilty hero'. But he has been successful only when he has created an autonomous character such as Harras; there is a dignity about the way such a character achieves redemption—but compare the cardboard Wolter's decision to confess.

Zuckmayer's best novels are *The Moon in the South* (*Salwàre*, 1937; tr. 1938), a long story about the love affair of an 'intellectual' with a peasant, and *Carnival Confession* (*Die Fastnachtsbeichte*, 1959; tr. 1961), in which immense vitality is once again partially undermined by a moral intensity that the author seems to be forcing upon himself against his creative will.

Zuckmayer's poetry (TCG, PGV) is traditional in form, as one would expect; it is relaxed, colloquial and unambitious—but whatever mood, small scene or event Zuckmayer describes is newly illuminated. In his poetry his voice is seldom analytical—and this suits him, since his natural way of seeing is more valuable than his thinking.

XIII

Nothing illustrates the nature of the German genius more clearly than the German novel. As Paul West has remarked, 'German writers mythologize easily and naturally'; there have tended to be in even the best of German novels 'too many possibilities'. An ordinary enough realistic tale can suddenly turn into a symbolic history of the human (or at least German) soul, or an ambitiously guilty account of the fatal split between Nature (*Natur*) and Spirit (*Geist*). This is why the rare miniaturists, such as Lampe or R. Walser (qq.v.), are so welcome and remarkable when they appear. Again, almost every German novel is vitiated by ponderousness, length and guilt. And yet who will now accuse such Germans or Austrians as the Manns, Hesse, Musil, Broch (qq.v.) of having, in their pre-1939 novels, something too big on their minds? The guilty sense of being German was shared by writers, from the communist Brecht to the conservative Thomas Mann; this demonstrated more than an irresistible tendency towards grandiosity. We grumble, justifiably, of there being a too grand, too suffering element in most of those great German novels. Perhaps they do share one specifically German characteristic possessed by the Third Reich: that was intended to endure for a millennium; they plan with similar ambitiousness to solve the whole mystery of human evil. . . . Yet the Third Reich in a dozen years performed evil on a scale unprecedented in history, and not a single writer of even near-genius gave them serious, continuous, unequivocal support.

Expressionism contained within itself elements that the Nazis transformed into reality; the Nazi episode itself may itself be seen as a 'formless scream'. The 'new objectivity' that succeeded expressionism and tried to modify its extremism even while remaining loyal to its real achievements was a reflection of a more than literary mood in Germany: but it was not strong enough to avoid the cataclysm of 1939–45. When literary activity started up again in 1945, when the older writers emerged from exterior or interior exile, and newer ones came into being, the situation was a fluid one. One German critic spoke of the literature of 'the Year Nought' (*Nullpunkt Literatur*). It was an understandable and popular concept; but a quarter of a century of writing has shown it to have been an invalid one. The post-war German writing is as recognizably teutonic as that produced by those who began before 1939. It would be surprising if it did not display some distinctively new features; but these features were not nearly as innovatory or drastic as those that began to appear in German literature in about the year 1910—and this in spite of the fact that post-1945 writers (especially poets) have been, for obvious reasons, much more open to foreign influences. As Rodney Livingstone has pointed out, the possibly unexpected 'continuity was provided by both the Inner and the Outer Emigration'. If I have chosen to deal with some older writers—such as Hans Erich Nossack—on this rather than on the other side of the historical watershed of 1945 then this is only because their work seems to me to belong to the later rather than to the earlier period: the work of their maturity comes after rather than before the final catastrophic realization of 1945. This is certainly true of Nossack (born 1901), Günter Erich (born 1907) and probably of Stefan Andres (born 1906); but it is not true of Anna Seghers (born 1900). That this decision as to who belongs to the later period and who does not has often had to be arbitrary makes its own point: the distinction is artificial and therefore not of great importance. A 'new' German literature came into being at the end of the first decade of this century; but it did not come into being in 1945. As a whole German literature is as it always was: 'philosophical', intensely and ambitiously over-anxious to probe colossal fundamentals (even when it begins with modest and solely realistic intentions), and simultaneously gloomy about the loneliness of the solipsist, the socially unengaged self and the threatening nature of society.

All this becomes evident in the retrospective consideration of the first postwar literary star in the (West) German firmament, WOLF-GANG BORCHERT (1921–47). Borchert was regarded as the spokesman of the *Nullpunkt*, and has been called 'a monument of unique artistry to the . . . disillusion of Germany in the immediate post-war years.' And in those years he did seem to Germans, and even to others, to be 'unique'.

Born in Hamburg, Borchert was whisked into the army almost before he had had time to grow up. He spent just over a year as a bookseller's assistant, during which time he lived unconventionally and marked himself out as a critic of the Nazi government. (The Gestapo arrested him for having had a homosexual affair with 'one Rieke': they meant Rilke.) He was happier when, between December 1940 and June 1941, he acted with a touring company. This came to an end when he was called up. He was severely wounded on the Russian front, and in addition suffered from jaundice and diphtheria in military hospitals. Acquitted of wounding himself in the hand, his letters home were intercepted and he was sentenced to death, pardoned (a Nazi strategy) and returned to the front—only to be arrested again, after discharge from the army, for displaying a defeatist and anti-Nazi attitude. He died only two years after the end of the war, on the day before his only extant play *The Man Outside* (*Draussen vor der Tür*, 1947; tr. in *The Prose Works of Wolfgang Borchert*, 1952), which had previously been broadcast, received its first highly successful performance. He wrote some poetry while he was in the army, but is remembered for his prose sketches and the single play.

Borchert was highly gifted, and in the case of at least one story, 'Billbrook', he showed genius; but, his brilliance notwithstanding, he was not original and he was, and by some still is, overrated.

The Man Outside, for all the angry satirical energy and the promise in manipulation of language that it shows, is a neo-expressionist *Heimkehrerdrama* (homecoming-drama). Negatively, that is to say satirically, this depiction of the return of a prisoner-of-war to his ruined homeland and ruined life is effective; positively it is a failure drawing upon outworn expressionist techniques and a torrent of what Rodney Livingstone rightly calls 'pompous' cliché. The fact is that, although the quality of Borchert's language is superior (and that of course is important), judged solely in terms of content his play is not intrinsically different from any typical late expressionist drama. The mood of *The Man Outside* oscillates between satirical nihilism and pseudo-ecstasy (with an understandable emphasis on the former); this successfully reflected the mood of 1947. No critical self-examination emanated from Borchert, whose fragile, three-quarters stifled genius operated only in established channels. One may even go so far as to say of *The Man Outside* that it is not only the old, but the old posing as the new, the different—and morally superior. There is nothing in it that is not in Toller's *Hinkemann* (q.v.), except that the latter pays some attention to reality whereas the former is not really more—not even in that smoking rubble!—than the familiar 'formless scream'.

Borchert's essentially miniaturist fiction—short, plotless, colloquial, evocative—is more modest, and achieves a good deal more. In

'Billbrook' a young Canadian pilot sets out joyfully to explore a district of Hamburg that bears his own name (Bill Brook), but he meets nothing but despair, rejection and emptiness. In this short story Borchert comes nearer than he did in his play to an understanding of the spiritual poverty of his own nihilism: here the genius of his ability, remarkable in his circumstances, to descry the truly human amongst the dehumanized, is intimated. Borchert's fiction is sensitive and poetic, but the large amount of attention it naturally received when it was published is misleading: judged by what he achieved, Borchert was a minor writer.

KARL WITTLINGER (1922) carried on the more or less expressionistic tradition of Borchert with *Do You Know the Milky Way?* (*Kennen Sie die Milchstrasse?*, 1956). As in a number of German novels and plays, the returning soldier finds himself superfluous. He ends up in a mental home, and his psychiatrist (in a twist that showed the influence of the theatre of the absurd), after acting out his patient's life-story, becomes a milkman. A later play, *Transmigration of the Soul* (*Seelenwanderung*, 1963) is a slick, but inoffensive and entertaining version of the Faust legend.

However, not all post-1945 German literature is as clearly traditional as that of Borchert, who reacted to the situation immediately and instinctively. For one thing the German language itself has been turned into a more straightforward instrument; to a large extent it has, literally, been cleaned up. The younger writers do not try to be inventive with language, only to employ it directly. (This is why such a writer as the linguistically reprehensible Ernst Jünger so clearly does not belong to the post-war period.) The hysteria, the sentimentality, the rhetoric—these at least have been purged away, even if their cause has not.

This cooling down and cleaning up of the language was in accord with the spirit of the movement—or, as appropriately, anti-movement—called *Gruppe 47*.

Many members of *Gruppe 47*, most notably the poet Günter Eich, have expressed themselves through the medium of the *Hörspiel*, the radio-play, which has been more fully developed in Germany than anywhere else in the world. Radio is an appropriate medium for the practitioners of expressionist and post-expressionist methods: there is no 'Aristotelian' formality, scenes ('sound-tableaux') follow one another in a succession rather than a progression, and different actions may be almost simultaneously presented. The first *Hörspiele* were written and broadcast in the mid-Twenties—there were similar efforts in Great Britain by Richard Hughes (q.v. 1) and Tyrone Guthrie—but the form did not come into its own until after the war.

The founder of *Gruppe 47*, HANS WERNER RICHTER (1908), the son of a North Prussian fisherman, is a writer of documentary fiction not unlike that of Plievier (q.v.), but more polished and less powerful. Richter, well known for his opposition to Hitler, fled to Paris in 1933 but was forced by poverty to return to Berlin in the following year; he unwillingly joined the army in 1940, and fell into American hands three years later. On release he edited a left-wing magazine, *Der Ruf*, until it was banned by the occupying forces; it was good enough to upset everyone. Richter himself is a comparatively crude realist, and his fiction is of little literary interest; but *Gruppe 47*, founded as a successor to *Der Ruf*, has accommodated many more versatile and gifted writers—a fact that does much credit to Richter.

Gruppe 47 has continued to meet every year for discussion and reading of new work. Its prize is the most coveted in West Germany. It is anti-programmatic, profoundly sceptical and tends to straight-forward language. The right wing is excluded, and has not tried to enter. Nothing, it seems, has been lost by this. Because *Gruppe 47* has been so eclectic—a Roman Catholic liberal, Heinrich Böll, is one of its most characteristic writers—allowing itself to represent what responsible German literature actually is rather than (beyond the insistence on 'clean', non-visionary language) trying to shape it, it has lasted. Its strength lies in the fact that one cannot be dogmatic about it. Few of those German writers who established themselves after 1945 who have not been associated with it could be described as fundamentally alien to its modest aims.

XIV

Borchert's was the only important new name in the German theatre in the immediate post-war years. Switzerland, where Brecht's plays were seen during and after the war, provided what continuity there was; two of the leading German dramatists of the post-war years, Max Frisch and Friedrich Dürrenmatt (qq.v.), are Swiss. The Austrian theatre survives in the works of Lernet-Holenia (q.v.) and FRANZ THEODOR CSOKOR (1885–1969); but the work of the Viennese Fritz Hochwälder (q.v.), who emigrated to Switzerland in 1938, is not in this tradition. It is only with Rolf Hochhuth (q.v.) and his few successors that new beginnings have been made.

MAX FRISCH (1911) was born in Zürich. During the Thirties he was a university student and reporter before he decided to become, like his father, an architect. He was a soldier (guarding the frontiers of his neutral country) for a short time at the beginning of the war. After he gained literary success Frisch gave up his architect's practice (he had been awarded a prize for the design of a municipal swimming bath); he now spends much of his time in Rome.

The Swiss have been unkindly described as 'typical Germans who escaped two world wars'; this is an unfair generalization, but is an aspect of Switzerland that deeply concerns both Frisch and Dürrenmatt. Bourgeois Switzerland is proud of its 'sensible' approach, its decision to remain 'minor', its financial solidarity, the perfect, tiny gloriousness of its watches, its neutrality. Its intellectuals, however, see its 'sense' and 'minority' as cruel and petty; its neutrality as a matter of luck and lack of commitment. Neutral Switzerland is a particularly apt vantage-point for the consideration of the possibility that the Second World War and its aftermath were caused, not by Germany alone, but by the whole world's failure to achieve a properly human sense of responsibility. This 'Swiss guilt', this refusal to smugly accept neutrality, pervades the work of both Frisch and Dürrenmatt, more particularly that of the former.

Frisch's first performed play, *Now They Sing Again* (*Nun singen sie wieder*, 1945), in which the dead mix with the living, was an unremarkable latter-day essay in expressionism, and showed no more promise than the autobiographical novel *Jürg Reinhart* (1934).

Frisch's chief theme, his serious handling of which gives him higher status than the cleverer Dürrenmatt, is the search for identity—for an authentic existence. It is not clear whether Frisch believes in the existence of a single, true identity for the individual; but he believes in the search for it. His attempts to define the nature of the love that makes it a possibility are sober and unsentimental.

Frisch made friends with Brecht while the latter was in Switzerland, and although he shares only Brecht's critical attitude towards the bourgeois, and not his communism, he was deeply influenced by him. This immediately showed itself in *When the War Came to an End* (*Als der Krieg zu Ende war*, 1949), in which the heroine steps out of her role to comment upon it. In 1951 came his best play to that date, *Count Öderland* (*Graf Öderland*, 1951, rev. 1956, 1961; FTP), a brilliant *tour de force* in which a public prosecutor suddenly becomes a terrorist—only to find himself, as dictator, obliged to rule. To escape —whether from fantasy or fact—he kills himself. This reveals the identity of prosecutor and gangster as well as hinting at the true nature of 'revolution'; but the central character is unfortunately not made convincing as either human being or 'stage person'.

The more comic *Don Juan or Love of Geometry* (*Don Juan oder Die Liebe zur Geometrie*, 1953) presents Don Juan as a misogynist devoted to mathematics and therefore irresistible to women. He arranges his own legendary 'death' in front of his assembled girl-friends, but is found out and trapped into a respectable marriage. As critics have pointed out, the basic form of Frisch's mature works is that of the parable, for the incidents he depicts make little sense detached from some kind of 'moral'. The moral here is that the image the world has of a man is actually more real than the man himself. At the end of the play a book about Don Juan the seducer is introduced: this legend will outlive the mathematician and even the trapped and domesticated married man. Thus, when we think of others as having a certain character, we withdraw love from them—and threaten the possibility of their free development—by clamping a mask upon them.

Frisch's most famous play, originally written for radio, *The Fire Raisers* (*Biedermann und die Brandstifter*, 1958; FTP), is certainly a parable, although its form owes something to the theatre of the absurd (q.v.). The bourgeois Biedermann is a cruel and relentless businessman, but, as his name ('honest man') implies, he regards himself as being a respectable and decent fellow. When sinister characters infiltrate his house and begin to pile up petrol he welcomes them and relies upon his good nature to prevent them from carrying out their intention. Finally he hands them the matches with which they fire his own property and the whole town. (An epilogue in hell, added later to the stage version, did not improve this short play.) Apparently the theme was originally suggested to Frisch by the Czech President Beneš's acceptance of the communist coup of 1948, whereby Gottwald was able to establish a dictatorship. But it applies equally to the German acceptance of Hitler and to mankind's possession of the atomic bomb. Furthermore, given the personality of Biedermann, the question arises as to who really is the 'fire raiser', and whether he deserves a better fate. . . . Frisch here represents the plight of modern man, trapped between the bourgeois viciousness of Biedermann and the true nature of 'revolution'.

Frisch's most substantial play is *Andorra* (1961; FTP), in which the country depicted is 'any country'—but most aptly neutral Switzerland, smugly aware of its virtue, and confident of its ability to dissuade the neighbouring 'Blacks' from invading it. The young hero Andri has been presented by his schoolmaster father as a Jew he adopted: actually he is his bastard son, the result of an affair with a 'Black' woman. He proposes to teach his countrymen the fallacy of racism by eventually revealing Andri as no Jew, but his son. But Andri's identity is shown as having been destroyed by the opinion of others, who impose upon him the 'image' of a Jew. Finally he dies as a Jewish scapegoat for the murder of his own mother by Andorrans. This is one of the most moving of all post-war dramas, and incidentally reveals what the modern theatre owes to Brecht in a technical sense: between the scenes each character (named only by his trade or profession) enters a dock and tries to excuse himself of the crime of Andri's murder.

Frisch has also written three novels. *I'm not Stiller* (*Stiller*, 1954; tr. 1961) deals with a sculptor's forced rediscovery of an identity he had successfully shed. In some respects this goes more deeply into the question of identity than Frisch's plays. Stiller refuses the image forced upon him by society; but fails to discover himself. Frisch seems to hint here, as he has elsewhere, that the only way of achieving 'authenticity' is to 'accept God'—but what he means by this he has not made clear. *I'm not Stiller* eventually resolves itself as yet another elaborate artist's expiation piece: Stiller, who can't be himself, therefore makes images. Is this, Frisch asks, 'responsible'?

Homo Faber (1957; tr. 1959) again explores the consequences of human creativity. The technologist hero (called Faber: 'maker') is trapped by various failures of intricate machinery (razors, engines) into marriage with his own daughter: he is thus inexorably an Oedipus, for all the brilliance with which he and his 'civilization' have distanced themselves from 'nature'.

Wilderness of Mirrors (*Mein Name sei Gantenbein* 1964; tr. 1965) is Frisch's most difficult and ambitious work, an attempt to deal truthfully with human lack of identity that, according to one bemused critic, is 'so uncompromising as to shatter the very foundations of the medium of the novel'. As in Musil's *The Man without Qualities* (q.v.), only more deliberately and systematically, and as a matter of structural policy, every conjecture and possibility is envisaged; characters are 'tried out' under different images. Gantenbein's marriage is 'happy' because he can be 'blind' while his wife deceives him with other men. . . . This is a contrived novel, which probably fails because of an absence of human richness. But, of course, in the state of affairs it reveals—the absence of fixed identity—human richness is not even possible. . . . Somehow Frisch's attempt to convey the poignancy of this—as a result of a residual, reluctant scepticism about 'God'?—fails. Yet he is a sensitive, acutely intelligent and never frivolous writer, who seemed one of those who carry the future of literature in their hands—his *Diary* (etc.) is another important book —but he has done little recently.

So far FRIEDRICH DÜRRENMATT (1921), son of a Berne pastor, has not revealed himself as of quite the calibre of Frisch. The difference between the two is apparent in their fiction: Frisch is the author of major novels, Dürrenmatt of highly competent, original and intelligent detective stories: *The Judge and His Hangman* (*Der Richter und sein Henker*, 1950; tr. 1954), *Suspicion* (*Der Verdacht*, 1954) and *The Pledge* (*Das Versprechen*, 1958; tr. 1959). But he is ten years younger than Frisch, and his flippancy is perhaps less natural to him than defensive.

Dürrenmatt, whose first aspiration was to be a painter, has withdrawn his first two plays, *It is Written* (*Es steht geschrieben*, 1947) and *The Blind* (*Der Blinde*, 1948), although they have been published. In *Romulus the Great* (*Romuluus der Grosse*, 1949, rev. 1957; FPD) and *The Marriage of Mr. Mississippi* (*Die Ehe des Herrn Mississippi*, 1951; DFP) he at last found his style. Both are comedies, and both overturn bourgeois values. Romulus, the (unhistorical) last Roman emperor before the invasion of the barbarians, is a clown who finally achieves human dignity by refusing to regard himself seriously as a martyr. Romulus is a convincing figure, who develops throughout the play, whose unobtrusive message is for mankind to give up self-esteem. The surrealistic *The Marriage of Mr. Mississippi* is brilliant but less successful, since its characters remain abstractions and it ultimately depends upon stage effects.

An Angel Comes to Babylon (*Ein Engel kommt nach Babylon*, 1953, rev. 1957; DFP) is again brilliant, but too much reflects its author's philosophical bewilderment—Dürrenmatt's profusion of tricks is not wholly successful in concealing his yearning (even if ironically qualified) for a 'system'. This play is supposed to have a sequel whose theme will be the construction of the Tower of Babel.

After this Dürrenmatt produced what is still probably the best of his plays, although it has not attained the international success of *The Physicists* (q.v.). The central character, a shopkeeper called Ill, attains much the same kind of dignity as Romulus does in the earlier play. In *The Visit* (*Der Besuch der alten Dame*, 1956; tr. 1962) an old millionairess, whom in youth Ill has seduced and impregnated, returns to her home town when it is running through a hard time. She offers a large sum of money—if the burghers will enable her to have her revenge on Ill by killing him. In the end they do it: they lose their integrity, but the ordinary little Ill achieves a stature he never previously had as he comes to accept his fate.

But it was *The Physicists* (*Die Physiker*, 1962; DFP) that provided Dürrenmatt with his greatest commercial success. It is, undoubtedly, one of the most sheerly skilful plays of its time, and is perhaps the most effective, literate and unpretentious of all the 'black comedies'. It is set in a mental home, where we encounter three apparent lunatics, who claim to be Newton, Einstein and the spokesman of

King Solomon. Actually, however, this third man is a brilliant physicist who has sought refuge, in the sanatorium, from the terrible power of his own discoveries. In the first act all three men murder their nurses: each has fallen in love with her patient and has discovered his sanity. The other two madmen are agents of the two main world powers, sent to abduct the genius, Mobius. While a police inspector investigates the murders, Mobius persuades the others to help him save the world by staying put. They agree, but unfortunately the female psychiatrist in charge of their 'cases' has taken copies of Mobius' manuscripts before he burned them; herself mad, she proposes to exploit them. Whether 'a certain flippancy about the treatment' actually 'introduces a note of insincerity' (H. F. Garten) or not, it is certain that Dürrenmatt fails to do full justice to his ingenious plot. An excellent play, *The Physicists* should also be a moving one—and for some reason it is not.

Dürrenmatt has written short stories and radio plays, one of which, *A Dangerous Game*, was translated (1960). An immensely gifted writer, it remains for him to do justice to the emotional seriousness he displays in his thoughtful criticism.

FRITZ HOCHWÄLDER (1911) was born in Vienna, but left for Switzerland in 1938. He has continued to write plays (for radio and TV as well as the stage) of a consistently high standard for over a quarter of a century, but has never repeated the commercial success of *The Strong are Lonely* (*Das heilige Experiment*, 1947; ad. 1954), which was first performed in 1943. This deals with the destruction of the theocratic Jesuit state in eighteenth-century Paraguay and with the conflict in the mind of the Father Provincial—between his own spiritual interests and the needs of his Church as a whole. Hochwälder was a friend of Georg Kaiser (q.v.), and based his second play *The Fugitive* (*Der Flüchtling*, 1945) on a scenario written by him just before his death in Switzerland. This story of the conversion of a frontier guard to a belief in freedom—a fugitive takes his wife from him—is his least convincing play; it was made into a successful film. *The Public Prosecutor* (*Der öffentliche Ankläger*, 1949; tr. 1958) is as good as anything he has written. Fouquier Tinville, the public prosecutor of the period after Robespierre's death, conducts a case against an anonymous enemy of the people: himself. *Donadieu* (1953), based on a ballad by C. F. Meyer (q.v.), is a convincing and dramatically effective account of a man's renunciation of the right to revenge himself upon his wife's murderer. In *The Inn* (*Die Herberge*, 1956), once again a finely constructed and highly effective play, the theft of a bag of gold brings to light a more serious crime. *The Innocent* (*Die Unschuldige*, 1958) is a comedy in which a man's life is changed when he is accused of a murder of which he is not, but—as he realizes—might have been, guilty. *Thursday* (*Donnerstag*, 1959), written for the Salzburg festival, is a miracle play, and one of the few in which Hochwälder has used a modern setting and drawn on the traditions of his native theatre. Pomfrit, an Austrian Faust, wins his struggle against the devil's temptation. *1003* (1963) is Hochwälder's most experimental play. It shows the author creating a character, and at the same time is concerned with his usual theme of the humanization of man: his awakening of conscience, and acquirement of qualities that entitle him to the definition of human: the transformation of '*Nichtmensch*' into *Mensch*. *The Raspberry-picker* (*Der Himbeerpflücker*, 1965), a farce, is based on Gogol's *Government Inspector*. *The Command* (*Der Befehl*, 1967) is for television.

Hochwälder is a prolific playwright, well known to the public for his Paraguayan success, but perhaps not enough heeded by critics. His technical skill extends, as *1003* demonstrates, to the nonconventional play; and it never conceals a superficial or sentimental approach.

WOLFGANG HILDESHEIMER (1916), from Hamburg, was originally a painter (he trained in England), but is probably best known as one of the comparatively few German so-called dramatists of the absurd. He emigrated to Palestine in 1933 and, an Israeli citizen, now lives in Switzerland. He is certainly the leader of such dramatists in German. He is also the author of short stories and radio plays and a radio opera (with music by Hans Werner Henze). His first stage success, *The Dragon Throne* (*Der Drachenthron*, 1955), was based on his *Hörspiel* on the Turandot story, *Prinzessin Turandot*, of the previous year. His first venture into the theatre of the absurd was the trilogy of one-act plays *Plays in Which Darkness Falls* (*Spiele in denen es dunkel wird*, 1958). His earlier radio plays were bizarre and witty variations on 'Ruritanian' themes. Now he consciously drew upon the techniques of the theatre of the absurd to depict the grotesque manner in which non-material values lay buried in the commercial details of the new prosperity. *Pastoral or Time for Cocoa* (*Pastorale order die Zeit für Kakao*), the first of the three 'darkness' plays, is very close to reality in its depiction of a number of men mixing business talk with sham culture—but condenses the action to expose its absurdity. Hildesheimer's use of the absurd has been characteristically German in that he has made it as didactic as possible—since (he says) 'life makes no statement' so the absurd play becomes a parable of life by itself making no statement. His first full-length play of the absurd is *The Delay* (*Die Verspätung*, 1961), which is set in a village inn. An old professor is waiting for the arrival of a fabulous bird, while all public services have ceased to function. This is a moving play, but owes much to Beckett and Ionesco. Hildesheimer is gentle rather than gloomy or savage. The use of this technique by RICHARD HEY (1926) is less convincing. As H. F. Garten implies, his plays *The Fish with the Golden Dagger* (*Der Fisch mit dem goldenen Dolch*, 1959) and *Woe to Him Who Doesn't Lie* (*Weh dem der nicht lügt*, 1962) are essentially romantic dramas conveniently cast into the fashionable form of the absurd.

PETER WEISS (1916), who was born near Berlin, and who is often referred to as Brecht's natural successor, was an early member of *Gruppe 47*, but did not attain his present high reputation until he was well over forty. Best known in the English-speaking world as the author of *Marat/Sade*, which was eventually filmed, Weiss is the author of several other plays and novels. His father was a Czech Jew (converted to Christianity), his mother Swiss. When Weiss was eighteen the family left for London, and he studied photography at the London Polytechnic. In 1936 he went to Prague to study at the Academy of Art. In 1938 he fled to Switzerland. He went to Sweden in 1939, to rejoin his parents, and eventually became a Swedish citizen. For the next twenty years he devoted himself mostly to visual arts: first as a painter and then as a film-maker. He published two small collections of poetry in Swedish in the Forties, but did not take up writing seriously until the late Fifties. Weiss met and was encouraged by Hesse (q.v.). Other influences are his experience in the documentary cinema, the gruesome alogical world of Grimms' tales and the Märchen, surrealism, Kafka, and Breughel and Bosch and their re-appearance in the work of Kafka's friend the painter, novelist and illustrator Alfred Kubin.

Weiss's first book in German, his 'micro-novel' *The Shadow of the Coachman's Body* (*Der Schatten des Körpers des Kutschers*, 1960), was written eight years before its publication. This is a child-narrator's account of the events in an isolated house in some undefined fairy-tale past; the cinema has influenced the descriptive terms, chiefly compounded of light and shadow; the atmosphere is menacing, the attitude of the narrator unmistakably paranoid. This is an experiment, not entirely successful because it becomes repetitious and boring; but it is a remarkable and original piece of writing.

The two autobiographical pieces, *Leavetaking* and *Vanishing Point* (*Abschied von den Eltern*, 1961; *Fluchtpunkt*, 1962; tr. 1967), usefully appear in English in a single volume. This narrative, covering the years 1916–47, makes evident the purely personal difficulties that account for Weiss's slow start: what his best English critic Ian Hilton describes as 'extreme alienation'. The partial attempt in his first prose work to describe the world in terms of 'scientific' perception failed because it did not correspond closely enough to Weiss's own alienated point of view. It was simply another, frozen, point of view. The autobiographical narrative, in which there is some excellently lucid and minutely observed detail (technically of a conventional sort), is more successful.

But Weiss was to find his true *métier*, and his first release from the severe feelings of alienation that afflicted him, in the drama. He has said that when he writes a book he feels alone; but when his work reaches the stage he feels 'alive'. His play, *The Persecution and Assassination of Marat as Performed by the Inmates of the Asylum of Charenton under the Direction of the Marquis de Sade* (*Die Verfolgung und Edmordung Jean Paul Marats, dargestellt durch die Schuaspielgruppe des Hospizes zu Charenton unter Anleitung des Herrn de Sade*, 1964; tr. 1965), known simply as *Marat/Sade*, is an original amalgam of the theatres of the absurd and cruelty (qq.v.), and of Beckett, Wedekind, Genet, Ionesco and Strindberg (qq.v.); but the strongest influence of all came from Brecht (q.v.), whose political ideas Weiss took with absolute seriousness. He was to offend many of his left-wing admirers in the West when, in the year following his greatest success, he announced his allegiance to East Germany. (Since he chooses to remain in capitalist Sweden, this is doubtless to be interpreted as a gesture within the Western camp—or perhaps as a kind of autobiographical alienation effect.)

Clearly, however, Weiss's requirements for feeling alive included widespread success as well as the dramatic form. His earlier plays) had been failures. In *The Tower* (*Der Turm*, 1963; tr. PWGT, 1967 and *The Insurance* (*Die Versicherung*, 1967), written in the late Forties and early Fifties respectively, there is insufficient dramatic element; and in *Night with Guests* (*Nacht mit Gästen*, 1963) the rhyming doggerel in which the play is written merely helps to emphasize its slightness. *Marat/Sade*, certainly superior to anything Weiss has done before or since, finely and inventively dramatizes the tension within him—and in history—between imagination and action, individualism and socialism. It lacks German ponderousness, and, like the plays of Brecht that were its main inspiration, it offers enormous possibilities to its director—and it has attracted distinguished directors, including the greatest of them all, Ingmar Bergman. Like its predecessors, *Marat/Sade* lacks true dramatic action; but it is a *tour de force* because it creates the illusion of it, smuggling in a good deal of almost Shavian discussion of ideas. Against a background of insane babbling Sade directs his play of the murder of Marat. The date is 13 July 1808, fifteen years after the actual event. Acting out Weiss's own conflict between what he felt to be creative solipsism and de-

sirable but unattainable revolutionary socialism, *Marat/Sade* mir-
rored a universal conflict. Every production, from Peter Brook's
simplistic one to the infinitely subtle, individualistic Ingmar Bergman's, added a new dimension. Significantly, Weiss preferred the
most 'committed' production in which Marat is made the revolutionary hero. He revised the script five times, each time in this
direction. From his own act of political commitment may be marked
—after all too brief an ascent—his creative decline, a decline that is,
however, gradual and, doubtless, not irreversible. This has nothing
to do with the merits of Marxism or the deficiencies of capitalism; it
is simply that nothing Weiss has written since *Marat/Sade* is on the
same imaginative level because it lacks its high tension.

In *The Investigation* (*Die Ermittlung*, 1965; tr. 1966), staged in
Germany by Erwin Piscator (q.v.) not long before his death, Weiss
allows a selection of facts to substitute for imagination. This oratorio
is a series of extracts, pretentiously broken up into free verse, from
reports of the proceedings at the Auschwitz trial at Frankfurt-on-
Main in 1964. It is, of course, unbearably moving; but attempts to
demonstrate that this is so because of Weiss's selective brilliance are
misguided. Almost any such juxtaposition would be equally effective.
Offered to us as a work of imagination, *The Investigation* is merely
impertinent. As one critic remarked, 'it wrote itself'. *My Place*
(*Meine Ortschaft*, 1965; GWT), a prose account of Weiss's visit to
Auschwitz, is superior. Of the three successors to *The Investigation*,
only the 'everyman' piece *How Herr Mockinpott Was Relieved of his
Sufferings* (*Wie dem Herrn Mockinpott das Leiden ausgetrieben wurde*, 1968),
although its situation is over-indebted to Kafka, is better: non-
documentary, it is more inventive and more vital in its detail. *The
Song of the Lusitanian Bogey* (*Gesang vom luritanischen Popanz*, 1967),
about the brutal Portuguese suppression of the Angolan uprising of
1961, and *Vietnam Discourse* (*Viet Nam Diskurs*, 1968)—the one in the
form of a song-and-dance revue for (ideally) an all-Negro cast, and
the other 'tub-thumping documentary' (Ian Hilton)—are slavishly
Brechtian in technique and have no claim at all as imaginative
works. Rather, they are political acts. Weiss has turned into a higher
middlebrow entertainer in the most fashionable modern manner of
left-wing conscience-stirrer. It does not much help his work that the
attack is really less on the capitalist West, admittedly as corrupt as
Weiss likes, than on the solipsistic tendencies of the author. Beneath
their superficially bang-up-to-date, fashionable appearance, Weiss's
propaganda pieces are curiously old-fashioned, and hark back to
the days of expressionist activism; furthermore, they tend increasingly to over-simplify matters, a risk often run by those who abandon

the objective function of the writer for the necessarily subjective one of changing the world (which is Weiss's avowed aim). His latest work, *Trotsky in Exile* (*Trotzki im Exil*, 1970), once again documentary, diminishes the humanity of Trotsky in the interests of its message. Weiss, a sincere man, remains desperately naïve about the nature of revolutions. He can hardly have carefully considered the state of his master Brecht's mind at the end of his life. He sees, he has written, 'no reason why artists in a Socialist state should be restricted in their own natural development'. One can only sadly append one's own mark of exclamation. He and literature would be better served if he concentrated more upon his natural—and not his intellectual— development. One may see in him another example, and in this case a victim, of *Künstlerschuld*: instead of, like Rilke, yearning to be a 'country doctor', he has decided to be a doctor to the world from which he cannot help feeling so distant. And yet the feeling for other people displayed in some of his prose of the early Sixties—for, say, the Swedish forestry workers in *Vanishing Point*—is stronger and purer and certainly more beautiful and natural than that displayed in the more or less cleverly manipulated puppets of his propaganda plays. The masters of Auschwitz itself regarded their charges as puppets; had they regarded them as people they could not have abused them as they did.

It is easy to understand why the post-war Germans evolved a documentary-drama form as a means of solving their problems: theoretically, in place of ecstasy, or mere interpretation, the facts would speak truthfully, would clarify the situation, and would deter the tendency to excess. The more 'documentary' such works are, of course, the less imaginative they are likely to be. But creativity itself has come under strong suspicion in Germany: better, therefore, to have facts than figments of the imagination.

This form is also, however, a logical development of epic theatre (q.v.), and the documentary drama has tended to become less an objective theatre—fulfilling the role of the good newspaper, which of course no commercially viable newspaper can for long fulfil—than either a theatre of protest or, as in the case of Peter Weiss, an agent for social change. Ours, furthermore, is an age of the 'directors' theatre'; as one critic has written, 'The play is no longer the thing; it is what producer and director make of it that counts'. The documentary drama, one might say, is one manner—and an important one—in which the authors connive at this arrangement. It mostly suits playwrights in whom the springs of invention or imagination are weak; but it might be a prelude to a genuinely co-operative phase in the theatre, in which individuals need not be distinguished.

The best known, or some would say most notorious, of the documentary-dramatists is ROLF HOCHHUTH (1931), who was born near Kassel in Northern Hesse. Hochhuth has written both short stories and a novel (neither are published in book form), but it was his play about the Roman Catholics and the Nazis, *The Representative* (*Der Stellvertreter*, 1963; tr. 1963) that made him famous. Appropriately in the age of director's theatre, the German text consists of much more than anyone has ever seen in any production: what goes in depends on the director. This play, first produced by Piscator in Berlin, is undoubtedly an indictment of Pope Pius XII for his indifference to the plight of the Jews and his failure to denounce Nazi persecution of them. It aroused much controversy, all of which tended to obscure the question of its dramatic merit. Pope John XXIII is supposed to have exclaimed, when asked what could be done to neutralize the effects of the play, 'Do against it? What can you do against the truth?' Hochhuth has been compared with Schiller, and this is apt so far as *The Representative* is concerned, for the structure is old-fashioned and 'plotted' as distinct from, say, Weiss's documentaries; but *Soldiers* (*Soldaten*, 1967; tr. 1969) his second play —again a textually massive work from which the producer must select—is more chaotic, and its dialogue is flatter and less effective. This is clearly intended as a condemnation of the inhumanity of war in general, based on Hochhuth's belief that history (tragically) expresses itself in a few strong personalities who make decisions; its effect is to suggest that the British were as morally culpable as the Germans. Now this point of view—if Hochhuth intended it—might no doubt convincingly be set forth in an imaginative work; here it functions simply as journalism. The question of whether or not Churchill connived at, or ordered, the death of the Polish General Sikorski has nothing to do with the literary value of *Soldiers*.

Hochhuth has written some powerful scenes; and his technique, in his first play, of interspersing heartless official cliché with concentrated verse does convey his indignation and his humanity. But *Soldiers* is more decisively a directors' play: furthermore, its imaginative worth seems to have been wilfully vitiated by polemical considerations. *The Representative* was a mixture of pamphlet and drama, displaying creative gifts of a high order; *Soldiers* is skilful journalism, and should be judged on that level.

XV

One of the most characteristic of post-war West German writers is the novelist, critic and playwright MARTIN WALSER (1927) born in Wasserburg. He is not a profound writer—but he is a useful one, a responsible and scrupulous social critic and satirist who knows his limitations. It is typical of him that, as a critic, he should approach drama as essentially historical. It is wrong, he asserts, to reinterpret any drama of the past. He does not, in other words, fully grasp the critical problem of the drama that is ephemeral and the drama that transcends its time: his own work, although not frenetic or over-programmatic like some of Weiss's, is written specifically for its time. A dialectical writer, and excessively intellectual, he lacks the confidence of inspiration—an understandable attitude in an intelligent German of his generation. But he rationalizes this into a critically unconvincing distrust of words' capacities. For Walser, the artist is not guilty but incapable: pressure to write in him is low. He first attracted wide attention with his novel *The Gadarene Club* (*Ehen in Philippsburg*, 1957; tr. 1959), a satire on business and the German 'economic miracle'. *Half-Time* (*Halbzeit*, 1960) is a more comprehensive satire on the same subject-matter. *The Unicorn* (*Das Einhorn*, 1966), his most amusing and psychologically pointed novel, deals with the experiences of a man commissioned by a woman publisher to write a novel about love. He gets his copy from an affair with her.

Walser, almost always an accomplished and argute writer, is at his most adroit in the *Hörspiel* and in stage drama. *The Rabbit Race* (*Eiche und Angora*, 1962; ad. 1963, with *The Detour, Der Abstecher*, 1961) is unoriginal inasmuch as it patchily draws on almost every dramatic source available in the half-century preceding its composition; but it is both intelligent and entertaining. The central character is Alois Grübel, representative of the exploited German, 'nice' but naïve, who submits to all manner of evil. *The Detour* is a sinister comedy which Walser subsequently turned into a radio play, heard in Great Britain in 1962. *The Black Swan* (*Der schwarze Schwan*, 1964) continues Walser's study of the German character and of German guilt in particular. A son tries to discover if he contains within himself the seeds of his father's guilt. Like nearly all Walser's work, the penetrating intelligence of this play is undermined by a failure to create—perhaps arising from a lack of interest in—individual character. In so far as Germany has produced a 'new writer' since 1945, the cool, non-incandescent Walser is typical. His workaday creative talent, operating in more or less 'intelligible' forms, stands in contrast to the paucity of that of many self-conscious, non-representational *avant gardists*. But recent work has been poor.

HANS ERICH NOSSACK (1901), from Hamburg, is older and, by contrast, wholly introspective; but, with his constant theme of self-renewal, he is indisputably a post-war writer. Forbidden to publish by the Nazis in 1933 on account of his left-wing views, he gave up the hand-to-mouth existence (factory-worker, salesman, clerk, reporter, unemployed) that he had deliberately chosen rather than continue to study law and philosophy at Jena, and joined his father's coffee-importing firm. His manuscripts were destroyed in the Hamburg air-raids of summer 1943, although it seems that an unfinished drama about Lenin written in the Thirties, *Elnin*, survives. Virtually all of the work—novels, plays, poems, essays—by which he is known arises not from early left-wing interests but from experiences of the war; and what started this off was his witnessing, from the country outside Hamburg, its destruction by Allied bombers. He felt that he was literally watching the destruction of his own past, and his subsequent writings are an account of his difficult rebirth: of his struggle to find himself as a real person and to survive as one. He has developed into one of the strangest of contemporary writers; and his writing, always difficult, has consistently gained in power.

His first works—they can be classified as short stories although English-speaking readers might call them autobiographical essays; and he himself calls them 'reports'—described the Hamburg raids, and were praised by Jean Paul Sartre. All these pieces were revised and collected together as *Dorothea* (1950). In his fiction Nossack uses surrealistic devices to express bewilderment, disgust and a Bergsonian (q.v.) disbelief in time. Like most German writers, he has directed his satirical attention at the *Wirtschaftswunder* society, the prosperous and smug perpetrators and maintainers of the 'economic miracle'. But he remains obsessed by what he saw from outside his native Hamburg; paradoxically, its chaos preserves him from the anti-human horrors of the *Wirtschaftswunder*. The first novel he published, *At Latest in November* (*Spätestens im November*, 1955) tells—from her point of view—of a woman torn between her husband, an industrialist, and a writer. The husband, a 'good fellow', uses her beauty as an advertisement for the firm; she meets the writer because he is the recipient of the firm's prize (more advertisement). Thus the writer depends on the crass businessman for cash, prestige and sex. Nossack shows relentlessly that the love between these two people sets up no authentic values in opposition to the industrialist's rosy materialism. Marianne, the wife, returns to her husband, but leaves him again—to meet death with her lover in a car crash. This, Nossack's most technically conventional work, is wholly pessimistic. *The Younger Brother (Der jüngere Bruder,* 1958) is an even sharper indictment of the capitalist present.

We Know That Already (Das kennt man, 1964) is the paranoid—or is it?—narrative of a dying prostitute of Hamburg's Reeperbahn district. She has been run over—by a genuine accident or by the machinations of the people who live 'over there', on the other side of the river? The surface of this multi-layered book is (for Nossack) a fairly straightforward account of the breakdown of a simple mind, which takes to paranoically interpreting kindness as hostility. But, ironically, this colloquial monologue, hardly surrealist in terms of the dying girl's delirium, has its sinisterly realistic side. The book has great distinction of style; the demotic nature of the girl's narrative does not so much question as cut through the parodistically teutonic sections of the plot (for example, 'over there', in a quiet glade, where time is non-existent, at the secret centre of the slave-run industrial complex, dwells the great mistress whose servant the narrator was in a previous incarnation).

Nossack's best novel, *The Case d'Arthez (Der Fall d'Arthez,* 1968), again deals, in a complex plot, with the problem of discovering an 'authentic' existence in a political state that regards such authenticity as treason. For Nossack there is no modern state that would be able to tolerate a truly free individual. The anonymous narrator, d'Arthez, and his friend Lambert, are all shown as in search of self: the narrator gives up his post with the security service, d'Arthez renounces name and fortune, Lambert (whose name is a pseudonym) refuses success. Nossack, in a novel that is surprisingly easy to read, makes the quest for self and truth mean something in psychological as well as mythical, or parabolic, terms. To a large extent it may be seen as what his earlier and sometimes recondite work was leading up to. He has also written poetry, criticism and plays.

EDZARD SCHAPER (1908) was born near Posen, now in Poland; he lived in Esthonia and Finland from 1930 until after the war, and finally settled in Switzerland. A Baltic background predominates in his work, which is unequivocally Christian. The solution he offers to the problems of terror and tyranny, to which he is acutely and honestly sensitive (as his background might suggest)—a solution involving the cultivation of a Christian stoicism in order to attain inner freedom—is not sufficiently worked out to be convincing to readers. But his accounts of the struggle to survive of an Orthodox Christian community in Esthonia in *The Dying Church (Die sterbende Kirche,* 1935) and its sequel *The Last Advent* (*Der letzte Advent*, 1949) are touching and always truthful. Nor are they without some humour. He is at his best, however, and least hortatory, in the novella. 'The Shipwrecked Ark' (1935), in which a cargo of circus animals perish in a storm as a young couple try to resolve their difficulties, is the most delicate example.

ALBRECHT GOES (1908), who was born in Würtemberg, is another Christian traditionalist, but one of greater power and range. He is a Lutheran pastor who served as an army chaplain on the Russian Front. His poetry (TCG) is traditional and occasionally achieves an impressive serenity in the manner of Mörike, of whom he has written a study (1938). He is well known as an essayist. His best work is contained in the two novellas *Arrow to the Heart* (*Unruhige Nacht*, 1949; tr. 1951) and *The Burnt Offering* (*Das Brandopfer*, 1954; tr. 1956). In the first a chaplain on the Russian Front has to comfort a young soldier who is going to be shot in the morning for desertion. *The Burnt Offering* describes how a butcher's wife becomes aware, through her work, of the true nature of the Nazi attitude towards the Jews. This admirably straightforward, brief tale is Goes's masterpiece.

STEFAN ANDRES (1906–70), a Roman Catholic from the Moselle valley, began as a trainee-priest, but abandoned this in favour of study at the university and extensive travel. He lived in Italy from 1937 until 1949. His simplistic first novel, *Brother Lucifer* (*Bruder Luzifer*, 1932), is autobiographical: a not extraordinary account of conflict between spiritual aspirations and physical instincts. He was a prolific author of plays, novels, novellas, poetry, short stories and *Hörspiele*: a competent writer whose lusty sense of humour and vitality continually redeem his books from dullness. The novella that made him famous after the war, *We are Utopia* (*Wir sind Utopia*, 1942; tr. 1954), is his best book, an example of ingenuity fully exploited. A monk, Paco, leaves his monastery in Spain to devote himself to the establishment of that heaven upon earth which his superiors have told him not even God has been able to create. Fighting against the fascists in the Civil War he is captured—and confined in his old cell in the very monastery from which he had fled. The officer in charge of the prisoners, a bullying rapist and killer, is terrified of dying unconfessed, and comes for help. Paco, with his knowledge of the place, could kill him and help his friends to escape. However, although knowing that the officer's intention is to machine-gun them all, he confesses him and allows him to carry out his murderous plan. Andres turned this powerful and unostentatious story into a moving and effective *Hörspiel*, *God's Utopia* (*Gottes Utopia*, 1950). The dystopian trilogy *The Deluge* (*Die Sintflut*, 1949–59) is about an ex-priest,

Moosethaler, who becomes a Hitler in an imaginary country. *The Journey to Portiuncula* (*Die Reise nach Portiuncula*, 1954) is a clever and amusing novel, full of Andres' love for the south, about a rich German brewer who revisits the place in Italy where thirty years before he betrayed a girl and his youthful ideals.

GERD GAISER (1908), the son of a Würtemberg priest, has been one of the leading writers of fiction since 1950. Like Andres, he began by training for the priesthood but abandoned this for art studies and travel. Then he was an art teacher until the war, when he joined the Luftwaffe. After being released from a British P.O.W. camp in Italy he became a painter; then an art teacher again. His creativity, too, was stirred by experience of war. His use of symbolism is effective in short stories, but sometimes obtrusive in his novels. *A Voice is Raised* (*Eine Stimme hebt an*, 1950), his first novel, on the ubiquitous theme of the returning soldier, was an unusually optimistic conclusion, and gives an honest portrayal of a man who regains his hold on life after devastating experiences. The dense style, however, vitiates much of the novel's effect: it appears pretentious. *The Falling Leaf* (*Die sterbende Jagd*, 1953; tr. 1956) relates the disillusion of a fighter squadron based in Norway with both their task and the war they are fighting. This is in a realistic style throughout. Gaiser, in what is possibly the most outstanding of all the German novels about the Second World War, has been accused of treating the question of moral guilt 'superficially'. But what he actually does is to give an unforgettable picture of what his bored and disgusted pilots actually do: go on fighting, although they know that they will lose, that there is no honour or chivalry left, and that their cause is worse than unjust. *The Ship in the Mountain* (*Das Schiff im Berg*, 1955) more ambitiously sets out to explore the relationship between man and nature, but succeeds only in some of its details: a poor community discover caves in the mountainside upon which they live and plan to make them a tourist attraction. *The Last Dance of the Season* (*Schlussball*, 1958; tr. 1960) satirizes the 'economic miracle' yet again; but one has only to compare this with, say, Martin Walser's competent *Half-Time* (q.v.) to see that Gaiser is a truly imaginative writer, whose language is richly suggestive. That he is not a moralist, and will not facilely condemn the behaviour of either his disillusioned pilots or even his bourgeois participants in the *Wirtschaftswunder* seems admirable: his committal is creative. Gaiser has achieved most, however, as a writer of short stories, in which he is better able—perhaps more intuitively and less consciously—to handle his extra-realistic impulses without becoming laboured. His best work arises from a self-exploration conducted by the means of writing; excellent novelist although he is at his best, the length of the form causes him to take too much thought in what, for him, is the wrong way. 'Antigone and the Garden Dwarf' (GSS) is an excellent example of his subtle humour and poetic sense of language. On the face of it a light-heartedly grotesque tale about a struggle between two men to buy a garden-dwarf from an unconfident florist, it is at the same time an account of the horrors and violent impulses that lie only just beneath the surface of 'civilized' life. It is witty and readable. Gaiser has attracted some hostile criticism from younger writers; but it is he, with his cautious modernism, who seems to have more to say than they, with their too often reckless and externally rather than internally dictated search for new forms.

GERTRUD FUSSENEGGER (1912) was born in Pilsen in Czechoslovakia, the daughter of an Austrian army officer. A distinguished writer, she has not had the critical attention she deserves. Many of her novels deals with the Czechoslovakian past: *The Brothers from Lasawa* (*Die Brüder von Lasawa*, 1948) is about two brothers in the Thirty Years War; and her two most substantial novels, *The House* (*Das Haus der dunklen Krüge*, 1951) and *The Masked Face* (*Das verschüttete Antlitz*, 1957) are dense sociological studies of the immediate Bohemian past. The short story 'Woman Driver' (GSS), about a bored and unhappily married woman who drives to her death, gives a good example of how, by means of a lyrical style, she can gain new insight into a commonplace theme.

ALFRED ANDERSCH (1914) was born in Munich; as a communist he spent six months in Dachau when Hitler gained power. He was an unwilling factory worker and then soldier, and deserted in 1944, preferring to be a prisoner-of-war in the U.S.A. Later he edited the eventually banned *Der Ruf*, helped with the founding of *Gruppe 47*, and worked for Stuttgart Radio. Andersch, who is now more of an anarchist than a communist, is the same sort of writer as Martin Walser—but on the whole he is less efficient as well as less satirical and sharp. After an autobiography describing his desertion from the army, he published *Flight to Afar* (*Sansibar oder Der letzte Grund*, 1957; tr. 1958). This describes how people could behave decently even under the hideous pressure of Nazidom, but is more journalistic than imaginative, and because of this makes unconscious concessions to its readers. Rodney Livingstone's charge that Andersch, for all his personal courage and fine record of resistance to the Nazis, provides fashionably vague solutions for fashionably vague guilts is difficult to answer. But Andersch, an intelligent and capable writer, took to fiction in the first place because the Allies stopped him running *Der Ruf*. The people in his novels are products of his thinking rather than of his imagination, which does not function autonomously. Lacking Martin Walser's satirical edge, his writing is transparently sincere (as the often impassioned style indicates) but remains vague in the very diagnoses it desperately wants to make. In *The Redhead* (*Die Rote*, 1960; tr. 1961) he portrays a woman, herself successful in business, who becomes suddenly nauseated, while on holiday in Italy, with her husband and the commercially comfortable Germany he stands for. So far so good. But Andersch can do nothing psychologically convincing with her: her love affairs, and final decision to work in a factory, are hopelessly contrived. Andersch is committed to the *avant garde*, but is himself an essentially conservative writer. His stories, some of which are collected in *The Night of the Giraffe* (tr. 1965), are at their best when autobiographical, or when describing events the author has witnessed. If Andersch cannot but simplify his material, however, he undoubtedly possesses genuine dramatic power; probably his best work has been done in radio-drama. His best known *Hörspiel*, *Driver's Escape* (*Fahrerflucht*, 1965), has been published, with three other volumes devoted to his work for radio.

The poet and short-story writer WOLFDIETRICH SCHNURRE (1920), a founder of *Gruppe 47* (q.v.) (which he later left), was born in Frankfurt-on-Main, but grew up in north-east Berlin, the setting of much of his work, from 1928. He spent over six years in the army. He is the author of some highly distinguished *Hörspiele*—indeed, certain critics see these, some of which have been collected in the volume *Furnished Room* (*Spreezimmer möbliert*, 1967), as his best work. Schnurre) who sometimes provides lively illustrations to his books, crosses bitter satire with humour both charming and 'absurd'. He thus combines, without pretentiousness, the traditions of Heine, Tucholsky and Brecht (corrosive satire), Busch (stolid nonsense) and Morgenstern (poetic humour). He became well known with his first novel *Stardust and Sedan Chair* (*Sternstaub und Sänfte*, 1953), the diary of a confidence-poodle who writes sonnets. The title story in the collection *People Ought to Object* (*Man sollte dagegen sein*, 1953) is one of his best known. A man reads an advertisement in the paper announcing that God has died, and goes to his funeral. Only the parson and the grave-diggers are there, and they are bored. Only the sordid and drab world remains. Perhaps the moral is Voltaire's 'Si dieu n'existait pas, ils faudrait l'inventer'. Schnurre's poetry (MGP, TCG, GWT) is compressed, satirical and frequently sinister, as in 'Denunciation', about the moon whose 'employer is known to us;/he lives on the far side of love'. However, he has also written straightforwardly lyrical poetry. The short story 'In the Trocadero' (GSS) offers an excellent example of this sensitive and original writer at his best. Comparison

of Schnurre with Swift—whom he has studied and written well about
—to the disadvantage of the latter has been attempted and is very
silly; but he is a powerful writer, whose anger is in no sense misanthropic, like Arno Schmidt's, but based rather in his intelligent humanitarianism.

ARNO SCHMIDT (1914) is the most thoroughgoing *avant gardist* in
Germany; he has no trace of teutonic ponderousness—on the contrary, there is something positively Gallic about his procedures,
whose excessively cerebral nature is, however, consistently modified
by his sense of humour and unfrivolous integrity of purpose. Because
it is difficult, his work has not attracted the attention it deserves outside Germany. Born in Hamburg, he was a mathematical child-
prodigy whose studies were forbidden by the Nazis. He was in the
army that occupied Norway as a cartographer (maps and map-
reading play a large part in his fiction). He has written many critical
essays, a book on the popular adventure-author Karl May, and
translations of such authors as Wilkie Collins and William Faulkner.
There is no doubt of his subtlety and brilliance; and whatever view
be taken of the success of his large-scale experiments, it is certain that
they have no pretentiousness. Schmidt is acutely self-critical, and
frequently parodies German writing of the 'magic realist' type—and
his own style. Only one passage—from his novel *Die Gelehrtenrepublik*
(1957)—seems to be available in English translation (GWT). The
novella *Leviathan* (1949) describes a train journey out of the ruins of
Berlin towards death. *Nobodaddy's Children* (*Nobodaddys Kinder*, 1951–
63) consists of three novels, series of diary entries by three progressively younger characters. The last book, *Black Mirrors* (*Schwarze
Spiegel*) consists of the writings of the last man in the world. Sardonic,
atheistic ('The "Lord", without Whose willing it no sparrow falls
from the roof, nor are 10 Million people gassed in concentration
camps: He must be a strange sort —if He exists now at all'), sceptical,
exceedingly clever, Schmidt attracts some critics but few book
reviewers, who find him 'perverse' and are horrified, as journalists
always seem to be, by his biting pessimism. Paul West (who admires
him) has said that for Schmidt life is a 'cheerless conundrum'—but he
might as well have written 'cheerful'. *From the Life of a Faun* (*Aus dem
Leben eines Fauns*, 1953), the first of the trilogy, evokes the atmosphere
of (civilian) wartime Germany as well as any book. The middle novel,
Brand's Heath (*Brands Haide*), describes an ex-POW's researches into
the life of an obscure author and his relations with a mistress who
eventually deserts him—but sends him food parcels from America.

Schmidt's most massive book is *Zettel's Dream* (*Zettels Traum*, 1970).
This breaks up and rearranges several languages (including English),

and was originally printed in facsimile, with handwritten corrections and additions—and parallel columns of typescript.

Schmidt is not a behaviourist; but he writes in constant awareness of modern scientific discoveries. Narratives that give the illusion of life being a continuously efficient process are, to him, inadequate. He seeks to build up a truthful picture out of the fragments of conscious perception. Essentially Schmidt is (like Joyce) a comic writer; he is an important one.

The Roman Catholic HEINRICH BÖLL (1917), born in Cologne, is, with Günter Grass, the most celebrated—and translated—of all post-war German novelists. He is a prolific, versatile and gifted writer, always sensible. Before being conscripted he was a bookseller. He served in the ranks of Hitler's army, and was wounded four times on the Russian front. Eventually he was taken prisoner. Soon after the war he began to write. His big public success came with *Acquainted with the Night* (*Und sagte kein einziges Wort*, 1953; tr. 1955). A satirical and humorous writer, Böll, although a moralist, is as undogmatic and undidactic as it is possible for a Roman Catholic to be. He is reticent and his Catholic point of view is only implied. He was never a Nazi; but neither has he been leftist (for example, he can express admiration for individual freedom and the dignity of poverty—compare another Catholic, Léon Bloy, q.v.—in Eire, where he has a home); his energy was and remains directed against war. Böll's starting point is, once again, desolation; but he is in a slightly different position from such a writer as, say, Gaiser (q.v.), who undoubtedly felt some kind of patriotism (if not sympathy for the Nazis themselves) at the very beginning of the war (as his early poetry shows).

A basic theme in all Böll's fiction is man's inability to change the course of his destiny. This is something Böll deals with without philosophical or (apparently) religious preconceptions. He is no determinist; but he does not provide the unconvincing solution, of Christian stoicism, of a Schaper (q.v.): that his powerless heroes must suffer is not accepted stoically by them, since he refuses to teach by manipulating them. Böll tries to proceed from human situations, and to record first of all what people actually feel and actually do. His use of relatively modern techniques—flashback, interior monologue and so on—is invariably functional. He won the 1972 Nobel Prize.

His first two books were about the war. In *The Train was on Time* (*Ser Zug war pünktlich*, 1949; tr. 1956) the hero is being taken by train to the Russian front; in *Adam, Where art Thou?* (*Wo warst du, Adam?*, 1951; tr. 1955) he is retreating from Rumania back into Germany. These do not have the meticulousness of Gaiser's study of disillusion,

The Falling Leaf (q.v.), but are more impressionistic accounts of men as so much rubble being carted back and forth to inevitable destruction. The horror of war struck deep at Böll, and few modern writers have conveyed it to their readers with such force.

Next, as well as writing short stories and radio-plays, Böll turned to writing novels about the effects of war on family life. *Acquainted with the Night* is devoted to a single weekend in the life of Fred Bogner, a poor and numbed survivor of the war. *The Unguarded House* (*Haus ohne Hüter*; tr. 1957) is more complex, contrasting the fate of two families, one rich and one poor, made fatherless by war. In *Billiards at Half-past Nine* (*Billard um halbzehn*, 1959; tr. 1961) his technique becomes yet more elaborate; and the time-span is now reduced to only one day. This tender and compassionate study of the concerns that keep generations apart and together was Böll's richest achievement to date, although with it he may have sacrificed some of his more facile readers. But his best novel is the simplest of all: *The Clown* (*Ansichten eines Clowns*, 1963; tr. 1965), a book in which his Catholicism is, if anything, even more radical than that of Graham Greene (q.v. 1). Hans Schnier, a clown, finds his work tolerable while he lives with Marie; but Catholic intellectual friends influence her to leave him, and she marries elsewhere. Now the time interval is reduced to a few fours, although (as always) there are many flashbacks. The anti-Catholic Hans is defeated, reduced from clown to beggar, in a process that reveals him as possessed of a grace that the Catholics of the book lack.

Böll admits to having been influenced by Dickens and Joseph Roth (q.v.). His short stories bear the influence of Hemingway (q.v. 1), whose terse style seemed like a tonic to the post-war Germans. An author to whom he is very close, although his techniques are more modern, is Graham Greene (q.v. 1). The reasons are obvious enough. Like Greene he is drawn to the sordid; he is also highly professional—although not to that point where, occasionally, the sense of art vitiates Greene's work, making the reader feel that everything is so well-tailored that, after all, it must only be a story.

Böll has been translated into at least seventeen languages, and is probably the most commercially successful of all the serious post-war German writers. But this success has been thoroughly earned, and none has been gained by making concessions—either consciously or unconsciously. He has written many memorable short stories, which some critics regard as his greatest achievement. Some of these are collected in *Traveller, if you Come to Spa* (tr. 1956) and in *Absent without Leave* (tr. 1967). Typical of his ironic but lusty humour is the story, contained in the latter collection, called 'Bonn Diary', in which a bunch of officers heartily prove that their former commander was responsible for more deaths than the official estimate. 'Pale Anna' (GSS) encapsulates in a few pages his attitude to war: the war veteran seeks for the physical equivalent of his own mental scars in a girl's face, ruined by bomb blast. One can discern Hemingway's influence here; but it has been wholly assimilated; and Böll in any case understands the possibilities of love (particularly heterosexual love) more profoundly and less histrionically than Hemingway. Another well-known story is 'Dr Murke's Collected Silences', from the volume of that title (*Doktor Murkes gesammeltes Schweigen*, 1958), in which an assistant radio producer collects snippets of silent tape in order to preserve his sanity. Böll has also written many *Hörspiele*, a stage play, and several volumes of essays, including an *Irish Notebook* (*Irisches Tagebuch*, 1957).

The Viennese ILSE AICHINGER (1921), wife of Günter Eich (q.v.), studied medicine for a time before taking up writing. Her first fiction was a novel, *The Greater Hope* (*Die grössere Hoffnung*, 1948); since then she has preferred the short story and *Hörspiel*, and has become one of the most outstanding practitioners of her generation. Some of her earlier short stories are collected in *The Bound Man* (*Der Gefesselte*, 1953; tr. 1957). Her novel, based on her own experiences of persecution during the war, deals with the short life of a young, partly Jewish girl from the *Anschluss* until her death in street-fighting seven years later. Ilse Aichinger's prose is lucid in the manner of Kafka, whom she also resembles in that she is less a surrealist than a fabulist. She will not accept the surface of life—what is ordinarily called 'reality'—and all she writes is permeated with wonder. Her style is lyrical, or at least semi-lyrical; and often her prose comes close to verse in its regular rhythms. 'Story in Reverse' (GSS) is characteristic, being on exactly the same theme as Günter Kunert's (q.v.) 'Film put in Backwards' (GWT)—the executed soldier wakes in the 'black/ of the box. . . . The lid flew up and I/Stood, feeling:/Three bullets travel/Out of my chest/Into the rifles of soldiers . . .'—except that the subject is a young girl suffering from a fatal disease. This is treated with great pathos.

WALTER JENS (1923) is a classics teacher who was born at Hamburg. He has had wide influence as a critic, in which capacity he is preferable as commentator on individual works to propagandist for postwar German literature. His fiction is less tendentious. *No—The World of the Accused* (*Nein—Die Welt der Angeklagten*, 1950) is a variation on Zamyatin's *We* (q.v. 4) and more directly, Orwell's *1984* (q.v. 1). It is one of the more effective of the many post-war dystopias. A future world-state has divided mankind into judges, witnesses and accused. The ruling terror is the Palace of Justice. The hero betrays his girl and becomes a witness; but when he refuses to become a judge he is killed. Owing much to Orwell, this nevertheless refined his vision and further defined the anti-human nature of the totalitarian state. *The Blind Man* (*Der Blinde*, 1951; tr. 1954), a novella, works well on both levels; as an account of a teacher suddenly overwhelmed by blindness, and an allegory of man lost in darkness. *Forgotten Faces* (*Vergessene Gesichter*, 1952) is a more realistic story about a home for retired actors. Jens's best novel, however, is *The Man Who did not Want to Grow Old* (*Der Mann, der nicht alt werden wollte*, 1954), which mixes satire and psychological analysis to produce a sad comment on the limitations of academicism and the differences between generations. A German student commits suicide in Paris, and his old professor investigates the reasons. He considers the young man's literary remains, part of a novel, to be outstanding, and analyses them accordingly. This gives Jens a chance to reveal the character of the professor; he never takes advantage of it to gain cheap effects, and the final impression is a tragic one, of an intelligence life-starved and wasted.

GÜNTER GRASS (1927), who was born of German-Polish parents in the Free City of Danzig (now Gdansk), has achieved the greatest success of all post-war German writers. Unlike Böll, who is a writer of similar status, he has not alienated the pseudo-progressive element, as powerful and vociferous in Germany as it is ignorant. Grass's integrity is hardly in doubt, but he has a more flamboyant and colourful personality than Böll; this keeps him in the newspapers and therefore in the forefront of the minds of reviewers. Grass, who fought in the army towards the end of the war and was captured by the Americans, began, like so many German writers (one needs to think only of Hauptmann, Arp, Weiss, Hildesheimer. . . .) as an artist: a sculptor. He had become known both for his art and his radio plays by the mid-Fifties. He wrote *The Tin Drum* (*Die Blechtrommel*, 1959; tr. 1961) in Paris in the latter part of the decade. *Gruppe 47* awarded him a prize for it before publication. Since then Grass has written three more novels, a full-scale stage play, poetry and several essays and speeches. Committed to the establishment of socialism in West Germany, he campaigned for the Social Democrats in 1965 and 1969 (when they were just successful); and in 1972 when they did well.

Grass is a linguistically exuberant, ingenious and highly inventive writer, whose work is a unique combination of vitality and grotesquerie. He is old enough to have taken part in Nazi activities and the war (he was a member of the Hitler Youth when Germany seized Danzig) without being responsible. This, as has been pointed out, makes him eager to probe the immediate past, an activity that puzzles those too young to have experienced Nazidom, but annoys those who once accepted it. Grass insists that the artist, however committed he may be in life, should be a clown in art. There is, however, much pained irony in this pronouncement—which not all his critics have realized. But Grass, an intelligent and sensible as well as a clever and amusing man, has made good sense of the division between his art (which is sceptical about human happiness) and his life (unequivocal political activity for a party of which he is critical). Such an arbitrary division must not, of course, be taken too literally; but Grass remains extraordinarily relaxed, a remarkable feat for a really gifted German writer.

The Tin Drum is a historically meticulous examination of the period 1925–55, narrated by the dwarf Oskar Matzerath. Fantasy of the specifically German sort is brilliantly counterpointed with historical detail. We can understand that Oskar's childhood need for tin drums, his glass-shattering screams if denied them, is not merely fanciful. *Dog Years (Hundejahre*, 1963; tr. 1965) begins in 1917, and, with three narrators instead of one, therefore takes in even more history. *Cat and Mouse (Katz und Maus*, 1961; tr. 1961) is a novella: the oversized Joachim Mahlke's schoolfriend tells the story of his successful military career. *Local Anaesthetic (örtlich betaubt*, 1969; tr. 1970) comes up to date to examine the nature of the student revolt. Characteristically, Grass spreads himself, or at least his inclinations, among the characters: Scherbaum, the boy who is going to burn his beloved dog in front of a Berlin cakeshop in protest against the Viet Nam war; Starusch, his liberal form-teacher who persuades him not to do so, and whose dental problems are (it is said) the same as Grass's; and the unnamed dentist, maker of 'corrective bridges', who lives on Senecan principles. This novel, part of which appeared as a play, *Davor*, early in 1969, solves nothing for Grass or anyone else; but it reveals the German conflict between activism and quietism as soberly—although ebulliently in terms of style—as it has ever been revealed. Grass has angrily parodied Rilke for his 'inwardness', but has never failed to acknowledge it in himself.

Grass is a charming, most often playful or satirical, minor poet (*Poems of Günter Grass*, tr. 1967). In the Fifties he wrote several violent comedies, certainly to be classified as of the absurd type; *The Plebeians Rehearse the Uprising (Die Plebejer proben den Aufstand*, 1966), which did not work well on the stage, is a Brechtian drama ironically depicting Brecht's refusal, as he rehearsed his adaptation of *Coriolanus*, to side openly with the East German workers in their uprising of 1953.

UWE JOHNSON (1934) was born in Pomerania. He left East Germany in 1959 to settle in the West. Once again, he is concerned with the problem of expressing truths in literature—and not with playing omniscient Balzacian games. This problem becomes—or seems to become—more acute when, as in Berlin, a community is artificially divided and the hapless individual is trapped by conflicting—and in the case of the East, politically directed—mores. Demotic in style, Johnson aims at a meticulous and detailed realism. He put his point of view in 'Berlin, Border of the Divided World' (GWT) before the Wall was built in August 1961. *Speculations about Jakob* (*Mutmassungen über Jakob*, 1959; tr. 1963) is a delicate exploration of the psychological facts about the death of a worker. This, written before he came to the West, remains his best novel. Its successors, *The Third Book about Achim* (*Das dritte Buch über Achim*, 1961; tr. 1966) and *Two Views* (*Zwei Ansichten*, 1965; tr. 1967), put more emphasis on technique and do not provide, except fleetingly, imaginative illumination.

OSKAR MARIA GRAF (1894–1967) was a left-wing, pacifist Bavarian who left Germany for Czechoslovakia in 1933, and then settled in the U.S.A. from 1938. There he wrote intellectually over-ambitious novels of the future, such as *The Conquest of a World* (*Die Eroberung einer Welt*, 1948). Much better, because in a more deliberately 'minor' tradition, were his coarse, comic novels about the Bavarian peasantry. As has been well said, these 'produce the effect of having been related by word of mouth over the beer and radishes to an eager circle of listeners, who bang the table with their fists in token of assent'. These include *The Stationmaster* (*Bolwieser*, 1931; tr. 1933), *The Wolf* (*Einer gegen alle*, 1932; tr. 1934) and *The Life of my Mother* (*Das Leben meiner Mutter*, 1947; tr. 1940). The best of his last work is to be found in his short story collections, where he reverts to his earlier subject-matter.

XVI

All post-war German literature is, naturally enough, one form or another of reaction to Nazism and its disastrous end: this necessarily entered into the very fibre of the thought or feeling of all Germans. Of a somewhat older generation, such poets as HANS EGON HOLTHUSEN (1913) and RUDOLF HAGELSTANGE (1912) continued to write in traditional styles, but devoted themselves entirely and consciously to the immediate situation. Even GÜNTER EICH (1907–72), author of the most distinguished and highly thought of *Hörspiele* of the age (all of them distinctly modernist in technique) has not abandoned regular syntax or employed surrealist effects.

Eich, born in Lebus near Frankfurt-on-Oder, is one of the most influential writers of his time. What makes his poetry (TCG, MGP, GWT) 'modern' is its laconic directness and conspicuous lack of rhetoric. He published a volume in 1930, but this may be regarded as juvenilia. Technically, his poetry is more conservative than his radio work, which is as *avant garde*—particularly in its use of dream situations—as anyone could require. But its content, like its tone of voice, is radical—a fact that its form brings out with an at times shocking force. In the famous 'Latrine', one of the best poems to come out of Germany in the last quarter of a century, he squats 'over a stinking ditch' over bloody, fly-blown paper, watching gardens, a lake, a boat. 'The hardened filth plops' and 'some lines of Hölderlin ring madly' in his ears: ' "But go now and greet the lovely Garonne".' The clouds are reflected in the urine, and swim away beneath his 'unsteady feet'. This is taking 'nature poetry' to its extreme limits, by juxtaposing the fleetingly beautiful—the poetry and the clouds— with the disgusting—the uncomfortable evacuation of hard 'filth' plopping into a pulp of bloody, fly-blown decay. It reflects ruined Germany, but only from a basis of keenly observed and honestly felt experience. Eich, than whom there is no better poet in modern Germany, was the true heir of Lehmann and Loerke (qq.v.).

Holthusen, from Schleswig-Holstein, was influential in the years immediately after the war, but has written little poetry since. He is well known as an intelligent critic, oriented to the earlier period of modernism. His chief concern, never obscurantist, is with the valid survival of the old values into the present. His 'Tabula Rasa' (TCG), written in a style reminiscent of early Rilke and influenced by T. S. Eliot, spoke for all sensitive Germans in 1948: 'What demon is this which, pitiless, grips us and wrings us and impels us to and fro! We pile our dead, bewildered, we grow poorer from year to year. O frenzied inferno!' (TCG, MGP, TCGV.)

The Prussian Rudolf Hagelstange wrote a series of anti-Nazi sonnets, which were widely circulated, while he was a serving soldier. He is, unusually, a poet who combines a deep religious faith of a traditional sort with a full awareness of modern atheistic tendencies. His *Ballad of the Buried Life* (*Ballade vom verschütteten Leben*, 1952; tr. 1962) is the outstanding modern narrative poem on a contemporary theme in Germany; it is about six German soldiers trapped underground for six years by an explosion. It is tendentiously Christian and somewhat predictable; but the material is impressively handled. (TCG, MGP.)

The poet FRIEDRICH GEORG JÜNGER (1898), like his brother Ernst Jünger (q.v.), has been fascinated by aristocratic, non-Nazi forms of totalitarianism. He was involved in Ernst Nickisch's 'National Bolshevism' with his brother, and had to fly to Switzerland in 1937 when he offended the Nazis with his clandestine but well-known poem 'The Poppy'. His opposition to the regime was considerably less equivocal than that of his brother, who gladly helped to fight Hitler's wars (if only because he believed in the war itself, and not its cause).

Jünger has written criticism and (latterly) fiction; but it is as a poet that he is chiefly known and respected. He has not eschewed modern concerns or sought refuge in inadequate or outmoded attitudes, but he has consistently made use of traditional forms (he has also revived some), of which he is a skilful practitioner.

In terms of content, Jünger's poetry is a fairly uninteresting—and unattractive—combination of aristocratic stoicism and emotionally unconvincing but accurate observation of nature. Like his brother's, his position seems an artificial one. But his hardness of style, elegant control of expression and intelligence give his poetry a certain distinction. Its intellectual spuriousness is somewhat compensated for by the fact that it reflects a genuine attempt to combat both disorder and sexual confusion. What is interesting is the nature of his failure to achieve this.

His best poem remains the anti-Nazi 'The Poppy' (TCG), in which he expresses his indignation at the Nazi betrayal of good-mannered totalitarian ideals. This is impressive and courageous.

KARL KROLOW (1915), born in Hanover, was originally closer in feeling and style to Lehmann and the tradition of nature poetry than Eich; but he has found it necessary to experiment with surrealism, and to attempt a more hermetic and impenetrable type of poetry than either Lehmann or Eich would write; Krolow has even been criticized, not altogether unjustly, in the sense that he is over-prolific and his experiments frequently fail, for following merely fashionable trends. He has translated much from Spanish and French (Apollinaire, the surrealists, Lorca) and one of the most powerful influences upon him has certainly been Lorca (q.v. 3), particularly in the way he uses colour. Krolow is a poet of great lyrical gifts and a charming surrealist; possibly his involvement with experimentation has caused him to be somewhat over-valued, and has led readers of his poetry to look for or to assume the existence of depths that are not in it. (TCG, GWT, MEP, MGP and *Invisible Hands*, tr. 1969.)

PAUL CELAN (ps. PAUL ANTSCHEL, 1920–70), who was born in Rumania and whose parents were murdered by the Nazis while he was sent to forced labour, is a conspicuously modern poet; but he is more certainly a substantial one than Krolow. He became a naturalized Frenchman, and made his living as a language-teacher in Paris. He is generally considered, despite the undeniable difficulties offered by his hermetic poetry, to be the leading German poet of his generation—and the most outstanding to appear since well before the Second World War. Without doubt he is Germany's foremost 'surrealist' poet. He made some distinguished translations from modern poets. Like Krolow he was deeply influenced by the French surrealists; also by Trakl and Goll. Another influence not so often mentioned was really a part of his Jewish background: that fabulous Jewish lore which figures so strongly in the paintings of Chagall and has been mentioned in connection with Kafka. Celan is profoundly serious, and seldom exhibitionistically frivolous in the manner one sometimes suspects in Krolow and recognizes in many others. His integrity is never in doubt: he desperately wants to communicate, but must confront the problems both of a cliché-ridden poetic language, and of the inefficacy of any language against the hideousness of such facts as the Nazi oppression of the Jews, which is one of Celan's main themes. This theme functions in his poetry as an acute sense of loss: that whole Rumanian community, with its irreplaceable lore, from which Celan came was wiped out. Only one thing, he said, was not lost: language. But even this 'had to pass through its own inability to answer'. Celan's most famous poem, 'Fugue of Death' (TCG, MEP, MGP, PPC), is a fitting representative of his genius. Unlike many of his poems, particularly the later, it is not in the least obscure—yet it is a poem that one can produce as evidence of the quality of the poetry of 'uprooted metaphor': autonomous poetry that uses language as an explorative instrument. Here we all drink the 'Coal-black milk of dawn', and 'Death is a master from Germany' who 'whistles his Jews'.

Towards the end Celan had serious difficulty in expressing himself in poetry, and doubtless would have done better to remain silent. He became derivative, and occasionally he even copied frivolous 'modernists', producing post-surrealist nonsense that had an air of desperation about it. He began to play with words: but his lack of humour made this an unsuitable activity for him. Yet his best poems express responses to life that are unusual:

> Gorselight, yellow, the slopes
> fester to heaven, the thorn
> woos the wound, bells ring
> in there, it is evening, the void

rolls its oceans to worship,
the sail of blood is aiming for you.
(GWT)

Responsible criticism has hardly yet come to terms with such poetry;
but it must and will do so. Celan killed himself.

ERICH FRIED (1921), a Viennese, has lived in London since 1938;
for some years he worked for the British Broadcasting Corporation,
and is well known for his efficient and sensitive translations into
German of Shakespeare, E. E. Cummings, Hopkins and Eliot (qq.v.
1). Fried is not a poet of the incantatory power of Celan, but he has
often, and fairly, been compared to him: he experiences the same
kind of difficulties with language as Celan did. The point has been
made that he writes his poems in a language which he does not use in
daily speech; they treat words with special reverence. He writes
densely and punningly, and exhibits a considerable sense of humour
(in contrast to Celan), and is strongly and openly committed to the
left (one of his books is called *and Vietnam and, und Vietnam und,* 1966).
Fried, like Krolow, has had a book of English translations devoted to
him: *On Pain of Seeing* (tr. 1969; also TCG, GWT, MGP).

Fried believes 'with Ernesto Che Guevara . . . that the main task
for art is the fight against alienation [in the Marxist sense of men being
alienated by capitalist forces from a meaningful and creative exist-
ence]'. This is what he means when he says that his poetry is 'committed' (he has been at the centre of a controversy on this subject in
Germany, where he is highly thought of). His use of language in
poetry is a fight against alienation, a fight he also (he says) wages
with himself. Latterly he has been experimenting with sounds and
word associations in the manner of the 'concrete' poets. This work,
while it may well be necessary to Fried, is no more convincing than
the later poetry of Celan. In English Fried's poetry tends to appear
trite, aphoristic or, sometimes, even gnomic; in the original German
it is clearer that he is trying to explore the nature of language itself.
Most effective in more recent work have been his protest poems.

The Prussian HELMUT HEISSENBÜTTEL (1921) is the most extreme
modernist, if we except 'concrete' poets such as Jandl, Mon or
Gomringer, whose work has perhaps less relationship to literature
than to the graphic arts, showmanship and entertainment. Heissenbüttel is an associate of these artists, but is altogether more literary.
Whatever his readers may think about his abandonment of syntax,
they must concede him intelligence and the fact that his is a genuine
rejection of traditional modes. Christopher Middleton, a shrewd and
well-informed enthusiast, dedicated to the *avant garde*, says of him:

'his so-called "texts" are a kind of linguistic spectral analysis of modern forms of consciousness, atomized, disoriented, admassed'.

Heissenbüttel, much influenced by Wittgenstein, has rejected the term 'experiment' in art and therefore calls his first novel, *D'Alembert's End* (*D'Alemberts Ende*, 1970), an *Ausprobieren* (test: trial and error). This extremely complicated fiction—it makes almost any French exponent of the *nouveau roman* seem elementary by comparison —requires both concentration and a high degree of previous admiration in order to read right through. It is a testament to Heissenbüttel's philosophical and critical acuteness, but more doubtfully to his imagination. This attacks the notion of story-telling, and simultaneously explores problems of identity and satirizes foolish or misguided intellectuals. Like Arno Schmidt (q.v.), Heissenbüttel takes note of the new physics, and distrusts conventional grammar because it establishes false relationships and hierarchies: like Schmidt again, but more thoroughgoingly and less comically, he presents reality in disparate fragmented parts (a 'master of discontinuous consciousness'). In himself Heissenbüttel may well be only a minor writer, of limited imaginative capacity; but he is a theorist and critic of whom it is necessary to take account (MGP, GWT, TCG.)

Of the several woman poets writing in German the Austrian INGEBORG BACHMANN (1926–1973) was the most highly regarded. A book of her stories, *The Thirtieth Year* (*Das dreissigste Jahr*, 1961; tr. 1964) has appeared in English; she has also written opera librettos and radio plays. She wrote her doctoral dissertation on Heidegger, and all her poetry is essentially a means of discovering 'authenticity' in his very special sense. She travelled a great deal. Her poetry, which has been described both as a skilful amalgam of many other poets' styles (Rilke, Trakl, Hölderlin, Goll, Benn, and very many others), and as highly original, is lyrical, tender in its allusions to nature, sporadically surrealist ('the fishes' entrails/have grown cold in the wind' is typical) and above all confessional. Bachmann is a fluent and always impressive poet, but often she seemed to be lost in her own rich flux, and to have discovered not authenticity but a self-induced trance. She set fire to herself in bed.

HANS MAGNUS ENZENSBERGER (1929) was born in Bavaria. Often referred to, in a foolish phrase, as 'Germany's angry young man', he is nevertheless a vociferous opponent of what he dislikes: the economic prosperity, uncommitted literature, the pseudo-*avant garde*. He lives in Norway. Enzensberger is a shrewd and sensitive critic torn between 'personal' poetic impulses, which he distrusts because he believes that the indulgence of them leads to political indifference of the kind exercised by Benn (q.v.), and 'public' impulses—the desire to share his poetry, not make it a dangerous esoteric mystery. Enzensberger's master is Brecht—but he responds to Benn. Unlike Brecht, Enzensberger cannot write poetry of the ballad type: poetry that can communicate with 'the people' and yet contain subtleties of which only more 'literary' folk would be likely to be aware. Brecht's slyness was built in. Enzensberger is honest, and a fine critic—his attack on the *avant garde* for trying to be new when for the time being 'newness' has exhausted itself is important. But his position is so ingenuous that his lyrical impulse has been at least half-strangled; indeed, he will resort to rhetoric, laboured satire and journalistic tricks in order not to indulge it. Michael Hamburger, who has introduced a selection of his poems in English translation (*Poems*, 1968) draws attention to this deadlock between 'public purpose and private impulse' and suggests it will have to be broken; but he considers the poetry to date to have been successful. Certainly it has a refreshing directness, and certainly it testifies to Enzensberger's poetic gifts. But his refusal to indulge his private impulses and concomitant lack of a Brechtian vein of balladry or the equivalent sometimes force him into writing a sort of poetry that he might not otherwise perpetrate. 'Foam', for example, reads like a parody of Ginsberg's *Howl* (q.v. 1); of course it is more intelligent, but the rhetoric and anger give the impression of having been manufactured as a substitute for other, politically more ambiguous, emotions. The later 'summer poem', another longish piece, is more successful in expressing the quality of Enzensberger's own emotion; but in it he does not yet dare to face, within himself, the threat (as one might put it) of his poetic impulse. An important critic, probably a gifted lyrical poet, his position is really only another version of that *Künstlerschuld* that in one way or another has assailed nearly every modern German writer. His attitude has been a significant one; his surrender to himself might have even more interesting consequences. So we still see him at his best only in such excellent satires as 'Middle Class Blues' or such exceedingly interesting poems as 'Lachesis Lapponica', where he nevertheless nervously distances himself from his motivations.

XVII

We have already seen that a number of writers committed to communism, eventually including Brecht, returned to East Germany (Deutsche Demokratische Republik) rather than to the West (Bundesrepublik Deutschland). In this country, one of the most repressive in the Russian bloc, literature and the press are under the direct control of the party. Therefore literature is defined as a weapon of the revolution, and is subject to the same kind of restrictions as have developed in Russia. East Germany is one of the communist countries where *avant garde* or 'formalist' art has small chance (like Bulgaria, but in contrast to Czechoslovakia, Poland and Hungary). The influential writers are not necessarily the officially recognized ones (Becher, q.v., has had no influence at all; and few have heard of the novelist HANS MARCHWITZA, 1890–1965, hailed as an important social realist). The authorities have to stomach Brecht's reputation; but they do not like him. The writers worthy of note are those who, in one way or another, manage to express themselves as well as toe the party line. As we see elsewhere, this is always difficult and sometimes impossible. For this reason the published fiction in the German Democratic Republic tends to be of a low quality; where it has strength this lies in depiction of facts or situations: in what may be called naïve realism.

The Leipzig-born BRUNO APITZ's (1900) *Naked Among Wolves* (*Nackt unter Wölfen*, 1958), set in Buchenwald concentration camp— Apitz, as a communist, spent nine years in various of these—has been highly praised. An account of the preservation of a smuggled baby, it is a moving book; but the plainness of its style amounts to crudity, and the psychology is unsubtle. This is not nearly as 'real' as even the comparatively crude Plievier (q.v.). It is not a book one would wish to dispraise; but a better one would have revealed the psychology of men under intolerable conditions in considerably more depth.

STEFAN HEYM (ps. HELLMUTH FLIEGEL, 1913) came from Chemmitz, and left Germany in 1933. He went to Prague and then to America, where he did military service. He returned to East Germany in 1953. He has written in English and German. Like many uncomplicated, straightforward communists, Heym's work is readable but crude in psychological detail. *Hostages* (1942; *Der Fall Glasenapp*, 1958), on resistance to the Nazis in Prague, is at least as exciting as a John le Carré thriller, and more intelligent; but it flourishes best in the mind of the indignant reader. Later novels became increasingly bombastic, and *The Eyes of Reason* (1951) dishonestly exploits Heym's considerable skill to give a false account of the communist takeover in Czechoslovakia. Recently he has taken a more critical line.

More interesting—and more cunning—are the Prussian ERWIN STRITTMATTER (1912), president of the East German Writers' Association and MANFRED BIELER (1934), both of whom work in the picaresque tradition, which in an atmosphere of social realism can cover a multitude of sinfully unpalatable truths. Strittmatter—who deserted from the Nazi army, became a communist civil servant and worked on newspapers before taking to writing—was first taken up by Brecht, who himself produced his first play, a comedy, *Katzgraben* (1954). The best of his novels, *Ole Bienkopp* (1963), is subversive of East German political procedures if not of communism; but not in any too obvious manner. It tells of a man who tried to get new methods adopted in his locality. He is destroyed by the party, and does not live to see his ideas accepted. This was accepted by Strittmatter's party as high comedy. . . . It would be preferable to have a translation of this rather than of Bieler's *The Sailor in the Bottle* (*Bonifaz, oder der Matrose in der Flasche* 1963; tr. 1965), for while this satire (mostly on the capitalist West) has its moments, it is not Bieler's best work. More effective are his short stories (GWT).

The East German theatre is almost destitute of significant new plays. Only PETER HACKS (1928), who was born in Breslau and went to East Germany to join Brecht's Berliner Ensemble in 1955, has dealt with the social problems of his adopted country with anything like a critical vigour. His *Moritz Tassow* (1965) satirizes collective farming.

But in poetry East Germany has produced at least two major talents and several minor ones. STEPHAN HERMLIN (ps. RUDOLF LEDER, 1915), who returned to Germany from Palestine in 1947, was criticized for writing 'personal' poems; his later work, more conformist, is less interesting. However, a poet such as PETER HUCHEL (1903) has seldom (hardly at all, in fact, except in 'Das Gesetz', on the East German agrarian reforms), in his poetry at least, appeared to be politically committed in any sense. Removed from the editorship of the important magazine *Sinn und Form* in 1962, he has at last been able to get to the West. Huchel has always written in the German nature tradition; but he is different from Lehmann or Eich (qq.v.) in that he is essentially, for all his realism and careful imagery, a meditative poet. For all his courage in developing *Sinn und Form* into an organ independent of mediocre sub-literary meddlers, Huchel is nearer to an independent nature-poet than a rebel. His poetry has in it something of the melancholy of Edward Thomas (q.v. 1), although it is freer in form. (TCG, MGP, GWT.)

JOHANNES BOBROWSKI (1917–65), who did not become well known until two or three years before his death, it no more typical a figure in the East German situation than Huchel. Bobrowski was a prisoner-of-war in Russia for eight years, until 1949, when he went to Berlin. Apart from a children's book, he did not publish a volume of poetry until 1961. He received a *Gruppe 47* prize in 1962. *Shadow Land*, his selected poems in English translation, appeared in 1966. He wrote some notable fiction.

Bobrowski is a brooding poet who writes of the landscapes and obscure or extinct folkways of Eastern Europe. His style is haunting and beautiful, and yet impersonal. He reminds one a little of a dark, non-Jewish, and un-gay Chagall. (GWT, TCGV).

WOLF BIERMANN (1936) was born in Hamburg and did not go to East Germany until 1953, the year of the workers' uprising. In 1965 his work was suppressed. The genius of this explosive balladeer is more doubtful than that of Bobrowski: but he belongs to a newer generation. GÜNTER KUNERT (1929) deserves to be called a minor successor to Brecht. He was helped by Becher (q.v.). He is the most gifted and subtle of a number of practitioners of what Michael Hamburger has called 'minimal poetry': they resemble Brecht in that they remain committed to the general direction their society is taking, but insist on retaining their freedom to criticize—and to be the best judges of what is good and what is bad for the progress of mankind. Kunert leaves the gaps to be filled in by intelligent readers. (GWT, MGP.)

Scandinavian Literature

I

There is controversy, into which I shall not enter, as to the exact meaning of the term Scandinavian. For the purposes of this book the following literatures are dealt with under the heading: Danish, Norwegian, Swedish, Finno-Swedish and Icelandic.

Scandinavia's literature offers as sharp a contrast to Latin as its climate. It is generally characterized by stoicism, seriousness, gloom, tragedy. This is to be expected in a region of long, severe winters—with their obvious consequences. But the compensatory aspect, mainly aesthetic, also exercises its influence: the landscape is majestic, and the bright sunlight that illuminates it for some of the year is of especial significance. The Scandinavians tend to be practical, and their contibution to philosophy has been small; they are disinclined to make abstractions. In terms of liberalism, modern Scandinavia is advanced and enlightened (the early abolition of capital punishment in Denmark is only one of many examples); the three chief nations have kept their monarchies, but these have for some scores of years been less anachronistic in form and function than their British counterpart. Illiteracy is negligible. To an educated Scandinavian the main languages are mutually intelligible in print if not in speech. There is a sharp division between 'town' and 'country' writing.

II

Just as no study of modern German literature is possible without taking Nietzsche into account, so must consideration of modern Danish, indeed, Scandinavian, literature begin with Georg Brandes (1842–1927), born of an unorthodox Jewish family in Copenhagen. Until Brandes lectured on him in 1888, the works of Nietzsche (q.v.) had been virtually ignored. This gives an idea of his intelligence and his influence. But he was probably more of a cultural agitator than a critic; and he was not original—despite aggressive assertions to the contrary by old-fashioned critics. Nevertheless, he introduced European literature to Denmark—and to the whole of Scandinavia—in his Copenhagen lectures of 1871. Brandes influenced and was influenced by all the important Scandinavian writers of his time, including Strindberg and Ibsen (qq.v.).

Before 1871 Danish literature had been complacently romantic and unrealistic; Brandes demanded a radical realism and a discussion of social problems. With his flamboyant positivism and his brilliant lecturing he introduced the spirit of naturalism into Denmark. There were inevitable reactions against his ideas, but he dominated the Danish scene until his death. Brandes, the inspirer of the Modern Awakening (*moderne Gennembrud*) movement in Denmark—nearly every European country, of course, has an equivalent—had an intuitive understanding of the needs of his time. He was called an atheist and a socialist; actually he was—or turned into—an anti-democrat, a right-wing disciple of Nietzsche, who preached an 'aristocratic radicalism': a sort of proto-fascism. But Brandes would never have supported a fascist government.

The most important creative writer of the Modern Awakening was J. P. Jacobsen, whose fiction fascinated Rilke (q.v.) so much. Jacobsen, who also left a few poems of high quality, should have lived into this century, but died of tuberculosis before he had reached the age of forty. Although his two novels can justly be called classics of Danish naturalism, they transcend genre: they are records of the struggle in the author's mind between a dreamy romanticism and a harsh, cynical realism. Three other important novelists did, however, live into this century.

HERMAN BANG (1857–1912), born on the island of Als, was influenced by the French naturalists and Jonas Lie (q.v.); but his naturalism, pervaded with *fin de siècle* gloom, is idiosyncratic. His impressionistic style, which employed much dialogue, was formed from the example of his compatriot Hans Andersen, but also from a desire to achieve a kind of modified version of the realism aimed at in Germany by Holz and Schlaf (qq.v.). This attempt at objectivity, the result of hatred of his own homosexual nature and desire to escape from it, was attended by a highly subjective approach to his material: Bang continually projected his own sense of gloom and alienation into his fiction, which is peopled by characters whose dreams have been smashed; his achievement was seriously weakened because he could not, in the circumstances of the time, deal with his own problem. His first novel, *Hopeless Generations* (1880), was banned (but only after it had achieved some success). He wrote many novels, of which the two best are *Time* (1889), about the Danish war with Austria and

Prussia, and the earlier *By the Wayside* (1886), a plotless saga of Danish provinical life and a woman's helpless suffering. The novel in which he recorded his own miseries most potently is *Denied a Country* (1906, tr. 1927), the story of a wandering violinist, clearly a projection of himself. This is a collection of glum vignettes, in which the meaningless conversations of the characters have a vaguely menacing effect. Bang eventually approached an almost expressionistic (q.v.) technique (*The Grey House*, 1901), consisting of dialogue interspersed with description; explanation is eschewed.

HENRIK PONTOPPIDAN (1857–1943), who was born in Fredericia in East Jutland, is regarded by some as Denmark's greatest novelist. He began as an idealist; he married a peasant girl and attempted to live a Tolstoian (q.v.) life. This experience is reflected in his first cycle of novels. *The Promised Land* (1891–5; pt. tr. E. Lucas, 1896), about a clergyman (the profession of Pontoppidan's father) who fails in his Tolstoian aspirations. He had previously written a number of naturalistic short stories. This manner is continued in the early stories of *The Apothecary's Daughters* (1886; tr. 1890). His later novel-cycles are the eight-volume *Lucky Peter* (1898–1904) and *Kingdom of the Dead* (5 vols., 1910–16). These are superior to the earlier cycle, but they remain untranslated into English despite his Nobel Prize (shared with Gjellerup, q.v.) of 1917. Pontoppidan's fiction massively and majestically portrays and analyzes Denmark between 1875 and the end of the First World War. For the first nineteen of these years progress and justice in Denmark were hindered by the governments of the malign J. B. S. Estrup, a fact that prompted Pontoppidan to increasingly eloquent denunciation. The early series deals with the neglect of the peasants and the disillusioned aftermath of the defeat of Denmark (when Jutland was annexed to Schleswig-Holstein, an event Pontoppidan witnessed). It presents a figure, satirically realized, who sacrifices everything and gets nothing in return except anguish and, finally, incarceration in a lunatic asylum. *Lucky Peter* is a subtler, more wide-ranging and more poetic book: its protagonist recalls Peer Gynt: Per Sidenius (a projection of the author) is one of those who finally discover themselves, but not without enduring a sceptical restlessness that for long alienates him from everything, including himself. It is a powerfully individualistic and socially pessimistic novel, in which Per at the end leaves his family in order to lead a hermit's life and to write down (rather than achieve in existential terms) his final, and fruitful, conclusions. *Kingdom of the Dead* is less autobiographical and even more socially pessimistic. It presents a number of characters all of whom fail in the realization of their fine ideas; it feels towards an indictment not merely of society but of man-

in-society: 'you have', he remarks elsewhere, 'the tyrants you deserve'. Pontoppidan's last novel, *Man's Heaven* (1927), is his most
morose and acrid indictment of the use made by his fellow-country-
men of the great opportunities offered to them; it is not convincing,
however, as fiction. Better are his memoirs, the fruits of old age,
called *On the Road to Myself* (1933–43): these are surprisingly good-
tempered and optimistic: the gloom came out in Pontoppidan when
he put his imagination to work. He wrote from a naturalist point of
view, but his imagination's subject is self-discovery and self-realization in a hostile environment.

KARL GJELLERUP (1857–1919) shared the Nobel Prize with Pontoppidan, but his work is of little interest. His Nobel Prize, in fact, came
as a shock to everyone, including the Danes. At first he was a
theological student; then he turned to Brandes and atheism. Not
long after that he became attracted by German idealism. He settled
in Germany and ultimately collapsed into a facile Christianity,
having, characteristically, passed through Buddhism in the mean-
time. He was a superficial writer and underwent hosts of influences
without assimilating, or really understanding, any of them. His first
novel, *An Idealist* (1878), is atheistic. *Minna* (1889; tr. 1913) is a
sickly paean to all things teutonic in the person of his wife. His only
remotely readable novel is *The Mill* (1896), which is set in Denmark
and imitates Dostoevski.

*

The history of Brandes' influence befits that of a theorist: the best
writers who came under it either broke away or transcended it.
HOLGER DRACHMANN (1846–1908), for example, who was born in
Copenhagen, was a true radical who mistakenly thought that
Brandes was. Drachmann was chiefly a poet; with Holstein and
Aakjær, he was the chief traditional poet of his generation. Too
happy and healthy to be a *poète maudit*, he was none the less a genuine
Bohemian and sincere denier of genteel values. He was conscious of
the socialist movement, and, unlike Brandes, shared its aspirations;
but as a poet he celebrated what he saw as the possibilities for individual anarchy inherent in it. His merit is all in his lyrical tone.
His lines 'I wear the hat I want to./I sing the songs I want to/And
can' sum up his early attitude. He dropped this pose, however, in his
mid-thirties, and wrote some introspective poetry of higher quality.
He was a master craftsman of a rather obvious type; almost all his
poetry is spoilt by Swinburnian pseudo-vitality (although his
sexuality was more robust than that of the English poet). As well as

plays and libretti for operettas, Drachmann wrote a long novel, *Signed Away* (1890), which is perhaps the best thing he ever did—his poetry having dated badly. Here he successfully represents the poles of his own personality as two characters: a vagabond poet and an industrious, aesthetic artist.

LUDVIG HOLSTEIN (1864–1943) is the lyrical celebrator of Denmark's natural scene. His pantheism is irrelevant, something he doubtless felt obliged—in his always sincere way—to affect; he is at his best when writing simply and directly of nature. Born on Zealand, the son of a count, he was an admirer of Jensen's (q.v.) materialism. Holstein was a simple materialist who desired above all to make the best of life, and this best he saw in the nature from which man comes and to which he returns. (TCSP).

JEPPE AAKJÆR (1886–1930) was born in Jutland, the son of a poor farmer, and wrote his best poetry in the Jutish dialect; he is often referred to as a Danish Burns. An autodidact and rabid socialist (he was gaoled), with a gift for epigram, he is still one of his country's most widely read poets. He began with crude socialist novels; but after spending some time in Copenhagen he developed intellectually and was able to devise a dialect poetry that is at once simple and subtle: it is held together by its original and haunting rhythms. He intelligently paraphrases Burns, and learnt much from him. As P. M. Mitchell has observed, he graduated from being a naïve (q.v.) to a sentimentive (q.v.) writer—but without, it must be added, losing his inspiration. (TCSP)

Aakjær's first wife MARIE BREGENDAHL (1867–1940) was one of the leading regional novelists; she attained fame with her descriptions of Jutland and its inhabitants. Her best book is a collection of short stories, *A Night of Death* (1912; tr. 1931). A later massive novel cycle of Jutland life is worthy but not of the same quality.

A group of regionalist writers, mostly from Jutland, gathered round Jensen (q.v.) and Aakjær; this was in part a reaction against Brandes (of whom Aakjær wrote: 'Sole giant in a field where critics perch/How much we revel in your deep research!/You write so finely of the mighty dead;/Why is so little of the living said?/Can Intellect not count you an apostle/Until its work is found to be a fossil?') and his positivist intellectualism. There was a similar reaction from the more cosmopolitan poets. In this group the so-called 'neo-romanticism' of the Nineties amounted to little more than a release of 'private' emotions that naturalism had seemed to proscribe. No one yet thought of eschewing realism—even if they did so. The three poets who represent this *fin de siècle* movement in Danish literature began as close friends: VIGGO STUCKENBERG (1863–1905),

JOHANNES JØRGENSEN (1866–1956) and SOPHUS CLAUSSEN (1865–1931). They were originally followers of Brandes, but became interested in French symbolism as a result of some lectures on the subject given in Copenhagen in 1892 by Léon Bloy (q.v.), whose wife was Danish.

Jørgensen may be dealt with briefly. He drew apart from the others when, in 1896, he became a Roman Catholic; soon afterwards he went to Italy, where he lived. He became famous as a writer of religious prose—lives of saints, memoirs, and so on—which has been of interest to Catholics, and has given him a reputation in Denmark as chief (lay) representative of Catholicism. He abandoned his early symbolist leanings for a well written, but dull, devout verse. Stuckenberg, less prone to dogma, was a more gifted poet. He wrote one percipient novel of adolescence, *Breaking Through* (1888). His wife Ingeborg acted as 'muse' to himself, the young Jørgensen and Claussen, but left him ten years later. Stuckenberg's poetry is symbolic only in the most simplistic way; his real merit lies in his directness, his tenderness and the nobility of his resignation.

Claussen, a friend of Verlaine's, deserves credit for being the first truly cosmopolitan Danish poet. He spent many years in France and Italy, and is the only out-and-out symbolic theorist his country, which remained largely impervious to the symbolist movement, knew. And yet, for all its attempts at a dutiful symbolism, most of his poetry remains explicit on a conventional level—as though it merely wanted to remind its readers that another kind of poetry existed. Because of his preoccupations with symbolism, which in retrospect seem academic, Claussen never resolved his own real problem, which was to reconcile his happily sensual love of life with his erotic guilt, which he recklessly and dishonestly rationalized as a hatred of technology. (TCSP) Another influential neo-romantic and symbolist, and friend of the Stuckenberg circle, was HELGE RODE (1870–1937), a religious mystic whose smoothly written, gentle poetry is usually spoiled by literary preciosity.

*

The conservative, neo-romantic, symbolic or regionalist reaction to Brandes attracted some undoubtedly reactionary figures. The poets HARALD BERGSTEDT (1877–1965) and the prolific VALDEMAR RØRDAM (1872–1946), whose early work has some small merit, ended up by collaborating with the Nazis. These would not be of interest to readers outside Denmark. (Both TCSP) The North Jutlander JOHANNES V. JENSEN (1873–1950), however, who was the leader of the counter-reaction to the Nineties neo-romanticism, was a writer of

European stature, whose Nobel Prize (1944) was possibly deserved. Jensen is Denmark's last definitely major author: he is also the first real modernist. He went to America when he was twenty-two, and fell under the influence of Whitman and the pushing and aggressive vigour of the new world. His first novel, *The Fall of the King* (1900–1; tr. 1933), about Christian II's defeat by the Germans, is in fact an indictment of Danish indecision and lack of vitality, which Jensen saw as a national disease. Apart from this aspect of it, it is a penetrating study of sixteenth-century people. Jensen's tales of his native Himmerland (North Jutland), *People of the Himmerland* (1898) and its two successors *New Tales* (1904) and *More Tales* (1910), are among the best of all modern regional literature. Jensen also invented a new form, which he called the myth: this was a short piece, without plot, concentrating upon essences. Here Jensen's best work may be found. Often Jensen begins with a description of a familiar object, but casts new light on it by applying to it a personal memory—or to his evolutionary philosophy. The results are poetic rather than merely odd. *The Myths* are in nine volumes (1907–44). Jensen, an inveterate traveller, was a convinced Darwinist: the huge novel for which he obtained the Nobel Prize, *The Long Journey* (1908–22; tr. 1922), treats of man's evolutionary journey from pre-glacial baboon to Columbus, whom Jensen makes into a teuton. His aim was to write a new Bible. This has isolated passages of great brilliance, revealing all the various influences on Jensen—Darwin, Kipling (q.v. 1), Heine, Wells (q.v. 1) and others—but it is imbued with the pseudo-Darwinist theory which he called 'Gothic expansion', according to which civilization began in the Scandinavian North. This dreary and charlatanic theory spoils the book as a whole—and many of its parts. 'Gothic expansion' has unpleasantly racist elements—but Jensen repudiated the Nazis. Jensen also wrote some poetry of quality; most clearly influenced by Whitman, it is nevertheless prophetic of a more modern American, urban tone. 'At Memphis Station' (TCSP) is the most famous example. It begins characteristically:

> Half-awake and half-dozing,
> In an inward seawind of dadaid dreams
> I stand and gnash my teeth
> At Memphis Station, Tennessee.
> It is raining.

Jensen was a naïve (q.v.) writer posing as a thinker; his philosophy is worthless. This adversely affects his later fiction, but is irrelevant to his finest work: the tales of Himmerland and the myths.

There was one other Danish novelist of European stature: MARTEN ANDERSEN NEXØ (1869–1954), born in a Copenhagen slum and Denmark's foremost Marxist writer. Nexø was first a social democrat, but after the First World War he became a convinced follower of the communist party line; he escaped to Moscow in the Second World War and travelled extensively in Eastern European countries after it. He died in Dresden. His two most important novel cycles, *Pelle the Conqueror* (1906–10; tr. 1913–16) and *Ditte* (1917–21; tr. 1920–22) depend on his sympathy for and knowledge of the poor and downtrodden—but not on his socialism. *Pelle* is largely autobiographical, featuring Nexø himself in the person of Morten. *Ditte* is a poignant study, from cradle to early grave, of an illegitimate woman, and is chiefly impressive for its convincing portraiture of goodness in the face of adversity. None of this has to do with socialist realism.

Nexø had the same kind of beginnings as Gorki (q.v. 1), and his first novel, *Life Drips Away* (1902) is Gorkian. His first outstanding book, however, was the remarkably sensitive account of his sojourn among the poor in the Mediterranean, where he had gone to recover from tuberculosis: *Days in the Sun* (1903; tr. 1929). His *Memoirs* (1932–9; pt. tr. *Under the Open Sky*, 1938) give a fascinating account of his early life and conversion to socialism. Nexø is a massive naturalist, and at his best—particularly in *Ditte*—he approaches Dreiser (q.v. 1). (His own poetic asides are only a little less beside the point than Dreiser's.) Two other well known shorter novels, *In God's Land* (1929; tr. 1933), an attack on the complacency of wealthy farmers, and *Morten the Red* (1945), a continuation of *Pelle*, are unsuccessful as fiction.

GUSTAV WIED (1858–1914) was the most humorous of Denmark's novelists. Moreover, he was the outstanding prose writer of the Nineties. Wied's ironic mask hid a bitter nihilism and sense of loneliness which finally led him, on the outbreak of the First World War, to suicide. He was in many ways a typical Dane: humorous, introspective, self-mocking but with a strong moralistic element. Wied was in some ways close to his compatriot Søren Kierkegaard (1813–55), that quintessential Dane who had no Danish followers: like Kierkegaard, he felt trapped between an 'either' and an 'or' (*Either/ Or*, 1843, is the title of one of Kierkegaard's most famous books), between an aesthetic and an ethical life. In his unfinished autobiography he speaks of himself as a divided man: '. . . any time I run into trouble "the other" takes care of the matter and says "of what importance is it to you?" and I feel relieved'. But Wied, unlike Kierkegaard, was not a religious man: he saw life as a meaningless farce. He began by writing Strindbergian (q.v.) dramas, but these failed. His best mature work may be divided into four genres: the bitter, humorous sketches of *Silhouettes* (1891) and other volumes; his so-called 'satyr' plays—designed for reading; his comedies, including *Skirmishes* (1901), which was a commercial success; and satire. Some of his novels such as *The Family* (1898)—his most seriously purposed book—and *The Fathers Eat Grapes* (1908), are good but not distinguished. He invented, however, a legendary character, Knagsted, in two satirical classics: *Life's Malice* (1899) and *Knagsted* (1902). One of Knagsted's recreations is the collection of famous Danish writer's commas. For nearly half a century, dating from a few years before his death, Wied's work was half-forgotten; during and since the Second World War it has enjoyed a deserved revival.

The two best known woman novelists of this period are AGNES HENNINGSEN (1868–1962) and, particularly, KARIN MICHAËLIS (1872–1950). Agnes Henningsen wrote a number of novels on the erotic problems of women that shocked the readers of their period; but her best work is her eight-volume *Memoirs* (1941–55). Karin Michaëlis, who was born at Randers in North-East Jutland, but spent much time outside Denmark, enjoyed an international reputation which she may not altogether have deserved: she was, it is true, a pioneer—but not a very distinguished one. She became famous through *The Dangerous Age* (1910: tr. 1911), which is in the form of a diary written by a woman during her menopause. Very much of her time, Karin Michaëlis was a good woman: intelligent, and psychologically accurate, and she opened up new territory for novelists; but her work is not distinguished as fiction. She is, however, an interesting writer, especially of volumes of memoirs. Other women writers included HÜLDA LÜTKEN (1896–1947) and THIT JENSEN (1876–1957), best known as a historical novelist. Possibly more distinguished than any of these was the wife of the poet Helge Rode (q.v.): EDITH RODE (1879–1956). Her poetry is skilful but has dated; her best fiction, mostly short stories, will last in a way that Michaëlis' cannot. Unfortunately nothing has been translated except one story, 'The Eternal Adorer' (tr. in *The Norseman*, 1950).

The Jutlander JAKOB KNUDSEN (1858–1917) was a minor novelist of the reaction against Brandes. He was an honest authoritarian: Christian, courageous, cruel, pigheaded, hero-worshipping, believing in inequality; the kind of proto-fascist who would never have supported a fascist government. He is often aptly called 'the Carlyle of Denmark'. (He would have loathed Christ, he said, as a gutless, repulsive, sexless and flabby type—but he happens to be the son of God.) Many of his novels are unpleasant in the manner of Carlyle: *Lærer Urup* (1909), for example, is an attack on the humane treatment of criminals. *Fear* (1912) is about Martin Luther. His best novel is *The Old Pastor* (1899), which boringly advocates society's right to kill bad men not legally guilty of any crime, but which portrays its degenerate beast-type with a certain romantic fascination. But Knudsen's only real virtue is the fine, homespun plainness of his prose. He was a priest, but when he divorced his wife and married again he was forced to become a lecturer.

The fiction of HARALD KIDDE (1878–1918), who came from Vejle in East Jutland, has its roots in the attitudes of J. P. Jacobsen and Herman Bang (qq.v.). Kidde was also clearly influenced by Kierkegaard. He is an introspective dreamer, but one who sounds a more hopeful note than either of his masters. *Aage and Else* (1902–3) and *The Hero* (1912) are his chief novels. The purpose of both seems to be to raise up forces stronger and more virile than Kidde felt himself to be. The first novel is too long; but it still has elements of a classic— not least because of the way in which it captures the *angst* and indecision of the central character, a self-portrait. As genuine if not as notable a precursor of the existentialist mood as Kierkegaard, Kidde's work is now attracting increasing attention. He died in the influenza epidemic that swept Europe in 1918 (claiming, too, Apollinaire, q.v.).

ALBERT DAM (1880), although of Kidde's generation, was not discovered until the early Fifties. He wrote two novels in the first decade of the century, another in 1934, and then, at the age of seventy, began to produce fiction that made the Danes feel that they had amongst them a major modernist writer, of great wisdom. His short stories, none of which has been translated, begin where Jensen in his 'myths' (q.v.) left off. His is a genius somewhat akin to that of his contemporary, Karen Blixen (q.v.).

*

The Danish social drama begins with the not very effective plays of the brother of Georg, EDVARD BRANDES (1847–1931) and of the more interesting OTTO BENZON (1856–1927). A Danish playwright of the genius of Strindberg or Ibsen (qq.v.) is lacking. The theatre of Wied (q.v.) comes nearest to Strindberg in versatility and general attitude. His *Dancing Mice* (1905), a clearly pre-expressionist piece, portrays human beings as mice in a treadmill. His series of small 'satyr' plays, collected together as *Nobility, Clergy, Burgher and Peasant* (1897) are witty. His most successful play is $2 \times 2 = 5$ (1906; tr. E. Boyd and K. Koppel, 1923). Among the more conventional talents that of the Jewish HENRI NATHANSEN (1868–1944) stands out. He fled from the Nazis to Sweden, where he jumped out of a hotel window.

He was for many years director of the Royal Theatre of Copenhagen. Many of his plays are about Danish Jews and their problems. The best of these was *Within the Walls* (1912). CARL ERIK SOYA (1896) is the natural successor to Wied, although he has been strongly influenced by Pirandello. Much of his work, particularly the more recent, is spoiled by a naïve desire to shock (he was almost fifty before he gained recognition). His most important dramatic work is the exuberant tetralogy called *Bits of a Pattern* (1940–8). Here his laconic dialogue and presentation are outstanding. His novel *Grandmother's House* (1943; tr. 1966) is an evocation of Copenhagen at the beginning of the century, distinguished for its psychological acumen and its creation of an eerie atmosphere.

The two most important modern Danish dramatists, however, are KAJ MUNK (1898–1944), a parson murdered by the Nazis, and KJELD ABELL (1901–1961). Munk was a publicist and journalist who set out to break up the polite theatre by a return to high, poetic drama. He was less unsuccessful in this difficult project than any other playwright of the century. His theme was power. He passed from an early admiration of fascism to a practical hatred of it that cost him his life. He, too, was deeply influenced by Kierkegaard. His most powerful play is *The Word* (1932; PKM), in which a madman, suddenly regaining his sanity, performs the miracle of raising the dead. This, which exploited the basic Romeo-Juliet theme, was freer than any other of his plays from his besetting sin of melodrama. Two other plays are *Herod the King* (1928; PKM) and *Cant* (1931; PKM) on Henry VIII of England. Munk, despite his heroism and martyrdom, has been somewhat overrated. But his plays made the Danes feel that they possessed a major dramatist—and the earlier ones do, for all their faults, have real power.

Abell is superior, both as craftsman and a thinker. His *The Melody that Got Lost* (1935; ad. 1939), which established his reputation, is a satire on the 'little man'; its technique is cinematic and impressionistic. His best play, *Anna Sophie Hedvig* (1939; tr. in *Scandinavian Plays of the Twentieth Century*, 1945), is about a seedy schoolteacher's murder of an unjust colleague. Abell presents this insignificant little woman as a symbol of resistance to Nazi tyranny; only the ending, where she is shot, along with an anti-Franco volunteer, jars. During the occupation Abell openly opposed the Nazis and was finally forced underground. Of his later plays *Days on a Cloud* (1947; tr. in *The Genius of the Scandinavian Theatre*, 1964) is the most outstanding. This, against a mythological background, portrays a scientist's apathy and retreat into cliché. Abell never wholly realized his gifts, but he is Denmark's best modern dramatist.

ERNST BRUUN OLSEN (1923) is Denmark's radical critic of society. His successful *Teenager Love* (1962) is an effective and scathing satire on the pop industry.

*

Of the poets who came into prominence between the wars one of the most important is PAUL LA COUR (1902–56), whose position in Denmark was something like Auden's (q.v. 1) in Great Britain—though he is a very different kind of poet. His real effect was on the poets of the post-1945 generation. He lived in Paris for many years, and wrote an influential critical book, *Fragments of a Diary* (1948), which is more important than his poetry. He began, a follower of Jensen (q.v.), with poems that showed his interest in painting. He had, in fact, started by trying to be a painter. His later manner was first manifested in the collection *I Demand All* (1938). It is not that he is a 'political' poet, but that he wants to find a valid reason why, in a disintegrating Europe, he and others should pursue the path of poetry. This is the theme of *Fragments of a Diary*, which acutely reflects the modern phenomenon I have called *Künstlerschuld* (q.v.). This is la Cour's main contribution, because in his actual poetry and fiction he seldom found the coherence, the method, he searched for. (TCSP)

More representative as a creative writer is NIS PETERSEN (1897–1943), better known as a novelist in the English-speaking world, but in fact more important as a poet. Petersen is Denmark's (rather late on the scene) *poète maudit*: a vagabond who has something (but not temperance) in common with Vachel Lindsay and, for metrical virtuosity, Roy Campbell (qq.v. 1). He is emphatically a naïve (q.v.) writer, very much hit or miss. *The Street of the Sandalmakers* (1931; tr. 1933) is a novel set in the Rome of Marcus Aurelius, but, in the German tradition, is really a comment on modern Denmark. *Spilt Milk* (1934; tr. 1935) is, curiously, about the Irish 'troubles'. Petersen also wrote readable, exaggerated accounts of his wanderings, in the form of prose sketches. But his poetry, in rigorous selection, shows him at his best; at times he can achieve the sultry eroticism of a D. H. Lawrence (q.v.).

TOM KRISTENSEN (1893), critic, poet and novelist, is the leading Danish expressionist, although his first master was Jensen (q.v.). Expressionism (q.v.) reached Denmark after the First World War; Kristensen used its violent techniques to express his own disillusion and programmatic modernism:

> In chaos I lift my rifle
> to take aim at the star of beauty

could serve as his motto. He has had little of his own to say, but has faithfully reflected the concerns of his generation; expressionism has come as naturally to him as it has, so to say, to his age. Between the wars he was the leading interpreter of writers such as Joyce and Hemingway (qq.v.). His poetry is exhilarated, basically traditional and simple despite the noise it makes and its sprawling presentation. His best novel, which is none the less somewhat tedious, is *Havoc* (1930; tr. 1968), a Hemingwayesque depiction of the Danish 'lost generation', in which 'drunkenness of the senses mingles with the dream of a revolution to come'. (TCSP)

Kristensen is a useful writer, an enthusiastic interpreter of foreign writers whom he does not always fully understand, but JACOB PALUDAN (1896) is a deeper one. He is an intelligent conservative, who resembles Aldous Huxley (q.v. 1), who has influenced him, in his loathing of the materialistic and the crass and the physical in modern life. In contrast to Kristensen, he deplores the modern— but in a consistently shrewd way. As a young man he went to America, which made him feel as disgusted and gloomy as it had made Kristensen ecstatic. After his major novel, *Jørgen Stein* (1932–3; tr. 1966), Paludan turned to criticism. *Jørgen Stein* is a pessimistic study of Denmark between wars. Jørgen Stein is in certain respects the kind of man Kristensen portrays (self-portrays?) in *Havoc*: he has lost direction; he has given up. In him Paludan symbolizes modern degeneration: he moves sceptically from one idea to another, and takes refuge in dreams. Here Paludan's conservatism vitiates his understanding of the conditions that produce scepticism, and he cannot see that in scepticism lies a hope for universal tolerance and understanding. But Jørgen himself is convincingly lost; Paludan has the warmth Huxley lacked.

KAREN BLIXEN (ps. Baroness BLIXEN-FINECKE, also known as ISAK DINESEN, 1885–1962) can hardly be related to the development of Danish literature; but to some tastes outside Denmark she has been the best modern Danish author—partly, no doubt, because her work has been consistently available. She ran a coffee-plantation in Kenya until 1931, and was remote from literary influences. *Out of Africa* (1937) is her account of this experience: a classic of tenderness and understanding. Her stories in *Seven Gothic Tales* (1934), in English, *Winter's Tales* (1942) and *Last Tales* (1957) are eccentric masterpieces; ostensibly Gothic pastiche, their outward form conceals epic wisdom, profound feminine sorrow, and a clean magic almost lost today. She is undoubtedly the princess of modern aristocratic storytellers, a delight and a revelation. Her style is in fact not pastiche but precise, sober, studied and often ironically epigrammatic, the product of a full experience. In these sad and lovely tales, as men and women go through the rituals of love, adventure and dying, we sense a poet's wisdom.

*

The work of minor rather than major poets reflects the influx into Denmark of surrealism, dada and nonsense. SIGFRED PEDERSEN (1903) mixes the clichés of bourgeois politicians and newspaper commentators with Copenhagen slang in a delightful verse. JENS AUGUST SCHADE (1903) is a disrespectful poet, amusing when he is thumbing his nose at everybody but dull when he essays Whitman-esque poems. His erotic poetry somewhat resembles Cummings' (q.v.), as does his whole *œuvre*: he has the same satirical impulses, the same tendency to destroy by false diminution of his satirical target, the same saving humour. *Sjov in Denmark* (1928) a series of poems in which the archetypal Dane fails ludicrously in all his aspirations (revolution, suicide, and so on) is his best and most char-acteristic book. PIET HEIN (1905) calls his poems 'grooks': brief, epigrammatic, resigned verses in which Hein displays a sharp humour. HALFDAN RASMUSSEN (1915), ten years younger, Denmark's leading proletarian poet, is also a writer of the best nonsense poetry in the language (published in a series of volumes under the title *Tomfoolery*).

A newer generation, immediately influenced by la Cour (q.v.), has been less interested in humour and the surrealist approach than in Eliot, Rilke (particularly) and the symbolists. The most impres-sive is THORKILD BJØRNVIG (1918), the joint editor of the most influential post-war magazine, *Heretica*. His first master was Rilke, of whom he has perhaps purged himself by making some excellent translations. He seems, like other contemporary Danish poets, to be more obsessed with discovering viable procedures than with the expression of his own sensibility; but he is helping to prepare the way for a more urgent writer. (TCSP) ERIK KNUDSEN (1922) is, by contrast, certainly more urgent; but his attitudes—of savage dis-illusion with pop culture and of general scepticism—are so far more attractive than his over-diffuse poetry. (TCSP) MORTEN NIELSEN (1922–44), a member of the resistance, was killed in an accident before he had time to fulfil his promise. But his lucid poetry is still read in Denmark, in the same way as Keith Douglas' (q.v. 1) is here. His participation in active resistance gave his doubtfulness an edge of lyricism. (TCSP)

TOVE DITLEVSEN (1918) is the best known contemporary woman

writer, for both poetry and fiction. From a Copenhagen working-class family, she writes of the proletariat and of women's difficulties: a modern equivalent of Karin Michaëlis, but with a lyrical poetic gift and a better developed imagination. She has written acutely and candidly of her own problems, which have included drug addiction.

*

Denmark's more recent novelists have achieved better results than her poets. This is not an unusual state of affairs: poetry requires not merely pressure to write, but a language to write in, and this is becoming increasingly difficult to create in the ultra-sophisticated atmosphere of the century.

HANS KIRK (1898–1962), a communist and a skilful novelist, provides an example of socialist realism (q.v. 4) operating freely: not under a tyranny of mediocrities. Kirk chose to adhere to the method; but no one 'directed' or 'corrected' him. He left the Danish Civil Service to join a group of Jutland fishermen, and wrote an excellent and vivid novel about the experience, *Fishermen* (1928), which transcends its conscious aims, and which incorporates elements of unanimism (q.v.) as much as of socialist realism. Kirk does not in the least share the fanatic religious faith (the 'Inner Mission' of the Danish State Church) of his fishermen, although he may admire it; but in any case he gives a remarkably objective presentation. Kirk never equalled this achievement. His two Thirties novels, *Labourers* (1936) and *New Times* (1939) are comparatively crude: here he presents a collective phenomenon of which he approves, rather than sympathetically studies one that he does not. *Son of Wrath* (1950), showing Jesus Christ as a Jewish proto-Marxist, contains some vivid passages.

An interesting contrast to Kirk's *Fishermen* is to be found in ERIK BERTELSEN's (1898) *Daybreak* (1937), which treats the 'Inner Mission' as a positive force; this is ultimately sentimental, but it is a useful complement to Kirk's book, and skilfully incorporates much dialect.

JØRGEN NIELSEN (1902–45), an outstanding psychological novelist, received no recognition in his lifetime, but is now regarded as an important writer. He wrote about the sullen, tough, solitary farming people of the Jutland heath. His first book was of short stories: *Low Land* (1929). He wrote several novels, of which the best is *A Woman at the Bonfire* (1933); it is an outwardly uneventful work, but possess-ed keen insight into the mental states of people who desire happiness but whose beliefs prevent them from attaining it. One novel, *The*

Haughty (1930), is set in a town: a study of provincial post-war disillusion that parallels and even excels Kristensen's *Havoc* (q.v.).

However, the two most important novelists of modern Denmark have been H. C. Branner and M. A. Hansen. HANS CHRISTIAN BRANNER (1903–66) was born at Ordrup. After failing as an actor he went into publishing; he first made his name with radio plays. Then he published *Toys* (1936), a novel about the power-struggle among the employees of a Copenhagen firm. This already displays his individualism; but his main preoccupations did not come to the fore until later. Like Jørgen Nielsen, he is essentially a psychological novelist; but he dwells particularly in the area of fear and solitude. He discovered his true métier in the story collection *In a Little While We Are Gone* (1939); *Two Minutes of Silence* (1944; tr. 1966) contains his best stories. No contemporary except perhaps Conrad Aiken (q.v. 1) can match Branner as the revealer of the child's psyche, with its irrational terrors and its incomprehension of its parents' world. In *The Child Playing on the Shore* (1937) fear of this world drives a boy to his death. Branner matured as a novelist with *The Riding Master* (1949; tr. 1951), which shows him to have fully absorbed Freud: now he reveals his characters' hidden motives. *No Man Knows the Night* (1955; tr. 1958) is the peak of his achievement.

MARTIN A. HANSEN (1909–55), who came from Zealand, enjoyed even greater prestige, at the time of his early death, than Branner. His first two novels, *Surrender* (1935) and *The Colony* (1937), are sober sociological examinations of farming life; the first tells of an experiment in collective farming. Then, forced by wartime conditions to write of apparently innocuous subjects, he wrote *Jonathan's Journey* (1941 rev. 1950), ostensibly a fairy tale about a smith who captured the devil in a flask and set out to visit the king. The whole is an allegory of the Nazi tyranny. *Lucky Christopher* (1945) is a historical novel, this time set in the sixteenth century. Then came his finest novel, *The Liar* (1950; tr. 1954), a subtle study of a contemporary Christian. Hansen was a romantic Christian (like Kierkegaard, he was interested not in dogma but in faith) who finally evolved a kind of subtle Christian nationalism, a synthesis of Christianity and Jensen's (q.v.) Norse fantasies.

The leading figure in Danish letters today is the over-prolific KLAUS RIFBJERG (1931), author of plays, poetry and novels. Rifbjerg can be superficial, sentimental and slapdash, but he is highly talented; lately (*Narrene*, 1971) he has been writing excellent plays, and this form may prove to be his true métier.

Several other novelists should be mentioned. AAGE DONS (1903), whose choice to write about alienated neurotics and bunglers of life links him with Bang (q.v.), first became well known with *The Soldiers Well* (1936; tr. 1940). This is a convincing account of the series of frustrations that lead a woman to a murder—which is not discovered. An important later novel is *The Past Is Not Gone* (1950). LECK FISCHER (1904–56) was a reliable realist, writing with insight about ordinary lives. His best book is the trilogy *Leif the Lucky* (1928–9 rev. 1935), about two friends—one lucky and bold, the other timid—both afflicted by an inner insecurity. Fisher was modest but never middlebrow: a fine professional writer. KNUD SØNDERBY (1909–66) began with a competent Hemingway novel—a Danish equivalent of *The Sun Also Rises* (q.v. 1)—*In the Middle of a Jazz Age* (1931). His best novel, which was later made into a highly successful drama, is *A Woman Too Many* (1935), a fine portrait of an interfering mother. The play was tr. in *Contemporary Danish Plays*, 1955. MOGENS KLITGAARD (1906–45) wrote proletarian novels in the Thirties; but the historical novels, *The Red Feathers* (1940) and *Trouble at Newmarket* (1940) are better. MARCUS LAUESEN (1907) is most famous for *Waiting for a Ship* (1931; tr. 1933), a story of prosperous merchants in the region of the German-Danish border. Its successors, more philosophically ambitious, have not been as good. HANS SCHERFIG (1905) is another unpretentious professional: *The Idealists* (1945; tr. 1949) is his most outstanding book.

*

The Faeroe Islands, of only 25,000 inhabitants, have preserved a literature in their own dialect. Two Faeroese have written fiction in Danish: WILLIAM HEINESEN (1900) and JØRGEN-FRANTZ JACOBSEN (1900–38). Heinesen's *Niels Peter* (1938; tr. 1939) is a psychological novel; *The Black Kettle* (1949) deals with the British occupation of the Faeroes in the Second World War; *The Lost Musicians* (1950) is an allegory. Jacobsen's *Barbara* (1938; tr. 1948), published posthumously, is a warm novel about a woman who likes men in and out of bed. The chief writer of fiction in the Faeroese language is HEDIN BRU (ps. H. J. JACOBSEN, 1901): *Mirage* (1930); *Firm Grip* (1936).

III

From the sixteenth century until 1814 Norway was a province of Denmark. The movement that led to breakage of the link with Denmark also gave the impetus to the creation of a national literature. It was during the nineteenth century that the synthetic literary language, *landsmål* (national, or country, language), was formed. The original *riksmål* (state language) still exists, and most Norwegian literature is written in it; but New Norwegian (as *landsmål* is now called) is employed by a number of important writers.

In the Seventies Norwegian literature was still dominated by Ibsen, Bjørnson, Kielland and Lie (qq.v.). All survived into the twentieth century; but all are essentially nineteenth-century figures: forerunners but not part of modern literature.

HENRIK IBSEN (1828–1906) admired Brandes (q.v.), who made himself as felt in Norway as in his native Denmark. His 'social' period begins with *Pillars of Society* (1877), towards the end of the decade of Brandes' greatest influence. He had already written his poetic dramas, *Brand* (1866) and *Peer Gynt* (1867). Ibsen's theatre transcends movements, but his development through *The Wild Duck* (1884) and *Hedda Gabler* (1890) to *The Master Builder* (1892) can be seen to reflect the concerns of the time. In Norway the period of 'social' writing did not persist as long as in Denmark, and the impulses behind the neo-romanticism and decadence of the Nineties (reflected in *Hedda Gabler*) were stronger. Ibsen's influence is to be seen in every important European dramatist who came after him. Pirandello (q.v. 3) was initially particularly affected. Acquaintance with his work makes it clear that no aspiring playwright could fail to react to it and to learn from it. Ibsen gave European drama the depth it lacked, both by his technique—the masterly recreation of the past in terms of the present; the invention of a truly realistic dialogue—and by the diversity of his approach. He is an entirely international figure, who has been accepted in the English-speaking world as though he were a part of it; his major plays have been translated into the idiom of succeeding generations.

BJØRNSTJERNE BJØRNSON (1832–1910) was a greatly gifted writer of plays, novels and poetry; but in all but a few works he was overshadowed by the more cosmopolitan Ibsen, who lived abroad for many years. Where Ibsen was internationally minded, Bjørnson was nationally minded. It is appropriate that he should have written Norway's national anthem. But the element of chauvinism and conservative morality that runs through his work did not affect *A Gauntlet* (1883), a play in which he attacked the blindness and hypocrisy of authority. His novels are ponderous and didactic, but he left much charming shorter fiction. Most likely to survive are his tales of peasant life.

ALEXANDER KIELLAND (1849–1906), born at Stavanger, was the great Norwegian radical novelist of the nineteenth century. His masterpiece, *Garman and Worse* (1880; tr. W. Kettlewell, 1885), set in Stavanger, ironic, elegant and bitter, is an attack on the social system of his day. His other work, apart from early stories, hardly comes up to this.

More important was JONAS LIE (1833–1908), the antithesis of Kielland. He was not interested in social problems as such, but in people. His really important work is contained in his perceptive treatment of Norwegian middle-class life. *One of Life's Slaves* (1883; tr. 1895) gives an account of a disintegrating marriage. He was affected by naturalism; but saw trolls, those Scandinavian mischief-makers, as responsible for most of life's mishaps. His genius came out most fully in *Weird Tales from the Northern Seas* (1891–2; tr. 1893), where he avoids, on the one hand, the crude spiritualism that mars his first novel, *The Visionary* (1870; tr. 1894), and on the other the sentimental and simplistic insistence on family harmony (never something to have a philosophy about) that renders *Life Together* (1887) commonplace.

*

ARNE GARBORG (1851–1924) was a quasi-naturalist who turned Tolstoian. He was profoundly affected by the suicide of his father, which had been brought about by an extreme piety. No Norwegian except Amalie Skram (q.v.) can be described as a true naturalist, but the implications of Garborg's first fiction are undoubtedly naturalistic. He was the first major Norwegian novelist to write in *landsmål* (whose opponents, it should be noted, were not and are not vicious pro-Danish anti-patriots, but objectors to what they see as its linguistically contaminating effects and its artificiality). His first two books, *Peasant Students* (1882) and *Menfolk* (1886) are on one level indictments of the circumstances under which young men had to acquire their education. But in reality they are desperately gloomy indictments of human circumstances. . . . Garborg, at this stage of his development, was Norway's Gissing (q.v. 1); he is consistently dour, and his would-be parsons are young men of infinitely unpleasant disposition. Laurits Kruse of *Menfolk* is one of the most outstanding young swine of the fiction of the latter part of the nineteenth century—and his callousness comes entirely naturally to him. By the time of *Peace* (1892; tr. 1930) Garborg had reached his Tolstoian phase. The hero kills himself, but not before he makes a gesture of practical Christianity in the best Tolstoian tradition. The hero is partly based on Garborg's father, and the novel holds a balance between approval and disapproval that makes it Garborg's tensest and best. The later work, including poems and plays, is nobler but less imaginatively convincing.

AMALIE SKRAM (1846–1905) was born Bertha Amalie Alver, married a sea-captain, left him, and married the Danish critic Erik Skram (1884). Subject to mental disturbance, she wrote an excellent exposé of the shortcomings of psychiatric medicine, based on her experiences in a Copenhagen hospital in 1894, in *Professor Hieronimus* (1895), a novel that has a secure place in at least the history of the ill-treatment of the mentally ill. The subject-matter of Amalie Skram's earlier novels (*Constance Ring*, 1885; *Madame Inès*, 1891; *Betrayed*, 1892) is women who 'cannot love', from which it has been concluded that her problem was 'frigidity', a province in which many male critics of the early part of this century liked to pronounce themselves expert. Such is not the case. Her subject is actually the difficulty sensitive and inwardly emancipated women found, in her day, in dealing with husbands who sexually repelled them by their demands. Amalie Skram was the kind of woman who sought, temperamentally, for extra-marital sexual satisfaction. (She had it and enjoyed it.) Her great achievement is her naturalistic cycle called *The Hellemyr Family* (1887–98), which traces the decline (but from no heights) of a poor fishing family through three generations. These are the grimmest of all naturalist fiction; they are also among the most vivid.

KNUT HAMSUN (originally KNUT PEDERSEN, 1859–1952), who came from the north of Norway, was a powerful and important writer who lived too long into this century to understand it. Recipient of the Nobel Prize (1920), he took up a strongly pro-Nazi attitude in the Second World War, and is only just now emerging from the shadow this cast upon him. His good work, which arose from complex instinct and not intellect, was done in the first half of his long life. But he is nevertheless one of the most important figures in Norwegian literature after Ibsen.

Hamsun began by attacking Ibsen's 'social' approach, and demanding a subjective literature. His first novel, *Hunger* (1888; tr. 1967), is a brutally egocentric account of the mental perceptions of its hero, a friendless wanderer. It foreshadows the unwitting egocentricity of the American poet Charles Olson (q.v. 1), himself of Scandinavian extraction, in its curious insistence—implicit rather than stated—that what Olson called 'the ego' must not come between the writer and the reader. Olson meant by ego, 'thought; invention; calculation; art'. Hamsun was not as polemic; but his insistence upon emphasizing his hero's perceptions—at the expense of all else—reveals a similar state of mind. *Hunger* is a repulsive book; but a powerful one.

Hamsun's best novel, which gets way beyond his always unpleasant intentions, is *Mysteries* (1892; tr. 1927); a new translation (1971) is becoming an American bestseller. This is a great novel, carrying within it the seeds of most of the experiments in fiction that have been made since. A young man spends a summer in a small resort. He ends by destroying himself. The 'mysteries' of the title are the mysteries of his contact with others, through whom he searches for himself and his own motives. *Pan* (1894; tr. 1956) explores similar territory, but more sporadically. Most of the rest of Hamsun's output, including his plays and verse, is of little intrinsic interest: it celebrates, with some incidentally beautiful impressions of nature, his self-love. But *Mysteries* reveals the young man's lyrical bewilderment at the human failure of his solipsism, and is a classic. Hamsun evolved his remarkable style by remaining insensitive to whatever appeared to threaten his perceptive faculties. Hamsun was an unpleasant man, but his primitivism, when it remains intuitive, is instructive; the result of his attempting to rationalize it into 'thought' was his fascism (he even visited Hitler in 1943).

HANS ERNST KINCK (1865–1926), born in Finnmark, is more attractive and intelligent than Hamsun, but lacks his power and instinctive depth. Nor did he realize his genius except in fragments—because, ironically, he took so much painful thought. But he remains Norway's finest writer of short fiction. His novels are marred by the didacticism of his purpose, which is to reveal the differences between, and hence find means of reconciling, the cultures of peasants and townfolk. But his short stories exhibit understanding and insight; their imaginative and artistic excellence undermine his noble hopes for his country.

OLAV DUUN (1876–1939), who wrote in a *landsmål* tempered by his native Trøndelag dialect, was a leading modern Norwegian writer. He recalls Lie (q.v.) in his emphasis on the *strangeness* of the fate that controls human existence—the unique quality in Norwegian writing, familiar to us in the trolls of Ibsen's *Peer Gynt*. His novel-cycle *The People of Juvik* (1918–23; tr. 1930–5) traces the history of a family from the Middle Ages to the twentieth century. Duun is interested in the difficulties of adaptation of relatively primitive peoples to modern conditions, a problem he treats with sensitivity and insight. In *The Present Time* (1936) he too cleverly symbolized the world situation in terms of peasant life, thus somewhat distorting the latter. *Floodtide of Fate* (1938; tr. 1960), his last novel, is a more successful allegory; it describes how the people of a small island overcome the natural disaster of flood. 'If we lift the earth from beneath our feet and the sky above us, we are still men all the same, we go on in spite of cold, we don't even know ourselves how much we can bear'. Duun's style, which owed much to the Norwegian tradition of oral story-telling, may in its 'seamlessness' be compared to that of George Moore (q.v. 1) for narrative effectiveness.

The prolific JOHAN BOJER (1872–1959), also from Trøndelag, was a conventional realist of some merit. His novels achieved a popularity abroad, especially in France, that is possibly out of proportion to their merits. He is most famous for *The Last of the Vikings* (1921; tr. 1936), about the codfishers of the Lofoten islands. His best books provide excellent examples of barely written, effective psychological regionalism—they usually deal with Trøndelag people; much of his work, however, is trite. Translations of good novels include: *The Power of a Lie* (1903; tr. 1908), a powerful novel about the consequences of a forgery, and *Treacherous Ground* (1908, tr. 1912), which is on the favourite Norwegian theme of idealism: Erik tries to make up for the ruthlessness with which his father has exploited the workers in building up his fortune—but events prove the falsity of his intentions. Bojer wrote some plays and poetry.

PETER EGGE (1869–1959), another Trøndelagander, is also firmly in the realist tradition. *Hansine Solstad: The History of an Honest Woman* (1925; tr. 1929), the story of a humble girl whose life is ruined by an unjust accusation of theft, is his most famous book. But incomparably his best is *Jægtvig and his God* (1923), a moving and exciting novel about a visionary young cobbler's fight to establish a new religion.

KRISTOFER UPPDAL (1878–1961), again from Trøndelag, was a more isolated and eccentric writer. He began his life as an itinerant navvy. Although the subject of Uppdal's massive novel-cycle *Dance Through a Shadowy Land* (1911–24) is the Norwegian technological revolution—occasioned by the development of hydro-electric projects—he is interested in the process of psychological transformation rather than in the social aspect. This is an example of a writer, as distinct from a politician, getting his priorities right. Uppdal worked out a grandiose philosophical system, involving Nietzschean recurrence, which is pretentious as a whole but incidentally interesting. This is presented in a large philosophical poem, *Cults* (1947), narrated by just such a navvy as he once was. It was written—and this is evident—under the cloud of madness, which afflicted Uppdal for the last twenty-five years of his life. Uppdal was certainly a proletarian writer; but he approached the problems of the proletariat less than ecstatically: he regarded the technological revolution as tragic. His verse is mostly trite; but the collection *Gallows Hill* (1930) is an exception.

JOHAN FALKBERGET (1879–1967) was born in the copper mining district of Røros (in South Trøndelag), and followed his father into the mines at the age of eight; he did not finally leave them until he was twenty-seven. An over-optimistic but good-hearted Christian whose first literary efforts were inspired by evangelistic tracts, his finest work is to be found in his unrelentingly truthful pictures of mining life at the end of the last century and the beginning of this: *When Life's Twilight Comes* (1902), *Black Mountains* (1907). His later historical novels have received higher praise, and this has been deserved—but the quality of the writing never quite comes up to that inspired by his early feelings of indignation. Of these *Lisbeth of Jarnfjeld* (1915; tr. 1930) has been translated. *Christianus Sextus* (1927–35), in six volumes, is an epic of the Røros mining industry from about 1800. *Bør Børson* (1920) is a novel about the tragic results of industrialization.

SIGRID UNDSET (1882–1949) was born in Denmark, the daughter of a famous Norwegian archeologist. When she got the Nobel Prize (1928) she told reporters: 'I have not the time to receive you. I am studying scholastic philosophy'. She had joined the Roman Catholic Church in 1924. When at home she wore national costume. Her third novel, *Jenny* (1911; tr. 1921), which gained her her first success, is a semi-naturalistic account of a sensitive girl's failure to achieve happiness; it is of no promise. She became internationally famous with *Kristin Lavransdatter* (1920–2; tr. 1930), set in medieval Norway. This was a pioneer work in the historical novel, in that it applied modern pseudo-psychology to circumstances in which modern psychology did not exist. This method proved to have enormous middlebrow possibilities. *Kristin Lavransdatter* is a skilful work, into which Sigrid Undset put much hard work; but it is not important as literature. It was followed by a less effective historical cycle. The tendentious Catholic fiction of her later years, all dealing with contemporary society, provided entertainment for bored middle-class ladies all over the world, but is worthless.

An incomparably superior and more serious writer was CORA SANDEL (ps. SARA FABRICIUS, 1880–1974), born in Kristiansand. Since 1921 she lived mostly in Sweden. Her studies of intelligent women trying to realize themselves are masterly in their subtlety and poetic qualities, as they are in the creation of atmosphere. She began late, with *Alberta and Jacob* (1926; tr. 1962), followed by *Alberta and Freedom* (1931; tr. 1965) and *Odd Alberta* (1939). Her masterpiece is *Krane's Café* (1945; tr. 1968), one of the century's most pitiless and accurate revelations of small-town nastiness and male selfishness. Katinka Stordal, deserted by her husband, supports her children by dressmaking. The women of the small Nor-wegian coastal town where she lives overlook her slovenliness and occasional tipsiness because she is superb at her job—and thus an ally of their vanity. But one day, in Krane's Café, the meeting place of the leading residents, a coarse but honest Swede shows an interest in Katinka for her own sake. She spends the day talking to him and then goes to bed with him. The town is scandalized—and put out by the fact that the dresses for a forthcoming ball may be delayed. Even Katinka's errant husband pleads with her. ... This great novel was successfully dramatized by Helge Krog (q.v.). *Leech* (1958; tr. 1960) is also excellent.

RONALD FANGEN (1895–1946), whose mother was English, is most important for *Duel* (1932; tr. 1934), an examination of the hostile friendship between two different types of men. In 1934 he joined the Oxford Movement (now called 'Moral Rearmament'), and his work lapsed into the kind of simplistic vulgarity (if not concealed authori-tarianism) that one associates with that unpleasant manifestation.

More gifted and important was SIGURD HOEL (1890–1960). Hoel was an intelligent and self-critical left-winger. He realized that 'social criticism and psychological analysis are aspects of the same pheno-menon. ... The fight for social, economic and moral liberation is the same fight on the same front'. He directed the 'Yellow Series', which presented such writers as Hemingway, Sherwood Anderson, Faulk-ner and Caldwell (qq.v. 1) to the Norwegian reading public. *Sinners in Summertime* (1927; tr. 1930) is a satire on members of the younger generation who imagine themselves emancipated but are in fact as bourgeois as the adults against whom they are in revolt. In *One day in October* (1931; tr. 1933) he made a penetrating analysis of bourgeois puritanism in a series of portraits of middleclass marriages. *The Road to the End of the World* (1933) returns to the world of childhood. *Two Weeks before the Glacial Nights* (1934) and *Meeting at the Milestone* (1947; tr. 1951), a study of treachery, are his best novels.

AKSEL SANDEMOSE (ps. AKSEL NIELSON, 1899–1965) was a Dane with a Norwegian mother. Having made his literary début in Denmark, he settled in Norway and made his entry into Nor-wegian literature in 1931 with *A Sailor Comes Ashore. A Fugitive Crosses his Tracks* (1933 rev. 1955; tr. 1936), which appeared in America with an introduction by Sigrid Undset, marks the beginning of his mature manner. It is a series of deep investigations into the mind of a murderer, a skilful assemblage of fragments. *Horns for Our Adornment* (1936; tr. 1939) and *September* (1939) return to the subjects of the sea and sailors. *The Coal-Tar Seller* (1945) is about a swindler. Sandemose, one of Norway's most interesting writers, concentrated in most of his mature fiction on Strindbergian (q.v.) themes of love and murder: *The Werewolf* (1958; tr. 1966) is characteristic.

JOHAN BORGEN (1902), born in Oslo, began by writing in the manner of Hamsun (q.v.). Since the war he has established himself as a leading novelist with *Days of White Bread* (1948), the ironic *News on the Subject of Love* (1952) and with the trilogy *Lillelord* (1955–7), whose main theme is the problem of preserving individual identity under the Nazi occupation. This is an extreme example of his central concern: people's means of achieving themselves in the web of deceit in the midst of which they live.

*

Ibsen was a world figure; his immediate Norwegian successor, GUNNAR HEIBERG (1857–1929), did not reach this eminence. He was unfortunate in having a repulsive physical appearance, which frustrated his ambitions to become an actor. He was, like Ibsen, a follower of Brandes (q.v.), and he broke with the conservative traditions of his family in order to know what friends—including bohemians—he wished to know. His radicalism and cosmopolitanism naturally led him to attack Bjørnson. Because he had necessarily to live in the shadow of Ibsen, Heiberg has not had his due outside Norway. His first play, *Aunt Ulrikke* (1883), is an Ibsenian exposure of social hypocrisy. *King Midas* (1890) attacked 'the uncrowned King of Norway', Bjørnson, the darling of polite society, and caused a fierce uproar: Heiberg was determined to make the best of physical ugliness. It is in fact an effective attack on Bjørnson's brand of moral purity, which could be unpleasant. His best plays, however, are *The Balcony* (1894; tr. 1922) and *The Tragedy of Love* (1904; CCD). The first act of the former is hilarious. A woman just manages to conceal her lover, with whom she has spent the night, from her unexpectedly early husband by getting him onto the balcony. He has then to explain his early presence by evincing a desire to buy the house. The husband agrees, says that the property is sound, and to prove it leaps onto the balcony—which collapses, precipitating him to his death. All this and the comic sequel is presented deadpan: in a lyrical prose. It was attacked by the moralists for its 'unsoundness'. More amusing still, the 'modernists' praised it. Played in the right way today it would bring the house down; nor would Heiberg turn in his grave. The balcony (through which a lover no. 2 gains entry, and through which husband no. 2—the original lover—then makes his departure) is not a 'crass' symbol (as it has been called) but a comic one—the whole thing, surely, anticipates Sternheim. To suggest that Heiberg is nearer to the truly crass Sudermann (q.v.) is to miss the point. *The Tragedy of Love* is on the theme of the artist as solitary as well as on that of woman-as-insatiable-lover (Heiberg had two bad marriages with only one satisfactory mistress between).

Lie, Kielland, Hamsun and Kinck (qq.v.) all made contributions to the theatre, as did other novelists, such as Bojer (q.v.), after them. But the modern Norwegian theatre belongs mainly to HELGE KROG (1889–1962) and NORDAHL GRIEG (1902–43). Krog, always a lively figure on the Norwegian scene, is in some ways the natural successor to Heiberg—but not in any narrow sense. He also achieved a more effective dialogue. Krog's social drama, all on the side of enlightenment and against bourgeois pseudo-morality, includes *On the Way* (1931; tr. 1939) and *Break Up* (1936; tr. 1939). He wrote *Don Juan* (1930) in collaboration with Sigurd Hoel. All these are very much in the Ibsenite tradition, and are well and unpretentiously done. His ostensibly light comedy, however, is also extremely good, and perhaps in this form he is more original. Typical of this genre is *Triad* (1933; tr. 1934). Krog was a useful man to have around: intelligent, tolerant, highly talented, skilful and, above all, an excellent polemicist who thoroughly enjoyed being the bad boy of Norwegian literature between the wars.

Nordahl Grieg was the most influential member of the younger generation in Norway between the wars. He had been to sea and to Oxford, and was active as a journalist. He travelled widely: China, Spain, Russia. He was one of the enthusiasms of Malcolm Lowry (q.v. 1), who also went young to sea. Grieg was a poet, novelist and dramatist—but his chief influence was certainly in the theatre. He was receptive to a host of influences, including those of Kipling (q.v. 1) and Marx. He did not have time to reconcile the man-of-action in himself with the intellectual. For a time he was a Marxist, as he demonstrated in the anti-war play *Our Honour and Our Might* (1935) and in *Defeat* (1937; tr. 1945), about the Paris Commune. The latter influenced Brecht (q.v.) in his own play on the Commune. He joined the free Norwegian forces in London, worked as a propagandist, and in 1943 was shot down on an American bombing mission over Berlin. Grieg wrote some lucid early poetry, a good novel about his experiences at sea, *The Ship Sails On* (1925; tr. 1927), and other excellent journalistic prose; but it is as a dramatist, especially in the two plays mentioned above, that he was most appreciated. His role as Norwegian hero is really less significant. A volume of his war poems, *War Poems*, appeared in English in 1944; but this gives no idea of his real creative capacities. His early work, though, is his best.

Two other Norwegian dramatists should be mentioned. ASLAUG

VAA (1889) is perhaps primarily a poet, but her lyrical plays, especially *The Stone God* (1938) are interesting and effective. The *landsmål* writer TORE ØRJASÆTER (1886), also primarily a poet, composed two notable expressionist plays: *Anne* (1933), and *Christophoros* (1948). The expressionism is of Strindberg's variety (both are dream-plays), but Ørjasæter uses that form only to put in a content very much his own. The younger TORMOD SKAGESTAD (1920) has tried to revive the verse drama, influenced by Eliot and, alas, Fry (qq.v. 1).

*

The first modernist in Norwegian poetry was a minor poet, the consumptive and mentally disturbed SIGBJØRN OBSTFELDER (1866–1900). Obstfelder was the first to recognize the importance of Edvard Munch, the painter who has already been mentioned in connection with expressionism (q.v.). He was a kindred spirit. He wrote, in a lyrical free verse, of his feelings of alienation from the world. Unlike such a poet as Campana (q.v. 3), however, his anguish is not resolved in even a handful of poems, and the final impression is of a sickly rather than a dynamic decadence. One seldom finds anything better than:

> The day it is passing in laughter and song.
> Death he is sowing the whole night long.
> Death he is sowing.
>
> (TCSP)

VILHELM KRAG (1871–1933) is less decadent, and some of his poetry about his native Sørlandet has an old-fashioned charm; but he is similarly weak. (TCSP)

More important are Olav Aukrust and Olav Bull. OLAV AUKRUST (1883–1929) wrote in *landsmål*. He combines love of the Norwegian peasantry and landscape with a mysticism that he acquired by reading Indian and Persian literature. He is a lyrical poet of much greater power than Krag, but his work has inevitably dated. (TCSP)

OLAV BULL (1883–1933), however, is the first really important modern Norwegian poet: he is ironic, sophisticated, capable of assimilating cosmopolitan influence, and an excellent technician. Bull was, one feels, the first Norwegian poet to really understand what modernism was about. In fact some of his work has been condemned for 'introspection' by critics who understand it less well than he did. He learned particularly from the philosophy of Bergson and the poetry of Valéry. But because he was an intellectual it must not be thought that he was not a lyrical poet: he was, but a fastidious one. Comparison with Valéry is a little far-fetched; but at his best—not in such poems as the popular 'Metope'—when he is self-critical and ironic but still moved, he is very good indeed. (TCSP)

The leading Norwegian poet in some people's minds was ARNULF ØVERLAND (1889–1968), who swung from a strongly pro-German attitude in the First World War to a socialism that led the Nazis, provoked by the clandestine circulation of his patriotic poems, to put him in a camp in 1942. When he was released in 1945 he was Norway's most honoured poet. But it must be admitted that his earlier individualistic poetry is on the whole his best. This is tragic, romantic, lonely—but tersely expressed, as though the form criticized the content. This is the poet of such collections as *The Hundred Violins* (1912). By the time of *Bread and Wine* (1924) he had become almost a socialist realist, and he continued in this vein. But in his post-war poetry—having witnessed Russian leaders' betrayal of communism—he has developed a new and stridently anti-modernist manner that is not wholly satisfactory: it seems to reflect the critical intentions of his intellect rather than those of his imagination. However, all his work is characterized by vitality, formal excellence and a poetic know-how that prevents it from declining into absolutely prosy diatribes. (TCSP)

Tore Ørjasæter's (q.v.) concerns are broadly those of Uppdal and Duun (qq.v.)—the impact of the industrial revolution on the peasantry—but he has increasingly incorporated his own metaphysics into his poetry, which frankly anthropomorphizes nature, as in 'The Kiss'. (TCSP)

HERMAN WILDENVEY (ps. HERMAN PORTAAS, 1886–1959) introduced a new and welcome note of insouciant humour into Norwegian poetry, which on the whole is ponderous, like their winter, rather than sparkling, like the dance of sunlight in their fiords. Like Bull, Wildenvey enjoyed living as he wished to live. This led the aged Bjørnson (q.v.) to say of his first volume, *Bonfires* (1907): 'I suppose he is not such a swine as he makes himself out to be'. Wildenvey genuinely developed, for while he retained his easy, colloquial tone (of which he was a master), his poetry deepened in thought and feeling. He seems to have developed his happy manner from having studied for a year within the grim confines of an American theological seminary. But in his later poems a concern with religion returns. A selection of his poetry (*Owls to Athens*, 1934) was translated by Joseph Auslander.

It is difficult to classify TARJEI VESAAS (1897–1970), who was a *landsmål* writer, born in Vinje, Telemark: he has done many good things in poetry, drama and fiction. He was an exceedingly live and versatile writer: the kind of intelligent, vital and curious author that no literature can afford to be without. Since 1946 he received a 'State Artist's Salary'—something which in Great Britain, if it existed, would betoken a mediocrity or an aristocrat, but which, in Norway, exercises few pressures, hidden or otherwise. He was an instrument sensitive to the developments of modern literature—and therefore to the developments of the world. His experimentalism amounted to no more than his desire to be this: to record his own complex reactions to life. His great gift was the consummately Norwegian one of relating people to landscape and of symbolizing their unconscious feelings for one another through descriptions of landscape. He begins a poem:

> Talk of home—
> Snow and fir forests
> Are home.
>
> From the very first
> It is ours.
> Before anyone ever said it.
> That it *is* snow and fir forests,
> It is here within us,
> And then it remains
> Always, always.
>   (TCSP)

His plays have not been as successful as other work, but he cultivated the radio play effectively. He realized himself most fully in his fiction, to the complexities of which his poetry is a useful index. A number of novels have now been translated including *The Ice Palace* (1963; tr. 1965) and *The Seed* (1940; tr. 1966), his best. *The Seed* describes an island in the grip of a collective madness, brought on by a madman, that affects animals and human beings alike. *The Ice Palace*, more ambitious, is about identical twins, one of whom attempts to explore a frozen waterfall (the ice palace of the title) alone. She is destroyed when it melts, and her sister tries to recreate her perfectly in her memory. Both these books—clearly, like much of Vesaas' fiction, influenced by Kafka—are full of possibilities. Unfortunately characterization would have strengthened the later one—and here the author fails. He succeeds magnificently in evoking the landscapes against which the dramas are played, but almost perversely neglects psychology. Since his fiction is almost exclusively devoted to trying to pinpoint the kind of bestiality that produces fascists and tyrants, and therefore war, this is a serious lack. As the history of German expressionism shows, neither a wholly instinctive nor a wholly intellectual reaction to the obscene processes by which men desire to acquire power over one another is adequate. Mankind needs a sense of psychology to deal with its Hitlers and Stalins—as we see in the unhappy cases of Pirandello (q.v. 3) and Mussolini, and Wyndham Lewis (q.v. 1) and Hitler. But Vesaas was none the less dedicated and, in his sphere, of remarkable authority. The early *The Great Cycle* (1967) is outstanding.

Norwegian poets since after the First World War have searched for new means of expression, means that would somehow reconcile and resolve their inner conflicts: between tradition and the new, order and anarchy, the collective and the individual. PAAL BREKKE (1922) translated *The Waste Land* (q.v. 1), which has had its effect—not a very impressive one, because it came more than twenty-five years after its appearance in English. TOR JONSSON (1916–51) is the chief representative of the neo-lyrical reaction to modernism. (TCSP) JAN-MAGNUS BRUHEIM (1914), a farmer, woodcutter and violinist from Gudbrandsdalen, in whose dialect he writes, is another lucid and deliberately unsophisticated poet (TCSP), as is GUNVOR HOFMO (1921), whose poems make an almost Platonic appeal to the secret world that resides in nature. (TCSP)

The leading modernist poets between the wars were CLAES GILL (1910), EMIL BOYSON (1900) and ROLF JACOBSEN (1907). In the Thirties Boyson wrote a love-poetry that reminds one more of the Victorian poet Coventry Patmore than of anyone else, although it is more genuinely philosophical than Patmore's, With *Hidden in Shadows* (1939) he became more self-consciously modernistic in style. (TCSP) Gill was much influenced by Boyson; his reading of Yeats has caused him to try to achieve a resonant, emotionally fully satisfying style that yet preserves the essentials of modernism. He has more recently been active in the theatre. (TCSP)

Jacobsen was Norway's violent and mindless modernist. An imitator of Whitman's technique, influenced by Jensen's (q.v.) more authentically Whitmanesque American verse, Jacobsen introduced this century's technological clatter into Norwegian poetry. He might have been a Cendrars (q.v.) or a Mayakovsky (q.v. 4), but instead joined the Nazis when they invaded Norway, and thus more resembled Marinetti (q.v. 3). Later poetry is anti-technological.

Much of GUNNAR REISS-ANDERSEN's (1896–1964) work was spoiled by over-fluency and preciosity, but he occasionally succeeded in recording his confusions in a memorable poem. His best work was written in the war in the spirit of Øverland's anti-Nazi poetry; he was able to escape to Sweden. (TCSP)

The outstanding post-war novelist is possibly AGNAR MYKLE (1915). He is known in English-speaking countries for his trilogy: *The Hotel Room* (1951; tr. 1963), *Lasso Round the Moon* (1954; tr. 1960) and *The Song of the Red Ruby* (1955; tr. 1961); and for *Rubicon* (1966; tr. 1966). In all these novels the same character (although in two of them under different names) appears. Mykle combines elements of Thomas Wolfe and D. H. Lawrence (qq.v. 1) with Norwegian earthiness and a troll-like humour. Mykle is a powerful writer, an idealistic, amorous, socialist vitalist; but he is not a satisfactory one. He does not do as much with his energy as he should—it does not hide his rather simplistic bewilderment.

TERJE STIGEN (1922) has written good short stories—*Dead Calm on the Way* (1956)—and some intelligent novels of adventure, such as *The Saga of Åsmund Armodsson* (1958). His latest novel, *Infatuation* (1970), displays deep psychological understanding of the love between a girl student and her schoolmaster. ODD BANG-HANSEN (1908) wrote two impressive anti-war novels, *The Midge and the Lamp* (1949) and *Fly, White Dove!* (1953), and followed these up with some well constructed novellas.

IV

Swedish letters would have taken a quieter course between the forces of conservatism and naturalism had it not been for the restless and frequently highly irritating genius of AUGUST STRINDBERG (1849–1912), the son of a shipping-agent. His mother was an ex-waitress, a fact that he chose to emphasize. Ibsen (q.v.) was a father of the modern theatre—he is indispensable—but Strindberg, who made his torment so much more evident to the world, is of equal historical importance. The founding-father of expressionism in the theatre, he is more obtrusive than Ibsen. One can confidently assign Ibsen to the century in which he lived most of his life; the same cannot apply to Strindberg. But this does not imply a judgement in favour of him; actually, the habit of postulating him as an alternative to Ibsen and then damning him is a wasteful exercise. He achieved less than Ibsen in the dramatic form—because he was too frenetic ever to relax into warmth of feeling—but the quality of his anguish none the less penetrates even into our own times. Ibsen is a classic, and carries the authority of a classic; Strindberg, not a classic, still worries us: we understand his difficulties too well.

Strindberg has rightly been described as 'incorrigibly subjective'; his self-absorption frequently appears and is perverse; but he had to clarify his motives and to explore himself. He became increasingly unstable in his personal life; for example, after his first marriage failed he imagined that European feminists had won his wife Siri over to their side and that they were persecuting him; he had a doctor come with him to a brothel to measure his erect penis in order to counter the rumour that he was 'not a man'. He had his gentle side, out of which came some fiction of charm and sweetness; but his major work is written not from a still centre of wisdom but from a whirling periphery of subjective torment. It does not cast a sober light on life, but illuminates it in lightning flashes. What is 'modern' about Strindberg is that he made no distinction whatever between art and life: he ignored the assumptions of the previous centuries. If expressionism (q.v.) is rightly characterized by a shriek, then Strindberg was the first to open his mouth.

Strindberg's brilliant first novel, *The Red Room* (1879; tr. 1967) was an exposure of social hypocrisy and city rackets—and an account of a young man's painful recovery from idealism. His *The Son of a Servant* (1886–1909; tr. 1967), with its characteristic title, retraces his spiritual development. Much of his prose (one cannot safely call it either autobiography or fiction) records the vicissitudes and major spiritual events of his troubled life: his first marriage (*The Confession of a Fool*, 1895; tr. 1912), the 'inferno' period in Paris, when he was experimenting with alchemy and the occult (*Inferno*, 1897; tr. 1962), the quieter time of his third marriage (1901–4), which ended less violently (*Ensam*, 1903). Other prose by Strindberg is strictly fiction and is, by his standards, objective. In *The People of Hemsö* (1887; tr. 1959) his sense of humour is most apparent, as is his gift for description. This is a story of the people of Stockholm skerries. Its successor, *In the Outer Skerries* (1890), disposes of a 'Nietzschean' (q.v.) superman, Borg, by the strict application of naturalist laws. It is typical of Strindberg that he should have been in the course of his life everything that it was then possible to be: socialist, aristocrat, feminist, anti-feminist, Nietzschean, anti-Nietzschean, Christian, democrat, occultist. . . . *In the Outer Skerries* is ambigous, and illustrates the conflict between his Nietzschean ideas and his Darwinist convictions (inspired in the first place by reading Zola).

But drama was the genre in which Strindberg excelled. His earlier naturalistic plays—*The Father* (1887; tr. 1964), *Miss Julie* (1888; tr. 1964)—mix morbid psychology, of which Strindberg had made himself a master, paranoid fear of women, and hereditary determinism. These do contain an element of Grand Guignol; we should protest at a classification of them as drama of the highest class if only because they exclude too much. But in technique they are nearly perfect, particularly so in their use of silence—and of the silences by which people torment one another.

Later, after his 'inferno' period, Strindberg became a Sweden-borgian—and consequently a symbolist. (Emanuel Swedenborg, 1688–1772, was a Swedish scientist and theologian whose later ideas —which were not mystical—had an important influence on symbolism. Very briefly, he taught that creation is dead, except through God's intervention, through whom man lives. His law of correspondences is popularized by Baudelaire's famous sonnet, q.v.) The first part of his symbolist-expressionist play *To Damascus* (1898–1901; tr. 1959), is considered by some to be the finest of all his work. Others prefer *A Dream Play* (1901; tr. 1963), a highly poetic evocation of human evanescence.

Strindberg exercised an enormous influence in the international theatre; he is also a crucial figure in the development of Swedish literature. He was the dominating figure of the Eighties, and the other writers of this period, who formed the rather amorphous group known as Young Sweden, are overshadowed. In Sweden even the ideas of Brandes filtered through largely by way of Strindberg.

In the Nineties there was the familiar neo-romantic reaction, which may of course be traced in Strindberg himself—as, in Norway, it can in Ibsen.

Sweden's great distinction in literature before Strindberg—whose own poetry is somewhat neglected outside his native country—had been in lyrical poetry. On the whole this has declined—diffusing itself into a number of minor writers rather than remaining in the hands of a few masters; the exceptions can hardly be described as lyric poets. The reaction to naturalism of the leaders of the Nineties, which took the form of a demand for wholesomeness and joy in life, rather than of decadence, were, however, mostly poets. (Count CARL SNOILSKY, 1841–1903, survived into this century but belongs to an earlier era; his attempts to reach the working classes in the early Eighties were not successful.) VERNER VON HEIDENSTAM (1859–1940), together with his friend, the Jewish OSCAR LEVERTIN (1862–1906), wrote *Pepita's Marriage* (1890), a manifesto satirizing naturalist gloom and exalting the role of the imagination. With Strindberg temporarily absent from the scene, this exercised a strong influence on a generation of poets. Heidenstam has been aptly called 'a great national poet *manqué*': he was an exquisite minor who inflated himself into a pretentious magnus rather resembling the later Hauptmann (q.v.), who was, however, a far better writer. His poetry, the best of which is to be found in *Poems* (1895), is visual, pagan and exuberant; he was skilled enough not to misuse the influence of Goethe. But as he developed he tended to cover up his Nietzschean feelings of loneliness and poetic arrogance with, first, a rhetorical patriotism, and later (*New Poems*, 1915) a concentrated classical style. Some of his poetry was translated into English in *Sweden's Laureate* (1919) after he had won the Nobel Prize (1916). His historical fiction contains fine isolated passages, but lacks any real direction: he was a minor writer suffering from a condition of self-appointed greatness. The Nobel award quietened his aspirations, and he lived the last quarter-century of his life in a majestic isolation broken only by the pilgrimages of young men.

Levertin was infinitely more intelligent, more sensitive, more interesting, rather less gifted: the perfect sentimentive (q.v.) foil to Heidenstam's naïvety. Until his early death he was Sweden's leading critic. He began as a social writer, but soon turned to a more personal and romantic style. He is less canny than Heidenstam in hiding his preoccupations. His Pre-Raphaelite interest in antiques, expressed in his poetry, seldom conceals his death-haunted sexuality. The song-cycle *King Solomon and Morolf* (1905) contains some of his best work. Anyone who understands Dante Gabriel Rossetti will understand Levertin.

GUSTAF FRÖDING (1860–1911), who was born in the province of Värmland, produced his poetry against the heavy odds of progressive mental illness and chronic poverty. He spent the last thirteen years of his life in confinement. Before that he had failed socially and academically; but *Guitar and Concertina* (1891; tr. 1930), his first collection of poems, made him Sweden's most popular poet. In it, in clear and charming verse, he writes of the people of his native province. *Splashes and Rags* (1896) contained 'Morning Dream', for whose honest eroticism he was prosecuted. Although acquitted, this experience helped to drive him towards total withdrawal. His finest poetry is collected in *Grail Splashes* (1898); these poems, written on the verge of mental collapse, cluster about the sinister symbol of the grail—a pagan grail. They usually retain the simple surface of the earlier regional ones, but reach more deeply into their author's disturbed mind, in which sexual guilt threatened a Spinozan serenity and faith in the ultimately divine unity of all things. Fröding, especially in his last phase, is a European as well as a Swedish poet; a late romantic who can evoke delight as easily as terror, and whose lyrics have at their most powerful an almost unbearable intensity of feeling. C. W. Stork translated a *Selected Poems* (1916).

ERIK AXEL KARLFELDT (1864–1931) is a modern paradigm of

Sweden's genius for lyrical poetry. He came from the province of Dalecarlia, and did for it what his friend Fröding had done for Värmland. He declined the Nobel Prize (he was on the committee for many years) in 1918, but was awarded it posthumously (1931). His early poetry was influenced by Fröding, but later he developed his own manner. His most popular collections, featuring his bachelor-poet Fridolin, are *Fridolin's Songs* (1898) and *Fridolin's Garden* (1901). These embody old peasant customs that he had noted as still prac- tised in contemporary Dalecarlia. He is more than a country poet, however, for he uses flora and country customs as symbols for his re- strained but ecstatic eroticism. His later poetry deepened in mood and texture: less overtly gay and carefree, it expresses moods of sadness and fear of death. Particularly notable are his versions of Biblical stories—set in Dalecarlia—which date from the turn of the century. These have the swing and verve of a Vachel Lindsay (q.v. 1), as in 'The Sea Voyage of Jonah'.

And they grab him without heeding
His insistent, frantic pleading:
'Can't you see I am a prophet and a holy man at that!'
But they answer: 'Where you're heading
You can practise water treading
Though undoubtedly you'll float, O prophet, on your priestly fat!'
Upside down is Jonah in the midst of his descent
With his frock coat round his head and flapping like a tent.
In the horrid depths below
We behold a double row
Of the gaping monster's gleaming teeth on bloody murder bent.

(TCSP)

BO BERGMAN (1869–1967) had a long and distinguished career as a good minor poet and dramatic critic in his native Stockholm. His predominantly melancholy mood is caught in his lines 'Not happi- ness but yearning/Desire for it makes us sing'. He developed from a decadent pessimist into a humanist wryly concealing his scepticism in an elegant, urban poetry. He is the poet, above all, of the Stockholm winter. He was in fact one of the earliest of the European urban poets—what his close friend Söderberg did in prose he did in verse— and his prime historical importance lies in his initiation of a poetry entirely stripped of rhetoric and the habit of poeticizing. He is among the first of the anti-romantics: in his early poetry he distrustfully chops down emotion to an ironic slightness. Later he modified his powerful sexuality in a series of restrained urban descriptions and nostalgias. His mood is often that of Fargue (q.v.), or, even more, of a Bacovia (q.v. 3)—but in place of Bacovia's instability of mood he substitutes a robust humour. Bergman is a very good minor writer; he wrote excellent novels and short stories, including *The Ship* (1915).

Two other poets may be associated with Bergman in initiating this new and more restrained mood, although the approach of each was entirely different. VILHELM EKELUND (1880–1949), who came from Skåne, was an eccentric and semi-mystical sage whose influence is yet to be felt—or not felt. From 1908 until 1921 he was out of Sweden; when he returned he lived poorly, supported only by a small group of admirers. His importance lies in his introduction into Swedish poetry, in his early collections, of a skillfully modulated free (perhaps irregular is the better word) verse. From the year of his voluntary exile he turned to an aphoristic prose that reflects his intelligent successive assimilations of various thinkers and writers (including Nietzsche, George, qq.v., and others more ancient) rather than any personal development. For all but devotees, his best work is contained in his seven collections of poetry, in which he seems to be more himself. They are not perhaps much more than Shelleyan hymns to ineffable beauty, and anyone who is familiar with the best of romantic poetry will recognize their unoriginality; but their free form and phraseology are, respectively, masterful and beautiful; they helped by their example to free Swedish poets from restrictions. (TCSP)

ANDERS ÖSTERLING (1884), at first a symbolist, later brought his understanding of Wordsworth to bear on his poetry, and thus contributed importantly to the new simplicity of diction of which Swedish poets were in search. He was more distinguished as translator than poet, but his own simple poems about the places and people of Skåne, in southernmost Sweden, have their modest place. He adapted Wordsworth's direct treatment of rural characters to his own environment with some success. (TCSP)

DAN ANDERSSON (1888–1920), born in Dalecarlia, was concerned with the proletariat in his poems and novels, and is one of the initiators of modern Swedish 'proletarian' literature; but he was no Marxist. He was concerned less with class-struggle than with what he could make of the actual lives of poor people, which he knew because he was one. He was himself a charcoal-burner in a region of Dalecarlia where impoverished communities of Finnish origin lived their own idiosyncratic and deprived lives: he was concerned with the mystery of this kind of existence rather than with social improvement. His autobiographical novels, *Three Homeless Ones* (1918) and

David Ramm's Heritage (1919), are clumsy but broodingly intense. *Charcoal-Burner's Ballad and Other Poems* (1915) was translated in 1943. *Black Ballads* (1917), however, contains his most achieved poetry. (TCSP)

BIRGER SJÖBERG (1885–1929) was an embryonic Brecht (q.v.), who in the years after the First World War sang his songs to his own guitar accompaniment. He began as an entertainer, but disgust with bourgeois society gradually drove him into a subversive attitude which he could not successfully integrate into his popular perform- ances. He ended by being driven literally to madness and death. *Frida's Book* (1922) contains his ballads of small town life; *Crises and Wreaths* (1926) some of his later, more important and more angry poetry. Three posthumous volumes appeared: work reflecting his rancour and rage against bureaucracy and complacency. His con- ventional verse is charming but somewhat *kitsch*; his more serious poetry incorporates elements of terror and rage expressed in a racy language that has had an influence on later poets. (TCSP)

Perhaps less important, but nevertheless immensely gifted and vital is EVERT TAUBE (1890), also a singer of his own songs. These are often about his early life as a sailor and his life in Argentina between 1910 and 1915. Taube is in a great Swedish tradition, running from Sweden's greatest poet Carl Michael Bellman to himself (with whom it seems it will die—falling into the hands of popsters and com- mercialities), of the singer-poet. He is a light poet, but an authentic one.

Little need be said of BERTIL MALMBERG (1889–1958) except that he was a skilful technician who varied from an inflated pseudo-philo- sophical poetry to jolly aphorisms. His late transformation to a modernistic style (which he attributed to the effects of a brain haemorrhage) is unconvincing and need not be taken seriously. He was for a time an adherent of the Oxford Movement: an indication of the quality of his mind, which did not match his capacities as a craftsman. Thus he could write: 'The one thing on earth/You may trust in still/Is not what you feel,/But what you will.' (TCSP)

HJALMAR GULLBERG (1898–1961), born in Malmö and for a long time a theatrical director of Swedish radio, had a more interesting development, rooted in his linguistic rather than in his emotional or intellectual reactions. His early poetry was traditional in form, con- cerning itself with themes both Christian and classical. He then used poetry to express a series of moods: he can be Hardyesque ('Someone from eternity/Arranges for his exalted pleasure/With comets and suns/A great display)', ironically sentimental, straightforwardly erotic, or, perhaps most characteristically, find a basis for his mysticism in the everyday. This early poetry is written in a deliberately conversational, anti-poetical style. It was extremely popular in the Thirties; but after the Second World War (in which of course Sweden remained neutral and unoccupied by the Nazis), the new generation not altogether fairly condemned it as tending to the middlebrow. He responded with three collections of poems in a new style: more highly charged, sceptical, closely packed. Gullberg was a translator from Sophocles, Lorca and other important European poets. (TCSP; sel. tr. F. Fleisher, *Seven Swedish Poets*, 1963)

*

By the beginning of the Thirties a 'culture debate' was in progress. Heidenstam's (q.v.) sentimental patriotism has been succeeded by a more socialistic and viable kind of nationalism. But this manifested itself in prose; it was insufficient for poets. Bourgeois culture was attacked by the proletarian Marxists, by the Freudians and by 'primitivism' (Martinson, Lundkvist, qq.v.). The most intelligent faction gathered around the magazine *Spektrum*.

KARIN BOYE (1900–41), a psychologist, Sweden's most outstanding modern woman poet, represented a synthesis of all three attitudes. Some of her earlier poetry—technically influenced by Ekelund (q.v.) —is over-idealistic and over-intense: a compost of unassimilated influences. Translating Eliot's *Waste Land* (q.v. 1) in the early Thirties helped her to find a manner of her own. Karin Boye's was a tragic personality. She abandoned Christianity for Freud and socialism, and ended as a desperate and reluctant Marxist; but the rise of totalitarianism disturbed her essentially religious nature so much that she killed herself. Her best poetry describes the mysteries of transformation and ageing; her poetry of political anguish is less good, although moving. This was more effectively expressed in the totalitarian novel *Kallocain* (1940; tr. 1966), which belongs, in intensity and horror, with Orwell's *1984* (q.v. 1). *The Seven Deadly Sins* (1941) is her final, posthumous collection. Her early fiction was unsuccessful, but *Too Little* (1936), a novel about a writer of genius destroyed by his domestic environment, deserves mention. But Karin Boye was above all a poet, whose best poems are among the most beautiful and original to have been written in Sweden in the present century. She inevitably reminds the English-speaking reader of Sylvia Plath (q.v. 1); but her work, while it matches Sylvia Plath's in intensity of manner, is more substantial and controlled. 'My Skin is Full of Butterflies' is characteristic:

My skin is full of butterflies, of flutterwings—
They flutter out over the field, enjoying their honey
And flutter home and die in sad little spasms,
No flowerdust is stirred by gentle feet.
For them the sun—hot, boundless, older than the ages . . .

But under skin and blood and within the marrow
Heavily heavily move captive sea-eagles
Spread-winged, never releasing their prey.
How would you frolic in the sea's spring storm
And cry when the sun brought yellow eyes to glow?

Closed the cavern! Closed the cavern!
Between the claws, writhing, white as cellar-sprouts, sinewy strands

Of my innermost self.

(TCSP)

*

ARTUR LUNDKVIST (1906) was a Marxist and a 'primitivist'; but in
the late Twenties Lundkvist, with Martinson (q.v.), treated here
primarily as a prose writer—together with GUSTAV SANDGREN (1904),
JOSEF KJELLGREN (1907–48), both now better known for their proletarian novels than for their verse, and ERIK ASKLUND (1908)—made
his début in the collection *Five Young Ones* (1929). This marked an
important stage in Swedish poetry, for it introduced to it such diverse
influences as D. H. Lawrence (q.v. 1), Whitman, Sandburg (q.v. 1)
and others, and drew attention to the neighbouring voice of Finnish-
Swedish poetry (Björling, Södergran, qq.v.). Lundkvist has great
energy and talent, but is derivative and has nothing of his own to say.
That he should have been regarded (1974) as a serious contender for
the Nobel Prize—not that he got it—is testimony to the Swedes'
habit of overrating their literature.

The poet regarded by most critics as Sweden's most original and
greatest of this century is GUNNAR EKELÖF (1907–68). Karin Boye
may have been neglected in this respect; but Ekelöf deserves his
reputation. He is a genuinely philosophical and mystical (rather than
existential) poet, of great persistence and integrity. He lived much of
the latter part of his life in seclusion. For Ekelöf thought and inner
feeling *are* experience, and his poetry is a continual attempt to define
his position. Ekelöf's poetry is primarily rooted in Swedish literature
—in Fröding and, technically, in Ekelund (qq.v.); but he became
aware of Rimbaud (whom he translated in the early Thirties) and
surrealism (q.v.) before most other Swedish poets. His work also has

affinities with the 'cubist' poetry of Reverdy (q.v.). There is also a strongly oriental—particularly Sufic—element in his poetry. His writing has always been exceedingly esoteric and personal, and none of it yields its meaning without long acquaintance. His first book, *Late Hour on Earth* (published by the Spektrum Press), surrealistic in manner, reflected his solipsist despair at being unable, as a person, to break through to the objects of his own perceptions, which consequently appear as hallucinated and menacing. The poet he is nearest to here is certainly Reverdy; though he most admired Desnos (q.v.). The poet's isolation affects the whole field of his contemplation. (Experience in an existential sense counts for nothing at all.)

> The nerves screech silently in the dying light
> which flows through the window grey and delicate
> the red flowers silently feel their wounds in the dying light
> and the lamp sings on lonely in a corner
> (tr. *Late Arrival on Earth: Selected Poems*, 1967)

On a less personal level, these first poems assail—with a highly sophisticated irony—what is petrified in the bourgeois culture. Ekelöf does not of course exempt or spare himself. He has called the collection 'a suicide book' because in it he set out to do no less than strip himself of all bourgeois illusion—and his approach is not political but highly personal—in at least a mental sense. He risked self-destruction. Like Ungaretti (q.v. 3) he seeks to return to the primitive, the real, the human situation; but he does not take Ungaretti's specifically verbal approach, and he also desires a more denatured—philosophical—version of the primitive. It makes him into a formidable poet; but a good deal of the early work is over-programmatic and repeats the content of surrealist manifestos ('To the overwhelming and general stupidity, to the state and the laws, the family and the Church, lies and fears, with hatred,/In order to violate false innocence, to ravage the lovely false-fronts . . .').

In his books of the next twenty years Ekelöf, with some lapses, tried to 'become like himself': in other words, to locate himself among the objects (including people) of his perception. Erik Lindegren (q.v.), in an informative essay, has described Ekelöf's division of people into three categories: the naïve, innocent, timid, wild people who have not been tempted by dualism; the committed moralists, who identify with what they believe in, 'partly enlightened, partly prisoners'; and those who reject rationalism, who see morality as 'totalitarian opium'. This third ('authentic'?) type is familiar enough, although Ekelöf's division is highly original—and valuable. Ekelöf's search for a valid identity reveals itself in the later collections: *Trash* (1955), *Opus Incertum* (1959), *A Night in Otočac* (1961), *Diwan* (1965) and *The Tale of Fatumeh* (1966).

Ekelöf is undoubtedly a major poet, and one who repays close study. If he is not a great one then this would be because nearly all his poetry deliberately deals in abstractions: seems to lack flesh and blood. But then, it may be argued, his is a poetry of abstraction: of how man is assailed by abstractions. ... 'Come and help me', he asks in 'Monologue with his wife'; 'I am vanishing./He has a grip on me, he transforms me, the god over there in the corner whispering'. He is a true modern metaphysical, and he will almost certainly prove to be a prophetic poet. (TCSP; *Selected Poems*, tr. 1967; another *Selected Poems*, 1971.)

Ekelöf's only slightly younger contemporary ERIK LINDEGREN (1910) was profoundly influenced by both him and surrealism; he is contemporary Sweden's foremost experimental poet. He first became known in the Forties, as one of those defenders of liberty (in a neutral country) who also assured the victory of modernism. Although Swedish compromise during the years 1939–45 was prudent in the circumstances, these writers (grouped around the magazine *40-tal*) nevertheless felt morally contaminated. The two most important members of this pessimistic group were Lindegren and Vennberg (q.v.). Others included RAGNAR THOURSIE (1919) and WERNER ASPENSTRÖM (1918), who founded and co-edited *40-tal*. Thoursie is a poet of menace, clearly influenced by Ekelöf but more on the attack: he arranges the familiar paraphernalia of everyday life in threatening patterns. (TCSP) Aspenström approaches the same material in a more lyrical manner. (TCSP) Lindegren, who feels that he is being 'fitted into the wall of hatred like the grey stone' even while he senses 'the community of stones', reacts to his predicament with a disjointed poetry, whose lyricism is only evident in fragments. His *The Man Without a Way* (tr. *New Directions*, 20, 1968; pt. TCSP) consists of forty 'broken sonnets', and is self-evidently a preparation for action: a concrete statement of commitment, made in this form because no other (say, a conventionally coherent one) would be adequate. This work eventually became a classic statement for the succeeding generations. It consists of an 'inner' poetry of surrealistic surface but carefully worked out internal structure. Lindegren does not have Ekelöf's intensity, and there is something lucubrated about his most indignant poetry; but the sincerity of the violent experience is unquestionable. By contrast KARL VENNBERG (1910) is both more accessible and tougher; his brand of socialism is also more straightforward. He is a polemicist (particularly for a 'Third World' attitude to the East-West conflict), and in his poetry a refreshing sceptic with an eye for the detail of the world of nature and sex that he loves and feels is being torn asunder by rigidly held ideas.

LARS FORSSELL (1928) is an experimentalist who blends together a specifically Swedish lyrical note, internationalism (sometimes glib and suspect), and a revival of old popular forms, and of the fable and idyll. In his earlier poetry he functioned behind the masks of a pathetic clown or a petrified bourgeois—for example, *F. C. Tietjens* (1954), a kind of Swedish Chaplin or M. Plume (q.v.). His later poetry is more mannered. Sheer virtuosity, versatility and a capacity for writing too irresponsibly in the vaguely surrealistic 'continental manner' are his worst enemies. (TCSP) Infinitely more serious in TOMAS TRANSTRÖMER (1931), a psychologist who has the rare ability to express his inner world in coherent external terms. Robert Bly has brilliantly translated *20 Poems* (1970).

*

The novelist SELMA LAGERLÖF (1858–1940) won the Nobel Prize (1909). She became in her later years stupid and out of touch; but the Swedish public loved her, and not too foolishly. Few of her books (most of which were translated into English) are without merit and insight into the ways of her native Värmland; but it is for her first novel, *The Story of Gösta Berling* (1891; tr. 1898) that she will be remembered. This is a book that will survive, as those by her Norwegian fellow Nobel Prize winner, Sigrid Undset (q.v.), will not. It is really a series of stories—rather than a novel—the hero of which is the womanizing Gösta, a defrocked priest, drunkard and poet. The time is an indeterminate past, the place, of course, Värmland. Selma Lagerlöf's style here is a mixture of rhetoric, inherited from Carlyle, and lucidity. *The Story of Gösta Berling* is epic in its range, shot through with real romance and vitality, and certainly a great book. Succeeding novels are often good, but lack the classic sweep of this. In *The Wonderful Adventures of Nils* (1906–7; tr. 1907) she wrote possibly the best educational book of all time: a geographical portrait of Sweden seen from the back of a goose. *Thy Soul Shall Bear Witness!* (1912; tr. 1921) should be mentioned as a good novel of the supernatural. Selma Lagerlöf is one of the last great naïve epic writers. Her intuitive genius enabled her to invent tales of great complexity from raw folk material.

PER HALLSTRÖM (1866–1960) remained in a conservative and moralistic tradition, but is perhaps neglected today. His self-conscious quest for beauty, in poems, novels and plays, is dull and dated; but his sincere pessimism (learned from Schopenhauer) and sense of the macabre emerge in certain short stories.

His contemporary HJALMAR SÖDERBERG (1869–1941), however, who went in the opposite direction, is a more important writer. He is a fascinating figure, whose sustained and systematic campaign against Christianity (mostly in his last, and creatively inactive, twenty-five years) has led to his work being undervalued. He was the friend of Bo Bergman (q.v.), and did in prose for turn-of-the-century Stockholm —where he was born—what Bergman did in verse: the city's atmosphere is conveyed more precisely and evocatively in *Marti Birck's Youth* (1901; tr. 1930) than in any other Swedish prose. Söderberg was a naturalist, but a Swedish naturalist: he believed in Darwinism and fate, but always at the back of his mind there lurked the more-than-suspicion that trolls, fairies and even more mysterious entities might be directing fate. He was ready, then, for Freud— whom he read and understood early. His fiction has a special glow, which comes out in his poetic and ironic short stories (*Selected Short Stories*; tr. 1935). *Doctor Glas* (1905; tr. 1963) is a neglected master- piece: one of this century's great novels—and one of the earliest to utilize Freud's discoveries in an intelligent and unsensational manner It was of course entirely passed by in its time. It tells of the murder, by the lonely Dr. Glas, of his attractive patient's husband, a repulsive and demanding Lutheran—a murder that brings him nothing. Cast in the form of Dr. Glas's own journal, it catches, inimitably, the moods of Stockholm in the early years of this century. Söderberg wrote one more novel, *The Evening Star* (1912), a love story, like his successful play, *Gertrud* (1906). His short stories have not been bettered by any Scandinavian writer. It is said that he lacks 'robust- ness'; but this judgement may well reflect a sly distaste for his un- sensational and persuasive pessimism. His anti-Christian essays are as superbly argued as his stand against Nazism in the Thirties was prophetically accurate. He learned from Jacobsen, Bang and Anatole France (qq.v.), but discovered his own manner early. He is certainly a more important writer than France, who merely served him, in his youth, as a model of scepticism. His second wife was Danish, and he spent the last twenty-four years of his life in Denmark. He is a major writer, and urgently due for reappraisal.

*

Swedish 'proletarian' literature is unique in Europe: a number of largely self-taught writers have investigated working-class life with- out any discipline imposed from above. GUSTAV HEDENVIND-ERIKSSON

(1880–1967) was one of the pioneers of this literature. He wrote with consistent intelligence about the lives of railway-constructors and, in the Fifties, of those employed in the modern Swedish timber industry. The self-taught MARTIN KOCH (1882–1940) was a more imaginative writer, whose silence in the last twenty years of his life is to be explained by his guilt at being more interested in the psychology of his proletarian characters than in their struggle to achieve social parity. Influenced by Upton Sinclair and Jack London (qq.v.), Koch was essentially an inspired chronicler of the dregs of Stockholm: *God's Beautiful World* (1916) is a memorable depiction of oppressed scum: it is a novel of despair, paradoxically contrasting an evil urban vitality with a benign, moribund pastoralism.

VILHELM MOBERG (1898–1973), another autodidact, belongs to the 'proletarian' school; he is a puzzling writer, since he has persisted in combining a facility for producing successful midcult fiction with literary qualities that cannot be ignored. *The Earth is Ours* (1935–9; tr. 1940), a trilogy, about Knut Toring who leaves his south Swedish home for the big city but then feels impelled to return to and come to terms with it, is probably his best novel. It is markedly successful in its depiction of Swedish social and economic problems of the time. Moberg's famous novels about Swedish nineteenth-century immigrants to the U.S.A.—*The Emigrants* (1949; tr. 1956), *Unto a Good Land* (1952; tr. 1957), *Last Letter Home* (1956–9; tr. 1961)—are less good. They have a pseudo-epic air; but at the same time they incorporate much valuable reportage.

More cosmopolitan than Moberg is EYVIND JOHNSON (1900), born at Boden. He is more aware of contemporary mental stress. *The Novel of Olof* (1934–7) is an autobiographical series, describing his adolescence and hard apprenticeship as a timberman. *Return to Ithaca* (1946; tr. 1952) is a modern version of the *Odyssey; The Days of his Grace* (1960; tr. 1965), is a dissection of the totalitarian spirit set in the time of Charlemagne. The massive but laboured *Krilon* (1941–3) trilogy should also be mentioned: an allegory of Nazism and neutrality. Johnson is an intelligent writer, prolific but sophisticated. He is, however, too restlessly experimental. He won the Nobel Prize (1974).

HARRY MARTINSON (1904) is internationally the best known of the Swedish 'proletarians'. Orphaned at six, he had a tough and nasty early life; eventually he became a sailor and continental wanderer. He has recorded some of his adventures in *Cape Farewell* (1933; tr. 1936). He began as an adherent of 'primitivism', and pretended to believe in the goodness of mankind and the imminent victory of the proletarian struggle; but actually he is and always has been a lyrical nihilist and loner. *The Road* (1948; tr. 1955), his best book, a novel about tramps, makes his position clear: the answer to industrialization and the technological plans of politicians is to preserve your individuality and freedom by taking to the road. Martinson's poetry in shorter forms is his best; the rest is spoiled by being inflated into grandiose statements of his 'philosophy', a tedious and pretentious mystical primitivism. *Aniara* (1956; tr. 1963), for example, a long poem in 103 cantos about a space-ship drifting irremediably into the void, is unfortunately as puerile in general conception as it is interesting in detail (one of its translators, Hugh McDiarmid, is himself a naïve polymath of the Martinson type). It should be added that this view of Martinson, although by no means new, is a minority one. The general consensus is that, in the words of Dr. Tord Hall, 'Martinson is a pioneer of the poetry of the Atomic Age. No poet before him has tackled the formidable task of studying Man with the aid of modern science ... observing him in the astronomical perspective of the two-hundred-inch reflector at Mount Palomar ... work whose symphonic breadth derives from one shuddering theme —Man's journey through his own emptiness, humanity's fall away from earth, into the trackless void'. Dr. Tord Hall deserves, as one of England's best living poets has remarked, to eat his own christian name. But Martinson shared the 1974 Nobel Prize with Johnson.

But this writer has been overrated only as a 'thinker'. Foe once it is realized that his ideas are merely tiresome, he may be read for his immediate insights; and he is one of the best of all Swedish nature writers. Far more important, in fact, than his 'mysticism' is his feeling for the wilderness and for fauna and flora. His intuitive linguistic innovations are also of importance. His best poetry is to be found in *Trade Wind* (1945); this is vigorous and of high quality.

IVAR LO-JOHANSSON (1901) is another writer who had a rough early life, and had to find his own education. He is associated in the mind of the Swedish reading public with Johnson, Martinson and Moberg as a proletarian writer; but most especially with Jan Fridegård (q.v.), as the leading portrayer of the grim lives of the Swedish farm labourers before the First World War. Lo-Johansson's father was an illiterate who eventually acquired his own small farm; he pays him high and moving tribute in *The Illiterate* (1951). His massive 'collective' novels of the Thirties—including *Good Night, Earth* (1933)— are aesthetically clumsy but impress by their sincerity and the accuracy of their portrayal of the labouring characters. He has also written of the city and of every kind of social problem: prostitution, old age, even sport. *Mana is Dead* (1932), a love story, sounds an entirely different note. *The Illiterate* was the first of a series of auto-biographical novels—this is a well established Swedish genre—which is of considerable value. Lo-Johansson is a shrewd observer of both the mores and the psychology of his contemporaries; his later work has been improved by its unexpectedly relaxed quality and its humour.

JAN FRIDEGÅRD (1897–1968) takes the same kind of subject-matter, but his approach is more indignant and cynical, and he concentrates on individual rather than collective fate. His best work is the tough *Lars Hård* (1935–42) tetralogy, showing how an ex-soldier is smashed down by the impersonal forces of society, and yet retains his own identity. It is a deidealized self-portrait—Fridegård had been a navvy, a soldier on the dole—which illuminates the lower end of Swedish society in the years before the Social Democrats came to power (1932) more fully than any historical or sociological work. *Lars Hård* is a latter-day naturalist novel of great power and depth, which Fridegård did not surpass. Fridegård's later fiction, some of it historical, is however consistently skilful and intelligent.

*

GUSTAF HELLSTRÖM (1882–1953), who worked for some time in England and U.S.A., published many interesting autobiographical novels; but his finest work is to be found in *Lacemaker Lekholm has an Idea* (1927; tr. 1930), a survey of a family over two generations. A grandson returns from the States to his grandfather's centenary, which gives the author his occasion. This has a naturalist programme —Hellström believed that character was determined by heredity— but its virtues lie in its psychological shrewdness, warmth and humour. *Carl Heribert Malmros* (1931) gets inside the skin of a chief of police.

LUDVIG NORDSTRÖM (1882–1942) had an English mother and knew English literature (as did Hellström) well. He was an uneven writer, whose advocation of a world-Utopia, which he called 'totalism' (based on a one-sided view of H. G. Wells, q.v. 1), vitiates most of his later work. But he was the first to write effective fiction about the Baltic region of Sweden (where he was born). Then he is racy, lushly comic and splendidly evocative of the quality of the people's lives. His finest work is undoubtedly to be found in his early tales: for example, *Fisherfolk* (1907) and *The Twelve Sundays* (1910).

The huge fictional output, much of it topical, of the popular author SIGFRID SIWERTZ (1882) is distinguished by intelligence and consistency of attitude; but two or three books stand out above the rest. He began as a decadent with atmospheric stories of Stockholm in the manner of Bo Bergman and Söderberg (qq.v.); but in 1907 he attended a series of lectures by Bergson (q.v.), and, as a critic has said, 'his *flâneurs* became activists'. *The Pirates of Lake Mälar* (1911) is a boys' adventure classic, and represented to its author a return to spiritual health. His masterpiece is *Downstream* (1920; tr. 1923), a savage and relentless attack on commercial values embodied in a selfish and profiteering family. *Jonas and the Dragon* (1928) dissects the world of journalism with almost equal skill. *Goldman's* (1926; tr. 1929) is about the world of big stores. His autobiographical books are excellent.

ELIN WÄGNER (1882–1949), Sweden's leading feminist, and the biographer of Selma Lagerlöf (1942–3), was a journalist and publicist as well as a novelist. Her feminism was quasi-mystical, and she was a strongly religious woman who found it exceedingly difficult to reconcile her convictions with her emancipated views on modern life. Her best book, *Åsa-Hanna* (1918), an evocation of Småland country life, is one of the finest of recent Swedish provincial novels. This evokes a whole culture at the same time as it re-creates the mind of childhood, and imaginatively explores the character of Hanna, who finds her way back to honesty from the life of crime into which she has innocently been lured. Elin Wägner's other novels are worthy but not on this high level.

HJALMAR BERGMAN (1883–1931), born at Örebro, the 'Wadköping' of his fiction, in central Sweden, offers a strong contrast to the other writers of his generation. 'Not always agreeable to conventional readers', Bergman is closer to Strindberg than any of his contemporaries, and he must certainly be treated as a fundamentally expressionist writer. A melancholic, much of his fiction presents a comic or tragi-comic surface. He attained great popularity in the last years of his life. A pessimist, hindered by his near blindness, ill health and depressive constitution, Bergman ironically took refuge in his own world; yet his gift for penetrating realistic writing is as great as anyone's. He found success with *God's Orchid* (1919; tr. 1923), the ninth of a series of re-creations (he lived mostly outside Sweden) of his home town. Markurell has advanced ruthlessly from inn-keeper to rich financier; he is obsessed with love for his son—who turns out not to be his. *Thy Rod and Thy Staff* (1921; tr. 1937) explores the same territory. *The Head of the Firm* (1924; tr. 1936) is a Freudian study in sexual fascination: a young man becomes obsessed with, and is destroyed by, his future mother-in-law. Finally Bergman showed himself, in *Clown Jac* (1930), as a clown haunted by fear and driven to his performance by it. Its object? To drive fear way by laughter. This is his greatest novel.

PÄR LAGERKVIST (1891–1974), who received (for his novels *The Dwarf* and *Barabbas*) the Nobel Prize (1951), is well known in Sweden for his lyrical poetry. His reputation is international; there are, one feels, other Swedish writers more deserving—for example, Söderberg, Hjalmar Bergman (qq.v.). Lagerkvist's very high philosophical intentions are more impressive than his creative solutions of them. His creative life was a project to heal the wound made in him by the First World War—his first book of poetry was called *Anguish* (1916), of which the title poem begins:

> Anguish, anguish is my heritage
> My throat's wound
> My heart's cry in the world.

The Dwarf (1944; tr. 1953) presents a hideous creature against a colourfully drawn Renaissance background. *Barabbas* (1950; tr. 1952) is his most tragic work, setting up Barabbas as a foil to the impossible Christ-figure, and presenting man as wounded by the loss of goodness but powerless to act in the interests of his own virtue. As good as this is the novella *The Hangman*, a medieval allegory of contemporary (Nazi) evil. Lagerkvist is a fine stylist, but as a whole his work is given too great a symbolic burden. He is lucky to enjoy the reputation he does.

OLLE HEDBERG (1899) is by contrast a realist whose work has no sense of ambitiously straining towards philosophic 'greatness'. He is a satirist and, latterly, a disenchanted moralist. He has been one of Sweden's most consistently probing and astute analysts of middle-class mores. *Animals in Cages* (1959; tr. 1962) consists of two stories, in both of which dialogue plays so large a part (cf. Ivy Compton-Burnett, Henry Green, qq.v. 1) as to give them an almost dramatic quality. The first, 'A Smiling Procession of Triumph', gives an ironic and subtle version of the conflict between rebellious youth and experienced conservatism; the second, 'Awake in a Dormitory Town', is a mellower study of youth and age.

LARS AHLIN (1915) is a younger and different type of proletarian writer, who emerged later (in *40-tal*, q.v.) than the group already dealt with—and underwent the hardship of unemployment during the Thirties, when they had already become writers. Ahlin is an anti-naturalist and anti-theorist inasmuch as he believes in the autonomy of his characters. One of Sweden's most important active contemporary novelists, he is also one of the few modern authors to make something of the ubiquitous influence of Dostoevski. The long *My Death is My Own* (1945) is sprawling and unsatisfactory in structure but undeniably powerful. Ahlin is intelligently concerned with the religious impulse in modern men and women, and has become a master of discovering this when it takes other forms, such as neuroses or moral intentions. *Night in the Market Tent* (1957) deals with a man's evasion of love on the grounds that he has not deserved it. It is a remarkable work, sometimes confused, but always powerful and acute.

LARS GYLLENSTEN (1921) is predominantly an intellectual; but this does not prevent him from using an at times highly evocative language. Gyllensten has tended to dissipate his energy in a series of restless experiments; but there is no denying his gifts. The early *Children's Book* (1952) remains one of his best novels: a description of a man's desire to cling to childhood's innocence, and therefore to childhood, which results in madness and—ironically—a stunted personality. *The Testament of Cain* (1963; tr. 1967) is an original and clever re-creation of the Genesis myth: there are only a few documents of the Cainites' literature available, and the reader is invited to piece them together. This is, however, more intellectually than imaginatively attractive.

The death of STIG DAGERMAN (1923–54), a leading and most original writer of the Forties—he was closely linked with *40-tal* (q.v.)—was a serious loss to Swedish literature. A latter-day expressionist who owed a large but not crippling debt to Kafka (q.v.), his energy was prodigious. His suicide meant as much to the intellectuals of his generation as that of Pavese had to Italians four years before. Other obvious influences on Dagerman included the tough or primitive American novel (Hemingway, Faulkner, q.v. 1), and, nearer home, the symbolic procedures of the Norwegian Vesaas (q.v.). His later novels, *Burnt Child* (1948; tr. 1950) and *Wedding Pains* (1949), are brilliant but so shot through with anguish that the final effect is of a half-muted shriek. Better is his first novel, *The Snake* (1945), an evocation of the menace of the outside world to the individual. Dagerman's finest work is contained in the short stories collected in *The Games of Night* (1947; tr. 1960), in which his tendency towards symbolism is more controlled. He distinguished himself in the theatre, and, especially, as a radio dramatist.

SARA LIDMAN (1923), who has spent a considerable time in Africa, has most recently written sensitive and subtle novels about the oppressed minority in South Africa (by whose government she has been persecuted). Her earlier fiction was regionalistic, and looked back to the Thirties. Sara Lidman is able to portray both the tenderly innocent and the brutally egocentric—nowhere better than in her only translated novel, *Rain Bird* (1958; tr. 1962), the record of a girl's bruised childhood and her evolution into a tough and selfish, but self-aware, woman.

*

No Swede since Strindberg has been a major dramatist, and no entirely serious writer has concentrated exclusively on the genre. But some Swedish writers have written notable plays. Per Hallström's (q.v.) *The Count of Antwerp* (1899) marked the beginning of a series of competent classical historical dramas. He translated most of Shakespeare into what may be described as a kind of Edwardian Swedish. Hjalmar Bergman (q.v.) was Strindberg's natural theatrical successor; in his first plays, tragedies, he chose Maeterlinck's (q.v.) cloudy manner but used it to demonstrate, often to sinister effect, how the unconscious mind rules behaviour. His last comedies are outstanding, especially *Patrasket* (1928), about a Jewish business man: here Bergman daringly and always entertainingly contrasts the commercial non-values of the business man with the conscientious ones of the Jew. Pär Lagerkvist (q.v.) is more expressionist in technique—and even more obviously indebted to Strindberg and Maeterlinck than Bergman. His least effective plays, however, belong to a period when he had tried to cast off these influences, and was trying for a 'magic realism', in which the fantastic is to be endowed with an everyday quality: *Victory in the Dark* (1939) and the dramatized version of his novel *Barabbas* (1953), which he also scripted for a movie directed by Alf Sjöberg (1953)—to be preferred to the more vulgar, better known, but not worthless Italian version directed by Richard Fleischer and starring Anthony Quinn, Silvana Magnano and Jack Palance. Lagerkvist's earlier technique has something in common, too, with the 'theatre of silence' (q.v.), although he hardly anticipated it as Bracco (q.v. 3) did. Stig Dagerman (q.v.) also wrote a remarkable adaptation of his story *The Condemned* (1948; tr. in *Scandinavian Plays of the Twentieth Century*, 1951).

V

Some 400,000 Finns, of Nyland and Åland islands, speak Swedish as well as Finnish—a language that has nothing in common with Scandinavian, and whose literature is of course treated separately.

The Swedo-Finnish literature is more international than the Finno-Finnish, simply because while the latter had only native traditions to fall back upon, the former had Swedish—and all that this had absorbed. Because of its peculiar situation, it has developed an interesting and unique kind of independence. Like other modern European literatures, it is divided, in the opening period, into the traditional and the modern, and like those other literatures which develop in predominantly rural environments the two strands have in common the love of the native landscape and its customs. It was undoubtedly EDITH SÖDERGRAN (1892–1923), who was born in Russia, who introduced modernism into Swedo-Finnish literature; she was also influential in Sweden and in Finno-Finnish literature. Strongly influenced by Nietzsche, her 'cosmic' philosophy is not today of much interest. But her free-associative technique and consumptive ecstasy (she died of tuberculosis, to which she succumbed after fifteen years of poverty and illness) about nature are a different matter. Particularly moving is the humble, humorous and unhysterical acceptance of early death that she manifests in her less philosophically pretentious poems, such as 'The Portrait':

> For my little songs,
> The funny plaintive ones, the evening purple ones,
> Spring gave me the egg of a water-bird.
> I asked my beloved to paint my portrait on the thick shell.
> He painted a young leek in brown soil—
> And on the other side a round soft mound of sand.
>
> (TCSP)

Too high claims have been made for Edith Södergran; but in the context of Scandinavian and Finnish poetry her importance should not be underestimated.

The aggressive ELMER DIKTONIUS (1896–1961), who studied music and originally wanted to be a composer, once nearly starved; it was from this experience that (he said) his lifelong socialism mostly stemmed. There is something almost of Mayakovsky (q.v. 4) in his explosiveness; but he is more personal and, when being himself, more melodious. He translated many poets into and from Finnish. Diktonius, founder of two modernist magazines, was perhaps more vitally important as a lively influence than as a poet in his own right—his own poetry is almost always over-excited; but it is also bold and has a Whitmanesque tang. Like Södergran, he had a strong influence, during the Thirties, on Swedish literature.

Later manifestations of modernism such as surrealism and dada

(qq.v.) were introduced into Swedo-Finnish poetry by GUNNAR
BJÖRLING (1887–1960), who was again extremely influential in
Sweden as well as in his own country. Björling remained resolutely
faithful to dadaist, grammar-smashing procedures; but, paradoxically, this was for him a method of expression rather than a means of
mental exploration. For he had a philosophy, an attempt to reconcile
naturalist with vitalist impulses, and he stuck to it. But this philosophy is less important in his poetry, which is at bottom one of
reification: objects of sense-experience are reconstituted and as such
raised to significant status:

> Hear me, bird of the night
> Take me day
> Arising!
> Speak, shadow,
> Fill with morning devotion
> China's land and Peking's alleys
> And that oasis
> And all the boats are rolling
> Like a morning over the peasant's cart.
>
> (TCSP)

Björling was a minor poet, but a consistent one.

Most of the early poetry of RABBE ENCKELL (1903) is impressionistic
and concerned with nature; although highly subjective and compressed, it is not notably modernistic; but he defended Björling and
the modernist cause, and published in *quosego* (1928–9), the vehicle
for the new poetry. He had studied art in Italy and France, and his
early inspiration was painting. Like a number of other failed painters
he tried to make poetry into a sort of painting. A little later he
turned to the verse drama with classical themes—*Orpheus and
Eurydice* (1938), *Jocasta* (1939). His later classical preoccupations,
which recall and were perhaps influenced by Ekelund's (q.v.), are
reflected in his collection *Copper Breath* (1946); a selection of his
poems was included with the two dramas in *Nike Fleeing in the Garb
of the Wind* (1947), which was introduced by Lindegren. Since then
he has written more classical verse plays, including *Agamemnon*
(1949), poetry, and intimate essays. His understanding of the
classical spirit is profound, and he is its chief exponent in the
Scandinavian languages. His later poetry is not pastiche; even
more than H.D.'s (q.v. 1), it re-creates Greek elegance and elegiac
calm for its own age. Enckell's voice is his own, but he has assimilated the lesson of Sappho:

O, sun
Thou who in the cobweb of thy rays
Weavest, weavest
Catching, tying hearts together,
Bind,
One morning before awakening
A heart
Closely to mine.

(TCSP)

But translation can give no impression of his stylistic achievement.

One of the most distinguished Swedo-Finnish novelists is TITO COLLIANDER (1904), who taught both art and (Greek Orthodox) religion in schools. His approach may well have been a decisive influence on Ahlin (q.v.), but his postulation of mystical Christian acceptance of suffering is more definite than Ahlin's. His characters are weak and passionate, and the spiritual peace they sometimes attain is convincing—but possibly more specious than Colliander intends.

WALENTIN CHORELL (1912), more modernist in outlook, although in his fiction stylistically conventional, is a leading playwright as well as a novelist. His plays, including *Madame* (1951), have been widely performed in Scandinavia and Germany. His most important fiction is the trilogy *Miriam* (1954–8). He chooses to deal, in an austere manner, with the world of people who have been stripped, by mental disorder, to their instinctive and primitive selves.

VI

In Iceland realism was inaugurated—under the influence of Brandes (q.v.), as elsewhere in Scandinavia—through the medium of *The Present* (1882–3), edited by students who had attended his lectures. But its impact was not quite as great—doubtless because the urban socialism that Brandes appeared to represent could have little appeal in a country of poor rural crofters and fishermen. It was not until the first two decades of this century that the drift to the towns took place. Its chief achievement was to decisively separate intellectual life from the gloomily narrow piety represented by the Lutheran State Church. Christianity reconstituted itself as the 'new theology', which threw out hell—doubtless sensing its unpopularity. (It is in this period, too, that the Icelandic vogue for

spiritualism and theosophy has its origin. This trend is still so
strong that it can co-exist with militant Marxism.) The movement produced no important writer; one of its leaders, the poet
HANNES HAFSTEIN (1861–1922), went on to react against at least
the pessimism inherent in Brandes' philosophy—and indeed, to
become prime minister (1904). STEPHAN G. STEPHANSSON (ps. STÉFAN
GUÐMUNDARSON, 1853–1927), who had left Iceland for the New
World in 1872, properly belongs to American-Icelandic literature,
which belongs to Canada, North Dakota, and neighbouring states.
He was the most important of the realists, among whom he belongs
by virtue of his social satires. But he was primarily a poet, and was
undoubtedly the dominant personality in the settlers' literature.
He was a crude but honest poet, who told vigorous stories, made
nostalgic descriptions of his homeland, and expressed generally
humanitarian beliefs. The pronouncement of one F. S. Cawley that
he was 'the finest poet of the Western world' belongs more to the
history of comedy than criticism; but he was a worthy figure.

Symbolism came to Iceland from Denmark, from whence it was
brought by EINAR BENEDIKTSSON (1864–1940). His five books of
verse are, however, less important than his influence in turning
Icelandic literature away from naturalism. His poetry is lofty, not
to say pompous; his notion of symbolism is extremely limited—as
is his notion of poetry itself, which he regards as the most suitable
means of expression of noble and idealistic emotions. But he helped
to prepare the way for better poets who were not, as he was, really
interested in the wave of nationalism that swept over the country in
the first years of the century.

HULDA (ps. UNNAR BJARKLIND, 1881–1946) went back to simple and
folk forms. (TCSP) JÓHANN GUNNAR SIGURÐSSON (1882–1906) was
probably the best of the neo-romantics. (TCSP) But more important
than these is ÞÓRBERGUR ÞÓRÐARSON (1889), who filled the traditional measures with nonsense and satirized the sentimentality of
more conventional poets, as in 'Futuristic Evening Moods':

> Rant thy treble rhyme from stable,
> Rarest child mid life's defiledness!
> Spy! what gibberish were you saying?
> Sprung white lilies on scarlet tongue then?
> Glycerine is a godly oozing.
> Gling-glang-glo! who's got the low wretch?
> Nybbari good and Noah the scrubber!
> *Nonsense! Chaos! Bhratar! Monsieur!*

> (TCSP)

Þórðarson is the best modern Icelandic poet. Like so many Icelanders, he has been involved with theosophy and Yoga as well as Marxism; he was also an Esperanto enthusiast. He was a prominent anti-Nazi. *The Eccentric* (1940–1) is a lively and interesting autobiographical novel, in which he displays remarkable self-awareness and a superb humour. His massive, Boswellian fiction, *The Life of Pastor Arni þorarinson* (1945–50) is a comic masterpiece. *The Hymn About the Flower* (1954–5) is written from the point of view of a child. Þórðarson is also important for *Letter to Laura* (1924), socialist and modernist essays that introduced much that was intelligent and new to Iceland. Considering the world reputation of Laxness (q.v.), who could never have got started without him, Þórðarson has been cruelly neglected outside Iceland; he is a superior writer.

The prolific GUNNAR GUNNARSSON (1889) made his reputation in Denmark as a writer in Danish, but returned to Iceland in 1939. He has been compared to Olav Duun (q.v.) as an interpreter of ordinary people. *Guest the One-Eyed* (1912–14; tr. 1920) is an over-romanticized historical novel about his own part of Iceland; nevertheless, it has enormous verve and descriptive skill. *Seven Days' Darkness* (1920; tr. 1930), set in Reykjavík, is really much better. It records the collapse into madness of a doctor during the influenza epidemic of 1918. This is Gunnarsson's best book; what has followed it—including plays and poetry—has been no more than worthy.

HALLDÓR LAXNESS (1902), born in Reykjavík, is Iceland's leading writer; in 1955 he was awarded the Nobel Prize. No Icelandic writer in the last century can be compared to him except Þórðarson (who is a superior poet and who began the process of freeing Icelandic prose from archaism, which Laxness completed). As a young man Laxness travelled and absorbed many cultures and influences: German expressionism (q.v.), Catholicism (he was in a Luxemburg monastery for a time), French surrealism (q.v.), and America. Finally he arrived at a communism (about 1927) from which he has not retreated. (It should perhaps be mentioned that communism is not eccentric in Iceland: the party have for some time held seats in parliament.) Laxness is a lyricist and a satirist who has shown the kind of development characteristic of major writers—and yet he is not quite one. The novel *The Great Weaver from Casmïr* (1927) marks his emergence from Catholicism, whose intransigence he savaged in his essays of 1929: *The Book of the People*. His fiction of the Thirties—*Salka Valka* (1931–2; tr. 1963), *Independent People* (1934–5; tr. 1945), *The Light of the World* (1937–40)—all dealt with the contemporary Icelandic scene. They are conceived on too grand a scale to entirely suit all tastes—one can understand this tendency, however, in the literature that produced the Eddas—but they must undoubtedly be accepted as landmarks in Scandinavian literature. The first deals with the fishing community, the second with farming, and the third with a folk poet. These are fiercely critical of society, but ultimately must be treated as expressionist rather than social novels. *The Atom Station* (1948; tr. 1961) satirized the American presence in Iceland; likewise the play *The Silver Moon* (1954). *Paradise Reclaimed* (1960; tr. 1962) is at the expense of the Iceland Mormons. Laxness' style has become more formal with time; but it always reflects his own turmoil: cynicism clashes with lyrical acceptance, anger with gentleness. Of his historical novels, in which he owes most to the traditional literature of his country, only the satirical *Happy Warriors* (1952) is available in English. *Iceland's Bell* (1943) is set in the early eighteenth century.

Select Bibliography

by the late F. Seymour-Smith

Reference books and other standard sources of literary information; with a selection of national historical and critical surveys, excluding monographs on individual authors (other than series) and anthologies.

Imprint: the place of publication other than London is stated, followed by the date of the last edition traced up to 1971. *OUP* = Oxford University Press, and includes departmental Oxford imprints such as Clarendon Press and the London OUP. But Oxford books originating outside Britain, e.g. Australia, New York, are so indicated. *CUP* = Cambridge University Press.

GENERAL AND EUROPEAN

Baker, Ernest A.: A Guide to the Best Fiction. *Routledge,* 1932.

Beer, Johannes: Der Romanführer. 14 vols. *Stuttgart, Anton Hiersemann,* 1950–69.

Benét, William Rose: The Reader's Encyclopaedia. *Harrap,* 1955.

Bompiani, Valentino: Dizionario letterario Bompiani delle opere e dei personaggi di tutti i tempi e di tutte le letterature. 9 volumes (including index volume). *Milan, Bompiani,* 1947–50. *Appendice.* 2 vols. 1964–6.

Chambers's Biographical Dictionary. *Chambers,* 1969.

Church, Margaret: Time and Reality: studies in contemporary fiction. *North Carolina;* OUP, 1963.

Contemporary Authors: an international bio-bibliographical guide. *In progress. Detroit, Gale,* 1962.

Courtney, W. F. (Editor): The Reader's Adviser. 2 vols. (Vol. 1: Literature). *New York, Bowker,* 1968–71.

Einsiedel, Wolfgang: Die Literaturen der Welt in ihrer mündlichen und schiriftlichen Uberlieferung. *Zurich, Kindler,* 1964.

Ellmann, Richard and Charles Feidelson (Editors): The Modern Tradition: backgrounds of modern literature. *New York, OUP,* 1965.

Esslin, Martin: The Theatre of the Absurd. *Penguin Books,* 1968.

Fleischmann, Wolfgang B. (Editor): Encyclopaedia of World Literature in the Twentieth Century. 3 vols. *New York, Frederick Ungar,* 1967–71. (An enlarged and updated edition of Lexicon der

Weltliteratur im 20 Jahrhundert. *Infra*.)

Ford, Ford Madox: The March of Literature. *Allen and Unwin*, 1939.

Frauwallner, E. and others (Editors): Die Welt Literatur. 3 vols. *Vienna*, 1951–4. *Supplement* (A–F), 1968.

Freedman, Ralph: The Lyrical Novel: studies in Hermann Hesse, André Gide and Virginia Woolf. *Princeton; OUP*, 1963.

Grigson, Geoffrey (Editor): The Concise Encyclopaedia of Modern World Literature. *Hutchinson*, 1970.

Hargreaves-Mawdsley, W. N.: Everyman's Dictionary of European Writers. *Dent*, 1968.

Harward, Timothy B. (Editor): Euopean Patterns: contemporary patterns in European writing. *Dublin; Dolmen Press; OUP*, 1963.

Hoppé, A. J.: The Reader's Guide to Everyman's Library, *Dent*, 1971.

Josipovici, Gabriel: The World and the Book: a study of the modern novel. *Macmillan*, 1971.

Kearney, E. I. and L. S. Fitzgerald: The Continental Novel: a checklist of criticism in English, 1900– 66. *New Jersey, The Scarecrow Press*, 1968.

Keller, Helen: The Reader's Digest of Books. *New York*; and *Allen and Unwin*, 1947.

Kindermann, Heinz and Margarete Dietrich: Lexikon der Weltliteratur. *Vienna, Humboldt*, 1951.

Kindlers Literatur Lexikon. 5 vols. *Zurich, Kindler*, 1965–9. (A–Ra; in progress.) Based on Bompiani *supra*.

Kronenberger, Louis and Emily Morison Beck (Editors): *Atlantic Brief Lives*: a biographical com-

panion to the arts. *Atlantic Monthly Press Book: Boston, Little Brown*, 1971.

Kunitz, Stanley J. and Howard Haycraft: Twentieth Century Authors. *New York, the H. W. Wilson Co.*, 1942. *Supplement*, 1955.

Laird, Charlton: The World Through Literature. *New York*; and *Peter Owen*, 1959.

Lexikon der Weltliteratur im 20 Jahrhundert. 2 vols. *Freiburg, Herder*, 1961–1.

Magnus, Laurie: A Dictionary of European Literature. *Routledge*, 1926.

Melchinger, Siegfried: Drama Zwischen Shaw und Brecht. Translated by George Wellwarth as: *The Concise Encyclopaedia of Modern Drama. New York*; and *Vision Press*, 1966.

Mondadori, Alberto: Dizionario universale della Letteratura contemporanea. 4 vols. *Verona*, 1959– 62.

Mukerjea, S. V.: Disjecta Membra: studies in literature and life. *Bangalore*, 1959.

Murphy, Rosalie (Editor): Contemporary Poets of the English Language. *St. James Press*, 1970.

The Penguin Companion to Literature. 4 vols. *Penguin Books*, 1969– 72.

Poggioli, Renato: The Theory of the Avant Garde. *Belknap Press, Harvard University Press*, 1968.

Priestley, J. B.: Literature and Western Man. *Heinemann*, 1960.

Smith, Horatio (Editor): Columbia Dictionary of Modern European Literature. *Columbia University Press*, 1947.

Steinberg, S. H. (Editor): Cassell's Encyclopaedia of Literature. *Cassell*, 1953.

Studies in Modern European Literature and Thought Series. *Bowes and Bowes* (*The Bodley Head*) and *Yale University Press*, 1952 . . .

Van Tieghem, Philippe and Pierre Josserand: Dictionnaire des Littératures. 3 vols. *Paris, Presses Universitaires de France*, 1968.

Ward, A. C.: Longman Companion to Twentieth Century Literature. *Longman*, 1970.

Wellwarth, George E.: The Theatre of Protest and Paradox: developments in the Avant Garde drama. *New York*; and *MacGibbon and Kee*, 1965.

West, Paul: The Modern Novel. *Hutchinson*, 1965.

Writers and Critics Series (British, European and American). *Oliver and Boyd*, 1960.

DUTCH

(*Dutch; Flemish*)

Backer, Franz de: Contemporary Flemish Literature. *Flemish PEN Centre, Bruxelles*, 1934.

Ridder, André de: La Littérature flamande contemporaine: 1890–1923. *Paris, Edouard Champion*, 1923.

Tielrooy, Johannes B.: Panorama de la littérature hollandaise contemporaine. *Paris*, 1938.

Weevers, Theodor: The Poetry of the Netherlands in its European Context: 1170–1930. *OUP*, 1960.

FINNISH

Havu, Ilmari: Finland's Literature. *Stockholm*, 1958.

Perret, Jean-Louis: Panorama de la littérature contemporaine de Finlande. *Paris, Editions du Sagittaire*, 1936.

FRENCH AND BELGIAN

Adereth, Maxwell: Commitment in Modern French Literature. *Victor Gollancz*, 1967.

Alden, Douglas W. and others (Editors): Bibliography of Critical and Biographical References for the Study of Contemporary French Literature: books and articles. *New York, French Institute*, 1949–69: *in progress*.

Austin, L. J., Garnet Rees and Eugène Vinever: Studies in Modern French Literature: presented to P. Mansell Jones by pupils, colleagues and friends. *Manchester University Press*, 1961.

Benn, T. V.: Current Publications on Twentieth Century French Literature. *ASLIB*, 1953.

Braun, Sydney D.: Dictionary of French Literature. *New York*; and *Peter Owen*, 1959.

Charlier, Gustave and Joseph Hanse: Histoire illustré des lettres françaises de Belgique. *Bruxelles, La Renaissance du livre*, 1958.

Clouard, Henri: Histoire de la littérature française du symbolisme à nos jours, 1885–1960. 2 vols. *Paris*, 1948–62.

Clouard, Henri and Robert Leggewie (Editors): French Writers of Today. *New York, OUP*, 1965.

Cocking, J. M.: Three Studies in Modern French Literature. *Yale University Press*, 1960.

Cruickshank, John (Editor): The Novelist as Philosopher: studies in French fiction, 1935–60. *OUP*, 1962.

Fletcher, John: New Directions in Literature: critical approaches. *Calder and Boyars*, 1968.

Girard, Marcel: Guide illustré de la littérature française moderne de

1918 à nos jours. *Paris*, 1962.

Guicharnaud, Jacques: Modern French Theatre: from Giradoux to Genet. *Yale University Press*, 1967.

Harvey, Sir Paul and J. E. Heseltine: The Oxford Companion to French Literature. *OUP*, 1959.

Lalou, René: Histoire de la littérature française contemporaine: de 1870 à nos jours, with a bibliography of representative works. 2 vols. *Paris*, 1947. (The second edition was translated into English as *Contemporary French Literature*, *New York*; and *Jonathan Cape*, 1925.

Lalou, René: Le Roman français depuis 1900. Dixième édition par Georges Versini. *Paris: Que Sais-je, No. 497*, 1966.

Lalou, René: Le Théâtre en France depuis 1900. *Paris: Que Sais-je, No. 461*, 1965.

Mallinson, Vernon: Modern Belgian Literature, 1830–1960. *Heinemann*, 1966.

Peyre, Henri: Contemporary French Literature. *New York, Harper and Row*, 1964.

Peyre, Henri: French Novelists of Today. *New York, OUP*, 1967.

Peyre, Henri: Modern Literature: Vol. 1: The Literature of France. *Princeton Studies, New York, Prentice-Hall*, 1966.

Rousselot, Jean: Dictionnaire de la poésie française contemporaine. *Paris, Larousse*, 1968.

GERMAN

Bithell, Jethro: Modern German Literature, 1880–1950. *Methuen*, 1959.

Closs, August and H. M. Waidson: German Literature in the Twentieth Century (with chapters on novels by H. M. Waidson). *Introductions to German Literature*, Vol. 4. *Barrie and Jenkins*, 1969.

Flores, John: Poetry in East Germany: adjustments, visions and provocations, 1945–70. *New Haven and London, Yale University Press*, 1971.

Forster, Leonard: German Poetry, 1944–8. *Cambridge, Bowes and Bowes*—now *Bodley Head*, 1949.

Garten, H. F.: Modern German Drama. *Methuen*, 1959.

Hamburger, Michael: From Prophecy to Exorcism. *Longman*, 1965.

Hamburger, Michael: Reason and Energy. *Routledge*, 1957.

Hatfield, Henry: Modern German Literature: the major figures in context. *Edward Arnold*, 1968.

Keith-Smith, Brian: Essays on Contemporary German Literature. *Oswald Wolff*, 1966.

Lange, Victor: Modern German Literature, 1870–1940. *Ithaca, New York*, 1945.

Morgan, Bayard Quincy: A Critical Bibliography of German Literature in English Translation; with supplement, 1928–55. *New Jersey, The Scarecrow Press*, 1965.

Robertson, J. G.: History of German Literature. *Edinburgh, Blackwood*, 1970.

Waidson, H. M.: The Modern German Novel, 1945–65. *University of Hull; OUP*, 1971.

Waterhouse, Gilbert: A Short History of German Literature: third edition with a continuation by H. M. Waidson. *Methuen*, 1959.

SCANDINAVIAN

(*Icelandic, Danish, Norwegian, Swedish*)

Beyer, Harald: A History of Norwegian Literature. Translated by Einar Haugen. *New York, The American Scandinavian Foundation, New York University Press*, 1956.

Bredsdorff, Elias: Danish Literature in English Translation. *Copenhagen* 1960.

Bredsdorff, Elias, Brita Mortensen and Ronald Popperwell: An Introduction to Scandinavian Literature. *CUP*, 1951.

Claudi, Jørgen: Contemporary Danish Authors: with a brief outline of Danish literature. *Det Danske Selskab, Copenhagen*, 1952.

Downs, Brian W.: Modern Norwegian Literature, 1860–1918. *CUP*, 1966.

Einarsson, Stéfan: A History of Icelandic Literature. *Johns Hopkins Press* (for the *American-Scandinavian Foundation*), *Baltimore*, 1957.

Gustafson, Alrik: A History of Swedish Literature. *University of Minnesota; OUP*, 1961.

Gustafson, Alrik: Six Scandinavian Novelists: Lie, Jacobsen, Heidenstam, Selma Lagerlof, Hamsun, Sigrid Undset. *University of Minnesota; OUP*, 1968.

Heepe, Evelyn and Niels Heltberg (Editors): Modern Danish Authors. Translated by Evelyn Heepe. *Copenhagen, Scandinavian Publishing Co.*, 1946.

Kärnell, Karl A.: Svenskt litteraturlexicon. *Lund*, 1964.

Mitchell, P. M.: A Bibliographical Guide to Danish Literature. *Copenhagen*, 1961.

Mitchell, P. M.: A History of Danish Literature. *Copenhagen, Gyldendal*, 1957.

Index

Aage and Else (Kidde), 372
Aakjær, Jeppe, **367**
'Abbaye, L', Group, France, 79, 80
'Abbaye' Group, Holland, 14
Abbaye d'Évolayne, L' (Régnier), 135
Abbé, L' (Bataille), 134
Abell, Kjeld, **373**
Abraxus (Audiberti), 181
Absent Without Leave (Böll), 348
Absurd, Theatre of, 59, 163*f.*
Abu Talfan (Raabe), 190
Achterberg, Gerrit, **9–10**
Acquainted With the Night (Böll), 347, 348
Across Paris (Aymé), 133
Action Française (p.), 33, 83, 84
Ad Astra (Larin-Kyösti), 22
Adam, Paul, **34–5**
Adam, Where Art Thou? (Böll), 347
Adamov, Arthur, **165–7**
Adepts in Self-Portraiture (Zweig), 283
Adventurous Heart, The (E. Jünger), 280
Aeon (Mombert), 248
African Confidence (Martin du Gard), 75
After War (Renn), 278
Against Nature (Huysmans), 31
Agamemnon (Enckell), 414
Age of Reason, The (Sartre), 125
Ahlins, Lars, **410–11**
Aho, Juhani, **19**
Aichinger, Ilse, **349**
Aimé Pache, Vaudois Painter (Ramuz), 74
Aimez-vous Brahms? (Sagan), 145
Aktion, Die (p. Germany), 235
Alain-Fournier, **96–7**
Alberta and Freedom (Sandel), 385
Alberta and Jacob (Sandel), 385
Alcestis (Euripides *adapt.* Von Hofmannsthal), 208
Alexis, Paul, **30**
'Alienation Effect', 314
Alienation (Van Oudshoorn), 3–4

Aline (Ramuz), 74
All Men Are Mortal (Beauvoir), 136
All Quiet on the Western Front (Remarque), 279
Altenberg, Peter, **217–18**
America (Kafka), 290
Amethyst Ring, The (France), 38
Amok (Zweig), 283
Amphitryon 38 (Giraudoux), 159
Anabasis (Perse), 120
Anatol (Schnitzler), 218
and Vietnam and (Fried), 356
Andersch, Alfred, **344–5**
Andersson, Dan, **398–9**
Andorra (Frisch), 329
Andreas or the United Ones (Von Hofmannsthal), 209
Andreas-Salomé, Lou, 210
Andres, Stefan, **342–3**
Angel Comes to Babylon, An (Dürrenmatt), 331
Anguish (Lagerkvist), 410
Anhava, Tuomas, **27**
Aniara (Martinson), 407
Animals in Cages (Hedberg), 410
Anja and Esther (K. Mann), 312
Anna Sophie Hedvig (Abell), 373
Annals of the Origin of the Twentieth Century (Sternheim), 224
Anne (Ørjasæter), 389
Anouilh, Jean, **160–1**
Answer of the Deep, The (Huelsenbeck), 308
Antarctic Fugue (Cendrars), 95
Antigone (Anouilh), 160
'Anti-Literature', 145
'Anti-Novel', The, 145, 146*f.*
Antoine, André, **61**
Anton Wachter (Vestdijk), 8
Antschel, Paul, *see* Celan, Paul
Apitz, Bruno, **359**

Apocalypse (Van Deyssel) 33
Apollinaire, Guillaume, **111–14**
Apothecary's Daughter, The
  (Pontoppidan), 365
Approximate Man (Tzara), 109
Aragon, Louis, **123–4**
Ardèle (Anouilh), 161
'Aristocratism', 179
Arp, Hans, **306–8**
Arrabal, Fernando, **168**
Arrabiata, L' (Heyse), 189
Arrow to the Heart (Goes), 342
Art: Its Nature and Its Laws (Holz), 194
Art Moderne, L' (p. France), 52
Artaud, Antonin, **168–70**
Åsa-Hanna (Wagner), 409
Ascension of Mr. Baslèvre, The
  (Estaunié), 34
Aspects of Love (Lilas), 175
Aspenström, Werner, **403**
Assassinated Poet, The (Apollinaire), 114
Assistant, The (Walser), 286
Assumption of Hannele, The (G.
  Hauptmann), 198
At Latest in November (Nossack), 340
Atom Station, The (Laxness), 418
Audiberti, Jacques, **181**
August (Streuvels), 12
Aukrust, Olav, **389**
Aunt Ulrikke (Heiberg), 387
Aurélien (Aragon), 123
Autumn Glory (Bazin), 33
Avarice House (Green), 100
Aymé, Marcel, **133–4**

Baal (Brecht), 314
Bachelors, The (Montherlant), 90
Bachmann, Ingeborg, **357**
Baden-Baden, Cantata of Aquiescence
  (Brecht), 315
Baga (Pinget), 156
Bahr, Hermann, **217, 235**
Baillon, André, **57–8**
Baker's Wife, The (Giono), 92
Balcony, The (Genêt), 141
Balcony, The (Heiberg), 387
Balcony in the Forest, A (Gracq), 143
Bald Prima-Donna, The (Ionesco), 165
Ball, Hugo, **308**
Ballad of the Buried Life, A
  (Hagelstange), 353
Balzac and His World (Marceau), 144
Bang, Herman, **364–5**

Bang-Hansen, Odd, **393**
Baphomet (Klossowski), 134
Barabbas (Ghelderode), 174
Barabbas (Lagerkvist), 410, 412
Barbara (J. F. Jacobsen), 379
Barbarian in Asia, A (Michaux), 177
Barbusse, Henri, **70–1**
Bark Tree, The (Queneau), 131–2
Barlach, Ernst, **224–6**
Barrault, Jean-Louis, 65, **157**
Barrès, Maurice, **36–7**
Bataille, Georges, **134**
Baudelaire, Charles-Pierre, **42–4**
Bazin, Hervé, **143**
Bazin, René, **33**
Beaumarchais (Wolf), 313
Beauvoir, Simone de, **135–6**
Beaver Coat, The (G. Hauptmann),
  198–9
Becher, Johannes, R., **266–7**
Beckett, Samuel, **137–40**
Becket, or the Honour of God (Anouilh)
  161
Beer-Hofmann, Richard, **219–20**
Before Dawn (G. Hauptmann), 198
Before the Decision (Von Unruh), 262
Beggar, The (Sorge), 258
Behind the Glass (Merle), 137
Being and Nothingness (Sartre), 125
Belgium, Languages of, 52
Bellemère, Jean, *see* Sarment, Jean
Bellman (Zuckmayer), 321
Bells of Basel, The (Aragon), 123
Belloc, Hilaire, 83
Benediktsson, Einar, **416**
Benkal the Consoler of Women
  (Schickele), 275
Benn, Gottfried, **252–7**
Benzon, Otto, **372**
Bergengruen, Werner, **274–5**
Bergman, Bo, **397–8**
Bergman, Hjalmar, **409–10**, 412
Bergroth, Kersti Solveig, **22, 28**
Bergson, Henri, xv
Bergstedt, Harald, **368**
Berlin (Plievier), 282
Berlin Alexanderplatz (Döblin), 304–5
Berlin, the Land of Cockaigne (H. Mann),
  226, 227
Bernanos, Georges, **84–6**
Bernard, Jean Jacques, **162–3**
Bertelsen, Erik, **377**

Bertin, Charles, **178**
Betrayed (A. Skram), 382
Betrayed People, The (Döblin), 305
Beyond the Distances (A. R. Holst), **7**
Bieler, Manfred, **359**
Bierbaum, Otto Julius, **220**
Biermann, Wolf, **361**
Big Net, The (Kasack), 289
Bigot, The (Renard), 40
Billiards at Half-Past Nine (Böll), 348
Bint (Bordewijk), 9
Birds (Perse), 120
Birds Fly Away and the Leaves Fade, The (Bourges), 32
Birds of Paradise (Martens), 17
Birds Were Hers, The (Vartio), 27–8
Bismarck (Von Unruh), 262
Bits of a Pattern (Soya), 373
Bitter Victory (Guilloux), 99
Bjarklind, Unnar, *see* Hulda
Björling, Gunnar, **414**
Bjørnson, Bjørnstjerne, **380**
Bjørnvig, Thorkild, **376**
Black Curtain, The (Döblin), 303
Black Ecstasy (Pekkanen), 23
Black Kettle, The (Heinesen), 379
Black Mirrors (Schmidt), 346
Black Mountains (Falkberger), 385
Black Rose, The (Montherlant), 90
Black Song (Bertin), 178
Black Swan, The (T. Mann), 234
Black Swan, The (Walser), 339–40
Blakeston Lizzie (Hémon), 74
Blanchot, Maurice, **154–5**
Blaue Reiter Group, 235, 307
Blind, The (Dürrenmatt), 331
Blind Man, The (Jens), 350
Blixen, Karen, **375–6**
Blood of Others, The (Beauvoir), 136
Blood Sweat (Jouve), 119
Bloy, Léon, **40–1**
Blue Angel, The (H. Mann), 227–8
Blue Bird, The (Maeterlinck), 60
Blue Boll (Barlach), 225
Blue Hussar, The (Nimier), 144
Blue Rider Group, *see* Blaue Reiter Group
Bobrowski, Johannes, **360–1**
Bodart, Roger, **178**
Bodiless Man, The (H. Tierlinck), 13
Body's Rapture, The (Romains), 80
Bojer, Johan, **384, 388**
Böll, Heinrich, **347–9**

Bölsche, Wilhelm, **195**
Bonaparte (Von Unruh), 262
Bonfires (Wildenvey), 390
Bonjour Tristesse (Sagan), 145
Bonnefoy, Yves, **184**
Book of Hours, The (Rilke), 210, 211
Book of Joachim of Babylon, The (Gijsen), 16–17
Book of the Age, The (Holz), 194
Book of the People, The (Laxness), **417**
Boon, Louis-Paul, **16**
Bør Børson (Falkberget), 385
Borchardt, Rudolf, **203**
Borchert, Wolfgang, **324–6**
Bordewijk, Ferdinand, **9**
Borgan, Johan, **387**
Bötticher, Hans, *see* Ringelnatz, Joachim
Boubourouche (Courteline), 62
Bouhélier, Saint-Georges de, **50–51**
Bouhélier-Lepelletier, Stephene-Georges de, *see* Bouhélier, Saint Georges de
'Boulangism', 36
Bound Man, The (Aichinger), 349
Bourges, Élémir, **32**
Bourget, Paul, **32–3**
Boutens, P. C., **4**
Boye, Karin, **400–1**
Boyhood and Youth (Carossa), 273
Boylesve, René, **33–4**
Boys in the Back Room, The (Romains), 80
Boyson, Emil, **392**
Braak, Menno ter, 8
Brains (Benn), 254
Brancovan, Anna Elizabeth, Comtesse Mathieu de Noailles, **52**
Brand (Ibsen), 380
Brand New Death, A (Dabit), 98
Brandes, Edvard, **372**
Brandes, Georg, **363–4**
Brand's Heath (Schmidt), 346
Branner, Hans Christian, **378**
Bread and Wine (Øverland), 390
Break up (Krog), 388
Breaking of the Ice, The (Halbe), 196
Breaking Through (Jørgensen), 368
Breasts of Tiresias, The (Apollinaire), 112
Brecht, Bertolt, **313–20**
Bregendahl, Marie, **367**
Brekke, Paal, **392**
Brenner, Dir (p.), 242

Breton, André, 109, **110–11**
Brieux, Eugène, **61**
Broch, Hermann, **294–7**
Brod, Max, **269**
Brofeldt, Juhani, *see* Aho, Juhani
Bronnen, Arnolt, **260**
Bronner, Arnold, *see* Bronnen, Arnolt
Brothel of Ika Loch, The (Van Ostaijen), 14
Brother Lucifer (Andres), 342
Brothers' Feud, The (Van Eeden), 4
Brothers From Lasawa, The (Fussenegger), 344
Bru, Hedin, **379**
Bruckner, Ferdinand, **312–13**
Bruheim, Jan-Magnus, **392**
Bruller, Jean, *see* Vercors
Bubu of Montparnasse (Philippe), 39
Buddenbrooks (T. Mann), 231
Bull, Olav, **389–90**
Bullfighters, The (Montherlant), 89
Bureaucrats, The (Courteline), 62
Bürger Schippel (Sternheim), 223
Burghers of Calais, The (Kaiser), 263–4
Burgomaster of Stilemonde, The (Maeterlinck), 61
Burlador (Lilar), 175
Burning Bush, The (Kokoschka), 258
Burnt Child, The (Dagerman), 411
Burnt Offering, The (Goes), 342
Burroughs, William, 111
Busch, Wilhelm, **190**
Butor, Michel, **151–2**
Buysse, Cyriel, **11–12**
By the Wayside (Bang), 365
By Way of Sainte-Beuve (Proust), 69

Cahiers de la Quinzaine (p. France), 108
Caligula (Camus), 128
Calligrammes (Apollinaire), **113**
Camus, Albert, **127–31**
Cant (Munk), 373
Canth, Minna, 19
Cape Farewell (H. Martinson), 406
Captain of Köpenick, The (Zuckmayer), 321
Cardboard Crown, The (Sarment), 163
Cardinal of Spain, The (Montherlant), 90
Carette, Albert, *see* Marceau, Félicien
Carl and Anna (Frank), 268
Carl and Rosa (Döblin), 305
Carl Heribert Malmros (Hellström), 408
Carmelites, The (Buanos), 86

Carnival Confession (Zuckmayer), 322
Carossa, Hans, **273**
Carrots (Renard), 39
Case d'Arthez, The (Nossack), 341
Case of Sergeant Grischa, The (Zweig), 276
Casper Hauser (Wasserman), 268
Castillo, Michel del, **145**
Castle, The (Kafka), 290, **292–3**
Castle of Argol, The (Gracq), 143
Castle to Castle (Céline), **94–5**
Cat and Mouse (Grass), 351
Cathedral, The (Huysmans), 32
Caucasian Chalk Circle, The (Brecht), **317**, 318
Cause of the Crime, The (Frank), 267
Céard, Henri, **30**
Celan, Paul, **354–6**
Céline, Louis-Ferdinand, **93–5**
'Cemetery By the Sea, The' (Valéry), 106–7
Cenci, Les (Artaud), 169
Certain Plume, Un (Michaux), 176
Cendrars, Blaise, **95–6**
César (Pagnol), 163
Chaminadour (Jouhandeau), 86
Chamson, André, **104–5**
'Chandos Letter' (Von Hofmannsthal), 169, 207
Chantecler (Rostand), 64
Chaos and Night (Montherlant), 90
Chapel Road (Boon), 16
Char, René, **182–4**
Character (Bordewijk), 9
Charcoal-Burner's Ballad, The (Andersson), 399
Charlatan, The (Kesten), 282
Charles Blanchard (Philippe), 39
'Charon' Group, Germany, 248
Cheeks on Fire (Radiguet), 97
Cheese (Elsschot), 15
Cheops (Leopold), 6
Chéri (Colette), 71
Chesterton, G. K., **83**
Chief, The (H. Mann), 228
Child and the Spells, The (Colette), 72
Child at the Balustrade, The (Boylesve), 34
Child Playing on the Shore, The (Branner), 378
Childhood (Carossa), 273
Children of Alsace, The (Bazin), 33
Children of Guernica, The (Kesten), 282–3
Children of the Game (Cocteau), 158
Children's Book, The (Gyllensten), 411

China Shepherdess, The (Marceau), 144
Chorell, Walentin, **415**
Christianus Sextus (Falkberget), 385
Christophoros (Ørjasæter), 389
Chronicles of Hell (Ghelderode), 174
Chronique (Perse), 120
Chumblerg, Hans, **311**
'Cimitière Marin, Le' (Valéry), 106
Circle of Chalk (Klabund), 271
City Beyond the River, The (Kasack), 288–9
Civilisation (Duhamel), 82
Clara d'Ellébeuse (Jammes), 51
Claudel, Paul, **64–6**
Claudia (Zweig), 275
Claus, Hugo, **17**
Claussen, Sophus, **368**
Clock Struck One, The (Zuckmayer), 322
Cloister, The (Verhaeren), 61
Closson, Herman, **175**
Clown, The (Böll), 348
Clown Jac (H. Bergman), 409–10
Coal-Tar Seller, The (Sandemose), 387
Cocteau, Jean, **157–9**
Coenan, Frans, **4**
Coiners, The (Gide), 68
Cold Light, The (Zuckmayer), 322
Colette [Sidonie Gabrielle], **71–2**
Colliander, Tito, **415**
Colonel's Children, The (Supervielle), 117
Colony, The (Hansen), 378
Combat (p. France), 127
Come and Go (Roelants), 16
Comédie-Française, 65, 157
Comic History of Klizer Karel, The (Ghelderode), 174
Command, The (Hochwälder), 333
Commerz und Privatbank (Schwitters), 308,
Concert, The (Bahr), 217
Concreter (Viita), 27
Condemned, The (Dagerman), 412
Confession, The (Adamov), 165
Confession of a Fool, The (Strindberg), 394
Confessions of Felix Krull, Confidence Man, The (T. Mann), 234
Confusions of Silence, The (A. R. Holst), 7
Confrontation, The (Guilloux), 99
Confusions of Young Törless, The (Musil), 300, 301
Congo Insurrection (Walschap), 16
Conquest of a World, The (Graf), 352
Conrad, Michael Georg, **195**

Constance Ring (A. Skram), 382
Constantinople (Loti), 35
Copeau, Jacques, **157**
Coppée, François, **45**
Copper Breath (Enckell), 414
Coral, The (Kaiser), 264
Coronal (Claudel), 66
Corydon (Gide), 68
Coster, Albert de, **53**
Count d'Orgel Opens the Ball (Radiguet), 97
Count Öderland (Frisch), 328
Count of Antwerp, The (Hallström), 412
Count of Charolais, The (Beer-Hofmann), 219
Country Doctor, The (Kafka), 291
Country of Origin, The (Du Perron), 8
Couperus, Louis, **3**
Courteline, Georges, **61–2**
Crime, A (Bernanos), 85
Crime of Sylvestre Bonnard, The (France), 38
Crime Passionel (Sartre), 127
Criminals, The (Bruckner), 312
Crises and Wreaths (Sjöberg), 399
Crommelynck, Fernand, **171–3**
Croquignol (Philippe), 39
Cruelty, Theatre of, 169–70
Csokor, Franz Theodor, **327**
'Cubism', 112
Cubist Painters, The (Apollinaire), 112
Cult of the Self, The (Barrès), 37
Cults (Uppdal), 384
Cure Through Aspirin (Walschap), 15–16
Curtis, Jean-Louis, **143–4**
Cyanide (Wolf), 313
Cyrano de Bergerac (Rostand), 64

Dabit, Eugène, **98–9**
'Dada', 109, 258, 306, 413
Dagerman, Stig, **411, 412**
Daily Bread (Boylesve), 23–4
Daisne, Johan, **16, 17**
D'Alembert's End (Heissenbüttel), 357
Dam, Albert, **372**
Damaged Goods (Brieux), 61
Dance Through a Shadowy Land (Uppdal), 384
Dancing Mice (Wied), 372
Dangerous Age, The (Michaëlis), **371**
Dangerous Game, A (Dürrenmatt), 332
Danton (Rolland), 41
Dark Journey, The (Green), 100

Dark Pilgrimage, The (Wassermann), 268

Dark Room of Damocles, The (Hermans), 10

Dark Stranger, A (Gracq), 143

Däubler, Theodor, **248**

Daumal, René, **169**

Dauthenday, Max[imilian], 203–4

David Ramm's Heritage (Andersson), 399

Davidsohn, Hans, *see* Hoddis, Jakob van

Davor (Grass), 351

Dawn Fiancée, The (Claus), **17**

Daybreak (Bertelsen), 377

Days in the Sun (Nex), 370

Days of Contempt (Malraux), 103

Days of His Grace (E. Johnson), 406

Days of Hope (Malraux), 103–4

Days of White Bread (Borgen), 387

Days on a Cloud (Abell), 373

Dead Calm on the Way (Stigen), 393

Dead Day, The (Barlach), 225

Dead Lake, The (Heyse), 189

Dead Letter (Pinget), 156

Dead Queen, The (Montherlant), 90

Death (Lemonnier), 59

Death and the Fool (von Hofmannsthal), 207–8

Death in Venice (T. Mann), 232

Death of a Doll (Bruckner), 313

Death of a Nobody (Romains), 80

Death of Angèle Degroux, The (Marsman), 7

Death of George, The (Beer-Hofmann), 220

Death of Virgil, The (Broch), 297

Death of Vitalism, The (Marsman), 7

Death on the Instalment Plan (Céline), 93

'Decadence', **XIII**

Decampment (Stadler), 241

Deception, The (Bernanos), 84

Decline (Trakl), 243

Decline of the West, The (Spengler), 254

Decorte, Bert de, **14**

Dedicated Life in Poetry, The (Du Pin), 187

Deeps of Deliverance, The (van Eeden), 4

Defeat (Grieg), 388

Degrees (Butor), 152

Deguy, Michel, **187**

Dehmel, Richard, **191–2**

Delattre, Louis, **57**

Delay, The (Hildesheimer), **333**

Deluge, The (Andres), 342–3

Demian (Hesse), 298–9

Demolder, Eugène, **56–7**

Demons, The (von Doderer), 284

Denied a Country (Bang), 365

Denmark, Literature of, **363–79**

Deruga Trial, The (Huch), 197

Desert Love (Montherlant), 90

Desert of Love (Mauriac), 77

Desnos, Robert, **124**

Desperate One, The (Bloy), 41

Destouches, Louis-Ferdinand, *see* Céline, Louis-Ferdinand

Detour, The (Walser), 339

Devil in France, The (Feuchtwanger), 273

Devil in the Flesh, The (Radiguet), 97

Devil's General, The (Zuckmayer), 322

Deyssel, Lodewijk Van, **2–3**

Diana (H. Mann), 227

Diary (Frisch), 330

Diary 1928–57 (Green), 100

Diary of a Chambermaid, The (Mirbeau), 60

Diary of a Country Priest, The (Bernanos), 85

Diary of My Times (Bernanos), 85

Dice Box, The (Jacob), 116

Dies Irae (Bergengruen), 275

Diktonius, Elmer, **413**

Dilthey, Wilhelm, **193–4**

Dinesen, Isak, *see* Blixen, Karen

Dinner Party, The (Mauriac), 153

Dionysus-Dithyrambs (Nietzsche), 192

Disciple, The (Bourget), 33

Discours sur la Méthode (Ponge), 180

Disque Vert, Le (p.), 176

Ditlevsen, Tove, **376–7**

Ditte, Nexø, **370**

Ditzen, Rudolf, *see* Fallada, Hans

Diwan (Ekelöf), 403

Do You Know the Milky Way? (Wittlinger), 326

Döblin, Alfred, **303–6**

Doctor Glas (Söderberg), 405

Doctor Faustus (T. Mann), 233

'Dr. Murke's Collected Silences' (Böll), 349

Doderer, Heimito von, **284–5**

Dog-Days (Claus), 17

Dog Years (Grass), 351

Dominici Affair, The (Giono), 92

Don Giovanni (Jouve), 118

Don Juan (Krog and Hoel), 388

Don Juan or Love of Geometry (Frisch), 328–9

Donadieu (Hochwälder), 332

Dons, Aage, **378–9**

Dorgelès, Roland, **71**

Dorothea (Nossack), 340

Down There (Huysmans), 32

Downstream (Siwertz), 409

Drachman, Holger, **366–7**

Dragon Throne, The (Hildesheimer), 333

Drayman Henschel (G. Hauptmann), 199

Dream, The (Montherlant), 89

Dream Play, A (Strindberg), 395

Dreamer, The (Green), 100

Drieu La Rochelle, Piere-Eugène, **87–8**

Drinker, The (Fallada), 277

Driver's Escape (Andersch), 345

Drogon (Van Schendel), 5

Droll Peter (Timmermans), 15

'Druidism', 179

Drums in the Night (Brecht), 314

Du Bouchet, André, **184–5**

Du Gard, Roger Martin, *see* Martin Du Gard, Roger

Dumarchais, Paul, *see* Mac Orlan, Pierre

Du Perron, Eddy, **7–8**

Du Perron, Charles Edgar, *see* Du Perron, Eddy

Du Pin, Patrice de la Tour, **186–7**

Du Plessys, Maurice, **49–50**

Duel (Fangen), 386

Duhamel, Georges, 79, **80, 82–3**

Duinese Elegies (Rilke), 210, 213

Dullin, Charles, **157**

Duo (Collette), 71

Dupin, Jacques, 184, **185**

Duras, Marguerite, **142–3**

Durch Group, Germany, 195

Dürrenmatt, Friedrich, **330–2**

Durtain, Luc, **80**

Duun, Olav, **383–4**

Dwarf, The (Lagerkvist), 410

Dying Church, The (Schaper), 341–2

Dying Man, The (Hermann-Neisse), 252

Each in His Darkness (Green), 100–1

Eagle With Two Heads, The (Cocteau), 158

Earth is Ours, The (Moberg), 406

Earth is Round, The (Salacrou), 161–2

Earth Spirit (Wedekind), 221

Easter in New York (Cendrars), 95

Eccentric, The (Þórðarson), 417

'École Romane' Group, 48

Ecuador (Michaux), 177

Edge of the World, The (Hyry), 25

Eeden, Frederik van, **4**

Eekhoud, Georges, **57**

Egg, The (Marceau), 144

Egge, Peter, **384**

Ekelöf, Gunnar, **401–3**

Ekelund, Vilhelm, **398**

Electra (Euripides, *adapt.* Von Hofmannsthal), 208

Elli, or the Seven Steps (Schaeffer), 203

Elizabeth of England (Bruckner), 312

Elsewhere (Michaux), 177

Elskamp, Max, **54–5**

Elsschot, Willem, 14, **15**

Eluard, Paul, **122–3**

Elnin (Nossack), 340

Emerald Road, The (Demolder), 56

Emigrants, The (Moberg), 406

Emil and the Detectives (Kästner), 287

Emmanuel, Pierre, **187**

Empire Builders, The (Vian), 167

En Route (Huysmans), 32

Enchantments (Valéry), 106

Enckell, Rabbe, **414–15**

End is Not Yet, The (Von Unruh), 263

End of Chéri, The (Colette), 71

End of the Bourgeois, The (Lemonnier), 56

Endgame (Beckett), 140

Enfants du Paradis, Les (film, Prévert), 180

Engländer, Richard, *see* Altenberg, Peter

Ensam (Strindberg), 394

Enzensberger, Hans Magnus, **357–8**

'Epic Theatre', 314, 337

Erasers, The (Robbe-Grillet), 150

Erasures (Leiris), 132

Ermine, The (Anouilh), 160

Ernst, Max, **307**

Ernst, Paul, **197**

Escapade (Ségalen), 73

Esch the Anarchist (Broch), 296

Estaunié, Édouard, **34**

Et Nunc Manet in Te (Gide), 67

'Eternal Adorer, The' (E. Rode), 371

Eulogies (Perse), 119–20

Eve (Péguy), 108

Evening Star, The (Söderberg), 405

Evenings (Van Het Reve), 11

Events of 1918 (Meri), 25
Everyday Life (Jotuni), 22
Ewald Tragy (Rilke), 210
Exercises in Style (Queneau), 132
Exile (Perse), 120
Exile and the Kingdom (Camus), 130
Existentialism, 125*f.*, 136
Experimental Novel, The (Zola), 29
'Expressionism', XIV, 109, 216*f.*,
    234*f.*, 257*f.*, 323, 374
Eye of God (Hellens), 58
Eyes of Elsa, The (Aragon), 123
Eyes of Reason, The (Heym), 359

F.C. Tietjens (Forssell), 404
Fabian, the Story of a Moralist, 287
Fabricius, Sara, *see* Sandel, Cora
Fackel, Die (p.), 270
Falkberget, Johan, **385**
Fall, The (Camus), 130
Fall of the King, The (Jensen), 369
Fallada, Hans, **276–7**
False Light (Closson), 176
Falling Leaf, The (Gaiser), 343
Family, A (Von Unruh), 262
Family, The (Wied), 371
Family Selicke, The (Holz and Schlaf),
    195
Fangen, Ronald, **386**
Fanny (Pagnol), 163
Fantastic Realities (Hellens), 58
Fantastic Tales (Bordewijk), 9
Fargue, Léon-Paul, 114–15
Farigoule, Louis, *see* Romains, Jules
Faroe Islands, Literature of, 379
Fat and the Thin, The (Zola), 30
Father, The (Strindberg), 394
Fatherland (Järnefelt), 20
Fathers Eat Grapes, The (Wied), 371
Fantastulus (Spielhagen), 190
Fear (Knudsen), 372
Fear and Misery in the Third Reich
    (Brecht), 316
Felybrief, J. K., *see* Oudshoorn, J. Van
Ferment, The (Estaunié), 34
Fermina Marquez (Larbaud), 116
Feuchtwanger, Lion, **272–3**
Feydeau, Georges, **62**
Fibrils (Leiris), 132
Field and Barracks (Haanpää), 23
Figaro, Le (p. France), 48
'Fin de Siècle', XIV
Finnegans Wake (Joyce), 131

Finnish Language, 19
Fire Raisers, The (Frisch), 329
Fire Within, The (Drieu la Rochelle), 87
Fireworks (Wedekind), 222
Firm Grip (Bru), 379
Fisrt Book of Schmol, The (Van
    Ostaijen), 14
Fish With the Golden Dagger, The (Hey),
    334
Fischer, Leck, **379**
Fisherfolk (Nordström), 408
Fishermen (Kirk), 377
Fishing for Shadows (Sarment), 163
Five Great Odes (Claudel), 66
Five Weeks in a Balloon (Verne), 41
Five Young Ones (Lundkvist, Sangren,
    Kjellgren, Martinson and another),
    401
Flanders Road, The (Simon), 153
Flax Field, The (Streuvels), 12
Flemish Language, 1
Flemish, The (Verhaeren), 55
Flesh (Benn), 253
Fliegel, Hellmuth, *see* Heym, Stefan
Flight to Afar (Andersch), 344
Flight to Arras (Saint-Exupéry), 102
Flood, The (Clézio), 156
Floodtide of Fate (Dunn), 383
'Floralism', 179
Flowers of Evil, The (Baudelaire), 42
Flutes and Daggers (H. Mann), 227
Flutterings of the Heart, The (Marceau),
    144
Fly, White Dove! (Bang-Hansen), 393
Follain, Jean, **186**
Fontane, Theodore, **189**
Fool in Christ, Emanuel Quint (G.
    Hauptmann), 199
Footsteps of Fate (Couperus), 3
Force of Circumstance, The (Beauvoir), 136
Forest of the Dead, The (Wiechert), 275
Forests of the Night, The (Curtis), 144
Forgeries (Kasack), 289
Forgotten Faces (Jens), 350
Forms (Nijhoff), 9
Forssell, Lars, **404**
Fort, Paul, **51–2**
40-tal (p. Sweden), 403, 410, 411
Forum Group, Holland, 8, 15
Four Seasons, The (Merrill), 46–7
Fournier, Henri-Alban, *see* Alain-
    Fournier
Fourteenth of July, The (Rolland), 41

Fragments of a Diary (La Cour), 374
France, Anatole, **37–8**
Frank, Leonhard, **267**, 311
'Free Stage, The', Germany, 195
Frénaud, André, **186**
French Diana, The (Aragon), 123
Frida's Book (Sjöberg), 399
Fridegård, Jan, **408**
Fridolin's Garden (Karlfeldt), 397
Fridolin's Songs (Karlfeldt), 397
Fried, Erich, **356**
Frisch, Max, **327–30**
Fritz Kocher's Compositions (Walser), 285–6
Fröding, Gustaf, **396**
From Morn to Midnight (Kaiser), 263
From Now On (p. Holland), 11
From the Dawn Angelus to the Evening Angelus (Jammes), 50–1
From the Heroic Life of the Bourgeoisie (Sternheim), 223
From the Life of a Faun (Schmidt), 346
Fruit of Nothing (Bruckner), 313
Fruits of the Earth (Gide), 67
Fugitive, The (Hochwälder), 332
Fugitive Crosses His Tracks, A (Sandemose), 386
Furnished Room, The (Schnurre), 345
Fussenegger, Gertrud, **344**

Gadarene Club, The (Walser), 339
Gaiser, Gerd, **343–4**
Gallows Hill (Uppdal), 384
Gallows Songs (Morgenstern), 239
Game of Patience, The (Guilloux), 99
Games of Night, The (Dagerman), 411
Garborg, Arne, **381**
Garden on the Orontes, A (Barrès), 37
Garden Where the Brass Band Played, The (Vestdijk), 8
Gardens and Rivers (Audiberti), 181
Garman and Worse (Kielland), 380–1
Garnier, Pierre, **179**
Gas, I and II (Kaiser), 264
Gauntlet, A (Bjørnson), 380
Gear (Leiris), 132
Gelehrtenrepublik, Die (Schmidt), 346
Genêt, Jean, **140–2**
Génétrix (Mauriac), 77
Genevoix, Maurice, **71**
George, Stefan, **200–2**
Germans in Provence, The (Jouhandeau), 87

Germinie Lacerteux (E. and J. de Goncourt), 30
Gertrud (Söderberg), 405
Gezelle, Guido, 11
Ghelderrode, Michel de, **173–4**
Gide, André, **66–8**
Gigi (Colette), 71
Gijsen, Marnix, **16–17**
Gill, Claes, **392**
Gilles (Drieu la Rochelle), 87
Giono, Jean, **91–3**
Giraud, Albert, **53**
Giraudoux, Jean, **159–60**
Girls, The (Montherlant), 89–90
Gjellerup, Karl, **366**
Glass Bead Game, The (Hesse), 300
Glass Bees, The (E. Jünger), 281
Goat Song (Werfel), 266
Goddesses, The (H. Mann), 227
God's Beautiful World (Koch), 406
God's Orchid (H. Bergman), 409
God's Utopia (Andres), 342
Goes, Albrecht, **342**
Golden Fruits, The (Sarraute), 149
Golden Guts (Crommelynck), 172–3
Goldman, Jean-Isidore, *see* Isou, Isidore
Goldman's (Siwertz), 409
Golem, The (Meyrink), 294
Golssenau, A. F. Vieth von, *see* Renn, Ludwig
Gomperts, H. A., **10**
Good Hope, The (Heijermans), 4
Good Night, Earth (Lo-Johansson), 407
Good School, The (Bahr), 217
Good Woman of Setzuan, The (Brecht), 317, 318
Goose Man, The (Wasserman), 269
Goris, Jan-Albert, *see* Gijsen, Marnix
Gorter, Herman, **5–6**
Gorz, André, **145**
Gracq, Julien, **143**
Graf, Oskar Maria, **352**
Grail Splashes (Fröding), 396
Grand Écart, Le (Cocteau), 158
Grandmother's House (Soya), 373
Grass, Günter, **350–2**
Gravitations (Supervielle), 117
Great Fear of the Well-Disposed, The (Bernanos), 84
Great Illusion, The (Waltari), 24
Great Miscellany (Ponge), 180
Great Risk, The (Brod), 269

Great Weaver from Casmir, The (Laxness), 417

Greater Hope, The (Aichinger), 349

Green, Julien, **100–1**

Green Disk, The (p. France), 176

Green Henry (Keller), 189

Green Mare, The (Aymé), 133

Greeta and His Lord (Järnefelt), 20

Grey Birds (Van Schendel), 5

Grey House, The (Bang), 365

Grieg, Nordahl, **388**

Griese, Friedrich, **311**

Grimm, Hans, **311**

Grindel, Eugène, *see* Éluard, Paul

Groaning Beasts (Bordewijk), 9

Gruppe 47 (Germany), 326–7, 334, 344, 345, 350, 360

Guest the One-Eyed (G. Gunnarsson), 417

Guignol's Band (Céline), 94

Guillevic [Eugène], **185–6**

Guilloux, Louis, **99–100**

Guitar, The (Castillo), 145

Guitar and Concertina (Fröding), 396

Gullberg, Hjalmar, **399–400**

Gunnarsson, Gunnar, **417**

Guðmundarson, Stefan, *see* Stephansson, Stephan G.

Haanpää, Pentti, **23–4**

Haarla, Lauri, **28**

Haavikko, Paavo, **27**, 28

Haavio, M., *see* Mustapää, P.

Hacks, Peter, **360**

Hafstein, Hannes, **416**

Hagelstange, Rudolf, **352**

Halbe, Max, **196–7**

Half-Time (Walser), 339

Hallström, Per, **404–5**, 412

Hamlet (Döblin), 306

Hamsun, Knut, **382–3**, **388**

Hangman, The (Lagerkvist), 410

Hansen, Martin, A., **378**

Hansine Solstad (Egge), 384

Happy Warriors (Laxness), 418

Hart, Julius, **195**

Harvard Advocate (Brecht), 315

Harvest (Giono), 92

Hasenclever, Walter, **259**

Haughty, The (J. Nielsen), 378

Haulleville, Eric de, **176**

Hauptmann, Carl, **198**

Hauptmann, Gerhart, 195, **197–9**

Havoc (Kristensen), 375

He Who Said Yes/He Who Said No (Brecht), 315

Head Against the Walls (H. Bazin), 143

Head of the Firm, The (Bergman), 409

Headmaster Kleist (Kaiser), 263

Heart of Alsace, The (Schickele), 275

Heart on the Left (Frank), 268

Heartbreak (Aragon), 123

Heaven and Hell (Kornfeld), 259

Hebrew Ballads (Lasker-Schüler), 248

Hedberg, Olle, **410**

Hedda Gabler (Ibsen), 380

Hedenvind-Eriksson, Gustav, **405–6**

Hedin, Sven, **278**

Heiberg, Gunnar, **387–8**

Heidenstam, Verner Von, **395**

Heijermans, Hermann, **4–5**

Hein, Piet, **376**

Heinesen, William, **379**

Heinrich Brothers, **195**

Heissenbüttel, Helmut, **356–7**

Heliopolis (E. Jünger), 281

Helka Songs (Leino), 20–21

Hellemyr Family, The (Skram), 382

Hellens, Franz, **58**, 176

Hellström, Gustav, **408**

Hémon, Louis, **74–5**

Henningsen, Agnes, **371**

Hennique, Léon, **31**

Henri IV (H. Mann), 229

Henry, King of France (H. Mann), 229

Henschke, Alfred, *see* Klabund

Hensen, Herwig, **14**

Herédia, José-Maria de, **45**

Heretic of Soana, The (G. Hauptmann), 199

Heretica (p. Denmark), 376

Hermans, Willem Frederik, **10**

Hermlin, Stephan, **360**

Hero, The (Kidde), 372

Herod the King (Munk), 373

Heroic Comedy (Bruckner), 313

Herr Puntila and His Man Matti (Brecht), 317

Hermann-Neisse, Max, **252**

Herzmanovsky-Orlando, Fritz Von, **294**

Hesse, Hermann, **297–300**

Hey, Richard, **334**

Heym, Georg, **239–40**

Heym, Stefan, **359**

Heyse, Paul, **189**

Hidden in Shadows (Boyson), 392
Hildesheimer, Wolfgang, **333-4**
Hille, Peter, **246**
Hinkemann (Toller), 261, 311
Hiroshima Mon Amour (film, Duras), 142
History of a Mary, The (Baillon), 57
Hochhuth, Rolf, **338**
Hochwälder, Fritz, **332-3**
Hoddis, Jakob Van, **236**
Hoel, Sigurd, **386, 388**
Hoffmann, Elisabeth, *see* Langgässer, Elisabeth
Hofmannsthal, Hugo Von, **204-209**
Hofmo, Gunvor, **392**
Hollo, Anselm, **25**
Holst, A. Roland, **6-7**
Holstein, Ludwig, **367**
Holthusen, Hans Egon, **352**
Holy Sinner, The (T. Mann), 233-4
Holz, Arno, **194-5**
Home for Our Adornment (Sandemose), 386
Homo Faber (Frisch), 330
Honour (Sudermann), 196
Hop Signor! (Ghelderode), 174
Hopeless Generations (Bang), 364
Hörspiele, 326, 339, 342, 345, 349, 352
Horrible Tango, The (Wolkers), 11
Hostage, The (Claudel). 65
Hostages (S. Heym), 359
Hot and Cold (Crommelynck), 173
Hotel du Nord (Dabit), 98
Hotel Room, The (Mykle), 393
Hothouses (Maeterlinck), 60
House, The (Fussenegger), 344
House in Haarlem, The (Van Schendel), 5
House of Assignation, The (Robbe-Grillet), 150, 151
House of the People, The (Guilloux), 99
House on the Canal, The (Coenen), 4
Houtekiet (Walschap), 15
How Herr Mockinpott Was Relieved of His Sufferings (Weiss), 336
How I Wrote Certain Books (Roussel), 73
How It Is (Beckett), 139
Huchel, Peter, **360**
Huelsenbeck, Richard, **308**
Huguenau the Realist (Broch), 296
Hulbeck, Charles R., *see* Huelsenbeck, Richard
Hulda, **416-17**

Human Voice, The (Cocteau), 158
Hundred Thousand Billion Poems, A (Queneau), 131
Hundred Violins, The (Øverland), 390
Hunger (Hamsun), 382
Hunger Artist, The (Kafka), 292
Hunting With the Fox (Renard), 40
Hussar on the Roof, The (Giono), 92
Huysmans, Georges Charles, *see* Huysmans, Joris-Karl
Huysmans, Joris-Karl, **31-2**
Hymn About the Flower (Þorðarson), 417
Hyry, Antti, **25**

I Am to Blame (Jotuni), 28
I Demand All (La Cour), 374
I, the King (Kesten), 282
Ibsen, Henrik, **380**
Ice Palace, The (Vesaas), 391
Iceland, Literature of, 415-18
Iceland Fisherman, An (Loti), 35
Iceland's Bell (Laxness), 418
Idealist, An (Gjellerup), 366
Idealists, The (Scherfig), 379
Illiterate, The (Lo-Johansson), 407, 408
Illuminating Window, The (Doderer), 284
I'm Not Stiller (Frisch), 330
Immaculate Conception, The (Éluard), 123
Immemorial, The (Ségalen), 73
Immoralist, The (Gide), 67
Impostor, The (Cocteau), 158
Impressions of Africa (Roussel), 72
Imprint, The (Estaunié), 34
In a Little While We are Gone (Branner), 378
In Alastalo's Room (Kilpi), 22
In Camera (Sartre), 126
In Danger (A. R. Holst), 7
In God's Land (Nexø), 370
In Sight of Chaos (Hesse), 299
In the Labyrinth (Robbe-Grillet), 150
In the Middle of a Jazz Age (Sønderby), 379
In the Outer Skerries (Strindberg), 394
Incredible Borgias, The (Klabund), 271
Indelible Seal, The (Langgässer), 250, 251
Independent People (Laxness), 417
Indipondi (G. Hauptmann), 199
Infatuation (Stigen), 393
Inferno (Barbusse), 70
Inferno (Strindberg), 394
Inn, The (Hochwälder), 332
Innocent, The (Hochwälder), 332-3

Innocents, The (Broch), 295
Insel, Die (p. Germany), 220
Insurance, The (Weiss), 335
'Integralism', 179
Interrogation, The (Le Clézio), 156
Intimacy (Sartre), 125
Intimate Journal of A. O. Barnabooth, The (Larbaud), 116
'Intimism', 179
Into the Labyrinth (Mallet-Joris), 171
Invasion, The (Adamov), 166
Investigation, The (Weiss), 336
'Investigations of a Dog' (Kafka), 291
Invisible Hands (Krolow), 354
Ionesco, Eugène, **164–5**
Irish Notebook (Böll), 349
Iron Gustav (Fallada), 277
Iron in the Soul (Sartre), 125
Is Mr. Larose the Killer? (Crommelynck), 173
Island, The (Merle), 137
Isolated, The (Meri), 25
Isou, Isidore, **179**
It Is Written (Dürrenmatt), 331

Jaccottet, Philippe, **187**
Jacob, Max, **115–16**
Jacob's Dream (Beer-Hofmann), 220
Jacobsen, H. J., *see* Bru, Hedin
Jacobsen, Jørgen-Frantz, **379**
Jacobsen, J. P., **364**
Jacobsen, Rolf, **392**
Jægtvig and His God (Egge), 384
Jahnn, Hans Henny, **271–3**
Jakob von Gunten (Walser), 286
Jakobowsky and the Colonel (Werfel), 266
Jammes, Francis, **50–1**
Järnefelt, Arvid, **20**
Jarry, Alfred, **62–3**
Jazz Player, The (Roelants), 16
Jealousy (Robbe-Grillet), 150
Jean Barois (Martin Du Gard), 75
Jean Santeuil (Proust), 69
Jean-Christophe (Rolland), 41
Jean-Jacques of Nantes (Sarment), 163
Jenny (Undset), 385
Jens, Walter, **349–50**
Jensen, Johannes V. **368–9**
Jensen, Thit, **371**
Jeune Belgique, La (p.), 52
Jeune Belgique Group, 56, 57
'Jeune Parque, La' (Valéry), 106
Jew Süss (Feuchtwanger), 273

Job (Kokoschka), 258
Job (Roth), 284
Jocasta (Enckell), 414
'*Johanna Maria*', *The* (Van Schendel), 5
Johnson, Eyvind, **406**
Johnson, Uwe, **352**
Johst, Hanns, **264**
Jonas and the Dragon (Siwertz), 409
Jonathan's Journey (Hansen), 378
Jonck-Heere, Karel, **14**
Jørgen Stein (Paludan), 375
Jørgensen, Johannes, 368
Joseph and His Brothers (T. Mann), 233
Joseph Breaks Free (Kesten), 282
Jotuni, Maria, **22, 28**
Jouhandeau, Marcel, **86–7**
Jour se Lève, Le (film, Prévert), 180
Journal (Ramuz), 74
Journal of Colonel Maumort, The (Martin du Gard), 75
Journals 1889–1949 (Gide), 66, 107
Journals (Green), 100
Journey to Portiuncala, The (Andres), 343
Journey to the End of the Night (Céline), 93
Jouve, Pierre-Jean, **118–19**
Jouvet, Louis, 157
Joy (Bernanos), 84
Joy of Man's Desiring (Giono), 92
Judge and His Hangman, The (Dürrenmatt), 331
Juha (Aho), 19
June Solstice, The (Montherlant), 88
Jünger, Ernst, **279–82**
Jünger, Friedrich Georg, **354**
Jungwein Group, 217, 219, 283
Jürg Reinhart (Frisch), 328
Just, The (Camus), 130
Juvonen, Helvi, **27**

Kafka, Franz, **289–94**
Kahn, Gustave, **46**
Kailas, Uuno, **25**
Kaiser, Georg, **263–4**
Kaiser Went, the Generals Remained, The (Plievier), 282
Kaiserreich, The (H. Mann), 228
Kaiser's Coolies, The (Plievier), 282
Kallocain (Boye), 400
Karl and Anna (Frank), 311
Karl and Rosa (Döblin), 305
Karlfeldt, Erik Axel, **396–7**
Kasack, Hermann, **288–9**

Kästner, Erich, **287–8**
Katerpoesie (Scheerbart), 190
Katzgraben (Strittmatter), 360
Kayenberg, Albert, *see* Giraud, Albert
Keller, Gottfried, 189
Kempner, Alfred, *see* Kerr, Alfred
Kerr, Alfred, **196**
Kesten, Hermann, **282–3**
Kestner, René, *see* Rehfisch, Hans José
Kidde, Harald. **372**
Kielland, Alexander, **380–1, 388**
Killer, The (Ionesco), 165
Kilpi, Volter, **22**
Kinck, Hans Ernst, **383**, 388
King Midas (Heiberg), 387
King Orpheus (Segalen), 73
King Solomon and Morolf (Levertin),
  396
King Wren (H. Mann), 229
Kingdom of Love, The (Brod), 269
Kingdom of the Dead (Pontoppidan),
  365–6
Kirk, Hans, **377**
Kiss for the Leper, A (Mauriac), 77
Kjellgren, Josef, **401**
Klabund, **271**
Klitgaard, Mogens, **379**
Kloos, Willem, **1–2**
Klossowski, Pierre, **134**
Knacker's ABC, The (Vian), 167
Knagsted (Wied), 371
Knickers, The (Sternheim), 223
Knock (Romains), 81
Knudsen, Erik, **376**
Knudsen, Jakob, **371–2**
Koch, Martin, **406**
Kokoschka, Oscar, **257–8**
Kolonne Hund (Wolf), 313
Kornfeld, Paul, **259**
Koskenniemi, Veikko Antero, **21–2**
Kostrowitsky, Guillaume-Albert-
  Vladimir-Alexandre-Apollinaire de,
  see Apollinaire, Guillaume
Krag, Vilhelm, **389**
Krane's Café (Sandel), 385
Kraus, Karl, **269–71**
Kretzer, Max, **195–6**
Krilon (E. Johnson), 406
Kristensen, Tom, **374–5**
Kristin Lavransdatter (Undset), 385
Krog, Helge, **388**
Krolow, Karl, **354**
Krönung Richards III, Die (Jahnn), 272

Küfer, Bruno, *see* Scheerbart, Paul
Kunert, Günter, 361
'*Künstlershuld*', **XVIII**, 96, 139, 155,
  320, 358, 374

La Cour, Paul, **374**
La Rochelle, Pierre-Eugène-Drieu, *see*
  Drieu la Rochelle, Pierre-Eugène
Labourers (Kirk), 377
Lacemaker Lekholm Has an Idea
  (Hellström), 408
Lærer Urup (Knudsen), 371–2
Lagerlöf, Selma, **404**
Lagervist, Pär, **410**, 412
Lament for Agnes (Gijsen), 17
Lampe, Friedo, **286–7**
Land Without Death (Döblin), 305
Langgässer, Elisabeth, **250–2**
Lanterne Magique (Fargue), 115
Larbaud, Valéry-Nicholas, **116**
Large and the Small Manœuvre, The
  (Adamov), 166
Larin-Kyösti, **22**
Lars Hård (Fridegård), 408
Larsson, Kyösti, *see* Larin-Kyösti
Lasker-Schüler, Else, **246–8**
Lasso Round the Moon, A (Mykle), 393
Last Advent, The (Schaper), 342
Last Captain of Horse, The
  (Bergengruen), 274
Last Dance of the Season, The (Gaiser),
  343
Last Days of Mankind, The (Kraus), 270
Last Letter Home, The (Moberg), 406
Last of the Vikings, The (Bojer), 384
Last Tales (Blixen), 375
Last Year at Marienbad (Robbe-Grillet),
  151
Late Hour on Earth (Ekelöf), 402
Lateur, Frank, *see* Streuvels, Stijn
Lattice, The (Schaeffer), 203
Lauesen, Marcus, **379**
Lautréamont, 'Comte de', 110
Laws of Hospitality, The (Klossowski),
  134
Laxness, Halldór, **417–18**
Le Fort, Gertrud Von, **273–4**
Le Roy, Grégoire, **54**
Léautaud, Paul, **52**
Leaves of Hypnos (Char), 183
Leavetaking (Weiss), 334
Lecavelé, René, *see* Dorgelès, Roland
Leech (Sandel), 386

Leg, The (Elsschot), 15

Legend of the Holy Drinker, The (Roth), 284

Léger, Marie-René Alexis Saint-Léger, *see* Perse, Saint-John

Lehmann, Wilhelm, **249–50**

Leif the Lucky (Fischer), 379

Leino, Eino, **20–1**

Leiris, Michel, **132–3**

Lemmonier, Camille, 53, **56**, 59, **98**

Leopold, Jan Hendrik, **6**

Leopold the Well-Beloved (Sarment), 163

Lerberghe, Charles Van, **54**

Lernet-Holenia, Alexander, **287**

Let's Face It (Kästner), 287

Letter of Lord Chandos to Francis Bacon, The (Von Hofmannsthal), 207

Letter to Laura (Þorðarson), 417

Letters (Ball), 308

Letters (Rilke), 210

Lettres, Les (p. France), 179

'Lettrism', 179

Levertin, Oscar, **395**

Leviathan (Schmidt), 346

Lewis, P. Wyndham, 83

Liar, The (Hansen), 378

Libertinage (p. Holland), 10

Lichtenstein, Alfred, **236–7**

Lidman, Sara, **411–12**

Lidoire (Courteline), 62

Lie, Jonas, **381**, **388**

Lie, The (Sarraute), 149

Lieder, Rudolf, *see* Hermlin, Stephen

Life and Death in Den Ast (Streuvels), 12

Life and the Sun (Sillanpää), 22–3

Life As We Dreamed It (Roelants), 16

Life Drips Away (Nexø), 370

Life Everlasting (Kasack), 288

Life of Galileo, The (Brecht), 317–18

Life of My Mother, The (Graf), 352

Life of Pastor Arni Þorarinson, The (Þorðarson), 417

Life of Samuel Belét, The (Ramuz), 74

Life Together (Lie), 381

Life's Malice (Wied), 371

Light (Barbusse), 70–1

Light of the World, The (Laxness), 417

Lilar, Suzanne, **175**

Liliencron, Detlev Von, **190–1**

Lillelord (Borgen), 387

Linde, Otto Zur, **248**

Lindegren, Erik, **403**

Linna, Väinö, **24**

Lisbeth of Jarnfjeld (Falkberget), 385

Little Dreaming King, The (Heijermans), 4–5

Little Man, What Now? (Fallada), 277

Little Novels (Schnitzler), 219

Little Prince, The (Saint-Exupéry), 102

Little Republic, The (Van Deyssel), 2

Little Saint, The (Simenon), 171

Little Town, The (H. Mann), 228

Local Anaesthetic (Grass), 351

Locus Solus (Roussel), 72

Loerke, Oskar, **250**

Lo-Johansson, Ivar, **407–8**

Lonely One, The (Johst), 264

Long Journey, The (Jensen), 369

Lönnbohm, Armas Eino Leopold, *see* Leino, Eino

Loser Wins (Sartre), 127

Lost Domain, The (Alain-Fournier), 96

Lost Musicians, The (Heinesen), 379

Lost Paradise, The (Jouve), 118

Loti Pierre, **35–6**

Love Colour of Paris, The (Romains), 80

Love Story, A (Van Deyssel), 2

Lovely Day, A (Céard), 30

Lovers are Never Losers (Giono), 91–2

Low Land (J. Nielsen), 377

Lucebert, **10**

Lucifer's Dream (Curtis), 144

Lucky Christopher (Hansen), 378

Lucky Peter (Pontoppidan), 365

Lundkvist, Artur, **401**

Lütken, Hülda, **371**

Mac Orlan, Pierre, **101**

Machine-Wreckers, The (Toller), 260

Mackay, John Henry, **195**

Madame (Chorell), 415

Madame Clapain (Estaunié), 34

Madame Inès (A. Skram), 382

Madame Lupar (Lemonnier), 56

Madame Marie (Soumagne), 175

Madame Meuriot (Alexis), 30

Madeleine (Gide), 67

Madwoman of Chaillot, The (Giraudoux), 159

Maeterlinck, Maurice, 60–1

Magi, The (Frénaud), 186

Magic Circle, The (Haanpää), 24

Magic Mountain, The (T. Mann), 232

Magnetic Fields, The (Breton and Soupault), 111

Magnificent Cuckold, The (Crommelynck), 172
Magpie on the Gallows, The (H. Teirlinck), 13
Maid Silja, or Fallen Asleep While Young (Sillanpää), 23
Maids, The (Genêt), 141
Maintenance of Order, The (Ollier), 154
Malady of Youth, The (Bruckner), 312
Malatesta (Montherlant), 90
Mallarmé, Stéphane, 42, **44–5**
Mallet-Joris, Françoise, **171**
Malmberg, Bertil, **399**
Malone Dies (Beckett) 139
Malraux André **102–4**
Man in the Mirror, The (H. Teirlinck) 13
Man Is Good (Frank) 267–8
Man of Straw (H. Mann), 228
Man Outside, The (Borchert), 325
Man Who Did Not Want to Grow Old, The (Jens), 350
Man Who Had His Hair Cut Short, The (Daisne), 16
Man Without a Way, The (Lindegren), 403
Man Without Qualities, The (Musil), 300, 302–3, 304
Mana Is Dead (Lo-Johansson), 407
Mandarins, The (Beauvoir), 136
Mandiargues, Andre Pieyre de, **186**
Manhood (Leiris), 132
Manifeste du Surréalism, 1924 (Breton), 110
Mann, [Luiz] Heinrich, **226–9**
Mann, Klaus, **312**
Mann, Thomas, **229–34**
Manner, Eeva-Liisa, **28**
Mannerkorpi, Juha, **27**
Manninen, Otto, **21**
Man's Estate (Malraux), 103
Man's Heaven (Pontoppidan), 366
Man's Rib (Jotuni), 28
Manual of Piety (Brecht), 320
Marat/Sade (Weiss), 334
Marceau, Félicien, **144**
Marcel and Elise (Jouhandeau), 87
Marchwitza, Hans, **359**
Maria Capponi (Schickele), 275
Maria Chapdelaine (Hémon), 74
Maria Speermalie (H. Teirlinck), 13
Marie Donadieu (Philipe), 39
Marinetti, Filipo Tommaso, 80, 235
Marital Chronicles (Jouhandeau), 86

Marius (Pagnol), 163
Marja, A., **10**
Marquis Von Keith, The (Wedekind), 222
Marquise Went Out at Five, The (Mauriac), 153
Marriage (Walschap), 16
Marriage of Mr. Mississippi, The (Dürrenmatt), 331
Mars in Aries (Lernet-Holenia), 287
Marsman, Hendrik, **7**
Martereau (Sarraute), 148–9
Marthe (Huysmans), 31
Martin Birck's Youth (Söderberg), 405
Martin du Gard, Roger, **75–6**
Martinson, Harry, **406–7**
Marxism, 127–9
Masked Face, The (Fussenegger), 344
Masses and Man (Toller), 260
Master Builder, The (Ibsen), 380
Master Builders (Zweig), 283
Master of Santiago, The (Montherlant), 90
Masterless Hammer, The (Char), 182
Mathieu, Noel, *see* Emmanuel, Pierre
Matter of Conscience, A (Bengengruen), 274
Mauriac, Claude, **153**
Mauriac, François, **76–8**
Maurizius Case, The (Wasserman), 268
Maurras, Charles, **48–9**
Max and Maurice (Busch), 190
May, Karl, **267–8**
Measures Taken, The (Brecht), 315, 316
Meek Heritage (Sillanpää), 23
Meeting at the Milestone (Hoel), 386
Meister Timpe (Kretzer), 196
Melody That Got Lost, The (Abell), 373
Mélusine (Hellens), 58
Memoirs (Henningsen), 371
Memoirs (Nexø), 370
Memoirs of a Dutiful Daughter, The (Beauvoir), 136
Memoirs of a Guardian Angel (Hermans), 10
Memoirs of a Secret Revolutionary (Plisnier), 59
Mémoires de Dirk Raspe (Drieu la Rochelle), 88
Memorial (Jouhandeau), 86
Memories of Happy Days (Green), 100
Memories of the Asylum (Éluard), 123
Men of Darkness (Salacrou), 161
Men of Good Will, The (Romains), 81

Men Without Mercy (Döblin), 305
Ménard, Louis, **45–6**
Mendès, Catulle, **45**
Mercure de France (p.), 39
Meri, Veijo, **24–5**
Merle, Robert, **136–7**
Merrill, Stuart, **46–7**
Merry Vineyard, The (Zuckmayer), 321
Merry-Go-Round (Schnitzler), 218
Merz (Schwitters), 308
Messager, Charles, *see* Vildrac, Charles
'Metamorphosis, The' (Kafka), 290, 291
Meyer, Gustav, *see* Meyrink, Gustav
Meyrink, Gustav, **294**
Michaëlis, Karin, **371**
Michaux, Henri, **176–8**
'Midcult', XIX
'Middlebrow', XIX
Midge and the Lamp, The (Bang-Hansen), 393
Mielants, Florent, *see* Hensen, Herwig
Miguel Manara (Milosz), 118
Mijnheer Serjanszoon (H. Teirlinck), 12–13
Mill, The (Gjellerup), 366
Millenium of Song, A (*Anth.*), 27
Milosz, Oscar Veneslas de Lubicz, **117–18**
Minerva (H. Mann), 227
Minna (Gjellerup), 366
Minne, Richard, **14**
Mira (Brod), 269
Miracle at Verdun (Chumblerg), 311
Miracles (Alain-Fournier), 96
Mirage (Bru), 379
Miriam (Chorell), 415
Miss Julie (Strindberg), 394
Mr. Ripon and Nemesis (Hémon), 75
Misunderstanding, The (Vildrac), 162
Moberg, Vilhelm, **406**
Mobile (Butor), 152
Mockel, Albert, **53**
Moderato Cantabile (Duras), 142
'Modern Awakening' movement, Denmark, 364
Mogin, Jean, **178–9**
Moineaux, Georges, *see* Courteline, Georges
Moïra (Green), 100
Molloy (Beckett), 139
Mombert, Alfred, **248–9**
Monks, The (Verhaeren), 55

Monsieur Godeau Married (Jouhandeau), 87
Monsieur Teste (Valéry), 106
Mont, Paul de, **17**
Montherlant, Henri de, **88–91**
Moon in the South, The (Zuckmayer), 322
Moonscape (Waltari), 24
Moraine (Viita), 27
Moravagine (Cendrars), 95
Moréas, Jean, **48**
Moreldieu (Hellens), 58
Morgenstern, Christian, **237–9**
Morgue (Benn), 253
Moritz Tassow (Hacks), 360
Morten the Red (Naxø), 370
Moscow (Feuchtwanger), 273
Moscow (Plievier), 282
Mother, The (Brecht), 316
Mother and Child (Philippe), 39
Mother Courage (Brecht), 317
Motorcycle, The (Mandiargues), 186
Mouji, A. T., *see* Marja, A.
Mountains, Seas and Giants (Döblin), 304
Mulisch, Harry, **11**
Munk, Kaj, **373**
Murder, Hope of the Women (Kokoschka), 257–8
Murder of a Buttercup, The (Döblin), 303
Murders (Plisnier), 59
Murphy (Beckett), 138
Music Hall (Ostaijen), 14
'Musicism', 179
Musil, Robert, **300–3**
Mustapää, P., **25–6**
My Blue Piano (Lasker-Schüler), 248
My Brother Yves (Loti), 35
My Childhood (Pekkanen), 23
My Conversion (Järnefelt), 20
My Death Is My Own (Ahlin), 411
My Friend From Limousin (Giraudoux), 159
My Heart (Lasker-Schüler), 247
My Life as German and Jew (Wasserman), 268
My Little War (Boon), 16
My Place (Weiss), 336
Mykle, Agnar, **393**
Mysteries (Hamsun), 383
Mysteries of Love, The (Vitrac), 170
Mystery of Crowds, The (Adam), 35
Mystery of the Charity of Joan of Arc, The (Péguy), 109

Mystery of the Holy Innocents, The (Péguy), 109
Myth of Sisyphus, The (Camus), 127, 163
Myths, The (Jensen), 369

Nadja (Breton), 111
'Naïve', XVI–XVIII
Naked Among Wolves (Apitz), 359
Nana (Zola), 29
Narrene (Rifbjerg), 378
Narziss and Goldmund (Hesse), 300
Nathansen, Henri, **372–3**
Natives of the Bordeaux Country (Audiberti), 182
'Naturalism', XIII, 29, 31, 50–2, 194
'Naturalists', German, 194
'Naturist' Group, France, 50–2
Nausea (Sartre), 125
Nave, The (Bourges), 32
Necessary Step, The (Durtain), 80
Nekrassov (Sartre), 127
'Neo-Romanticism', XIII
Nepveu, André, *see* Durtain, Luc
'Neue Sachlichkeit' Movement, Germany, 310
New Book of Martyrs, The (Duhamel), 82
New Carthage, The (Eekhoud), 57
New Guide, The (p. Holland), 2, 4, 11
'New Objectivity' Movement, Germany, 310
New Poems (Rilke), 210, 211
New Reich, The (George), 200
New Tales (Jensen), 369
New Times (Kirk), 377
News on the Subject of Love (Borgen), 387
Nexø, Martin Anderson, **370**
Niels Lyhne (Jacobsen), 214
Niels Peter (Heinesen), 379
Nielsen, Jørgen, **377–8**
Nielsen, Morten, **376**
Nietzsche, Friedrich, **192–3**
Night Flight (Saint-Exupéry), 102
Night in Otocac, A (Ekelöf), 403
Night in the Market Tent (Ahlin), 411
Night is Darkness (Bernanos), 85
Night of Death, A (Bregendahl), 367
Night of the Giraffe, The (Andersch), 345
Night With Guests, A (Weiss), 335
Nights Without Night (Leiris), 132
Nijhoff, Martinus, **9**
Nike Fleeing in the Garb of the Wind (Enckell), 414
Nimier, Roger, **144–5**

No Answer (Pinget), 155–6
No Laughing Matter (Salacrou), 161
No Man Knows the Night (Branner), 378
No – the World of the Accused (Jens), 349–50
Nobel Prize, 37, 41, 45, 60, 67, 75, 76, 120, 125, 189, 197, 297, 347, 365, 369, 382, 385, 396, 397, 404, 410, 417
Nobility, Clergy, Burgher and Peasant (Wied), 372
Nobodaddy's Children (Schmidt), 346
Nocturnal (Hellens), 58
Noontide (Claudel), 65
Nordström, Ludwig, **408**
Norge, Jean, *see* Mogin, Jean
North Light, The (Däubler), 248
Norway, Literature of, 379–93
Nossack, Hans Erich, **340–1**
Notebook of Malte Laurids Brigge, The (Rilke), 210, 213, 214
Notebooks (Camus), 130
Notebooks (Valéry), 106
Nothing to Chance (Plisnier), 59
'Nouveau Roman', 73, 85
Nouvelle Revue Française (p.), 69, 88
Novel of My Parents, A (Järnefelt), 20
Novel of Olaf, The (E. Johnson), 406
November 1918 (Döblin), 305–6
Now They Sing Again (Frisch), 328
'Nullpunkt Literatur', 324
Nuptials (Camus), 127
Nuptials (Jouve), 119

Oberon and Madame (Van Schendel), 5
'Objective Correlative', XIV–XV
Oblate (Huysmans), 32
Obstfelder, Sigbjorn, **389**
Occupied City, The (Van Ostaijen), 14
Odd Alberta (Sandel), 385
Œdipus and the Sphinx (Von Hofmannsthal), 208
Of the Abyss and Aerial Man (Lucebert), 10
Of the Movement and Immobility of Douve (Bonnefoy), 184
Old House, The (Van Schendel), 5
Old Jan (Streuvels), 12
Old Pastor, The (Knudsen), 372
Old People and the Things That Pass (Couperus), 3
Old Tune, The (Pinget), 156
Ole Bienkopp (Strittmatter), 360
Ollier, Claude, **154**

Olsen, Ernst Bruun, **374**
On Earth As It Is in Heaven
   (Bergengruen), 274
On Pain of Seeing (Fried), 356
On the Edge of Night (Lampe), 287
On the Marble Cliffs (E. Jünger), 281
On the Road to Myself (Pontoppidan),
   366
On the Shores of My Finland (Pekkanen),
   23
On the Way (Krog), 388
One Day in October (Hoel), 386
One of Life's Slaves (Lie), 381
Open Mind, The (Bernanos), 85
Opus Incertum (Ekelöf), 403
Ordeal (Walschap), 16
Ørjasæter, Tore, **389, 390**
Orpheus (Cocteau), 158
Orpheus and Euridice (Enckell), 414
Orpheus and Euridice (Kokoschka), 258
Ostaijen, Paul Van, **14**
Österling, Anders, **398**
Other Messiah, The (Soumagne), 174–5
Oudshoorn, J. Van, **3–4**
Our Honour and Our Might (Grieg), 388
Our Lady of the Flowers (Genêt), 141
Out of Africa (Blixen), 375
Outsider, The (Camus), 127
Øverland, Arnulf, **390**
Owls to Athens (Wildenvey), 390

Paemel Family, The (Buysse), 12
Pagnol, Marcel, 92, **163**
Palace, The (Simon), 154
Pallieter (Timmermans), 15
Paludan, Jacob, **375**
Pan (p. Germany), 220
Pan (Gorter), 6
Pan (Van Lerberghe), 54
Pan: Hill of Destiny (Giono), 91–2
Panama (Cendrars), 95
Pandora's Box (Wedekind), 122
Pantagleise (Ghelderode), 174
Panu (Aho), 19
Paolo Paoli (Adamov), 166–7
Papa Hamlet (Holz and Schlaf), 195
Papadiamantopoulos, Iannis, *see*
   Moréas, Jean
Paracelsus (Schnitzler), 218
Parade (ballet) (Cocteau), 158
Paradise Reclaimed (Laxness), 418
Paradise Regained (Marsman), 7
Paris Pedestrian, The (Fargue), 115

Paris Soir (p.), 127
Park, The (Sollers), 156
Parnasse contemporain, Le (*Anth.*), 42
'Parnassian' Poets, 42
'Parnassianism', XIV
Parpagnacco (Guilloux), 99
Parricide (Bronnen), 260
Parson's Wife, The (Aho), 19
Part of Myself, A (Zuckmayer), 321
Parti Populaire Français, 87
Pasenow and Romantic (Broch), 296
Pasquier Chronicles, The (Duhamel), 80,
   82–3
Passage of Angels (Périer), 176
Passage of Kites (Butor), 151
Passage of Orpheus (Decorte), 14
Passing Time (Butor), 151–2
Past Is Not Gone, The (Dons), 379
Pastor Ephraim Magnus (Jahnn), 271–2
Pastoral or Time for Cocoa (Hildesheimer),
   333
Pastoral Symphony, The (Gide), 67
Path of Life, The (Streuvels), 12
Patrasket (H. Bergman), 412
Patrioteer, The (H. Mann), 228
Paulina 1880 (Jouve), 119
Peace (Garborg), 381
Peace, The (E. Jünger), 281
Peace at Home (Courteline), 62
Peasant Hymn (Timmermans), 15
Peasant of Paris, A (Aragon), 123
Peasant Students (Garborg), 381
Peasants, Bosses and Bombs (Fallada),
   276–7
Pedersen, Knut, *see* Hamsun, Knut
Pedersen, Sigfred, **376**
Pedigree (Simenon), 171
Peer Gynt (Ibsen), 380
Péguy, Charles, **108–9**
Pekkanen, Toivo, **23**
Pelle the Conqueror (Nexø), 370
Pelléas and Mélisande (Maeterlinck), 60
Penal Colony, The (Kafka), 291
Penguin Island (France), 38
People of Hemsö, The (Strindberg), 394
People of Juvik, The (Duun), 383
People of the Himmerland (Jensen), 369
People Ought to Object (Schnurre), 345
People Without Room (Grimm), 311
Pepita's Marriage (Von Heidenstam and
   Levertin), 395
Père Perdrix (Philippe), 39
'Perfecting of a Love, A' (Musil), 301

Pèrier, Odilon-Jean, **176**
Perrudja (Jahnn), 272
Perse, Saint-John, **119–20**
Persecution and Assassination of Marat (Weiss), 335
Personal Record 1928–1939 (Green), 100
Peter Camenzind (Hesse), 298
Peter Hille Book, The (Lasker-Schüler), 246
Peter the Czar (Klabund), 271
Petersen, Nis, **374**
Philippe, Charles-Louis, **38–9**
Physicists, The (Dürrenmatt), 331–2
Picnic on the Battlefield (Arrabel), 168
Pilgrim of the Absolute, A (Bloy), 41
Pillars of Society (Ibsen), 380
Pinget, Robert, **155–6**
Ping-Pong, Le (Adamov), 166
'Pippo Spano' (H. Mann), 227
Pirandello, Luigi, 280
Pirates of Lake Malar, The (Siwertz), 409
Pitoéff, Georges and Ludmilla, 157, 158
Place in the World, A (Sternheim), 223
Plague, The (Camus), 128
Planetarium, The (Sarraute), 149
Play (Beckett), 140
Play of Everyman, The (Von Hofmannsthal), 209
Playing With Fire (Vailland), 137
Playing With Love (Schnitzler), 218
Plays in Which Darkness Falls (Hildesheimer), 333
Pleasure and Regrets (Proust), 69
Plebeians Rehearse the Uprising, The (Grass), 351
Pledge, The (Dürrenmatt), 331
Plievier, Theodor, **282**
Plisnier, Charles, **59**
Podium (p. Holland), 10
Poë, Aurélien Marie Lugne, **157**
Poems and Words During the Thirty Years' War (Claudel), 66
Poems in English (Beckett), 138
Poems of a Multi-Millionaire (Larbaud), 116
Poems of A. O. Barnabooth (Larbaud), 116
Poems of a Rich Amateur (Larbaud), 116
Poet Lore (Stramm), 237
Point of Departure (Anouilh), 160
Poirier, Louis, see Gracq, Julien
Ponge, Francis, 179–80
Pontoppidan, Henrik, **365–6**
Poor, The (H. Mann), 228

Poor Flanders (H. Teirlinck and Stijns), 12
'Populism', 97–8
Port Royal (Montherlant), 90
Portaas, Herman, see Wildenvey, Herman
Portrait of a Man Unknown (Sarraute), 146, 148
Possessed, The (Dostoevski, dram. Camus), 130
Postman, The (Martin du Gard), **75**
Potomak, The (Cocteau), 158
Power of a Lie, The (Bojer), 384
Powers (Stramm), 237
Praise of Life (Elskamp), 54
Prayer for a Good End (Roelants), 16
Present, The (p. Iceland), 415
Present Time, The (Duun), 383
Prévert, Jacques, **180–1**
Primal Vision (Benn), 255
Prime of Life, The (Beauvoir), 136
Princess Maleine (Maeterlinck), 60
Private Life of the Master Race, The (Brecht), 316
Private Suhren (von de Vring), 279
Prix Goncourt, 71
Problems of the Lyric (Benn), 256
Professor Bernhardi (Schnitzler), 218
Professor Hieronimus (A. Skram), 382
Professor Mamlock (Wolf), 313
Professor Taranne (Adamov), 166
Promised Land, The (van Eeden), 4
Promised Land, The (Pontoppidan), 365
Prompter, The (Klossowski), 134
Proserpina (Langgässer), 251
Proust, Marcel, **68–70**
Provence, Marcel, see Jouhandeau, Marcel
Proverb, The (Aymé), 133–4
Prudhomme, René-Francois-Armand, see Sully-Prudhomme
Public Prosecutor, The (Hockwälder), 332
Pucelle (Audiberti), 182
Puthoste, Roger, see Thérive, André
'Pythie, La' (Valéry), 106

Quay of Shadows (Mac Orlan), 101
Queneau, Raymond, **131–2**
Querelle of Brest (Genêt), 141
Quest, The (Langgasser), 251
Quest for Joy, The (Du Pin), 187
Qu'est que le Surréalism? (Breton), 110

Quoat-Quoat (Audiberti), 181

Quoirez, Françoise, *see* Sagan, Francoise

Quosquo (p. Sweden), 414

Raabe, Wilhelm, **190**

Rabbit Race, The (Walser), 339

Raboliot (Genevoix), 71

Race and Culture (Leiris), 132

Races (Bruckner), 313

Radetzkymarsch (Roth), 284

Radiguet, Raymond, **97**

Radvanyi, Natty, *see* Seghers, Anna

Railway, The (Aho), 19

Rain Bird (Lidman), 412

Rains (Perse), 120

Rampart (Audiberti), 182

Ramuz, Charles-Ferdinand, **73–4**

Rape of a City, The (Plievier), 282

Rarahu: the Marriage of Loti (Loti), 35

Rasmussen, Halfdan, **376**

Raspberry-Picker, The (Hochwälder), 333

Rasputin (Klabund), 271

'Realism', XII–XIII, 2

'Réage, Pauline', 135

Rebatet, Lucien, **135**

Rebel, The (Camus), 128

Red Feathers, The (Klitgaard), 379

Red Lily, The (France), 38

Red Room, The (Strindberg), 394

Redemption of Tycho Brahe, The (Brod), 269

Redhead, The (Andersch), 345

Refuges (Fargue), 115

Régnier, Paule, **135**

Rehfisch, Hans José, **311**

Reign of the Evil One, The (Ramuz), 74

Reiss-Andersen, Gunnar, **392–3**

Remark, Erich Paul, *see* Remarque, Erich Maria

Remarque, Erich Maria, **279**

Remembrance of Things Past (Proust), 69–70

Renard, Jules, **39–40**

René Lys (Ségalen), 73

Renn, Ludwig, **277–8**

Representative, The (Hochhuth), 338

Reprieve, The (Sartre), 125

Return From the Front (Döblin), 305

Return to Ithaca (E. Johnson), 406

Reve, Gerard Kornelis van, **11**

Reverdy, Pierre, 112, **121–2**

Revocation of the Edict of Nantes, The (Klossowski), 134

Revolt of the Fishermen, The (Seghers), 278

Rhineland Heritage, The (Schickele), 275

Rhinoceros (Ionesco), 165

Richter, Hans Werner, **327**

Riding Master, The (Branner), 378

Rifbjerg, Klaus, **378**

Rigadon (Céline), 94

Rigaut, Jacques, 110

Right of the Strongest, The (Buysse), 11–12

Rilke, Rainer Maria, **209–16**

Rimbaud, Arthur, 42, 44

Ring Round the Moon (Anouilh), 160

Ringelnatz, Joachim, **309**

Ripe Corn, The (Rebatet), 135

Rise and Fall of the Town of Mahagonny, The (Brecht), 315

Road, The (Chamson), 105

Road, The (Martinson), 407

Road to the End of the World, The (Hoel), 386

Road to the Open, The (Schnitzler), 219

Roads to Freedom, The (Sartre), 125

Robbe-Grillet, Alain, **149–51**

Robber Band, The (Frank), 267

Robber Band, The (Romains), 80

Roberte, This Evening (Klossowski), 134

Rode, Edith, **371**

Rode, Helge, **368**

Roelants, Maurice, **16**

Rogue of Bergen, The (Zuckmayer), 321

Rolland, Romain, **41–2**

Romains, Jules, **78–82**

Romance of a Spahi, The (Loti), 35

Romance of National Energy, The (Barrès), 37

Romulus the Great (Dürrenmatt), 331

Ronde, La (film, Schnitzler), 218

Rørdam, Valdemar, 368

Rose Bernd (G. Hauptmann), 199

Rose of Flesh, A (Wolkers), 11

Rostand, Edmond, **64**

Roth, Joseph, **283–4**

Round Heads and Pointed Heads (Brecht), 316

Roussel, Raymond, **72–3**

Roux, Pierre-Paul, *see* Saint-Pol-Roux

Roux the Bandit (Chamson), 105

Royal Game, The (Zweig), 283

Rubbish, The (Rebatet), 135

Rubicon (Mykle), 393

Ruf, Der (p. Germany), 327, 344

Rule of the Game, The (Leiris), 132

Rumanian Diary, A (Carossa), 273

S.S. Tenacity (Vildrac), 162
Sackcloth Glove, The (Reverdy), 122
Sacred Hill, The (Barrès), 37
Saga of Åsmund Armodsson, The (Stigen), 393
Sagan, Françoise, **145**
Sailor Comes Ashore, A (Sandemose), 386
Sailor From Gibraltar, The (Duras), 142
Sailor in the Bottle, The (Bieler), 360
Sailors of Cattaro, The (F. Wolf), 313
Saint, The (von Unruh), 263
Saint-Denis, Michel, **157**
Saint-Exupéry, Antoine de, **101–2**
Saint-Genet (Sartre), 140
St. Joan of the Stockyards (Brecht), 315–16
Saint-Pol-Roux, **47–8**, 111
Sainte Europe (Adamov), 167
Salacrou, Armand, 13, **161–2**
Salavin (Duhamel), 82
Salka Valka (Laxness), 417
Salmon, André, **97**
Salonen, Frans Uuno, *see* Kailas, Uuno
Samain, Albert, **47**
Sancta Susanna (Stramm), 237
Sandel, Cora, **385–6**
Sandemose, Axel, **386–7**
Sandgren, Gustav, **401**
Saporta, Marc, **179**
Sardou, Victorien, **63**
Sarment, Jean, **163**
Sarraute, Nathalie, **146–7**
Sartre, Jean-Paul, 78, **124–7**, 128
Satin Slipper, The (Claudel), 65
Sauser, Frédéric, *see* Cendrars, Blaise
Scenters-Out, The (van Lerberghe), 54
Schade, Jens August, **376**
Schaeffer, Albrecht, **203**
Schaper, Edzard, **341–2**
Scheerbart, Paul, **190**
Schendel, Arthur van, **5**
Scherfig, Hans, **379**
Schickele, René, **275**
Schlaf, Johannes, **194–5**
Schlageter, Johst, **264**
Schmidt, Arno, **346–7**
Schnitzler, Arthur, **218–19**
Schnurre, Wolfdietrich, **345–6**
School for Jesters, The (Ghelderode), 174
School of Poetry, The (Gorter), 5–6
School of the Dictators, The (Kästner), 287

School of Uznach, The (Sternheim), 312
Schröder, Rudolf Alexander, 220
Schweik in the Second World War (Brecht), 319
Schwitters, Kurt, **308–9**
Sea Ringed with Visions, A (Kokoschka), 258
Seamarks (Perse), 120
Seated Woman, The (Apollinaire), 114
Second Sex, The (Beauvoir), 136
Second Thoughts (Butor), 152
Secret Life, The (Estaunié), 34
Secret Life, The (Lemonnier), 56
Secret of the Kingdom, The (Waltari), 24
Seduction, The (Kornfeld), 259
Seed, The (Vesaas), 391
Seespeck (Barlach), 225
Ségalen, Victor, **73**
Seghers, Anna, **278–9**
Selected Essays (Montherlant), 91
Senora Carrar's Rifles (Brecht), 316
'Sentimentive', XVI–XVIII
September (Sandemose), 386
September Bees (Vandercammen), 178
September Storm (Lampe), 287
Set Purpose of Things, The (Ponge), 180
Setting, The (Ollier), 154
Seven Days' Darkness (G. Gunnarsson), 417
Seven Deadly Sins, The (Boye), 400
Seven Gothic Tales (Blixen), 375
Seventh Cross, The (Seghers), 279
Seventh Ring, The (George), 202
Séverin, Fernand, **56**
Sfaira der Alte (Mombert), 248
Shadow Land (Bobrowski), 360
Shadow of the Coachman's Body, The (Weiss), 334
Shame (Claus), 17
Shavings (Aho), 19
She Came to Stay, 136
Ship, The (Bergman), 398
Ship, The (Jahnn), 272
Ship in the Mountain, The (Gaiser), 343
Ship Sails On, The (Grieg), 388
Shoreless River (Jahnn), 272
Siddharta (Hesse), 299
Side of the Angels, The (Curtis), 144
Siegfried (Giraudoux), 159
Sightless, The (Maeterlinck), 60
Signal, The (Ostaijen), 14
Signed Away (Drachmann), 367
Signwriter, The (Kretzer), 196

Sigurðsson, Jóhann Gunnar, **416**
Silence, Theatre of, 412
Silence (Sarraute), 149
Silence of the Sea, The (Vercors), 136
Silent One, A (Martin du Gard), 75
Silhouettes (Wied), 371
Siljo, Juhani, **25**
Sillanpää, Frans Eemil, **22–3**
Silver Moon, The (Laxness), 418
Sim, Georges, *see* Simenon, Georges
Simenon, Georges, **170–1**
Simon, Claude, **153–4**
Simon the Pathetic (Giraudoux), 159
Singers, The (Frank), 267
Sinn und Form (p. Germany), 360
Sinners in Summertime (Hoel), 386
Sinuhe the Egyptian (Waltari), 24
Siwertz, Sigfrid, **408–9**
Sjoberg, Birger, **399**
Sjov in Denmark (Schade), 376
Skagestad, Tormod, **389**
Skirmishes (Wied), 371
Skram, Amalie, 382
Sleep and Death (Kailas), 25
Sleepwalkers, The (Broch), 295, 296
Slow Motion Picture (H. Teirlinck), 13
Small Souls (Couperus), 3
Small Town Tyrant, A (H. Mann), 227
Snake, The (Dagerman), 411
Snob, The (Sternheim), 223
Snoilsky, Carl, **395**
So Fatal a Desire (Klossowski), 134
Soap (Ponge), 180
Söderberg, Hjalmar, 405
Södergran, Edith, 413
Soft Soap (Elsschot), 15
Soldiers (Hochhuth), 338
Soldier's Tale, The (Ramuz), 73
Soldier's Well, The (Dons), 379
Sollers, Philippe, **156**
Somewhere Myself (Baillon), 57
Son, The (Hasenclever), 259
Son of a Servant, The (Strindberg), 394
Son of Wrath (Kirk), 377
Sønderby, Knud, 379
Song of Bernadette, The (Werfel), 266
Song of Eve (Van Lerberghe), 54
Song of Songs, The (Sudermann), 196
Song of the Lusitanian Bogey, The (Weiss), 336
Song of the Red Ruby, The (Mykle), 393
Song of the Scaffold, The (Le Fort), 274
Song of the World, The (Giono), 92

Songs of Maldoror, The (Lautréamont), 110
Songs of Man (Leino), 20
Sonnets to Orpheus (Rilke), 210, 213, 216
Sons (Benn), 253
Souls of the Soulless, The (Supervielle), 117
Soumagne, Henri, **174–5**
Soupault, Philippe, **111**
South (Green), 100
Southern Mail (Saint-Exupéry), 102
Soya, Carl Erik, **373**
Speculations About Jakob (U. Johnson), 352
Spektrum (p. Sweden), 400
Spengler, Oswald, 254
Sphinx and Strawman (Kokoschka), 258
Spielhagen, Friedrich, **189–90**
Spilt Milk (N. Petersen), 374
Spirits (Apollinaire), 113
Splashes and Rags (Fröding), 396
Sponger, The (Renard), 40
Spring Evening in the Latin Quarter (Koskenniemi), 21
Spring Hummings of This Fellow, The (Larin-Kyösti), 22
Spring's Awakening (Wedekind), 221
Square, The (Duras), 142
Square (von Unruh), 262
Squire Hellman (Aho), 19
Stadler, Ernst, **240–1**
Stain on the Snow, The (Simenon), 171
Stairway of Stone and Clouds, The (Daisne), 16
Stalingrad (Plievier), 282
Standard, The (Lernet-Holenia), 287
Stanzas (Moréas), 48
Star of Satan (Bernanos), 84
Stardust and Sedan Chair (Schnurre), 345
State of Siege, The (Camus), 130
Static Poems (Benn), 255
Stationmaster, The (Graf), 352
Steles (Ségalen), 73
Stephansson, Stephan G., **416**
Steppenwolf, Der (Hesse), **299–300**
Sternheim, Carl, 172, **222–4**, 312
Stigen, Terje, **393**
Stijns, Raimond, **12**
Stone Bridal Bed, The (Mulisch), 11
Stone God, The (Vaa), 389
Stopfkuchen (Raabe), 190
Stories of a Lifetime (T. Mann), 230, 233
Storm of Steel (E. Jünger), 280

Story of Gösta Berling, The (Lagerlöf), 404

Story of O., The (Réage), 135

Story of Rope, A (Meri), 25

Story of the Eye, The (Bataille), 134

Story of the Hare, The (Jammes), 51

Strait Is the Gate (Gide), 67

Stramm, August, **237**

Strange Mr. Curtois, The (Soumagne), 175

Straw Man, The (Giono), 92

'Stream of Consciousness', XV–XVI

Street of the Sandalmakers, The (N. Petersen), 374

Streuvels, Stijn, **12**

Strindberg, August, 216, **393–5**

Strittmatter, Erwin, **359**

Strong Are Lonely, The (Hochwälder), 332

Strudlhof Steps, The (Doderer), 284

Struggle With the Angel, The (Malraux), 104

Struggle With the Angel, The (H. Teirlinck), 13

Stuckenberg, Viggo, **367**

Stud, A (Lemonnier), 56

Sturm, Der (p. Germany), 235, 237, 240, 246, 258, 303, 307

Such Is Life (Toller), 261

Such Is Life (Wedekind), 222

Suderman, Hermann, **196**

Sulky Fire, The (Bernard), 162

Sully-Prudhomme, **45**

Sum of Our Days, The (Chamson), 105

Summa of Poetry (Du Pin), 187

Summer in Ter-Muren (Beon), 16

Sunday of Life, The (Queneau), 132

Superb, The (Chamson), 105

Supermale, The (Jarry), 63

Supervielle, Jules, **116–17**

Supplication of Christ, The (Saint-Pol-Roux), 47

Surrealism, 109*f.*, 123, 258, 307, 309, 401, 403, 413

Surrender (Hansen), 378

Suspicion (Dürrenmatt), 331

Sutter's Gold (Cendrars), 95

Swaanswijk, L. J., *see* Lucebert

Swann's Way (Proust), 69

Sweden, Literature of, 393–418

Sylva (Vercors), 136

'Symbolism', 43*f.*, 201, 217

'Synthesism', 179

Tagger, Theodor, *see* Bruckner, Ferdinand

Tailhède, Raymond de la, **48, 49**

Tale of Fatumeh, The (Ekelöf), 403

Tale of 672. Night (Von Hofmannsthal), 209

Tale of the Love and Death of Cornet Christopher Rilke, The (Rilke), 210

Tales for Yesterday's Children (Mockel), 53

Tanker, The (Elsschot), 15

Tanner Family, The (Walser), 286

Tardieu, Jean, **167**

Tardiveau, René, *see* Boylesve, René

Taube, Evert, **399**

Tears of the Acacias, The (Hermans), 10

Teenager Love (Olsen), 374

Teirlinck, Herman, **12–13**

Teirlinck, Isidoor, **12–13**

Tel Quel (p. France), 156

Telemachus in the Village (Gijsen), 17

Temple and Cross (Marsman), 7

Temps et la Vie, Le (Adam), 35

Temps Modernes, Les (p. France), 128

'Temptation of Silent Veronica, The' (Musil), 301

Tempter, The (Broch), 295, 296

Ten Year Exile (Wolfskehl), 203

Tentacular Cities, The (Verhaeren), 55

Ten-Thirty on a Summer Night (Duras), 142

Terror on the Mountain (Ramuz), 74

Testament of Cain, The (Gyllensten), 411

That Is the Question (Crommelynck), 173

Theatre and Its Double, The (Artaud), 169

Théâtre Alfred Jarry, 168

Théâtre, Antoine, 62

Théâtre d'Art, 52

Théâtre de l'Atelier, 157

Théâtre de l'Œuvre, 52, 62, 157

Théâtre du Vieux-Colombier, 157

Théâtre Libre, 61

Theatre of Cruelty, The (Artaud), 169

Theatre of the Absurd, *see* Absurd, Theatre of

Thérèse: a Portrait in Four Parts (Mauriac), 77

Thérèse Desqueyroux (Mauriac), **77**

Thérèse Raquin (Zola), 29

Thérive, André, **98**

Thésée (Gide), 68

Thibault, Anatole-François, *see* France, Anatole

Thief's Journal, A (Genêt), 141

Thiery, Herman, *see* Daisnes, Johan

Thijm, J. L. A., *see* Deyssel, Lodewijk van

Third Book About Achim, The (U. Johnson), 352

Third Walpurgis Night, The (Kraus), 270

Thirtieth Year, The (Bachmann), 357

This Quarter (Beer-Hofmann), 219

Thomas the Obscure (Blanchot), 155

Those of Verdun (Genevoix), 71

Those One Holds in One's Arms (Montherlant), 90

Thoursie, Ragnar, **403**

Three Comrades (Remarque), 279

Three Homeless Ones (Andersson), 398–9

Three Leaps of Wang-Lun, The (Döblin), 303

Three Masters (Zweig), 283

Three Months of Prison (Vildrac), 162

Three Novels (Beckett), 139

Three Women (Musil), 301

Threepenny Opera, The (Brecht), 314–15, 319

Thursday (Hockwälder), 333

Thus Spake Zarathustra (Nietzsche), 192

Thy Rod and Thy Staff (Bergman), 409

Thyl Ulenspiegel (De Coster), 53

Tidings Brought to Mary, The (Claudel), 65

Tiger at the Gates (Giraudoux), 159

Time (Bang), 364

Time Confounded (Salacrou), 161

Timmermans, Felix, **15**

Timon (Bruckner), 312–13

Timon and the Gold (Bruckner), 313

Tin Drum, The (Grass), 350, 351

To Damascus (Strindberg), 395

To Each According to his Hunger (Mogin), 179

Toller, Ernst, **260–1**, 311

Tomfoolery (Rasmussen), 376

Tonka (Musil), 300

Too Little (Boye), 400

Topaze (Pagnol), 163

Torch, The (p. Germany), 270

Torchbearer Group, Finland, 24, 25, 26

Torso, The (Langgässer), 252

'Totalism', 179

Tower, The (Von Hofmannsthal), 209

Tower, The (Weiss), 335

Town Where the Prince is a Child, The (Montherlant), 91

Toys (Branner), 378

Trade Wind (H. Martinson), 407

Tragedy of Love, The (Heiberg), 387

Train Was on Time, The (Böll), 347

Trakl, Georg, **241–6**

Transfiguration (Toller), 260

Transient Evil, The (Audiberti), 182

Transmigration of the Soul, The (Wittlinger), 326

Tranströmer, Tomas, 404

Trash (Ekelöf), 403

Traveller, If You Come to Spa (Böll), 348

Traveller Without Luggage (Anouilh), 160

Treacherous Ground (Bojer), 384

Triad (Krog), 388

Trial, The (Kafka), 290, 292

Trial of Our Lord, The (de Mont), 17

Triangle in the Jungle, The (Lucebert), 10

Trickster, The (Simon), 153

Trifles for a Massacre (Céline), 94

Triumph of Reason, The (Rolland), 41

Trojan Women, The (Euripides, *adapt.* Werfel), 266

Trophies, The (Herédia), 45

'Tropism', 148

Tropisms (Sarraute), 146

Trotsky in Exile (Weiss), 337

Trouble at Newmarket (Klitgaard), 379

Try at a Description of a Dinner . . . (Prévert), 181

Turm, Der (Von Hofmannsthal), 208, 209

Turn of the Century, The (Halbe), 196–7

Turner, Georg, *see* Rehfisch, Hans José

Twelve Sundays, The (Nordström), 408

Twenty Poems (Trakl), 243

Twilight of the Gods, The (Bourges), 32

Twins of Nuremberg, The (Kesten), 283

$2 \times 2 = 5$ (Wied), 372

Two Executioners, The (Arrabal), 168

Two Flags, The (Rebatet), 135

Two Minutes of Silence (Branner), 378

Two Views (U. Johnson), 352

Two Weeks Before the Glacial Nights (Hoel), 386

Tynni, Aala, **27**

Tzara, Tristan, **109**

þóðarson, þórbergur, **416–17**

Ubu Roi (Jarry), 62–3, 157

'Unanimism', 14, 78 *f.*

Unanimous Life, The (Romains), 80

Unconquered Love (Huch), 197
Under Fire (Barbusse), 70, 71
Under the Axe (Bourges), 32
Under the Polar Star (Linna), 24
Understudy, The (Roussel), 72
Undset, Sigrid, **385**
Unguarded House, The (Böll), 348
Unicorn, The (Walser), 339
Unknown Quantity, The (Broch), 295
Unknown Soldier, The (Linna), 24
Unknown Woman of Arras, The
    (Salacrou), 13, 162
Unnameable, The (Beckett), 139
Unruh, Fritz von, **261–3**
Unto a Good Land (Moberg), 406
Uppdal, Kristofer, **384**
Uprooted, The (Barrès), 37
Urujac (Audiberti), 181

Vaa, Aslaug, **389**
Vaché, Jacques, **110**
Vagabond, The (Colette), 71
Vailland, Roger, **137**
Vala, Katri, **26–7**
Valéry, Paul, 44, **105–8**
Van Ermengem, Frédéric, *see* Hellens,
    Franz
Vandercammen, Edmond, **178–9**
Vanishing Point (Weiss), 334
Vartio, Marja-Liisa, **27**
Vatard Sisters, The (Huysmans), 31
Vatican Cellars, The (Gide), 67
Veni Creator Spiritus (Werfel), 265
Vennberg, Karl, **403–4**
Venus (H. Mann), 227
Vercors, **136**
Verdi: a Novel of the Opera (Werfel),
    266
Verhaeren, Emile, **55–6**, 61, 79
Verne, Jules, **41**
Vers et Prose (p. France), 52
Verwey, Albert, **2**
Vesaas, Tarjei, **390–2**
Vestdijk, Simon, **8–9**
Vian, Boris, **167–8**
Viaud, Louis Marie Julien, *see* Loti,
    Pierre
Victory in the Dark (Lagervist), 412
Viélé-Griffin, Francis, 46
Vietnam Discourse (Weiss), 336
View, The (Roussel), 72
Viita, Lauri, **27**
Vildrac, Charles, 79, **162**

Viljanen, Lauri, **26**
Villa Aurea (Kaiser), 264
Villa Oasis (Dabit), 98
Vinzenz and the Girl Friend of Important
    Men (Musil), 300
Viper in the Fist, A (H. Bazin), 143
Vipers' Tangle, The (Mauriac), 77
Virgin of Paris, The (Jouve), 119
Visionaries, The (Musil), 300
Visionary, The (Lie), 381
Visit, The (Dürrenmatt), 331
Visit to Godenholm (E. Jünger), 281
'Vitalism' Group, Holland, 7
Vitrac, Roger, **170**
Voice in the Crowd, A (Merrill), 47
Voice Is Raised, A (Gaiser), 343
Voices of Blood (Thérive), 98
Voices of Silence, The (Malraux), 103
Votre Faust (Butor), 152
Voyage of Patrice Périot, The (Duhamel),
    83
Voyeur, The (Robbe-Grillet), 150
Vring, Georg von der, **279**

Wadenström, Alice, *see* Vala, Katri
Wadzek's Struggle with the Steam Machine
    (Döblin), 304
Wagener, Henri, *see* Soumagne, Henri
Wagner, Elin, **409**
Waiting for a Ship (Lauesen), 379
Waiting for Godot (Beckett), 138
Walk, The (Walser), 285
Wallenstein (Döblin), 304
Wallonie, La (p. Belgium), 53
Walnuts of Altenburg, The (Malraux), 104
Walschap, Gerard, **15–16**
Walser, Martin, **339–40**
Walser, Robert, **285–7**
Waltari, Mika, **24**, 28
Waltz of the Toreadors (Anouilh), 161
Wanderer in Love, A (Van Schendel), 5
Wanderer Lost, A (Van Schendel), 5
Wandering Jew, The (Apollinaire), 114
Wandering Palaces (Kahn), 46
War (G. Hauptmann), 198
War (Renn), 278
War in the White Desert (Haanpää),
    23–4
War Poems (Grieg), 388
Wassermann, Jakob, **268–9**
Waterman, The (Van Schendel), 5
Way of Sacrifice (Von Unruh), 262–3
Way of the Stars, The (Däubler), 248

Way Through the Marshland, The (Langgässer), 251
We Are Utopia (Andres), 342
We Know That Already (Nossack), 341
We Two (Michaux), 178
Weavers, The (G. Hauptmann), 198
Wedding Pains (Dagerman), 411
Wedekind, Frank, 220–2
Weekend at Dunkirk (Merle), 137
Weird Tales from the Northern Seas (Lie), 381
Weiss, Peter, 334–7
Weissen Blätter, Die (p. Germany), 306
Werewolf, The (Sademose), 387
Werewolf, The (Vitrac), 170
Werfel, Franz, 265–6
When Life's Twilight Comes (Falkberget), 385
When Love is Young (Halbe), 196
When the Mountain Fell (Ramuz), 74
When the War Came to an End (Frisch), 328
Who Weeps for Juckenack? (Rehfisch), 311
Wiechart, Ernst, 275
Wied, Gustav, 370–1
Wild Duck, The (Ibsen), 380
Wildenvey, Herman, 390
Wilderness of Mirrors, A (Frisch), 330
Will-o'-the Wisp (Elsschot), 15
Wind (Simon), 153
Wind, Sand and Stars (Saint-Exupéry), 102
Winds (Perse), 120
Winter (Griese), 311
Winter By the Sea, A (A. R. Holst), 7
Winter's Tale (Blixen), 375
Wisdom of the Sands, The (Saint-Exupéry), 102
With Doriot (Drieu la Rochelle), 87
With Wit, Light and Guts (Huelsenbeck), 308
Within the Walls (Nathansen), 373
Without a Country (H. Mann), 228
Without Soul (Thérive), 98
Wittlinger, Karl, 326
Woe to Him Who Doesn't Lie (Hey), 334
Woestijne, Karel van de, 13–14
Wolf, Friedrich, 313

Wolf, The (Graf), 352
Wolf Among Wolves (Fallada), 277
Wolfskehl, Karl, 202–3
Wolkers, Jan Hendrik, 10–11
Wolves, The (Rolland), 41
Woman at the Bonfire, The (J. Nielsen), 377
Woman of the Pharisees, A (Mauriac), 78
Woman Too Many, A (Sønderby), 379
Woman Who Was Poor (Bloy), 41
Woman Without Sin, The (Lemonnier), 98
Wonderful Adventures of Nils, The (Lagerlöf), 404
Wooden Crosses, The (Dorgelès), 71
Word, The (p. Holland), 10
Word, The (Munk), 373
Words (Prévert), 181
Worker, The (E. Jünger), 280
World of the Thibaults, The (Martin du Gard), 75–6
World of Yesterday, The (Zweig), 283
Wrong Side and the Right Side, The (Camus), 127

Year of the Soul, The, 201
Year of the Vanquished, The (Chamson), 104
Yellow Laughter (Mac Orlan), 101
Yester Year (Elsschot), 15
Yesterday (Von Hofmannsthal), 209
Young David (Beer-Hofmann), 220
Young Doctor's Day, The (Carossa), 273
Young Eagle, The (Rostand), 64
'Young Fate, The' (Valéry), 106
Young Girl in the Rose Garden, The (Jotuni), 22
Young Viennese Group, see Jungwien Group
Young Woman of 1914, A (Zweig), 276
Younger Brother, The (Nossack), 341

Zazie (Queneau), 132
Zettel's Dream (Schmidt), 346–7
Ziaux, Les (Queneau), 131
Zola, Émile, 29–30, 79
Zuckmayer, Carl, 321–3
Zweig, Arnold, 275–6, 283

GUIDE TO MODERN WORLD LITERATURE
Martin Seymour-Smith

19505 3   **Volume 1**   £2·25
American, Australian, British-Canadian,
New Zealand, South African literature.

20230 0   **Volume 3**   £1·75
Greek, Italian, Jewish, Latin American,
Portuguese, Rumanian, Spanish, Turkish,
Western minor, Yugoslavian literature.

20231 9   **Volume 4**   £1·75
African and Caribbean, Albanian, Arabic,
Bulgarian, Chinese, Czechoslovakian,
Eastern minor, Hungarian, Indian and
Pakistani, Japanese, Polish, Russian literature.

TEACH YOURSELF BOOKS

POETRY

Robin Skelton

When Boswell said to Dr. Johnson, 'Then, sir, what is poetry?', Dr. Johnson replied, 'Why, sir, it is much easier to say what it is not. We all *know* what night is, but it is not easy to tell what it is.'

Poetry has always been regarded with awe; in this excellent and penetrating book Robin Skelton brings understanding of it beyond Dr. Johnson's honest but evasive answer.

All those who respond to poetry in any form will benefit from reading the book. To the perception of the general reader it gives the added knowledge of the structure, the attitudes and the creative processes in poetry; to the student it offers an invaluable and comprehensive approach to the subject.

TEACH YOURSELF BOOKS

CREATIVE WRITING
Victor Jones

How can one learn to write creatively, for, as the author of this book writes, 'to suggest that a book on creative writing can create a creative writer is equivalent to suggesting that a book on divinity can create God.'

But what the aspiring writer can do is to recognise that he, like everyone else, enjoys the essential attributes of the writer—experience of life and native talent.

This book demonstrates how to shape and control this talent, drawing on one's own personal experience. It covers every form of writing, from the novel and the short story to poetry, drama and writing for radio and television.

The result is an approach to creative writing, packed with practical advice on how to find both success and satisfaction in one's own work.

Also available from Teach Yourself Books

GUIDE TO MODERN WORLD LITERATURE
Martin Seymour-Smith

19505 3	**Volume 1**	£2·25
20230 0	**Volume 3**	£1·75
20231 9	**Volume 4**	£1·75
17886 8	**Analytical Psychology** David Cox	95p
18256 3	**Creative Writing** Victor Jones	50p
05577 4	**Ethics** A. C. Ewing	70p
05645 2	**Logic** A. A. Luce	50p
05690 8	**Poetry** R. Skelton	40p
17887 6	**Political Thought** C. Wayper & W. Parkin	50p
19498 7	**Psychology Today** ed. B. Gillham	95p
19819 2	**Sociology** J. Abraham	75p
05747 5	**Zen** C. Humphreys	50p